POLITICS AND TRADITION BETWEEN ROME, RAVENNA AND CONSTANTINOPLE

The *Variae* of Cassiodorus have long been valued as an epistolary collection offering a window into political and cultural life in a so-called barbarian successor state in sixth-century Italy. However, this study is the first to treat them as more than an assemblage of individual case studies and to analyse the collection's wider historical context. M. Shane Bjornlie highlights the insights the *Variae* provide into early medieval political, ecclesiastical, fiscal and legal affairs and the influence of the political and military turbulence of Justinian's reconquest of Italy, and of political and cultural exchanges between Italy and Constantinople. The book also explores how Cassiodorus revised, updated and assembled the *Variae* for publication and what this reveals about his motives for publishing an epistolary record and for his own political life at a crucial period of transformation for the Roman world.

M. SHANE BJORNLIE is Assistant Professor of Roman and Late Antique History at Claremont McKenna College. His research interests include ethnography, late antique letter collections, ancient political culture and the 'decline and fall' of the Roman Empire.

Cambridge Studies in Medieval Life and Thought
Fourth Series

General Editor:
ROSAMOND MCKITTERICK
Professor of Medieval History, University of Cambridge, and Fellow of Sidney Sussex College

Advisory Editors:
CHRISTINE CARPENTER
Professor of Medieval English History, University of Cambridge

JONATHAN SHEPARD

The series *Cambridge Studies in Medieval Life and Thought* was inaugurated by G. G. Coulton in 1921; Professor Rosamond McKitterick now acts as General Editor of the Fourth Series, with Professor Christine Carpenter and Dr Jonathan Shepard as Advisory Editors. The series brings together outstanding work by medieval scholars over a wide range of human endeavour extending from political economy to the history of ideas.

This is book 89 in the series and a full list of titles in the series can be found at:
www.cambridge.org/medievallifeandthought

POLITICS AND TRADITION BETWEEN ROME, RAVENNA AND CONSTANTINOPLE

A Study of Cassiodorus and the Variae, *527–554*

M. SHANE BJORNLIE

CAMBRIDGE
UNIVERSITY PRESS

CAMBRIDGE
UNIVERSITY PRESS

University Printing House, Cambridge CB2 8BS, United Kingdom

Published in the United States of America by Cambridge University Press, New York

Cambridge University Press is part of the University of Cambridge.

It furthers the University's mission by disseminating knowledge in the pursuit of education, learning and research at the highest international levels of excellence.

www.cambridge.org
Information on this title: www.cambridge.org/9781107028401

© M. Shane Bjornlie 2013

First published 2013

A catalogue record for this publication is available from the British Library

Library of Congress Cataloguing in Publication data
Bjornlie, Michael Shane, 1969–
Politics and tradition between Rome, Ravenna and Constantinople: a study of Cassiodorus and the Variae 527–554 / M. Shane Bjornlie.
p.   cm. – (Cambridge studies in medieval life and thought: fourth series; 89)
Includes bibliographical references.
ISBN 978-1-107-02840-1 (hardback)
1. Cassiodorus, Senator, ca. 487–ca. 580. Variae.   2. Cassiodorus, Senator, ca. 487–ca. 580 – Political and social views.   3. Rome – History – Germanic Invasions, 3rd–6th centuries.   4. Italy – Politics and government – 476–1268.
I. Title.
PA6271.C4V23   2012
945´.01 – dc23   2012024346

ISBN 978-1-107-02840-1 Hardback

For Atia, Aisling, Adelheid and Michelle

CONTENTS

Contents

Contents

ABBREVIATIONS

Att. Sett.	S. Leanza, ed., *Atti della Settimana di Studi su Flavio Magno Aurelio Cassiodoro* (Soveria Mannelli, 1986)
Cassiod.	S. Leanza, ed., *Cassiodoro: dalla Corte di Ravenna al Vivarium di Squillace, Atti del Convegno Internazionale di Studi* (Soveria Mannelli, 1993)
CC Just.	M. Maas, ed., *Cambridge Companion to the Age of Justinian* (Cambridge, 2005)
CCSL	*Corpus Christianorum. Series Latina*
Cités Ital.	M. Ghilardi, C. Goddard and P. Porena, eds., *Les cités de l'Italie tardo-antique (IVe–VIe siècle): Institutions, économie, société, culture et religion* (Rome, 2006)
CIC	*Corpus Iuris Civilis*
CIL	*Corpus Inscriptionum Latinarum*
Crisis Oik.	C. Chazelle and C. Cubitt, eds., *The Crisis of Oikoumene: The Three Chapters and the Failed Quest for Unity in the Sixth-Century Mediterranean* (Turnhout, 2007)
CSEL	*Corpus Scriptorum Ecclesiasticorum Latinorum*
CSHB	*Corpus Scriptorum Historiae Byzantinae*
LCL	*Loeb Classical Library*
MGH AA	*Monumenta Germaniae Historica. Auctores Antiquissimi*
MGH CM	*Monumenta Germaniae Historica. Chronica Minora*
MGH Form.	*Monumenta Germaniae Historica. Formulae Merovingici et Karolini Aevi*
MGH Poet.	*Monumenta Germaniae Historica. Poetae Latinae Aevi Carolini*
MGH SRM	*Monumenta Germaniae Historica. Scriptores Rerum Merovingicarum*
MGH SRG	*Monumenta Germaniae Historica. Scriptores Rerum Germanicarum*
Ostrogoth.	Barnish, S., and F. Marazzi, eds., *The Ostrogoths from the Migration Period to the Sixth Century: An Ethnographic Perspective* (Woodbridge, 2007)

List of abbreviations

PG	*Patrologia. Cursus Completus, Series Graeca*
Phil. Soc.	A. Smith, ed., *The Philosopher and Society in Late Antiquity* (Swansea, 2005)
PL	*Patrologia Cursus Completus, Series Latina*
PLRE	*Prosopography of the Later Roman Empire*
Teoderic.	*Teoderico Il Grande e I Goti d'Italia: Atti del XIII Congresso Internazionale di Studi sull'Alto Medioevo* (Spoleto, 1993)
TLRE	A. Jones, *The Later Roman Empire, 284–602: A Social, Economic, and Administrative Survey, AD 284–395* (Baltimore, 1964)
TTH	*Translated Texts for Historians*

Unless otherwise noted, all primary sources have been translated by the author.

ACKNOWLEDGEMENTS

This book began with an interest in explaining the dramatic departures of Cassiodorus' epistolary collection, the *Variae*, from other paradigms for the publication of letter collections in ancient and late antique writing. Doing so has required questioning the validity of a number of trusted models for the political, literary and social context of the *Variae*. As a result, this book offers a substantial departure from the *communis opinio* concerning Cassiodorus, the *Variae* and sixth-century Italy. However, for all that is new in this book, much derives from steadily accumulated advances in the understanding of how the ancient literate elite wrote and read epistolary collections, the impact of literature on political culture and the sensitivity of communities to the transmission of political ideas and ideology. Even with the support of new scholarly approaches to old problems, suggesting a new model for understanding Cassiodorus and the *Variae* has required the interest, generous encouragement and frank criticisms of a good many people.

The many accumulated debts incurred while writing this book began with a doctoral thesis at Princeton University, where I benefited immeasurably from the mentorship of Peter Brown and Bob Kaster. Peter Brown combined scholarly wisdom with indefatigable patience in a manner worthy of the very best late antique bishops. Bob Kaster managed the difficult feat of clothing red ink with kindness and respect, and was always available to read Cassiodorus' Latin with me. For their willingness to continue reading and commenting on the book manuscript, I owe a professional debt; for the *humanitas* and friendship, I am grateful at a more personal level. Others read and offered valuable comments on substantial portions of the dissertation, subsequent articles or the manuscript itself. Among these, I am especially grateful to Clifford Ando, Celia Chazelle, Gerda Heydemann, Bill Jordan, Michael Maas, Volker Menze, James O'Donnell, Ralph Mathisen, Michele Salzman, Bryan Ward-Perkins and Ian Wood. For conversations, comments on more specialized points and friendly encouragement, I should also like to thank Jonas Bjørnebye, Kim Bowes, Thomas Brown, Averil Cameron, Maurizio Campanelli,

Acknowledgements

Alexandra Chavarría, Christopher Chinn, Kate Cooper, Damian Hernandez, Kristine Iara, Rita Lizzi, Barbara Naddeo, Manu Radhakrishnan, Andrew Riggsby, Carly Steinborn and Philipp von Rummel.

The American Academy at Rome provided funding and incomparable hospitality during the last year in which I worked on the manuscript; the Arthur and Janet Ross Library at the Academy, and the many friendly denizens of that library, were particularly indispensable. During the year in Rome I was also fortunate enough to benefit from audiences at a number of colloquia where I presented work from the manuscript. I should like to thank Bryan Ward-Perkins and Volker Menze for generous invitations to speak, respectively, at Trinity College, Oxford, and at the Central European University, Budapest. I am also especially grateful to Turid Seim and Katariina Mustakallio for organizing an excellent series of seminars at the Norwegian and Finnish Institutes of Rome, where I was able to present research.

The completion of this book owes as much to the careful attention that it received in its final stages as it does to those who provided initial advice and inspiration: Rosamond McKitterick has been a tireless editor, an insightful commentator and, more importantly, a persuasive source of encouragement without whom this book would probably still languish under the tyranny of Horace's dictum.

Finally, I dedicate this book to my four Muses – my wife and our three daughters. There is no proper recompense for the time that they cheerfully sacrificed that I might write this book.

PART I

The Variae *as windows onto painted curtains*

INTRODUCTION

Sometime in the late 560s a group of artisans carefully removed, tessera by tessera, the portraits of more than a dozen people from the mosaics flanking the nave of Sant'Apollinare Nuovo in Ravenna. These mosaics portray, on the south wall, the palace (*palatium*) of the Amal king Theoderic conflated with a profile of the urban landscape of Ravenna and, on the north wall, a profile of the nearby suburb of Classe. The figures removed from the two mosaics originally held ideologically key positions before the city gates of Ravenna and Classe and within the colonnaded arches of the *palatium*. In their stead, the mosaicists filled the vacancies of the portals and arches with mosaics portraying draperies and coloured brick. Only disembodied hands, extending beyond the altered zones, and palimpsest shadows of the former figures remained to remind the audience that earlier associations had been expunged from the church.[1] These new empty spaces represent carefully arranged fields of rhetorical communication that have much to tell about the political, religious and cultural realities confronting their contemporary audience.

Built and consecrated early in the reign of Theoderic (491–526), a so-called barbarian king of the Arian Christian sect, Sant'Apollinare Nuovo was a monumental public space that would accumulate contradictory associations over the course of the first half of the sixth century.[2] Through its physical proximity to the *palatium* of Theoderic in the heart of Ravenna, the church in the first stage of its history contributed to the celebration of Amal governance in Italy. The figures previously visible in the architectural spaces of the nave mosaics (including a portrait of Theoderic and a dedicatory inscription bearing his name) signified the close association between political and religious conceptions of the late

---

[1] On this function of *damnatio memoriae*, Hedrick, *History*; Urbano, 'Donation', 71–110; Flower, *Forgetting*.

[2] In general on Sant'Apollinare Nuovo, Deliyannis, *Ravenna*, 146–74; on the deletions of iconography and portraits sponsored by the Amals, 164–72.

antique state.[3] After 540, when Justinian's soldiers entered Ravenna and initiated what would become a long period of eastern imperial control of the city, it became necessary to detach the church from the obvious celebration of the political successes of the Amal dynasty. The need for this intervention in public memory did not become imperative until after 554, when Justinian's *Constitutio Pragmatica* finally declared eastern imperial victory in what had been nearly two decades of war in Italy (the Gothic War). Thus, late in the 560s, the bishop of Ravenna, Agnellus, rededicated the church in the name of St Martin and systematically removed images identifiable with Amal rule.[4] For those who might have remembered the significance of the original figures, such a *damnatio memoriae* served as a reminder that the Amals, despite their success under Theoderic, had ultimately failed as a political and dynastic regime. The erasure privileged a competing interpretation of the Amals by which they were understood as heterodox Christians who had subjected Italy to 'barbarian' rule. The curtained empty zones of mosaic in Sant'Apollinare Nuovo illustrate how the clear stamp of Theoderic's success as a ruler, visible elsewhere throughout the city in its architectural fabric, was reimpressed on Ravenna as the legacy of barbaric despotism that had been conquered by the eastern Roman Empire.

The nave mosaics at Sant'Apollinare Nuovo testify to the ability of late antique media to present communicative silences. They offer an interesting analogue to the proper subject of this study – the collection of legal and administrative letters that Cassiodorus compiled as the *Variae*. The altered mosaics of Sant'Apollinare and the letters of the *Variae* have much in common as 'windows onto painted curtains'. Each in its own way represents a response to the polemic surrounding the postwar reputation of Amal rule in Italy. In fact, this study will argue that the *Variae* act as a piece of polemical literature in a manner comparable to that of the visual medium of the mosaics. Where the mosaics literally opened windows onto painted curtains to obscure a previous ideological message, the individual letters of the *Variae* operate as tesserae in the production of a composite image that also functions as an ideological curtain or screen. In the preface to his heavily abridged translation of the *Variae*, Thomas Hodgkin in 1886 vented his frustration at attempting to penetrate the opacity of the letters by stating, 'The curtain is the picture.'[5] This description characterized for Hodgkin the difficulty entailed in understanding, in its own terms, the performance of sixth-century history that he encountered in the *Variae*. What Hodgkin wanted in

[3] Agnellus, *Liber Pontificalis Ecclesiae Ravennatis* 85–9.
[4] Wood, 'Theoderic's monuments', 252–60; Deliyannis, 'St. Martin'.   [5] Hodgkin, *Letters*, vi.

the *Variae* was a window into the day-to-day operation of the state in sixth-century Italy. What he found was a culturally specific performance. This study suggests that reading the *Variae* is considerably more complicated than translating the surface rhetoric and bureaucratic jargon of a late antique chancery. Rather, the collection represents Cassiodorus' attempt to construct a composite image of Amal rule in Italy for a particular audience. In this sense, the *Variae* are an attempt at literary portraiture which responds to events and conditions at a particular moment in Cassiodorus' career. Much as the later artisans of Sant'Apollinare preserved some features of the original mosaic programme (the architecture of the *palatium* and urban profiles of Ravenna and Classe), introduced features to create a new programmatic statement (twin processions of martyrs and saints) and effaced other elements entirely (Theoderic and members of his court), Cassiodorus too engaged in a revisionist presentation of Italy under the Amals by selectively preserving, enhancing and deleting from the historical reality that the letters purport to represent.

The *Variae* comprise 468 documents that Cassiodorus arranged in twelve books.[6] As a collection of dispositive letters (legal judgments and administrative directives), the *Variae* treat an almost panoptic range of official activities: appointment to public offices, the collection of taxes and the management of state property, criminal cases and civil disputes, the maintenance of urban amenities, and the diplomatic correspondence of Amal rulers to eastern emperors and other so-called barbarian rulers. Taken as a whole, the *Variae* span more than thirty years of Cassiodorus' activities as an intimate member of the palatine service attached to the Amal court.[7] The presumably official nature of the collection, its chronological breadth and the rich range of materials contained within the individual letters have made the *Variae* a prized source for scholars concerned with early sixth-century Italy. The *Variae* have been prominent in studies of political and ecclesiastical affairs, fiscal and legal administration, urban life and rural production, barbarian ethnogenesis and the transmission of classicism. Yet it must be emphasized that the *Variae* are also among the most idiosyncratic of late antique epistolary collections.[8] Typical epistolary collections take the form of personal letters directed by a

---

[6] See Fridh, *Opera*; O'Donnell, *Cassiodorus*; Pferschy, *Formular*; Krautschick, *Cassiodore*; Viscido, *Studi*; MacPherson, *Rome*; Barnish, *Cassiodorus*, xiv–liii; Jouanaud, 'Pour qui Cassiodore', 721–41; Gillett, 'Cassiodorus' *Variae*', 37–50; Kakridi, *Cassiodors Variae*; Giardina, *Cassiodoro*; Bjornlie, 'A reappraisal', 143–71.

[7] The letters purportedly represent Cassiodorus' official correspondence as quaestor, *magister officiorum* and praetorian prefect under, successively, the rulers Theoderic, Athalaric and Amalasuntha, Theodahad and Witigis.

[8] Note the apt description of O'Donnell, *Cassiodorus*, 86.

single author to members of a wider community of correspondents. The *Variae*, however, contain presumably official governmental documents. The edicts, judicial responses, diplomatic letters and administrative *formulae* written in the names of various Ostrogothic rulers have the appearance of a résumé of the Ravenna chancery. As an additional departure from the norm, Cassiodorus addressed two prefaces (opening Books I and II) to the audience of the *Variae* and he attached to the collection a treatise on the soul (the *De anima*), the preface of which continues Cassiodorus' previous address to the audience of the *Variae*.[9] This level of direct interaction with an intended audience is not found in earlier epistolary collections. The combination of documentary material with what is essentially a philosophical inquiry into the source of wisdom (the *De anima*) similarly lacks a precedent. Furthermore, Cassiodorus embedded within the letters of the *Variae* an encyclopaedic range of digressive material. Individual letters contain excursuses pertaining to everything from the behaviour of animals, the motion of stars and the nature of music, to the origins of writing, the history of law and the accomplishments of engineering. In terms of their formal structure as a collection and the content of individual letters, the *Variae* are as unprecedented among epistolary collections as they are among bureaucratic writing and legal literature. Cassiodorus' authorship is uncontested. What remains problematic and debatable is the extent to which the letters represent the mode of expression characteristic of the Ostrogothic chancery rather than Cassiodorus' own agenda.[10]

This book suggests that the letters represent a documentary record of the Ravenna chancery which Cassiodorus later subjected to heavy revision reflecting the political exigencies that attended the fall of the Amal court during the Gothic War. In particular, this book suggests that Cassiodorus drew heavily upon themes of the political discourse of Constantinople at a time when it seemed that the eastern imperial control of Italy was imminent and his own social and political position had suddenly become quite precarious.[11] From Cassiodorus' perspective during the opening stages of the Gothic War, the protraction of the conflict to almost two decades (535–54) and the total fragmentation of political power in Italy in the aftermath could not have been foreseen.

It was in this period, during the late 530s and early 540s, that the *Variae* were politically relevant, not during the preceding decades when Cassiodorus first penned the original letters in fulfilment of various

---

[9] Cassiodorus later referred to the *De anima* as the thirteenth book of the *Variae*, *Expositio Psalmorum* 145.2.
[10] See Fridh, *Terminologie*, 1–5.　　[11] Compare McKitterick, 'Roman history', 21–9.

public offices. It was as a collection that the *Variae* had the potential to make an intervention in how eastern imperial victory in Italy might impose a reinterpretation of the previous fifty years of Ostrogothic governance. This book will suggest that the object of the *Variae* was the political rehabilitation of the Italian elite who had served as the palatine bureaucracy of the Amals. The book will claim that, in essence, the *Variae* are an apologetic work intended to counter the notion that the former palatine elite served a 'barbarian' regime. The collection aimed to demonstrate their suitability to return to a role in the government at Ravenna. This study examines how Cassiodorus positioned a number of ideologically charged themes in the letters of the *Variae* to demonstrate that suitability. These were themes deployed in a contemporary moral and legal discourse concerning proper governance at a time when it appeared that there was still a possibility of creating a political framework in Italy that would include the former bureaucratic elite of Ravenna. More importantly, this study will suggest that Cassiodorus' portrayal of western palatine service in the *Variae* engaged in a debate about the proper definition of imperial rule emerging from the polemical discourse surrounding the reign of Justinian. The sources that Cassiodorus drew upon in order to construct an idealized persona of state service originated not only in Italy, but also in Constantinople. As we shall see, much of the digressive material that Cassiodorus included in the letters (for which the collection received its name) provided anchor points for the polemical themes of an apologetic project that was responsive to political conditions at the eastern capital.

Therefore, rather than a collection of entirely genuine artefacts from the Ostrogothic chancery, this book argues that the *Variae* represent a literary enterprise. At a point when it became clear that the Gothic War would irrevocably alter the terms by which the palatine elite of Ravenna enjoyed its status, Cassiodorus selected, edited and arranged letters from a pre-existing assemblage in order to represent his contribution to the government at Ravenna. He interpolated select letters with thematic digressions and, in some cases, even invented new letters. Thus, although much of the material in the collection does indeed correspond to the actual political and cultural conditions of Ostrogothic Italy, specific themes found in the collection represent Cassiodorus' later intervention in the public record of the Ostrogothic regime and more properly correspond to the period when the Gothic War was drawing a new social, economic and political map for Italy. Rather than a privileged window into the experiment of a post-Roman 'barbarian' regime, the *Variae* are, in fact, a window into the impressive range of cultural and political communication between the new sixth-century states of the western

Mediterranean and the continued embodiment of the Roman Empire at Constantinople.[12] The differences between Italy and the eastern empire (social, political, economic, religious) were substantial enough at the advent of the Gothic War that Cassiodorus could only offer a favourable portrayal of western palatine service by adapting that portrayal to certain norms of the eastern imperial capital, such as had not been current in Italy. Thus the *Variae* also offer a lens through which to observe the interaction of politics, religion, philosophy and literature between the eastern and western Mediterranean.

[12] For a recent example of the range of Mediterranean communications in this period, Conant, 'Mediterranean communications', 1–46.

Chapter 1

CASSIODORUS AND ITALY IN THE FIFTH AND SIXTH CENTURIES

EMPIRE IN THE SIXTH CENTURY

In the early 590s a late contemporary of Cassiodorus, Gregory of Tours, reflected on the events of the previous three centuries and observed that 'a great many things have been happening', both matters that were well ordered by traditional probity (*rectae*) and those unacquainted with the guidance of virtue (*improbae*).[1] Gregory deplored the capricious savagery of kings, the impudence of heretics and the penury of learning that had come to replace the attainments of a former age. In this way, he viewed his own society as a consequence of dramatic decline. Gregory used this grim portrayal of decline, found in the preface of his *Decem libri historiarum*, to realize a new definition for sixth-century society based on the church and the vigour of orthodox faith which, for him, represented the last strand of continuity with former times. Gregory's capacity for rhetorical hyperbole has been duly noted in modern scholarship and his history stands as but one of many literary projects in a long tradition extending from Livy and Sallust that portrayed cultural crisis.[2] At the same time, Gregory's rhetorical stage-setting also captures something very real in what it meant for Mediterranean society in the sixth century to have been the heir to centuries of Roman *imperium*. For many of the post-classical elite like Gregory, the sixth century was a vantage point from which the peak of past grandeur and the uglier senectitude of that past were both visible. Of course, the same may also be said of nearly any period within the long sweep of Roman history. Cato, Tacitus and Boethius probably all thought themselves equally justified as 'the last of the true Romans', albeit Romans defined in very different terms. Thus Gregory and his contemporaries were a part of a truly *longue durée* in which the portrayal of cultural decline was a stock piece of the cultural performance by which a literate elite promoted themselves as

---

[1] Gregory of Tours, *Decem Libri Historiarum, praefatio.*
[2] Goffart, *Narrators*; James, 'Gregory of Tours'; Heinzelmann, *Gregory of Tours*; Mitchell and Wood, *World of Gregory.*

conservators of an authentic *romanitas*. However, it is important to note that interpreting the significance of over 1,000 years of Roman past was a contentious activity. Contemporaries did not doubt that their society was in some significant way a legacy of Roman empire, but the terms defining what it meant to be a society in the tradition of Roman Empire was open to challenge.

In the east, Constantinople stood in the fullest flower of its role as an imperial capital, boasting the largest urban population in the Mediterranean and drawing on the resources of an economy that could trace lines to commercial contact with Persia, India and China.[3] Eastern Mediterranean cities shared common elements of a largely Christian Hellenic culture and the urban elite classes accepted, and even competed for, a participatory role in the political rituals of an imperial state that was still ideologically Roman. Indeed, the eastern Mediterranean society of the early sixth century had achieved the kind of cultural and political integration not even found under emperors of the Pax Romana. The emperor who received acclamation in the *kathisma* of the Hippodrome, in the great churches and in the palace of Constantinople represented an idea that was still universally accepted in the Mediterranean as the apex of political rule in the civilized world. So-called barbarian peoples, including the sophisticated Sasanian Empire to the east, regularly submitted gestures of deference to this sublime realization of perfect empire. This, of course, is the perspective regularly promoted by the imperial court. The reality of eastern Mediterranean society was decidedly more complicated. For example, it is hardly possible to speak of the eastern empire as a unified Christian empire. Although the emperors had long forsaken traditional Roman cults, many Christians in the east (including the emperor) had difficulty agreeing on who was properly Christian.[4] So-called paganism, which had not enjoyed a legal face since Theodosius in the late fourth century, throve in surprisingly public quarters. Above all, the so-called barbarians, especially the Sasanians, applied far more leverage on the imperial court than any self-respecting emperor could admit. Even the so-called Roman army of the east was regularly composed of Goths, Herulians, Huns, Isaurians and Armenians. What made these soldiers Roman was the regular receipt of the emperor's gold solidus.[5] The portrayal of a monolithic eastern imperial culture in the historical sources for the early sixth century is often quite distinct from

---

[3] Daryaee, 'Persian Gulf', 1–16; Morony, 'Economic boundaries', 166–94; Whittaker, *Rome*, 163–80.

[4] Chazelle and Cubitt, *Crisis Oik.*; Menze, *Justinian.*

[5] Lee, 'Empire at war', 113–33; Rance, 'Narses', 424–72; Heather, '*Foedera*'.

how the societies of the eastern Mediterranean actually behaved. Yet the governing elite of predominantly Greek-speaking Constantinople would call themselves Romans with enthusiastic confidence well into the four-teenth century, perpetuating a very rhetorical performance of imperial power.

In the west, by contrast, the Roman Empire had followed a different trajectory. After becoming an effectively separate empire with the death of Theodosius in 395, the western provinces accommodated themselves to changing social, economic and political conditions in a complex pro-cess once commonly (and misleadingly) referred to as 'decline and fall', although now more often discussed in more nuanced terms of the 'trans-formation' of the Roman world.[6] Throughout the course of the fifth century, the direct influence of imperial power in Italy contracted and local provincial elites negotiated the formation of independent regional forms of political power. These new regimes were often based on ele-ments of the fragmented western Roman military or on concentrations of immigrant settlers ('barbarians') who at some point had assumed the role of the Roman military.[7] By the end of the fifth century, Italy itself would bear the indelible stamp of these processes of social, economic and political change. Where once the great villas of elite landowners marked Italy as the epicentre of trans-Mediterranean consumerism, the countryside of the late fifth century was increasingly fragmented by new patterns of abandonment and resettlement that often lacked the tradi-tional orientation toward urban markets.[8] Where the local *curiae* of Italian cities and towns had played an integral role in maintaining a fiscal econ-omy and in sustaining a vibrant habit of endowing the urban fabric, the local church and its bishop were increasingly the focus of urban organi-zation, economic activity and local patronage.[9] Where Roman legions had previously defined imperial frontiers beyond the Alps with their encampments, immigrant settlers recruited for military service (federated soldiers) now lived as ad hoc militias in both towns and the countryside.[10]

---

[6] MacMullen, *Corruption*; Ward-Perkins, 'Continuists, catastrophists', 157–76; Liebeschuetz, *Decline*; Heather, *The Fall*; Ward-Perkins, *The Fall*; O'Donnell, *The Ruin*.

[7] Halsall, 'Childeric's grave'.

[8] For bibliography, Cavarría and Lewit, 'Bibliographical essay', 3–51; also Christie, 'Landscapes', 256–75; Marazzi, 'Late antique Italies', 119–59; Francovich and Hodges, *Transformation*; Christie, *Archaeology*.

[9] Pietri, 'Aristocratie', 417–67; Ward-Perkins, *Building*; Lizzi, *Vescovi*; Wataghin, 'Christianization', 209–34; Liebeschuetz, *Decline*, 104–36; Barnish, 'Religio', 387–402; Christie, *Archaeology*; Cooper and Hillner, *Religion*; Bowes, *Private Worship*; Lizzi, *Conversione*.

[10] Barnish, 'Taxation', 170–95; Heather, 'Fourth-century'; Durliat, 'Cité', 153–79; Heather, 'Foed-era', 292–308; note also Vegetius, *Epitoma rei militaris* 1.7, 1.20, 1.21, 2.3 and 2.18, on the disappearance of field training indicative of a standing army.

In Rome, the Senate still presided over local public life and an annually appointed consul celebrated public games at the Circus and Colosseum, but the urban population had long since contracted to well under half that of its height and the political governance of Italy had long since passed to Ravenna, where the last in a series of federated soldiers (today referred to as the Ostrogoths) held power.[11]

The Ostrogoths arrived in Italy in 489 after well over a generation of previous service as immigrant recruits to the eastern imperial army.[12] The stage for their expedition to Italy had been set by the complicated and fluid military culture of the eastern empire in which military commanders in the provinces competed for the preferment of the emperor in Constantinople. Negotiations with the eastern emperor Zeno cleared the way for Theoderic the Amal to enter Italy with a substantial contingent of Goths. After deposing the previous military ruler of Italy (Odoacer) in 491, the Goths settled throughout northern and central Italy with Theoderic as their king at Ravenna.[13] The social, political and economic landscape of Italy was substantially different from that of the Balkans and Constantinople, not least because Italy had two cultural and political capitals: Rome and Ravenna. Nonetheless, the Goths attempted to erect a regime that maintained the rhetorical style of Roman imperial government.[14] They were assisted in this endeavour by selectively recruiting from the Italian landowning elite to serve at the palatine court of Ravenna, where they received office and status. In most cases, these palatine Italians were drawn from municipal origins.[15] By contrast, the Amal court at Ravenna showed a studied deference to the senatorial aristocracy of Rome and, for the greater part, relegated the senatorial elite to the maintenance of the ancient capital.[16] It is important to note

[11] Ruggini, *Economia*; Chastagnol, review, 210–12; Chastagnol, *Le Sénat*; Wes, *Kaisertums*; Cecconi, *Governo*; Wickham, review, 238–9; Honoré, *Law*, 1–29; Marazzi, 'Rome in transition', 21–39; MacGeorge, *Warlords*; Ghilardi, Goddard and Porena, *Cités*; Halsall, *Migrations*, 220–83; McEvoy, 'Imperial office'.

[12] On Goths in the eastern empire, Wolfram, *Goths*; Heather, *Goths*; Heather, 'Roman Balkans', 163–90.

[13] On the arrival of Ostrogoths in Italy, Ennodius of Pavia, *Panegyricus* 6.23–8.47; Procopius, *Wars* 5.1.2–31; *Excerpta Valesiana* 36–57; Jordanes, *Getica* 268–95; on their settlement, Bierbrauer, *Italien*; Settia, 'Fortificazioni'; Vera, 'Proprietà'.

[14] Momigliano, 'Italian culture', 207–36; Jones, 'Odoacer and Theoderic', 126–30; Burns, *Ostrogoths*; Brown, *Byzantine Italy*, 77–99; Moorhead, *Theoderic*; Barnwell, *Roman West*; Heather, 'Ostrogothic Italy', 317–53; Heather, 'Theodoric', 145–73; Amory, *Ostrogothic Italy*; Heather, 'Roman and Goth', 86–134; Halsall, *Migrations*, 284–338; Barnish, '*Cuncto Italiae*', 317–37; Kitchen, 'Italia and Graecia', 116–19.

[15] Barnish, '*Cuncto Italiae*', 328.

[16] Cassiodorus, *Variae* 7.31, indicates that the *princeps urbis romae* and his staff served in residence at Rome as the representatives of Amal authority; the core of the administrative and military apparatus of the Amals was housed in Ravenna.

that for many living in Italy in the early sixth century, although the ruler
in Ravenna was a king of the Goths, he was also a Christian, a former
Roman general from the Balkans, a former consul in Constantinople,
and an adopted son of the emperor with patrician status who spoke
Latin and probably understood Greek; in other words, there was very
little to differentiate him from many previous emperors of the fourth and
fifth centuries.[17] If the governmental apparatus of sixth-century Ravenna
seemed decidedly different in comparison with the eastern empire, this
was the result of nearly a century of political and economic change in
Italy which the Ostrogoths inherited; it was not the result of Ostrogothic 'barbarization'. It is true that the Amal government in Ravenna
would institute a number of their own governmental innovations, but
these merely formalized previous adaptations in the political and economic environment of Italy that were already well advanced.[18] From the
account of evidence pertaining to late fifth- and early sixth-century Italy,
although the political arrangements between the senatorial aristocracy
of Rome and the Amal court of Ravenna could be strained at times,
Theoderic and his immediate successors, Athalaric and Amalasuntha,
maintained a remarkably stable political regime.

CASSIODORUS AND THE GOTHIC WAR

When sixth-century Italy did finally experience sudden and disruptive
upheaval, it was the result of a startlingly aggressive vision of imperial
power that had taken shape in Constantinople with the accession of Justinian as the new eastern emperor.[19] As a continuation of his recently successful campaign against the Vandals in North Africa, Justinian attempted
to restore territory controlled by the Amals to the Eastern Empire.[20]
In 535, the eastern commander, Belisarius, crossed to Italy from North

---

[17] On Theoderic's political background, *PLRE II*, 1077–84; concerning Greek, Ennodius of Pavia,
Panegyricus 3.11, 'educavit te in gremio civilitatis Graecia praesaga venturi'; Cassiodorus, *Variae*
11.1.6, notes that Theoderic's daughter was learned in Latin, Greek and Gothic; for Theoderic as
an emperor, the triple-solidus medallion of Theoderic bears the inscription '*Rex Theodericus Pius
Prin(ceps) I(nvictus) S(emper)*'; epigraphic evidence from Terracina refers to Theoderic as *Princeps*
and *Augustus*, *CIL* 10.1, 690–1.

[18] For example, the frequent use of Gothic *saiones* as agents with unusually diverse competence,
Cassiodorus, *Variae* 2.4, 2.13, 2.20, 3.20, 3.48, 4.14, 4.27, 4.32, 4.34, 4.47, 5.5, 5.10, 5.19, 5.20,
5.23, 5.27, 8.24, 8.27, 9.2, 9.14, 9.18, 12.3; on the *saiones*, Morosi, '*Saiones*', 150–65; on other
administrative changes, Sinnigen, 'Administrative shifts', 457–66; Morosi, '*Comitiaci*', 77–111;
Barnish, '*Cuncto Italiae*', 322–4; Lafferty, 'Law', 337–64.

[19] For the ideological purpose of Justinian's military, legal and religious activities, Meier, *Zeitalter
Justinians*; Millar, 'Rome, Constantinople', 62–8.

[20] Hannestad, 'Guerre Gothique', 136–83; Evans, *Justinian*, 126–82; Amory, *Ostrogothic Italy*, 165–
92; Bodel, 'Asbadus', 91–100.

Africa and initiated a series of victories that included accepting, or in some cases forcing, the submission of Sicily, Bruttium and Naples.[21] The Gothic nobility responded to these successes by murdering the current Amal king, Theodahad, whose lack of decisiveness they attributed to negotiations with Justinian for a private settlement.[22] Afterwards, the army elevated Witigis as the new king of the Goths.[23] Witigis formalized his association with the Amal dynasty by marrying the granddaughter of Theoderic (Matasuntha) at Ravenna, despite the fact that, as Procopius claims, Matasuntha was not a willing bride. By this time, Belisarius had already entered Rome and accepted the submission of the remaining southern Italian provinces and Samnium. Belisarius entered Rome in December of 536.

When Witigis arrived at Rome with his army in February of 537, he initiated what would become a year-long siege in an attempt to dislodge Belisarius' army.[24] The siege of Rome represented the first consequential event in Justinian's protracted attempt to restore Italy to eastern imperial control and it was one of the more dramatic and perhaps symbolic events of the eighteen-year war. It is only by accident that the forces who defended Rome were Byzantine soldiers and citizens of the city. It could easily have been the Gothic army in Rome which previously, during the course of nearly fifty years, had maintained stability in Italy by defending Rome against Byzantine aggression. The irony of the situation was certainly not lost on the event's chief narrator, Procopius, who found a rich opportunity to reduce the siege to one of the timeless heroic conflicts between Roman and barbarian that had all the ideological consequence of the famous sieges of the Gauls of Brennus in 390 BC or Alaric's Goths in AD 410. Procopius reported that for a year and nine days the Goths conducted operations against nearly twelve miles of Rome's mural fortifications.[25] In keeping with the tradition of ancient historiography, the drama of cultural conflict between Romans and barbarians was inflated with grossly exaggerated numbers. According to Procopius' *Wars*, scarcely more than 5,000 Byzantine troops managed to repel over 150,000 Goths from sagging and hastily rebuilt mural fortifications. Procopius noted that no less than sixty-nine armed engagements tested the martial vigour of Belisarius' soldiers.[26] Procopius further mobilized a number of stock motifs recognizable to his audience from earlier episodes of Rome's past that communicated how this siege represented but one conflict in an extended history in which Roman

---

[21] Procopius, *Wars* 5.4–7.   [22] Procopius, *Wars* 5.11.1.   [23] Procopius, *Wars* 5.11.5.
[24] Procopius, *Wars* 5.14–21.   [25] Procopius, *Wars* 6.10.13.
[26] Procopius, *Wars* 5.5.2–5, 5.14.15, 5.16.11, 5.24.3, 6.2.37.

culture weathered the threat of barbarism. For example, in contrast to their overwhelming numbers, the Goths possessed little knowledge of military science, one of the staples of past Roman successes. According to Procopius, the personal armature of the Goths was inferior and the king was ridiculously ignorant of siegecraft.[27] Further emphasizing the antiquity of this cultural struggle, Procopius claimed that anxiety over the Gothic threat to the city compelled a number of the Roman citizens to prize open the doors of the Temple of Janus and some even attempted to consult the long-inefficacious Sibylline texts. The parallel to similar events during Alaric's siege of 410 are probably not incidental.[28] The fact that Procopius dedicated more space to describing the year-long siege at Rome than to any other conflict in the Persian, Vandalic or Gothic wars suggests that the event was ideologically significant and warranted literary embellishment.[29] The rhetorical handling of the conflict presents but one example in a wider assemblage of sixth-century literature of how the precarious military situation in Italy encouraged witnesses and later commentators to rewrite the character of the Amal state.

For witnesses of these events such as Procopius and Cassiodorus, the rapid breakdown of old compromises upon which the political stability of Italy had been based only confirmed how the idea of previous prosperity under the Amals was now open to reinterpretation. The rejection of Witigis' overture for peace during the siege of Rome provoked the Gothic king to order the slaughter of Roman senatorial hostages held at Ravenna, an act that would have deepened the rift between supporters of the Amals and those sympathetic to eastern imperial power in Italy. Complicating lines of loyalty even further, Milan and Liguria seceded to the eastern imperial cause and Matasuntha reportedly offered a treasonous proposal to one of Belisarius' commanders.[30] When Witigis finally withdrew from Rome in March of 538, the theatre of war had expanded throughout central and northern Italy. In the following year, siege warfare continued as the primary pattern of conflict and Italian towns committed to the cause of both the Goths and the eastern empire experienced privation and reversals of loyalty. Tuscany, Ariminum, Pavia, Milan, Urbino and Aemilia each in turn became the focus of siege operations.[31] Procopius described the impact of the war's

---

[27] Procopius, *Wars* 5.21.1–5.22.11; also 5.27.15–29.

[28] Cf. Procopius, *Wars* 5.24.28–31 and 5.25.18–25; Rutilius Namatianus, *De reditu suo* 2.52; Zosimus, *Nova Historia* 5.38.

[29] Procopius allocated twenty-three chapters to the siege of Rome, *Wars* 5.17–6.10; cf. much shorter treatments of the sieges of Edessa, 2.12–13; Daras, 2.27–28; Nisibis, 2.18–19; Mount Papua, 4.6–7; Naples, 5.8–11; Ravenna, 6.28–29.

[30] Procopius, *Wars* 6.10.11 and 6.28.26.   [31] Procopius, *Wars* 6.11–20.

expansion in vivid detail, noting the disruption of cultivation, the displacement of urban populations and famine.[32] The combination of famine and military defeats at Auximum and Dertona eventually confined Witigis to Ravenna, where he capitulated in 540.[33] Soon after, Belisarius transported Witigis and his followers to Constantinople, where captured Goths featured in the choreography of Belisarius' triumphal procession. Having received the patrician dignity from Justinian, Witigis lived as an honoured guest in Constantinople until his death a few years later. Matasuntha likewise maintained honoured status at the eastern capital and later married Justinian's cousin Germanus, a union that some at the eastern capital regarded as having the potential to improve the current political climate.[34]

Even after the capture of Ravenna and the end of the Amal dynasty, the Goths of Italy could still produce an effective king after the stamp of Theoderic. The accession of Totila in 541 dramatically reversed eastern imperial successes throughout the Italian peninsula. These reversals, which included the complete sack of Rome in 546, prevented political boundaries and loyalties from stabilizing for the next decade until the Gothic defeat at Busta Gallorum in 552.[35] Social, political and economic dislocation became recurrent in Italy. Justininian's *Constitutio Pragmatica* indicates just how troubled this period had been. In addition to declaring the final eastern imperial victory in 554, the *Constitutio Pragmatica* also attempted to resolve widespread confusion concerning property ownership, one of the surest indications of societal instability.[36] Without a doubt, many of these problems were the direct result of military conflict. However, equal culpability lay with the eastern magistrates sent to Italy who extorted the Italian population in order to pay the eastern army.[37] As a result, loyalties that recurrently shifted to either the Gothic or imperial cause were another feature of the war.[38] In the face of such dramatic social, political and economic change to the landscape of Italy, it is hardly surprising that members of the former palatine elite such as Cassiodorus should have concern for the manner in which

---

[32] Procopius, *Wars* 6.20.   [33] Procopius, *Wars* 6.23–30.

[34] On Germanus, *PLRE III*, 527; referring to the son of Matasuntha and Germanus, Jordanes, *Getica* 314, 'in quo coniuncta Aniciorum gens cum Amala stirpe spem adhuc utriusque generi domino praestante promitit'.

[35] On Totila and the war, *PLRE III*, 1328–33; Rance, 'Narses', 424–72; Procopius, *Wars* 7.2–40.

[36] Moorhead, 'Totila', 385–6, on the *Constitutio* as an indication of social dislocation during the war; Amory, *Ostrogothic Italy*, 149–51, on the problems of property ownership during the war; for a more summary description of the economic disruption, Everett, *Literacy*, 15–19.

[37] Procopius, *Anecdota* 18.13–22.

[38] Procopius, *Wars* 7.4.13–18, 7.5.19, 7.9.1–6, 7.11.1–10, 7.23.1, 7.36.7, 7.39.21–24.

the war would distort the memory of their contribution to a previous era of relative prosperity in Italy.

This, at least, was how Cassiodorus viewed matters. Less than a decade after the conclusion of the Gothic War, while writing the introduction to his *Institutions*, Cassiodorus recalled the 'raging wars and violent struggles' that had prevented him, in collaboration with Pope Agapetus, from founding a school dedicated to Christian and secular teaching at Rome. Cassiodorus' pointed remembrance reveals how the Gothic War had been a genuine cultural crisis for many people in sixth-century Italy:

When I realized that there was such a zealous and eager pursuit of secular learning, by which the majority of mankind hopes to obtain knowledge of this world, I was deeply grieved, I admit, that Holy Scripture should so lack public teachers, whereas secular authors certainly flourish in widespread teaching. Together with blessed Pope Agapetus of Rome, I made efforts to collect money so that it should rather be the Christian schools in the city of Rome that could employ learned teachers [of secular learning] . . . from whom the faithful might gain eternal salvation for their souls and the adornment of sober and pure eloquence for their speech . . . But since I could not accomplish this task because of raging wars and violent struggles in the kingdom of Italy – for a peaceful endeavour has no place in a time of unrest – I was moved by divine love to devise for you, with God's help, these introductory books to take the place of a teacher.[39]

Distance and loss are palpable elements of Cassiodorus' lament. Rather than providing an institution that would have allowed the synthesis of two ancient sources of wisdom at Rome, Cassiodorus could only offer the *Institutions* as a token voice from his remote exile at Vivarium, where he founded a monastic community on his family estates in southern Bruttium (on the seashore near Scyllaceum, modern Squillace).[40] The sense of cultural crisis becomes even more profound given that Cassiodorus had been praetorian prefect at the time of his plans to found the school with Agapetus. For Cassiodorus, the school represented a lost opportunity for the political and religious elite to agree upon a programme of renewed learning. Instead, the eastern imperial intervention forcibly redefined Italy as a post-Roman region that had succumbed to 'barbarization' as opposed to a state capable of realizing a cultural ideal.[41]

The very notion that the eastern empire should reclaim Italy implied that the governmental and religious traditions of the western empire had

---

[39] Cassiodorus, *Institutiones, praefatio* 1, trans. Halporn, *TTH*, 105.
[40] On Vivarium, Cappuyns, 'Cassiodore', 1359–61; O'Donnell, *Cassiodorus*, 177–222; Barnish, 'Cassiodorus after conversion', 157–87.
[41] Cf. Amory, *Ostrogothic Italy*, 135–47.

fallen into desuetude. Justinian's broader programme of imperial restoration (*renovatio*) required the repatriation of Italy to an original source of imperial authority. In a very real sense, Italy faced an event in which its recent past was to be reinterpreted by the rival imperial narratives of Constantinople.[42] Indeed, propaganda emerging from Justinian's court prior to the Gothic War went so far as to assign the moment of the western political 'fall' to the deposition of Romulus Augustus in 476, a designation that made Justinian's conquest long overdue.[43] This justification for war posed a direct threat to the legitimacy of a full generation of the Italian elite who had maintained the state by working with rulers who styled themselves according to the traditions of the late Roman political and military culture.

It is true that a dramatic transition to a post-classical society had definitely occurred in Italy prior to the Gothic War. But this was an incremental process of concessions and adaptations initiated well before the arrival of the Ostrogoths in 489. The previous century had witnessed a nearly continuous process in which the Italian peninsula accommodated itself to narrower political, economic and social horizons. That process of accommodation involved adopting new political, economic and social forms that would eventually distance Italy as a society, in many ways strikingly so, from Constantinople and the eastern empire.[44] It is important to emphasize, however, that the sundering of Italy from the imperial culture of the east had not been the result of 'barbarian' settlement in Italy, nor was it a result of the form of government established by the Amals in Ravenna. Nevertheless, the reconquest of Italy initiated by Justinian in 535 exposed Italy's departure from its earlier imperial past at a moment when those actors who had participated in the accommodation of Italy to a new political environment under the Ostrogoths were at their most vulnerable.

Cassiodorus was prominent among the Italian elite who had worked closely with the Amal regime in Ravenna. His biography as a public figure and later as a Christian exegete has already received considerable scholarly attention, but it will be helpful briefly to sketch the outlines here.[45]

---

[42] The process by which local identities and narratives become renegotiated through exposure to powerful external sources of authority is described in postcolonial literature: Said, *Orientalism*; and Hobsbawm and Ranger, *Tradition*; more recently, in a Roman context, Dench, *Romulus' Asylum*; Andrew Wallace-Hadrill, *Revolution*; Woolf, *Barbarians*.

[43] Croke, '476', 81–119.

[44] On the *longue durée* of these processes, Ruggini, *Economia*; Marazzi, 'Late antique Italies'; Mac-George, *Warlords*; Christie, *Archaeology*; Wickham, *Framing*; Cooper, *Household*.

[45] For Cassiodorus' biography, Van de Vyver, 'Cassiodore', 244–92; Löwe, 'Cassiodor', 420–46; Cappuyns, 'Cassiodore', 1349–1408; Momigliano, 'Cassiodoro'; Fridh, *Opera*; O'Donnell,

Born sometime around 485, Cassiodorus' entry into palatine service had probably already been decided by his affiliation with a prominent local family of Bruttium that had pre-existing ties to state service.[46] At a young age Cassiodorus served in ex officio capacity as *consiliarius* to his father, who was praetorian prefect for Theoderic from 503 to 507. Cassiodorus then advanced to hold the three offices most intimate with the policies of the Amal government. From 507, he acted as quaestor, reviewing legal cases and drafting the official pronouncements of Theoderic's court. As master of offices (523–8), he managed the palatine staff and daily affairs at court for Theoderic's heirs, Athalaric and Amalasuntha. Later, as praetorian prefect (533–38/40), Cassiodorus held the highest-ranking public office in Italy, granting him authority over the appointment of magistrates throughout Italy and over the state's fiscal apparatus.[47] It was quite probably this last office which allowed Cassiodorus to accept patrician status, much as it had his father. The loyalty of his family to the Amal court at Ravenna earned him a consulship in 514 and possibly the governorship of his native province of Bruttium. By all appearances his career was exemplary in its advancement through the palatine *cursus*, good fortune no doubt influenced by the early promise of Cassiodorus' literary talent. Early in his public vocation, the Amal court honoured Cassiodorus with several literary commissions, including a panegyric to Theoderic, an ethnographic history of the Goths that traced the rise of the Amal family and a chronicle annotating the consulships of the Roman Empire.[48]

At the close of the first phase of the Gothic War in 540, when Witigis surrendered Ravenna to Belisarius, the public life enjoyed by Cassiodorus and other members of the western palatine elite came to an abrupt end. At the time, Cassiodorus still held the position of praetorian prefect and it is generally accepted that when Belisarius delivered Witigis to

Cassiodorus; Krautschick, *Cassiodore*; Barnish, 'Cassiodorus after conversion', 157–87; Barnish, *Cassiodorus*, xxxv–liii; Leanza, *Cassiodoro*; Halporn and Vessey, *Cassiodorus*, 13–19; Giardina, *Cassiodoro*.

[46] Cassiodorus, *Variae* 1.4.4–6, notes that his father served as *comes rei privatae* and *comes sacrarum largitionum* under Odoacer and praetorian prefect under Theoderic; *Variae* 1.4.10, that his grandfather served as *tribunus et notarius* under Valentinian III; and *Variae* 1.4.14, that his great-grandfather held *illustris* rank and exercised some military authority in Bruttium and Sicily; also Barnish, *Cassiodorus*, xxxvii–xxxix.

[47] On Cassiodorus' political career, *Variae* 9.24.3–9; *Ordo generis Cassiodororum* 1–3 and 27–9; Cappuyns, 'Cassiodore', 1351–5; O'Donnell, *Cassiodorus*, 33–54; Barnish, *Cassiodorus*, xxxix–liii.

[48] Cassiodorus mentions his panegyric and the *History of the Goths* in *Variae*, *praefatio* 1.11; the *Ordo generis Cassiodororum* 29–37 mentions the panegyric, the *History of the Goths* and the *Variae*; on Cassiodorus' *Chronica*, Mommsen, *MGH CM XI.2*, 111–19.

Constantinople, Cassiodorus was among the officials included in the king's entourage.[49] The sources do not permit a precise narrative for Cassiodorus' activities leading up to or following this decisive moment. Fragments of the epithalamium written on the occasion of Witigis' marriage to Matasuntha, the granddaughter of Theoderic, place Cassiodorus in early 537 at Ravenna, where he clearly served in official capacity as the author of the celebratory piece.[50] Procopius noted that later in 538, during the siege of Rome, Witigis agreed upon a three-month armistice in which time envoys would request terms of peace from Justinian in Constantinople. Letters which Cassiodorus wrote on behalf of Witigis and later included in the *Variae* (10.32–35) may be the very same letters dispatched with the envoys, locating Cassiodorus in the entourage of Witigis during the siege.[51] Throughout these episodes, Cassiodorus continued to act as praetorian prefect for Witigis, despite the fact that Belisarius had appointed Fidelius as a new praetorian prefect of Italy.[52] Given that the Goths abandoned the cordon around Rome suddenly and in the midst of battle, it seems unlikely that Cassiodorus negotiated a means of remaining at Rome when Witigis returned to Ravenna.[53] Indeed, had Cassiodorus returned to Ravenna with Witigis, the same diplomatic letters written in Witigis' name in the *Variae* could also pertain to renewed attempts to negotiate peace during the Byzantine siege of Ravenna.[54] Whether Cassiodorus vacated his office at Rome in 538 or after the siege of Ravenna in 540, it is difficult to imagine how a former consul serving the Amals as senior magistrate during the first years of the war could have escaped Belisarius' attention. Although later in date, the *Gothic History* of Jordanes and a letter from Pope Vigilius (*Epistula ad Rusticum et Sebastianum* 14) provide firm evidence for Cassiodorus' presence at the eastern capital as late as 550.[55] However limited, the evidence seems to suggest that Cassiodorus arrived at Constantinople in 540 with the Amal household and remained there probably until the close of the war in 554, when Justinian issued the *Constitutio Pragmatica* outlining the incorporation of Italy into the eastern empire and permitting Italian émigrés to return home.

---

[49] O'Donnell, *Cassiodorus*, 104–7; Amici, 'Cassiodoro', 221–6.
[50] On the epithalamium, Mommsen, *MGH AA XII*, 459–63; According to Procopius, *Wars* 5.11.10–27 and 5.17.13, Witigis departed Rome for Ravenna in December 536 and returned for the siege in February 537.
[51] Cassiodorus, *Variae* 10.31–35; cf. Procopius, *Wars* 6.7.13–15, on the armistice and envoys.
[52] Procopius, *Wars* 5.20.20.
[53] Procopius, *Wars* 6.10.1–20.   [54] Procopius, *Wars* 6.28.23 and 6.29.1–6.
[55] On the connection between Jordanes and Cassiodorus in Constantinople, see Christensen, *Jordanes*; Amici, 'Cassiodoro'.

It is in this period of fourteen years (540–54) that Cassiodorus began his most productive period of writing. The Gothic War continued to run its course across the Italian peninsula, now in a contest between imperial forces and Goths under the substantially more energetic and resourceful Totila. The majority of Cassiodorus' work from this period reflects his interest as a Christian exegete. The post-Ravenna corpus of Cassiodorus' work includes the monumental *Expositio psalmorum*, which provided the fullest exegetical treatment of the Psalms to date; the *Institutions*, a bibliographical treatise for the secular and religious reading appropriate to a lettered Christian; an ecclesiastical history known as the *Historia Tripertita* which combined the previous Greek histories of Socrates, Sozomen and Theodoret; a number of other biblical treatises; and, finally, at the age of 93, well after the conclusion of the Gothic War, a treatise on orthography.[56] Most of these works may be located in the period of Cassiodorus' retirement from public life at Vivarium. Well before then, however, at some point between the end of his praetorian prefecture (either 538 or 540) and his retirement in southern Italy (possibly 554), Cassiodorus also compiled the collection of letters which he called the *Variae*, to which he subsequently appended the *De anima*.

LOCATING THE *VARIAE*

Precisely when Cassiodorus revised his letters and assembled them as the *Variae* is a matter of some importance. The *opinio communis* has Cassiodorus compiling the *Variae* sometime between 538 and 540, immediately after the latest datable letter and prior to Belisarius' capture of Ravenna.[57] Within this time frame, studies have suggested that Cassiodorus may have compiled the *Variae* during his last days at Ravenna or after his removal from prefectural office, either at Rome or perhaps even on his family estates in southern Italy. Much of the scholarly consensus for this reconstruction can be traced to the work of Theodor Mommsen.[58] When Mommsen completed his edition of the *Variae* in 1894, he was still four years away from bringing an end to the thirteen-volume *Auctores Antiquissimi*, a mammoth contribution to the *Monumenta Germaniae Historica* that would attach late Roman sources to the nineteenth-century study of barbarian history. In addition to his own scholarly contributions to the project, Mommsen focused his prodigious organizational talents

[56] Cappuyns, 'Cassiodore', 1364–88; O'Donnell, *Cassiodorus*, 131–222; Halporn and Vessey, *Cassiodorus*, 13–19.
[57] On the latest letter, Krautschick, *Cassiodore*, 108; Goffart, review, 991.
[58] Mommsen, *MGH AA XII*, xxx–xxxi; Fridh, *Opera*, x; O'Donnell, *Cassiodorus*, 103; Krautschick, *Cassiodore*, 11; Barnish, *Cassiodorus*, xiv; Gillett, *Envoys*, 175; Amici, 'Cassiodoro', 221.

on directing the collaborative efforts of over a dozen other scholars editing manuscripts for the *Auctores Antiquissimi*. By 1898, when the project
was finished, Mommsen had come to call it his 'chronische Krankheit'.[59]
Such was the magnitude of Mommsen's accomplishment that, since the
publication of his edition, every piece of scholarship either attempting
to interpret the ideology of the *Variae* or using them as an evidentiary
source accepts 538–40 as a general time of publication.[60] The subject of
the collection's date of publication amply demonstrates this. It is important to recognize that Mommsen's interest in the *Variae* at that time
was mainly codicological and philological, and understandably so. The
exhaustive procedure that Mommsen employed required examining and
collating 111 manuscripts into a catalogue of six groups of transmission.[61]
The technical authority of his editorial procedure appears in 140 pages
of the introduction to his edition.[62] By contrast, explanation for the
date when Cassiodorus published the collection received scarcely two
pages.[63] According to Mommsen, Cassiodorus would have produced the
entire corpus of the *Variae* sometime between 537 (the date to which he
ascribed the latest letters with confidence) and 540, when Amal authority
in Ravenna ended. His explanation rests on two assumptions that have
been followed by subsequent modern studies.

First, because it was assumed that the letters were entirely authentic to
the occasions of original composition and hence the collection required
little in the way of revision or composition, they could have surfaced as a
complete collection as early as the autumn of 537. Mommsen supported
537 as the *terminus post quem* by noting Cassiodorus' use of the past tense
in reference to his prefecture in the first preface to the *Variae*, which he
assumed ended in 537 when Procopius states that Belisarius appointed
a new praetorian prefect for Italy. It should be noted that Belisarius
appointed Fidelius the new praetorian prefect during the siege of Rome.
At that time, any authority that Belisarius had over administrative matters
was strictly delimited by the mural fortifications of the city. Procopius is
silent with regard to Cassiodorus, who still served as praetorian prefect
for the Goths outside the walls of Rome; despite this silence, it is nevertheless difficult to imagine how Belisarius' new appointment would have
compelled Cassiodorus to abdicate his position (Fidelius' later death at
Pavia certainly indicates that his appointment did not enjoy the consent

---

[59] 'Chronicle headache'. Croke, 'Mommsen', 173.
[60] Most recently, Kakridi, *Cassiodors Variae*; Giardina, *Cassiodoro*, 25.
[61] For the *conspectus codicum*, Mommsen, *MGH AA XII*, lxxviii–cviii.
[62] Mommsen, *MGH AA XII*, xxxix–clxxviii.   [63] Mommsen, *MGH AA XII*, xxx–xxxi.

of the Goths).[64] More recently, the date ascribed to the latest letter of
the collection has been adjusted to the autumn of 538, confirming the
fact that Cassiodorus continued to serve in an official capacity despite
Fidelius' appointment.[65] Most studies have since adjusted the earliest possible date of publication to 538, although the opinion that Cassiodorus
concluded his public life when Fidelius claimed the praetorian office has
remained current.[66]

Second, Mommsen also assumed that Cassiodorus' ex officio interest
in the political life of Ravenna would have ceased with Witigis' capitulation in 540. This position was taken in part because of a statement
from the preface to Cassiodorus' *De anima* that mentions 'two great
peoples' in the past tense, which Mommsen interpreted as a reference
to a decisive separation of the Goths and Romans in 540.[67] Because
Cassiodorus clearly indicated that he had written the *De anima* following his completion of the *Variae*, Mommsen assigned the capitulation
of Ravenna as the *terminus ante quem* for the publication of the letters.
O'Donnell and Halporn have both observed that Cassiodorus' statement
(*tam magnis populis, cum duo essent*) is too obscure to refer definitively to
Ravenna in 540.[68] Even if Mommsen's reading of *tam magnis populis* as
a reference to Ravenna is correct, it does not identify precisely when
after 540 Cassiodorus finished the *De anima*; a post-540 publication of
the *De anima* would not necessarily exclude the *Variae* from also having been published sometime after 540. Nevertheless, Mommsen located
the publication of the *Variae* between Cassiodorus' abdication from the
prefecture and the capitulation of Ravenna. Subsequently, most studies
of Cassiodorus and the *Variae* have followed, either tacitly or explicitly,
Mommsen's determination of the date.

The designation of 540 as a *terminus ante quem* for the *Variae* becomes
even more tenuous when reckoned against the problematic dating of
Cassiodorus' later works. Calculating backwards through Cassiodorus'
corpus permits only an approximate chronology for the order in which

[64] Procopius, *Wars* 6.12.34–35, the Goths kill Fidelius outside a church; *Wars* 6.21.40, the Goths
feed the pieces of Fidelius' successor as praetorian prefect, also appointed by Belisarius, to dogs
during the sack of Milan.
[65] Reydellet, *Royauté*, 188; Krautschick, *Cassiodore*, 108; Goffart, review, 991.
[66] For references to the appointment of Fidelius in connection with the dating of the *Variae*,
Hasenstab, *Variensammlung*, 34; Van de Vyver, 'Cassiodore', 252; Jones, *TLRE*, 18; Cappuyns,
'Cassiodore', 1369; Fridh, *Opera*, x; Krautschick, *Cassiodore*, 11; O'Donnell, *Cassiodorus*, 103;
Barnish, 'Cassiodorus after conversion', 157; Giardina, 'Progetto delle *Variae*', 55; Gillett, *Envoys*,
175.
[67] Cassiodorus, *De anima* 18.
[68] O'Donnell, *Cassiodorus*, 127–8; Halporn, *Cassiodorus*, 281, note 88.

he completed individual projects. The preface to *De orthographia*, written in his ninety-third year and therefore probably just before his death, lists the sequence of previous works attributed in part or in whole to his years at Vivarium. The first mentioned and therefore the earliest written is the *Expositio psalmorum*, followed by the *Institutions*, a commentary on the letters of Paul, a *Codex de grammatica*, the *Liber memorialis* annotating the chapter headings of the Bible, the *Complexiones* on the New Testament and, finally, the *De orthographia* itself. Cassiodorus did not include works written prior to the *Expositio* in this list.[69] Internal and external evidence is insufficient to date precisely any of the texts listed in the *De orthographia*. Assigning an indisputable date to the *Expositio psalmorum*, or even to the *Institutions* which followed, would certainly assist in dating the *Variae* and the *De anima*, but the dating of these works can only be approximated. The most recent examination of the later Cassiodorian corpus annotated in the *De orthographia* suggests, with broad consensus, that Cassiodorus began the *Expositio psalmorum* sometime in the late 540s in Constantinople and later completed the work at Vivarium after his return from the eastern capital.[70] It seems more than probable that Cassiodorus moved to Vivarium permanently after 554, when Justinian's *Constitutio Pragmatica* allowed the return of Italian émigrés formerly detained in Constantinople.[71] After completing the *Expositio*, Cassiodorus turned to the *Institutions* and his discussion within the *Institutions* firmly locates their production at the monastery of Vivarium (hence after 554).[72] However, the *Institutions* may not have been finished until the early 560s. Such a late date of completion for the *Institutions* could mean that Cassiodorus engaged in only preliminary work on the *Expositio* at Constantinople in the 540s and then completed it at Vivarium after 554.[73] Shifting Cassiodorus' work on the *Institutions* and *Expositio* to a later period creates a wider window of opportunity in which he may have revised the letters of the *Variae* and then composed the *De anima*. Indeed, the *Expositio* refers to the *De anima* as the

---

[69] On the *De orthographia*, Keil, 129–42; Cassiodorus, *De orthographia, praefatio*, begins his discussion of previous works with the *Expositio Psalmorum*.

[70] Cappuyns, 'Cassiodore', 1369, placed the germination of the *Expositio* in Italy *c.* 538; the majority of scholarship has Cassiodorus working on the *Expositio* during his residency at Constantinople between 540 and 554: Mommsen, *MGH AA XII*, ix–xi; Van de Vyver, 'Cassiodore', 247–9; Walsh, *Cassiodorus*, 5; Gillett, 'Cassiodorus' *Variae*', 40; Halporn and Vessey, *Cassiodorus*, 35–6; however, Momigliano, 'Cassiodoro', 4, dated it after 554 at the Vivarium, while Barnish, 'Cassiodorus after conversion', 164, offers the solution that the *Expositio* may have been drafted in Constantinople and later revised at Vivarium.

[71] *Constitutio Pragmatica* 4 and 24, on the property rights of returning émigrés; also Moorhead, 'Totila', 382–6.

[72] Cassiodorus, *Institutiones* 1.29.1.   [73] Halporn and Vessey, *Cassiodorus*, 39–42.

thirteenth book of the *Variae*, confirming the completion of both works, although once again the date for this is elusive.[74]

Interestingly, the opening statement of the *Expositio* makes a firm declaration that, by the time of its composition, Cassiodorus had abandoned his previous ambitions for public office.[75] The statement clearly marks a boundary beyond which the *Variae* would not have had relevance. But once again, the moment when Cassiodorus abandoned all hope for a return to public life at Ravenna and decided to begin the *Expositio* could have happened anytime in the 540s. Indeed, it is even possible that this moment did not arrive until as late as 550. It was in this year that the death of Germanus, the husband of Matasuntha and nephew of Justinian, may have collapsed ambitions to rehabilitate the memory of the Amals in Constantinople. This would mean that Cassiodorus may have arranged and revised the *Variae*, and then composed the *De anima*, almost anytime during the 540s. Nothing from the *Variae* or *De anima* contradicts a later date of publication. The second preface of the *Variae* merely indicates Cassiodorus' intention to write the *De anima* as the next project. The *De anima*, in turn, merely confirms the completion of the *Variae*.[76] Neither statement draws attention to the capitulation of Ravenna in 540 as a concrete *terminus ante quem*. Given the manner in which the *Variae* and the *De anima* refer to each other, it is reasonable to assume that Cassiodorus conceived of writing the *Variae* and the *De anima* as a whole and that the *De anima* followed closely upon the completion of the *Variae*.[77] Given the fact that the *De anima* is itself a complicated philosophical treatise, the completion of which would have required a degree of detachment from the demands of public office and the exigencies of warfare, it seems more probable that the closely connected publication of the *Variae* and *De anima* occurred after the capitulation of Ravenna; that is, sometime in the 540s. Because Cassiodorus also commenced the *Expositio psalmorum* in Constantinople, it would seem likely that he finished the *Variae* and *De anima* sometime between the capitulation of Ravenna and the mid-540s. This would mean that Cassiodorus had ample time to prepare the *Variae* with careful consideration given to how the political discourse of Constantinople might have an impact on the postwar settlement of Ravenna.

The reason why a later date has not been previously considered has to do with another tenacious view in the modern historiography of Cassiodorus' writing. For a long time it was thought that Cassiodorus' writing belonged to two neatly divided spheres of interest: the political

---

[74] Cassiodorus, *Expositio Psalmorum* 145.2.   [75] Cassiodorus, *Expositio Psalmorum, praefatio* 1.
[76] Cassiodorus, *Variae, praefatio* 11.7; *De anima* 1.   [77] Cassiodorus, *Variae, praefatio* 11.7.

interests of Cassiodorus' public career at Ravenna and the later religious interests associated with Vivarium.[78] This view imagined that the capture of Ravenna in 540 had truncated Cassiodorus' political opportunities and therefore represented the crucial moment when Cassiodorus 'converted' to more purely religious pursuits. The sentiment of the opening passage of the *Expositio* certainly seems to suggest that Cassiodorus eventually embraced the pursuit of religious studies to the exclusion of interest in a public life, but it is impossible to say with certainty when between 540 and 554 this moment would have taken place. More recent studies have emphasized how the spiritual and the profane were equally part of Cassiodorus' intellectual and public life irrespective of whether he held political office.[79] Cassiodorus had well-developed religious interests throughout his public life. Cassiodorus' own *Chronica* suggests his involvement in resolving some manner of religious controversy at Rome in the very year of his consulship.[80] His preparation to found a school of sacred and secular letters with Pope Agapetus, undertaken while praetorian prefect, similarly illustrates his simultaneous engagement in political and religious matters.[81] The clearly religious tone of letters written in his name as praetorian prefect also indicates that the religious and the political were not mutually exclusive influences on Cassiodorus.[82] Additionally, recent studies of both the *Expositio psalmorum* and the *Institutions* have drawn attention to how Cassiodorus engaged with polemical and political issues even when writing about explicitly religious matters.[83] The fact that Jordanes had access to Cassiodorus' *Gothic History* in Constantinople undermines the view that Cassiodorus' interests at the eastern capital were strictly theological.[84] Nonetheless, studies have been late to recognize how this dichotomy, even after being rejected, has had an impact on the dating of the *Variae* and, ultimately, how the *Variae* have been read as a text.

The assumption that Cassiodorus' complete corpus reflects two profoundly different spheres of literary activity has contributed to the view that he published the *Variae* as a final departure from his political life at

---

[78] O'Donnell, *Cassiodorus*.

[79] Lamma, *Oriente e Occidente*, 180; Cameron, 'Cassiodorus deflated', 183; Barnish, 'Cassiodorus after conversion', 162–4; Silvestre, 'Uso politico', 83; Halporn and Vessey, *Cassiodorus*, 24–37; Amici, 'Cassiodoro', 221–31.

[80] Cassiodorus, *Chronica* 514.   [81] Cassiodorus, *Institutiones, praefatio* 1.

[82] For example, *Variae* 11.2, 11.3, 11.4, 11.8.

[83] Barnish, 'Cassiodorus after conversion', 157–87; Halporn and Vessey, *Cassiodorus*, 24–37; Amici, 'Cassiodoro', 215–31; Chazelle, 'Three Chapters', 161–205; Heydemann, 'Christian *gentes*'.

[84] Barnish, 'Cassiodorus after conversion', 157–87, extends Cassiodorus' polemical interests well into the period of his religious writing; Amici, 'Cassiodoro', 221–31, contests the view of Cassiodorus in Constantinople as *vir religiosus*.

the advent of the Gothic War.[85] Without a doubt, the Gothic War was an event of the greatest possible cultural and political consequence for a magistrate of the Amal court. But it is precisely for this reason that it should *not* be assumed that Cassiodorus retreated into religious retirement. Many other Italian émigrés resident in Constantinople, like Cassiodorus, used their proximity to the eastern court to further personal political interests. Members of the senatorial aristocracy of Rome certainly found ample opportunity during the Gothic War to advance personal ambitions by appealing to Justinian. Furthermore, the assumption that the *Variae* represent political interests that ended in 540 has favoured the use of the *Variae* as 'documentary' evidence and reduced its literary and polemical complexity to stylistic self-indulgence on Cassiodorus' part. On the contrary, this study takes the position that it is mistaken to view the letters of the *Variae* as unfiltered artefacts of a defunct political career.[86] Rather, as this study argues, Cassiodorus had the opportunity and incentive to revise and arrange the *Variae* as an idealizing model of western palatine service under the Amals.

This study also argues that Cassiodorus fashioned that idealizing model against an active polemical discourse that attempted to define the appropriateness of both the Gothic War and Justinian's reign. Obviously, the dimensions of this discourse would have been consequential to Cassiodorus and other members of the former western palatine elite whether they were at Rome, Ravenna or Constantinople. In other words, regardless of whether Cassiodorus compiled the *Variae* under house arrest or in relative freedom at any of the three Roman capitals, after 540 all three locations were under eastern imperial control and each could have offered Cassiodorus access (both official and unofficial) to channels of the eastern political polemic. Of course, affairs in Constantinople were equally consequential to Cassiodorus and his political dependents before the capitulation of Ravenna and it is certainly possible to imagine the troubled context of Ravenna's relations with Constantinople in the late 530s as an incentive to publish the *Variae*. In either case, before or after 540, the events of the Gothic War would eventually require a statement that could mediate the postwar settlement on behalf of the western palatine elite. However, given the level of Cassiodorus' commitment to the Gothic cause leading up to the capitulation of Ravenna, it seems more probable that a text such as the *Variae* that

---

[85] Löwe, 'Cassiodor', 432–45; Cappuyns, 'Cassiodore', 1355–6; Fridh, *Opera*, vii–viii; O'Donnell, *Cassiodorus*, 103–7; Krautschick, *Cassiodore*, 11; MacPherson, *Rome*, 7–8; Paratore, 'Cassiodoro nella cultura', 20–22.

[86] Contra Barnish, *Cassiodorus*, xviii, and Gillett, *Envoys*, 184.

̃acilitate political rehabilitation would not have become neces-
̃fter 540.

THE *VARIAE* IN A CONTEXT OF POLITICAL URGENCY

The previous discussion has already alluded to Cassiodorus' continued
close affiliation with the Amal regime at the opening stages of the Gothic
War. A more thorough reprise of the circumstances that would have
inflected a post-540 interpretation of Cassiodorus' involvement with the
Amal regime makes it clear that his decision to produce the *Variae* was
not simply a matter of optimism; it was a matter of extreme political
urgency. Cassiodorus' continued service to Witigis after Belisarius had
appointed Fidelius as the new praetorian prefect of Italy would have
raised questions concerning Cassiodorus' respect for eastern imperial
authority in a post-540 context. Although not explicit in the collection
because of the deletion of dates and protocols from individual letters, the
Variae strongly suggest that Cassiodorus maintained steadfast support for
the Gothic regime even in the stages of the war leading to the capture of
Ravenna. The diplomatic letters written on behalf of Witigis (10.32–35)
indicate Cassiodorus' involvement in attempts to negotiate peace with
Justinian. Letter 10.32 even mentions damage to the city of Rome and
Witigis' marriage to Matasuntha as reasons for reconciliation between
the two 'republics'.[87] The mention of conflict at Rome suggests that
the envoys departed Italy either sometime during the siege of Rome
or possibly even later, during the siege of Ravenna.[88] Letters 10.33 and
10.34 ask for the intercession of an anonymous master of offices (probably the eastern *magister officiorum* in Constantinople) and unspecified
bishops in order to arrange peace. And finally, letter 10.35, addressed to
the Byzantine prefect of Thessalonica, sought permission for the unhin-
dered passage of envoys between Witigis and Justinian. Presumably the
full dossier of letters (10.32–35) accompanied the Gothic envoys and
Italian bishops sent to address Justinian. And again, as suggested, letters
10.32–35 may equally correspond to a diplomatic mission arranged during the final stages of the siege of Ravenna in 540.[89] In either case, the
letters are an indication that Cassiodorus remained committed to the
Gothic cause at least until the capitulation of Witigis.[90]

The last letter of the collection similarly provides an indication of
Cassiodorus' involvement with the Gothic regime toward the end of
Witigis' reign. Written in Cassiodorus' own name as praetorian prefect,

---

[87] Cassiodorus, *Variae* 10.32.1 and 10.32.3. [88] Cassiodorus, *Variae* 10.32.1.
[89] Procopius, *Wars* 6.28.23. [90] Contra Sirago, 'Goti nelle *Variae*', 120.

the letter is an edict authorizing the remission of taxes in Liguria and Aemilia.[91] Although not explicitly naming Witigis, the edict claims to have been written on behalf of a prince 'whose excellence [was] tested in the capacity of a soldier'.[92] The only Ostrogothic king to take to the field of battle since Theoderic was Witigis, whose soldiers literally elevated him to the kingship on their shields. The description in the edict of recent incursions of the Burgundians and Alamanni as the cause of famine agree with Procopius' account of the last stages of Witigis' reign.[93] Cassiodorus also alludes to the wider theatre of war with eastern imperial forces, 'I could easily enumerate for you how many hosts of the enemy will have fallen in other places.'[94] His reticence in naming Justinian or the eastern empire directly as the enemy conforms to a habit found throughout the *Variae* for referring to conflicts with the east only obliquely.[95] It was a precaution probably taken during the revision of letters to be included in the collection.

Cassiodorus' indebtedness to the Gothic regime can also be understood in terms of the general outline of his political career. Cassiodorus has often been portrayed as enjoying a life that alternated between public office and literary leisure, the ancient paradigm of interchanging periods of *negotium* and *otium* that formed the traditional *cursus honorum* for a senator.[96] The gaps between Cassiodorus' tenure in various magistracies lend themselves quite attractively to this portrayal. Nevertheless, the consistency of subjects addressed in individual letters throughout the collection suggests an unusual lack of differentiation in Cassiodorus' duties at court. Whether he was writing as quaestor, master of offices, or praetorian prefect, the letters of the *Variae* continued to meet the same essential needs of state, implying a uniformity of duties undifferentiated by official competences. That dispositive letters, letters of appointment, and diplomatic correspondence should all issue from the same pen over the course of thirty years suggests a more permanent political position than the traditional alternation between court duties and scholarly leisure. This is particularly curious given that such correspondence should have been entrusted to a quaestor when Cassiodorus held the posts of master of offices or praetorian prefect. Instead, Cassiodorus continued to handle the official correspondence of the Amals at the same time that a succession

[91] Cassiodorus, *Variae* 12.28.
[92] Cassiodorus, *Variae* 12.28.2, 'rectorem, quem sub militis nomine probaverat singularem'.
[93] Procopius, *Wars* 5.13 and 6.25.
[94] Cassiodorus, *Variae* 12.28.4, 'possem quidem vobis dinumerare, quanta in aliis locis hostium turba ceciderit'.
[95] Cassiodorus, *Variae* 2.38.2, 8.10.9–10, 9.25.10, 11.1.10.
[96] For example, Mommsen, *MGH AA XII*, ix–xi; Reydellet, *Royauté*, 185.

of contemporary quaestors (Decoratus, Honoratus, Ambrosius, Fidelis) could have filled that role.[97] That Cassiodorus continued to write for the Amals in essentially the same capacity has been attributed to the dependence of the court on his literary talent. However, studies of the intellectual culture at the Amal court and among the Italian aristocracy during the late fifth and early sixth centuries suggest that Cassiodorus was not exceptional with respect to his learning.[98] Compared to his contemporaries, it is certain that Cassiodorus' literary attainments could be equalled or surpassed by others such as Ennodius of Pavia, Arator or Boethius.

It is more probable that Cassiodorus was a member of a core of trusted individuals who formed a royal household living at court.[99] Cassiodorus' connection to the Amals had probably been understood in terms of a lifelong commitment, perhaps something closer to the role of a *patricius* in Frankish Gaul, which seems to have been a permanent position held at the pleasure of the king.[100] This highly personal element of service to the Amal regime becomes particularly apparent in the light of three letters of the *Variae* that have received little attention.[101] Each letter requests the presence of a former public official at the Amal court. These were not summonses in answer to legal suits, nor do they promise appointment to office – two more frequent causes for summoning individuals to court. In the case of the letters addressed to Cassiodorus' father and Artemiodorus, it is clear that the recipients had already attained the highest appointments possible.[102] The third recipient, Carinus, shared the rank of *vir illustris* with Artemidorus and Cassiodorus senior and had presumably held similarly high office. Rather than requests to attend court in official capacity, these letters express a sense of personal gratitude for services previously rendered and explicitly mention the interest of the king in the recipients' wellbeing.[103] Such letters recall the ideal of kingship served by close association with trusted advisers. These glimpses into the highly personal nature of state service suggest that Cassiodorus' *cursus* may not have included intermittent spates of leisured retirement; it seems more probable that he remained attached to the Amal court even

---

[97] For quaestorships held during Cassiodorus' tenure in other offices, Cassiodorus, *Variae* 5.3, 8.13–14 and 8.18.

[98] Cavallo, 'Cultura a Ravenna', 29–51; Heather, 'Ostrogothic Italy', 320–38; Petrucci, *Writers*, 1–35; Polara, 'Letteratura', 11–36.

[99] Cassiodorus, *Variae* 8.21.6, notes the household of Cyprian, whose sons were trained in the Gothic language and customs at court from an early age; cf. Amory, *Ostrogothic Italy*, 152–65.

[100] For example, Gregory of Tours, *Decem Libri Historiarum* 4.42, 'Mummolus a rege . . . patriciatum promeruit'; also, 4.44–45, 5.13, 6.1, 6.26 and 6.35.

[101] Cassiodorus, *Variae* 3.22, 3.28, 5.28.   [102] Cassiodorus, *Variae* 1.3, 1.42, 1.43 and 2.34.

[103] Cassiodorus, *Variae* 3.22.1, 3.28.1, 5.28.

while out of office. That this would have required extensive absence from his familial estates actually agrees with the established convention for elite land management in late antiquity.[104] Cassiodorus also provides some sense of how his own career in palatine service had become a lifetime occupation of personal intimacy with the royal court. On the occasion of his elevation to the praetorian prefecture, Cassiodorus described how Theoderic's presence educated him in his youth and how, when an adult, he shared philosophical inquiry with that same king.[105] Hence it is quite possible to envisage Cassiodorus' presence at the Amal court as continuous up to the point when Belisarius dissolved the Gothic government at Ravenna. This was a record of political affiliation from which Cassiodorus and others could not casually detach themselves.

The close association that Cassiodorus had with the Amal court became particularly problematic in light of several events occurring before 540. As previously mentioned, Cassiodorus played a rather intimate role in the marriage of Witigis and Matasuntha.[106] His epithalamium for the occasion must have been delivered sometime between Witigis' accession in December of 536 and his departure for Rome in February of 537.[107] So long as Witigis remained in power, the perception of complicity in coercing an Amal bride to wed would have had little impact on Cassiodorus. However, after 540, and later the death of Witigis, Matasuntha's proximity to Justinian's court had the potential to cause serious problems. Similarly, the senatorial elite were in a position to cast Cassiodorus' involvement with the Gothic regime in an entirely unfavourable light. When negotiations with Justinian's court had failed during the siege of Rome, Witigis became so incensed that he ordered the execution of a large number of senators being held hostage at Ravenna. The precise number is not known, but Procopius claims that it was the 'majority' of senators. This occurred quite possibly while Cassiodorus still acted as praetorian prefect.[108] Just as problematic for pro-Gothic loyalties, soon after Witigis abandoned the siege of Rome, a Gothic army sacked Milan and razed the city as punishment for having favoured the eastern imperial cause. Procopius noted that the Goths executed all civilian males, regardless of age, and enslaved the women, thereby eliminating an urban population of more than 300,000.[109] It is hardly probable that the population of late antique Milan had ever become as

[104] A point emphasized by Grey, 'Revisiting *agri deserti*', 362–76.
[105] Cassiodorus, *Variae* 9.24.3 and 9.24.8.
[106] Martindale, *PLRE IIIB*, 851; Procopius, *Wars* 5.11.27.
[107] See Mommsen, *MGH AA XII*, 463; Sanfilippo, 'Cassiod. Orat.', 460–4.
[108] Procopius, *Wars* 5.11.26–29 and 5.26.1–3.   [109] Procopius, *Wars* 6.21.39.

numerous as Procopius reports and it is probably best to regard the scale as an exaggeration. Nevertheless, the execution and enslavement of the entire population of Milan was perhaps the most brutal spectacle of the entire war and, as praetorian prefect, Cassiodorus had presided over it, regardless of whether or not he had been directly involved.

These episodes set the stage for a very clear division of loyalties within the political elite of Italy. Upon arrival in Constantinople, members of the palatine bureaucracy of Ravenna came under the scrutiny not only of Justinian, but also of other Italian émigrés opposed to the Amal regime. Constantinople had become a haven for Italian refugees since the beginning of the war. Many among the dislocated elite were surviving members of the senatorial class of Rome for whom Amal rule had become emblematic of the oppression of 'Roman liberties'. Of particular concern to Cassiodorus were members and associates of the Anicii who resided in high favour at the eastern capital.[110] Although Theoderic's execution of two prominent members of the Anicii, Boethius and Symmachus, occurred much earlier, in 524, the memory of these deaths had become the ideological touchstone for the struggle of 'Roman liberties' against 'Gothic barbarity'.[111] The death of Boethius was especially prejudicial to Cassiodorus.[112] Prior to his trial, Boethius had been master of offices and Cassiodorus advanced to this office as an immediate consequence of the philosopher's death. In his *Consolation of Philosophy*, Boethius blamed 'palatine dogs' for his political downfall and although he did not name Cassiodorus, succession to Boethius' post would not have endeared him to the conservative enclave of the senatorial elite at Rome.[113] According to his own testimony in the *Variae*, Cassiodorus' later nomination as praetorian prefect in 533 met with decided opposition.[114] And another letter clearly states that Cassiodorus encountered resistance in the exercise of his duties as praetorian prefect; again, possibly as a consequence of Theoderic's handling of the senatorial class.[115] Later, the execution of senatorial hostages at Ravenna and of Roman civilians at Milan probably activated the memory of Boethius' death to an even greater extent, no doubt furthering the damage to the reputation of the palatine ministry that served Cassiodorus. Cassiodorus' continued support of the Gothic

---

[110] On the senators Petronius Nicomachus Cethegus and Petrus Marcellinus Felix Liberius in Constantinople, Martindale, *PLRE II*, 281–2 and 677–81; more generally on Italian émigrés, Croke, *Marcellinus*, 86–8; Brown, *Byzantine Italy*, 28–9; note also John Lydus, *De magistratibus* 3.28.4.

[111] On the execution of Boethius, Procopius, *Wars* 1.5.32–39 and 5.1.27–35; *Excerpta Valesiana* 2.87; Boethius, *De consolatione philosophiae* 1.4.70; also, Moorhead, 'Libertas', 161–8.

[112] Bjornlie, 'A reappraisal', 150–2; more generally on this theme, Barnish, 'Maximian', 16–32.

[113] Boethius, *De consolatione philosophiae* 1.4.34–75.

[114] Cassiodorus, *Variae* 11.1.18.   [115] Cassiodorus, *Variae* 10.28.1.

regime after the onset of war doubtless confronted him when Belisarius dissolved the Amal government and transported Witigis, Amalasuntha and the remnants of their court to Constantinople.[116]

After 540, eastern imperial channels of authority conferred all political appointments in Italy. Because of the war's exaggeration of the social and political divide that separated the senatorial and former palatine elite, integrating Cassiodorus and his political dependents into the new political structure was extremely problematic. Even if Cassiodorus did not arrive at Constantinople until later in the 540s, control of Rome and Ravenna by eastern imperial officials opened new channels of communication between Italy and Constantinople and presented ripe opportunities for political detractors. The reputations of Cassiodorus and those members of the western palatine elite who had worked most closely with the former Amal regime would have required careful rehabilitation. Responsibility for the reputation of the former palatine bureaucracy of Ravenna naturally weighed heaviest on Cassiodorus, who, as the former praetorian prefect, had occupied the apex of a network of political patronage. Resonances of this concern appear in the first preface of the *Variae*, where Cassiodorus stated that he had compiled the collection for the edification of those who would enter palatine service in future generations and, more importantly, to rectify the reputations of those who served with him under the Amals. Indeed, Cassiodorus places this sentiment in the voice of those associates at court who had purportedly urged him to compile the *Variae*:

Then will your work be able to educate, without offence and by means of a studied eloquence, those unlearned men who must be prepared for public office, and it will happen that those who are situated in more tranquil circumstances will more happily obtain the habit that you practised while tossed about amid the dangers of various altercations ... We entreat you not to permit that those who merited receiving illustrious honours by your endorsement should be recalled to the obscurity of silence ... If you would pass on to the following generation the record of those who must be honoured, you will have postponed, after the custom of the ancients, the annihilation of those who perished becomingly.[117]

---

[116] Procopius, *Wars* 7.1.1–2; cf. Mommsen, *MGH AA XII*, xxx–xxxi.
[117] Cassiodorus, *Variae, praefatio* 1.8–9, 'deinde quod rudes viros et ad rem publicam conscia facundia praeparatos labor tuus sine aliqua offensione poterit edocere, et usum, quem tu inter altercantium pericula iactatus exerces, illos, qui sunt in tranquillitate positi, contingit felicius adipisci ... Noli, quaesumus, in obscurum silentii revocare, qui te dicente meruerunt illustres dignitates accipere ... Quos si celebrandos posteris tradas, abstulisti, consuetudine maiorum, morientibus decenter interitum'; cf. Barnish, *Cassiodorus*, 2–3.

Cassiodorus' role as patron of palatine officials is particularly apparent in the last two books of the *Variae*, where he arranged a dossier of letters written in his own name to various subordinates, both the staff of his personal *officium* and the officials whom he assigned throughout the provinces. Often these letters have less to do with concrete administrative concerns than they do with a portrayal of governmental morality as it flowed from the praetorian prefect to his agents. Indeed, moral accountability is the common refrain in all letters of the *Variae*.

Assuming that Cassiodorus would not respond in some way to the potential consequences of the Gothic War underestimates the hopes that the bureaucratic elite held for a successful return to a share of governance in Italy. Even after Ravenna's fall in 540, the likelihood that Italians might shape the postwar government would have seemed tangible at least until Justinian's *Constitutio Pragmatica* of 554 settled matters. Provisions in the *Constitutio Pragmatica* concerning the ownership of private property in Italy indicate the sustained interest of elite Italians in how the outcome of the war would be decided at Constantinople.[118] It was for this abiding concern that Cassiodorus undertook the revision of a significant portion of chancery documents representing his public career. Signs of heavy revision and adaptation appear throughout the *Variae*, including two extensive prefaces, the deletion of epistolary protocols, the substitution of *ille et ille* for the names of persons within letters and the inclusion of two books of *formulae*.

Within this context of extreme political uncertainty for a representative of the Italian elite who had been heavily invested in the Amal regime, the production of the *Variae* as a text that depicts a government entirely in continuity with the laws, with the political and administrative culture, and with the social mores of Roman tradition becomes a matter with much more political immediacy than has previously been assumed. Rather than a backward-looking reflection of Amal government and Ostrogothic society, the *Variae* represent a dynamic attempt to shape the as yet undecided political present. Cassiodorus did so by constructing a model that communicated the suitability of the palatine elite of Ravenna to resume an active public life in Italy after the upheaval of Justinian's invasion. Cassiodorus was able to fashion that model by drawing from the contemporary cultural discourse concerned with good governance. The most prominent contributors to this discourse were influenced by the political climate of what had become the ultimate model for a 'Roman' society in the early sixth century – Constantinople. Examining the *Variae* within an expanded context that takes into

---

[118] *Constitutio Pragmatica* 4 and 24; cf. Moorhead, 'Totila', 382–6.

account communication exchanged at all levels (social, political, intellectual, and religious) between Rome, Ravenna and Constantinople permits an understanding of the *Variae* as a dynamic literary and political enterprise. Indeed, this study will argue that the *antiquitas*, or traditionalism, represented in the *Variae* has a very selective semiotic formulation. It marks Cassiodorus' attentiveness to eastern political conditions and his awareness of a highly differentiated audience involved in political processes in both Constantinople and Italy.

PART II

Cassiodorus and the circumstances of political survival

INTRODUCTION

The years that Cassiodorus spent in Constantinople constitute the period of his life about which the least is known. The scattered biographical details that Cassiodorus supplied in his writing permit a slender yet nearly continuous reconstruction of his progression in public office prior to the siege of Ravenna. These same works also supply the sequence of his literary enterprises. The greater portion of biographical material survives in the *Variae* and in works from Cassiodorus' later activity at Vivarium. For this reason, Cassiodorus is known most intimately through the record of his public career in Ravenna and his later retirement on family estates in Bruttium. By contrast, only two fleeting glimpses of Cassiodorus survive from the intervening period at the eastern capital, both of which surfaced toward the end of his residence there.[1] It is not possible to say with certitude whether Cassiodorus arrived at Constantinople in the entourage of the Gothic court which capitulated at Ravenna in 540 or later with other elite refugees fleeing Totila's siege of Rome in 545–6. Cappuyns hazarded the suggestion that Priscian, whom Cassiodorus possibly met in Constantinople, did not live much later than 540, although the date of Priscian's death is itself difficult to confirm.[2] It is clear, however, that Cassiodorus experienced the eastern capital during the aftermath of what had been the most serious challenge to Justinian's legitimacy as emperor. The 530s had been a decade fraught with difficulties for Justinian's court, and by the time of Cassiodorus' arrival those difficulties remained submerged within a discontented element of the bureaucracy. Thus the

---

[1] Pope Vigilius, *Ad Rusticum et Sebastianum* 14; and Jordanes, *Getica, praefatio* 1, place Cassiodorus in Constantinople around 550; Barnish, 'Cassiodorus after conversion', 157–8; Amici, 'Cassiodoro', 215–31; Croke, 'Jordanes', 473–94.

[2] Cassiodorus refers to Priscian in *De orthographia* 12, 'qui nostro tempore Constantinopoli doctor fuit'; Cappuyns, 'Cassiodore', 1356–7.

period in which Cassiodorus found himself a resident at Constantinople was crucial to the consolidation of Justinian's political position.[3] The various forms of social and administrative reform enacted by Justinian, the costly and conspicuously advertised building programmes undertaken in the wake of the Nika Revolt, the authoritarian measures taken to impose religious orthodoxy over a mosaic of eastern Christianities, and the continued military contests for control over North Africa and Italy, were all components of Justinian's bid to remain in power in the 530s and 540s. These earlier years of Justinian's reign were an arena for acting out a new relationship between imperial authority and the established social order of the political elite. It was particularly Justinian's response to an intransigent bureaucratic culture that provided grist for the mill of an emergent political discourse at Constantinople. The dynamism of this discourse manifests itself in an impressive range of literature to which Marcellinus Comes, Agapetus, Procopius, Junillus Africanus, Corippus, John Lydus, Jordanes and others contributed. It is precisely in the period of this literature that interaction between Constantinople, Rome and Ravenna would determine Cassiodorus' future as a political participant.

Yet Cassiodorus moved ghostlike through this landscape of political change and literary riposte. In spite of his holding the office of praetorian prefect of Italy at the onset of Justinian's reconquest, Cassiodorus' name surfaced in the works of the major eastern commentators only as a brief reference.[4] As a result of this seeming lack of interest, many studies have been content to treat what was for Cassiodorus a period of acute political turmoil as a decade of quiet scholarly preparation for his later religious vocation at Vivarium. It bears repeating that, as a former praetorian prefect (possibly in the entourage of Witigis and Matasuntha), Cassiodorus was a visitor of consequence at Constantinople. Although not mentioning Cassiodorus specifically, Procopius noted with a certain disdain the amount of influence that western émigrés enjoyed at Justinian's court, mentioning in particular Liberius, who had also served as a former praetorian prefect of Amal appointment.[5] Even if Cassiodorus' presence in Constantinople did not entail direct political participation, at the very least it would have been conspicuous owing to his previous appointments, not only in the eyes of those employed in the administration of the capital, but also among those Italian émigrés anxiously awaiting the outcome of the Gothic War. An unavoidable corollary of the offices that Cassiodorus had held under the Amal regime was his

[3] Maas, 'Roman questions', 8.
[4] Marcellinus Comes, *Chronicon* 514; Jordanes, *Getica*, *praefatio* 1–2.
[5] Procopius, *Wars* 7.36.6 and 7.37.26–27.

role as a political patron.[6] Maintaining a credible reputation required that Cassiodorus bear some amount of responsibility for the Italian bureaucratic elite and he could hardly have remained inattentive to the discourse shaping politics in Justinian's capital. Of course, the exact nature of Cassiodorus' residence at the eastern capital – whether as honoured guest, political hostage or exile seeking benefaction – would permit a better understanding of his reception of this literature. Such a reconstruction is not possible given the extant evidence. For the moment, it is important simply to note the contemporary currents of political thought to which Cassiodorus was exposed. Although this discourse first becomes visible in the literature of the 540s, it was initially germinated by the imperial reaction to earlier events at the beginning of Justinian's reign. The politically charged nature of communication between Rome, Ravenna and Constantinople prior to the Gothic War would have ensured that Cassiodorus, who had maintained an arguably consistent presence at the Amal court, had access to opinions circulating around the events of the imperial court.[7] Iconographic correspondences in the architecture of Ravenna and Constantinople, particularly in the monumental gateways of Ravenna that would have provided a central stage for the arrival of envoys from the east, suggest that diplomatic exchange between the two capitals was highly regular.[8] Whether Cassiodorus' thoughts on the nature of governance were formed earlier at Ravenna in reaction to news received through diplomatic channels (official or unofficial) or later at Constantinople, their origin can be traced to this energetic polemic. The themes that Cassiodorus threaded through his collection reflect his exposure (either direct or indirect) to the discourse active at the eastern imperial capital.

The following section will provide a Constantinopolitan context for understanding the purpose of themes present in the *Variae* and for reconstructing Cassiodorus' intended audience. The first chapter will describe in broad strokes the key events and political culture that set the tone of Justinian's responses to problems in the first years of his reign. The following chapters will trace the development of a polemical discourse concerning Justinian and the imperial court, with particular attention to the literature that was roughly contemporary with Cassiodorus' residency in Constantinople. With few exceptions, this literature

---

[6] On patronage, Garnsey, 'Roman patronage', 33–54.

[7] Blair-Dixon, 'Memories', 59–74, notes a parallel context for the *Collectio Avellana*; on communication between Ravenna and Constantinople during Theoderic's reign, Kitchen, 'Italia and Graecia', 116–30; more generally on the transformative agency of political communication in this period, Gillett, *Envoys*; and Canepa, *Two Eyes*.

[8] On iconographic correspondences, Malmberg, 'Above the gate'.

proceeded from the experiences of authors active in the complex social and political world of the administration of the eastern empire. While each author presents a different perspective of imperial governance, taken as a whole the writing from this period reveals an interactive dialogue centring on Justinian's policies. It is, above all, a discourse of complaint, one that surfaces almost universally in either carefully constructed criticism or defence of Justinian's court. The autocratic nature of Justinian's rule was particularly pronounced within the confines of the city walls of Constantinople and the censorship that attended his style of governance had a specific creative agency, forcing commentators to veil their criticisms in inventive ways.[9] Writers such as Procopius and John Lydus were capable of communicating a critique of Justinian's regime to a target audience that was attentive to coded criticism which, because of its oblique style, was still able to deflect the accusations of less sympathetic readers. Plausible deniability was an essential ingredient in the political critique of the sixth century. The final chapters of this section will consider how a significant segment of Cassiodorus' own Italian countrymen – the senatorial circle of the Anicii – were among the most dangerous of his potential detractors at Justinian's court. This was the group whose criticism Cassiodorus wished to deflect. The memory of Theoderic's culpability in the deaths of Boethius, Symmachus and Pope John confronted Cassiodorus while he and his associates bided their time under the scrutiny of Justinian's court. By fortifying the *Variae* with themes drawn from the Constantinopolitan discourse that criticized Justinian's regime, Cassiodorus was able to appeal to the sensitivities of the eastern bureaucracy as his target audience and still retain a certain degree of plausible deniability with respect to having been corrupted by collusion with a 'barbarian' government.

---

[9] On authoritarian rule and censorship, Honoré, *Tribonian*, 1–30; Cavallo, 'Circolazione libraria', 211–15; Cameron, *Procopius*, 19–22; McCormick, *Eternal Victory*, 47–78 and 124–9; Brown, *Power and Persuasion*, 128–43; Maas, *John Lydus*, 3–19; Kelly, 'Later Roman bureaucracy', 161–76; Kaldellis, 'Dissident circles', 1–4; Kelly, *Ruling*.

Chapter 2

THE AGE OF BUREAUCRACY

IDEOLOGY AND LEGITIMACY

Modern historians regularly bracket periods of Roman history with imperial reigns of unusual longevity.[1] The reigns of Augustus (ruled forty-three years) and Constantine (ruled thirty-one years) have each defined the initial terms by which historians assess imperial rule during the Principate and late antiquity respectively. Similarly, the reign of Justinian (thirty-eight years) has been seen as a departure toward a distinctly Byzantine stage of eastern Mediterranean history. Although this runs the risk of discounting the debt that these reigns owed to preceding *longue durée* trends, it is also the case that periods of long imperial tenure allowed the formulation and implementation of policies that may have been only partially imagined in previous reigns of shorter tenure. Holding the imperial office for an extended period tended to efface mistakes made earlier in public memory and, more importantly, allowed the development of an ideological language that complemented long-term, legitimizing strategies. Both Augustus and Constantine shifted gradually from posing as traditionalists dedicated to the preservation of existing cultural currents to rulers capable of transforming the language and idea of empire.[2] Thus Augustus assumed the mantle of autocratic rule by affecting a role as the conservator of senatorial privilege. The accretion of a language of the restoration of tradition was something that developed gradually and which only incrementally masked the social and political rupture that was the beginning of his reign. Similarly, Constantine adopted the position of a Christian ruler only gradually and in tandem with an incremental detachment from associations with the older tetrarchic order.

Change to the social and political status quo, such as occurred under Augustus and Constantine, inevitably involved redefining channels of political power and delineating who participated in and benefited from

---

[1] For example, Galinsky, *The Cambridge Companion to the Age of Augustus*; Lenski, *The Cambridge Companion to the Age of Constantine*; Maas, *The Cambridge Companion to the Age of Justinian*.
[2] Syme, *Roman Revolution*; Zanker, *Augustus*; Van Dam, *Constantine*.

39

empire. The problems associated with interpreting degrees of agency enjoyed by or refused to social groups close to the process of reimagining empire at specific moments are notorious. It is unlikely that a *communis opinio* will ever emerge concerning Augustus' relation to the Senate or Constantine's relation to Christians. Although it is known from later opinion that the innovative nature of emperors such as Augustus and Constantine provoked hostility from those who benefited the least from the development of a new political culture, those criticisms are often safely removed to periods under emperors with a less personal stake in preserving the image of an earlier regime's legitimacy (for example Suetonius and Zosimus as distant critics of Augustus and Constantine respectively). Only rarely does a contemporary critique survive the reigns of these emperors, and when it does it is usually oblique and muted, much as could be suggested for Livy's *Ab urbe condita* as a commentary on Augustus.[3]

The reason why a contemporary critique of these rulers does not survive may have to do with the success and longevity of successors who supported the policies of their predecessors as a foundation for their own legitimacy. In essence, the new languages of imperial legitimacy that developed out of these long reigns outlived the generation of disenfranchised groups. Thus Tiberius' twenty-three years of rule ensured sixty-six years of more or less Augustan policy and the twenty-four years of Constantius II extended the basic framework of Constantinian policy for fifty-five years. By contrast, contemporary criticism aimed at Justinian seems to have flourished enough to survive well beyond his reign. This may have to do with his successor, Justin II, whose reign seems to have lacked the kind of stability or success that would have represented a continuation of Justinianic policy. Like the reigns of Augustus and Constantine, that of Justinian faced substantial resistance. However, the historical record of Justinian's reign that remains exposed to modern view reveals a fascinating polemical contest waged between political elements favourable to Justinian's policies and those oppositional interests confronted with the loss of privilege and influence that attended a redefinition of the ideology of imperial rule.

Like Augustus and Constantine, Justinian's reign began with considerable challenges to the imperial tradition as it was perceived by particular interest groups. Unlike other rulers who enjoyed exceeding longevity, the success of Justinian's policies did not extend beyond his own reign to that of his successor. As a result, the lively polemical literature of the kind

---

[3] Petersen, 'Livy and Augustus', 440–52.

that did not survive the reigns of Augustus or Constantine outlived Justinian. The characterization of Justinian that survives in various sources is
contradictory and any attempt to render a composite from these sources
inevitably produces a rather Janus-faced figure, making him exceedingly
difficult to assess. Contemporary witnesses such as Procopius and John
Lydus incline the modern reader to see in Justinian an interloper and
innovator in traditions of government, someone whose blind ambition
and distrust of the elite set the empire on a trajectory of financial and
military ruin. Other witnesses, such as Marcellinus Comes and Junillus Africanus portrayed Justinian as a source of imperial renovation that
reclaimed lost imperial provinces, defended the unity of Christianity and
curbed elite corruption. What concerns the assessment of Cassiodorus
and the *Variae* is the visibility of themes contested in the polemical discourse that developed around Justinian's attempts to make the empire his
own. In order to appreciate how salient these themes were, it will first
be necessary to survey how political life was acted out at Constantinople
and to understand how a Justinianic style of governance developed out
of that background.

STRUCTURES OF POLITICAL POWER AT CONSTANTINOPLE

From its inception, Constantinople had the purpose of demonstrating
imperial legitimacy.[4] As a new capital, Constantinople provided a stage
for imperial prestige that did not depend on association with the traditions of the senatorial establishment at Rome.[5] The capital was quite
conspicuously a 'new Rome' with seven hills, fourteen city districts and
the annonarial contribution of Egypt which had been diverted from 'old
Rome'. The creation of a new Senate and a new core of palatine service
during the fourth century shaped the city's initial urban topography.[6]
The city was planned with an eye toward imperial ceremonial, with
thoroughfares linking basilicas, theatres, baths, a senatorial Curia and, of
course, the palace and Hippodrome – all of which would serve as stational points in the political pageantry of the capital. Constantinople was
also a city of churches where imperial power was articulated through the
new relationship of the emperor with the church.[7] By the sixth century,
the development of a language of political legitimacy at Constantinople

---

[4] Dagron, *Naissance*; Mango, *Constantinople*; Croke, 'Constantinople', 60–86; Canepa, *Two Eyes*,
7–11, 130–44, 154–87.
[5] On Constantinople as a 'new Rome', Zosimus, *Nova Historia* 2.31; also Dagron, *Naissance*, 43–7.
[6] Bowes, *Private Worship*, 103–16.
[7] On this relationship, Curran, *Rome*, for Rome; Van Dam, *Constantine*, 221–353, for
Constantinople.

that was both Christian and imperial had an entrenched past and had come to play a significant role in the interaction between the emperor's authority and that of other political constituencies at the capital – the military, the senatorial aristocracy and the bureaucracy.

The culture and function of these other political constituencies were substantially the result of social reorganization initiated by Diocletian and his tetrarchic successors (including Constantine) in response to the political instability that had wracked much of the third century.[8] The fragmentation of military and provincial administration that attended the reforms of the late third century necessitated the expansion of the imperial bureaucracy beyond any dimension formerly known in the Roman world. Where previously the Roman Empire had functioned with a truly minimalist administrative apparatus, from the fourth century over 40,000 would be employed in a systematically structured bureaucracy.[9] Members of the new late antique imperial bureaucracy received salaries (often in the form of both gold specie and a portion of the *annona*) and, at the end of a full career of service, pensions. These emoluments were also better than those received by equivalent military ranks, as befitted enrolment from the literate classes whose skills were necessary for administration. As a result, the empire of the fourth century experienced a new level of elite competition for imperial positions. Now more than ever, local elites and their families from across the provinces had access to an elaborate hierarchy of advancement and to enrichment in imperial service.

Early fourth-century changes to the structure of the imperial state had a profound impact on the distribution of political power at the new capital. From Diocletian and Constantine on, it had become a matter of policy to exclude the senatorial elite from positions with a potential for wider political influence.[10] With higher military offices held in reserve for men with extended military experience, the senatorial elite became limited to holding only a select group of senior magistracies attendant upon the emperor or fixed at the capital (*praesentalis*), thereby insulating the wider administration of the empire from the fractious involvement of aristocratic families. Even when expanded in number to about 2,000 members, the constrained nature of their political participation and the new source of their recruitment from the provincial *curiales* ensured that the Senate at Constantinople would represent an aristocracy increasingly entrenched in the local network of the capital and subject to the will

[8] For a conspectus of tetrarchic reforms, Jones, *TLRE*; and Potter, *Empire at Bay*.
[9] For the administration before Diocletian, Kelly, *Ruling*, 183–200; Ando, 'Administration', 177–92.
[10] On the new relationship of the senatorial aristocracy to the military and civil service, Jones, *TLRE*; Dagron, *Naissance*; Potter, *Empire at Bay*.

of the emperor. Even in the realm of economic influence, senators in the east lacked the same leverage as their western counterparts. Because the majority had been recruited from cities scattered throughout the Mediterranean, their patrimonial lands were distant and did not allow the exercise of influence over local markets and the urban populace in the same manner as the senatorial elite at Rome. In this way, although the increased size and hereditary exclusivity of the eastern Senate reinforced the new capital as the symbol of a centralized state, the eastern Senate ceased to have a directly participatory role in imperial government.[11]

In the absence of the traditional advisory role served by the Senate, late Roman emperors interacted closely with a small body of both civilian and military magistrates attendant on the person of the emperor (the *consistorium*). This core of senior officials was actively involved in debating and advising matters of state and the diversity of its members could range from popular professors of rhetoric to 'barbarian' nobility having served in the military for scarcely a generation.[12] The *consistorium* also contained those select members of the Senate periodically appointed to higher civilian magistracies. Although such appointments would more often be made from the ranks of the civil bureaucracy or the military, emperors regularly granted higher magistracies to senators as a *dignitas* or *honor*, underscoring the control that the emperor had over access to any public prestige enjoyed by members of the Senate. Emperors conferred these senior magistracies as one- to five-year appointments, allowing them to rotate a fair number of both senatorial and provincial elites through the upper levels of government while at the same time limiting dependence on their participation.[13] Many of these offices (such as quaestor, *magister officiorum* and praetorian prefect) commanded departments of the palatine secretariats, meaning that these senior posts exercised a kind of serial leadership over the most stable element of the Roman state – the bureaucracy.

The growth of the late antique bureaucracy represented a crucial shift in the governmental culture of the Roman state. Where once the administrative personnel serving the state had consisted of the private household of the emperor (for example during the Principate), the late antique civil service enjoyed a substantially independent institutional identity. With the expansion of the civil administration to over 20,000 positions in the

---

[11] On the senatorial order at Constantinople, Dagron, *Naissance*, 147–90; Heather, 'New Constantines', 12–18; Vanderspoel, *Themistius*, 51–70.
[12] On the *consistorium*, Jones, *TLRE*, 49–50; cf. 'Flavius Arbitio 2' and 'Themistius 1' in *PLRE I*, 94–5 and 889–94, respectively.
[13] On senior *dignitates*, Heather, 'New Constantines', 18–21.

east alone, the growth of a distinctive institutional identity was a gradual and natural process visible at both eastern and western capitals. This development, however, was more continuous and deeply entrenched in the east, where the largest apparatus of the bureaucracy was fixed from an early date to the city of Constantinople.[14] By contrast, in the west during the fourth and fifth centuries, the imperial court shifted between Trier, Rome, Milan and Ravenna. For this reason and others, the western bureaucracy seems to have become a comparatively reduced institution before the end of the fifth century. By the time of Justinian's accession, the bureaucracy of Constantinople maintained an even stronger position at the capital than it had under Constantine. The civil service styled itself with the perquisites and trappings of the military – adopting the name *militia officialis*, recruiting through documented enlistment (*probatoria*) and conferring a ceremonial badge (the *cingulum*). In terms of collective function, the civil service assessed and facilitated the collection of taxes, stored and distributed goods to be paid as salaries to military and civil service, answered petitions, issued legal verdicts, maintained official records, recruited new members and managed the physical and ceremonial infrastructure of the capital. Any function of imperial government involving finance, manpower and property fell under the competence of the civil service. Perhaps the more important function of bureaucracy was the role it played in socializing the disparate elite communities of the Mediterranean to the idea of imperial rule. The bureaucracy drew its members from a broad swathe of the provincial urban elite and from the extended families of existing *milites*, creating nodes of heterogeneously compacted elites at both the centralized departments of Constantinople and the various offices dispersed throughout the provincial capitals. As such, the bureaucracy was a primary means by which the broad stratum of middling urban elite in the eastern Mediterranean related to and participated in the eastern Roman empire.

THE STRUCTURE OF THE EASTERN BUREAUCRACY

Bureaucratic officials (*milites* or *palatini*) were organized into bureaus or departments (*scholae*, *officia* or *scrinia*) dedicated to a variety of administrative functions. Internally, departments had an elaborate structure mediated by chains of command under intermediary ranks of officers. The *scholae* initially had real military function, performing the role of the palace guard (referred to variously as *scholares*, *domestici* and *protectores*)

---

[14] Jones, *TLRE*, 563–606; Carney, *Bureaucracy*, 89–115; Heather, 'New Constantines', 18–25; Lendon, *Honour*, 176–236; Kelly, *Ruling*; Haldon, 'Economy', 42–7.

commanded by a college of junior officers (*comites* and *tribuni*). By the reign of Justinian, an honorary role had come to replace the military function of the *scholares* and their recruitment from the provincial urban elite reflects the function of the imperial court as a locus for socialization to central governmental authority. The purely military function of protecting the palace and the person of the emperor transferred to a complementary body of palace guards, actual soldiers called the *excubitores*. On the administrative side, departments called *scrinia* maintained correspondence and records. *Milites* within the *scrinia* were organized into grades according to function (*memoriales*, *epistulares* and *libellenses*) under departmental officers (*magistri* and *primicerii*). By far the most important departments, which probably also possessed the greatest number of personnel, were the *officia*. The *officia* were divided into categories that possessed judicial, financial and sub-clerical functions. Sub-clerical *officia* were diverse and typically pertained to public works and menial functions. Judicial matters were handled by the *officia* of legal experts and clerks called *exceptores*. Easily the most tradition-bound and educated cadre of civil service, the *exceptores* were also possibly the most hierarchically stratified. Each *officium* of legal clerks (*beneficiarii*) was supervised by a college of *speculatores* and *commentarienses*, a *cornicularius* and a *princeps*. These *officia* of legal experts typically enjoyed greater prestige than offices of the *scriniarii*, the cohorts of less educated accountants who managed financial affairs under the separate direction of *numerarii* and *tabularii*.

Although the various intermediary officers within departments had contact with respective senior magistrates (holding *dignitates*) of the *consistorium*, the bureaucracy did not constitute a part of the imperial court in the sense of operating in close contact with the emperor. Members of the emperor's *consistorium*, his personal guard (*excubitores*), palace pages (*silentiarii*) and the servants of the private imperial chambers (*cubicularii*) constituted the imperial 'court'. The sheer size of the bureaucracy also contributed to ensuring that it was an institution that functioned independently of the person of the emperor. Although impossible to reconstruct in precise numbers, John Lydus' *De magistratibus* discusses six public offices of the *consistorium* that each commanded *scrinia* and *officia*.[15] Additionally, there were *dignitates* (such as the *comes rei privatae* and *comes sacrarum largitionum*) that fell under the authority of the praetorian prefect, but which maintained independent hierarchies of *scrinia* and *officia*.

---

[15] John Lydus, *De magistratibus* 1.14, the praetorian prefecture; 1.24, the quaestorship; 1.34, the urban prefecture; 1.39, the censor; 1.50, the prefect of the watch; 2.23, the master of offices; Boak and Dunlap, *Administration*, 30–40, on independent competences and staffs of senior offices; also, Haldon, 'Economy', 42–7.

Each such department could enrol between four hundred and six hundred members.[16] Procopius claimed that the *scholares* of Constantinople numbered at 5,500, and this does not include the *domestici* and *protectores* (who held higher status among the titular ranks).[17] In total, the service elite of the eastern capital must have numbered in the many thousands, perhaps as high as 20,000.

The attractions that drew such numbers to civil service were various. By the fifth century, officials engaged in palatine service, like senators, had been granted immunity from most forms of decurial *munera*.[18] As mentioned earlier, having access to regular distributions of the *annona* (including rations of grain, wine and other foodstuffs, clothing and animal fodder, all at state-controlled prices), in addition to an annual salary and discharge pensions in gold, was a lucrative enticement to serve at the capital. The almost exclusive access to gold coinage enjoyed by the magistrates and personnel of state service conferred enormous prestige. Access to gold specie also granted the benefit of allowing the payment of taxes through *adaeratio*, the advantageous commutation of tax payments by coin as opposed to payment in kind.[19] The patron–client relationship that developed within departments of the bureaucracy also secured distinct advantages through connection with elite networks and patronage. Cementing clientage within bureaucratic culture, higher officials within each bureau enjoyed the privilege of *suffragium*, which granted authority to appoint recruits to their departments.[20] Such officials were also positioned to recommend subordinates for promotion outside their particular bureau. The privilege of *praescriptio fori* provided that in cases of legal censure members of civil service would face the judgement of their own superior, granting the bureaucracy considerable leverage in dealing with the civilian population.[21] Thus the various emoluments of state service ensured a premium on intimate connections within bureaus and generated an administrative culture of corporatism. If the demographic trends of enrolment in late antique schools also correspond to professional vocations in civil service, then at any given moment the bureaucracy tended to siphon recruits more heavily from certain regions than from others.[22] Although these regional recruitment pools tended to shift location from one generation to the next, representing the dynamic and fluid nature of

---

[16] Jones, *TLRE*, 583, notes over 400 in the *scrinia* of the prefecture of Africa; 593, about 600 for the *officium* of the city prefect.
[17] Procopius, *Anecdota* 24.15–20 and 24.24–26.   [18] *Codex Theodosianus* 6.26.14.
[19] Banaji, *Agrarian Change*, 56–65; on the prestige of gold coinage, cf. the use of gold coins as jewellery, Bruhn, *Coins*.
[20] On *suffragium*, Jones, *TLRE*, 391–6.   [21] On *praescriptio fori*, Jones, *TLRE*, 484–94.
[22] For this trend in schools, Watts, 'Student travel', 13–23.

how the empire interacted with a wider Mediterranean population, the inevitable tendency for a strong regional flavour in the bureaucracy also strengthened patronage and institutional corporatism.[23]

Although members of the bureaucracy could reach the highest peaks of civil government with appointment to the emperor's *consistorium* and senatorial rank, for the greater part the institution represented a career path separate from that of the *consistorium* and the Senate. Whereas the offices of the *consistorium* generally conferred tenures of limited duration, enrolment in one of the departments of the *militia officialis* required between fifteen and twenty years of service.[24] *Milites* graduated within the ranks of individual departments and often progressed laterally to bureaus with different administrative functions before advancing to more senior positions (not unlike the manner of military advancement in the traditional legion).[25] This level of mobility in civil service meant that men of relatively modest backgrounds experienced a dense network of professional attachments in the course of achieving distinction in service. Because advancement through the ranks of the bureaucracy could constitute a lifelong career, corporate solidarity set the tone for civil service at every stratification of the late antique bureaucracy.

John Lydus offers the most intimate glimpse of how the bureaucratic elite negotiated the different sources of power in Constantinople. Lydus' *De magistratibus* offers a view of palatine service from within subaltern solidarity, not from the spectacular height of one of Justinian's associates at the imperial court. The degree to which Lydus' perspective of government at Constantinople was detached from the imperial court becomes apparent when he talks about his early career. Lydus described how, upon arriving at Constantinople, he chose to pursue a civil career that was separate from attachments with the court. 'As I expected that things would go far better for me as time went on, I held back from forming keen attachments towards the court and made the whole of my life over to the service.'[26] The statement reveals the presence of a bureaucratic career path with a basis for solidarity that was independent of the closer confines of the imperial court. The 'attachments' that Lydus avoided were probably those with families that had become entrenched over generations in higher offices and that naturally gravitated toward closer affiliations with the *consistorium*. These great families more than probably

---

[23] Consider John Lydus, *De magistratibus* 1.20.1–7, on the relationship between patronage and office holding.
[24] Heather, 'New Constantines', 18–21, notes that by 400 AD members of the *agentes in rebus* and *scrinia* served for fifteen years and those of the *privatiani* and *largitionales* for twenty.
[25] Carney, *Bureaucracy*, 102–8.
[26] John Lydus, *De magistratibus* 3.28.2, trans. Carney, *Bureaucracy*, 83.

included the senatorial elite, who occupied a tight orbit around the imperial court. By the time of Justinian's reign, the Senate at Constantinople
had been pared down to include only those members possessing the rank
of *illustris*.[27] Absent the intermediary ranks of *spectabiles* and *clarissimi*, the
gulf between senatorial status and palatine service was prohibitive. The
life which attracted Lydus was a middling, clerical status. Removed from
the lofty manoeuvrings of court politics, a member of the bureaucracy
could claim membership in an institution with its own self-defining
culture and predictable dynamic for advancement.[28]

Lydus furthermore articulated his distance from the upper strata of
familial aristocracy by noting his separation from the traditional lifestyle
of alternating *otium* and *negotium*, a cultural ideal that allowed the senatorial elite to explain their separation from anything other than only
intermittent political activity. Much as it appears in Cassiodorus' preface
to the *Variae*, Lydus too noted this distinction between a civil servant and
an aristocrat:

A man could gather many things of this nature [examples from history] together
at his leisure, if his lot should chance to be to live his life through in a carefree
fashion without having work to do and if he did not indulge in the sort of
foolish pastimes over which I toil away night and day, despite my being involved
in countless worries.[29]

Like Cassiodorus, Lydus seems to have marked his distance from the
leisured elite status of the senatorial class.

BUREAUCRATIC INTELLECTUAL CULTURE

The corporatism and patronage of the bureaucracy ensured that it would
develop a distinctive and insulating institutional culture. The bureaucracy expressed its institutional and cultural distinctiveness principally
as an enclave for classical traditionalism.[30] This attachment to classical
tradition is understandable in several contexts. Beginning with the Second Sophistic, the entry of talented provincials to imperial service had
been, traditionally, through the demonstration of intellectual training –
the declamation of philosophers, the recitations of poets and the dedication of literary works had always opened avenues by which the educated

[27] Haldon, 'Economy', 39, on the *illustres* as the only senatorial rank at Constantinople; similarly,
Evans, *Justinian*, 41, on the mutual exclusivity of the senatorial and palatine elite.
[28] Kelly, *Ruling*, 36–44.
[29] John Lydus, *De magistratibus* 1.23.3, trans. Carney, *Bureaucracy*, 22; see Chapter 7 below for
comments on this same distinction made by Cassiodorus.
[30] What Michael Maas, *John Lydus*, has called 'antiquarianism'.

provincial elite gained the attention of the imperial court, often on behalf of fellow townsmen in provincial communities. With the interest of obtaining imperial favour, communities increasingly selected men with literary training to plead local causes. Emperors keen to demonstrate their own cultural attainments frequently granted audience to and publicly associated themselves with an emerging class of touring literati who could draw crowds with readings at private elite residences, public lecture halls, libraries and even theatres.[31] From the second century onward, the presence of such learned advisers in the imperial consistory was commonplace.[32] In some cases, positions in the imperial secretariat provided springboards to even greater responsibilities.[33] By the fourth century, the literary scholar Themistius provided the model for a *politikos philosophos*, a philosopher and disciple of *paideia* who was fully engaged in the political life of the imperial court.[34]

The classical intellectual interests of the late antique bureaucracy were also an extension of how elites had always positioned themselves in local municipalities as morally suitable representatives of a wider imperial world. It was a long-accepted trope that education, or more specifically an education grounded in wisdom of the ancients (*paideia*), was a civilizing force that provided the mind with order and symmetry, raised it above the native state of primal impulses and attached the individual to the received collective wisdom of civilization through the digesting of ancient texts.[35] Engagement with the classical literary education conferred transcendence above nature and stored the accumulated wisdom of the past, both of which made the recipient more perceptive in the identification of virtue. In short, the traditional education grounded in Latin and Greek literature was thought to make people morally superior as repositories of an ancient and tested knowledge. This was a highly conservative pedagogical and intellectual culture which, more than any other aspect of the history of Romanization, had provided homogeneity for disparate elite classes. Participating in this literary culture was the chief means by which an individual assumed membership of an imperial community irrespective of their ethnic or geographical origin. In a polity that was a mosaic of languages and indigenous cultures, elites trained in the ethos of *paideia*

---

[31] Wright, *Select Letters of Jerome*, xv–xix; Philostratus, *Lives of the Sophists*, especially *Favorinus* 1.8.489–494; *Dionysius of Miletus* 1.22.522–527; *Polemo* 1.25.530–545; *Herodes Atticus* 2.1.546–566; *Aspasius of Ravenna* 2.33.627–628.

[32] For example, Philostratus, *Alexander of Seleucia* 2.5.571; *Adrian of Tyre* 2.10.590.

[33] For example, Philostratus, *Antipater of Hierapolis* 2.24.607.

[34] For Themistius' explanation for a politically active philosophical life, *Oratio* 17 and 34; also, Vanderspoel, *Themistius*, 1–13 and 27–30, on the politically active philosopher.

[35] Kaster, *Guardians*, 50–69; Brown, *Power and Persuasion*, 35–70; Watts, *City and School*, 1–23.

could relate to one another other across distances at a cultural level in a way that less literate classes could not. In this sense, too, the literate elites could relate to the state with a degree of personal interest and intimacy that the less literate could not. The Graeco-Roman educational formation had long been grafted onto the idea of an imperial society, meaning that the lower orders (other than perhaps those active in the military) were effectively excluded from close assimilation to the idea of the imperial Roman state.

By the sixth century, the imperial bureaucracy had become an enclave for traditionalism and classical learning as a natural course of recruiting the intellectual elite from across the eastern Mediterranean. *Paideia* cemented the bureaucratic institutional culture and became a benchmark for participation in its patron–client circles. For many in civil service, the shared intellectual background lent bureaucratic corporatism the aspect of a quasi-religiosity. Quintilian in the first century noted that the shared educational experience could produce personal bonds that had a quality of 'almost religious feelings of attachment'.[36] Within the bureaucratic elite, the solemnity of ritual and ceremony that attended public life provided further expression for deference to the traditions of antiquity that demarcated the bureaucratic elite from a wider 'unlearned' culture. It would be careless to describe this veneration of antiquarianism in terms of a formal cult. However, the maintenance of a spirit of corporatism probably did involve some symbolic aspects that could have been experienced as religiosity. There was already a long history, extending from the second century to the sixth, in which the quasi-religious expression of fidelity and solidarity in administrative service had developed.[37] It is worth noting that Q. Aurelius Symmachus did not champion the cause of a 'pagan' deity when he petitioned Theodosius to restore the Altar of Victory; rather, he decried the repudiation of established practices for serving the state: 'The love of established practice is a powerful sentiment'.[38] Despite its innocuous nature as sentimental observance, the perspective of Christians such as Damasus, Ambrose and Prudentius took a less than compromising view, revealing the potential conflict not between religions, but between two groups claiming to guard the portals to appropriate tradition.

---

[36] Quintilian, *Institutio Oratoria* 1.2.20, 'Mitto amicitias, quae ad senectutem usque firmissime durant religiosa quadam necessitudine inbutae: neque enim est sanctius sacris isdem quam studiis initiari', trans. Russell, *LCL*, 91.

[37] Nelis-Clément, *Beneficiarii*, 269–88.

[38] Symmachus, *Relationes* 3.4, 'Consuetudinis amor magnus est', trans. Barrow, *Prefect*, 37; on Symmachus' conception of tradition, Salzman, 'Reflections',

The *amor consuetudinis* of Symmachus' sentiment can similarly be read throughout Lydus' treatise. Describing his entry into the corps of civil service, Lydus noted that he had 'made his whole life over to the service', suggesting a deeply transformative commitment. He furthermore recalled with some nostalgia how matters of state were 'once cautiously undertaken after prayer by men of the greatest experience'.[39] Again, it is not necessarily the vestigial spore of 'pagan' practices that surfaces here, but the expression of a profound sense of devotion to a way of life that had become traditional for educated public officials of middling status. The social environment of the late antique grammarian which Robert Kaster has brought to life sheds light on several salient aspects of the interaction between bureaucratic intellectual culture and status. Like *grammatici*, the social life of the bureaucrat was determined by participation in deeply ideological structures of conservative tradition; and like *grammatici*, the liberally trained bureaucrat was both a marginal and a liminal figure, granting access to hierarchies of power which overshadowed his own status.[40] Unlike grammarians, whose status depended on constant interaction with their social superiors rather than through association with a college, the late antique bureaucrat both was insulated by membership of a confraternity and possessed the educational background to claim a higher form of morality.[41]

In some ways, the intense corporatism of bureaucratic service may have been a response to the emergence of Christianity as the dominant religion of the Mediterranean. Although it is not possible even in the sixth century to declare Christianity triumphant, especially in as much as there was not one but many Christianities, it is certainly true that as a broadly construed religious form Christianity had exerted considerable pressures on the evolution of social life of the Mediterranean elite. Christianity began to gain traction in the Roman Empire at precisely the time when the social and cultural identity of a large swathe of the Mediterranean population was in transition. As the imperial state drew more and more provincial elites into active political roles, a vibrant source of cohesion to local identity (the local elite class) was gradually drained away to play a role in an empire to which the non-elite could less easily relate.[42] In an imperial world where elite identity had become more dependent on lateral connections to other elites scattered across the Mediterranean urban network, participation in those traditions that

---

[39] John Lydus, *De magistratibus* 3.28.2 and 2.18.2 respectively, trans. Carney, *Bureaucracy*, 83 and 54.
[40] Kaster, *Guardians*, 15–31; also Gillett, 'Olympiodorus', 1–29.
[41] Kaster, *Guardians*, 50–69 on the moral claims of the educated, 123–32 on grammarians entering palatine service.
[42] Brown, *Late Antiquity*, 60–8.

had staged local identity and been safeguarded by the stewardship of local elites necessarily weakened. The drain on local cultural capital is nowhere more apparent than in local euergetistic practices, where a dramatic decline in epigraphic dedications (and, by extension, elite interest in benefaction to local communities) is evident beginning in the third century and culminating in the fifth century.[43] This did not mean the extinction of local identity, but rather it was a period in which local identities retrenched themselves with new patrons. The new religious movements of late antiquity were founded on the need of groups for whom the empire was conceptually too large to be reinscribed in some form of communal identity. Christianity's basis as a religion that required the mediation of texts – and texts accessible to a lower level of literacy – lay partly in the attempt of local non-elites to appropriate the element crucial to the identity of an elite that was increasingly less involved in local affairs. Faced with the glass ceiling of *paideia*, which elite tradition had touted as the only route granting access to true knowledge and moral living, Christian converts found themselves in the possession of a text-based doctrine that granted the same claim of moral superiority to a disenfranchised clientage. The reorganization of elite class identity that occurred in reaction to the claims of this new source of moral excellence from the third century to the sixth would prove to be one of the most transformative to occur in the ancient world.[44] Writing by Christian authors was increasingly interested in appropriating the prestige of 'classical' linguistic and literary habits.[45] The presentation of the Christian ascetic in the fourth century could adopt formal aspects from the literary portraiture of secular philosophers with as much ease as monastic thinkers of the sixth century could infuse Christian doctrine and liturgy with elements of Neoplatonic spirituality.[46] It is important to note here that boundaries between concepts that contributed to the formation of elite identity had become porous. Concrete definitions would typically surface only at specific moments when the political and social order was publicly contested.

With Christianity waxing as an alternative form of moral instruction, with the support of Constantine's official recognition and with the continued support of succeeding emperors, the Christian church soon became a new trans-Mediterranean institution open to elite colonization. The interaction between new patrons of the marginalized and the old

[43] Ward-Perkins, *Building*, 14–37; Liebeschuetz, *Decline*, 11–19.
[44] Brown, *Power and Persuasion*, 71–117.
[45] McKitterick, *History and Memory*, 218–64; Chin, *Grammar and Christianity*.
[46] On Christian ascetic and secular philosophical biography, Watts, 'Three generations', 117–33; on the sixth-century Dionysius as a Platonizing Christian, Perl, *Theophany*.

patrons of establishment created a language of religious authority which allowed each to play a role in the emerging Christian church.[47] In precisely the same period of Mediterranean history, the bureaucracy became one of the last bastions of traditional secularism. Although it would be inaccurate to designate the bureaucracy as a 'pagan' institution given the prosopographical evidence for Christians in the civil service, it is certainly the case that the culture of the bureaucracy was weighted toward the cultivation of traditional, secular *paideia*. Both Christian and Hellene *milites* accepted literary antiquarianism as a facet of the institutional culture because it provided bureaucratic culture with its distinctiveness from the other institution with which it competed for prestige – the Christian church.[48] Members of the *militia officialis* were expected to have a classical literary education and recruitment into the bureaucracy was often channelled through patronage networks associated with important centres of classical learning – Rome, Athens, Antioch, Alexandria.[49] This aspect of bureaucratic corporatism was probably nowhere more vibrant than in the ranks which recruited from higher provincial nobility and more middling urban provincials who required classical training as a matter of course in the performance of administrative duties – the *scholares* on the one hand and the *exceptores* on the other.

NEOPLATONISM AND BUREAUCRATIC CULTURE

The culture with which members of the bureaucracy insulated themselves from other competing forms of elite expression received at least superficial exposure to Neoplatonism.[50] The Middle Platonism of the preceding centuries had striven to reconcile the teachings of Plato and Aristotle, and the Neoplatonism of late antiquity that subsequently developed and continued well into the sixth century advanced the synthesis of these two traditional sources of wisdom.[51] Additionally, Neoplatonism developed a sustained interest in describing a political order that was in harmony with both the sensible and intelligible aspects of the universal

---

[47] Brown, 'Elites', 335–45.

[48] For the burgeoning debate concerning 'pagan' and Christian conflict, Momigliano, *Conflict*; O'Meara, *Neoplatonism*; Barnish, 'Martianus Capella', 98–111; Rike, *Apex Omnium*; Salaman, *Paganism*; Ando, 'Pagan apologetics', 171–207; Athanassiadi and Frede, *Pagan Monotheism*; Salzman, 'Rethinking violence', 265–85; Schott, *Christianity*; Mitchell and Van Nuffelen, *One God*; Mitchell and Van Nuffelen, *Monotheism*; Cameron, *Last Pagans*.

[49] Watts, *City and School*, 24–78.

[50] On the development of Neoplatonism from the third century to the sixth, Wallis, *Neoplatonism*; Hadot, *Néoplatonisme*; Edwards, *Neoplatonic Saints*, vi–lv; O'Meara, *Platonopolis*; Baltussen, *Simplicius*, 140–71; Remes, *Neoplatonism*, 1–33; Siniossoglou, *Theodoret*.

[51] Baltussen, *Simplicius*, 1–14.

'soul'.[52] By the end of the fifth century, Neoplatonic thought had articulated a fully matured conception of government that paralleled a universal conception of cosmology and natural order.[53] In as much as the philosophy emphasized hierarchical progression and harmony within hierarchy, it was particularly well suited as an ethos complementing bureaucratic corporatism.[54] This aspect of bureaucratic culture, rather than being viewed as religious attachment per se, is better understood as part of the educational background that formed a basis for group identity for many in state service.[55] The fullest possible exposure to *paideia* ideally included familiarity with rhetorical and philosophical instruction.[56] Moreover, Neoplatonism dismissed sources of wisdom with claim to antiquity only reluctantly. Pythagoreanism, Stoicism, Aristotelianism, Chaldean Oracles and even myths were almost indiscriminately examined as possible sources granting access to universal truth. Both syncretic and exegetical in its literary habits, Neoplatonic thought often aimed at locating agreement between the accepted core teachings of Plato and alternative sources of wisdom.[57] As such, Neoplatonic thought had an attachment to a particularly cosmopolitan conception of authentic antiquity. For palatine officials drawn from a wide range of regional backgrounds who shared a veneration for the traditions of antiquity, Neoplatonic thought was ideal as a complementary political theology. Although few palatine officials would devote themselves to the full rigour of philosophical study, many would affect a 'Platonic–Aristotelian *koine*' as a part of their social identity.[58] Only the wealthier members of the bureaucracy could have acquired this philosophical patina in the course of their education, but these were also the most influential members of the bureaucratic hierarchy who set the tone of bureaucratic culture for their subalterns.[59]

Neoplatonic thought had much to offer civil servants in terms not only of prestige, but also of the specifically Neoplatonic conception of moral governance.[60] Neoplatonic thought was distinctive in that it

---

[52] Remes, *Neoplatonism*, 77–8.   [53] Siorvanes, *Proclus*, 6–20; O'Meara, *Platonopolis*, 39–48.
[54] On the unity of hierarchy in Neoplatonism, Siorvanes, *Proclus*, 6–20; O'Meara, *Platonopolis*, 46–7; Baltussen, *Simplicius*, 68–87.
[55] For similarities to late antique religious patronage, Bowes, *Private Worship*, 21–37.
[56] On pedagogical developments in the sixth century, Cameron, 'Education'; Greatrex, 'Lawyers', 148–61.
[57] Remes, *Neoplatonism*, 10–19.   [58] Lanata, *Legislazione*, 225–6.
[59] On the exclusivity of a literary education, Rapp, 'Literary culture', 379–82.
[60] For example, Hadot, *Néoplatonisme*, 153–56, on the correspondence between the soul and civic virtue; and Siorvanes, *Proclus*, 6–20, on the similarity between the Neoplatonic metaphysical hierarchy and civil service.

provided a place for the public virtues of civil service (justice, restraint, wisdom and fortitude) in a hierarchy of higher, contemplative virtues. In essence, Neoplatonism anchored the practical virtues associated with public service in a more comprehensive system for elaborating moral good.[61] The belief that political activity furthered moral improvement was an ethos that could activate personal conviction, as represented in a statement by Boethius: 'I wanted the chance to take an active part in affairs of state, so that what powers for good I possess might not wither with age unused.'[62] Disseminated from senior departmental officers to their staff in the course of exercising authority on a daily basis, the precepts of a Neoplatonic theology of state service would encourage discipline and cultivate a deeper understanding of corporatism. The process of disseminating a form of moral instruction, in particular, would strengthen the bonds of patronage upon which an official's reputation depended.[63]

The intersection between Neoplatonic thought, civil service and the corporatism that developed as a part of bureaucratic culture had a very specific locus in the early sixth century – the Academy at Athens.[64] Marcus Aurelius made the first connection between the state and philosophical studies at Athens by granting an imperial donation that supported professors of the Academy with a state stipend.[65] By the fourth century, Neoplatonic philosophers of the Academy had strong ties to the imperial bureaucracy at Constantinople. In the case of one provincial family from Apamea, three generations traced its membership in imperial service and involvement in Neoplatonic philosophy to Iamblichus at Athens.[66] Olympiodorus of Thebes, the historian and imperial official at Constantinople, maintained firm connections with the intellectual community at Athens.[67] The family background of one of the celebrated philosophers of the Academy in the fifth century, Proclus, extended to the imperial bureaucracy at Constantinople.[68] Proclus himself certainly had access to imperial political channels.[69] Not surprisingly, a distinguished list of politically active men benefited from this network and could trace their intellectual genealogy through Athens – emperor Anthemius; Severianus, a provincial governor under Zeno; Pamprepius,

[61] As described by Marinus, *Life of Proclus* 18; Van den Berg, 'Neoplatonic politician', 106–11; Remes, *Neoplatonism*, 190–6.

[62] Boethius, *De consolatione philosophiae* 2.7.3–5, trans. Tester, *LCL*, 215–17; also on this, O'Meara, *Platonopolis*, 48.

[63] Chin, *Grammar and Christianity*, 110–38, on pedagogy as socialization.

[64] Watts, *City and School*, 87–128.   [65] Cassius Dio, *Historia Romana* 72.31.3.

[66] O'Meara, 'Neoplatonist ethics', 91–3.   [67] Gillett, 'Olympiodorus', 14–18.

[68] Remes, *Neoplatonism*, 27–8.   [69] Marinus, *Vita Procli* 15.

the *magister officiorum* under Zeno; Marcellinus, the *magister militum* and governor of Dalmatia; Pusaeus, the eastern praetorian prefect of 465; and Messius Phoebus Severus, prefect of Rome and consul in 470.[70] There is no reason to assume that the distinction of this list indicates that John Lydus, who spent a year studying under a scholar from the Academy before taking his first post in the *officium* of the praetorian prefect at Constantinople, was precocious among lesser public officials for having listened to the lessons of the Academy's hallowed porticoes; it is probable that many such as John followed this course of instruction in the hope of attaining similarly high offices. Athens served as a catchment area where a wide distribution of the eastern Mediterranean elite could receive instruction in what purported to be a universal political philosophy.[71] Nor would eventual recruitment into civil service sever ties with Athens. The Neoplatonic ideal dictated that philosophers offer their advice on correct living to the politically active.[72] Bureaucrats trained at the Academy could expect to maintain connections with their intellectual patrons, enhancing their own cultural capital in daily interactions with a younger generation of subalterns.

Although the Academy at Athens was not a cultic site (nor did it screen Christian pupils), the instruction available there had a definite religious tone that complemented the veneration of tradition and antique wisdom. The 'philosopher sage' was widely characterized in Mediterranean literature as having been directed by the will of gods, and their reputations could become visibly associated with urban temple cults.[73] The third-century wellsprings of Neoplatonism, Porphyry and Plotinus, formulated a set of principles that established traditional, 'pagan' notions of communal religion as the foundation of the political state.[74] By the sixth century, many intellectual centres, such as Alexandria, approached Neoplatonism with more circumspection as a warehouse of antiquarian knowledge.[75] Athens, however, proved more tenacious and the curriculum of the Academy emphasized oracular spirituality in combination with the practice of theurgy.[76] Introduced by Iamblichus, theurgy comprised

---

[70] O'Meara, *Platonopolis*, 21.

[71] Cameron, 'Ancient universities', 664, notes students from Cilicia, Phrygia, Lydia, Phoenicia and Gaza at the Academy just prior to its closure in 529.

[72] On this, Van den Berg, 'Neoplatonic politician', 106–11; Remes, *Neoplatonism*, 190–6.

[73] Fowden, 'Sages', 145–70.

[74] Siorvanes, *Proclus*, 6–20; Digeser, 'Religion', 68–84; Remes, *Neoplatonism*, 194.

[75] Westerink, 'Philosophy', 176.

[76] On Chaldaean Oracles and Neoplatonic philosophy, Saffrey, 'Neoplatonist spirituality', 250–65; Athanassiadi, 'Apamea', 117–43; on the development of soteriological interests in Neoplatonic thought as a reaction to Christianity, Siniossoglou, *Theodoret*, 34–47.

a set of divinatory rituals used to bridge the divine universe and human understanding.[77] In essence, theurgy was a form of ritualized meditation intended to activate revelation concerning the mysteries of the natural and cosmic world. The Iamblichan brand of Neoplatonic thought, unlike other schools, was deeply entrenched in speculation on the role of nature in a wider cosmic harmony and natural symbolism figured prominently in theurgic practices.[78] As a result, the school at Athens drew from across the eastern Mediterranean elites who self-identified with non-Christian traditions.[79] Evidence abounds for the continuity of traditional non-Christian religious practices in the Greek east that would have supplied the school at Athens with a receptive audience.[80] The *Dionysiaca* of Nonnos of Panopolis portrays a vigorous 'pagan' religion in the fifth century, and Hellene communities were active in the early sixth century at Edessa, Baalbek and Aphrodisias. John of Ephesus reportedly converted 70,000 so-called pagans in the towns and countryside of sixth-century Asia Minor.[81] As previously noted, Procopius suggests that a latent veneration for the traditional religion of the empire was observable in sixth-century Rome.[82] Even when dismissed as exaggeration, Procopius' comments still suggest an (eastern) audience that was receptive to the religious traditions of state service.

In contrast, the Alexandrian school tended to eschew direct engagement with the non-Christian tradition and probably for this reason had earned substantial emoluments from the eastern capital at a time when the doctrine of the Athenian school rendered it susceptible to imperial censure.[83] Despite its vulnerability to imperial disfavour, the Athenian school experienced a renewal of popularity and prestige from 515 until

---

[77] Described by Porphyry, *De regressu animae*, and Iamblichus, *On the Mysteries of the Egyptians* 2.11.96–97; Fowden, 'Pagan holy man', 33–59; Shaw, 'Theurgy', 1–28; Remes, *Neoplatonism*, 171–3.

[78] Clark, 'Cosmic sympathies', 310–18, how the teachings of Iamblichus ran cross-current to most Neoplatonic tenets, which expressed a dismissive attitude toward the natural world.

[79] Lanata, *Legislazione*, 223; Blumenthal, 'John Philoponus', 62; Fowden, 'Pagan holy man', 38, notes how adherence to Plato, especially through its connection to Iamblichan theurgy, made Neoplatonism at Athens more 'aggressively pagan' than at Alexandria.

[80] Bowersock, *Hellenism*, 41–4; Whitby, 'John of Ephesus', 111–31; Jones, 'Apollonius of Tyana', 49–64; Baltussen, *Simplicius*, 50. For the archaeology of 'pagan' communities surviving into the sixth century, Johannes, 'Zerstörung', 203–42; and Chaniotis, 'Aphrodisias', 243–73.

[81] John of Ephesus, *Ecclesiastical History* 3.27.

[82] Procopius, *Wars* 5.7.6–8 and 5.24.28–37, on the Sibyl; 5.25.18–25, on the temple of Janus.

[83] Cameron, 'Ancient universities', 670–1; on polemical debate between the Hellene Neoplatonic teaching of Athens and the Christianized Neoplatonism at Alexandria, Sorabji, 'Ammonius', 203–13, and Baltussen, *Simplicius*, 176–88; on the sensitivity of Neoplatonism at Alexandria to the local Christian community, Blumenthal, 'John Philoponus', 54–63; also Sorabji, 'John Philoponus', 1–40.

529 under the direction of Damascius.[84] The prestige of Damascius' school at this time is traceable through the social networks that drew students from across the east.[85] As indicated by the career of John Lydus, this prestige contributed to the increased importance of an Athenian education as a component of the profile of public officials at Constantinople. This is not to suggest that Athens was directly responsible for the practice of 'pagan' religion at the eastern capital. Only a few of the most devoted students would have reached a study of the more overtly 'pagan' aspects of Neoplatonic mysteries. For the most part, those who attended the Academy constituted a wide circle of 'listeners' who transmitted the reputation of the school and the antiquarian ethos to Constantinople, but who did not necessarily subscribe to the religious practices cultivated at the school.[86]

The transmission of an ethos formed through the veneration of *paideia* and Neoplatonic precepts created the culture of bureaucratic corporatism that allowed members of the *militia* to insulate themselves against the intrusion of senior magistrates from the *consistorium* holding temporary tenure over various bureaus of the civil service. By the sixth century, the bureaucratic departments had coalesced into an institution capable of weathering the vicissitudes of imperial succession and, importantly, capable of acculturating to its own defining mores the steady flow of educated elite drawn to Constantinople.[87] The relative ease with which the eastern bureaucracy made the transition from one emperor to the next reveals much about stability within the institution. The essence of this institutional stability was the transfer of primary allegiance away from the emperor and toward an abstracted conception of the state. Given that the bureaucracy numbered in the thousands, most of whom would never have intimate access to the emperor, this was a perfectly natural development. Whereas in the earlier imperial period, palatine freedmen had formed a powerful faction whose personal influence depended on access to the emperor, the sixth-century civil service had, to a certain extent, successfully detached itself from that dependence, and this seems to have remained the case at least until the reign of Justinian.[88]

---

[84] Watts, 'AD 529', 169–70, more fully in Watts, *City and School*, 118–28; also Wildberg, 'Philosophy', 329–30.
[85] On social networks and patronage extending from the Academy at Athens to various other cities in the east, Watts, 'Student travel', 14–21; also Fowden, 'Pagan holy man', 40–5; O'Meara, 'Neoplatonist ethics', 91–100.
[86] On 'listeners', Fowden, 'Pagan holy man', 39.
[87] Carney, *Bureaucracy*; Lendon, *Honour*, 222–32; Nelis-Clément, *Beneficiarii*, 269–88; Kelly, *Ruling*, 26–30.
[88] Brown, *Late Antiquity*, 156.

Insulated by its own profound veneration of elite tradition, its *reverentia antiquitatis*, the bureaucracy enjoyed an institutional identity that had greater continuity than the reigns of individual emperors. The combination of an established tradition for civil service, the shorter tenures of senior magistrates from the *consistorium* and historical volatility in the reigns of emperors created the ideal environment for a shift in the ideological loyalties of the bureaucracy. For members of the bureaucracy, civil service as an institution, not the emperor, embodied the state. Indeed, emperors had come to depend on partnership with the bureaucracy not only for the administrative functioning of the empire, but to lend nascent or troubled regimes legitimacy. Claiming authority over and staging the deference of an enduring institution that symbolized the Roman state could substantiate the most tenuous claims to legitimacy. Receiving that deference in a real sense was a matter that required careful negotiation between the emperor and prominent elements of the bureaucracy. Conversely, the bureaucracy became regarded as the guardian of a legitimating tradition that could potentially curb (particularly in the sphere of law) the unlimited prerogative of the emperor. The bureaucratic role in interpreting law derived in part from its daily function as an administration. More importantly, the bureaucracy came to view the law as its own domain on the basis of the traditional study of classical literature prized in bureaucratic culture. Literary exegesis and the moral explication that was the product of exegesis had traditionally formed the basis of forensic and legal training. From the perspective of the bureaucratic elite, this was the singular and indisputable source of legal expertise. From the perspective of the emperor, it was a potential rival to imperial authority.

Chapter 3

THE REIGN OF JUSTINIAN

REGIME CHANGE

Exactly why Justinian viewed the continuity and almost institutional independence of the bureaucracy as a source of rivalry has to do with the insecurity of his accession to the imperial throne. Historical precedents warranting a new emperor's mistrust of the palatine service were certainly at hand as practicable advice.[1] While corporatism was advantageous to members of the civil service in terms of maintaining cohesiveness and blunting the potentially disruptive nature of internal competition for distinction, it could also appear presumptuous and threatening from the perspective of emperors with only recently minted legitimacy.[2]

Justinian's own political career began through the agency of two conditions active in eastern imperial successions since the death of Theodosius II – the continued recruitment of relatively marginal provincials into state service at Constantinople and the factionalized process of negotiating imperial succession among parties holding active political roles. Justinian's uncle, Justin, arrived in Constantinople from Thrace during the 460s at a time when the Balkan and Danubian provinces shouldered the burden of accommodating Gothic *foederati* conscripted after the collapse of Attila's Hunnic confederacy. Despite the unsympathetic portrayal in later sources depicting his illiterate and semi-barbaric origins in Thrace, Justin's career under three emperors advanced him to a position of considerable influence at the imperial court.[3] Under Leo and Zeno, Justin ascended through the ranks of the *excubitores* during the

---

[1] Cassius Dio, *Historia Romana* 77.6.2 and 77.10.5, on Septimius Severus and the imperial freedmen; Aurelius Victor, *De Caesaribus* 39 and 42, on Diocletian and the *frumentarii*; Ammianus Marcellinus, *Res Gestae* 22.4.1–2 and 26.4.4, on Julian and Valentinian, respectively.

[2] On earlier imperial successions and the court, Jones, *TLRE*, 217–37; Cameron, *Claudian*; Lenski, *Failure of Empire*; Croke, 'Dynasty'; Haarer, *Anastasius*.

[3] On Justin, *PLRE II*, 648–51; descriptions of his origins as a Thracian peasant may be found in Procopius, *Anecdota* 6.2; John Malalas, *Chronographia* 410; Evagrius, *Historia Ecclesiastica* 4.1; Zonaras 14.5.1.

same period that Theoderic the Amal resided at the palace as *magister militum praesentalis* (483–7). Later, Anastasius appointed Justin *comes* of the *excubitores*, granting him full authority over the only functionally military cohort of the imperial palace. When Anastasius died in 518, Justin became the focus of attention among rival palace factions. Apparently the Senate and ministers of the *consistorium* proved dilatory in nominating a successor and, as a result, two factions of the palace personnel (the *excubitores* and *scholares*) assembled at the Hippodrome with a large portion of the urban populace to settle the matter. When each faction proposed a different candidate, Anastasius' former chief chamberlain (*praepositus sacri cubicularii*) Amandus attempted to suborn Justin for the purpose of distributing one pound of silver to each palace guard in order to secure their support for Theocritus, a prominent *domesticus* of the palace. Justin distributed the bribe in his own name, thereby securing the support of the *excubitores*, the Senate and the people assembled at the Hippodrome. Only the *scholares* showed displeasure with the arrangement and this may be important as their social status and function at court was closely analogous to the *domestici*, possibly indicating that Theocritus had had support from the *scholae*. In any case, Anastasius' nephews are not mentioned in the narrative, indicating that the dominant elements of the court were leaning away from dynastic succession.[4]

Justin's advanced years (aged perhaps sixty-six or sixty-eight) at the time of his accession also suggest that his candidacy had been calculated to avoid another imperial dynasty that would inevitably challenge the ascendancy of court factions. Perhaps on account of this and the contested nature of his accession, almost immediately after gaining the throne Justin began grooming his young nephew Justinian (also a native of Thrace) as his heir. Justin had introduced Justinian to court earlier under Anastasius, during which time Justinian served as an attendant to the *magister officiorum*. After his uncle's elevation, Justinian advanced to the rank of *comes et magister militum praesentalis* from 520 and attained a consulship in 521. In 527, Justin proclaimed Justinian his colleague in government, thus ensuring the full transfer of imperial powers, soon after which he died.

Justinian's succession was unstable in several respects. First, Justin had commenced his reign with the execution of Amandus, Theocritus and, under separate circumstances, the influential military commander Vitalian (along with numbers of his attendants).[5] Justinian was reported to

---

[4] For Justin's accession, Marcellinus Comes, *Chronicon* 519; Procopius, *Anecdota* 6.1–16; John Malalas, *Chronographia* 410–11.

[5] On Vitalian in court politics, Haarer, *Anastasius*, 164–81; Ruscu, 'Vitalianus', 773–85.

have had a hand in several of these proscriptions.[6] Second, members of Anastasius' family continued to prosper visibly even after being excluded from imperial office.[7] The reluctance of the *scholares* to accept Justin probably also compounded the insecurity that Justinian experienced in the early years of his reign. The public execution of a prominent member of the *domestici* and the similarity in social and intellectual backgrounds shared between the *scholares* and influential elements in the bureaucracy (particularly the *exceptores*) no doubt coloured Justinian's perception of the bureaucracy, causing him to question the loyalty of any form of corporatism that did not centre directly on the imperial seat. Additionally, the bureaucracy had profited from a number of Anastasius' administrative reforms and the test of loyalties at Justin's accession may have alienated Justinian in his subsequent dealings with this group.[8] Justinian's understanding of the political dynamic that had brought his uncle to power may explain why, during the thirty-eight years of his reign, the emperor never ventured beyond the capital.

BUREAUCRACY UNDER SIEGE

From the outset of his reign, Justinian seemed determined to contest the institutional independence of the bureaucracy. He did so through a series of administrative reforms which, according to A. H. M. Jones, were concerned to excise corruption from the exercise of law and from the management of fiscal resources.[9] Tony Honoré, taking a different perspective, attributed Justinian's administrative reforms to his peculiarly provincial defects of personality and his lack of sensitivity to the functioning norms of public culture at Constantinople.[10] More probably, the simple politics of self-preservation motivated the policies that would challenge the social and political traditions of the bureaucracy. In particular, the judicial branch of the bureaucracy (the *exceptores*) wielded considerable influence in Constantinople and their traditional role as stewards of legal processes made them targets of Justinian's ideological programme.[11] Justinian entrusted the implementation of these reforms to John the Cappadocian, who received appointment as praetorian prefect early in

---

[6] Procopius, *Anecdota* 6.27–28; Zachariah of Mytilene, *Historia Ecclesiastica* 8.2; Victor, *Chronica* 523.
[7] On the continued prominence of relatives of Anastasius, Cameron, 'Anastasius', 259–76.
[8] Haarer, *Anastasius*, 193–229, for Anastasius' administrative reforms.
[9] Jones, *TLRE*, 269–96.   [10] Honoré, *Tribonian*, 1–30.
[11] Kelly, 'Later Roman bureaucracy', 167–75, expanded on in Kelly, *Ruling*, 191–203; Maas, *Exegesis*, 2–11; Pazdernik, 'Justinianic ideology', 185–212; Haldon, 'Economy', 49.

February of 531. Promoted to the senatorial rank of *illustris* from his previous position as *scriniarius* on the staff of a *magister militum*, John's abrupt elevation presented a stark contrast to channels of measured advancement in the bureaucracy.[12] Although the post was a dignity of limited tenure, the praetorian prefect held authority over the entire palatine service and John used his position to enforce internal reform. He revoked *suffragium* on the grounds that practices for promoting within the bureaucracy had become corrupt. Instead of advancing eligible members of the *exceptores*, John personally directed the placement of *scriniarii* (accountants from the financial branch of bureaucracy) in choice positions typically reserved for men of educated distinction.

The imposition of the *scriniarii* was perhaps the most disruptive breach in bureaucratic culture.[13] It allowed men lacking the appropriate exposure to *paideia* to hold positions that presumably called for a deep respect for antique tradition (*reverentia antiquitatis*), breaking the chain of adherence to the dominant institutional culture. Of course, this was a complaint that had been voiced in previous generations and reflects a seemingly age-old conflict. Libanius and Julian criticized Constantine's record for the preferment of less polished clerks over rhetorically trained scholars, even though it may have been in Constantine's better interest to disrupt previous channels of patronage.[14] The narrow technical expertise of the *scriniarii* and their distance from an education in liberal letters that implied elevated social status made them tractable and more useful.[15] From the perspective of *exceptores* and other bureaucrats trained in the precepts of the classical tradition, the preferment of simple accountants threatened to discredit the intellectual elite's cultural capital and their authority to acculturate new members and to govern the progression of their careers. These traditionalists were witness to the initial stages in the dismantling of the cultural basis of patronage and solidarity that had cemented the institution and, from their perspective, the state.

John Lydus summed up the grievance by noting that, previously, men had received high honors in state service by virtue of an education in the liberal arts, experience in the courts of law and carefully regulated advancement; the more recent trend under John the Cappadocian signalled a break in bureaucratic custom.[16] Lydus emphasized the customary role of patronage and also the moral qualifications received through a traditional education as necessary to advancement in office. The claim that

[12] *PLRE IIIA*, 627–35.   [13] Carney, *Bureaucracy*, 158; Kelly, *Ruling*, 30.
[14] Libanius, *Oratio* 62.8–9; Ammianus Marcellinus, *Res Gestae* 21.10.7–8, noted that Julian had criticized Constantine for advancing a man who was 'inconsummatum et subagrestem'.
[15] Cf. Kaster, *Guardians*, 47–70, for an identical scenario with respect to the *notarii*.
[16] John Lydus, *De magistratibus* 2.18.1–3, 3.35.1–36.2.

law prescribed waiting nine years before advancing to a higher appointment speaks to a concern that members of a bureau should become thoroughly acculturated to the traditions of civil service.[17] Lydus also lamented how literary and legal inquiry died away in the bureau offices and this should be understood in terms of the erosion of a cultural identity that had supported bureaucratic corporatism.[18] The revocation of *suffragium* furthermore threatened to undermine corporatism within the bureaucracy by challenging the right of civil servants to refer suits against them to the official of their *schola* or *officium*, a serious blow to bureaucratic patronage. John Lydus referred to the destabilization of patronage in the bureaucracy when he complained that of the 'liberal treatment of friends . . . a dim trace of this practice was preserved until recently among the Romans'.[19] Clearly, for John Lydus, tampering with practices concerning the appeal of legal cases and allowing *scriniarii* to usurp posts normally reserved for the *exceptores* disrupted established channels of bureaucratic patronage.[20] The reforms enacted by John the Cappadocian attempted to force a realignment of the network that had granted a substantial degree of institutional independence to the bureaucracy.[21]

Anxiety over the decline of Latin in bureaucratic chanceries was complementary to a more general concern for the loss of the bureaucratic intellectual culture.[22] Both concerns are traceable to the shift in social background of administrative personnel. Lydus in particular deplored poor Latinity as symptomatic of moral failure in public life.[23] The Latin literature of late fifth- and early sixth-century Constantinople flourished within the carefully guarded confines of the political elite, testifying to the importance of Latinity to maintaining not only ideas of empire but group identity.[24] Authors writing in Constantinople such as Priscian, Marcellinus Comes, Jordanes, Junillus, and Corripus (not to mention the initial publication of Justinian's own *Corpus Iuris Civilis*) attest to

---

[17] John Lydus, *De magistratibus* 2.18.1–3; Ammianus Marcellinus, *Res Gestae* 21.16.3, expressed a similar concern that appointments to court should wait ten years to ensure good character.

[18] John Lydus, *De magistratibus* 3.13.1–15.1.

[19] John Lydus, *De magistratibus* 1.20.3–5, trans. Carney, *Bureaucracy*, 19.

[20] John Lydus, *De magistratibus* 2.15, 2.17, 3.9, 3.35–36; on this, Carney, *Bureaucracy*, 184.

[21] Haldon, 'Economy', 49–51; Pazdernik, 'Justinianic ideology', 187 and 195–8.

[22] Honoré, *Tribonian*, 124–38; Cameron, 'Old and new Rome', 29.

[23] John Lydus, *De magistratibus* 2.12 and 3.42, twice repeats an oracle from 'the Roman Fonteius' predicting Fortune's desertion of the Romans 'at the time when they shall themselves forget their ancestral tongue', trans. Carney, *Bureaucracy*, 50 and 94; Auerbach, *Literary Language*, 252–4, notes the enduring use of Latin in chanceries as a sign of bureaucratic conservatism.

[24] Cavallo, 'Circolazione libraria', 203–20, locates sustained interest in the production of Latin texts at Constantinople in the civil service; also on Latinity in the east, Nicks, 'Literary culture', 183–203; Rapp, 'Hagiography', 1228–77; Cameron, 'Old and new Rome', 15–36; on the cultural authority of Latin and its imperial associations, Smith, *Europe after Rome*, 28–40.

an active Latin readership at the capital. The fact that Latin fell into desuetude as the dominant medium of political communication under Justinian and yet retained its primacy in ecclesiastical communication at the capital suggests not a general cultural shift toward Greek in the circles of the literate, but a specific policy aimed at the cultural prestige of Latin in governing.[25] The administrative shift from Latin to Greek originated in Justinian's *consistorium* and parallels the eclipse of an aristocratic bureaucracy that had generated its own imperial traditions in order to maintain cultural cohesion.[26] In essence, John the Cappadocian attempted to create a cadre of civil servants unaffected by notions of the moral superiority of *paideia* and more devoted to the emperor than to membership in bureaucratic culture.

This attack on the culture of bureaucratic corporatism also targeted the influence of Neoplatonic teaching on bureaucratic social networks. Neoplatonism provided the framework for a bureaucratic political ideology and offered traditionalists a set of philosophical tenets with which to contest a new style of government.[27] This prong of Justinian's contest with bureaucratic ideology would not have threatened all members of the civil service, but for many it represented the crisis point of a culture under siege. In 529, just two years after his accession as emperor, Justinian passed legislation targeting the Hellenes – those non-Christians educated in a classicizing tradition, many of whom were members of the bureaucracy.[28] The edict of 529 forbade so-called pagans from drawing state salaries for teaching, confiscated the property that had supported the Academy at Athens and, more tellingly, purged public officials of a 'Hellenic' disposition from civil service in Constantinople.[29] The later account of John Malalas paints a broad picture of proscription.[30] The list of proscribed is impressive in that it included officials holding prominent positions in the administration of Constantinople. Pseudo-Dionysius of Tel-Mahre, discussing the event later in the eighth century, noted that the persecution targeted nobles, philosophers, grammarians, physicians

---

[25] Millar, 'Greek and Latin', 92–103, notes that the transcripts of the Synods of 536 and 553 were originally written in Latin for the subscription and then subsequently copied in Greek, the copies of which retained specific Latinate vocabulary.

[26] Honoré, *Tribonian*, 124–38, that after 541 all imperial *Novellae* are written in Greek; Kelly, *Ruling*, 32–6, that John the Cappadocian required all prefectural constitutions to be issued in Greek.

[27] Brown, *Power and Persuasion*, 69.

[28] *Codex Iustinianus* 1.11.9, 1.11.10, 1.5.18, 2.11.10; commented on by John Malalas, *Chronographia* 18.42 and 18.47; Agathias, *Histories* 2.30.3–32.1; Procopius, *Anecdota* 26.35; Theophanes 1.276.

[29] For the lively discussions, Cameron, 'Ancient universities', 653–71; Maas, *John Lydus*, 68–76; Hällström, 'Neoplatonic school', 145–57; Watts, 'AD 529', 168–82; Watts, *City and School*, 128–41; Corcoran, 'Anastasius, Justinian', 183–208.

[30] John Malalas, *Chronographia* 18.42.

and civil servants – precisely those members one would expect to find in a politically active intellectual network.[31] In addition to prohibiting non-Christians from teaching, the confiscation of properties that had been allocated to the support of the school at Athens effectively closed its doors for want of professors and financial support.

A statement from Junillus, an émigré from North Africa who contributed to the formulation of Justinian's legal and political theology, suggests that Hellenes in the bureaucracy and Neoplatonic teaching at Athens were linked in the eyes of the imperial court. Junillus denigrated 'adversaries [to his ideological conception] such as the Sibyls and the philosophers'.[32] The coupling of Sibyls and philosophers as 'adversaries' reveals much about official animosity toward a non-Christian orientation. That such invective against paganism and philosophy should surface in a treatise on political and legal ideology points concern in the direction of the bureaucracy. John Malalas later acknowledged the connection between Athens and state service more directly, stating that 'the emperor issued a decree and sent it to Athens ordering that no-one should teach philosophy *nor* interpret the laws'.[33] That the edict of 529 debarred teaching both Neoplatonic philosophy and law at Athens has direct bearing on politics at Constantinople.[34] Both religion and law were intimately connected to Justinian's political ideology and the edict of 529 targeted the influence of Athens in both arenas. Edward Watts interprets the closure of the Academy as Justinian's reaction to the casting of dice in Constantinople, a practice connected to traditional *sortes*. It seems that the imperial court reacted to a concern that non-Christian religious rites traceable to Neoplatonic doctrine had conflated with administrative procedures.[35] Whether Hellenes in state service were practising 'pagans' or not, 'the ambiguities surrounding the definition of paganism' were easily exploitable and allowed one of the cornerstones of elite pedagogical culture, *reverentia antiquitatis*, to be confused with non-Christian religious practice.[36] From the imperial perspective, the accusation of sorcery was a tried and proven method (practised, for example, in the purge of philosophers and their sympathizers by Valentinian and Valens in the 370s) for removing the leading figures of a culture that did not fit the

[31] Pseudo-Dionysius of Tel-Mahre, *Pseudo-Dionysius of Tel-Mahre*, 71.
[32] Junillus, *Instituta Regularia* 2.29, trans. Maas, *Exegesis*.
[33] John Malalas, *Chronographia* 18.47, trans. Jeffreys, Jeffreys and Scott, *John Malalas*, 264, emphasis mine; on the link between the closure of the school and the practice of law, Hällström, 'Neoplatonic school', 146–7.
[34] Hällström, 'Neoplatonic school', 145–7; Wildberg, 'Philosophy', 331.
[35] Watts, 'AD 529', 171–4.
[36] Quote from Maas, *John Lydus*, 68–76; also Kaldellis, *Procopius*, 99–112.

image of a Christian imperial world.[37] From the traditionalist perspective, the closure was provocative enough that the leading figures from the school embarked, at least temporarily, on a self-imposed exile to Persia (a truly political statement given the eastern Roman Empire's current state of war with the Sasanian Empire).[38]

The tandem closure of the Academy at Athens and censure of Hellenes in Constantinople were related to the confluence of tradition, religion and law in the bureaucracy. It was in Constantinople, not Athens, where Justinian came in contact with a bureaucratic matrix of philosophical and political ideals that could challenge his interest in establishing a specifically Christian ideology and language of legitimacy. Significantly, Justinian's policy with regard to Athens did not extend to other communities with active 'pagan' communities such as Edessa, Baalbek and Aphrodisias.[39] Rather, the policy was rooted in Justinian's interest in replacing the corporatism of the civil bureaucracy with a cult of autocracy centred on the emperor. The end of the Academy in Athens and the repression of Hellenes in Constantinople had been calculated to undermine both the source and the representatives of the traditionalism that had sustained institutional identity for many in the bureaucracy. It was part of a wholesale attempt to impose a shift in governmental ideology and resistance must have been substantial. Although the Academy never again instructed students, the pogrom against Hellenes at the capital required additional iterations in 534 and 545, with effects reaching deeper into the ranks of the bureaucratic corps and employing more brutal methods. Unrepentant Hellenes were publicly humiliated and executed. Not surprisingly, it was across the span of these pogroms, from 529 to 545, that a stridently polemical literature developed and it was shortly after either the second or the third pogrom that Cassiodorus found himself in Constantinople.

CONTESTING LAW AND RELIGION IN CONSTANTINOPLE

In addition to undermining the intellectual foundation of bureaucratic corporatism, Justinian contested bureaucratic privilege with respect to the interpretation of law. Justinian's codification of the most comprehensive body of Roman law to date often receives attention as one of the great accomplishments of his reign and is typically discussed in terms of the

---

[37] For the trials against *maleficium*, which seems to have targeted mainly the philosophically minded elite, Lenski, *Failure of Empire*, 211–34; note also the comments of Markus, *Signs*, 126.

[38] On the exile of Damascius, Simplicius and others, Watts, 'Philosophical life', 285–302; Baltussen, *Simplicius*, 13–14.

[39] Liebeschuetz, *Decline*, 241–2, suggests that the anti-Hellene legislation was enacted in response to circumstances specific to the political climate at the capital.

project's continuity with earlier advances in the systematization of Roman law.[40] What has not received enough consideration is the extent to which Justinian's legal project had been calculated to reduce dependence on a bureaucracy that considered its purview to be the interpretation of law and the unravelling of legal discrepancies.[41] Justinian entrusted the project to his court quaestor, Tribonian, who replaced the prominent Hellene Thomas (who was probably executed as a result of the pogrom of 529).[42] Tribonian's task was to simplify imperial law by removing or reconciling contradictions present in all extant statutes and judgements. The resultant *Corpus Iuris Civilis* was a massive overhaul of the Roman legal tradition never before attempted on this scale. The previous attempt, the *Theodosian Code*, had merely attempted to gather, arrange and edit the edicts of emperors since Constantine. Justinian's *Corpus* would collect and simplify the scattered sources of public and private law and render them systematically in order to arrive at a single, universally applicable, body of law.[43] Begun in 528 and completed in the final version in 534, the project falls within the time frame of Justinian's early engagement with bureaucratic independence. As a project that aimed to simplify law, the production of the *Corpus* promised to eliminate dependence on the recondite literary skills formerly needed for legal interpretation. In effect, the new *Corpus* had the potential to undermine yet another source of bureaucratic prestige, which was the assumption that only an education in the classical literary heritage equipped one to weigh the meaning (and morality) of law.[44]

From the bureaucratic perspective, the literary elite trained in classical letters, rhetoric and law were the only social group properly instructed to understand the spirit of the law where its letter often proved inadequate.[45] Indeed, the extent to which education in late antiquity increasingly combined training in classical letters with legal training had been a direct consequence of the growth of an imperial bureaucracy.[46] The new legal

---

[40] Although note more recently the distinctions made by Ando, 'Religion', 126–45; for a concise summary of the production of the Justinianic Code and its constituent parts, Sirks, 'Code', 265–302; Liebs, 'Roman law', 244–52; Corcoran, 'Anastasius, Justinian', 184–6.

[41] Humfress, 'Law and legal practice', 164–7, suggests that Justinian's legal enterprises were more concerned with bolstering the authority of his regime than with general utility to the state but does not draw specific reference to the importance of law in Justinian's conflict with the bureaucracy.

[42] *PLRE III B*, 1314–15, on Thomas; 1335–9, on Tribonian.

[43] *Codex Iustinianus, De novo codice componendo*, praefatio, and *Codex Iustinianus, De Iustiniano codice confirmando* 1, elaborate Justinian's decision.

[44] Marrou, *Education*, 418–21; Honoré, *Law*, 7–9.

[45] Humfress, 'Law in practice', 383, on the tension between the interpretative training of legal experts and the imperial court.

[46] Greatrex, 'Lawyers', 148–61.

codification obviated (in theory) the need for such sensitive expertise, so much so that what were perceived as underqualified accountants (*scriniarii*) could now hold higher positions in civil service. From the perspective of the imperial court, the personal discretion of men trained in classical letters and rhetoric had held the law hostage for too long.[47] Eliminating the need for the bureaucracy to interpret law returned jurisprudence to the close confines of the imperial court and elevated Justinian as the singular *fons legis*, a role which Junillus carefully attempted to articulate in his *Instituta Regularia Divinae Legis*.[48] That the preface to the *Codex Iustinianus* celebrates the high rank of jurists commissioned to undertake the work (notably the quaestor, praetorian prefect and men of patrician status, all satellites of the *consistorium*) underscores the exclusion of bureaucratic officials from the formulation of law.[49] Although the bureaucracy worked with law on a daily basis, henceforth their role would be strictly one of maintaining process and procedure. The closure of the school at Athens, where legal and philosophical training had been combined, was an act closely related to the promulgation of the *Corpus Iuris Civilis*. Pogrom and promulgation each attempted to ensure Justinian's primacy as the chief exegete of the law, a role that would reinscribe his legitimacy as emperor and weaken rival claims.

Justinian's attack on the cultural traditions of the Hellenes and his dismissal of specialized expertise for the interpretation of law were also intimately connected to the rhetoric of Christian empire. Many scholars have noted the acutely triumphalist court propaganda that portrayed Justinian as the defender of the legal, political and religious unity of Christianity.[50] The triumphalist aspect of this unity is particularly evident in the opening address of Justinian's new legal *Corpus*, where military conquest is explicitly linked to the ecumenical exercise of justice.[51] That this new unity should include religion is evident in the *Novellae*, where Justinian claimed ultimate authority over matters of state and religion

[47] On the role of legal experts to provide advice to magistrates and emperors concerning the interpretation and limits of law, Honoré, *Law*, 7–9.
[48] On this function of the *Instituta*, Maas, *Exegesis*; also *Codex Iustinianus, De Iustiniano codice confirmando* 1, for an expression of Justinian as the singular source of law; Procopius, *Anecdota* 14.5, gives the same impression, albeit in disapproving terms.
[49] *Codex Iustinianus, De novo codice componendo* 1. Of the ten jurists named, seven were either current or former members of the imperial *comitatus* and two of the three not having served in the *comitatus* held senatorial rank; only Tribonian held a lesser status of 'virum magnificum magisteria dignitate inter agentes decoratum'.
[50] Hunger, *Prooimion*; Humfress, 'Law and legal practice', 162–71; Haldon, 'Economy', 49; Ando, 'Religion', 142–5; Markus and Sotinel, 'Introduction', 1–14; Millar, 'Rome, Constantinople', 62–8.
[51] *Codex Iustinianus, De Iustiniano codice confirmando, praefatio*; similar terms repeated again in *Institutiones Iustiniani, praefatio*.

precisely because the two were inseparable. The claim is perhaps most plainly articulated in the preface to Justinian's sixth *Novella*:

In truth the greatest gifts brought together for humanity by the heavenly indulgence of God are the priesthood and imperial rule, the one attending to matters divine, and the other taking care and presiding over human affairs, both issuing from one and the same source provide for human life. And so nothing will be of greater concern to emperors than the good character of priests, when they continuously pray to God on the behalf of emperors. For if the priesthood should be everywhere free of blame and fully faithful before God, and imperial rule moreover should manage the state entrusted to it justly and correctly, the blessings will be proportionate, conferring on humanity whatever is appropriately useful.[52]

The idea of an emperor acting as an agent of the divine on earth was nothing new. As early as Augustus, the association between divine favour and political power is visible in one manifestation or another. In Justinian's articulation, however, the emperor's position as the one whom God had made chiefly responsible for the security of Christianity negated the customary gestures with which one negotiated and built consensus with other political constituencies.[53] The imperial ambition that so relentlessly involved Justinian in matters of Christian doctrine and theology was the exercise of a vocabulary adopted from earlier imperial public personae. In a sense, Justinian's repressive measures against Hellenes, Manichaeans and Jews were simply more aggressive than religious policy enacted by previous emperors. The difference now was that the official rhetoric, at least at the capital, prescribed submission to Christianity as a prerequisite to political participation in a way that did not allow traditionalists to hold dual identities. There would be no crypto-pagans or Platonizing Christians in the autocratic Christian empire that Justinian envisaged. For Justinian, flexibility in identity represented potential flexibility in loyalty.

Justinian's aggressive involvement with the Christian church was similarly motivated. The exercise of truly autocratic authority required that the Christian church should represent a unity that would correspond to the legal and political unity of empire. Imposing a universal doctrine on the mosaic of Christian traditions and practices was a formidable task that had confounded every previous emperor to make the attempt. Indeed,

---

[52] Justinian, *Novella* 6, *praefatio*, 'Maxima quidem in hominibus sunt dona dei a superna collata clementia sacerdotium et imperium, illud quidem divinis ministrans, hoc autem humanis praesidens ac diligentiam exhibens; ex uno eodemque principio utraque procedentia humanam exornant vitam. Ideoque nihil sic erit studiosum imperatoribus, sicut sacerdotum honestas, cum utique et pro illis ipsis semper deo supplicent. Nam si hoc quidem inculpabile sit undique et apud deum fiducia plenum, imperium autem recte et competenter exornet traditam sibi rempublicam, erit consonantia quaedam bona, omne quicquid utile est humano conferens generi.'

[53] Canepa, *Two Eyes*, 100–21.

70

the christological controversy current in Justinian's day could be traced
to the Council of Chalcedon in 451, a synod originally convened through
the orchestration of the Empress Pulcheria.[54] Chalcedon attempted to
reconcile the teachings of Eutyches, a monk at Constantinople who had
opposed the very public and popular role of religious leadership adopted
by Pulcheria. In response to Pulcheria's identification with the mother
of Christ, Eutyches held that Christ was purely divine and untainted
by the stain of mortal parentage. Although Eutyches' formulation found
traction with a wide audience, it was problematic for church leaders and
imperial authority in that it contravened the duality ascribed to Christ
at the Council of Nicaea. As the first ecumenical council, Nicaea had
laid the foundation for the institutionalization of the church and had also
set the stage for the intimate codependence shared between the church
and the Roman Empire. Challenging the tenets of Nicaea risked much.
As a consequence, the Council of Chalcedon in 451 ruled in favour
of a dual christological interpretation, resulting in a schism between
Chalcedonian and miaphysite (non-Chalcedonian) Christian communities across the eastern empire. The synod proved additionally divisive
between the east and west through the inclusion of a canon which sought
to raise Constantinople to an ecclesiastical stature equal with Rome.

By the sixth century, the division between Chalcedonian and miaphysite church leadership was deeply entrenched and proved resistant
to Justinian's realization of a doctrinally seamless empire. Even while
Justin reigned, Justinian had been involved in an attempt to resolve the
religious difficulties between Rome and Constantinople. In 519 he sent
John Maxentius and the so-called Scythian monks to Rome, where they
attempted to persuade Pope Hormisdas to accept an amended Chalcedonian statement of faith.[55] Early in Justinian's reign, while he initiated
the contest with bureaucratic independence, the emperor continued his
efforts to find some form of rapprochement between the two christological positions. In 533, Justinian issued two edicts attempting to rede-
fine the Chalcedonian formulation in order to bridge the rupture with
non-Chalcedonian Christians in the east.[56] It was perhaps in an attempt
to neutralize opposition from the two bastions of theological leadership in the west that in the same year Justinian initiated the reconquest
of Carthage and then Rome.[57] Finally, in 543 or 544, Justinian issued

[54] Gray, 'Chalcedon', 215–38; Haarer, *Anastasius*, 89–100 and 116–24; Price, 'Three Chapters', 17–24; Menze, *Justinian*.
[55] Rapp, 'Hagiography', 1275–7.   [56] Gray, 'Chalcedon', 227–33.
[57] For the reaction of Justinian's doctrinal position in Italy, Barnish, 'Cassiodorus after conver-sion', 157–87; Sotinel, 'Emperors and popes', 267–90; Sotinel, 'Three chapters', 85–120; for the reaction in North Africa, Modéran, 'Afrique reconquise', 39–82.

an edict condemning the works of three fifth-century exegetes whom the miaphysite church leaders had found particularly objectionable – Theodore of Mopsuestia, Theodoret and Ibas of Edessa.

These so-called Three Chapters would fuel disputation between Justinian's court and Christian leadership of the east, Rome and Carthage throughout the period of, and well after, Cassiodorus' residency at the eastern capital. Although not directly related to his dealings with the bureaucracy, it is worth noting that Justinian's ambition for religious unity provided the justification needed to adulterate the customs of bureaucratic administration and legal tradition. According to his most trenchant critics, Justinian's vision of Christian autocracy propelled the eastern empire on a course of military conflict with North Africa and Italy, the events of which shaped Cassiodorus' representation of bureaucratic service in Ostrogothic Italy. Officials persecuted because of their attachment to Neoplatonism and Hellene traditions viewed Justinian's doctrinal interventions as the obverse of the same coin. Probably for this reason, both Procopius and Agathias took a dim view of the contemporary religious discourse in general, 'the sort of inconclusive hair-splitting which results neither in persuasion nor in enlightenment'.[58] The comparative lack of interest in matters of religion characteristic of the *Variae* may be a result of Cassiodorus' awareness of the latent hostility that many officials in Constantinople harboured. According to the *Variae*, Amal rulers addressed men of the church only concerning matters that touched upon the administration of the state, never concerning proper belief. Scholars have generally attributed this to a desire not to draw attention to the schismatic Arian beliefs of the Goths. However, the letters written in Cassiodorus' name (Books 11 and 12) express overtly religious sentiments and open with appeals to Italian bishops for divine support. Cassiodorus here may have intended to demonstrate the correct political place for religion in state service – an inversion of Justinian's governmental policies in which rulers do not involve themselves in religion, but where religion nonetheless shapes the morals of public servants.

THE NIKA REVOLT

The first years of Justinian's reign reveal a concerted effort to articulate the emperor's authority at the centre of law, religion and imperial administration. It was in the midst of these changes that a powerful element

---

[58] Agathias, *Histories* 2.29.2–5, trans. Frendo; also, Procopius, *Wars* 5.3.5–9, against the 'insane folly' of the Christians.

in the bureaucracy of Constantinople attempted to resist the momentum of the emperor's policies in a dramatic uprising in 532.[59] The Nika Revolt began with the arrest of five prominent members of the circus faction responsible for recent violence at the Hippodrome.[60] When the populace appealed to Justinian for clemency, he imprudently disregarded their pleas, sparking six days of massive insurrection.[61] Rioters emptied prisons of the incarcerated and set the monumental centre of the capital to flame, including portions of the palace and the original Hagia Sophia.[62] Justinian retreated to inner portions of the palace with the *consistorium* and attending members of the Senate. In the absence of direct intervention from the emperor, the seemingly random spread of violence developed a purposeful political character. The crowd assembled in the Hippodrome articulated particularly specific demands, including the deposition of Eudaemon the urban prefect, John the praetorian prefect and Tribonian the quaestor. Hostility toward Eudaemon is explained by his role in the initial arrest of faction members. John and Tribonian, however, are linked mainly by their roles as agents of Justinian's new policies. Justinian's response was conciliatory and he promised to remove both John and Tribonian from their offices. On the fifth day, however, the populace seized upon two nephews of Anastasius, Hypatius and Pompeius, and elevated Hypatius as emperor. Thus encouraged by popular acclaim, Hypatius secured the approval of those members of the senatorial order not sequestered in the palace and assembled with much of the urban populace in the Hippodrome. After nearly a week of vacillation and inaction on Justinian's part, the indiscriminate brutality of his reprisal could not have been anticipated. The generals Belisarius and Mundus assembled a force of soldiers outside the city and, after briefly testing the entrances to the Hippodrome, attacked the populace assembled there. Procopius claims that more than thirty thousand were slain in that one day and that both heirs of Anastasius were arrested and executed on the following day.[63]

---

[59] 14–19 January 532; Procopius, *Wars* 1.24.32–41.
[60] On violence associated with urban spectacle, Cameron, *Factions, passim*; Haas, *Alexandria, passim*; Whitby, 'Violence', 229–53; Liebeschuetz, *Decline*, 203–20; for accounts of previous spectacle violence in Constantinople, Marcellinus Comes, *Chronicon* 501, 507 and 512.
[61] On the political role of the Hippodrome, MacCormack, *Ceremony*, 242; Dagron, *Naissance*, 314–47; Greatrex, 'Nika', 63; for a fuller treatment of the political role of the theatre in an earlier imperial context, Edwards, *Politics*, 110–36.
[62] On the zone of urban destruction, John Lydus, *De magistratibus* 3.70; the new subterranean cistern later built by Justinian incorporated much material spoliated from areas destroyed during the riots.
[63] Procopius, *Wars* 1.24.54.

The Nika Revolt represents a crucial breakdown in the social and political order of Constantinople within five years of Justinian's accession and it has understandably received much attention in modern scholarship. The revolt has been read as an opportunity for senatorial families (those supporting Hypatius) to express their resentment of Justinian's protégés.[64] Geoffrey Greatrex has even suggested that Justinian allowed the riots to unfold as a means of luring a latent senatorial coup to the surface.[65] Alexandra Cekalova has already noted that Justinian's early policies provoked the revolt and that the uprising precipitated the adoption of even stauncher policies in the following years.[66] Christian Gizewski is certainly correct to describe the revolt as an opportunistic popular movement which factions attempted to harness for their own political demands.[67]

What seems consistently clear from the narrative presented in the primary sources is that the revolt mobilized a considerable segment of the population at Constantinople and that the actions taken during the later stages of the revolt required the direction of some form of political leadership. The specificity of demands made at the Hippodrome in the midst of widespread opportunistic violence would have required an organizing element. The spontaneous reaction of a mob against an unpopular measure is a common enough feature of ancient urban life for it not to require much explanation. Urban insurrection could often be the result of pervasive and unfocused discontent with the status quo. Ammianus Marcellinus' account of riots at Rome in 355 offers interesting comparanda in which urban unrest focused initially on the arrest of a popular charioteer by the urban prefect.[68] When the crowd's demand for the release of the charioteer was refused, discontent continued to surface. However, Ammianus noted that subsequent demands were of a trivial nature (the distribution of better wine to the urban populace) and that the disturbance was easily handled because of the insubstantial character of leadership within the crowd.[69] By contrast, the articulation of specific political demands, as occurred during the Nika Revolt, indicates the involvement of organized leadership.

Although previous scholarship has examined the potential roles played in the riot by the senatorial elite and circus factions, similar consideration has not been given with respect to the bureaucracy. By 532

---

[64] Cameron, *Factions*, 280; Honoré, *Tribonian*, 54.
[65] Greatrex, 'Nika', 60–86, esp. 77–8. [66] Cekalova, 'Nika-Aufstand', 12–16.
[67] Gizewski, *Normativität und Struktur*, 148–206, points to racing factions, although Cameron, *Factions*, 20–3 and 258–61, notes that the faction demarch, as an institutionalized political office, does not appear in sources until 602.
[68] Ammianus Marcellinus, *Res Gestae* 15.7. [69] Ammianus Marcellinus, *Res Gestae* 15.7.2.

members of the civil service had witnessed obvious evidence of the threat to their institutional culture. Leading figures within the bureaucratic corps had both the motive to exploit the riots and the means to co-ordinate the demands of protesters. In its favour, the bureaucracy had regularly assumed a visible role in political ceremonial and their familiarity before the public would have made it relatively easy for members of the civil service to manipulate the uprising as it unfolded. Furthermore, the grievances of the bureaucratic corps were far more immediate than those of the senatorial elite or the general populace. The emperor had lavished attention on the great families, for example, in his refurbishment of the Hippodrome which provided members of the Senate with conspicuously honoured seating.[70] Justinian had also been shrewd to keep members of particularly prominent families close to the imperial court.[71] On the other hand, members of the bureaucracy had been drawn from the middling elite, and the emperor had chosen to diminish, rather than elevate, their distinction as a means of elevating his own authority.

Prior to the outbreak of violence on 14 January, a cascade of events had escalated the anxieties of the bureaucratic elite, ensuring their participation in the riots. Tribonian's appointment to a leading role in the new codification of law on 13 February 528 had been followed soon after in 529 by laws targeting Neoplatonism in Athens and Hellenes in Constantinople. John the Cappadocian was soon after (20 February 531) appointed to the praetorian prefecture, where he enacted a series of measures curbing bureaucratic privilege at precisely the same time that the exodus of philosophers from Athens occurred.[72] That the leaders of the Academy did not depart earlier in 529 suggests that there may have been some attempt to negotiate the survival of the school which ultimately failed when John received his appointment. This failure of the philosophers to secure a *modus vivendi* also coincided with intensified communication between Justinian's court and leaders of miaphysite Christian communities.[73] These exchanges culminated in a synod at Constantinople in 532 after the Nika Revolt, but the communication that brought both miaphysite and Chalcedonian leaders together began

---

[70] Marcellinus Comes, *Chronicon* 528.
[71] Gizewski, *Normativität und Struktur*, 166, stresses the loyalty of the Senate to Justinian; Corcoran, 'Two tales', 202–3, notes judicial concessions granted to senators by Justinian in appeals to either the *silentium* or the *conventus*.
[72] On the exile of Neoplatonic philosophers in 531, Watts, 'Philosophical life' 285–6.
[73] On the discussions with miaphysites, Brock, 'Conversations', 87–121; Gray, 'Chalcedon', 229–30; Menze, *Justinian*, 58–75. Millar, 'Rome, Constantinople', 68–70, cites the anonymous Syriac continuator of Zachariah of Mytilene's *Ecclesiastical History* 9.15 for a meeting between miaphysite clerics of Syria and Justinian in 532.

much earlier and would have moved through chancery channels. The message of Christian unity in the face of Hellene persecution was voluble. The final piece of kindling may have been set with Justinian's negotiations for the *pacem cum Persis in aeternum*, by which the imperial court paid an indemnity of 11,000 pounds of gold to Chosroes.[74] Such a sum was sufficient to feed almost 200,000 people for a year and the conclusion of the settlement was widely unpopular.[75] For a tradition-oriented bureaucracy, the payment of an indemnity was a symbolic inversion of Rome's imperial role and the ultimate humiliation for men who understood their culture as the definition of empire. Although most historians date the final arrangements between Justinian and Chosroes after the Nika Revolt, Procopius' narrative makes it clear that Justinian's initial agreement to pay the massive sum was common knowledge in court during the last months of 531 – within weeks of the Nika Revolt.[76] Procopius furthermore suggests that, as a result of the Peace, both rulers immediately thereafter dealt with serious insurrections, 'Straightway it came about that plots were formed against both rulers by their subjects.'[77] For Procopius, the indemnity was clearly a causal factor in the insurrection. Procopius also draws attention to three factors which support a reconstruction of the revolt around bureaucratic dissatisfaction: John the Cappadocian was hated because 'he was entirely without the advantages of a liberal education'; Tribonian was similarly despised because, 'everyday, as a rule, he was repealing some laws and proposing others'; and a substantial contingent of the palace guard, quite possibly the *scholares*, had joined the rebellion and had positioned themselves to obstruct Belisarius at the Hippodrome.[78]

While it would be precipitous to suggest that the riots had been planned by a united bureaucracy, it seems more than reasonable to conclude that the most discontented faction within the bureaucracy seized upon a moment that was evidently ripe for ending Justinian's rule. The outbreak of urban violence afforded this contingent of the bureaucracy the singular opportunity to effect change amenable to their interests. Some modern studies of the event have assumed that the bureaucracy

---

[74] On the Eternal Peace, Greatrex, *Rome and Persia*, 215–18; for a vivid account of the challenges of maintaining the frontier with Persia, Johsua the Stylite, *Chronicle* 33–100.

[75] For the valuation of gold, Kenneth Harl, *Coinage*, 270–89.

[76] Procopius, *Wars* 1.21.17–28 and 1.22.7, that Justinian received and agreed upon the initial proposal within seventy days of the accession of Chosroes on 13 September 531.

[77] Procopius, *Wars* 1.23.1, trans. Dewing, LCL, 209; for the plot against Chosroes, *Wars* 1.23.1–29.

[78] Procopius, *Wars* 1.24.11–16, on John the Cappadocian and Tribonian; 1.24.44–46, on the betrayal of the palace guards, trans. Dewing, LCL, 223 and 225.

was the target of urban unrest rather than its organizational element by misreading John the Cappadocian and Tribonian as representatives of the civil service.[79] This grossly underestimates the rancour that public officials (especially the *exceptores*) felt for the administrative changes executed by John and for the role played by Tribonian in the adulteration of Roman legal tradition. The call for their deposition patently illustrates the leadership that a faction of the bureaucratic elite assumed during the riot. Once it appeared that the downfall of John and Tribonian had been secured and that Justinian was impotent to refuse demands made by the urban populace, it probably became clear that an opportunity for even more radical change was at hand – the elevation of a new emperor. During the third century, the military equivalent of the civil service, the Praetorian Guard, had exercised the prerogative of electing an emperor time and again. To assume that men who had earned their distinction through the toil of education would be any less tenacious than men girt with the *cingulum* of battle would be a miscalculation. It is perhaps a testament to the prevailing conservatism of the bureaucracy that a surviving relation to Anastasius was thrust forward to claim Justinian's place and not a member of their own ranks. Only after Hypatius' elevation did a significant portion of senatorial elite support the revolt, a further indication that more than mob volatility had directed matters. With a coalition of senatorial and bureaucratic elite enjoying popular support, it may be the case that only the terrible spectacle of 30,000 dead had the potential to restore Justinian to his position as emperor.

THE AFTERMATH

After the conclusion of the riot, Justinian acted to fortify the apparent vulnerability of his position by continuing the systematic reduction of bureaucratic independence. Hypatius and Pompeius were executed; John the Cappadocian was rehabilitated as praetorian prefect; Tribonian continued working on the *Corpus Iuris Civilis* in ex officio capacity until his reappointment as quaestor in 535; and more punitive restrictions were levelled against the bureaucracy, including further iterations of the pogrom against the Hellenes in 534 and 545.[80] Even the decision to

---

[79] Cekalova, 'Nika-Aufstand', 16.

[80] *PLRE IIA*, 628, John the Cappadocian was restored to office on 18 October 532 and would remain in this post until 7 May 541. *PLRE IIB*, 1336–8, Tribonian was appointed *magister officiorum* on 21 November 533 and then reappointed quaestor on 3 January 535; he would remain in this post until possibly 1 May 542. For the pogrom of 534, *Codex Iustinianus* 1.11.10.

invade North Africa in 533 and then Italy in 534 was, in part, a deliberate attempt to counter political discontent at the capital with military victory abroad.[81] More tellingly, Justinian had become sensitized to the volatility of public favour. As a result, he became much more restrictive in terms of how other constituencies at Constantinople enjoyed the display of public prestige.

The tenth-century *De ceremoniis* serves as a manual for the ceremonial conduct that had developed at the eastern court during the course of the early Byzantine centuries.[82] The text describes a ritualistic culture in which most ceremony occurred within the palace, with the bureaucracy serving as both participants and audience.[83] The aspect to note in this description is the restrictiveness of the ceremonial environment and its removal from the public eye. Many of the traditions mentioned in the text originate in the late fifth century to the early sixth and it may be possible to locate the point when the ceremonies practised by civil servants were removed from a public audience in the reign of Justinian.[84] John Lydus' lament about the disregard for the formerly observed protocols and regalia certainly indicates that a rupture had occurred in the bureaucracy's public visibility in Justinian's reign.[85] Regalia and uniform visibly defined hierarchical relationships and Lydus' complaints about the present-day disregard for such matters confirm a decrease in the ceremonial visibility of the bureaucracy.[86] Prior to the sequestering of bureaucratic ceremonial, moments of privileged ritualistic participation would have affirmed hierarchies of authority within the bureaucracy in addition to distinguishing civil service in the eyes of a wider public. If the identification of archival *officia* conjoined to the Hippodrome is correct, the bureaucratic corps maintained a substantial ceremonial presence at public spectacles prior to Justinian's accession.[87] Given how the prominence of the bureaucracy in public ceremonial events would have celebrated the long continuity of the institution through the performance of tradition and would have signalled, by comparison, the recent mint of Justinian's own reign, it may be the case that Justinian had begun to curtail

---

[81] Merrills and Miles, *Vandals*, 228–52; note the tone of divine justification offered for war in a *Novella* of 534, *Codex Iustinianus* 1.27.1.1–2.
[82] Cameron, 'Court ritual', 121–2.   [83] Cameron, 'Court ritual', 130–1.
[84] On the sixth-century provenance of material in *De ceremoniis*, MacCormack, *Ceremony*, 240; Dagron, *Emperor and Priest*, 84–124; Canepa, *Two Eyes*, 8–11.
[85] John Lydus, *De magistratibus* 1.7–8, 1.12.5, 1.17, 1.28.5, 1.32, 1.37, 2.2, 2.4, 2.13–14, 2.21.
[86] On ceremony and regalia as elements of political prestige among public officials, Boak and Dunlap, *Administration*, 98–100; and Kelly, *Ruling*, 18–26; as elements of political communication in the reign of Justinian, Cameron, *Factions*, 249–51, and Canepa, *Two Eyes*, 188–204.
[87] Kelly, 'Later Roman bureaucracy', 163.

the public visibility of the bureaucracy even before the Nika Revolt.[88] According to Marcellinus Comes, Justinian had ordered changes to the architecture of the Hippodrome just a year before the purge of 'Hellenes' from civil service.[89] John Lydus and Procopius both commented on how Justinian curried the favour of the circus factions (and, by extension, the public). It seems that Justinian had attempted to diminish the public presentation of civil servants and this may be another dimension of his attempt to redirect the focus of ceremony at the Hippodrome, which had always been a crucial arena for political communication.[90] Even after Justinian's death, the Hippodrome remained an arena for the drama of imperial succession and perspicacious emperors knew how to direct that drama.[91]

Justinian reinforced his control of political communication at the Hippodrome immediately after the Nika Revolt. The riots had destroyed much of the zone north of the palace, including the older Hagia Sophia of Theodosius II. The new Hagia Sophia begun in the immediate aftermath of the riot dwarfed the older church and dramatically altered the orientation of traditional imperial ritual.[92] The sheer rapidity of its construction (it was dedicated on 27 December 537) attests to the urgency involved in controlling public ceremonial. From the vantage of the Hippodrome, where the church was plainly visible, the size of the new edifice erected at Justinian's command dominated the landscape of the city. It was a tacit reminder to the political elite and the urban populace who assembled at the Hippodrome that Justinian held a divinely sanctioned mandate as emperor that none could contest.[93]

Justinian's control of public presentation at the capital extended well beyond the bureaucracy. When Belisarius returned to the capital after conquering the Vandals and leading their captive court in his train, instead of receiving a traditional triumph that would have marked Belisarius as a person of political consequence, Justinian allowed him only a

---

[88] Brown, *Power and Persuasion*, 12–20, on the confluence of ceremony, the distribution of authority and anxieties derived from political factionalism and conflicts of interest at court; McCormick, *Eternal Victory*, 47–78, on the shift from large-scale public triumphal celebrations to circus-related celebrations in the period from Theodosius to Justinian, which implies a devolution of ceremony attendant upon the military and a concomitant increased focus on the civil service.

[89] Marcellinus Comes, *Chronicon* 528.

[90] John Lydus, *De magistratibus* 2.15.2; Procopius, *Anecdota* 10.16–18; Evagrius, *Historia Ecclesiastica* 4.32; Canepa, *Two Eyes*, 100–53, in general on how the control of political ritual in Constantinople related to a wider sphere of diplomatic competition between the eastern Roman Empire and the Sasanian Empire; 18–19 and 167–74 on the importance of the Hippodrome as stage setting for political ritual.

[91] Gregory of Tours, *Decem Libri Historiarum* 5.30.   [92] Canepa, *Two Eyes*, 15.

[93] Procopius, *Buildings* 1.1.27, refers to it as a 'watchtower' that dominated the rest of the city.

simple procession on foot.[94] Belisarius' next victory over the Ostrogoths at Ravenna earned even less acclamation; similar to the restricted venue of court ceremonial described in the *De ceremoniis*, Justinian presided over the viewing of spoils from that campaign in a private chamber at court.[95] What should have warranted a triumph had been reduced to the emperor's own private spectacle. Similarly, Justinian reduced another traditional means of celebrating shared public prestige first by reducing the scale and duration of consular games in 537.[96] In this case, Justinian's insecurity seems justified by several occasions where rebellions had formed around the candidacy of consuls as potential imperial rivals, notably Basiliscus and Illus under Zeno and then Hypatius and Pompeius under Justinian.[97] The careful rationing of the public aggrandizement enjoyed by individuals other than the emperor would culminate in the year 541, when Justinian ended the tradition for the appointment of consuls. Thus with Justinian ended a political tradition that had allowed the Mediterranean elite to mark the passage of more than eleven centuries with their names.[98]

The consequences of Justinian's attempt to weaken the solidarity of bureaucratic corporatism would not have failed to impress Cassiodorus when he arrived in Constantinople in the 540s. By that time, the initial shock resulting from the decree of 529 and the outcome of 532 had given way to a wide range of oblique criticisms that carefully avoided provoking additional censure. Cassiodorus' exposure to this discourse of complaint is particularly evident in the manner with which he portrayed Neoplatonic thought and an ideology of state service in the letters of the *Variae*.[99] Given Cassiodorus' political position after the capture of Ravenna, it may seem like a miscalculation on Cassiodorus' part that he would appeal to eastern bureaucratic sensitivities, but even as late as the 540s Justinian's control of Constantinople could not have seemed a *fait accompli*. One could well imagine how news of the very active political discontent in Constantinople might have been received by audiences at Rome and Ravenna, where the temperament of the eastern imperial court had

---

[94] For a discussion of processionals as political dialogue between the governing class and the populace, MacCormack, 'Adventus', 721–52; McCormick, *Eternal Victory*, 47–78, with attention to Belisarius' triumphal procession at 124–9.

[95] Procopius, *Wars* 4.9.3, on Belisarius' return from Libya; *Wars* 7.1.3, on Belisarius' return from Italy.

[96] Justinian, *Novella* 105.   [97] Cameron and Schauer, 'Basilius', 140.

[98] Note the traditionalist sentiment of Ammianus Marcellinus, *Res Gestae* 29.2.15, 'consulares post scipiones et trabeas et fastorum monumenta mundana'.

[99] On the *Variae* as a Neoplatonic document, Lanata, *Legislazione*, 228–31; Fridh, '*Variae* II.40', 49; Barnish, 'Religio', 396; Mauro, 'Cassiodoro', 222; also Halporn and Vessey, *Cassiodorus*, 20, on the overt Platonism of the *De anima*.

frequently been a matter of some consequence. The possibility that the powerful eastern bureaucracy would survive Justinian and, indeed, that it seemed a far more stable source of political power needs to be taken into account in light of Cassiodorus' access to diplomatic channels as praetorian prefect at Ravenna and his exposure to political rumour as an émigré in Constantinople.

Chapter 4

VOICES OF DISCONTENT IN
CONSTANTINOPLE

THE LITERARY PUBLIC OF POLITICAL COMPLAINT

The great events of the first half of the sixth century in the Mediterranean were inescapably linked to policies formulated at, and the politics
of, the imperial court of Constantinople. The fluctuating Persian frontier
that at times consumed and then disgorged entire communities, the displacement of urban and military aristocracies that attended the conquest
of Vandalic North Africa and Ostrogothic Italy, the growth of a new
religious culture in the Arabian peninsula, the continued autonomous
settlement of 'barbarian' peoples in formerly Roman provinces, the
polarization of eastern Christian communities and the rise of Rome
as the centre of western Christendom – all of these long-term processes
were influenced by the policies and politics of the eastern imperial capital. Nowhere were those policies more vigorously discussed, and at times
disputed, than in Constantinople. The consequence of every diplomatic
mission, military expedition and legal or administrative reform in the
eastern empire sounded in the corridors of state service. Civil servants in
Constantinople knew about the forfeiture of cities on the eastern frontier
before the citizens of those communities received the order to abandon
native hearth and home. The sixth-century historians involved in state
service at the capital were aware of regions and events in a way that other
witnesses of the sixth century were not. The literary culture that was
the inheritance of a cosmopolitan elite class of Constantinople (broadly
defined to include provincial recruits and senatorial families) ensured that
the exchange of both Greek and Latin texts communicated these events.

The involvement of the literate class in various aspects of the political
culture and their lack of monolithic social cohesion ensured that the
literary rendition of contemporary events would be deeply encoded
with diverse ideological perspectives.[1] The senator, the bishop and the
legal clerk of late antiquity each portrayed the present as a consequence

---

[1] On literacy in this period, Greatrex, 'Lawyers', 148–61; Rapp, 'Literary culture', 376–97.

of different interpretations of the past and for different purposes. The malleability of *mos maiorum* as a vehicle for traditionalism and political legitimacy ensured that competing contemporary ideologies frequently contested the interpretation of the past. The awareness of opposed views meant that the literary representation of past and contemporary events was dynamic and polemically charged. Given its frequently ideological basis, engagement in literary activity in the sixth century could be seen as an urgent and morally justified obligation.[2] Constantinople in particular was a social and political environment where literary activity had become reactionary. When social groups lost influence in the political process, literary discourse inevitably became polemical. The traditionalist elite of the bureaucracy, as an alienated group, were particularly well equipped to mount a sustained literary campaign.[3] The bureaucratic elite possessed an intimate connection with expressions of *paideia*, a secure corporate identity strengthened by institutional continuity and sheer numbers and, from their perspective, justified indignation.

The polemical literature that developed during Justinian's reign is the topic of the current chapter. The manner in which the authors of this period referred to each other either explicitly, indirectly or thematically betrays a definite pattern of critique and polemical riposte, suggesting a dynamic political environment in which writers were aware of the consequences of political ideology. Communicating through the correspondences of themes was a particularly important style of writing for authors of sixth-century Constantinople. It allowed them to respond to each other without attracting official censure. For authors such as Junillus and Marcellinus Comes who were intimate participants in the imperial court's production of a language of legitimacy, subtlety was often unnecessary. For others, however, such as Procopius and John Lydus, the consequences of critique weighed more heavily and their literary projects were correspondingly more elaborate. Much literary creativity found in the more noted authors of the Justinianic period may be attributed to the adoption of literary strategies that sought to communicate different messages to different audiences. Authors of sixth-century Constantinople were by no means engaging in literary innovation. Literature produced throughout the Roman Empire had the potential to disguise and misdirect intended meaning.[4] Submerging political critique in oblique references and

[2] Greatrex, 'Lawyers', 157–61; Cooper, *Household*, 68–76.
[3] In general on literary disputation, Cameron, 'Old and new Rome', 16–17.
[4] Petersen, 'Livy and Augustus', 440–52; Schouleer, 'Déguisement', 257–72; Edwards, *Politics*, 117–19; Bartsch, *Actors in Audience*, 100–1, 115–16, 145–6 and 156–7; Malosse, 'Libanius', 519–24; Hedrick, *History*, 131–70; for ancient discussions of disguised meaning, Quintilian, *Institutio Oratoria* 1.11.3, and Gregory of Nazianzus, *Epistulae* 51.4.

allusions that could invite unfavourable comparisons had been a feature of Latin and Greek literature at least since the early empire. The classicizing historians of the sixth century inherited this sophisticated rhetorical palette with which to tint their own productions of the past. Even the most obvious ploy of embedding fictional speeches in narratives could be used to subtle effect, allowing the author to voice personal opinions indirectly.[5]

The refined use of evasive literary techniques in the sixth century is a direct corollary of an active polemical discourse in which criticism of imperial policies had already resulted in several pogroms of the literary elite. But rather than extinguish the critical impulse, censure ensured its vitality by forcing authors to adopt more oblique, less detectable forms of expression. Out of this suppressed polemic certain themes emerged which signalled the emperor as the intended target. For example, discussion of the contemporary rejection of tradition often pointed to Justinian as the *agent provocateur* and reigning innovator. The themes that emerge from the extant commentary suggest a political and social dialogue that was probably more pronounced and audible in the daily interaction of public officials than is visible in the written word. In a sense, the extant literature is just the tip of a polemical iceberg, the buoyancy of which was sustained by the day-to-day gossip and complaint exchanged within various departments of the bureaucracy.

In the course of surveying authors contemporary with Justinian's reign, it is worth keeping in mind that the fundamental causes of complaint had been set in motion by the policies of Justinian's early years as emperor, between 527 and 540. It is inconceivable that Cassiodorus' thoughts on how best to present a record of the Italian bureaucratic elite would not have taken Constantinopolitan affairs into account. Even if Cassiodorus compiled the *Variae* between 538 and 540, as is regularly assumed, Belisarius was at that time already in possession of Rome and Ravenna's capitulation to eastern imperial rule would have seemed highly probable. The diplomatic and cultural channels connecting Italy and Constantinople would have informed Cassiodorus about the political climate at the eastern capital much earlier in the course of his official duties at Ravenna, at least since holding the praetorian prefecture in 533, by which time Constantinopolitan affairs had become particularly volatile. Priscian provides just an example of the kind of cultural and political communication regularly sustained by the literary elite between Rome and Constantinople.[6] Envoys sent between Ravenna and Constantinople

---

[5] Frendo, 'Three authors', 123–35, notes this as a persistent evasive technique.
[6] On Priscian's connections in Rome, Nicks, 'Literary culture', 189–90.

for matters as routine as the annual appointment of eastern and western consuls supplied officers at the Amal court (such as Cassiodorus) with information about the eastern capital right up to the outbreak of war in the Italian peninsula. Assessing the political climate in Constantinople would have been acutely consequential for Cassiodorus as he prepared the *Variae*. Taking into account the polemical currents present in contemporary Constantinopolitan discourse therefore becomes essential to understanding how the *Variae* function as a text.

ZOSIMUS AT THE THRESHOLD OF THE DEBATE

The exchanges of political polemic may be profitably traced starting with the *Nova Historia* of Zosimus. Although it is generally considered that Zosimus wrote the *Nova Historia* somewhat earlier than Justinian's accession, certain themes that he emphasized are mirrored in the political commentary emerging out of Justinian's reign, most notably in the works of Procopius and John Lydus.[7] Zosimus' public position placed him within the orbit of a general political perspective shared by many officials at Constantinople.[8] As *advocatus fisci*, Zosimus was a legal expert who had devoted an entire career to the bureaucracy, probably among the *exceptores* of Constantinople, before receiving a customary two-year appointment in the *comitiva consistoriana* prior to retirement.[9] As such, concerns about the emperor's responsibility for preserving political tradition which fill the *Nova Historia* very likely represent the contemporary political views of the bureaucracy. A slightly later generation of elite readers in Constantinople found Zosimus' history particularly relevant to current political conditions. This relevance may be what allowed his history to remain in popular circulation, as it did throughout the better part of the sixth century. The *Nova Historia* certainly retained its currency long enough to provoke a response from Evagrius, who spent time in Constantinople in 588 and later wrote his own history. Evagrius addressed a rhetorical disputation directly to Zosimus, indicating that Zosimus' work had achieved some degree of authority with the educated class of the capital.[10] It is worth noting that Evagrius was writing

---

[7] Cameron, 'Zosimus', 106–10, offers a *terminus post quem* of 498; for an *ante quem* of 501, Treadgold, *Historians*, 107–14; for later dates, Goffart, 'Zosimus', 421, suggested anytime between 498 and 518; Paschoud, *Zosime*, ix–xvi, allows for a date even later than 518.

[8] Jeffreys, 'Writers', 135–6.

[9] On Zosimus, *PLRE II*, 1206; Treadgold, *Historians*, 108, as a Constantinopolitan author; on the *advocatus fisci*, Jones, *TLRE*, 508–10.

[10] Evagrius, *Historia Ecclesiastica* 3.40–41.

85

an ecclesiastical history that continued the work of earlier church historians who had covered the same period treated by Zosimus.[11] It would be difficult to claim that material from Zosimus' political history was in some way essential to Evagrius' ecclesiastical history.[12] Nevertheless, his refutation of Zosimus received a full chapter. The topic that Evagrius disputed was one tied closely to the critique of Justinian – the contest between traditionalism and innovation.

The *Nova Historia* discloses a deep concern for the correct character of political governance and its relation to past tradition, a bundle of cultural and political concerns that Michael Maas has termed 'antiquarianism' in describing the work of John Lydus.[13] The *Nova Historia* provided a road map to historical cause and effect, demonstrating how innovation in political traditions had brought the Roman Empire to a state of collapse.[14] Innovation manifests itself in many forms in Zosimus' history: it entailed the introduction of new practices in public life, opened the door to the rise of usurpers and upset the competence of public offices and the administration of the empire as a whole.[15] Although the *Nova Historia* ends well before Zosimus' own contemporary day, he threaded the theme of the present-day consequences of past innovation throughout the text.[16] According to Zosimus, past innovation in government was responsible for the end of the Roman Empire in his own time. Some of the topics that Zosimus found particularly corrosive to the state, such as public spectacles and frivolous building projects, would retain their notoriety as politically charged and polemical issues during the reign of Justinian.[17] Central to the issue of innovation was the vulnerability of tradition to the prerogative of a single ruler. Zosimus noted that the empire had been productive and expansive when governed by an aristocracy, but that the appointment of a single ruler had subjected the course of the state to the cast of dice.[18] Although the affairs of the state would abide harmoniously so long as imperial authority resided in the hands of a just and moderate ruler, it was inevitable that the state would eventually be entrusted to someone with a less scrupulous concern for custom and result in common catastrophe for

[11] Evagrius, *Historia Ecclesiastica, praefatio* 1.
[12] On Evagrius' sources, Whitby, *Evagrius*, xxvi–xxviii; Treadgold, *Historians*, 299–308.
[13] Maas, *John Lydus*.   [14] Goffart, 'Zosimus', 416–17.
[15] Zosimus, *Nova Historia* 1.1.2, for a statement on historical causation and imperial decline; 1.6.1, for innovation in public life; 1.18.3, 1.20.5, 1.23.4, 1.38.3, 1.49.4, for susceptibility to innovation resulting in the elevation of usurpers; 2.32.3–33.10, for innovation in public offices.
[16] For innovation noted as the cause of present-day problems, Zosimus, *Nova Historia* 1.6.1, 2.7.6, 2.34.2, 3.33.9.
[17] Zosimus, *Nova Historia* 1.6.2, 2.34.3–4, 3.2.8, on public spectacles; 2.32.2, on inappropriate building projects.
[18] Zosimus, *Nova Historia* 1.5.4–6.

all. The full realization of Zosimus' construction of historical inevitability became manifest in the reign of Constantine, 'the first cause of the affairs of the empire declining to their present miserable state'.[19] This caustic view of Constantine obviously was informed by Zosimus' non-Christian sympathies, but it is important to note that these were sympathies at least tolerated within the bureaucracy until the accession of Justin, quite probably when Zosimus began writing.[20]

For Zosimus, adherence to the traditional forms of religious expression was fused to the political health of the state. Deviation from the prescribed religious habits of the state was the worst form of innovation.[21] Constantine's innovation in matters of religion was perhaps among the greatest and, by Zosimus' time, a body of Christian literature had mythologized Constantine's role in the formation of a new Christian empire.[22] The traditionalist response was, naturally, to denigrate Constantine and to demonstrate the subsequent deterioration in Roman imperial affairs. As noted by Lellia Ruggini, the *Nova* in Zosimus' title signalled a rejection of what had become the dominant Christian construction of the past.[23] It should also be noted that the title signalled decline as a consequence of innovation. By ending his history with the Visigothic sack of Rome in 410, Zosimus rendered the Constantinian innovation pointedly symbolic and he engaged with a contemporary debate that had already provoked responses from Augustine and Orosius.[24] It was precisely this criticism of Constantine and the Christian role in imperial history that elicited the extended refutation from Evagrius.[25]

Procopius and Lydus seem to have engaged with the currency of Zosimus' critique of Constantine in a more abstract and diffuse manner, particularly by commenting upon the contemporary affairs of the eastern empire precisely as though they had become the fulfilment of Zosimus' history. Zosimus sought to demonstrate at every turn that Constantine was untutored by *mos maiorum* and for this reason every matter in which he involved himself became a disruptive departure from custom. As will be treated in more detail below, Procopius and Lydus

---

[19] Zosimus, *Nova Historia* 2.34.3–4, trans. Green and Chaplin; Speck, 'Zosimus', 5, notes that the transition from the incompetence of Constantine to the problems of Constantinople was carefully constructed.

[20] Evagrius, *Historia Ecclesiastica* 3.40, calls Zosimus a Hellene.

[21] Goffart, 'Zosimus', 416–17; Lieu and Montserrat, *Constantine to Julian*, 13.

[22] On Eusebius and the Christian mythologizing of Constantine, Williamson, *Eusebius*, xiv–xvi; Barnes, 'Panegyric', 114; Lieu, 'Constantine's *Vita*', 136–76; Drake, *Constantine*, 9–34, 358–92; Van Dam, *Constantine*, 310–53; Drijvers, '*Vita Constantini*', 11–27.

[23] Ruggini, 'Publicistica', 146–83.

[24] On Zosimus' deliberate intention to end at 410, Goffart, 'Zosimus', 418; Speck, 'Zosimus', 1–14.

[25] Evagrius, *Ecclesiastical History* 3.40–41.

criticized Justinian (albeit obliquely) chiefly through illustrating 'innovation' as a general tendency of their age, and more specifically by describing Christian disputation, public building, the deterioration of administrative traditions and the political role of public spectacles as symptoms of Justinianic innovation – precisely the same arenas in which Zosimus criticized Constantine.[26] Zosimus' treatment of public spectacle, in particular, would have resonated clearly with an audience that had witnessed the political role of the Hippodrome in Justinian's reign. Zosimus used public spectacle as a medium to contrast the moral dispositions of Constantine and Julian, two emperors already contrasted in the popular imagination as embodying opposed religious cultures of empire. According to Zosimus, Constantine rendered his soldiers effeminate by habituating them to entertainments, while Julian provoked the hostility of the citizens of Antioch with his abstemious attitude toward spectacles.[27] In contrast to Constantine, Julian angered the populace by adopting a philosophical disposition and avoiding the games. Zosimus plainly considered the involvement of emperors in public spectacles to be 'the first cause' of the decline of the empire. Perhaps to reinforce this fact, he prefigured Constantine's innovation with the seemingly innocent introduction of pantomime to public theatre under Augustus, thus creating a causative trajectory that spanned from Augustus to Constantine to Zosimus' current day.[28] It is difficult to imagine an audience of the eastern empire in the sixth century that would not immediately associate a commentary on the political aspect of public entertainment with Justinian's involvement in the Hippodrome at Constantinople.

Thus, even if the date assigned to the *Nova Historia* prevents it from engaging directly with the reputation of Justinian, Zosimus' work nevertheless participated indirectly in a political discourse that informed the expression of later commentators. Of course, it is also possible to imagine Zosimus writing his *Nova Historia* in reaction to the reign of Justin, with whom Justinian had very early assumed a close partnership.[29] Procopius rather famously described the dangers, 'the vigilance of multitudes of spies', that prevented his recounting events as he truly saw them.[30] Procopius' reticence suggests that the potential for harsh censure at the time may have forced other writers similarly to adapt to the political climate

---

[26] Zosimus, *Nova Historia* 2.7 and 2.29, on abandoning ancient rites; 2.30, on the creation of Constantinople; 2.32.1, on building projects; 2.32.2–2.33.10, on administrative competences; 2.34.3–4, on spectacles.

[27] Zosimus, *Nova Historia* 3.12.1.   [28] Zosimus, *Nova Historia* 1.6.2 and 2.34.3–4.

[29] Procopius, *Anecdota* 6.20–25, portrays Justinian as managing the affairs of state on behalf of a senile Justin.

[30] Procopius, *Anecdota* 1.2, trans. Dewing, *LCL*, 3.

with a variety of literary ploys, everything from obvious silences to double entendre. In the case of Zosimus, it may be the case that he submerged the elaboration of contemporary problems in a historically polemical persona (Constantine), although doing so in terms easily recognizable as referring to either Justin or Justinian. The oracle that Zosimus claims prophesied that Constantine's new capital at Byzantium would be the cause of present-day misfortune for the empire may, in fact, have been intended to presage the arrival of Justin and Justinian:

> Thrace shall ere long a monstrous birth produce,
> baneful to all by course of time and use:
> a swelling ulcer by the sea shall grow,
> which when it breaks, with putrid gore shall flow.[31]

Although Justin and Justinian both originated from the region surrounding Naissus, in the province of Illyricum, many sources (perhaps pejoratively) claimed that they had come from Thracian stock.[32] The oracle could be taken to intimate the arrival of Justin and Justinian at Constantinople from a Balkan background, in which case the condemnation of Constantine and his new city becomes conflated with invective tacitly directed at the successors of Anastasius. The identification of Zosimus as a Hellene in the civil service writing sometime after 498 would mean that he advanced to the rank of *comes* under Anastasius and then began his history after retirement. Given the reluctant reception that Justin received from the *scholares*, one could imagine Zosimus reworking the contradictory tradition of Constantine in order to vent his own disapproval. The fact that the populace assembled in the Hippodrome had acclaimed Justin a 'new Constantine' may even have provided the spark to ignite Zosimus' literary project.[33] Such an acclamation made in the Hippodrome and in the presence of the *excubitores* would certainly explain Zosimus' statement that Constantine had enervated the soldiers by allowing them to attend public entertainments. As a piece of invective directed against Justin, the *Nova Historia* may have also sensitized Justinian to the problematic nature of Constantine's reputation and may explain why Justinian did not attempt to adopt more overt associations with the memory of the emperor who, by the sixth century, embodied the ideology of Christian empire.[34]

---

[31] Zosimus, *Nova Historia* 2.37.5–6, trans. Green and Chaplin.
[32] Evagrius, *Historia Ecclesiastica* 4.1; John Malalas, *Chronographia* 410; *Chronicon Paschale* 518; *Suda* 3796; Zonaras, *Epitome historiarum* 14.5.1.
[33] Whitby, 'Images', 87; Canepa, *Two Eyes*, 10.   [34] Whitby, 'Images', 89–90.

MARCELLINUS COMES ON ZOSIMUS AND EMPIRE

Whether or not Zosimus intended to map Justin and Justinian onto a negative tradition for Constantine, the currency of the *Nova Historia* in the eastern discourse suggests at the very least that a later readership probably adopted it for that purpose. The most immediate and direct reaction to the *Nova Historia* came from Marcellinus Comes, an author with intimate knowledge of the imperial court at Constantinople who attempted to correct the negative assessment of the recent imperial past. Cassiodorus mentioned in his *Institutions* that Marcellinus served as a *cancellarius* (personal aide) in Justinian's employ during the reign of Justin and that he was promoted when Justinian later attained the throne.[35] The position of *cancellarius* implies privileged access to Justinian. Furthermore, his appointment in 527 to *comes* seems to have been titular (not holding competence over a bureaucratic department) and the rank of *vir clarissimus* did not grant attendance in the Senate. This means that Marcellinus was a member of Justinian's innermost court, not the senatorial aristocracy or bureaucracy. It has been generally assumed that Marcellinus received his advancement as an expression of Justinian's gratitude for having written the *Chronicon*, although the fact that Marcellinus noted his rank in the preface may imply an earlier promotion.[36] In either case, Marcellinus held a privileged position in close proximity to Justinian and confirmation of his political importance again comes from Cassiodorus, who noted that the bishop of Alexandria, Athanasius II, dedicated a book on the Psalms to Marcellinus after he recovered from an illness.[37] Because Athanasius II was patriarch in Alexandria from 490 to 497, it should probably be assumed that Marcellinus was a person of some consequence even before Justin's accession. Marcellinus' political advancement under Justin and Justinian seems to coincide with stages of the production of the *Chronicon*. The first portion of the chronicle extending to 518 was probably written during the reign of Justin while Marcellinus served as *cancellarius* on Justinian's staff. Later, while a *comes* of Justinian's court, he continued the account to 534. An anonymous author with sympathies

---

[35] Cassiodorus, *Institutiones* 1.17.2; Croke, 'Misunderstanding Cassiodorus', 225–6.

[36] Marcellinus Comes, *Chronicon, praefatio*; *PLRE II*, 710; Treadgold, *Historians*, 27–35.

[37] Cassiodorus, *Institutiones* 1.4.3, 'Legendus est etiam libellus Athanasii, Alexandrinae civitatis episcopi, quem Marcello post aegritudinem in locum refectionis dulcissimae destinavit'; because Cassiodorus refers to Marcellinus as 'supradictus Marcellinus' later at *Institutiones* 1.17.2, the statement at 1.4.3 must refer to Marcellinus Comes, in which case the Athanasius mentioned must be Athanasius II, patriarch of Alexandria from 490–7; on Athanasius II, Neale, *Eastern Church*, 24–5.

very similar to those of Marcellinus later continued the chronicle to 548, indicating that Marcellinus had probably died and that court propaganda had changed hands.[38] All editions were written in Latin and composed using an annalistic framework. In comparison to the complex narratives of many classical forebears, Marcellinus' spare narrative invites the audience to assume that the material reported was the most important. Themes were to be noted immediately, rather than uncovered through studied consideration.

The *Chronicon* contests a whole complex of themes that Zosimus had used to portray the imperial past in the *Nova Historia*. Given the well-attested presence of Zosimus' history in the capital after the death of Anastasius in 519, its contribution to the political melange could well have demanded a propagandistic riposte from those such as Marcellinus who were sensitive to the more overtly polemical elements in the history. Marcellinus' *Chronicon* contests the anti-Constantinian thrust of the *Nova Historia* first with respect to the subject of public spectacles. Marcellinus punctuated his annalistic narrative with notations of periodic public dissidence centred on various spectacles (including the Hippodrome) at Constantinople.[39] With but one exception, the regular occurrence of public dissent at the capital prior to Justinian would seem at first to confirm Zosimus' belief that the games had been one of the formative evils in the decline of the empire.[40] However, as unlikely as it may seem, not only does Justinian fare well in this respect, but Marcellinus portrays him as a restorer of public discipline. According to Marcellinus, Justinian made his first consulship in 521 the most famed by virtue of the celebrations offered to the populace in the amphitheatre and Hippodrome.[41] Later, the *Chronicon* takes great care to indicate how Justinian reformed the public disorder associated with spectacles. The single entry for 528 discusses several measures that Justinian took immediately after his elevation: remodelling the imperial box with the intention of increasing the visibility of the imperial presence, renovating the porticos where the senators traditionally attended, and in general improving the discipline of the audience.[42] The final disassociation of Justinian from Constantine's reputation with respect to public spectacles appears in Marcellinus' account of the Nika Revolt. The entry for 532 entirely ignores the

---

[38] On Marcellinus' public position and the dates of the *Chronicon*, Ruggini, 'Nobilita', 77; Croke, 'Misunderstanding Cassiodorus', 225–6; Croke, *Marcellinus*, 19–35.
[39] Marcellinus Comes, *Chronicon* 445.2, 473.2, 491.2, 501.1, 507.1, 512.6.
[40] Marcellinus Comes, *Chronicon* 439.1, for the exception.
[41] Marcellinus Comes, *Chronicon* 521.　　[42] Marcellinus Comes, *Chronicon* 528.

Hippodrome as the focus of popular discontent.[43] Instead, the account focuses on the attempt of the heirs of the former emperor, Anastasius, to stage a coup.[44] While Marcellinus' account remained true to certain particulars, it occluded aspects of the story that might have allowed 532 to be seen as the fruition of Zosimus' prophecy in which the volatility of a failing empire was acted out on a stage traditionally reserved for the *infames*.

Marcellinus also addressed the relationship between Christianity and the Roman Empire which, for Zosimus, had been a cause of imperial decline. Whereas the *Nova Historia* tends to make the sack of Rome in 410 read as a consequence of political and religious innovation initiated earlier by Constantine, Marcellinus instead commenced the *Chronicon* with the year 378, when the Goths make a dramatic (although not the first) appearance in imperial history, with the destruction of Valens and the Roman legions at Adrianople. In essence, Marcellinus replaced innovation with the Goths as the central threat to the state, thereby rejecting Zosimus' claim that Constantine's reckless governance had precipitated the sack of Rome. According to Marcellinus' history, the Goths plagued the state, not the legacy of Constantine's innovations.[45] By commencing his history with 378, Marcellinus was able to overwrite the sack of 410 as the symbolic ruin of the state and the culmination of Constantine's poor policies.

By 534, when Marcellinus began revising and extending the original version of the *Chronicon*, Justinian's reign had already weathered its most controversial events and had entered the initial stages of conflict with the Ostrogothic government in Italy. In addition to rectifying Zosimus' image of an imperial world destined to suffer Constantinian 'decline and fall', Marcellinus pursued a line of Constantinian triumphalism in two thematic strands that were complementary to Justinian's own policies: the twin concerns of imperial relations with 'barbarian' peoples (primarily the Goths) and religious orthodoxy. Both themes receive studied attention from the beginning of the history with the accession of Theodosius, 'a singularly religious man and propagator of the Catholic church', who pacified the Goths in the aftermath of Adrianople.[46] At times, the pacification of the Goths and religious orthodoxy were interrelated issues, as

---

[43] Cf. the role of the Hippodrome in other accounts, Procopius, *Wars* 1.24, and *Anecdota* 12.12 and 19.12; John Lydus, *De magistratibus* 70.1–70.6; John Malalas, *Chronographia* 18.71.473–477; Evagrius, *Historia Ecclesiastica* 4.32.

[44] Marcellinus Comes, *Chronicon* 532.

[45] On Marcellinus' handling of the Goths, Croke, *Marcellinus*, 61–9.

[46] Marcellinus Comes, *Chronicon* 379.1, trans. Croke, 1.

when Theodosius' conquest of the 'Scythian tribes' permitted the expulsion of Arians from the church at Constantinople.[47] Imperial relations with the Goths follow a steady development from Theodosius until the announcement of the Gothic War in 534.[48] At the same time, imperial intervention in ecclesiastical politics continues on a steady (albeit troubled) course.[49] The two narrative threads seldom stray. For example, Theoderic is consistently shown in the least-favourable light: plunderer, grasping and untrustworthy ally, and treacherous invader of Italy.[50] But his barbarism is nowhere more apparent than as a ruler who would suborn the Pope to voyage to the east and petition for tolerance toward Arians in the east.[51]

What emerges is a narrative that concedes the necessity of Justinian's intervention in religious affairs and of armed conflict with the Goths. When Justinian finally did initiate the reconquest of Italy, Marcellinus had already constructed a narrative such that it would be understood not as the conquest of Roman Italy, but as the rebirth of a tradition for Christian empire possible only under Justinian. The narrative structure was particularly well prepared for this interpretation by the entry for 476. For this year, Marcellinus recorded no less than the end of imperial rule in the west, noting that after the deposition of the child-emperor Romulus Augustus by the *magister militum* Odoacer, 'old' Rome henceforth remained under the rule of Goths.[52] Thus Marcellinus constructed the tragic end of the western Roman empire as a foil to the sack of Rome in 410, a moment all the more propagandistic in that neither Odoacer nor his soldiers were, strictly speaking, Gothic. The truth of the matter was that 476 only became the end of the western empire at precisely the moment that it suited the propagandistic purposes of the eastern court.[53] Eastern and western commentators had never before seen 476 as anything except another in a series of fifth-century imperial depositions and the accession of another military commander. Nevertheless, Marcellinus' spurious claim concerning the end of the western empire was important in several respects. First, it contested the claim of Zosimus that Rome fell because Constantine had allowed traditional religious observances to

---

[47] Marcellinus Comes, *Chronicon* 380.
[48] On encounters with or news pertaining to the Goths, Marcellinus Comes, *Chronicon* 379, 380, 381.2, 382.2, 400, 410, 414.2, 419.2, 481.1, 482.2, 483, 487, 488.2, 489, 505, 514, 517, 525, 530.
[49] On the contest for religious orthodoxy, Marcellinus Comes, *Chronicon* 381.1, 398.3, 403.3, 416.2, 428.1–2, 430.3, 449.2, 451, 453, 458, 459, 463, 466, 494, 495, 511, 512.2–9, 513, 525; on imperial intervention in church affairs, 380, 458, 476.1, 494, 495, 511, 512.2–9, 513, 516.2–3, 519.2.
[50] Marcellinus Comes, *Chronicon* 482, 487, 488–9.   [51] Marcellinus Comes, *Chronicon* 525.
[52] Marcellinus Comes, *Chronicon* 476; MacGeorge, *Warlords*, 276–83.
[53] Croke, '476', 81–119.

lapse. Rather, Marcellinus' chronicle had been at pains from the very first year to demonstrate the Goths as the true destructive force in the empire. Second, the fall of 476 characterized Ostrogothic Italy as a 'barbarian' nation and provided Justinian with the proper ideological justification for its reconquest.

The fact that Procopius later repeats the significance of this date is testimony to its currency in the political discourse of the eastern capital.[54] The consistent attention that Marcellinus paid to the reputation of Constantine was more than a nostalgic concern to correct the image of the 'great' Christian emperor. The popular image of Constantine in the sixth century had the potential to deconstruct Justinian's own legitimacy as an emperor involved in theological controversy. When Pope Agapetus found himself an ill-treated guest of the emperor in 535 and in reaction called Justinian a 'Diocletian', it may be that the Pope had availed himself of a potent piece of the political discourse circulating in Constantinople.[55] The accusation was two-pronged: not only was Justinian persecuting a Christian leader, but he was most certainly not behaving like a Constantine.

THE *ANONYMUS VALESIANUS* AS IMPERIAL PROPAGANDA

The importance of Constantine's reputation to sixth-century governance should not be underestimated. The same interest that Marcellinus had in contesting Zosimus' characterization of Constantine appears again in a slightly later text, the *Excerpta Valesiana* or, as it is better known, the *Anonymus Valesianus*. The *Valesianus* combines two biographies, that of Constantine and that of Theoderic the Amal. Stylistic differences suggest independent authorship for the two biographies in the *Valesianus*, but it seems fairly certain that both biographies were eventually combined at Ravenna sometime during the 550s.[56] For a later compiler to pair these two rulers makes perfect sense in the context of a polemical discourse flowing freely between Constantinople and Ravenna. More than likely the two lives were combined in Ravenna as a result of the administrative relationship between Constantinople and the newly formed Exarchate

---

[54] Procopius, *Wars* 5.14.14, noted that with Belisarius' seizure of Rome in December of 536, Rome had again become an imperial possession after sixty years; in other words, Procopius is repeating the propaganda which suggested 476 as the terminus of the western empire.
[55] *Liber Pontificalis* 59.
[56] Rolfe, *Ammianus Marcellinus*, vol. III: 506–7; Barnish, '*Anonymus Valesianus*', 572–8; Vitiello, 'Cassiodoriana'.

of Ravenna.[57] Since the removal of the Amal court in 540, the administration of Ravenna operated under the direct control of the eastern court, making Ravenna a challenging political environment in the 540s and 550s. Eastern authority demanded legitimization in the same urban landscape where the Amals had left the indelible mark of prosperity. Positive associations with Theoderic as a builder and administrator required repudiation, or at least qualification, in order to justify the new imperial regime. Given that imperial and Gothic forces were contending for the rest of Italy at this time, the *Valesianus* makes perfect sense as a text that sought to polish the image of imperial rule and impugn that of the Amals. The currency of the *Nova Historia* and its potential impact on Justinian's public image required an effective propagandistic riposte that would restore Constantine's reputation. The *Valesianus* did so by contrasting Constantine with a portrayal of the 'barbarian' Theoderic. It was an effective inversion of the comparison that Zosimus had made between Constantine and Julian, with Constantine now lauded for correct religious belief (the first Christian emperor) and Theoderic portrayed as the aberrant ruler (a heretical king of Italy). Portraying Constantine as a founding father and Theoderic as the heretic who ruled after the 'end of empire' not only justified the position of the Byzantine Exarchate in Ravenna, it also furthered the notion that Justinian's war of conquest was a means of restoring Italy to its 'tradition' as a seat of Christian empire.

Although not as laudatory as the extant panegyrics offered to Constantine, the *Valesianus* makes a studied effort to rehabilitate Constantine's memory and provides an indication of how the eastern polemical discourse was informed by Zosimus' portrayal of Constantine. The reader finds Constantine born to a woman of humble origins (*matre vilisima*) as opposed to a harlot as stated by Zosimus.[58] Where Zosimus offered a deeply flawed domestic life as Constantine's reason for conversion to Christianity, the *Valesianus* ignores the executions of Crispus and Fausta and claims that Constantine became the first Christian emperor in order that 'the one-thousandth year of Rome might be dedicated to Christ rather than pagan idols'.[59] And, as may be expected, the *Valesianus*

---

[57] Moorhead, *Theoderic*, 261–3; note also *Excerpta Valesiana* 7.36, which attributes a reign of ten years to Romulus Augustus, a glaring error which is difficult to reconcile with a Ravennate origin where the author would have access to documents or a tradition, such as Cassiodorus' *Chronica*, that could correct such misinformation.

[58] *Excerpta Valesiana* 2; Zosimus, *Nova Historia* 2.9.2.

[59] *Excerpta Valesiana* 33, 'ut millesimus Romae annus Christo potius quam idolis dicaretur', trans. Rolfe, *LCL*, 529; contrast with Zosimus, 2.7.6, where Constantine neglected the celebration of an important date.

removes all stain of innovation from Constantine's name; instead, the changes wrought by Constantine were 'just and humane'.[60]

In contrast, the *Valesianus* subjects Theoderic's reputation to systematic dismantling.[61] Several internal narrative features suggest that Theoderic's biography was directly concerned with the propaganda of the eastern court. First, Theoderic's biography includes a lengthy (and rather fanciful) excursus on how Anastasius determined through prodigies and dreams that his nephews were unsuitable as his successors. According to the *Valesianus*, Anastastius was relieved to find that Justin would fulfil that role in their stead.[62] As the only glimpse of Anastasius' reign present in the *Valesianus*, the main concern of the story is apparently the legitimacy of Justin's accession and, by extension, that of Justinian; it seems that even in Ravenna in the 550s the notional legitimacy of the coup attempted by Hypatius and Pompeius required conditioning. Linked to this concern is the well-known story of Theoderic's illiteracy and his use of a stencil to sign his name on official documents.[63] Barnish was quite correct to propose that the reference to Theoderic's illiteracy had originally derived from a description of Justin, about whom eastern sources make the same claim.[64] But where Barnish suggested that a scribal error had substituted Theoderic's name for Justin's (the passage concerning Theoderic's illiteracy follows directly after the discussion of Justin's accession), it seems more likely that the author of the *Valesianus* purposefully reassigned the story to Theoderic as a means of contesting the popular portrayal of Justinian's predecessor as an illiterate emperor. Thus the author of the *Valesianus* intended Theoderic's biography to play a role in controlling certain elements of the eastern political discourse that had reached Ravenna.

Pairing Constantine and Theoderic had the obvious rhetorical thrust of comparing the first Christian emperor with the heretical 'barbarian.' The comparison also brought into higher relief a particular vulnerability of Amal propaganda, which had maintained a distance from associations with Constantine. Constantine's reputation understandably proved difficult for the Amal court to be associated with given that emperor's role in condemning Arian Christianity.[65] It even seems that Cassiodorus had expunged material pertaining to Constantine's contest with Arianism from his *Chronica*, which depended heavily on material from Jerome's *Chronicle* (itself a continuation of Eusebius).[66] Amal

[60] *Excerpta Valesiana* 34, 'Item Constantinus iusto ordine et pio vicem vertit.'
[61] Barnish, '*Anonymus Valesianus*', 584–95. [62] *Excerpta Valesiana* 74–8.
[63] *Excerpta Valesiana* 79. [64] Barnish, '*Anonymus Valesianus*', 573.
[65] Whitby, 'Images', 88; Vitiello, 'Cassiodoriana', 120–3. [66] Aiello, 'Cassiodoro', 146.

propaganda had instead favoured associations with Trajan and Valentinian.[67] It should be noted that the author of the *Valesianus* expected the contrasts of Theoderic's portrayal to communicate the extreme ideological contradiction of a 'barbarian' *imperium*. A measure of that confusion is visible in the maxims attributed by the *Valesianus* to Theoderic's 'unlettered wisdom'. Among these sayings, one in particular stands out: 'The poor Roman imitates the Goth, while the wealthy Goth imitates the Roman'.[68] Although the statement may be understood as a seemingly harmless observation concerning the role of wealth in ordering the ranks of society, it also encapsulates a complete inversion of a sixth-century social ideal in which the Goth cultivated the military virtues necessary for empire and the Roman preserved the arts of peace. Cassiodorus went to great lengths in the *Variae* to communicate the continuity of that ideal.[69] Theoderic's supposedly casual acknowledgement of the liberal transgression of social and political boundaries in the *Valesianus* was a refutation of the kind of society that Cassiodorus claimed existed between Romans and Goths in Italy.

JUNILLUS AFRICANUS AND THE BIBLICAL BASIS FOR EMPIRE

Marcellinus' chronicle and the *Valesianus* attempted to justify political theocracy in different ways. Marcellinus portrayed the historical necessity of governance after the model of Constantine by demonstrating the destructive force of the Goths and disunity in the church. The *Valesianus* similarly relied on Constantine as a referent which cast in sharper relief the departure of Theoderic's reign and, by extension, the providential nature of Justinian's. Another text contemporary with Marcellinus' *Chronicon* aimed to construct (albeit rather unsystematically) a different framework in support of theocratic political authority. Written in Greek, the *Mirror of Princes* was dedicated to Justinian by Agapetus, a writer who may have served as a deacon of the Hagia Sophia.[70] His treatise was written sometime after the Nika Revolt of 532, perhaps in gratitude for the

---

[67] *Excerpta Valesiana* 60; Cassiodorus, *Variae* 8.3.5; on this, Vitiello, 'Cassiodoriana', 113–33.

[68] *Excerpta Valesiana* 61, 'Dum illitteratus esset, tantae sapientiae fuit, ut aliqua, quae locutus est, in vulgo usque nunc pro sententia habeantur; unde nos non piget aliqua de multis eius in commemoratione posuisse. Dixit . . . "Romanus miser imitatur Gothum et utilis Gothus imitatur Romanum."'

[69] For example, Cassiodorus, *Variae* 8.3.4, 'iuvante domino custodire et Gothis Romanisque apud nos ius esse commune nec aliud inter vos esse divisum, nisi quod illi labores bellicos pro communi utilitate subeunt, vos autem habitatio quieta civitatis Romanae multiplicat'; 8.10.11, 'Convenit gentem Romuleam Martios viros habere collegas'; on Cassiodorus' cultivation of the idea of a bipartite society, Moorhead, 'Cassiodorus on Goths', 241–59.

[70] Bell, *Political Voices*, 27–49, for a detailed introduction to Agapetus.

emperor's attention to reconstruction of the church. Although clearly didactic in nature, Agapetus' work bears little resemblance to a formal and systematic philosophical treatise. Nonetheless, a single purposeful theme is apparent throughout the text. The various anecdotes and maxims of the text all served to emphasize the absolute and uncontested rule of the emperor in matters both secular and spiritual. For Agapetus, the emperor was quite patently appointed by God to rule the earth. The text was modelled on the received Eusebian conception in which the emperor's competence on earth mirrored the heavenly kingdom, justifying his uncontestable authority in all matters.[71]

Similar to Agapetus' exposition of a Constantinian triumphalism, although written with considerably more theoretical subtlety and sophistication, the Latin *Instituta Regularia Divinae Legis Libri Duo* of Junillus Africanus was another contemporary treatise that attempted to articulate imperial theocracy. In particular, Junillus' work was concerned with biblical exegesis and imperial law, both subjects of central importance at Justinian's court. Although Junillus served the imperial court later than Marcellinus, both wrote from the same perspective of close intimacy with Justinian's policies. Junillus' formulation of a theory that would support Justinianic *renovatio* may be understood in the simple terms of his social and political dependence on the emperor's court.[72] Junillus was numbered among the influential population of North African émigrés who arrived in Constantinople either before or immediately after Belisarius' conquest of the Vandalic kingdom. The rank of *vir illustris* probably indicates that he had held high social standing even before leaving North Africa.[73] Although the *Instituta* reveal Junillus' background as educated, he apparently knew very little Greek. All these factors – his social standing in newly conquered North Africa, his literary training and his dependence on the patronage of the emperor in a foreign city – probably made him an ideal candidate for the post of quaestor, which he held from 542 to 549, following the death of Tribonian. This position brought him in close contact with the processes of policy making. In fact, Junillus produced the *Instituta Regularia* while holding the quaestorship, and his exegetical interests are inseparable from his role as court propagandist.[74] Cassiodorus read the *Instituta Regularia* and referred to it in his own *Institutions*.[75] Although Cassiodorus recommended Junillus' work, among others, as an introductory manual

---

[71] Bell, *Political Voices*, 35–45.   [72] Maas, *Exegesis*, 1–83; Becker, 'Theodore', 30–8.
[73] *PLRE IIIA*, 742.   [74] Stein, 'Deux questeurs', 379–82, dates the text at 542.
[75] Cassiodorus, *Institutiones* 1.10.1.

for approaching the understanding of scripture, the *Instituta* does not actually engage in biblical exegesis directly; rather it explains the validity and importance of exegesis as an intellectual practice.[76] The context of the work is ostensibly a response to a 'cordial conversation' between Junillus and Primasius, bishop of Hadrumetum, who expressed interest in the Greek zeal for divine understanding during his delegation to the eastern capital.[77] However, embedded within the series of questions and answers that follows is a political position predetermined by the political environment of Justinian's court – the demand for doctrinal orthodoxy and justification for legal change.[78] The *Instituta Regularia* integrated concepts pertaining to the understanding of Christian scripture with concepts pertaining to the understanding of natural law (an emerging interest at Justinian's court significant to the codification of universal law and the formulation of doctrinal uniformity in the church). Junillus' text ascribed the right of the emperor to intervene in human affairs to an abstract conception of natural law that complemented biblical interpretation.[79] By articulating a theoretical framework for the convergence of Roman jurisprudence and Christian cosmology, the *Instituta Regularia* provided a foundation for Justinianic theocracy.[80] The *Instituta Regularia* thus supplied a definition for the will of the emperor that was based on biblical interpretation and a particular understanding of natural law. The *Instituta Regularia* also supplied a riposte to the charge of malign innovation on Justinian's part. In essence, no act of an emperor could be construed as innovation if his will proceeded from biblical antecedent.

THE ANONYMOUS *DIALOGUE ON POLITICAL SCIENCE*

That Justinian's court was sensitive to a contested political discourse is seen in the manner that both the *Chronicon* of Marcellinus and the *Instituta Regularia* engage in the production of a new language of imperial legitimacy. In fact, the projects of Marcellinus, Agapetus, Junillus and the *Valesianus* were each parallel approaches to the same problem of legitimating an emperor in the face of substantial opposition from a political group that had the advantage of institutional tradition. The *Mirror of Princes* and the *Instituta*, however, were not written in direct response to the history of Zosimus as was the *Chronicon*. Instead, it is more probable that Agapetus and Junillus responded, at some level, to ideas about aristocratic consensus in imperial governance that were current at the

---

[76] Maas, *Exegesis*, 83.   [77] Junillus, *Instituta, praefatio* 15–19.
[78] Maas, *Exegesis*, 4–18.   [79] Maas, *Exegesis*, 12.   [80] Maas, *Exegesis*, 67–70.

capital during the early years of Justinian's reign and found concentrated expression in an anonymous treatise written in Greek. This text, entitled the *Dialogue on Political Science*, explores the philosophical nature of temporal governance and attempts to address the issue of what form secular authority ought to take. The text adopts a more moderate stance in the political discourse: it does not offer what might be considered a criticism responding to specific policies of Justinian, but rather suggests in its own way a governmental posture that would ameliorate the impact of those policies for the most discontented social groups.

Now fragmentary, only one and a half books of an original six survive from the *Dialogue*. The extant fragment of Book 4 deals with military matters, while Book 5 sketches the ideal state and the ruler's role in that state. The treatise has been dated on circumstantial grounds to early in Justinian's reign, possibly sometime between 529 and 535.[81] The *Dialogue* takes the form of a philosophical dialogue between Menodorus and Thaumasius. If the extant text corresponds to a very similar one described by Photius, in which the interlocutors are identified as Menas the patrician and Thomas the *referendarius*, then the extant copy represents one version of the original which had used classicizing names for persons of genuine historical significance.[82] Both individuals held prominent positions in Justinian's early administration. Menas (or 'Menodorus') was a senator with patrician status who held an urban prefecture and a praetorian prefecture under Justin and later held the office of praetorian prefect under Justinian from 528 to 529. Thomas (or 'Thaumasius') held the post of quaestor, in which capacity he had acted as an original member of the commission to draft the *Codex Iustinianus*. Thomas was executed for his Hellene leanings in 529 and the sources are silent regarding Menas after his short prefecture which also ended in 529.[83] That an elegiac poem from this period praises a certain Menas as a philosophically inclined rhetorician lends weight to the assumption that Menas too had been condemned during the purge. The coterminal dates in which these two officials held office offers perhaps the most compelling reason for dating the *Dialogue* earlier rather than later. The use of 'Menodorus' and 'Thaumasius' expresses sensitivity to the potential for incurring official censure by circulating a philosophical treatise that essentially eulogized prominent public officials who had fallen as a result of Justinian's policies. Thus the author probably began composing the text sometime immediately after

[81] On the date, Fotiou, 'Dicaearchus', 534; Fotiou, 'Philosopher king', 17; Cameron, *Procopius*, 250; O'Meara, 'Justinianic dialogue', 49; Bell, *Political Voices*, 18–19.
[82] O'Meara, *Platonopolis*, 174; similarly, Bell, *Political Voices*, 9–13.
[83] PLRE II, 755, for Menas; PLRE IIIB, 1314–15, for Thomas.

529 (that is, in immediate response to the purge of Hellenes but before the retaliation of the Nika Revolt).[84]

The content of the text certainly claims inspiration from Neoplatonism, as would befit a Hellene in public office who had survived the purge of 529. The text bears the stamp of the tradition of political philosophy established by Plato, the hallmark interest of contemporary Neoplatonic thinking.[85] A theme of paramount importance in the *Dialogue* is the limit of autocracy. Consideration is given to the theoretical source of a ruler's right to exercise absolute power and to the role played by advisory bodies. Although the treatise considers temporal governance to be an imitation of the divine, the *Dialogue* offers a conceptualization that is more sensitive to Neoplatonic thinking, which had a long-standing interest in describing government as a divine instrument. The *Dialogue* is also keenly interested in describing a 'hybrid' political constitution that combines imperial, aristocratic and democratic characteristics of government.[86] Natural law is invoked as the prime governing agency which determines the scope of power exercised first by the ruler, then the Senate and optimates, the priesthood and, finally, the highest magistracies.[87] Chief among the interests of the text is the ruler's receptiveness to the consensus of an educated elite (optimates) which would play a role in preventing the capricious elevation of successors, restraining the arbitrary exercise of imperial power and ensuring respect for law (issues that troubled the reputation of Justinian's reign).[88] Predictably, the qualification of this elite class was its possession of *paideia*.[89] Additionally, a thinly veiled spirit of meritocracy seems to govern membership of the ruling elite – those who lacked the necessary natural gifts should find appointments in 'other orders of the city, whether military or civilian', while, conversely, those found to possess the appropriate natural gifts should be inducted into 'a second, separate college of optimates' to prevent promiscuous mixing of the two orders.[90] The provision made for natural talent, while seemingly generous, levels an implicit critique against Justin and Justinian, who should not have ascended beyond a lower grade of optimates.[91] In stark contrast to the elevation of Justin, the *Dialogue* prescribes a process in which the leaders of each order in society nominate three members of

---

[84] Fotiou, 'Dicaearchus', 547, suggests that anxiety over official censure is a factor in the anonymity of the text.
[85] Bell, *Political Voices*, 49–50.
[86] *Dialogue on Political Science* 5.1; Fotiou, 'Dicaearchus', 539–47; O'Meara, *Platonopolis*, 181.
[87] *Dialogue on Political Science* 5.17–21, esp. 5.21.
[88] *Dialogue on Political Science* 5.49; on this, Fotiou, 'Dicaearchus', 539–43.
[89] *Dialogue on Political Science* 5.23–26.
[90] *Dialogue on Political Science* 5.28–33, trans. Bell, *TTH*, 151–2.
[91] *Dialogue on Political Science* 4.73.

the optimates as candidates for the imperial office. The emperor would then be selected from among these candidates by lot. The 'lesser' optimates were explicitly excluded from imperial office.[92] Although critical of Justin's legitimacy and autocratic policies, the text shows evidence of a preference for the senatorial order that aligns well with the choice of Menas and Thomas (members of the *consistorium*) as interlocutors.[93] And while the *Dialogue* clearly does not represent the interests of a middling bureaucratic elite (the 'lesser' optimates), it does show sensitivity in responding to the divisive policies of Justinian's early years as emperor. Ultimately, like the *Mirror of Princes* of Agapetus, the *Dialogue* sought to provide a didactic model, but one that asserted a Neoplatonic (not Constantinian) conception of governance. Like the fourth-century orations of Themistius, the *Dialogue* attempted to carve out a role for traditional philosophical thought in the conception of just governance and the text's potential as advice to the emperor may have had the intention of curbing the prosecution of public officials (high and low) educated in the classical tradition of *paideia*.[94]

PROCOPIUS AND THE 'SECRET' RIPOSTE

A decidedly more aggressive and comprehensive critique of the imperial political structure appeared with Procopius of Caesarea. Procopius wrote in Constantinople at a time when most scholars would agree that Cassiodorus was a resident at the eastern capital. The discourse in which Procopius was embedded provided the political culture that Cassiodorus encountered with its distinctive contours of propaganda, polemic and reprisal. More than any other writer from the eastern Mediterranean, Procopius has had a profound influence on the modern understanding of the Justinianic period.[95] As a writer and frequent witness of events of his own day, Procopius' various works have allowed scholars to appreciate the dynamic of authority and communication that connected Constantinople to a wider Mediterranean world. Procopius' rich geographical scope (covering Persia, Arabia, North Africa, Greece, the Balkans and

---

[92] *Dialogue on Political Science* 5.50–53 and 5.55–57.
[93] On the restraint of the contemporary critique in the *Dialogue*, Bell, *Political Voices*, 64–75.
[94] Cf. Themistius, *Oratio* 1.3d and 5.64b; on the role of the philosopher in public life advocated by Themistius, Heather and Moncur, *Themistius*, TTH, 1–19.
[95] On Procopius, Rubin, *Prokopios*; Cameron, 'Scepticism', 466–82; Cameron, *Procopius*; Whitby, 'Historical writing', 25–37; Greatrex, 'Procopius'; Greatrex, 'Lawyers', 148–61; Greatrex, 'Recent work', 45–67; Codoñer, 'Prokops', 47–82; Kaldellis, *Procopius*; Kaldellis, 'Dissident circles', 1–17; Croke, 'Secret History', 405–31; Rance, 'Narses', 424–72; Treadgold, *Historians*, 176–226; Kaldellis, 'Secret History', 585–616.

Italy) has made his work a chief source for understanding the social, political, cultural, economic and even environmental history of the eastern Mediterranean for the fifth and sixth centuries. As an actor in the social and political drama spiralling out of Constantinople, Procopius was keenly aware of the dynamic interplay of polemic shaping the literary and political culture of the eastern capital. A glimpse of this awareness is visible on a number of occasions when he rejects the methodological bases by which his contemporaries have interpreted historical events.[96] Procopius could hardly restrain his distaste for specific contributors to the Constantinopolitan discourse. Well after the *Instituta Regularia* had been in circulation, Procopius labelled Junillus as ill-suited to hold the position of quaestor because of his ignorance of legal matters and his lack of Greek.[97] Procopius' own contribution to the polemical debates of his day can hardly be overemphasized. Because the histories of Procopius take centre stage in the modern understanding of the eastern empire during the first half of the sixth century, there has always been a potential for his perspective of Justinian's reign to have a distorting effect. It is certainly true that Procopius had a distinct influence on later eastern commentators. A small constellation of post-classical writers including Agathias, Menander, Theophylact and Evagrius consulted Procopius' work in the course of fashioning their own renditions of the past.[98]

Procopius' background, social standing and political position naturally played a role in how he filtered events for his audience. Although knowledge of Procopius' biographical details is slight, his own writing firmly attests to the kind of literary education that prepared him for a public position.[99] As a native of Caesarea in Palestine, famed for the library founded on Origen's collection and hence a destination for scholarly travel, it is probable that Procopius' education was of the highest order. Despite the fact that Procopius wrote his works in Greek, his training in law and the services that he provided on military campaign suggest that his education had imparted a firm command of Latin.[100] His proficiency in Latin had probably been a factor commending him to Belisarius, the rising commander in whose service he had been engaged exclusively, as far as is known, prior to writing his histories.[101] Later sources attribute to

---

[96] For example, Procopius, *Wars* 1.1.4–5, 2.22.1, 7.15.23, 7.32, 8.6.9.
[97] Procopius, *Anecdota* 22.17–20.
[98] Whitby, 'Historical writing', 25–37.
[99] *PLRE IIIB*, 1060–6; Cameron, *Procopius*, 5–8; Greatrex, 'Lawyers', 149–52; Greatrex, 'Recent work', 58; Kaldellis, *Procopius*, 1–4.
[100] For example, Procopius, *Wars* 3.14, 6.4.1–2 and 6.4.19.
[101] On his promotion under Belisarius, Procopius, *Wars* 1.12.20–24.

him the title of *rhetor* and this more than likely refers to the legal scope of his services as *consiliarius* to Belisarius.[102] The long period in which Procopius acted as *consiliarius* to Belisarius (from 527 to 542) suggests personal attachment and patronage. The contrasting origins and backgrounds of the two men, one with a military career begun as a Danubian recruit and the other with liberal-arts training in urban Palestine, suggests that the opportunities available at Constantinople had brought them together.[103] It may be that, similar to John Lydus, Procopius had been constrained at an early stage of his public career to choose between the bureaucracy and forming a close attachment to a rising patron.[104] The title *consiliarius* is rather uninformative but probably implies a wide range of duties after the manner of a personal aide. Procopius no doubt was selected because of his literacy and legal training, which may suggest that his official function entailed aspects of accountancy and correspondence for the army. Where Procopius recorded his own activities, a picture emerges of the personal attendant to whom Belisarius entrusted delicate diplomatic and administrative matters.[105] Procopius appears to have followed Belisarius consistently through a number of military appointments, at least until 542. Whatever his previous involvement in state service at Constantinople, the personal and continuous nature of his service as *consiliarius* to a prominent military commander effectively removed him from the more regularized manner of advancement available to officials at the capital. That said, it would be inaccurate to portray Procopius as having had a military career in terms of formal enlistment in the army or even as one of the *bucellarii* who acted as Belisarius' personal military household.[106] Rather, Procopius should be understood as one of the many middling provincial elite who initiated a career at some level of state service at Constantinople (probably during the early reign of Justin) and then made the transition to a career more intimately connected with a prestigious individual. Procopius' success depended on that of Belisarius and this had probably provided him with some personal advantages until 542, when Belisarius fell under official censure. Procopius recounted the bitter scene when Justinian discharged Belisarius from service after John the Cappadocian accused him of speculating on the emperor's recent illness. Favoured officials and eunuchs of the court were allowed to cast lots for the reassignment of Belisarius' loyal attendants. Others 'who had been

---

[102] *PLRE IIIB*, 1060 and 1066.   [103] Procopius, *Wars* 1.11.21.
[104] John Lydus, *De magistratibus* 3.28.2.
[105] Procopius, *Wars* 3.12.3, 3.14.3–15, 4.14.39–41, 6.4.1–4.
[106] On the *bucellarii*, Procopius, *Wars* 1.24.40, 3.11.19, 3.16.9–11, 3.17.1–5, 3.19.11–13, 3.23.5, 4.1.7.12–25, 4.8.20–23, 7.1.20–21.

his friends or had previously served him in some way' were forbidden from visiting Belisarius.[107]

Procopius' education and previous position probably accorded him somewhat too much self-determination to fall into the hands of a new 'master' after 542. However, the episode did effectively close access to a patron who had supported him for fifteen years and may have left Procopius with perhaps fewer options than a man of his experience would like. Procopius' comment in the *Anecdota* that Justinian had abolished the vocation of *rhetor* more than likely indicates that pursuing a career in legal advocacy had been closed to him after Belisarius' fall.[108] It may very well be the case that Procopius had been dismissed from one employment and denied access to another within the space of a year. When Belisarius finally regained Justinian's confidence and had his previous position rehabilitated, the fact that Procopius did not accompany Belisarius during his return to Italy probably implies that the restriction against association with former attendants remained in force as well.[109] It is generally agreed that Procopius began writing his histories sometime in 544 or 545 and that he worked continuously until he finished early in the 550s.[110] The dates on which Procopius began writing nearly coincide with the renewal in Constantinople of the proscription against certain professions (grammarians, physicians and philosophers) in 545.[111] It is possible that the debarment of professors of rhetoric from legal careers may have coincided with this latest Hellene purge of 545. Given his legal background, which had presumably warranted a later generation of authors to call Procopius a *rhetor*, this event may have consigned Procopius to permanent 'literary' retirement. If Procopius' previous position under Belisarius had insulated him from the dissatisfaction experienced earlier by the bureaucratic elite (Procopius would have been in Belisarius' employ when the general quelled the Nika Revolt in 532), by 545 his social and political opportunities had changed dramatically. The trenchant critique of Justinianic rule that Procopius constructed and which would engage a wider discourse of political complaint may not have been written as a member of the bureaucratic elite, but it certainly drew from a salient perspective housed within that group.

As previously mentioned, the threat of official censure was serious enough to prevent Procopius from directly and explicitly portraying

---

[107] Procopius, *Anecdota* 4.13–15, trans. Dewing, *LCL*, 47.
[108] Procopius, *Anecdota* 26.2.   [109] Cameron, *Procopius*, 50.
[110] *PLRE IIIB*, 1062–4; Cameron, *Procopius*, 8–10; Croke, 'Secret History', 430–1; Kaldellis, *Procopius*, 46, and 'Secret History', 585–98; Treadgold, *Historians*, 184–92.
[111] Maas, *John Lydus*, 70–2; Pseudo-Dionysius of Tel-Mahre, *Chronicle*, trans. Witakowski, *TTH*, 71.

Justinian in a spirit of invective and this determined the necessity of an alternate strategy for writing his history. Averil Cameron has noted that a characteristic feature that Procopius had in common with John Lydus was a penchant for expressing tacit support for the emperor while at the same time excoriating the policies of his government.[112] Anthony Kaldellis has elaborated on this by demonstrating how obscurity and allusion to texts from classical historiography (especially Herodotus and Thucydides) could deliver a kind of oblique critique of the emperor.[113] Procopius' commentary on the emperor closely follows the division of *ad rem* and *ad hominem* invective.[114] The scope of the *Wars* prevents the immediate impression that the history was written about Justinian, but the treatment of individual events served well enough to illustrate the failings, as Procopius saw them, of the emperor's policies. In contrast, Procopius supplied his audience with the full, direct force of invective against the personality of Justinian in his *Anecdota*. The policies of Justinian's administration, as they appear in the *Wars*, received fresh attention in the *Anecdota*, where they were invariably linked *ad hominem* to short-comings in the character of the emperor. In a sense, Procopius wrote a single history, separated into layers of interpretation. To recite the full list of Procopius' complaints would serve little purpose at this point, but a number of the more prominent complaints correspond to the general discourse challenging the official image of the emperor that the court sought to generate.

Justinian's conduct of the various wars waged by the state received carefully prepared treatment from Procopius. The narrative of the *Wars* gradually assembles a commentary that frames Justinian's military ambitions as the central cause of misfortune in the eastern empire. Procopius made it clear in his preface, stated with reserved neutrality, that the central purpose of his history was to capture Justinian's wars for all time.[115] He also stated that he deemed this subject of great importance to posterity in that such a narrative would reveal, 'at least for those who are most prudent... what outcome present events will probably have'.[116] The final outcome of Justinian's conquests was available to the attentive reader who noted the jarring contrast in how Procopius treated discrete moments of the various wars. The peace concluded by Justinian with Persia in 532 hardly met the criteria required of a laudable victory and the entire narrative constructed around the Eternal Peace casts the character

---

[112] Cameron, *Procopius*, 243; similarly Maas, *John Lydus*.   [113] Kaldellis, *Procopius*, 18–36.
[114] For parallels, LaFleur, 'Horace', 1790–7; Ahl, 'Safe criticism', 174–208.
[115] Procopius, *Wars* 1.1.1.   [116] Procopius, *Wars* 1.1.2, trans. Dewing, *LCL*, 2.

of Justinian in doubt.[117] By demonstrating the emperor's willingness to pay tribute, Procopius indirectly contrasted the firm resolve of Chosroes to the wavering disposition of Justinian.[118] Similarly, according to Procopius, Justinian later agreed to pay additional tribute from the wealth that Belisarius had acquired from the Vandal conquest, thereby sapping the glory of that campaign.[119] More condemning, though, is the manner in which Procopius made it clear that this treaty provoked the Nika Revolt. After concluding the matter of the Eternal Peace, Procopius immediately followed by describing the two revolts in Persia and Constantinople that were to be understood as a direct consequence of the treaty: 'Straightway it came about that plots were formed against both rulers by their subjects.'[120] Where Procopius described the revolt against Chosroes quite clearly as a political coup, he portrayed the Nika Revolt as popular unrest stemming from public spectacle. These two narratives were intended primarily as a means to compare and contrast the qualities of the two rulers. Chosroes is not simply assertive and capable of quelling the revolt with decisive action, as compared to Justinian, who sought refuge in the imperial palace and so protracted the riots that wholesale slaughter was necessary; rather, Procopius discusses Chosroes in terms that are virtually identical to those in which he will later characterize Justinian in the *Secret History*. According to Procopius, Chosroes almost lost power because he was 'a man of unruly turn of mind and strangely fond of innovations'. Similarly, those who opposed Chosroes 'were men of action . . . in vexation at his administration [who] were purposing to establish for themselves another king'.[121] Any audience familiar with the current political discourse at Constantinople and aware of the bureaucracy's role in the Nika Revolt would instantly recognize that Procopius was recounting different versions of the Nika Revolt in two separate episodes.

Just as condemnatory was the manner in which Procopius handled the decision to wage wars in both the east and the west. In a pair of speeches purportedly offered on separate occasions, envoys of the Goths and the Armenians asked Chosroes for assistance, citing the same conviction that, by attempting to wage war simultaneously in the east and the west, Justinian had caused a rupture in the natural order of things. Safely couching his opinion in the words of 'barbarian' envoys, Procopius was able to focus attention on Justinian's destructive nature as an

[117] Procopius, *Wars* 1.22.   [118] Procopius, *Wars* 1.22.9–14.
[119] Procopius, *Wars* 1.26.1–4.   [120] Procopius, *Wars* 1.23.1, trans. Dewing, *LCL*, 209.
[121] Procopius, *Wars* 1.23.2–4, trans. Dewing, *LCL*, 209.

innovator.[122] According to the envoys, Justinian's military policies were born of a kind of mental imbalance, not from concern for the good of the state. While Procopius safely distanced himself from censure by enclosing this opinion within speeches, the vagueness of the official reason provided for the wars falls just short of denouncing Justinian. The reason initially offered by Procopius (speaking as the historian) for involving the eastern empire in war with the Vandals was Justinian's interest in resolving Gelimer's disputed succession to the throne in Carthage.[123] But only slightly later, Procopius dramatizes the decisive moment with a speech from John the Cappadocian, who urges against the difficulties involved in undertaking an expedition to Africa. Justinian initially accepts John's advice, although Procopius then claims that a nameless bishop disclosed in private to Justinian a dream describing his victory on behalf of the Christians, an ambition reminiscent of Constantine's reputation.[124] In stark contrast to his earlier promise to narrate the wars that the state waged gloriously, Procopius later related the final outcome of the Vandalic war: 'Thus it came to pass that those of the Libyans who survived, few as they were in number and exceedingly poor, at last and after great toil found some peace.'[125] The narration of the war in Italy follows the same rhetorical pattern. Procopius offered an ambivalent melange of diplomatic and religious reasons for attacking the Goths. Any unscrupulous intentions that may have played a role in provoking the war were carefully devolved upon Justinian's disingenuous agent Peter.[126] In the end, the cost of conducting the war in Italy would resemble the outcome in Africa, 'As for the Italians, the result of the situation for them was that they all suffered most severely at the hands of both armies.'[127] Later, in Books 7 and 8 of the *Wars*, Procopius insinuated that the protraction of the war in Italy had been the result of Justinian's poor judgement in relieving Belisarius and his indecisiveness in appointing another commander.[128] In the *Anecdota*, Procopius ascribed the wars to Justinian's corrupt character, an accusation only indirectly discernible in the *Wars*.[129]

In regard to policies of civil administration, Procopius adopted a similar stratagem by which the blame invariably fell not upon Justinian, but upon those whom he had appointed – John the Cappadocian being Procopius' favourite.[130] In contrast, the *Anecdota* provide a more personal, *ad hominem*

[122] Procopius, *Wars* 2.2.6 and 2.3.37.   [123] Procopius, *Wars* 3.9.15–19.
[124] Procopius, *Wars* 3.10.18–21.   [125] Procopius, *Wars* 4.28.52, trans. Dewing, *LCL*, 459.
[126] Procopius, *Wars* 5.3.   [127] Procopius, *Wars* 7.9.2–6, trans. Dewing, *LCL*, 223.
[128] Procopius, *Wars* 7.36.5–6, 7.37.24–27, 8.5–7.
[129] Procopius, *Anecdota* 7.25; more generally, 18.1–24.
[130] Procopius, *Wars* 1.25, 2.3, 3.13, 3.8.

view of administrative and social problems in which the corruption of senior imperial administration points directly to Justinian's predilection for innovation and his general disregard for trusted custom.[131] Likewise in the *Wars*, Procopius initially restrained his criticism for Justinian's interventions in the affairs of the church, noting only how disputes over Christian doctrine had detained him from settling affairs in Italy.[132] In the *Anecdota*, Procopius suggests a deeper psychological understanding for what appears in the *Wars* as a simple preoccupation with religious matters. Rather than an interest in religious unity, Justinian's obsession with religion was a symptom of madness – his involvement in Christian doctrinal controversy was nothing less than a deliberate desire to set the disputants at odds with one another.[133] Finally, the *Anecdota* reveal a harsher indictment of Justinian with regard to his role in the spectacles. Although Procopius provided a thorough account of the Nika Revolt in the *Wars*, Justinian participates only enough to demonstrate his lack of decisiveness.[134] In the *Anecdota*, the emperor plays a much more active role where his devotion to the games and to the popularity of the factions 'thereby brought the Roman State to its knees'.[135] According to Procopius, Justinian's patronage of spectacles at the Hippodrome inspired lawlessness in the capital. This is a direct contradiction of the account of Marcellinus and a reading of the event that applied a dominant theme of Zosimus' *Nova Historia* to Justinian's reign.[136]

Procopius reveals the extent to which the literate elite in Constantinople were concerned about Justinian's policies abroad and the impact of those policies in the capital. Affairs in the western Mediterranean and their ideological interpretation were clearly consequential. More importantly, these concerns activated and shaped communication between eastern and western elites at the capital and between Constantinople and Italy.

THE GOTHIC HISTORIES OF JORDANES AND CASSIODORUS

Another author writing at precisely the same time as Procopius who explicitly acknowledged Cassiodorus was Jordanes. In 551 Jordanes finished a Latin history of the Goths (the *Getica*) in fulfilment of a request from a friend who had interrupted Jordanes' completion of another work – a chronicle that embedded the history of the Roman people in a

---

[131] Procopius, *Anecdota* 6.6, 6.21, 8.26, 9.51, 11.1–2, 14.1, 18.12, 20.15, 25 *passim*, 28 *passim*, 30.2.
[132] Procopius, *Wars* 7.35.11.
[133] Procopius, *Anecdota* 10.15; Kaldellis, 'Secret History', 606–15.
[134] Procopius, *Wars* 1.24.   [135] Procopius, *Anecdota* 7.1–2, trans. Dewing, *LCL*, 77–9.
[136] Procopius, *Anecdota* 18.31–35.

more 'universal' narrative called the *Romana*.[137] Because events recorded in the *Romana* end in 547 and his preface to this work mentions the previous completion of the *Getica* in 551, it is probable that Jordanes had completed the bulk of the *Romana* by 547, by which time Procopius' work on the *Wars* would have been well established. The few details that Jordanes provides for his background suggest that, like Procopius, his literary enterprises were somehow connected to the events and policies of Justinian's reign. Jordanes mentions that he had previously served as the *notarius* to a *magister militum* named Gunthigis Baza. According to Jordanes, this Gunthigis claimed a familial connection to the Ostrogothic royal household (*de prosapia Amalorum*) through his father's line, and that through his mother he was descended from the family of Candac, a leader of the Scirians and Alans who settled in Moesia after the end of Attila's Hunnic confederation. Jordanes also noted that his grandfather Paria had served as a *notarius* to the same Candac.[138] The obvious pairing of the family lines suggests that Jordanes' family had served a prominent house of the late Roman military aristocracy for several generations. The marriage of Candac's sister to a member of the Amal household was a relatively normal procedure by which *foederati* of diverse ethnic origins negotiated stability in a social and political environment where Roman imperial influence was prone to capitalize on divisiveness. The family of Jordanes, which was also Gothic, had probably served as members of a hereditary military household (possibly similar to what Cassiodorus calls a *condama* in reference to Gepid subjects of the Ostrogoths).[139] Because Jordanes wrote in Constantinople and the office of *magister militum* was unused in Ostrogothic Italy, it is possible to conjecture that Jordanes arrived in Constantinople after service to a federated military commander in Moesia, where many Goths had settled in the east.[140] The attention, however, that Jordanes gives to the Amal connection suggests that he was a Goth from Italy. In this case, Gunthigis probably arrived in Constantinople as a result of the Gothic War (whether through negotiation or capitulation) and received appointment as *magister militum* in the normal course of diplomacy, by which the empire secured viable military talent. Like the *bucellarii* of Belisarius, Jordanes may have been

---

[137] Jordanes, *Romana*, *praefatio* 4; on Jordanes in Constantinople, Croke, 'Getica', 117–34, and Croke, 'Jordanes', 473–94; for a summary of the debates concerning Jordanes, Amory, *Ostrogothic Italy*, 291–307.

[138] Jordanes, *Getica* 265–6.

[139] On Jordanes' Gothic origins, Jordanes, *Getica* 316; on the *condama*, Cassiodorus, *Variae* 5.10.2 and 5.11; on the personal military following of non-royal Gothic leaders, Heather, 'Amals', 122–6.

[140] The Ostrogoths awarded the title of *comes* to military leaders, presumably because only Theoderic held the title *magister militum* through the appointment of the eastern emperor.

detached from Gunthigis' service when his former patron received the new appointment, leaving Jordanes to pursue a religious vocation at the capital. The reference that Jordanes twice makes to his conversion may indicate that he had adopted orthodox (as opposed to Arian) belief as a precondition for his new vocation.[141] As the personal attendant of a Goth of some former prominence in Italy, Jordanes was probably confined to a monastic vocation. And, of course, perhaps the most compelling argument that Jordanes was a Goth from Italy living in exile is the simple fact that the *Getica* serves as a stage for the Amal dynasty. It is less likely that a Goth from Moesia in the continual service of the eastern empire would display as much interest in the affairs of Italian Goths.[142]

This reconstruction of Jordanes' background suggests, importantly, that he would have arrived in Constantinople under the same circumstances as Cassiodorus, and in fact this is the simplest possible explanation for Jordanes' familiarity with the former praetorian prefect of Italy. In a notoriously problematic statement, Jordanes claimed in the preface to his *Getica* that he had set out 'to condense in my own style in this small book the twelve volumes of Senator on the origin and deeds of the Getae from olden time to the present day'.[143] Jordanes then continues, 'But worse than every other burden is the fact that I have no access to his books that I may follow his thought . . . I have in times past read the books a second time by his steward's loan for a three days' reading. The words I recall not, but the sense and the deeds related I think I retain entire.'[144] That Jordanes stated that he had previously read Cassiodorus' *Gothic History* 'a second time' may suggest that he had first encountered the work during a public reading at the Amal court and then borrowed a copy from Cassiodorus' secretary. His inability to access the books again has sown a generation of debate concerning the extent to which Jordanes actually depended on Cassiodorus' now lost *Gothic History* as a source for the *Getica*. Several strong cases have been made in favour of Jordanes' independence from Cassiodorus' direct influence.[145] More

---

[141] Jordanes, *Romana, praefatio* 3; *Getica* 266; the view of Momigliano, 'Italian culture', 221–2, that Jordanes was the eponymous bishop of Crotone who visited Constantinople with Pope Vigilius in 550 does not take into account how the prosopography pertaining to *Getica* 266 casts Jordanes in a social context strikingly different from what would be expected for a papal envoy; also contra this view Barnish, 'Gothic History', 347–54.

[142] By comparison, consider Isidore of Seville, who in the late sixth century maintained close contacts with Italy and held a position intimate with Gothic rule in Hispania and yet only vaguely touches upon Gothic affairs in Italy in his *Historia Gothorum* 36 and 40.

[143] Jordanes, *Getica, praefatio* 1, trans. Mierow, 51.

[144] Jordanes, *Getica, praefatio* 2, trans. Mierow, 51.

[145] Barnish, 'Gothic History', 355; Croke, 'Getica', 117–29; Goffart, *Narrators*, 23; Wood, 'Review', 481–2; and now Goffart, 'Jordanes' *Getica*', 386–97; for the view that Jordanes copied Cassiodorus, Momigliano, 'Italian culture', 223; Heather, 'Amals', 127.

recently, careful examination of the *Getica* has traced the influence of a rich foundation of ancient Greek and Roman sources, although these are admittedly sources with which Cassiodorus was also familiar.[146]

Regardless of the degree of dependence on Cassiodorus' text, it is more important that Jordanes drew upon Cassiodorus' reputation in order to further his own political agenda.[147] Walter Goffart believes that Jordanes' 'commission' had been to refute Cassiodorus' *Gothic History* by diminishing the venerable past of the Goths and to shift the focus to the more recent fall of Ostrogothic Italy in 540.[148] While describing Jordanes as 'one of the obedient agents of Justinian's campaign of destruction' overstates what is known about the possible collusion between Jordanes and the eastern court, Jordanes' use of Cassiodorus does indeed locate the former praetorian prefect at the centre of a specific strand of polemic in Constantinople. Jordanes reveals the agenda that brought him to mobilize Cassiodorus' name as political capital in his brief references to Germanus Posthumus, the son of Justinian's nephew (also Germanus) and the Amal heiress Matasuntha whom Belisarius brought to the east after the fall of Ravenna.[149] One of the more compelling interpretations suggests that Germanus' preparations to attack Totila in 550 had inspired a party of émigrés from Italy to hope to establish a modus vivendi between Goths and Romans.[150] Matasuntha's marriage to Germanus may very well have encouraged this party to entertain thoughts of a politically stable dynasty in Italy and, possibly, repatriation to Italy.[151] However, with the unexplained death of Germanus, Jordanes' hopes shifted to the young son, whom the historian clearly regarded as the promise of political reconciliation: 'This union of the race of the Anicii with the stock of the Amali gives hopeful promise, under the Lord's favor, to both peoples.'[152] In this sense, it may be that Jordanes recognized Cassiodorus as a prominent agent working for the repatriation of Italians and capitalized on Cassiodorus' reputation through his former work on the *Gothic History*.

[146] Mierow, *Gothic History*, 19–37, for a cursory survey of Jordanes' sources; Blockley, *Fragmentary Classicizing Historians*, vol. II, *passim* 223–77, on the use of Priscus; Christensen, *Jordanes*, 52–155 and 200–20, with particular attention to Jordanes' use of Ammianus Marcellinus; Festy, 'Histoire Auguste', 184, on the use of the *Historiae Augustae*.
[147] For recent emphasis on the importance of the connection between Cassiodorus and Jordanes in Constantinople, Amici, 'Cassiodoro', 226–30.
[148] Goffart, 'Jordanes' *Getica*', 394–6.
[149] Jordanes, *Getica* 60.314.
[150] Van de Vyver, 'Cassiodore', 258; Momigliano, 'Italian culture', 218–22; Wes, *Kaisertums*; Ruggini, 'Nobilita', 79; MacCormack, *Ceremony*, 230; Barnish, 'Gothic History', 358; cf. also Procopius, *Wars* 7.39, for a description of the event.
[151] On the marriage of Germanus and Matasuntha, Jordanes, *Getica* 81, 251 and 314.
[152] Procopius, *Wars* 7.40.9; Jordanes, *Getica* 314, trans. Mierow, 141; on this view Momigliano, 'Italian culture', 222–3.

Where Cassiodorus' *Gothic History* could not have extended much later than the life of Theoderic, Jordanes adopted the very traditional practice of writing in continuation of a noted predecessor.[153] Jordanes was also capable of hewing close to official court propaganda in order to obtain that goal, as is visible in his willingness to copy Marcellinus Comes, almost verbatim, in the *Romana* concerning potentially polemical subjects such as the Gothic end to the western empire in 476 and the Nika Revolt in 532.[154] Jordanes wrote at an intersection of polemical interests at the capital: clearly attuned to the potential for official censure at the capital in the *Romana*, his *Getica* speaks to a particular urgency concerning the resolution of the Gothic War. More importantly, the *Getica* provides the single firmest indication of Cassiodorus' involvement in the political discourse at Constantinople.

JOHN LYDUS AT THE CENTRE OF CONFLICT

Although Procopius and Jordanes finished their respective works in the early 550s, the polemical element present in each responded to a discourse that had gained momentum among the educated governmental elite ever since the cascade of unpopular events initiating Justinian's reign. In both cases, the engagement of these authors was in some ways peripheral to the central contest between Justinian and the bureaucracy. Procopius, although not a member of the bureaucratic establishment, proved remarkably attentive to the key themes of the bureaucratic invective against Justinian and he used them to his own ends. Similarly, Jordanes was not a voice sounding from within either bureaucratic ranks or Justinian's court, but his history responded directly to one of Justinian's most disruptive endeavours – the Gothic War. The bureaucracy did, however, produce its own representative voice in the person of John Lydus, whose Greek *De magistratibus* was finished slightly later than the more traditional histories of Procopius and Jordanes in 553–4.[155]

---

[153] On 533 as the *terminus ante quem* by which Cassiodorus composed his *Gothic History*, Croke, 'Getica', 120–2; Goffart, *Narrators*, 32, rejects the opinion that Cassiodorus had written the *Gothic History* as early as 519, but Cassiodorus, *Variae, praefatio* 1.11, notes that he had written the history earlier while serving the Amals.

[154] Jordanes, *Romana* 345–6; Marcellinus Comes 476; similarly, Jordanes, *Romana* 364, does not copy Marcellinus' diction as much as follow his emphases in relating the Nika Revolt – Justinian is absent from the narrative about the conspiracy of Hypatius and Pompeius.

[155] Carney, *Bureaucracy*; Maas, *John Lydus*; Kaldellis, 'Religion', 300–16; Kelly, *Ruling*, 11–26; Kaldellis, 'Dissident circles', 1–17; Kaldellis, 'Republican theory', 1–16; Treadgold, *Historians*, 258–64; for the date of publication of the *De magistratibus*, Kaldellis, 'Secret History', 606.

Unlike Procopius, John Lydus followed a professional trajectory that
was more traditional for educated provincials filling the bureaucratic *officia* and *scholae*.[156] Rather than attaching himself to a military entourage,
Lydus arrived in Constantinople in 511 and spent a year there studying
Aristotle and Platonic philosophy under Agapius, a noted 'disciple of the
great Proclus' from Athens. When a fellow provincial from Philadelphia
provided Lydus with the appropriate entrée in 512, he assumed a post
in one of the departments of the praetorian prefecture under Anastasius,
whom he praised as 'the most mild of all emperors'.[157] Lydus held this
post continuously under Justin and Justinian until 532, when he became
a victim of the administrative reorganization of John the Cappadocian.[158]
Lydus may have attempted to salvage a career that would have otherwise
culminated in the traditional pension by presenting an encomium to
Justinian at court, but it seems that the peak of the normal bureaucratic
cursus had been withheld from him, at least until 543, when he received
reappointment as an academic holding a professorial chair in Latin.[159] By
this time, a professorship in Latin at Constantinople may have been little
more than a sinecure and it clearly did not deliver the kind of emoluments to which Lydus had aspired as an official in a praetorian *officium*.[160]
Between 532 and 543, Lydus composed two works – *De mensibus* on the
calendar and the traditional significance of festivals, and *De ostentis* on
the explication of natural portents. Neither text engages in criticism of
Justinian, although both align Lydus' interests with those of a broader
group of the bureaucratic elite whose Neoplatonist proclivities included
the continuity of political traditions and natural history.[161] The text that
offers the clearest reaction to Justinian's reform policies is Lydus' *De
magistratibus*, a history of public offices composed sometime after Lydus'
reappointment outside the bureaucracy. The fact that Lydus referenced
De mensibus in this treatise but mentioned nothing of *De ostentis* even
when the subject matter was particularly relevant probably indicates that
he composed *De magistratibus* after the persecution of Hellenes in 545.
By this time, public discussion of matters such as portents and Neoplatonic interest in natural history would have been, quite understandably,
muted.[162] In this case, both John Lydus and Procopius embarked on
literary projects that concealed trenchant critiques of the Justinianic

[156] John Lydus, *De magistratibus* 3.26.1–30.10.
[157] John Lydus, *De magistratibus* 3.26.1–4, trans. Carney, *Bureaucracy*, 81.
[158] John Lydus, *De magistratibus* 3.28.3.   [159] John Lydus, *De magistratibus* 3.26.1–3.30.10.
[160] John Lydus, *De magistratibus* 3.30.1–2.
[161] Maas, *John Lydus*, 61–66 on *De mensibus*; and 105–13 on *De ostentis*; Kaldellis, 'Religion', 300–16,
on Lydus as a Neoplatonist in light of *De mensibus* and *De ostentis*.
[162] Carney, *Bureaucracy*, 11.

regime at precisely the same time and after an eastern imperial administration in Italy had become the expected outcome of the Gothic War for Italians in exile such as Cassiodorus.

John Lydus' *De magistratibus* exposes the systemic faults plaguing Justinian's management of the civil administration and at the same time constructs an indirect critique of the emperor himself. While the *Anecdota* leave little doubt that Procopius held Justinian personally responsible for the failures of government, Lydus avoided direct criticism by heaving the full burden of responsibility onto John the Cappadocian. In one sense, Lydus' complaints may be understood in the context of his experiences working in praetorian *officia* under John the Cappadocian prior to 532.[163] But it is also true that John the Cappadocian was the ideal proxy for Justinian. Long-standing difficulties between Theodora and John the Cappadocian eventually resulted in 541 in his exile to Egypt, where he was confined to life in a religious order.[164] Nonetheless, even after his fall from favour, Lydus targeted John the Cappadocian as a direct extension of the Justinianic policies that had had such a dramatic impact on the traditions of state service. Any criticism levelled against John was officially sanctioned by his exile, although it is just as true that the policies he had pursued while enjoying the emperor's pleasure had official approval. Just as in Procopius' *Wars*, Justinian is rarely the subject of discussion, his absence in the face of rampant corruption nonetheless rendered him passively blameworthy with every aspersion that Lydus cast on John the Cappadocian.[165]

De magistratibus professes to offer a history of the development of public offices from early Roman origins until the present day, and Lydus used that framework to illustrate where current administrative practice had departed from traditions of the past. Interestingly, Lydus began with Etruscan divinatory practices as the first 'public office'.[166] Although Lydus' discussion thereafter maintains a very secular course, the initial connection between 'pagan' religion and public office should call to mind the history of Zosimus, then circulating in Constantinople.[167] Following the introduction, the treatise systematically exposes the degradation of the most esteemed public offices and the concomitant dissolution of the way of life enjoyed by public officials. As with Zosimus and Procopius, the theme of innovation holds central importance. In discussing the early

---

[163] For example, John Lydus, *De magistratibus* 2.21 and 3.68.
[164] Procopius, *Wars* 1.25.3–5, 1.25.13–44; John Malalas, *Chronographia* 18.89.
[165] For example, John Lydus, *De magistratibus* 3.69.2; on Lydus' praise of Justinian in *De magistratibus* as *pro forma*, Maas, *John Lydus*, 92–6, and Kaldellis, 'Republican theory', 9–12.
[166] John Lydus, *De magistratibus*, *praefatio* 1.
[167] John Lydus, *praefatio* 4; cf. also, Maas, *John Lydus*, 50.

office of *princeps*, Lydus provided an antique definition for governance that bears striking similarity to the prescription for ruler's respect for consensus found in the *Dialogue on Political Science*:

A characteristic peculiar to a *princeps* is that he never disturbs a single one of the laws of the state but sedulously preserves the status of his own constitution through the principate. He does nothing arbitrarily outside the law, and ratifies by his own vote policies that are favored by the best men in the state, displaying for the citizenry the affection of a father as well as that of a leader. He is the sort of statesman that God and the prosperity of the age have granted our generation.[168]

Perhaps with intended irony, Lydus shortly after noted that where the term *dominus* had once meant 'tyrant', its current usage had come to replace that of *princeps* and that Justinian accepted its application as an indication of his fatherly standing.[169] It should be noted that while Lydus professed to maintain a chronological narrative, he found, like Zosimus, several occasions to interject commentary on the current day. Examples include the current confusion of ranks between military and civil officials, the recent withering of clientage as an institution in public office and the deterioration of decurial status in Lydus' own lifetime.[170]

In Books 2 and 3, where Lydus surveyed public offices since Constantine, the subject of trampled custom invariably finds its way into the discussion. As might be expected of a traditionalist bureaucrat writing in Constantinople, some of the sentiment of Zosimus seems to have filtered into the history of public offices: 'But everything fated to begin has an end... For when Constantine, and fortune too, had gone from Rome... it came to be necessary for the prefect no longer to exercise control over the court and the forces under arms.'[171] Maintaining a careful distance from an overt interest in non-Christian sources of divine wisdom, Lydus pointed out that an oracle from antiquity had predicted the eventual subjection of ancient custom: 'Prophecies of this sort have assuredly come to fulfilment.'[172] Lydus' more open lament that ancient wisdom and the magisterial competences preserved by law had been shorn by the 'devil' should call to mind the characterization of Justinian as a possessed demon in Procopius' *Anecdota*.[173] References to the corruption of magisterial tradition have the cumulative effect of casting

---

[168] John Lydus, *De magistratibus* 1.3.5, trans. Carney, *Bureaucracy*, 10.

[169] John Lydus, *De magistratibus* 1.6.2–4.

[170] John Lydus, *De magistratibus* 1.12.5, 1.20.4–5, 1.28.5.

[171] John Lydus, *De magistratibus* 2.10.1–2, trans. Carney, *Bureaucracy*, 48.

[172] John Lydus, *De magistratibus* 2.12.1–2.

[173] John Lydus, *De magistratibus* 3.11.1–2 and 3.12.1; cf. Procopius, *Anecdota* 12.14.27, 18.1–4, 18.36–37, 30.34 for Justinian's demonic nature; on Lydus' probable knowledge of the *Anecdota*, Kaldellis, 'Dissident circles', 4–12.

Justinian's role as *dominus* in stark relief against the earlier depiction of the benevolent *princeps*. More pointedly, the transition from emperor as *princeps* to *dominus* challenges, if implicitly, the notion of *renovatio* that formed the core of propaganda promoted at Justinian's court.

According to Lydus, the only remission from this continuous decline was the temporary appointment of Phocas to the praetorian prefecture as a result of the Nika Revolt in 532. In addition to his replacing John the Cappadocian, Phocas' prefecture represented a new dawn for the rule of law, the open courting of ancient wisdom and a relaxation of censorious scrutiny: 'Orators began to be famous for their speeches; the publishing of books and keen rivalry about them began recurring as part of the whole life-style of the state.'[174] Although internal evidence places the completion of *De magistratibus* over two decades later, Lydus ended his treatise abruptly after announcing the brief tenure of Phocas, whom Justinian had nominated as a political concession to placate the agitators of the Nika Revolt. Concluding the evident optimism of Phocas' appointment with the sudden end of the treatise perhaps reveals the deep sense of betrayal that had been the experience of bureaucrats when Justinian reappointed John the Cappadocian less than a year later. Lydus discussed the Nika Revolt in *De magistratibus*, where he openly blamed John the Cappadocian for the revolt.[175] Attention to urban riots in a treatise on public offices suggests that what had been an unruly urban uprising had quickly become complicated by the widespread dissatisfaction of those whose careers depended on the preservation of magisterial tradition. Ultimately, the *De magistratibus* was an instrument fashioned in continued contestation of governmental policies that had incited the Nika Revolt.

JOHN MALALAS

The last contributor to the extant literature reflecting the polemical discourse of Constantinople who had first-hand experience of the emperor's governance is John Malalas. Educated in Antioch, Malalas probably entered imperial service at Constantinople sometime between 532 and 540.[176] The general lack of hostility to Justinian in his *Chronographia* implies that he had avoided falling under official censure, while the quality of his Greek may even suggest a lower level of education more befitting

---

[174] John Lydus, *De magistratibus* 3.76.10, trans. Carney, *Bureaucracy*, 124.
[175] John Lydus, *De magistratibus* 3.57.1–69.3, 3.70.1–6, 3.72.1.
[176] Jeffreys, Jeffreys and Scott, *John Malalas*, xxi–xxii; Kokoszko, *Descriptions*, 6–8; Treadgold, *Historians*, 235–56.

the *scriniarii* who had profited from Justinian's reforms.[177] In any case, his official position at Constantinople remains only vaguely discernible. The content of his *Chronographia*, however, which he concluded with the death of Justinian in 565, bears the stamp of official propaganda originating in the imperial court.[178] Malalas structured his work using selective criteria for topics, many of which served as polemical co-ordinates the interpretation of which both the discontented commentators of the day and Justinian's court attempted to control.[179] In Malalas' hands, the interpretation of those co-ordinates became purposefully inventive.

Paralleling Marcellinus Comes' engagement with the history of Zosimus, John Malalas grappled with the political ramifications of Constantine's reputation for Justinian's government. The attention given to Constantine's reign is not coincidental to Justinian's own reputation.[180] Malalas entitles his work in an awkward yet telling manner: 'A report of John, descended from the time of Constantine the Great, beginning from the time of creation of the world.' Apparently, for Malalas, both creation and Constantine were coterminous as beginning points for tracing 'events that took place in the time of the emperors'.[181] To that effect, the *Chronographia* traces in summary fashion the course of biblical empires arising from Adam until reaching the Roman Empire and finally, in Book 13, the reign of Constantine. The treatment of the first Christian emperor is effusive with praise and Malalas even adulterated the legend of Constantine in order to cast him more fittingly as Justinian's predecessor. For example, with respect to the famous struggle with Maxentius for which Constantine received a sign from God, Malalas reported that Constantine 'went out against barbarians', not an emperor supported by the Senate. In thanks to God for his victory, Constantine 'immediately . . . destroyed the shrines of the Hellenes and opened up the Christian churches'. The reference to Hellene worship was misplaced, as Constantine, at least according to Malalas' narrative, was in Rome at the time. His use of 'Hellene' as a generic term for 'pagan' clearly underscores a subject topical in sixth-century Constantinople. Afterwards, Malalas further altered Constantine's tradition by proposing that Silvester had baptized the emperor at Rome, thus conflating imperial and Christian *imperium* with the symbol of Rome, another theme contemporary to Malalas' day integral to justifying the Vandalic and Gothic

---

[177] On Malalas' Greek, Treadgold, *Historians*, 235–56.   [178] Scott, 'Malalas', 99–109.

[179] Scott, 'Malalas', 99–100, on Malalas' tendency to reinterpret events in contestation of the anti-imperial critique.

[180] On the comparison between Malalas and Zosimus, Jeffreys, 'Writers', 135–6; also, Scott, 'Image of Constantine', 57, notes Constantine as 'idealized and a focal point' in the chronicle of Malalas.

[181] John Malalas, *Chronographia*, *praefatio*, trans. Jeffreys, Jeffreys and Scott, *John Malalas*, 1.

wars.[182] In order to emphasize Constantine as the outstanding Christian emperor through comparison with other emperors, Malalas manipulated the length to which he treated certain imperial reigns. The lengthy reign of Constantius (an Arian Christian) was truncated and the shorter reign of Julian that followed received a treatment disproportionately long, a rhetorical ploy that allowed Malalas to contest Zosimus' treatment of the two emperors by portraying Julian at equal length to Constantine as the ideological antithesis of good imperial governance.[183] As previously noted, the same ploy had structured the *Excerpta Valesiana*.

After Constantine's founding of the eastern capital, Malalas' narrative becomes far more concentrated on Constantinople and the east. The fact that Malalas contracts the remit of his chronicle from the initial scope of a 'universal history' to one narrowly focused in the last book on the imperial capital suggests that, for Malalas, world history reached its necessary conclusion in Justinianic Constantinople.[184] Although this is understandable given that Malalas wrote in Constantinople (and possibly for a period in Antioch), the consistent attention given to specific themes in the description of successive imperial reigns has the effect of making Justinian's involvement in the events of his reign far more normative than is found in the dissenting literature of the day. In essence, Malalas contests the image of Justinian as an innovator by demonstrating the continuity of his policies with an imperial tradition that originated with Constantine. Thus, in opposition to the contemporary negative interpretation of Justinian's costly construction projects, Malalas traced imperial building projects commenced at Constantinople and throughout the eastern Mediterranean from the time of Constantine to Justinian.[185] In the area of religion, where Justinian also faced criticism, Malalas attempted to demonstrate how 'correct' Christianity was indelibly intermeshed with the integrity of the state. According to his narrative, only good Christian emperors had divine support in defending the state.[186] As a matter of demonstrating their piety, Justinian's predecessors regularly suppressed the Hellenes, making Justinian's confrontation with non-Christians a

---

[182] John Malalas, *Chronographia* 13.2; cf. Eusebius, *Vita Constantini* 4.61–64.

[183] John Malalas, *Chronographia* 13.1–14, on Constantine; 13.17 on Constantius; 13.18–23, on Julian; on the paired portrayals of Constantine and Julian, Scott, 'Image of Constantine', 59–62.

[184] Only with the final book treating Justinian does Malalas reckon the total number of years since Adam, *Chronographia* 18.8.

[185] John Malalas, *Chronographia*, 13.3, 13.7–8, 13.29, 13.37, 14.11, 14.12–13, 14.29, 16.8, 18.5, 18.11, 18.12, 18.17, 18.94.

[186] John Malalas, *Chronographia* 13.17 and 13.20–25, Constantius the Arian and Julian the Hellene respectively suffered defeat at the hands of the Persians; 13.34–35, Valens suffered defeat not at the hands of the Goths, but en route to inspect an arms factory.

matter of tradition.[187] Another sign of divine favour for such emperors was their ability to resist the Persian Empire. In fact, when read against the progression of Malalas' narrative, any ill repute that Justinian acquired for the Eternal Peace becomes erased by a long succession of emperors who (like Justinian) either compelled, or were entreated by, the Persians to arrange peace.[188] However costly the peace, Malalas ensured his audience that Christian Roman emperors always played the assertive role.

The contrastingly muted role of Goths in Malalas' imperial history suggests that the resolution of the Gothic War had also become a polemical issue in Constantinople which required careful handling. Malalas' adulteration of events involving the Goths may have attempted to counter the emergence of ideas in the capital concerning Gothic parity with the Roman state (as is clearly visible in the *Getica*). Thus, according to the *Chronographia*: Valens was not killed in battle with the Goths at Adrianople; it was Honorius who brought Alaric to Gaul to punish senators at Rome for conspiring against him; Galla Placidia did not marry Alaric's successor Athaulf, rather she remained a virgin until her marriage to the patrician Constantius; and Justinian's protracted, eighteen-year conquest of Italy required only a short, tersely narrated year.[189] The manner in which Malalas related the end of the Gothic War is particularly interesting. Contrary to the explicit statement of Procopius that Totila's body was never recovered at Busta Gallorum, Malalas recorded that the Gothic king's bloodstained garment had been publicly displayed in Constantinople.[190] Provided that a bloody garment (whether Totila's or not) was actually displayed at the capital, Procopius' heroicizing treatment of Totila in *Wars* and the conflicting versions offered by Procopius for his death had probably complicated what should have been a clear political message. Malalas' account attempted to communicate the political importance of that message in far simpler terms. Malalas' willingness to adulterate the past, especially in relation to the Goths, demonstrates how sensitive a subject Gothic Italy had become in political conversations at higher levels of the capital.

Malalas also used silence and misdirection to negotiate the damage done to Justinian's reputation by his putative involvement with the circus factions. According to Malalas, a long line of emperors made prominent public use of the Hippodrome (particularly the *kathisma*) and even

---

[187] John Malalas, *Chronographia* 13.2, 13.13, 13.27, 13.37, 13.48, 14.38, 17.9, 18.42 and 18.136.
[188] John Malalas, *Chronographia* 13.3, 13.27, 13.29, 14.23, 16.9, 17.9–10, 18.44 and 18.68.
[189] John Malalas, *Chronographia* 13.35, 13.49, 13.49, 18.88.
[190] Procopius, *Wars* 8.32.22–35; John Malalas, *Chronographia* 18.116; this version is repeated in the ninth-century chronicle of Theophanes the Confessor, *Chronica* 6044.

supported favourite racing factions. Interestingly, Justinian's reputed preference for the Blues is not mentioned, indicating that the association
between Justinian and the factions did indeed have some leverage in
the contemporary invective directed against the emperor.[191] The Nika
Revolt, where Justinian was most notoriously associated with the Hippodrome, received full treatment in the *Chronographia*. Malalas, however,
noted that the event had been prompted by the 'evil counsels' of 'aveng-
ing demons'.[192] An additional detail not present in earlier commentators
is that a substantial portion of the populace supported Justinian in opposition to the attempted elevation of Hypatius.[193] That the narrative of
such a late text would concern itself with ameliorating the emperor's
role in the Nika Revolt indicates that the event was widely regarded
as the pivotal moment that revealed the failings of and discontent with
Justinian's reign.

ECHOES OF CONTROVERSY

Although the production of this polemic centred on Constantinople,
responses to Justinian's policies are detectable in literature as far away
as the Persian frontier. The Syriac *Julian Romance* (completed *c.* 532)
superimposed upon the fourth-century emperor Julian contemporary
criticism of the fresh outbreak of war with Persia, interference with the
established legal tradition and new interventions in Christian doctrinal
disputes all attributable to Justinian.[194] Well into the late sixth century and
beyond, authors at or influenced by Constantinople would be exposed to
the polemical radiation of this earlier sixth-century discourse, even when
a particular assessment of Justinian's reign had ceased to have immediate
significance. It is quite probable that Agathias' decision to follow the
history recorded by Procopius was motivated by a sense of nostalgia
for bureaucracy's contest with the emperor. Born around 532 and the
son of a lawyer, Agathias received the traditional education preliminary
to state service (rhetoric and philosophy in Alexandria) and he studied
law in Constantinople.[195] Although his early social life was shaped by
close proximity to prominent members of Justinian's court, Agathias did

---

[191] John Malalas, *Chronographia* 13.7, on Constantine and the Hippodrome; 13.31, on Valentinian
and the Hippodrome; 14.2, Theodosius II favoured the Greens; 14.34, Marcian and the Blues;
15.5, Zeno; 16.2, 16.4 and 16.19, Anastasius; cf. Procopius' report of Justinian's involvement
with the factions, *Anecdota* 7.1–42.
[192] John Malalas, *Chronographia* 18.71.474.   [193] John Malalas, *Chronographia* 18.71.475–476.
[194] Wood, *Christian Political Thought*, 157–61.
[195] Cameron, *Agathias*; Frendo, *Agathias*; Whitby, 'Historical writing', 25–37; Treadgold, *Historians*,
279–90.

not begin writing his history until well into the reign of Justin II and he deliberately selected Procopius as his inspiration.[196] While Agathias could reflect on the inequities of Justinian's reign, in his purpose for writing he did not have the same immediacy as did earlier authors associated with the civil administration.[197] Another author, Theophanes of Byzantium, wrote a history that continued from Book 8 of Procopius' *Wars*, and he may have occupied a position in the civil service similar to John Lydus, although nothing more is known about the work.[198] As late as the reign of Justin II, a Hellene (Hesychius of Miletus) could still be found composing a *Chronica Historica* that demonstrated both a polite lack of interest in Christianity and a debt to the circulation of Procopius' *Anecdota*.[199] For an author such Evagrius, writing even later (between 588 and 594), only a vague impression of Justinianic tyranny persisted. The polemical construction of Justinian's reputation certainly resonated in Evagrius' account, although by this time the potency of the invective had become filtered and diluted by Evagrius' interest in the controversial nature of Justinian's involvement with the church.[200] Even further removed from the original discourse, a Coptic ecclesiastical historian writing as late as the 690s in Islamic Egypt still recalled the events of 532 in Constantinople through the words of Procopius.[201]

The voluble presence of this extended discourse is important in several respects. The polemical response to attempts by Justinian's court to fashion a language of imperial legitimacy suitable to the needs of his reign broadcast in no uncertain terms that the discontented who found themselves disenfranchised by the conditions of the newly fashioned imperial language could resist. Despite repeated pogroms of those holding public office in Constantinople, the assault on an intellectual tradition at Athens, the violent suppression of a revolt and the threat of further censure, voices could contest and even temper imperial will. Although one might identify different social and political contexts and aims for Zosimus, Procopius, John Lydus and Jordanes, the tangible recurrence of specific themes in their works attests to a political culture that was not entirely submissive to the idea of the emperor as the embodiment of the state. These voices of criticism were quite well equipped to imagine

---

[196] Agathias, *Historiarum libri quinque, praefatio* 16–22.
[197] Cameron, *Agathias*, 31–55.
[198] The *Chronica* of Theophanes are known through the literary summary of Phocas; Treadgold, *Historians*, 290–3.
[199] On Hesychius, Kaldellis, 'Works and days', 381–403; Treadgold, *Historians*, 270–8.
[200] Evagrius, *Historia Ecclesiastica* 4.30, 4.32, 5.1; on Evagrius, Whitby, *Evagrius*; Treadgold, *Historians*, 299–308.
[201] John of Nikiu, *Chronicle* 92.19–21.

their own political agency. The fact that so many other authors – Marcellinus Comes, Agapetus, Junillus and John Malalas – found it necessary to respond to precisely the same themes as their polemical interlocutors reveals just how much political agency remained beyond the emperor's immediate control. It also demonstrated how audible the protest was to extended audiences. To any politically sensitive observer, Justinian's will was not uncontested, nor was his reign entirely secure. For someone like Cassiodorus, the obvious political drama at Constantinople would have presented multiple opportunities and channels by which to pursue his own agenda, particularly one in support of his political dependents. And because political activity in Constantinople was often acted out through Latin literature, it should come as no surprise that Cassiodorus would wade into these troubled waters with his own contribution.[202]

---

[202] On Constantinople as a centre for the production of Latin literature, Cavallo, 'Circolazione libraria', 219–20; Garzya, 'Cassiodoro', 119–30; Rapp, 'Hagiography', 1230–75; Cameron, 'Old and new Rome', 17–29; Millar, 'Greek and Latin', 92–103.

Chapter 5

THE ANICII BETWEEN ROME, RAVENNA
AND CONSTANTINOPLE

The political culture of Constantinople provided its literary elite with fertile material for the production of a dynamic polemical discourse. As has been seen, the discourse is most visible in certain thematic strands that recur in sources both hostile and favourable to the rule of Justinian: the political aspect of public spectacles and public building, the legitimacy of wars and the right of the emperor to challenge traditional modes of conduct exercised by the bureaucracy. Even with the threat of imperial censure curbing the lengths to which critics might openly voice their opinion, a steady stream of complaint percolated to the surface of contemporary literature, polarizing the channels of political patronage. But polarizing political channels also presented new opportunities. Protesting in literature the exercise of the emperor's prerogative was an attempt to build consensus and solidarity around a vision of Roman governance in which social and political structures favourable to the traditional elite constrained the emperor. For the audience of this discourse, the act of protest in literature presumed that regime change was viable. It was not a given in the 540s that Justinian's reign would last. As the following chapters will illustrate, the potential for this discourse to represent regime change in the near future impressed Cassiodorus enough for the themes embedded in the polemic of Constantinople to permeate his presentation of the administrative culture of Ostrogothic society in the *Variae*. In essence, Cassiodorus oriented the *Variae* as an appeal to the political sensitivities of the traditionalist elite of Constantinople who stood poised to intervene in the restructuring of postwar Italy. The obvious contrast between the sophistication of Constantinople's tradition-bound political culture and the relatively innovative adaptations of the Ostrogothic state required that Cassiodorus attempt to correct the image of Italian administrative service. More importantly, access to political redress through the emperor was problematic for Cassiodorus, requiring that he attempt to encourage the good faith of the eastern bureaucratic elite as an alternative. The robustness of the political discourse at Constantinople had all but ensured a viable alternative for Cassiodorus.

The present chapter delineates the particular circumstance that determined the eastern bureaucratic elite, and not Justinian's court, as the channel through which Cassiodorus sought to further the interests of the western palatine elite (both those members in exile at Constantinople and those still in Italy awaiting the outcome of the war). That circumstance was the presence at Constantinople of a large number of North African and Italian émigrés who played a visible role in the pageantry of Justinian's reign. It is true that, with a few notable exceptions, eastern sources tend not to expose in great detail the activities of émigrés in residence at Constantinople. Most sources, however, do indicate that the eastern capital housed a large number of elites who had fled there in order to await the outcome of the Vandalic and Gothic wars. Indeed, a pattern for accommodating political refugees at the eastern capital had been established even before Justinian's reign. It is not always easy to see in what manner Justinian accommodated these new arrivals and the sources indicate that the presence of potentially influential actors (especially from 'old Rome') had a mixed reception among those involved in the political life at 'new Rome'. For example, Procopius' portrayal of Liberius as an interloper betrays an attitude that anticipated the presence of officials from the former Amal regime as a disruptive element in the dynamic of court politics.[1] The tenth-century *De ceremoniis*, which derived at least some of its substance from the practices of the fifth and sixth centuries, prescribed that representatives visiting from the west should be accorded privileges of rank equivalent to their eastern counterparts and in many cases it is apparent that Justinian's court did just this.[2] This particular injunction of the *De ceremoniis* concerning the former western empire may have been intended to blunt the hostile reaction of eastern court officials.

Indeed, Justinian's diplomatic protocol seems to have included vaunting the reputation of nearly anyone who bowed to his vision of an imperial society, including captive 'barbarians'. A number of the Gothic elite received the coveted status of patrician after capitulating to Belisarius and then submitting to Justinian in Constantinople, where the award became a part of the imperial court's performance of power.[3] It is apparent from fifth-century sources that eastern officials regarded representatives from the western court as agents of a foreign state, not as interchangeable

---

[1] Procopius, *Anecdota* 27.17–19 and 29.1–11.
[2] Gillett, *Envoys*, 224; more generally, Cameron, 'Court ritual', 106–32.
[3] Procopius, *Wars* 5.8.3; Jordanes, *Getica* 313.

counterparts.[4] For someone concerned about the orderly progression of public servants through the ranks of the state bureaucracy (such as John Lydus), the appointment of Italian 'free agents' to office from outside the requisite network would not have received a warm reception.[5] This in itself was a powerful incentive for Cassiodorus to model his portrayal of administrative culture in Italy after that of Constantinople. The impression that the western bureaucratic elite shared the same cultural mores as their eastern counterparts was an assurance that westerners would not expect to circumvent normal political advancement through access to the emperor.

Whether they had arrived as refugees fleeing 'barbarians' or as captives of eastern imperial conquest, the western elite in exile at the eastern capital would have received a range of reactions from different audiences and their social and political opportunities at the eastern capital would have been correspondingly differentiated. Prior to Cassiodorus' arrival in Constantinople, the eastern capital had become the home to North African elites fleeing the new regime of the Vandal king Thrasamund between 508 and 523. These North African exiles played a definite role in urging Justinian to topple the later regime of Gelimer in 533.[6] Junillus and Corippus represent, respectively, North African émigrés who had risen to prominent stations in Constantinople before the eastern imperial conquest of North Africa and after its administrative reorganization.

Elites from Rome and Italy had also preceded Cassiodorus at the eastern capital, some having arrived a generation earlier at the beginning of Theoderic's reign and others fleeing Gothic reprisals under Witigis and then Totila.[7] In particular, the exile of a large number of the senatorial aristocracy to Constantinople during the Gothic War has been taken as a potent ingredient in modern accounts of the political culture of the eastern capital. Although this population is not quantifiable, they certainly compensated with rank what they may have lacked in numbers.[8] As mentioned earlier, the witness of contemporary eastern sources tends to avoid specific names but generally points toward individuals in high position. Those émigrés whom Procopius did name as residing in

---

[4] Potter, 'Unity of Empire', 13–32.   [5] John Lydus, *De magistratibus* 3.28.4.

[6] On North Africans in Constantinople, Merrills and Miles, *Vandals*, 196–233; note also Procopius, *Wars* 4.5.8; Zachariah of Mytilene, *Historia Ecclesiastica* 9.17; *Collectio Avellana* 131, 230 and 231.

[7] Priscian, *In laudem Anastasii Imperatoris* 239–45: exiles from Italy had already arrived in Constantinople before the reigns of Justin and Justinian.

[8] For discussion of elite Italian émigrés in Constantinople, Cappuyns, 'Cassiodore', 1357; Brown, *Byzantine Italy*, 28–9; Croke, *Marcellinus*, 86–8; Maas, 'Roman questions', 11; Sotinel, 'Three Chapters', 87–90; Troncarelli, 'Boezio', 211–31; Cameron, 'Old and new Rome', 23–4.

Constantinople had often had previous public appointments in Italy.[9] Even the anonymous visitor from 'old Rome' mentioned by John Lydus seems to have held a senior magistracy and received a corresponding share of Justinian's attention.[10] That Justinian would ask a lower-ranking official such as Lydus to recite an encomium in the presence of such a visitor says much about how the emperor used exiled Italians to his advantage, possibly as a check against the presumptions of his own officials. The presence of members of the western senatorial elite of Rome was a visible reminder to the eastern bureaucratic elite that theirs were traditions of a newer mint in comparison to families that claimed to trace their public status to that of forebears who had governed the Roman Republic.[11] Their presence also opened channels of communication with the west by which Justinian attempted to advance his agenda for doctrinal unity.[12]

It would be mistaken, however, to assume that Justinian received all arrivals from Italy with equal favour. The senatorial elite from the city of Rome presented Justinian with different propagandistic opportunities than did those who had previously served as the palatine bureaucracy of the Amal court. Like the household of Gelimer, which was paraded in Constantinople in 534, the captive Ostrogothic court arriving in 540 included a large number of officers and functionaries of state service (those who had remained at Ravenna in advance of Belisarius' siege). It is unlikely that, in the course of negotiating a new role in postwar Italy with Justinian, the displaced senatorial elite from Rome would have reserved its hostility only for the Goths in Witigis' entourage. Even prior to the Gothic War, the distinction between palatine service at Ravenna and senatorial status at Rome had been a source of friction between two potentially different categories of Italian elites.

THE WESTERN SENATORIAL AND PALATINE DIVIDE IN CONSTANTINOPLE

Probably the most intractable difficulty for Cassiodorus in Constantinople was the social divide between the senatorial elite of Rome and the 'municipal' elites of the Italian peninsula that the Amal court had actively recruited as members of a palatine bureaucracy. This division is the political context least taken into account in modern considerations

---

[9] *PLRE II*, 281–2, on Cethegus; 677–81, on Liberius; *PLRE IIIA*, 174–5, on Basilius; 391, on Decius.
[10] John Lydus, *De magistratibus* 3.28.4.   [11] Brennan, 'Gentilician strategy', 335–9.
[12] Pietri and Pietri, *Prosopographie*, 1710–14; Sotinel, 'Emperors and popes', 277–84.

of Cassiodorus' political activities in Constantinople.[13] Studies have suggested that the elite social and cultural environment of sixth-century Italy was far more complex than a simple Roman and 'barbarian' dichotomy. Where senatorial families certainly dominated Rome and Campania, another social group composed of wealthy, landowning families of Italian municipalities had different opportunities in palatine service.[14] Cassiodorus belonged to a broad social stratum of families whose distinction depended on proximity to the state administrative apparatus and on the patronage of the Amal family for access to that apparatus.[15] The control that these families had over ample portions of the productive landscape of Italy ensured that the Amal court had an interest in apportioning political participation to them. The picturesque tableaux that Cassiodorus provided in the *Variae* of his native southern Italy remind the reader that what municipal Italian elites may have lacked in an ancestral political relationship with the city of Rome they more than made up for as proprietors of the economic hinterlands that allowed Rome and Ravenna to maintain their political importance.[16] Cassiodorus noted that he himself had defended the state (the Amal regime) in a time of military emergency with his personal patrimonial resources.[17] The Amal rulers of Italy learned very quickly that they could limit their dependence on the one class that had a more extended tradition for legitimate rule in Italy by increasing the loyalty of another class already estranged from the senatorial elite of Rome. The nature of estrangement between senatorial and palatine aristocracies was social, political and economic. At the social level, the still significant size of the urban population of Rome required that the senatorial order continually justify its station. Although the aristocracy at Rome was historically fluid in its social composition, elevated status required the pretension of pedigree.[18] Those pretensions were typically maintained through an ideology of continuity that advertised the mastery of the 'great families' over the city. That mastery was enacted in public building, control of the church, patronage of public spectacle and, most importantly, control of the apparatus by which key annonarial

[13] For example, Croke, '*Getica*', 132–4.
[14] Ruggini, 'Nobilita', 81–95; Demougeot, 'Boèce', 100; Matthews, 'Boethius', 26–31; Martino, '*Gothorum laus*', 39; Ruggini, 'Societa in Cassiodoro', 247–55; Barnish, 'Transformation', 133–50; Everett, *Literacy*, 29; Hen, *Roman Barbarians*, 40–53; Deliyannis, *Ravenna*, esp. 3 and 116.
[15] Pietri, 'Ravenne', 643–73.
[16] Cassiodorus, *Variae* 8.31, 8.33, 11.39, 12.12, 12.15.
[17] Cassiodorus, *Variae* 9.25.9, 'Nam deputatos Gothos propriis pavit expensis, ut nec provinciales percelleret nec fiscum nostrum expensarum oneribus ingravaret'; cf. Barnish, *Cassiodorus*, 127–30.
[18] Brennan, 'Gentilician strategy'.

commodities were acquired and distributed to the urban populace.[19] The administrative designation of provinces within Italy as providers of the *annona* for Rome (and, by extension, of the senatorial elite who administered the *annona* at Rome) would have imposed a social hierarchy on municipal elites. Enrolment in palatine service was a possible route to alleviate tributary status.[20] It is not without significance that the first visit, and one of the only visits, that Theoderic ever made to Rome was attended by a distribution of annonarial provisions to the urban populace – a pointed reminder that a political order existed close at hand that could out bid the senatorial elite.[21] The contraction of territories directly governed by the western empire during the fifth century had entailed the loss of far-flung senatorial properties in North Africa, Gaul and Spain. This in turn meant that by the sixth century the aristocracy of Rome had redrawn the social and cultural map of what defined centre and periphery.[22] The involvement of the municipal Italian aristocracy in provisioning increasingly militarized (and, from the cultural perspective of the senatorial elite, 'barbarian') zones of northern Italy from the mid-fourth to the late-fifth centuries made such distinctions easier to make.[23] To a certain extent, such distinctions had always been made by the aristocracy of Rome. Prosopographical studies of the *apparitores* of the early empire demonstrate how low-born professionals engaged in administrative vocations could constitute themselves as an *ordo* in reaction to the animosity of higher social and political orders.[24] The history of Ravenna as an imperial residence attests the need for a political focal point that was, as Deborah Deliyannis has described it, 'disembedded' from the senatorial establishment. This detachment had long-term effects on how the aristocracy of Rome interacted with other Italian elites intimate with the palatine halls of Ravenna.[25]

The record of official appointments found in the *Variae* attests to degrees of division in the political opportunities enjoyed by these two

---

[19] On the relationship of the senatorial order with Rome, Salzman, *Christian Aristocracy*, 19–68, for the fourth century; Pietri, 'Sénat', 123–39, for the fifth and sixth centuries.

[20] Giardina, 'Due Italie', 1–30.

[21] Cassiodorus, *Chronica* 500; *Excerpta Valesiana* 67.

[22] Wes, *Kaisertums*; Matthews, *Western Aristocracies*, 12–28 and 352–76; Pietri, 'Aristocratie', 417–67; Lendon, *Honour*, 222–32; Brown, 'Elites', 324–45.

[23] On the creation of northern Italy as a militarized zone that was distinct socially and economically from central Italy, see especially Ruggini, *Economia*; MacGeorge, *Warlords*.

[24] Purcell, '*Apparitores*', 125–73; Purcell, '*Ordo scribarum*', 633–74; similarly on the animosity of the upper social and political orders toward the social status of bureaucratic functionaries, Nichols, 'Social status', 113–21.

[25] For the history of Ravenna from Diocletian to Valentinian III, Deliyannis, *Ravenna*, 41–105; for the description of Ravenna as 'disembedded', Deliyannis, *Ravenna*, 3.

aristocratic groups. Posts with true administrative competence tended to be awarded to a non-senatorial elite while members of the senatorial class at Rome, for the most part, received awards of a more titular nature.[26] The poet Priscian, who maintained close ties with the senatorial elite of Rome, echoed the dissatisfaction that the senatorial aristocracy had with this arrangement in his *In laudem Anastasii Imperatoris*:

generously supporting those sent by old Rome by favoring them in every conceivable way . . . You gladly promote them through the ranks of distinguished appointments so that they may not feel pain at the loss of their homeland. Therefore they owe you their prosperity and safety and they offer prayers for you night and day.[27]

Anastasius' court provided distinction for those nobles whom the Gothic court had restricted to titular status and thereby cultivated what had been an enduring relationship between the elite of Rome and the eastern imperial court. In many ways, this would have been a comfortable relationship for the senatorial elite, who had dominated the political landscape of Rome for centuries, both in periods when emperors resided in Rome and especially in the frequent periods of the fifth century when emperors resided elsewhere. That this relationship between the senatorial elite and the eastern imperial court had preceded Theoderic's arrival in Italy underscores the need of the Amals to detach themselves from dependence on the great families of Rome and to foster a level of social and political comfort with an alternative source of elite talent and loyalty that was specifically oriented toward the Amal regime. No doubt exacerbating the rift between the two elite groups was the perception that the senatorial elite had elevated aspirations and more cosmopolitan connections through the eastern court and that the municipal elites, by colluding with the Goths, had obstructed the senatorial order from the level of political participation that was their traditional right.

The outlines of this cultural division and its tensions come into focus, if only faintly, in the *Variae*. A substantial component of Ostrogothic public relations was a manner of addressing the Senate at Rome that articulated the deference that had been its due since time immemorial. Expressions of the honour and prestige of the Senate fill the *Variae* like broken bits of linguistic *spolia* pasted to a rhetorical edifice.[28] The Ostrogothic policy that permitted the mint of coins at Rome (despite the presence of mints

[26] Moorhead, 'Boethius' life', 17–18.
[27] Priscian, *In laudem Anastasii Imperatoris* 239–53, trans. Coyne, 60.
[28] For example, Cassiodorus, *Variae* 1.13.1, 1.23.1, 1.41.1, 1.43.1, 3.11.3, 3.12.1; cf. Gillett, 'Rome, Ravenna', 131–67, for an overview of the relationship between the court at Ravenna and the Senate at Rome.

at Ravenna and Milan) also speaks to a posture of deference visible in the iconography of coins. Unlike the coins produced at Milan and Ravenna, the senatorial types were entirely lacking in reference to the eastern empire and to Gothic royalty.[29] However, beneath the protestations of respect for the reverend body of the Curia flows a refrain of censure and distrust. It is clear from the *Variae* that the concern of the Amal regime for the goodwill of the Senate extended only as far as the obedience of its senators. Individual letters remind the Senate, in strident tones, of its role as a body of model citizens. These epistolary rebukes portray the need of the Amal rulers to assert authority over a distant and distrusted enclave of political elite.[30] This tacit mistrust was evident in the regular supervision of the Senate by an official appointed from the palatine ranks serving the Amals.[31] More obviously, letters of the *Variae* that patently deal with the confinement of senatorial sons to Rome (in essence, as political hostages) make it clear that the senatorial elite occupied a rather paradoxical position that was both publicly honoured and regarded with intense suspicion.[32]

The tensions that could develop between the Senate and the Amal court were more normally relieved through the periodic nomination of a member of the senatorial *ordo* to public office. The high offices attained by senators such as Liberius and Boethius were exceptional and more regularly the domain of men intimate with the culture of the Amal court, not the Senate at Rome. The *Variae* maintain a studied ambivalence with respect to offices conferred by virtue of noble birth.[33] This in itself may signal as the target audience of the *Variae* a bureaucratic elite for whom an auspicious pedigree was the exception rather than the norm. On the one hand, the *Variae* could acknowledge noble birth as a source of excellence – 'we more fittingly seek a colleague for nobility from the veins of nobles, one who abhors that worthlessness in his conduct which he avoids in his blood'.[34] On the other hand, however, good birth unaccompanied by tried merits also caused circumspection in awarding public honours – 'If nobility of birth alone decorated you . . . we would perhaps suspend these dignities about to be conferred with understandable delay, lest a great

---

[29] On the continuity of the mint at Rome, Grierson and Blackburn, *Medieval Coinage*, 31–2; Arslan, 'Monetazione', 17–59; Metlich, *Coinage*.

[30] For example, Cassiodorus, *Variae* 1.44.1, 2.24.1, 4.43.1, 10.13.1.

[31] Cassiodorus, *Variae* 3.11.2 and 4.16.2.   [32] Cassiodorus, *Variae* 1.39 and 4.6.

[33] On this aspect of the *Variae*, Vitiello, *Principe*, 117–18 and 313–15.

[34] Cassiodorus, *Variae* 1.41.1, 'quapropter unde melius nobilitati collegam quaerimus quam de vena nobilium, qui se promittat abhorrere moribus, quam refugit sanguine, vilitatem?'; similarly, 2.15.2 and 3.6.1.

tribute become debased at the same time that it would be poured forth.'[35] In cases of appointment where lineage was the chief recommendation, the post could be, as in the case of Liberius' son, titular and devoid of real authority.[36] An office such as *comes primi ordinis*, granted to Maximus by Theodahad in 535, allowed the conferment of a public distinction that did not entail delegating real authority. This habit of allocating only titular offices to members of the senatorial aristocracy may have complemented the strategy of conservative elements within the senatorial elite who resisted serving the government at Ravenna. It allowed the senatorial nobility to demonstrate their nominal allegiance to a political tradition without being implicated in the policies of the current government. The *formula* for such a post at least paints a picture of happy agreement – 'It indeed seems great to many men to be claimed for alternating public duties on account of their upright actions; but how much more fortunate is it to take a splendorous honour and not to have the difficulties of conflicts?'[37] Titular appointments allowed the senatorial elite to preserve the face of tradition upon which their status depended but clearly did not allocate the kind of authority that would allow them to operate beyond the confines of the immediate region of Rome.

Although the *Variae* acknowledge the place of such appointments in the political culture of the Amal court, the administration of the state depended on actual, not honorary, service. The court actively encouraged the services of men dissociated from the senatorial elite of Rome and promoted the loyalty of those who would accept the culture of the court as the dominant arbiter of social standing. Correspondingly, the preference for officials educated under the tutelage of the court is found throughout the *Variae*.[38] This overt preference had a tendency to

---

[35] Cassiodorus, *Variae* 3.5.1, 'Si te aut nobilitas sola decoraret aut meritorum tantum laude polleres, conferendas forsitan dignitates dilatione probabili libraremus, ne magna vilescerent, cum simul omnia funderentur'; similarly, 4.2.1.

[36] Cassiodorus, *Variae* 2.16, on Venantius' elevation; note the presence of titular offices among the formulae, *Variae* 6.10, 6.11, 6.12, 6.20.

[37] Cassiodorus, *Variae* 6.12.1, 'Magnum quidem multis et inter vices videtur esse geniatum publicae utilitati probes actionibus occupari; sed quanto felicius honorem splendidum sumere et cogitationum molestias non habere?'; similarly, *Variae* 6.10, 'Formula qua per codicillos vacantes proceres fiant.'

[38] Cassiodorus, *Variae* 3.16.1, 'exploravimus efficaciam tuam per diversos industriae gradus, sed uni parem meruisti gratiam, variis actionibus aequaliter approbatus'; 4.4.3, 'In ipso quippe adulescentiae flore palatia nostra meritis maturus intravit'; 5.3.3, 'evaluit, inquam, ac se honoribus palatinis iudicio nostro laudatus immiscuit'; 5.40.4–5, 'didicisti, ut credimus, iudicare nostris serviendo iudiciis; ita; quod efficacissimum discipulatus genus est, agendo potius instructus es quam legendo'; 8.10.3, 'qui mox inter parentes infantiam reliquit, statim rudes annos ad sacri cubiculi secreta portavit, agens non ut aetas, sed ut locus potius expetebat'; 8.16.1, 'Solent quidem venientes ad aulicas dignitates diutina exploratione trutinari, ne imperiale iudicium aliquid probare videatur ambiguum'; 8.19.2, 'Hinc est quod vobis aggregare cupimus quem

exacerbate chauvinism with both the senatorial and palatine elite, with results that inevitably reflected on the government itself.[39] The case in point, as will be discussed later, is Boethius' conflict with personalities that had been a regular feature of the Ostrogothic court during his tenure as *magister officiorum*. The *Variae* express concerns about undue alienation while at the same time displaying a clear preference for elites trained in palatine service.[40] It is important here to consider the distinction that Cassiodorus makes in his second preface to the *Variae* between the *occupati* and the *otiosi* as factional elements of the Amal court. The *occupati*, as readers sensitive to the public record present in the *Variae*, represent those members of palatine service who had risen in station through dedicated service to the state. The *otiosi*, by contrast, could easily represent members of the senatorial elite who enjoyed only temporary association with the Amal regime at particular moments of their public careers. Nor were such distinctions peculiar to the western elite. In a statement from *De magistratibus* that has striking similarity to the sentiment from Cassiodorus' second preface, John Lydus made a distinction between those enjoying leisured privilege and those who 'toiled away night and day' and were involved in 'countless worries', clearly meaning the bureaucratic elite.[41]

The senatorial aristocracy (with its claims to a familial history that was coeval with the imperial state) and the elite recruited from large landowning municipal families probably had much in common. Senators of Rome and palatine officials both based their right to elite status on the ownership of large estates. Members of both groups could and did participate, to varying degrees depending on the individual, in the elite literary culture that connected them to the extended tradition of *mos maiorum*. And when distinctions were not enforced, a titular consulship could carry as much political prestige as a praetorian prefecture. Patterns of patronage, group affiliation and kinship formation also tend to confirm that elites across Italy in the fifth and sixth centuries constituted a comfortably self-aware social stratum where the flexibility, rather than harshness, of social distinctions was probably more common.[42] It is also true that the senatorial elite did not consistently represent a unified front. Factionalism within the senatorial order is a well-documented phenomenon

repererimus ubicumque praecipuum. Nam licet apud vos seminarium sit senatus, tamen et de nostra indulgenia nascitur, qui vestris coetibus applicetur. Alumnus cunctae vobis pariunt aulicae dignitates'; similarly, 1.4.3, 1.12.1–3, 1.42.2, 3.12.2–3, 5.3.1, 5.4.2, 5.21.1, 5.28.1, 8.9.8, 8.21.6, 9.7.2, 9.24.3–8.

[39] For examples of similar concerns about conflict over privileged proximity to the ruler, Cassius Dio, *Historia Romana* 69.20.2–3, and *Historia Augusta, Vita Pertinacis* 6.10–11.

[40] Cassiodorus, *Variae* 6.12.3, 8.21.4, 9.24.10.

[41] John Lydus, *De magistratibus* 1.23.3; trans. Carney, *Bureaucracy*, 22.

[42] See, for example, Smith, *Europe after Rome*, 83–114; Cooper, *Household*, 152–60.

in the fifth and sixth centuries, much as surfaced during the Laurentian Schism from 498 to 506.[43] However, the contrast between senatorial and palatine elites was always a potential conflict that could emerge whenever social standing and prerogatives were challenged. This was certainly the case with the deaths of Boethius and Symmachus, which brought latent factionalism to the surface and polarized relations between the palatine bureaucracy and a family network of the senatorial elite (the Anicii) who maintained strong connections with the eastern imperial court.[44]

THE POLITICAL IMPORTANCE OF THE ANICII

As an extended family, the Anicii were the product of the lucrative imperial opportunities that had become available to prominent provincial families across the Mediterranean. The Anicii traced their origins to families from Antioch and North Africa for whom imperial service in the first century had opened the doors to increasingly advantageous marriage opportunities. Continued imperial service eventually brought them into close association with the city of Rome, where the *gens* celebrated its first consulship (C. Anicius Cerialis) in AD 65.[45] By the fifth century, the Anicii could boast numerous collateral branches which, as a whole, dominated the political scene of Rome. Particularly from the fourth century onwards, the Anicii enjoyed an illustrious record of consulships and other high offices. In 474, Anicius Olybrius briefly became emperor of the west.[46] Olybrius was connected to the western and eastern branches of the imperial Theodosian dynasty through his marriage to Placidia, the daughter of Valentinian III. In his own branch of the family, Boethius' grandfather held a praetorian prefecture under Valentinian III, and his father held a consulship, urban prefecture and praetorian prefecture under Odoacer. Boethius' marriage to Rusticiana sometime before the end of the fifth century joined the Anicii with yet another venerable Roman family, the Symmachi, who traced their relationship with the western capital to magistracies from the early fourth century. Prior to Theoderic's arrival in Italy, the Anicii had already heavily invested in the successful regime of Odoacer. Boethius' father had fared well under Odoacer's governance of Italy, enjoying what presumably amounted to the full public *cursus* of the late fifth century, including the last praetorian prefecture held prior to the arrival of the Ostrogoths. Similarly,

---

[43] *Liber Pontificalis* 53.
[44] On the Anicii and Boethius' more immediate family, Galonnier, *Boèce*, 32–55.
[45] *PLRE I*, 'Sex. Cocceius Anicius Faustus Paulinus', 680–81; cf. also the stemma of the Anicii for the third and fourth centuries, 1133.
[46] *PLRE I*, 796–8.

Boethius' future father-in-law, Symmachus, showed at least tacit support of Odoacer's government by holding an urban prefecture (possibly from 476 to 491) and the consulship in 485.[47] The favour that the family clearly enjoyed under Odoacer probably has to do with the role that it played in negotiating a modus vivendi between Odoacer, the senatorial elite of Rome and the eastern court.

The extent to which the Anicii continued to cultivate imperial associations after Theoderic's arrival probably contributed to their detachment from the new Amal government at Ravenna. The cult of Saint Severinus promoted by Eugippius at Castellum Lucullanum, where the deposed Romulus Augustus resided in retirement, enjoyed the patronage of the Anicii.[48] Eugippius dedicated his anthology of Augustine's writings to Proba, a relative of Boethius, strengthening the association between the Anicii and a saint's cult, located at the estate of a former emperor, which developed during the reign of Odoacer.[49] Eugippius dedicated the *Vita Severini* sometime between 509 and 511, almost thirty years after the death of Severinus and during the peak of Theoderic's reign.[50] The *Vita's* favourable portrayal of Odoacer as the humble servant of the holy man speaks to a certain nostalgia for the period prior to Amal rule.[51] The settlement of a property dispute at Castellum Lucullanum by Liberius probably indicates that the cult had the capacity to attract wide senatorial support.[52]

Associations between Anicii and imperial rule in Italy certainly provided an uneasy background for interactions between the family and the Amal court. The long-term connection between the Anicii and the eastern court, however, particularly when sustained in periods of strained relations between the Amals and the eastern emperors, was cause for an even more fragile relationship with the Amals at Ravenna. Indeed, the connections of the Anicii to Constantinople were tentacular. The eastern court poet Priscian dedicated three of his grammatical treatises to Q. Aurelius Memmius Symmachus, the father-in-law of Boethius.[53] Priscian also trained Theodorus, who later assisted Boethius with his translation of Aristotle's *Categories* and seems to have been a regular intermediary for the Anicii between Rome and Constantinople.[54] Although

---

[47] *PLRE II*, 232–3 and 1044–5.
[48] Ruggini, 'Nobilita', 93–5; Marcellinus Comes, *Chronicon* 476.2.
[49] Momigliano, 'Italian culture', 211.   [50] Bieler, *Consolatio*, 9.
[51] Eugippius, *Vita Severini* 7.1, 32.1–2, 44.4–5.
[52] Cassiodorus, *Variae* 3.35, perhaps dating between 507–11, discusses the property dispute.
[53] On the friendship between Symmachus and Priscian, Momigliano, 'Italian culture', 212; Kirkby, 'Scholar', 59–61; Nicks, 'Literary culture', 189–90; also Chauvot, *Panégyriques*; and Coyne, *Priscian*.
[54] *PLRE II*, 1098.

the Acacian Schism had held many noble families of Rome at a distance from Anastasius' court since 484, Priscian's familiarity with the Anicii seems to indicate the cultivation of affability in spite of the prevailing political current. This same Priscian later composed his panegyric to Anastasius between the years 511 and 515, when the eastern court's relations with Theoderic had reached the brink of open war. The relations of the Anicii with the eastern court were certainly not trivial in light of eastern imperial raids along the coast of Italy.[55] Theoderic's own engagement with the east was equally aggressive and, in addition to seizing Sirmium in 504, it seems very likely that he also supported Vitalian's revolt against Anastasius in 514, probably when Priscian delivered his panegyric at the eastern court.[56] Nonetheless, Amal rulers recognized the long-standing familiarity of the Anicii with the eastern court. The regular and selective honouring of key Roman families was a normal aspect of diplomatic relations with the eastern court and the Anicii could boast of thirteen consular appointments from 480 to 541. Not surprisingly, members of the Anicii also figured prominently in embassies sent to the eastern court.[57]

The Anicii probably also served as points of contact for eastern missions to Rome. The consul of 438 and praetorian prefect Anicius Acilius Glabrio presented the *Theodosian Code* to the Senate when first received from the east and presided over its confirmation by the western Senate in his own home.[58] Almost a century later, the Anicii still served as the point of contact in eastern communication with Rome. In 519, when Justin and Justinian sent John Maxentius and the so-called Scythian monks to Rome in order to repair the breach caused by the Acacian Schism, the Anicii offered them a warm reception, despite their potentially heretical stance.[59] Although the Amals actively attempted to cultivate the eastern connections of the Anicii, doing so also exposed the Anicii to the mistrust that characterized the uneasy settlement that the Amals had reached with the eastern imperial court.[60] This may have to do with the fact that the eastern branch of the family was entrenched in the political life of the

[55] On Byzantine raids along the Italian coast at this time, Cassiodorus, *Variae* 1.16.2; Marcellinus Comes, *Chronicon* 508.
[56] On possible Gothic involvement with Vitalian, Marcellinus Comes, *Chronicon* 514.3; on Theoderic's campaign in Pannonia and relations with Anastasius, Moorhead, *Theoderic*, 173–200.
[57] Cameron and Schauer, 'Basilius', 128–31.
[58] *Codex Theodosianus, Gesta Senatus Urbis Romae* 1.
[59] On the Anicii, Dionysius and the Scythian monks, Chadwick, *Boethius*, 186–90; also, Rapp, 'Hagiography', 1275–7.
[60] On the involvement of the Anicii in eastern imperial politics and its consequence for Boethius, Demougeot, 'Boèce', 97–108; Obertello, 'Morte', 59–70.

capital and probably regarded as sharing the sympathies of the emperor's court. In 519, an eastern Symmachus from Constantinople was delegated to the task of acting as an envoy to Italy.[61] His counterpart in Rome (Symmachus, consul of 485) owned property in Constantinople which was later destroyed during the Nika Revolt.[62] Furthermore, by 527 at the latest, Justinian's nephew Germanus had married a daughter of the Anicii.[63]

The influence of the eastern Anicii was clearly visible in Constantinople, where Anicia Juliana rebuilt the church of Saint Polyeuktos between 524 and 527 and had completed the construction of a church dedicated to Saint Euphemia by 528.[64] Anicia Juliana was the daughter of the late western emperor Anicius Olybrius and, according to Gregory of Tours, her patronage of Saint Polyeuktos was of particular interest to Justinian, who visited the church.[65] Letters exchanged between Anicia and Pope Hormisdas concerning matters of religion attest to the value of the Anicii to the emperor as conduits of communication with the west.[66] In a political climate where direct communication from an eastern emperor to the Pope of Rome could provoke suspicion of interventionist tendencies, maintaining the loyalty of cultivated and respected intermediaries was a real asset. It is also worth noting that the columns recovered from the archaeological site of Saint Polyeuktos which were originally inlaid with laminated glass jewels are only seen elsewhere as depicted in the later apse mosaic of Justinian at San Vitale in Ravenna. If the mosaic does portray Justinian and his court at Saint Polyeuktos, it was a pointed reminder to the community of Ravenna that Justinian and the Anicii were in the ascendant in postwar Italy.[67] This reminder was certainly visible in the completed mosaic before the conclusion of the Gothic War, in the 530s and 540s, when the overt triumphalism of the mosaic's iconography signalled the culmination of political and military affairs between Ravenna and Constantinople.[68] Several of the last letters attributed to Theodahad

---

[61] *Collectio Avellana* 221 and 229.   [62] *PLRE II*, 1212.

[63] This was Passara, Germanus' first wife before marrying the Amal heiress Matasuntha in 541; the eldest child of Germanus and Passara (Iustina) was born in 527; *PLRE II*, 505–7; Procopius, *Wars* 3.39.14.

[64] Harrison, *Temple*, 15–40; Brubaker, 'Helena', 56.

[65] Gregory of Tours, *Gloria martyrum* 102, discusses Justinian's visit to the church.

[66] *Collectio Avellana* 164, 179, 198.

[67] Harrison, *Temple*, 78–9, for images of the columns from Saint Polyeuktos now held at the Istanbul Archaeological Museum (catalogue numbers 3908 and 5078); Janes, *God and Gold*, 60, notes the stylistic connection between the columns of Saint Polyeuktos and the columns depicted in the mosaics of San Vitale; on the importance of Saint Polyeuktos as a locus of political communication between Anicia Juliana and Justin–Justinian, Canepa, *Two Eyes*, 211–16.

[68] Alchermes, 'Art', 346–8.

in the *Variae* make it clear that diplomatic relations between Ravenna and Constantinople involved Justinian's interest in a construction project at Ravenna.[69]

THE FALL OF BOETHIUS AND THE AMALS

The career of Boethius had every outward sign of the Amal court's approval. His appointment to the consulship in 510 marked him as a person of consequence in relations between the Amal court and the senatorial elite of Rome. Similarly, the appointment of his two sons (Boethius and Symmachus) to the consulship in 522 signified the Amal court's continued interest in the prominence of the Anicii.[70] Given that the twin consulships traditionally symbolized the parity of the two Roman states, their paired appointment also signalled the potential role of the Anicii in restoring relations between the Amal court and the eastern court under Justin. Beyond his public career, the *Variae* also portray Boethius as the literary prodigy of his generation and the letters of the collection addressed to him make explicit reference to his handling of the Greek intellectual tradition.[71] The consulships and the celebration of Boethius' intellectual habits could be enjoyed by the Anicii without complicating the image that the family enjoyed as the last of respectable Romans. In a sense, these overtures may have been preparation to restore relations with the Anicii which had probably suffered during Theoderic's extended conflict with Odoacer from 489 to 493. The public careers of both Boethius' father and father-in-law came to an abrupt end with the arrival of the Ostrogoths. When Boethius accepted the appointment as *magister officiorum* in 522, it was the first non-titular office conferred upon one of the Anicii in almost thirty years. His new position inevitably brought him into a tighter orbit within politics at Ravenna and the concomitant celebration of his sons' consulships may have represented the culmination of careful diplomacy between Rome and Ravenna.[72] Boethius celebrated the occasion by delivering a panegyric to Theoderic before the Senate.[73] That this was one of the few documented occasions on which Theoderic visited Rome indicates the importance of the moment for the Anicii,

---

[69] Cassiodorus, *Variae* 10.8 and 10.9.

[70] For a concise treatment of Boethius' career and works, Magee, 'Boethius', 788–812.

[71] Cassiodorus, *Variae* 1.10, 1.45, 2.40.

[72] Moorhead, 'Boethius' life', 17–18, that conferring the master of offices on Boethius represented a change of policy; Demougeot, 'Boèce', 99–101, similarly notes the break in public office-holding for the Anicii after Odoacer.

[73] *Ordo generis Cassiodororum* 10–11.

for the senatorial elite and for the Amals.[74] Nonetheless, the potential for friction between senatorial and palatine dignity and the latent Amal distrust of the pedigree and eastern connections of the Anicii proved to be insurmountable obstacles.

The exact circumstances of Boethius' downfall have received considerable scholarly treatment. It is entirely likely that Justinian's policies against eastern Arian Christians, which immediately preceded accusations against Boethius, played a significant role in provoking Theoderic's hostility toward a Roman senator with influential connections with the eastern court and with the church of Rome.[75] Indeed, Boethius' own involvement in supporting a doctrinal formula that would bring the Acacian Schism to a close and unite the churches of Constantinople and Rome may have been viewed as having a political dimension.[76] Additionally, the premature death of Theoderic's son-in-law, Eutheric, may have amplified tensions concerning the dynastic stability of the Amal regime. At the same time, rapprochement between the Roman aristocracy and the religious policies of the imperial court had the potential to be viewed as opportunistic from the perspective of Ravenna.[77] But it is apparent, particularly in Boethius' final testament (*De consolatione philosophiae*), that the latent rivalry and egotism that characterized differences between senatorial and palatine elites had become a factor in politics at Ravenna almost immediately after his appointment as *magister officiorum*.[78]

In 522, the patrician Albinus (of the noble Decii family) was accused of exchanging treasonable communication with the eastern court by Cyprianus, a court official (*referendarius*) at Ravenna who had risen to office through an earlier military career.[79] Boethius elected to provide legal defence for his fellow senator and soon after found himself accused of treason through association with Albinus. According to the *De consolatione*, Boethius championed the cause of senatorial liberty in his capacity as master of offices.[80] In the course of doing so, he probably aggravated the sensitivity of municipal elites at Theoderic's court, resulting in open condemnation from of a group of men with a vested interest in maintaining a status quo favourable to non-senatorial elites. Men

---

[74] *Excerpta Valesiana* 67 and 80 mention two occasions when Theoderic visited Rome in 500 and 519.

[75] Obertello, 'Morte', 59–70.

[76] Chadwick, *Boethius*, 185–90; Sotinel, 'Emperors and popes', 273–5; Moorhead, 'Boethius' life', 30–2; Amory, *Ostrogothic Italy*, 206–16.

[77] On the dynastic insecurity of the Amals as an aspect of Boethius' downfall, Demougeot, 'Boèce', 103–6; Vitiello, *Principe*, 181–3.

[78] Moorhead, 'Boethius' life', 18–22.   [79] *PLRE II*, 332–3.

[80] Boethius, *De consolatione philosophiae* 1.4.16–21.

such as Conigastus, Traguilla, Cyprianus, Opilio and Gaudentius (whom Boethius labelled collectively the 'palatine dogs') received their senatorial rank only by holding offices conferred by Amal patronage. Hence their loyalty to the Senate was provisional.[81] Boethius, on the other hand, was a member of the senatorial order through family tradition, currently isolated in Ravenna where political deference followed unaccustomed channels. For Boethius, defending a colleague who shared his social background against the presumed arrogance of palatine officials was a matter of public honour.[82] As a result of these rivalries for public honour, and mutual mistrust, Boethius was arrested late in 523, tried in Pavia and then imprisoned near Milan (*in agro Calventiano*). His later execution in 524 was followed soon after (in 525) by the arrest, trial and execution of his father-in-law, Symmachus, who, in his turn, had attempted to offer a defence for Boethius.[83] Strangely, the fate of Albinus was never recorded.

The deaths of Boethius and Symmachus were a public-relations blunder of gross proportions for the Amals.[84] Even emperors with fully acknowledged imperial legitimacy such as Hadrian and Marcus Aurelius had been keen to avoid the alienation of the governmental elite by executing prominent members of the senatorial order.[85] For a 'barbarian' king ruling from distant Ravenna with only nominal approval from the eastern emperor, such an event had the potential to expose open hostility and disrupt the careful equilibrium that facilitated the governance of Italy. A comparison between this case and earlier cases where Theoderic had dealt with the transgressions of members of the senatorial order is instructive. Letters 4.22 and 4.23 of the *Variae* detail how Theoderic arranged for a panel of five senators to judge several of their peers (the otherwise unknown Basilius and Praetextatus) who had been accused of practising magic. The first letter is addressed to the urban prefect, Argolicus, and directs him to conduct the trial with five colleagues of patrician status (Decius, Volusianus, Caelianus, Maximianus and Symmachus, the father-in-law of Boethius). It clearly concerned Theoderic to appoint

---

[81] For the background of Boethius' accusers, Moorhead, 'Boethius and Romans', 609–11.

[82] Boethius, *De consolatione philosophiae*, 1.4.34–75, 'palatinae canes'; 1.4.41–43, 'Provincialium fortunas tum privatis rapinis tum publicis vectigalibus pessumdari non aliter quam qui patiebantur indolui'; more generally, on circumstances of the trial, Demougeot, 'Boèce', 101–6; Chadwick, *Boethius*, 46–68; Gruber, *Kommentar*, 119–38; Vitiello, *Principe*, 181–3; Galonnier, *Boèce*, 55–95; Goltz, *Barbar*, 355–76 and 388–400.

[83] On the execution of Boethius, Procopius, *Wars* 1.5.32–39 and 5.1.27–35; *Excerpta Valesiana* 87; on the execution of Symmachus, *Excerpta Valesiana* 92.

[84] For the aftermath of Boethius' fall, Barnish, 'Maximian'.

[85] *Historia Augusta*, *Vita Hadriani* 7.1–12 and *Vita Marci Antonini* 25.1–12 and 26.10–13.

the *quinqueviri* in order to avoid recrimination in condemning senatorial defendants, 'so that the authority of our piety may more confidently recommend what should happen... we who know not how to differ from the laws and in whose every action restrained justice is observed'.[86] Cassiodorus did not record the outcome of this trial, although Gregory the Great later mentioned that Basilius (and presumably Praetextatus) was found guilty and burned to death in Rome.[87] That Theoderic's reputation was unscathed by the event has much to do with how he had managed the appearance of consensus with leading members of the senatorial community. By comparison, Boethius had been charged with a crime (*maiestas*) that also carried capital punishment and there is a strong indication that he may have also been charged with sorcery (*maleficium*) during the course of his trial.[88] In Boethius' case, however, sentence was passed without a proper trial.[89] The difference lay in the fact that Boethius was a member of the Anicii and for that reason (from the Amal perspective) his trial could not be allowed to galvanize senatorial opposition to Ravenna.

Theoderic died in 526, shortly after the execution of Symmachus. In the months to follow, Amalasuntha and the Amal court attempted to amend the disruption of political harmony by restoring properties to Boethius' family that had been seized as a result of his condemnation. The appointment of one of the Anicii (Flavius Anicius Olybrius) as western consul for 526 may indicate that Theoderic recognized the necessity of a conciliatory gesture even before his death.[90] Despite the overture, the executions continued to raise problems for the Ostrogothic regime and, as previously discussed, cast a shadow on Cassiodorus' advancement as master of offices and probably later as praetorian prefect. Although Boethius had not indicted Cassiodorus as one of the 'palatine dogs' responsible for instigating the case against him, his later preferment under the Amals agitated some form of factional opposition.[91]

Relations with the senatorial elite deteriorated even further under Theodahad, whom Amalasuntha appointed as her ruling colleague in 534 after the death of her son (Athalaric). Theodahad depended upon Amalasuntha not only for legitimacy, but also for the rehabilitation of a

---

[86] Cassiodorus, *Variae* 4.22.2–3, 'ut confidentius fiat quod pietatis nostrae mandat auctoritas. Sed nos, qui nescimus a legibus discrepare, quorum cordi est in omnibus moderatam tenere iustitiam'; cf. Barnish, *Cassiodorus*, 77–8.

[87] Gregory the Great, *Dialogues* 1.4.

[88] Matthews, 'Boethius', 36; Robinson, 'Dead Boethius', 2–5; Boethius, *De consolatione philosophiae* 1.4.135–139.

[89] *Excerpta Valesiana* 87. [90] *PLRE II*, 798. [91] Cassiodorus, *Variae* 10.28.1 and 11.1.18.

personal reputation that had been tarnished by accusations of disregard for law and personal property.[92] Perhaps because she was an influential check on his political ambitions, Theodahad soon arranged to have Amalasuntha murdered.[93] The act proved unpopular with the senatorial elite, presumably out of appreciation for Amalasuntha's tactful interventions as a ruler, and her death increased tension between Theodahad and Rome.[94] It is under Theodahad that the mint at Rome, which had previously only struck coins bearing traditional Roman iconography, began producing bronze *folles* bearing the image of a Gothic king – a clear departure from the Amal court's previous policy toward Rome.[95] The marriage at this time of an unknown woman of the royal Amal line to Maximus, a former consul of the Anicii, may have been intended to ameliorate senatorial discontent, although even this appears to have been fruitless.[96] Later resorting to more severe measures, Theodahad summoned members of senatorial families to Ravenna as hostages and afterwards billeted a Gothic garrison at Rome.[97] Anxiety over Theodahad's intentions eventually reached such a pitch that he issued an oath of good faith to the Senate and the people of Rome.[98]

Compounding matters, or perhaps as a result of Theodahad's failure to secure the confidence of the Roman elite, diplomatic relations between the Ostrogothic court and Justinian also foundered.[99] The eventual outbreak of hostilities between the eastern court and Ravenna naturally activated the opposition that the senatorial elite felt toward the Ostrogoths and which had lain dormant. Belisarius invaded Ostrogothic territory late in 535 and in the following year a Roman aristocracy welcomed him into Rome, as Procopius claims, with gratitude for the expulsion of the

---

[92] Concerning property disputes involving Theodahad, Cassiodorus, *Variae* 3.15, 4.39, 5.12; and Procopius, *Wars* 5.3.2–3 and 5.4.1–3; for an expression of Theodahad's dependence on Amalasuntha, *Variae* 10.4.2–5.

[93] For the full account, Procopius, *Wars* 5.2.1–4.31; for the details of Amalasuntha's death, 5.4.12–29; also, Fauvinet-Ranson, 'Amalasonthe', 267–308.

[94] Note Procopius, *Wars* 5.2.3–5, on Amalasuntha's equity in dealing with the Romans and her control over the less-restrained among Gothic nobility; 5.4.27–29, on the grief shown by Romans at her death; for discussion of Amalasuntha as the agent of reconciliation between the Senate and the Amal court, Fauvinet-Ranson, 'Amalasonthe', 267–308.

[95] Grierson and Blackburn, *Medieval Coinage*, 33.

[96] On Maximus of the Anicii, Vitiello, *Principe*, 218–22.

[97] On the marriage of Maximus to an Amal bride, Cassiodorus, *Variae* 10.11.3 and 10.12.3; senatorial hostages, 10.13.5; discontent over the presence of a Gothic garrison at Rome, 10.14; Millar, 'Rome, Constantinople', 65, notes evidence for Theodahad's strained relationship with the Senate in Liberatus' *Breviarium causae Nestorianorum et Eutychianorum* 21.

[98] Cassiodorus, *Variae* 10.16 and 10.17.

[99] Evident in the content of Cassiodorus, *Variae* 10.19–24; similarly, Procopius describes the 534–5 period as one of deteriorating diplomatic relations between the courts of Ravenna and Constantinople.

Gothic garrison. Importantly, Belisarius encountered significant opposition, not only from the Goths but also from non-senatorial Italians who had benefited from the Amal regime.[100] Theodahad was dethroned and assassinated by the Gothic soldiery who interpreted his lack of action against Belisarius as an indication that he had forfeited Italy to Justinian at a price.[101] Witigis was immediately after elevated in his stead. With Cassiodorus still acting as praetorian prefect, Witigis rashly ordered the execution of senatorial hostages in response to Belisarius' seizure of Rome. This no doubt furthered the damage to the reputation of the palatine ministry serving Cassiodorus.[102] His continued tenure in this office after the onset of war would have confronted him when Belisarius later dissolved the Amal court at Ravenna and transported its remnants to Constantinople in 540.[103] Accompanying Witigis to Constantinople was his wife, Matasuntha, whose nuptials at Ravenna in 536 had been celebrated in a panegyric by Cassiodorus, an indication of his commitment to the political status quo in the face of regime change in the Italian peninsula.[104]

Upon arrival in Constantinople, members of the Italian bureaucracy came under the scrutiny not only of Justinian, but also of other Italian émigrés opposed to the Amal regime. Constantinople had become a haven for Italian refugees since the beginning of the war, a trend set earlier by refugees from Vandalic North Africa which Justinian no doubt encouraged to the increase of his own prestige. Prominent among the dislocated elite were members of the senatorial class of Rome whom the Amals had recklessly alienated from Ostrogothic rule. Of particular concern to Cassiodorus were members and associates of the Anicii, who held high favour at the eastern capital. Control of Ravenna and Rome by eastern imperial officials after 540 would have opened new channels of communication between Italy and Constantinople and presented new opportunities for political detractors. Matasuntha's marriage in Constantinople to Germanus (the emperor's nephew and a relation of the Anicii) is a firm indication of the closure of political channels to Cassiodorus and the palatine ministry that had witnessed her earlier marriage to Witigis. Matasuntha had accompanied the Amal court to Constantinople in 540 and Witigis died shortly after in 542. The period between the death of Witigis and Matasuntha's remarriage (probably in 549 or 550) was a crucial period for the western palatine bureaucracy

---

[100] Consider Procopius' account of the extent to which Naples resisted Belisarius, *Wars* 5.8–10.
[101] Procopius, *Wars* 5.11.1–9.
[102] On the slaughter of senatorial hostages, Procopius, *Wars* 5.26.1.
[103] Procopius, *Wars* 7.1.1–2.　　[104] *PLRE IIIB*, 851; Procopius, *Wars* 5.11.27.

residing at Constantinople in which political futures were still undecided and the ascendancy of the Anicii had not been formally signalled.[105]

WESTERN ANICII IN CONSTANTINOPLE DURING THE GOTHIC WAR

The senatorial elite held centre stage among Italians at Constantinople during the Gothic War. Perhaps the best-documented senator to embrace exile at Justinian's court was Liberius. Although not a member of the Anicii, his case demonstrates how easily prominent members of the senatorial elite at Rome could be grafted onto the political culture of the eastern court. Unlike those Anicii who had supported Odoacer and then found themselves excluded from preferment by the new Ostrogothic regime, Liberius managed to flourish after the change of government.[106] Liberius first held public office under Odoacer, and then under Theoderic he acted as praetorian prefect of Italy from 493 to 500, later holding the praetorian prefecture of the newly conquered provinces of southern Gaul from 510 to 529. As praetorian prefect of Italy, Liberius received initial acclaim for his role in negotiating the property settlement of Goths in Italy, for which Theoderic granted a consulship to his son, Venantius, in 507. Despite what would seem an intimate level of collusion with the Amals, when Theodahad sent Liberius to Constantinople in 534 with a group of senators to excuse the king for Amalasuntha's murder, Liberius' report to Justinian was decidedly unfavourable to Theodahad's cause. Rather than return to Italy, he remained at the emperor's court as a prominent and trusted guest, surely an indication that the invasion of Italy was now a certainty. Soon after, Liberius received the prefecture of Alexandria for his change of loyalty.

Procopius' account of Liberius, ambivalent in the *Wars* and hostile in the *Anecdota*, makes it clear that the Roman patrician was both active and controversial at Justinian's court.[107] After acting as prefect of Alexandria from 538 to 542, Liberius returned to Constantinople, where he played a substantial role in planning postwar Italy. The *Constitutio Pragmatica* (554), which details the provisions of the eastern imperial administration of Italy, illustrates Liberius' intimacy in policy formation. The first article of the document designated Liberius and Maximus (the same Maximus of the Anicii married to an Amal bride with Theodahad's consent) recipients of

---

[105] On Matasuntha, *PLRE IIIB*, 851–2; on Witigis, *PLRE IIIB*, 1382–6.
[106] For Liberius' career, see O'Donnell, 'Liberius', 32–71.
[107] Procopius, *Wars* 7.36.6, 7.37.26–27, 7.39.6–8; *Anecdota* 27.17–19 and 29.1–10.

the properties of Theodahad after the conclusion of the war.[108] Maximus appears to have remained in Italy, where he was eventually killed in 552 as a result of the war. However, the appearance of his name on the *Constitutio* designated his heirs and Liberius recipients of the property and indicates that even though Maximus was detained in Italy, his representatives in Constantinople had an active part in drawing up the final settlement of the *Constitutio*.

Prominent members of the Anicii would also eventually find their way to Constantinople, where their presence became a factor in the politics of the Gothic War. Petronius Nicomachus Cethegus was among the western Anicii who eventually arrived at Constantinople under these circumstances. In Italy, the Amals honoured Cethegus with a consulship in 504, although he appears not to have had a more active public role under the Ostrogoths.[109] By 545, after Rome had fallen under eastern imperial control, Cethegus assumed the role of president of the Senate (*caput senatus*). Procopius relates that when Totila breached the Asinarian Gate at Rome in 546, a group of senators and patricians (including a certain Decius and Basilius) escaped the sack.[110] The *Liber Pontificalis* provides a slightly more comprehensive account, noting that the senators Cethegus, Albinus and Basilius fled to Constantinople, where they 'were presented before the emperor Justinian in their affliction and desolation'. The *Liber* continues, noting that 'the emperor consoled them and enriched them as befitted Roman consuls'.[111] Procopius too took note of the favour that Cethegus enjoyed with Justinian.[112] Although Cassiodorus nowhere mentions Cethegus in the *Variae*, he addressed the *Ordo generis* to Cethegus while in Constantinople and it is only in this text that Cethegus bears the attribution *magister officiorum*.[113] Because it is known that Peter the Patrician held the office of *magister officiorum* in the east from 539 to 565, it seems very probable that the emperor appointed Cethegus *magister officiorum* of the west at a time when he was interested in securing the support of Rome's most prominent senatorial families for the postwar restructuring of Italy. Sources also identify Cethegus in the company of senior eastern members of Justinian's court (Belisarius, Peter

---

[108] *Constitutio Pragmatica* 1, 'excepta videlicet donatione a Theodato in Maximum pro rebus habita Marciani, ex quibus dimidiam portionem Liberio viro gloriosissimo dedisse meminimus, reliqua dimidia Maximo viro magnifico relicta, quas apud utrumque firmiter manere censemus'; note *PLRE IIIB*, 748–9, that the Maximus in question was the same slain in 552 by men of Totila in Italy and that his name in the *Constitutio* probably refers to his heirs.

[109] On Cethegus, *PLRE II*, 281–2.   [110] Procopius, *Wars* 7.18–20.

[111] *Liber Pontificalis* 61.7; trans. Davis, *TTH*, 60; on the *Liber*, McKitterick, 'Roman history', 19–34.

[112] Procopius, *Wars* 7.35.10.

[113] *Ordo generis Cassiodororum* 2–3, 'ad Rufium Petronium Nicomachum ex consule ordinario patricium et magistrum officiorum'.

the Patrician, an ex-consul Justin and the quaestor Marcellinus), which suggests that Cethegus held office as western master of offices *praesentalis*; that is, as a member of the emperor's court in Constantinople.[114]

The senatorial exiles who accompanied Cethegus from Rome included other prominent members of the Anicii. Basilius is particularly conspicuous for appearing in the accounts of both Procopius and the *Liber Pontificalis*. His full name, Anicius Faustus Albinus Basilius, suggests that (like Boethius) the marriage of his parents had conjoined two powerful family lines, in this case the Anicii and Decii.[115] Unlike the Decii, who were often entrusted to higher offices by the Amals, Basilius followed the more regular public profile for Anicii under the Ostrogoths and had been content with a titular appointment as *comes domesticorum*. His fortunes changed, however, in Constantinople, where Justinian eventually bestowed upon him the consulship of 541, the last to be held in the east or west.

Procopius and the *Liber Pontificalis* also place Cethegus in the company of Decius and Albinus during the flight to Constantinople. Although not one of the Anicii, the Decius in question also seems to have maintained a profile under the Amals that was befitting a member of the Roman aristocracy – that is, honoured but lacking authority within the Amal regime. He celebrated a consulship at Rome in 529, presumably through Amalasuntha's arrangement as Athalaric could not have been aged more than thirteen at the time. In Constantinople, however, his public profile changed dramatically and he appears to have played some role in forming the eastern imperial administration of Italy at Ravenna after the Gothic War. It is distinctly possible that either this Decius or a son had assumed the title of *exarchus Italiae* by 584.[116] The Albinus mentioned by the *Liber Pontificalis* has proven more difficult to identify. Martindale suggested that the Albinus mentioned in the *Liber* is the same Anicius Faustus Albinus Basilius who became consul in 541, although claiming that the *Liber* mistook the senator to be two individuals is problematic.[117] It is quite possible that the Albinus in question was a relation of, or was the very same, Albinus who fell under suspicion of treason at Ravenna and whom Boethius defended.[118] The fate of Albinus was not disclosed, either by

---

[114] Vigilius, *Epistola Encyclica ad Universam Ecclesiam* 15, 'id est calendis Februarii, gloriosos judices suos ad nos destinare dignatus est, id est Belisarium et Cethegum exconsules atque patricios, nec non et Petrum exconsulem patricium atque magistrum, sed et Justinum exconsulem et curapalatii et Marcellinum quaestorem', dated 552.

[115] On Basilius, *PLRE IIIA*, 174–5.

[116] *PLRE IIIA*, 391, notes the possibility that Decius (cos. 529) was also the later *exarchus Italiae* of 584.

[117] *PLRE IIIA*, 38.   [118] Boethius, *De consolatione philosophiae* 1.4.51–53.

Boethius in his *De consolatione* or by the *Valesianus*, which clearly states that Albinus and Boethius were imprisoned together in the baptistery of a church.[119] Given the propensity of the *Valesianus* to sensationalize Theoderic as a tyrant, it hardly seems likely that Albinus' death would have escaped attention unless he eventually received a pardon. The fact that this Albinus was one of the Decii, and hence a member of one of the few senatorial families to which the Amals had entrusted offices of genuine consequence, may have provided him with some leverage in the final days after Boethius' death. This particular Albinus had himself served the Amals as praetorian prefect and received attention, like Boethius, in Cassiodorus' *Variae*.[120] Given the lack of mention concerning Albinus' death and his shared confinement with Boethius, it seems likely that Albinus was responsible for the subsequent publication of Boethius' *De consolatione*. Finally, the fact that the *Variae*, the *Valesianus* and the *Liber Pontificalis* refer to an Albinus as *patricius* should indicate that the Albinus of each text is, in fact, the same man. If this is the case, then the specific reference made in the sources about Albinus in the company of prominent Anicii suggests that the Anicii had embraced Albinus for his association with the memory of Boethius. Preserving Boethius' last testament for later dissemination may have provided Albinus with the leverage needed to secure the friendship of the Anicii.

MEMORIES OF BOETHIUS AND THEODERIC DURING THE GOTHIC WAR

It would, then, appear that the senatorial elite who received the most obvious signs of Justinian's favour were intimately attached to the memory of Boethius and Symmachus, either as Anicii or, in the case of Albinus, as an actual actor in the tragedy of Boethius. At an ideological level, the fate of Boethius shaped both the war in Italy and the political influence of exiles in Constantinople. In one of his more colourful stories pertaining to Totila's sack of Rome in 546, Procopius recounted that the deacon Pelagius begged the Gothic king to spare the citizens of the city.[121] The citizen most in danger was Rusticiana, the daughter of Symmachus and widow of Boethius, whom the Gothic soldiery threatened with gang rape because she had been responsible for the destruction of Theoderic's public statues as revenge for the deaths of her husband and father.[122] Rusticiana managed to avoid the wrath of the Gothic soldiers through the intervention of the deacon Pelagius. Nevertheless, it is instructive

[119] *Excerpta Valesiana* 87.   [120] *PLRE II*, 51–2; Cassiodorus, *Variae* 1.20, 1.33, 4.30, 4.41.
[121] Procopius, *Wars* 7.20.22–25.   [122] Procopius, *Wars* 7.20.27–31.

that more than twenty years after the fact, the death of Boethius was a factor in the unresolved memory of Theoderic and, by extension, a factor in the discourse that attempted to settle the validity of Ostrogothic rule in Italy. The instability of loyalties during the Gothic War meant that the interpretation of ideologically charged events had particular significance. Procopius' history is full of episodes in which Goths, Italians and eastern imperial representatives change allegiance during the course of the war. In such a fluid environment, signifying attachment to a specific memory carried even more weight. In another story, Procopius provides an indication of how Theoderic's reputation had become a touchstone for representing the success or failure of Amal rule. Procopius reported that the decline of the Amal kingdom had been foretold in the disrepair of a mosaic of Theoderic in Naples which deteriorated gradually over time, culminating in its total ruin when the Goths laid siege to Rome.[123] The idea of a golden age under Theoderic which rapidly lost its lustre under successive kings is implicit, although the negative interpretation of Theoderic's reputation was by no means dominant.[124] The satirical treatment of Boethius by the poet Maximian in the mid-sixth century suggests that the public memory of the philosopher, too, was contentious.[125] The fact that Gregory the Great later recorded the fate of Symmachus but failed to mention Boethius may be an indication of how polemical Boethius' memory had become.[126]

The contestation of Amal successes had a clear pathway to Constantinople through the Anicii, whose own involvement in shaping reputations was based on self-interested concern for the restoration of a non-'barbarian' government in Italy. It seems that the deaths of Boethius, Symmachus and Pope John formed the ideological core of Justinian's justification for war very early in the Gothic War. Procopius reported that an attempt to negotiate Theodahad's submission to Justinian's authority after the defection of Liberius had included the stipulations that the Gothic king should 'have no authority to kill any priest or senator, or to confiscate his property for the public treasury except by the decision of the emperor'.[127] These were terms that answered to the downfall of Boethius, Symmachus and John.

---

[123] Procopius, *Wars* 5.24.22–27.
[124] Goltz, *Barbar*, surveys the sources discussing Theoderic from the late fifth century to the ninth and convincingly demonstrates the polemic of Theoderic's reputation.
[125] Shanzer, 'Ennodius, Boethius', 183–95; Barnish, 'Maximian', 16–32.
[126] Gregory the Great, *Dialogues* 4.31.4.
[127] Procopius, *Wars* 5.6.2–3, trans. Dewing, *LCL*, 49–51; on Liberius' diplomatic mission to Justinian, *Wars* 5.4.15–24.

The deacon Pelagius also played a role in facilitating this ideological justification for war. Pelagius had been a regular interlocutor in church affairs at Justinian's court and Procopius noted that he was a personal favourite of Justinian.[128] At Pelagius' request Totila restrained his soldiers from assaulting Rusticiana, but he then required Pelagius and a certain Theodorus to encourage Justinian to consider the Gothic king's terms for resolving the war.[129] This Theodorus had particular symbolic capital. He was probably the Theodorus who was son of the Basilius already in Constantinople and, perhaps more importantly, he had been arrested with Pope John in 525 as part of the cascade of arrests (Albinus, Boethius, Symmachus) following from Theoderic's distrust of senatorial intentions.[130] His value as a member of the Anicii family and as an intermediary with an imperial court that was already sensitized to the polemical value of Boethius' death was obvious. Presumably Rusticiana accompanied Pelagius and Theodorus to Constantinople, where her two sons were already in residence. By sending Rusticiana to Constantinople, Totila's overture to Justinian underscores how the memory of Boethius mediated negotiations for the exercise of power between Rome, Ravenna and Constantinople – three arenas with distinct political interests. Indeed, since the beginning of the Gothic War and the rupture between the senatorial elite and the Ostrogoths, association with the names of Boethius and Symmachus had supplied social and political cohesion for the Anicii as they prepared to retrench in a Mediterranean world governed by the eastern Roman empire. The extended future fortunes of the family suggest as much. Of Rusticiana's sons, Boethius (consul of 522) certainly fared well on eastern shores and eventually received from Justinian the praetorian prefecture of Africa (c. 556–61).[131] By the early seventh century, prominent descendants of Boethius and Rusticiana are still attested at Constantinople with collateral family members in Rome, Ravenna and Egypt.[132]

The death of Boethius and the memory of that event was a potent piece of the ideology that the Anicii assembled as an appeal to Justinian's

---

[128] Procopius, *Wars* 7.16.5; see also Pietri and Pietri, *Prosopographie*, 1710–14, Pelagius.

[129] Procopius, *Wars* 7.21.18.

[130] *PLRE II*, 1097–8, Theodorus the son of Basilius; *PLRE IIIB*, 1249, adviser to the deacon Pelagius; Boethius had dedicated the second, third and fifth tractates of his *Opuscula Sacra* to Pope John (then a deacon) and this may in part explain Theoderic's harsh treatment of the bishop of Rome.

[131] *PLRE II*, 961, Rusticiana; *PLRE IIIA*, 236–7, Boethius.

[132] On the Anicii in the late sixth and early seventh centuries, Brown, *Byzantine Italy*, 28–9; Sarris, *Economy*, 21–2; Cooper, *Household*, 84; *PLRE IIIB*, 1101–2, on a Rusticia at Ravenna c. 591 and a Rusticia, granddaughter of Boethius the philosopher, at Constantinople c. 592–603, whose daughter Eusebia married into the prominent Apion family of Egypt.

court and it was furthermore conveniently complementary to Justinian's own agenda. Nothing provided justification for the Gothic War so well as the example of Roman *libertas* having suffered the injustice of 'barbarian' tyranny. Boethius' own *De consolatione*, whether intended as such or not, supplied a scathing indictment of the government at Ravenna.[133] It is generally assumed that the *De consolatione* circulated among a discrete circle in the period immediately following his death.[134] Eventually, Boethius would find a posthumous audience in Constantinople.[135] Although Boethius constructed the concept of 'liberty' for the express purpose of demonstrating its ephemeral nature in the face of a more profound philosophical truth, this message was probably lost on those who would later make Boethius a martyr to the cause of the western Senate.[136] The strident language of Boethius' contest with philosophical truth was easily transferable to a condemnation of the Amal state: 'Do you think that this is the first time that Wisdom has been attacked and endangered by a wicked society?'[137] By expressing the frustrations that Boethius experienced while attempting to exercise virtue and justice as a magistrate, he drew from the kit of cultural assumptions held by the senatorial elite concerning the low characters of those involved in royal service, making the inevitable contrasts between the senatorial and palatine elite.[138] Although this was a part of the rhetorical apparatus of the *De consolatione* that would eventually bring Boethius around to acknowledging that genuine philosophical truth was not embedded in earthly activities, his final estimation that state service was incompatible with the exercise of moral judgement had considerable consequences.[139] This was precisely the type of indictment needed to support regime change in Italy. Importantly, the *De consolatione* contested a fundamental parity between natural moral order and moral government found in Neoplatonic thinking. Boethius claimed that moral government could not exist because of its essential concern with ephemeral matters of the external world, particularly concern for fame and reputation, which caused men

---

[133] On Boethius' portrayal in the *De consolatione* of Theoderic as a tyrant bent on the destruction of the Senate, Robinson, 'Dead Boethius', 7–13; Vitiello, *Principe*, 176–81 and 203–9; Goltz, *Barbar*, 381–7.

[134] Troncarelli, *Tradizioni*, 82–97. [135] Troncarelli, 'Boezio', 201–37.

[136] The qualification to Boethian liberty made by Magee, '*Consolatio*', 348–64; in general on the literary and philosophical nature of the text, Chadwick, *Boethius*, 225–47; Troncarelli, *Tradizioni*; Starnes, 'Boethius', 27–38; Shanzer, 'Death', 352–66; Frakes, *Fate*; Vitiello, 'Anti-Boethius'; Shanzer, 'Interpreting', 228–54.

[137] Boethius, *De consolatione philosophiae* 1.3.15–17, trans. Tester, *LCL*, 141.

[138] Boethius, *De consolatione philosophiae* 1.4.34–75.

[139] Boethius, *De consolatione philosophiae* 1.4.165.

to deviate from the path of virtue.[140] As will be discussed in full detail, the *Variae* countered this claim by demonstrating how the personal reputations of public servants and the wider reputation of the government were interdependent and equally bound to a natural order which dictated public deportment.

Boethius' preliminary characterization of a government that had failed at a moral level resonates particularly in the *Valesianus* (as already noted, this was a text indebted to the Constantinopolitan political discourse). Almost in a manner reminiscent of Procopius' *Anecdota*, the *Valesianus* dwells on the personality of Theoderic as the root of governmental failure, an indication of the Theoderic–Boethius polemic in extended development. Barnish has cautiously rejected the notion that Boethius' *De consolatione* influenced the *Valesianus*, although it should be noted that the sentiments of the *De consolatione* may have reached a Constantinopolitan audience in the form of reworked themes rather than actual text.[141] The frequency with which the Anicii maintained communication between Rome and Constantinople supports such a model. The sustained development of social and political tensions between palatine court and the senatorial elite is certainly a theme that the *Valesianus* bears in common with Boethius' final testament.[142] As already discussed, the pithy saying attributed to Theoderic concerning Roman Goths and Gothic Romans sought to demonstrate how Theoderic had confused the natural social order.[143] But like the *Anecdota*, the *Valesianus* dwells on the lurid and sensational. The actual execution of Boethius forms the final enactment of injustice. Details such as the binding of Boethius' eyes with a cord until the sockets burst and his final death under blows from a cudgel portray the death of a common thief, not the scion of an ancient family.[144] The audience hears nothing of his care during confinement – care that at least permitted enough furnishings and contemplative quietude for him to compose the *De consolatione*. The overall effect was intended to exploit antipathy toward Amal governance. Even so, the vitriol spilled in opposition to the Amal regime did not claim a captive audience at Constantinople. Procopius provided a view of the fall of Boethius and Symmachus decidedly more sympathetic to Theoderic.[145]

---

[140] Boethius, *De consolatione philosophiae* 2.7 and 3.4.

[141] On the rhetorical construction of Theoderic in the *Excerpta*, Barnish, '*Anonymus Valesianus*', 587–95; contra the influence of Boethius, 590; Robinson, 'Dead Boethius', 12, on the similarity of the basic Boethian narrative found in the *Valesiana* to the account provided by Procopius in *Wars*.

[142] Barnish, '*Anonymus Valesianus*', 572.   [143] *Excerpta Valesiana* 61.   [144] *Excerpta Valesiana* 87.

[145] Procopius, *Wars* 1.5.32–39; on Procopius' sympathy, Greatrex, 'Recent work', 66; and Kaldellis, *Procopius*, 102.

The difference can only be explained by considering the intended audiences of the respective texts – on the one hand, an audience sensitive to the production of propaganda at Justinian's court, and on the other hand, an audience receptive to the political benefits of 'barbarizing' the memory of Amal governance.

The strikingly dissonant portrayals of Theoderic found in sources that emerged either during or in the wake of the Gothic War also suggest the intensity of the polemic attempting to characterize Ostrogothic rule as either the preservation of a *res publica* or the failure of a 'barbarized' state. Indeed, as already suggested, the posthumous portrayal of Theoderic's personality and government was contingent upon the political polemic emerging both in Italy and in the eastern empire during the Gothic War. Cassiodorus, Marcellinus Comes, the *Anonymous Valesianus*, Jordanes and even the seventh-century Frankish chronicler Fredegar illustrate how the contradictory portrayals of Theoderic actually represent an interactive and dynamic political polemic. Ultimately, the various *personae* of Theoderic represent the extent of political uncertainty and social dislocation that attended the nearly twenty years of continuous war in Italy.

Before considering how Theoderic's posthumous reputation appeared in literary works, it is important to keep in mind that the *persona* that he bore in his own lifetime was multifaceted, but not necessarily conflicting. It is true that, to the soldiery which followed him to Italy from the Balkans, he was *rex Gothorum*, and that, to citizens of the continued Roman state in Italy, he was *princeps* and *augustus*. Theoderic would have learned to manage these aspects of his political identity not as competing Janus-like faces, but as complementary political facets. Theoderic had experienced a childhood that alternated between these roles. As the son of a Gothic leader who had crossed the Danubian frontier in the wake of the Hunnic confederacy's fall, Theoderic had known military life in the encampment of Gothic federated soldiers who served the eastern empire. The importance of maintaining the loyalty of these federated soldiers to the emperor had also required Theoderic to spend a significant period of his childhood (ten years) as a political hostage at the imperial court in Constantinople. The roles of Gothic federated soldier of the empire and courtier at the imperial capital had not been mutually exclusive for Theoderic. Furthermore, the Arian Christianity which he followed was a marker less of his barbarism than of his membership in the Roman military, where Arianism had long been tolerated in the eastern empire. His experiences in the imperial court and the military encampment had equipped Theoderic to navigate in the socially mobile world of the late Roman elite in both Latin and Greek. His later appointment as patrician, *magister militum* and consul of the east only reinforced his identity as a political leader of the Roman state who had risen from the military caste of late Roman society.

The portrayal of Theoderic as either 'barbarian' Goth or Roman ruler was contingent on political circumstances and the impact that such a portrayal was intended to have on a particular audience. Andreas Golz has already provided a comprehensive overview of many of the sources describing Theoderic which suggests a wide range of portrayals that were variously hostile, sympathetic or neutral toward Theoderic.[146] What has not received emphasis, however, is that much of the variation in handling Theoderic's reputation may be traced to the polemic of the Gothic War.

In many ways the range of literary testimony left by Ennodius of Pavia probably serves as a benchmark for the manner in which Theoderic projected himself in political communication. The laudatory terms in which Ennodius referred to Theoderic in his *Vita Epiphanii*, in the *Panegyricus* written for Theoderic and in various letters correspond with the fragmented epigraphic evidence of Theoderic's reign. Not surprisingly, according to his *Panegyricus*, Theoderic's governance followed in the imperial tradition of Alexander the Great, republican consuls and the best of emperors.[147] His virtues were both military and political: he both possessed the martial excellence of Gothic strength and shone with the virtues of peace.[148] The fact that Ennodius referred to Theoderic in very similar terms (*princeps invictus*, *dominus libertatis*, *imperator noster*) when writing to, presumably, very different audiences in his personal letters and the *Vita Epiphanii* suggests that, Goth or not, the political and religious elite of Italy preferred to refer to their ruler in an imperial style.[149] The *Variae* of Cassiodorus, many written in Theoderic's name, have much in common with the rhetoric found in Ennodius' writing, suggesting that the production of the image of the Gothic imperial ruler was a dialogue between the court and the governed. Of course, as will be demonstrated, the context in which Cassiodorus later published the *Variae* generated departures from the native Italian literary culture that Cassiodorus shared with Ennodius. It is enough, however, to point out that both Ennodius and Cassiodorus expressed Theoderic's reign in terms that emphasized the continuity of legitimate imperial rule.

By contrast, the perspective prevailing at the eastern imperial court emphasized the illegitimacy of Theoderic's political power. For

---

[146] Goltz, *Barbar.*   [147] Ennodius, *Panegyricus* 4.18, 17.78–81, 19.83–86.
[148] Ennodius, *Panegyricus* 19.83–86 and 21.89–93.
[149] Ennodius, *Vita Epiphanii* 125 and *Epistulae* 270.2 and 437.1, 'princeps invictus'; *Epistulae* 159.1, 'dominus libertatis'; *Libellus pro synodo* 74, 'imperator noster'.

Marcellinus Comes, the Gothic rule of Italy represented an extension of the end of the western empire. His history provided a narrative that framed Justinian's conflict with the Goths not as the conquest of Roman Italy, but as the rebirth of the imperial tradition possible only under Justinian. The attention that Marcellinus focused on Theoderic's earlier activities in the eastern empire was particularly well adapted to this teleology. Marcellinus consistently showed Theoderic in the least-favourable light: plunderer, grasping and untrustworthy ally and, finally, treacherous invader of Italy who acted without the eastern emperor's sanction.[150] It is noteworthy that Marcellinus made no mention of Theoderic's role in the deaths of Boethius, Symmachus or Pope John, all of which occurred within the chronological span of his *Chronicle*. These were deaths, like that of Theoderic himself, which acquired new significance during the course of the Gothic War, not in the preceding period.

The accounts of Procopius and the *Anonymus Valesianus* demonstrate perhaps better than any other sources how the contested nature of Theoderic's reputation emerged out of the Gothic War. Of particular interest is the manner in which Theoderic's involvement in the deaths of Boethius, Symmachus and Pope John surfaces in the political polemic as an evaluative criterion during the course of the Gothic War. The deaths of Boethius and Symmachus were particularly useful in inflecting the interpretation of Theoderic's reputation. The conflicting reputations of Theoderic are particularly evident in the competing versions of his death. According to Procopius, Theoderic perceived the injustice that he had committed by observing the face of the recently executed Symmachus in a fish served to him one evening at dinner. Theoderic read in this portent the end of his own life, for which reason he retired to bed and, after confessing his sin to his physician, quietly died.[151] In contrast, the *Excerpta Valesiana* claimed that he died of dysentery after the fashion of Arius (in the act of evacuating his bowels).[152] This version of Theoderic's death has a certain symbolic economy that assured the readers that 'barbarian' heretics could not expect spiritual ascent. Both narratives probably indicate that Theoderic died after eating a spoiled fish. Procopius' version, however, lent the king a certain prophetic, as opposed to heretical, quality. Indeed, his foreknowledge of the event and his willingness to retire to bed and await death in the company of an intimate witness resonate with a number of hagiographical narratives.[153]

---

[150] Marcellinus Comes, *Chronicon* 479.2, 482.2, 487–9.   [151] Procopius, *Wars* 5.1.34–39.
[152] *Excerpta Valesiana* 16.95; death of Arius described in Socrates Scholasticus, *Historia Ecclesiastica* 1.38.
[153] For example, Ennodius, *Vita Epiphanii* 190; Gregory the Great, *Dialogorum* 2.37.

Of particular interest to understanding what Procopius and the *Anonymus Valesianus* attempted to communicate is the attention focused on Theoderic's unlettered state of education. The *Valesianus* twice refers to Theoderic as *illiteratus*, and in the second instance this is a statement intended to condition the audience's understanding that Theoderic lacked a proper grasp of justice.[154] In essence, it was his condition as *illiteratus* which made him a 'barbarian' capable of condemning two senators and a pope. However, Theoderic as *illiteratus* meant something different to Procopius, who specifically paired his unlettered state of education with his innate sense of justice.[155] Just as in traditions pertaining to Christian saints who, like Antony and Martin, eschewed formal education, Procopius depicted a 'barbarian' king whose sense of justice derived from an innate understanding of *natura*.[156] This construction should not be mistaken for genuine sympathy for 'barbarians'; rather, it is an indication that Procopius profiled Theoderic in parody of Christian sainthood as a means of contesting the rhetoric of Justinian's military and political policies, which depended for their legitimacy upon the contrast between imperial and 'barbarian' government.

Cassiodorus' *Variae* similarly responded to the currents of this polemical discourse. As will be considered in greater depth in later chapters, Theoderic appears in the *Variae* explicitly as the purple-clad philosopher king who observed the truths of justice in the natural world. In fact, the relationship between the physical natural world and the metaphysical spiritual world forms a cornerstone of how Cassiodorus portrayed the legitimacy of Theoderic's reign. As the digressions of numerous letters in the *Variae* make plain, Theoderic's legal and administrative decisions were in harmony with a broader conception of the natural law that governed the affairs of men, the natural world and a more abstract embodiment of morality only perceived by a soul of pure moral conscience. Interestingly, Cassiodorus' attention to the relationship between nature and governance is not something for which a parallel exists in the works of Ennodius. Instead, this appears to be an aspect of a persistent eastern discourse pertaining to the proper definition of natural law. In other words, although the individual letters of the *Variae* do reflect much of the original Amal propaganda produced at Theoderic's Ravenna, Cassiodorus' publication of the collection during the Gothic War betrays yet another

---

[154] *Excerpta Valesiana* 12.61 and 14.79; see the discussion in Chapter 4 above and Barnish, '*Anonymus Valesianus*', 573.

[155] Procopius, *Wars* 5.1.26, emphasizes Theoderic's understanding of justice; 5.2.14, Theoderic's lack of education.

[156] For the paradigmatic example of a saint with 'unlettered' wisdom, Athanasius, *Vita Antonii* 1, 72, 73.

personality for Theoderic that was contingent upon the very specific historical conditions of the Gothic War.

Obviously the *Getica* of Jordanes also belongs in a consideration of this polemic. Jordanes provided one of the fullest and most detailed accounts of Theoderic's life – his early years in the Balkans and at Constantinople, the imperial sanction he received for seizing Italy and his campaigns there and the manner by which he fortified his kingdom of Italy with warfare and marriage alliances.[157] Absent from Jordanes' narrative is any notice of the Boethian affair. Unlike other narratives that derived from the period of the Gothic War or after, Theoderic's death was unattended by the disgrace of having condemned Boethius, Symmachus or Pope John. Unlike Marcellinus, who ignored the Boethian affair because it had not yet attained importance as a part of the discourse of the Gothic War, Jordanes' silence on the matter is exceptional given that he was writing in the last years of the Gothic War and had access to Italian exiles in Constantinople. This reticence may be explained by the fact that Jordanes' history provides a framework for the union between prominent representatives of the Anicii and Amals – Germanus and Matasuntha. In essence, Jordanes' history culminated a history of Ostrogothic interaction with the Roman state with a marriage between representatives of the noblest families of Roman and Goth. Drawing attention to the single most spectacular failure of diplomacy between Theoderic and the Anicii would have been, at the very least, awkward to explain.

By comparison, other texts originating from the period of the Gothic War and later consistently draw attention to the Boethian affair. Indeed, the manner of describing Theoderic's own death was inseparable from this narrative. The *Liber Pontificalis*, a text located squarely in the context of the Gothic War, condemned Theoderic as a heretical and tyrannical king for the deaths of Boethius, Symmachus and John.[158] It is not inconceivable that the *Liber Pontificalis* played a significant role in germinating the discourse concerning Theoderic's reputation to which both Procopius and the *Anonymus Valesianus* responded in very different ways. This was certainly the case for Gregory the Great. His *Dialogues* expanded the narrative of Theoderic's death with interesting detail. The *Dialogues* report that a certain holy man in Sicily learned of Theoderic's death in distant Ravenna through a dream.[159] In this vision, Pope John and the patrician Symmachus led a disrobed and barefoot Theoderic with chained hands to the brink of a volcano, where they cast him into the flaming abyss of Hell. Gregory claimed to have received this information

---

[157] Jordanes, *Getica* 52.270–59.304.   [158] *Liber Pontificalis* 55.5–6.
[159] Gregory the Great, *Dialogues* 4.31.

from the *defensor ecclesiae* at Rome, who had heard the story from the father of his son-in-law, placing him within the generation that had been an audience to the political discourse of the Gothic War.

Sometime in the mid-seventh century, the Frankish chronicler Fredegar composed a world history to frame Frankish affairs.[160] Fredegar cited a host of well-known histories, which he often used verbatim to bring his account to its fourth and final book, where he assumed responsibility for the narrative.[161] At the end of the second book, Fredegar appended two sizeable narratives to a portion taken from Hydatius, bringing his account to the late fifth and early sixth centuries. These narratives pertain to Theoderic and the court of Justinian, drawn respectively from a now lost *Gesta Theoderici* and the *Anecdota* of Procopius.[162] The material pertaining to Theoderic, in particular, seems to have derived from a milieu that was sensitive to the polemic of Theoderic's memory. Counter to the tendency prevailing in sixth-century eastern sources to emphasize the 'barbarian' foreignness of the Amals, the text elaborates in a rather lengthy and fabulous tale how Theoderic was, in fact, not a Goth, but a Roman from Macedonia. The text explains how Theoderic had been legally adopted by a noble Roman family in Macedonia, formally educated and enrolled in palatine service at Constantinople, where he evaded the various plots of the senatorial elite, and, finally, how the emperor Leo awarded him the *patriciatus Romanis seo Gothis* (patrician status over both Romans and Goths) so that he might lead an army of federated soldiers to restore order in Italy.[163] To emphasize his Roman origins, the text differentiates between Theoderic the Amal and Theoderic Strabo, 'who was a Goth'.[164] The portrayal of Theoderic as a Roman from Macedonia probably derived from the narratives in which Jordanes and

---

[160] On Fredegar, Wallace-Hadrill, *Fredegar*; Wood, 'Fables', 359–66; Diesenberger, 'Symbolic capital', 173–212; Collins, *Fredegar-Chroniken*.

[161] Krusch, *MGH SRM II*, 4–7; Book 4 was Fredegar's own composition.

[162] Fredegar, *Chronica* 57, explicitly attributes his chapter on Theoderic to a *gesta*, 'sicut huius libri gesta testatur'; on the *Gesta Theoderici*, Krusch, *MGH SRM II*, 200–14, demonstrated that relevant portions of the *Vita Fuldensis* and the *Vita ex Aimoino Hausta* derived from the same *Gesta Theoderici* as found in Fredegar; on the *Anecdota* as the provenance of the chapter pertaining to Justinian, Scheibelreiter, 'Justinian und Belisar', 267–80.

[163] Fredegar, *Chronica* 2.57, 'Theudericum, qui diligenter nutritus, Idacio et Eugeniae praesentatur, quem secum esse iusserunt, tanta in eum amplectentes amorem, ut ipsum sibi adoptarent in filium'; 'Defuncto Idacio et Eugenia, praeceptum imperatoris Leonis Theudericus iussus est militaris'; 'quidam ex senatoribus huius consiliae tacite contrarius, vehementer cum Theuderico amicicias inians'; 'Theuderico Romam direxit, qui a Romanis seo Gothis patriciati honorem gloriose susceptus est.'

[164] Fredegar, *Chronica* 2.57, 'Nam ille alius Theudericus, Theudoris regi filius, natione Gothus fuit. Nativetas Theuderici regis ex genere Macedonum ita fuit, qui in Aetalia Gothis et Romanis regnavit.'

Cassiodorus both attempted to demonstrate Gothic parity with the eastern state.[165] Interestingly, the *Gesta* of Theoderic also contains elements of the hostile tradition. Explicitly citing Gregory's *Dialogues*, the *Gesta* relates that the unwarranted executions of Pope John and Symmachus precipitated Theoderic's own downfall. According to the *Gesta*, the pair cast Theoderic's soul into a vat of fire. Nonetheless, the text is curiously silent concerning Boethius.[166]

Fredegar's interest in the *Gesta Theoderici* and the *Anecdota* is unusual and has to do with his interest in developing themes in Frankish kingship. Given the eastern provenance of the material pertaining to Justinian, it is entirely likely that materials from the *Gesta Theoderici* which Fredegar used were also eastern in origin.[167] It is certainly true that the Frankish courts maintained a frequent dialogue with the eastern imperial court during the sixth century, particularly as a foil to Ostrogothic intervention in Gaul.[168] Like all diplomatic relations in this period, the exchange of texts was an integral component of political communication. One nobleman, Amalafrid, the great-nephew of Theoderic and a cousin of the Frankish queen Radegund, had been in residence at Ravenna when Belisarius captured the city. His transfer to Constantinople in 540 was but one channel of communication between the eastern capital and the Frankish kingdoms.

The later Carolingian period accepted the Boethian affair as a chief feature of the narrative of Theoderic's life, although it had clearly become deracinated of propagandistic significance. Paul the Deacon's *Historia Romana* claimed that Theoderic, 'excited by the madness of his own iniquity', was responsible for the deaths of the two senators. Paul repeated Gregory's story that Symmachus and John later led the tyrant's soul to a fire-and-brimstone bath.[169] Nonetheless, Paul constructed a history of the Roman Empire that spanned from Aeneas to the end of the Gothic War; for Paul the Deacon, the Roman Empire ended when

---

[165] Viscido, 'Barbarus', 338–44, notes that Cassiodorus never attributes the term *barbarus* to the Goths.

[166] Fredegar, *Chronica* 2.59, 'Theudericus cum papa Romensis apostolicum virum Iohannem sine culpa morte damnassit et Symmacum patricium nullis causis extantibus itemque trucitare fecisset, ira percussis divina.'

[167] On the influence of eastern sources and affairs on Fredegar's *Chronica*, Wallace-Hadrill, *Fredegar*, xiii; Wander, 'Cypress', 345–6; Simoni, 'Memoria', 359–75; Borchert, 'Bild Theoderichs', 435–52.

[168] Wood, *Merovingian Kingdoms*; Gillett, *Envoys*, 17–26; Gregory of Tours, *Decem libri historiarum* 2.38, for diplomatic exchanges between Clovis and Anastasius; similarly, *Decem libri* 6.2 for the return of Chilperic's envoys from the eastern imperial court; similarly, Fredegar, *Chronica* 4.6, 4.9, 4.40.

[169] Paul the Deacon, *Historia Romana* 16.9–10, 'stimulatus rabie suae iniquitatis'.

Justinianic reconquest extinguished Gothic rule in Italy.[170] Apparently a similar nostalgia animated Charlemagne when, according to Agnellus and Walahfrid Strabo, he laid claim to an equestrian statue of Theoderic at Ravenna and had it transported to the new imperial capital at Aachen.[171]

In summary, the current picture of Theoderic is based on a composite of sources which were polemical and in competition with one another. Political tensions between the eastern imperial court and Ravenna set the stage for conflicting accounts of Theoderic, while the Gothic War in particular brought the issue of the Boethian affair into sharper focus than the attention it had previously received in sources would suggest. It was not until a later reception, beyond Italy and beyond the turmoil of the Gothic War, that the polemical aspects of Theoderic's reputation were fused into a single presentation. Most importantly, it should be recognized that the current preoccupation of modern scholarship to characterize Theoderic either as a Roman or as 'barbarian' engages in a debate that the sources attempted to influence in the sixth century. The ideological contest between 'barbarian' Ravenna and 'imperial' Constantinople was chiefly a topic developed in the context of the Gothic War. The sixth-century North African historian Victor wrote a chronicle of the years 444 to 563 and ignored the deposition of Romulus Augustus by Odoacer, Theoderic's assumption of power in Italy and the Gothic War.[172] Although he noted the overbearing corruption and peculation of the prefect of Africa (Boethius), it was of no interest to Victor that this was the son of the dead philosopher.[173]

THE *ORDO GENERIS* OF CASSIODORUS

For Cassiodorus, living in Constantinople, where the shape of post-war Italy would be decided and where future participation in that Italy would depend on which ideological interpretation of Ostrogothic Italy prevailed, the discourse concerning Boethius was an urgent matter. Responsibility for the reputation of the former palatine bureaucracy of Ravenna would have weighed most heavily on Cassiodorus, who, as the praetorian prefect, had occupied the apex of a network of political patronage. Resonances of this concern appear in the first preface of the *Variae*, where Cassiodorus stated that he had compiled the collection to rectify the reputations of those who had served with him under the

---

[170] Paul the Deacon, *Historia Romana* 16.23.
[171] Agnellus, *Liber pontificalis ecclesiae Ravennatis* 94; Walahfrid Strabo, *De imagine tetrici*.
[172] Victor Tonnennensis, *Chronica* 476, 489–3, 534–52.
[173] Victor Tonnennensis, *Chronica* 552, 'sed Boethio primate Byzaceni . . . validissimis persecutionibus impugnavit fidelibusque calumnias generando eorumque substantias auferendo'.

Ostrogoths.[174] This seems to be a concern that was directly responsive to the condemnation of state service seen in Boethius' *De consolatione*.[175] Indeed, Cassiodorus' concern for how he would be viewed with respect to the memory of Boethius (and for how a negative association could have an impact on his political prospects) seems to be the source of another text that surfaced in Constantinople. The *Ordo generis Cassiodororum*, or the *Anecdoton Holderi* as it is otherwise known, is a text that has been heavily disputed in modern scholarship. Most scholars agree that the *Ordo* is an abridgement of a work that Cassiodorus wrote while living in Constantinople.[176] The extent to which a later epitomizer may have altered the original is a matter of conjecture and it is entirely likely that the only difference between the extant text and the original is the addition of a protocol naming the author and its recipient, respectively Cassiodorus Senator and Rufus Petronius Nicomachus (Cethegus). It is precisely this line of address that has led scholars to suspect common interest between Cassiodorus and Cethegus, although it needs to be stressed that Cethegus appears nowhere in the *Variae* and seems to have been, at least politically, a nonentity until his arrival in Constantinople. Pope Vigilius mentions Cassiodorus and Cethegus together in the letter from 550, but the actual nature of the relationship is not clear. Vigilius' letter deals, in general terms, with attempts to negotiate the 'Three Chapters' controversy.[177] It was certainly in Vigilius' interest that the two émigrés work together for the benefit of the church at Rome, but Cassiodorus' interest in Cethegus is more aptly described by the content of the *Ordo*.

The *Ordo* provides a biographical sketch for Symmachus, Boethius and Cassiodorus. Some scholars have seen this as evidence that Cassiodorus was tied to the Anicii and their political interests. However, it is not clear that Cassiodorus was even a peripheral member of the family. His paternal properties in Bruttium, the lack of epigraphic and literary reference to Cassiodorii at Rome and the particularly palatine *cursus* of his public career all suggest otherwise. The titular statement of the text (which may well be attributed to the later redactor) seems to express some uncertainty about the relationship between the three subjects: 'The order of the family of Cassiodorii, those authors prominent either in their familial relations or [*vel*] in their erudition.'[178] The later redactor attempted to describe the *Ordo* based on possible commonalities between

---

[174] Cassiodorus, *Variae, praefatio* 1.8–9.   [175] Similarly, Vitiello, 'Anti-Boethius', 466–7.

[176] Momigliano, 'Italian culture', 215; Ruggini, 'Nobilita', 79; Vanderspoel, 'Cassiodorus', 500; Giardina, 'Progetto delle *Variae*', 45–6.

[177] On this in general, Barnish, 'Cassiodorus after conversion', 157–87.

[178] *Ordo generis Cassiodororum* 6–8, 'Ordo generis Cassiodororum: qui scriptores exstiterint ex eorum progenie vel ex quibus eruditis.'

the three subjects and assumed 'either familial ties or erudition' to be the common element. The content of the *Ordo* leans heavily in favour of the latter choice in as much as the *Ordo* provides a résumé of the public and literary attainments of three statesmen. In each case, public offices and literary works are noted. The parallel structure locates the three patricians within a similar cultural and professional orbit.[179] According to the *Ordo*, Symmachus appears not to have accepted anything other than titular offices. The opposite is true of Boethius and Cassiodorus. Both advanced politically by composing (and publicly reciting) orations in praise of Theoderic. The 'bucolic songs' composed by Boethius may refer to his inclusion of Menippean verse in the *De consolatione*, but any reference to the eventual execution of Symmachus and Boethius is nonexistent. Similarly, the text makes no reference to Boethius' *De consolatione*. If Cassiodorus had close ties with the Anicii, it would have been a simple matter to mention their deaths as an overture of sympathy and political affiliation. Instead, the *Ordo* reveals how politically charged the memory of Boethius and Symmachus had become in Constantinople. By representing Cassiodorus as if he shared a common political and literary culture with Boethius and Symmachus, the *Ordo* attempted to efface the kind of ethical distinctions made between the senatorial and palatine aristocracies in the *De consolatione*.[180] Because all three shared the same intellectual interests and received public prestige from the Amal court, with only degree of success separating them (Cassiodorus holds more important offices), all can be shown to have colluded with the Amal regime. This was precisely the kind of statement that would have diluted a critique of the Italian bureaucratic elite in Constantinople.

How the text was read can only be guessed at. Given its truncated form, it probably arrived in the hands of its later editor in the form of a pamphlet, a document offering little more explanation than its bare content, for which reason the editor added an introductory protocol. Substantial evidence attests to pamphleteering in the ancient world. Pamphlets in the form of short, slanderous books and epigrams are attested in contests of reputation in the Roman Republic and the Principate.[181] The *Historia Augusta* records how Hadrian, out of contempt for professors and philosophers, would 'often debate by means of pamphlets or poems issued by both sides in turn'.[182] The practice certainly continued into late antiquity. Sidonius Apollinaris commented on how 'untitled papers'

---

[179] *Ordo generis Cassiodororum* 9–37; discussed more fully in O'Donnell, *Cassiodorus*, 259–66.

[180] Similarly, Hedrick, *History*, 172.

[181] On the rampant use of *famosi libelli* during the Roman Republic and the Principate, Daube, 'Infamandi', 415; Bauman, *Crimen*, 246–65.

[182] *Historia Augusta*, *Vita Hadriani* 15.11, trans. Magie, *LCL*, 49.

circulated at the western court of Majorian and targeted the reputations of prominent men.[183] The habit of distributing pamphlets to shape
polemical discourse was even adopted in early ecclesiastical politics.[184]
Portions of the *Collectio Avellana* pertaining to the controversial papal
election of Damasus have been identified as forgeries that probably circulated in Rome as fourth-century pamphlets prior to inclusion in the
collection. Ennodius is similarly known to have distributed pamphlets for
papal electioneering during the Laurentian Schism at the beginning of
the sixth century.[185] Finally, political unrest at Constantinople later in the
tenth and eleventh centuries was frequently attended by an increase in
the volume of protest literature, including the distribution of slanderous
pamphlets.[186]

As a passive pamphlet that did not antagonize but rather mediated
the memory of Boethius, the *Ordo* offered a substantial contradiction to
the polemic that dramatized Boethius as a victim of 'barbarian' tyranny.
Whether Cethegus actually received the text is not verifiable and, in
fact, irrelevant. The fact that the *Ordo* was addressed to Cethegus and
then distributed with that association in mind is more important as such
a pamphlet might have been intended to neutralize any role of leadership that Cethegus enjoyed among the Anicii in Constantinople. Just as
important, the *Ordo* advertised Cassiodorus' two other contributions to
the Constantinopolitan polemic. The first was the *Gothic History*, which
clearly influenced Jordanes' portrayal of Roman and Gothic parity. The
second was a thorough exoneration of the Italian bureaucratic elite in
the *Variae*. An audience still in doubt about Cassiodorus' position with
respect to Boethius and Symmachus was encouraged by the *Ordo* to read
the *Gothic History* and the *Variae*.

---

[183] Sidonius Apollinaris, *Epistulae* 1.11.2, 'Temporibus Augusti Maioriani venit in medium charta
comitatum, sed carens indice, versuum plena satiricorum mordacium, sane qui satis invectivaliter
abusi nominum nuditate carpebant plurimum vitia, plus homines.'
[184] For example, Janson, *Prefaces*, 158, for pamphlets used by Cyprian, Rufinus and Ennodius;
Moorhead, *Theoderic*, 122–3, on the use of forged documents in 'pamphlet warfare' at Rome
during the Laurentian Schism.
[185] On the *Collectio Avellana* as polemical fragments, Blair-Dixon, 'Memories', 59–74, esp. 70–4 on
the Damasan dossier; on the Laurentian Schism more generally, Townsend, 'Forgeries', 165–74;
Moorhead, *Theoderic*, 114–39.
[186] Holmes, 'Political literacy', 141–2.

Chapter 6

THE MEMORY OF BOETHIUS IN THE
VARIAE

REWRITING FAMILY HISTORIES

Letters of the *Variae* addressed to Boethius and other senatorial elite indicate how Cassiodorus used the *Variae* to respond to the negative portrayals
of the Amal court and to shape the image of palatine service during the
Gothic War. It is worth noting that sources of the sixth and seventh
centuries written after Boethius' death mention him chiefly in connection with the celebrity of his execution. With the exception of a letter
from Ennodius congratulating him for the consulship of 510, Boethius
is nowhere mentioned for his importance as a political figure.[1] Other
letters that Ennodius addressed to Boethius, much like those addressed to
him in the *Variae*, celebrate his scholarly attainments.[2] In the case of both
Ennodius and the *Variae*, it seems that attention was paid to Boethius
merely in the interest of establishing close connection with a family of
great importance. Prior to the reputation Boethius gained for the *De consolatione* in the Carolingian period, his posthumous reputation had been
almost entirely constructed around the narratives concerning his death.[3]

One such narrative adaptation, minor in point of fact but significant as
an indication of the political considerations that motivated Cassiodorus'
handling of the *Variae*, deals precisely with the memory of Boethius'
execution in a Constantinopolitan context. As previously mentioned,
Marcellinus Comes did not take note of Boethius' death in his *Chronicon*
because he had begun writing the history in 518, before the outbreak
of the Gothic War when it became particularly relevant. Marcellinus
did, however, make the interesting claim that the antecedent to the
deterioration of the western empire was the death of the great general
Aetius. Curiously, Marcellinus also noted that Aetius had perished with
his friend, a certain Boethius:

---

[1] Ennodius, *Epistulae* 8.1.3.   [2] Ennodius, *Epistulae* 6.6, 7.13, 8.1, 8.31, 8.36, 8.37, 8.40.
[3] Robinson, 'Dead Boethius'.

Aetius, the main salvation of the western empire and a scourge to king Attila, was cut down in the palace, together with his friend Boethius, by the emperor Valentinian, and with him fell the western kingdom and it has not as yet been able to be restored.[4]

The designation of a Boethius as a former associate of Aetius, although obscure, does appear elsewhere.[5] However, the attribution of the fall and subsequent barbarization of the western empire to the event was something new. By default, this elder Boethius also became a prop of the former western empire. Although not incontrovertible, it is possible that Marcellinus included this detail in the course of revising the *Chronicon* in 534, when it became particularly potent as a piece of anti-Gothic propaganda. By this time, Marcellinus had joined Justinian's personal staff as *cancellarius*, Belisarius had just celebrated his triumph against the Vandals, Liberius had defected to the eastern court and the emperor was on the threshold of moving the theatre of war to Italy. Emphasizing the historical significance of the death of this elder Boethius naturally served a rhetorical purpose in barbarizing the Amals.

More importantly, the polemical potential of this stray historical fact resonated with Cassiodorus and it must be remembered that Cassiodorus had read Marcellinus' history while in Constantinople.[6] Cassiodorus too had included the deaths of Aetius and the earlier Boethius in his own *Chronica*.[7] At the time, however, Cassiodorus could not have conceived of the murder of a second Boethius at the hands of an Amal. Some twenty years after composing the *Chronica*, the political climate shaped by the Gothic War was very different and the signature of that change appears in the *Variae*. As in the *Ordo*, Cassiodorus sought opportunities in the *Variae* to create parity between his own career and that of Boethius. Thus letter 1.4, addressed to the Senate and announcing the promotion of Cassiodorus' father to patrician status, finds a previous Cassiodorus who had fulfilled a similar role as *sociatus* to Aetius on an embassy to Attila:

For the father of this candidate bore the praiseworthy dignity of tribune and secretary under Valentinian . . . But as the similar of spirit are always accustomed to prefer each other, he was the greatly cherished associate to the patrician Aetius in the governance of the state, to that Aetius whom the emperor at that

---

[4] Marcellinus Comes, *Chronicon* 454.2, trans. Croke, 22.

[5] *PLRE II*, 231, cites the episode in the *Fasti Vindobonenses Posteriores*, the Annals of Ravenna, Prosper of Tiro, Hydatius, Victor Tonnennensis.

[6] Cassiodorus, *Institutiones* 1.17.2.

[7] Cassiodorus, *Chronica* 1260, 'His conss. Aetius patricius in Palatio manu Valentiniani imp. Extinctus est, Boetius vero praefectus praetorio amicus eius circumstantium gladiis interemptus.'

time followed in every portion of counsel on account of his wisdom and [his] glorious labours undertaken on behalf of the state. Therefore not in vain was he sent in the capacity of a legate to the formidable warrior Attila with Carpilio, the son of Aetius. He beheld without fear one whom the empire feared and relying on truth he remained above those terrible glares and threats, nor did he hesitate to stand in the path of argument with that man, who, overcome with I know not what fury, seemed to expect the lordship of the entire world. He found a proud king, but left him pacified and he overturned the king's false accusations with such honesty that the king sought to ask for clemency, when it was advantageous not to have peace with such a wealthy realm . . . He brought back a peace thought untenable.[8]

Rather than death and the inexorable ruin of the western empire, the elder Cassiodorus' association with Aetius had achieved (quite fantastically) the salvation of the state. The implication is that the grandfather of Boethius fell under evil times while Cassiodorus' grandfather managed to serve the state splendidly. It furthermore suggests to the audience of the *Variae* that the disparate fortunes of Boethius and Cassiodorus under the Amals could be interpreted as something other than tyranny. The revision of this letter is evident in the fact that Cassiodorus' *Chronica* only mentions the death of the elder Boethius. The *Chronica* nowhere mentions the glorious accomplishments of Cassiodorus' grandfather, despite the fact that he found other opportunities to vaunt his own reputation in the *Chronica*.[9] The sudden recollection of his grandfather's association with Aetius in the *Variae* clearly has more to do with the memory of Boethius' death in the political context of the 540s.

REWRITING THE *DE CONSOLATIONE* AND THE ANICII

This is only one of several instances in which Cassiodorus used the *Variae* to condition a particular interpretation of the past. As previously noted, the *Variae* advertise the willingness of the Amal court to show at least superficial deference to the Senate. However, letters concerning

---

[8] Cassiodorus, *Variae* 1.4.11–12, 'Sed ut se pares animi solent semper eligere, patricio Aetio pro iuvanda re publica magna fuit caritate sociatus; quem tunc rerum dominus propter sapientiam sui et gloriosos in re publica labores in omni consilii parte sequebatur. Ad Attilam igitur armorum potentem cum supra dicti filio Carpilione legationis est officio non irrite destinatus. Vidit intrepidus quem timebat imperium; facies illas terribiles et minaces fretus veritate despexit nec dubitavit eius altercationibus obviare, qui furore nescio quo raptatus mundi dominatum videbatur expetere. Invenit regem superbum, sed reliquit placatum et calumniosas eius allegationes tanta veritate destruxit, ut voluisset gratiam quaerere, cui expediebat pacem cum regno ditissimo non habere . . . Pacem retulit desperatam'; cf. Barnish, *Cassiodorus*, 8–12.
[9] Compare Cassiodorus, *Chronica* 1356: 'Me etiam consule in vestrorum laude temporum adunato clero vel populo Romanae ecclesiae rediit optata concordia.'

the Senate also implicitly depict its moral deterioration as a body vested with social and political authority. The inability of the Senate to cope with social and religious ruptures in the city of Rome is a theme that Cassiodorus developed with purpose in the *Variae*.[10] This portrayal saps strength from the celebrated statement made by Boethius that he had been condemned for championing the freedoms of the Senate.[11] Boethius' claim certainly found forceful expression later in the *Valesianus*, indicating its potential for causing harm to palatine reputations.[12] In contrast, the *Variae* portray the Senate not as an oppressed institution, but as one continually in need of the admonition and moral guidance of an upright ruler.

In the same way that the *Ordo* blunted accusations by showing Cassiodorus' affinity with Boethius and Symmachus at a cultural and political level, the *Variae* also attempted to condition the later appraisal of actors close to the downfall of the two Anicii. The same Cyprianus named by Boethius in the *De consolatione* received prominent attention in the *Variae*. Letters 5.40 and 5.41 announce his appointment to the *comitiva sacrarum largitionum*, a post he held conspicuously from 524 to 525 after accusing Albinus and during the trial against Boethius. Letters 8.21 and 8.22 announce his receipt of patrician rank and his admission to the Senate, an honour that his services as *comes sacrarum largitionum* justified. Cassiodorus displayed each elevation in dignity with paired letters, one directed to Cyprianus and the other to the Senate. Thus the audience of the *Variae* had before them an abstract of the consensus between the Amal court and the Senate that attended Cyprianus' elevation, 'Just as it was fortunate for him to be elevated by us, so will it be praiseworthy for him to be associated with your assembly in the rule of offices.'[13] Similarly, the *Variae* illustrate the accomplishments and favours shown to Opilio, the brother of Cyprianus whom Boethius claimed had offered false witness against him. Letters 8.16 and 8.17 announce, to Opilio and the Senate respectively, his appointment as *comes sacrarum largitionum* from 527 to 528. Bolder still, letter 8.17 contradicts the *De consolatione* by claiming that Opilio had a reputation that was unblemished by slandering others, 'Therefore in what way might these who knew not how to ridicule colleagues be

---

[10] For example, Cassiodorus, *Variae* 1.44.1, 2.24.1, 4.43.1, 10.13.1.

[11] Boethius, *De consolatione philosophiae* 1.4.70, 'At cuius criminis arguimur summam quaeris? Senatum dicimur salvum esse voluisse.'

[12] *Excerpta Valesiana* 87.

[13] Cassiodorus, *Variae* 5.41.1, 'Cui sicut fortunatum fuit a nobis erigi, ita laudabile erit vestro coetui honorum lege sociari'; cf. Barnish, *Cassiodorus*, 89–90.

unable to serve their masters with pure intention?'[14] Publishing letters
that honoured the individuals chiefly responsible for Boethius' downfall
would seem to be unnecessarily provocative, and in a pre-war context
it would have been. However, after the fall of Amal rule in Italy, a bold
measure was needed to undermine the damage that the executions of
Boethius and Symmachus had done to the reputation of palatine service.
By publicly extolling the virtues that had allowed Cyprianus and Opilio
to rise in office, the *Variae* not only challenged the notion that the Anicii
had been the victims of unjust tyranny, they also attempted to vitiate
those elements of the *De consolatione* that had impugned the bureaucratic
elite of Ravenna. The narrative offered in the *Variae* was clearly meant
to supersede the narrative of Boethius' last testament.

Select members of the senatorial elite from Rome received the same
revisionist treatment in the *Variae* by advertising their complicity in
Ostrogothic rule. More importantly, like the *Ordo*, the *Variae* portray
the senatorial elite not only enjoying the benefits of the political culture
under the Ostrogoths but also as prominent actors in its production. The
Variae reserve a position for Liberius that could be interpreted as com-
mensurate with his prominence in the Amal regime, although this portrayal probably responds more to his later involvement with the imperial
court at Constantinople. In fact, Liberius' treatment in the *Variae* seems
carefully conditioned as a subtle reproach for infidelity. First appearing
in a pair of letters nominating his son Venantius as *comes domesticorum*,
the letters use his son's appointment as an opportunity to extol Liberius'
attainments (to the absolute exclusion of any substantive material pertaining to the son).[15] In a pair of letters (2.15 and 2.16) addressed to Venantius
and to the Senate, Cassiodorus described in some detail Liberius' services as praetorian prefect and, rather purposefully, drew attention to his
shifting fidelity to political patrons.[16] With full irony, Cassiodorus suggested that Liberius' faithfulness was manifest in the fact that he remained
loyal to Odoacer up to the point when his patron's defeat became
undeniable.[17] Perhaps a greater indictment, Cassiodorus then demonstrated the depth of Liberius' complicity with the Amals by describing
measures that he took as praetorian prefect to settle the Gothic army on
Italian property, for which 'the Roman republic owes its tranquility to the

[14] Cassiodorus, *Variae* 8.17.4, 'quomodo ergo sub puritate non serviant dominis, qui nesciunt
illusisse collegis?'
[15] Cassiodorus, *Variae* 2.15.2, 'Hinc est, quod te magnifici patris meritis aestimatum comitivae
domesticorum vacantis honore provehimus, ut qui es clarus stemmate, splendeas dignitate.'
[16] Cassiodorus, *Variae* 2.16.4, 'Probavimus hominis fidem.'
[17] Cassiodorus, *Variae* 2.16.2–3.

aforementioned Liberius'.[18] It is worth mentioning that Cassiodorus generally reserved addresses to the Senate for offices of higher distinction than an appointment as *comes domesticorum*, particularly since this appointment was only titular and internal to the palatine court.[19] Other letters of the Liberius 'dossier' similarly insinuate the investment that the statesman had made in the Amal regime, bringing his duplicity into higher relief. Letter 3.35 confirming a property settlement made on behalf of Romulus Augustus certainly advertised an association that ran counter to the patronage he had received from Odoacer.[20] The issue of Liberius' loyalty appears again in letter 8.6, where Athalaric asked him to formally pledge the fidelity of Gaul to the Goths in his capacity as the praetorian prefect of that region. And finally, in the letter announcing Cassiodorus' appointment as praetorian prefect of Italy, which expands into an elaborate panegyric to Amalasuntha, Cassiodorus generously recounted the rewards that Liberius had received for his service to the Amals.[21] Given the nature of the mission to Constantinople that had provided Liberius with his opportunity to defect, a letter featuring the virtues of Amalasuntha and the benefits of Liberius' service to the Amals delivered a pointed indictment against Liberius' perfidy.

The *Variae* also seem to colour the reputation of Albinus with a particular light, probably owing to his close association with the fate of Boethius. Interestingly, the *Variae* offer a picture of Albinus as someone who had often assumed the role of patronage for others. Letters 1.20 and 1.33 request Albinus to assume the patronage of the Green faction and to preserve public order at the spectacles at Rome. Similarly, the *Variae* portray Albinus as the sponsor of a building project that would renovate a portion of the Forum Romanum for the benefit of the lower classes living in the area and as a patron providing legal defence for a Roman physician harried by lawsuits.[22] In contradiction to the *De consolatione*, where Albinus figures as the obscure and defenceless object of Boethius' sense of moral duty and obligation, the *Variae* demonstrate that Albinus

---

[18] Cassiodorus, *Variae* 2.16.6, 'debet ergo Romana res publica et memorato Liberio tranquillitatem suam, qui nationibus tam praeclaris tradidit studia caritatis'; cf. Barnish, *Cassiodorus*, 28–30.

[19] Cassiodorus, *Variae* 2.15.2. Compare to other appointments addressed to the Senate: 1.4, the patriciate; 1.13, mastership of the offices; 1.43, the urban prefecture; 2.3, the consulship; 3.6, the patriciate; 3.12, the urban prefecture; 4.4, count of the patrimony; 4.16, president of the Senate; 5.4, quaestorship; 5.22, secretary of records; 5.41, count of the sacred largesse; 8.10, the patriciate; 8.14, quaestorship; 8.17, count of sacred largesse; 8.19, quaestorship; 8.22, the patriciate; 9.23, consulship; 9.25, praetorian prefecture.

[20] Ruggini, 'Nobilita', 77 and 93–5.   [21] Cassiodorus, *Variae* 11.1.16–17.

[22] Cassiodorus, *Variae* 1.20 and 1.33, concerning Albinus and the Greens; 4.30, concerning the renovation of the Forum Romanum; 4.41, to defend the physician Johannus.

had himself been so adept at representing the interests of the subaltern that the Amal court had frequently referred clients to his custodianship.

The treatment that Symmachus received in the *Variae* was considerably more calculated. Symmachus never held an office that could be considered close collusion with the Amal regime. Even under Odoacer, his consulship in 485 was a diplomatic gesture to the eastern imperial court where Symmachus maintained close contacts. Nonetheless, his portrayal in the *Variae* assumes definite intimacy between the Anicii and the palatine court. The first letter mentioning Symmachus requests that several patrician intermediaries investigate claims made by Symmachus and Festus against another patrician (Paulinus).[23] The interest of the letter seems to be in ending the controversy before the reputations of patrician litigants suffer. Similarly, letter 4.22 asks Symmachus to serve on a panel with four other patricians to judge the accusation of sorcery against Basilius and Praetextatus. Such letters could be understood in the context of the Amal court's interest in managing the balance of prestige among the senatorial elite where competition had historically been a source of disorder at Rome. However, several other letters insinuate a deeper level of collusion with the Amal regime. Containing an extended disquisition concerning manifestations of parental duty in nature, *Variae* 2.14 orders Symmachus to arrest and bring to trial a certain Romulus accused of murdering his father. The jurisdiction that Symmachus would have in such matters is dubious, particularly when other letters of the *Variae* delegate such missions to agents of the Amal court such as *comites* or *saiones*. Nor is a relationship between Symmachus and Romulus offered other than the former's sense of justice, 'Thus we have chosen your probity, since you would not be able to spare the cruel, not when it is a kind of piety to confound those who are shown to have involved themselves in crimes against the order of nature.'[24] The next letter (4.6) offers an additional dimension to Symmachus' interaction with the Amal court, requiring that he sequester at Rome the young sons of a senator (Valerianus) currently acting as the Amal ambassador to the Vandalic court. The letter makes it clear that senatorial children were political hostages at Rome whose confinement was enforced by other members of the Senate. The *Variae* demonstrate how a senator such as Symmachus, rather than being detached from and unblemished by the Amal

---

[23] Cassiodorus, *Variae* 1.23.
[24] Cassiodorus, *Variae* 2.14.5, 'Quia ideo elegimus mores vestros, quia crudelibus parcere non potestis, quando genus pietatis est in illos distringere, qui contra naturae ordinem sceleratis se docentur actionibus miscuisse'; cf. Barnish, *Cassiodorus*, 27–8.

government, colluded with Ravenna's wishes even when not bound by the obligations of public office.

The most famous letter directed to Symmachus in the *Variae* is the one that offers the most studied rebuttal of the illustrious patrician's reputation. Letter 4.51 was directed to Symmachus with a request to restore the ageing fabric of the Theatre of Pompey. Unlike other letters concerning elite patronage of the urban environment (such as 4.30 to Albinus), this letter does not respond to a request from a patron to under-take public construction. Instead, 4.51 directs Symmachus to assume the responsibility for a rather vague reason that may conceal an indictment of Symmachus' overgrown influence:

Since you will have thus devoted your attention to private buildings, so that you might behold a kind of city to have been made in your own home, it is right that you should be known to have clothed Rome in its own marvels, which you have adorned with the pleasantness of homes.[25]

The statement suggests the transgression of boundaries between pub-lic and private as might befit Amal suspicions of Anicii connections in Constantinople. The letter then continues with one of the lengthiest digressions in the collection on the likeness of a theatre to the natural world and on the development of the arts practised in the theatre. In the course of elaborating on the subject, the letter points out that as a man versed in the arts, Symmachus was the most suitable for the appoint-ment: 'Buildings indicate your character, since no man is acknowledged for being attentive to them, except one who is found the most steeped in their nature.'[26] The statement correlates the nature of the building project with the character of the patron. This is significant because it quickly becomes clear from the letter that the history of theatre arts was to be understood as one of continuous moral decline. From tragedy and comedy to pantomime and finally the mime, the letter creates a prob-lematic space in which to judge both the reputation of the monument and that of its proposed patron:

Here the subsequent age has dragged this to vice, mixing the invention of the ancients with obscenities, and impelled what was discovered for the sake of honourable delight to the bodily pleasures of rash minds. The Romans, inanely incorporating these rites, just as other customs, into their republic, founded an

---

[25] Cassiodorus, *Variae* 4.51.1, 'Cum privatis fabricis ita studueris, ut in laribus propriis quaedam moenia fecisse videaris, dignum est, ut Romam, quam domuum pulchritudine decorasti, in suis miraculis continere noscaris'; cf. Barnish, *Cassiodorus*, 79–82.

[26] Cassiodorus, *Variae* 4.51.2, 'Mores tuos fabricae loquuntur, quia nemo in illis diligens agnoscitur, nisi qui et in suis sensibus ornatissimus invenitur.'

edifice conceived from a lofty idea and wondrous generosity. It is rather from this that Pompey is not undeservingly believed to have been called the Great.[27]

The letter maintains a tone that is consistent with respect to the distrust that the Amal court had for public spectacles.[28] The *formula* for appointing a tribune of spectacles (*tribunus voluptatem*) clearly assumes that the post is degraded by the nature of public entertainment:

Although arts of the slippery sort would seem removed from honourable habits and the wandering life of actors would seem prone to bring forth dissoluteness, nonetheless antiquity has provided [them] a governess, so that they may not give way to every vice when they endure a judge of those affairs . . . Let this business be tempered by a kind of law, as if nobility could command the ignoble, and those who ignore the road of correct living might live by some measure of rule.[29]

Whether Symmachus actually received the letter pertaining to the Theatre of Pompey must be doubted. The hint of accusation and the association between the character of the would-be patron and a degraded profession was an insult only thinly veiled by the claim to shared participation within elite intellectual culture. With its clearly satirical construction, the letter's reference to Pompeius Magnus would have also invited consideration concerning that man's significance in history – civil strife at Rome, extended military contest between the eastern and western Mediterranean and the assassination of Rome's first emperor.

THE CONSTRUCTED MEMORY OF BOETHIUS

The manner in which the *Variae* interact with the *memoria* of Boethius seems similarly designed to demonstrate not only a shared cultural background between the Amal court and Boethius, but also Boethius' involvement in the Amal regime and the deep trust that Theoderic's court had

---

[27] Cassiodorus, *Variae* 4.51.11–12, 'Ubi aetas subsequens miscens lubrica priscorum inventa traxit ad vitia et quod honestae causa delectationis repertum est, ad voluptates corporeas praecipitatis mentibus impulerunt. Hos ritus Romani sicut ceteras culturas ad suam rem publicam inutiliter trahentes aedificium alta cogitatione conceptum magnanimitate mirabili condiderunt. Unde non inmerito creditur Pompeius hinc potius Magnus fuisse vocitatus.'

[28] For a profile of the various difficulties caused by public spectacle, Cassiodorus, *Variae* 1.20, 1.27, 1.30–33, 1.44, 3.39, 3.51, 5.25, 5.42.

[29] Cassiodorus, *Variae* 7.10.1, 'Quamvis artes lubricae honestis moribus sint remotae et histrionum vita vaga videatur efferri posse licentia, tamen moderatrix providit antiquitas, ut in totum non effluerunt, cum et ipsae iudicem sustinerent. Amministranda est enim sub quadam disciplina exhibitio voluptatum. Tenet scaenicos si non verus, vel umbratilis ordo iudicii. Temperentur et haec legum qualitate negotia, quasi honestas imperet inhonestis, et quibusdam regulis vivant, qui viam rectae conversationis ignorant.'

invested in him.[30] Similar to letter 4.51 to Symmachus, the letters to Boethius in the *Variae* were, in fact, fictive elaborations loaded with rhetorical strategy.[31] The dossier of Boethian letters follows a pattern consistent with the rhetorical purpose of the *Ordo generis* and demonstrates how Cassiodorus responded to the potential threat of political enemies at Justinian's court. They also provide insight into how the Constantinopolitan milieu shaped the composition of a collection of letters generally assumed to reflect the cultural and political context of Italy in the early sixth century.

Cassiodorus addressed three letters to Boethius in the name of Theoderic.[32] These letters provide some of the most elaborate disquisitions present in the collection, digressions that have more to do with demonstrating Theoderic's affability as a patron of the arts than with any real administrative function. Two of the letters to Boethius (1.45 and 2.40) request that he arrange expensive gifts for diplomatic envoys to present to the Burgundian court of Gundobad and the Merovingian court of Clovis. In each of these letters, Cassiodorus addressed Boethius as *patricius*, an honorary title usually awarded only after the completion of high office.[33] This presents a particular problem because, at least in the case of letters 1.45 and 2.40, the circumstance supposedly requiring the letters is datable only before Boethius' tenure in offices that would have warranted conferring patrician status upon him (that is, his consulship in 510 and master of offices from 522 to 523).[34] However, if these two letters are indeed genuine, they could not represent diplomatic activities occurring later than 507. Diplomatic relations with the Burgundian and Merovingian courts collapsed with the death of the Visigothic king Alaric II in 507, after which the Ostrogoths were engaged in a war against both Clovis and Gundobad to further Amal ambitions in southern Gaul. It is doubtful that Theoderic would bother to satisfy Gundobad's curiosity for water clocks and Clovis' passion for the cithar in such circumstances; a genuine diplomatic context for these letters could have occurred only before 507.[35]

The sequence of other letters in the *Variae* supports a narrative that emphasizes this break in diplomatic relations, particularly the terminal letters concluding Book 2 and commencing Book 3. The final letters of Book 2 (letter 2.40 to Boethius and letter 2.41 to Clovis on the same

---

[30] Similarly, Pizzani, 'Lettere', 141–61.   [31] As treated in Bjornlie, 'A reappraisal', 150–2.
[32] Cassiodorus, *Variae* 1.10, 1.45, 2.40.
[33] On the patriciate in the fifth and sixth centuries, Mathisen, 'Patricians', 35–49.
[34] This problem first noted in Bjornlie, 'A reappraisal', 150–2.
[35] On the date of these letters, Shanzer, 'Two clocks', 245–8.

subject) express cordial relations between Theoderic and Clovis, an affability maintained by the bonds of marriage that tied the two houses.[36] Book 3, however, commences with a letter advising Alaric II of the Visigoths (another marriage alliance) not to engage Clovis in war. The three letters that follow attempt to warn members of a diplomatic consortium (Franks, Burgundians, Herules, Warni and Thuringians) about impending military intervention in Gaul.[37] Cassiodorus emphasized the conclusiveness of these last diplomatic overtures with a subsequent series of letters pertaining to the reorganization of southern Gallic provinces that occurred under Ostrogothic military occupation.[38] After 508, the conditions that warranted letters 1.45 and 2.40 simply did not exist.[39] It is certainly possible to posit that the court at Ravenna made diplomatic overtures of the kind represented in these letters prior to the military actions of 507, but attempting to claim the authenticity of these letters in an earlier context would necessitate placing weighty diplomatic writing in the hands of Cassiodorus prior to his having held the office of quaestor.

Evidence from within the *Variae* also suggests that Boethius could not have had the title *patricius* before holding a suitably elevated public office. Other letters of appointment in the *Variae* award the patriciate only after conspicuous office holding – Cassiodorus' father after a governorship and praetorian prefecture, Inportunus after the consulship, Cyprian after a succession of military and minor civil posts culminating in the *comitiva sacrarum largitionum*, and Tuluin after serving as *comes* and possibly *magister militum* on several campaigns.[40] Boethius is not known to have held public office prior to 510, when he became consul, and Cassiodorus' use of *patricius* in letters pertaining to events prior to 510 is highly suspect.[41] If Boethius held patrician status in 507 when the diplomatic letters would have been relevant, it did not impress Ennodius of Pavia, whose letters fail to acknowledge Boethius as having patrician status.[42] Ennodius did recognize Boethius as *patricius* in the *Paraenesis Didascalia*, but this was

---

36 Cassiodorus, *Variae* 2.41.1, 'Gloriosa quidem vestrae virtutis affinitate gratulamur'; Theoderic was married to Clovis' sister, Audefleda.

37 Cassiodorus, *Variae* 3.1, to Alaric of the Visigoths; 3.2, to Gundobad of the Burgundians; 3.3, to unspecified rulers of the Herulians, Varni, and Thuringians; 4.4, to Clovis of the Franks.

38 Cassiodorus, *Variae* 3.16, 3.18, 3.32, 3.41, 3.42, 3.43, 3.44, 4.5, 4.19, 4.21, 4.26.

39 On the Ostrogothic war in southern Gaul from 507 to 511, Wolfram, *Goths*, 243–46.

40 Cassiodorus, *Variae* 1.3.5–6, on the offices of Cassiodorus' father; 3.5.5, the consulship of Inportunus; 8.10.4–6, the campaigns of Tuluin; 8.21.5, the offices of Cyprian; on Tuluin as *comes* and *magister militum*, Amory, *Ostrogothic Italy*, 425–6.

41 Boethius became consul in 510 and *magister officiorum* in 522.

42 Ennodius refers to Boethius with a number of appellative creations, *Epistulae* 6.6.1, 'magnitudo tua'; 7.13.2, 'emendatissime hominum'; 8.37.2, 'eminentia vestra'; 8.37.3 and 8.40.1, 'culmen vestrum'.

a work written after Boethius' consulship.[43] Even more problematic, Mommsen noted that in the best manuscript containing the *Didascalia*, the copyist had written *patricius* above the line, indicating that the attribution was possibly a later interpolation.[44] It is, furthermore, questionable whether the Ostrogothic court would entrust sensitive diplomatic matters to Boethius, who at that time was a young senator untested in public life.[45]

Only letter 1.10 of the *Variae* seems justified in referring to Boethius' patrician status. It asks Boethius to intervene in abuses concerning coin payments to the palace guard, something that would have fallen under his competence as *magister officiorum*, by which time Boethius may have received the honorary title as a result of his new palatine post.[46] Unfortunately, the letter studiously avoids drawing attention to Boethius' official capacity. It is less likely that Boethius would have been asked to intervene in financial matters as consul in 510. The arena for the honorary pageantry associated with the consulship is more properly located in Rome, not Ravenna, and even if the mint at Rome had been responsible for issuing payments to the palace guard at Ravenna (which is highly unlikely), the matter would have fallen under the purview of the urban prefect.[47] If authentic, the letter must refer to action taken by Boethius while serving as master of offices in 522 or 523, but even this authentication is problematic. Boethius' short tenure as master of offices fell during a period when Cassiodorus did not hold an office that would warrant his penning letters for the Amal chancery. Since Boethius could have been involved with the mint only as *magister officiorum*, this means either that Cassiodorus composed the letter while serving in an ex officio capacity at Ravenna, or that he wrote the letter after the fact and based it on knowledge of a case involving Boethius, or that the letter was a completely fictive intervention in the documentary record of the chancery intended to appeal to the memory of Boethius' academic interests. Whatever the case may be, Cassiodorus deliberately positioned letter 1.10 in the first book of letters among others that he supposedly wrote as quaestor, politely suppressing the memory of Boethius' tenure as master of offices and quite possibly Cassiodorus' presence at court during the trials leading to Boethius' execution.

---

[43] On the date, *PLRE II*, 234.   [44] Mommsen, *MGH AA XII*, 490.

[45] Shanzer, 'Ennodius, Boethius', 186–95, suggests that Boethius led a dissolute lifestyle in addition to his reputation as a scholar, something that may not have inspired confidence at a governmental level.

[46] On the competence of the *magister officiorum* over palatine personnel, Cassiodorus, *Variae* 6.6.1.

[47] On the Ostrogothic mints at Rome, Ravenna and Milan, Hendy, 'Barbarian coinages', 29–78; Arslan, 'Monetazione', 17–59.

In addition to the problematic use of *patricius*, the two diplomatic letters addressed to Boethius present other problems of authenticity. The arrangement of these letters follows an epistolary pattern seen throughout the *Variae*. It is often the case that Cassiodorus positioned diplomatic letters at the beginning and end of a book in order to 'bracket' letters concerning the internal administration of Italy with letters demonstrating Amal foreign policy. It was a strategy for arranging letters that lent Amal governance a semblance of *imperium*.[48] Of the diplomatic letters included in the collection, none actually names the envoys involved. The Amal court is known (from sources other than the *Variae*) to have employed men of outstanding qualifications on such occasions – Ennodius, Liberius, several popes, and a number of Italian bishops.[49] In the *Variae*, however, Cassiodorus simply denotes the legates as *ille et ille* (so-and-so).[50] This is not to suggest that Cassiodorus invented the diplomacy that structured relations between the Amal court and neighbouring western courts; steady diplomatic communication was doubtlessly necessary for the array of political marriages that provided the Amals with leverage among the Visigoths, Franks, Vandals and Thuringians. The substitution of *ille et ille* for the names of envoys does, however, call into question how and for what purpose Cassiodorus reconstructed the event of each diplomatic overture. Cassiodorus' use of *ille et ille* occurs not only with reference to legates, but also with indiction dates, the names of properties and the identity of various officials at the Ostrogothic court. A number of explanations have been offered for this curious habit.[51] It could be assumed that the use of *ille et ille* corresponds to Cassiodorus' wish to provide *formulae* for future officials. However, when compared to the wholesale use of *ille* in a true formulary, such as the eighth-century formulary of Marculf, Cassiodorus' lacunae are perplexingly specific.[52] Perhaps the most compelling suggestion is that he did not know the

<hr/>

[48] Cassiodorus, *Variae* 1.1, to Anastasius; 1.46, to Gundobad; 2.1, to Anastasius; 2.41, to Clovis; 3.1, to Alaric; 3.2, to Gundobad; 3.3, to the Herulians, Warni and Thuringians; 3.4, to Clovis; 4.1, to Hermanfrid and the Thuringians; 4.2, to the Herulians; 5.1, to the Warni; 5.2, to the Haesti; 5.43 and 5.44, to Trasimund and the Vandals; 8.1, to Justin; 9.1, to Hilderic and the Vandals; 10.1, to Justinian; 10.2, to Justinian.

[49] Cf. Gillett, *Envoys*, *passim*.

[50] Cassiodorus, *Variae* 1.1.4, 1.46.1, 2.41.3, 3.1.4, 3.2.3, 3.3.4, 3.4.4, 4.2.4, 5.1.3, 5.2.1, 5.43.4, 5.44.4, 8.1.5, 9.1.3, 9.16.3, 10.8.2, 10.14.5, 10.16.1, 10.17.1, 10.20.5, 10.22.1, 10.22.3, 10.23.2, 10.24.1, 10.32.4, 10.33.1, 10.35.1, 11.14.6.

[51] O'Donnell, *Cassiodorus*, 93, that it lent the collection a timeless quality; Conso, 'Formula', 280–1, that Cassiodorus considered these names of no consequence to posterity.

[52] The Formulary of Marculf, *MGH Form.*, substitutes every person, place and document with *ille*, including the name of the king, 'ille rex', and that of the subject of the letter, 'vir apostolicus ille'.

specific information.[53] Attempting to reconstruct an epistolary record
of the Amal regime over a span of thirty years, and quite possibly lacking access to original documents at the time, Cassiodorus relied on his
innate capacity to elaborate and reconstruct as he saw fit. The use of *ille
et ille* may have simply allowed him to avoid the embarrassment of later
encountering individuals, perhaps in Constantinople, who might recol-
lect the facts a bit more precisely. But that same lack of command over
the events also provided Cassiodorus with enough latitude to reinvent
particular moments embedded within an epistolary narrative.

The cultural content of the Boethian letters deserves attention as well.
In the case of the first letter (1.10), Cassiodorus established a pattern for
most of the extensive disquisitions in the collection. After a *proemium*
introducing the subject of the letter as an abstracted principle, the letter
then restates the problem in more concrete terms, when it is learned
that the palace guards have complained about payments received in adulterated coin. The nature of the complaint presents Cassiodorus with an
opportunity to expatiate on the purity and perfection of arithmetic and
the antiquity of the principle behind the denominations of coinage. The
disquisition almost disregards the real problem of fraudulent payments
to the palace guard; only the last line of the letter offers a solution,
'Therefore, see to it that the custodian of the coffers should hold his
own just practices and that what we intend for those deserving well,
they should obtain by uncorrupted reward.'[54] The real subject of the
letter is Boethius' eminence in liberal studies. Letter 1.10 allowed Cassiodorus to court Boethius' reputation as a scholar through the voice of
Theoderic. Any recrimination faced by Cassiodorus for the execution
of Boethius would have been associated with the posthumous reputation of Theoderic. By demonstrating affiliation between Theoderic and
Boethius at a cultural level, the implication of a 'barbarized' court at
Ravenna becomes more difficult to sustain.

Letters 1.45 and 2.40 provide similar opportunities to extol Boethius'
learning in the liberal arts and, by responding to his learned reputation positively, to construct a cultural alignment between the memory
of Boethius and the reputations of Theoderic, Cassiodorus and the Italian palatine bureaucracy.[55] Letter 1.45 celebrates the prestige Boethius

[53] Garzya, 'Cassiodoro', 118, in reference to Cassiodorus' use of *ille* in place of the name of a
particular Greek text.
[54] Cassiodorus, *Variae* 1.10.7, 'Providete itaque, ut et arbiter arcae habeat iustas consuetudines suas,
et quod bene meritis impendimus, incorrupto munere consequantur'; cf. Barnish, *Cassiodorus*,
12–14.
[55] Cassiodorus, *Variae* 1.45.3, 'Hoc te multa eruditione saginatum ita nosse didicimus, ut artes, quas
exercent vulgariter nescientes, in ipso disciplinarum fonte potaveris.'

enjoyed from intellectual habits learned from the Greek tradition which, in turn, illuminated the literary works that Boethius gave to a grateful Italy.[56] The letter then matches the reputation of Theoderic (and Cassiodorus) to that of Boethius by elaborating on the very matters in which Boethius found his fame – in this case a digression on natural history, astrology and engineering.[57] An identical compositional structure is found in letter 2.40, where Theoderic asks Boethius to select a citharist to accompany legates to the Frankish court of Clovis. Important details such as the payment of the citharist and whether the citharist should be considered a permanent 'gift' to Clovis (a slave) or whether the citharist should only accompany the embassy for a single performance are not mentioned. Equally curious, the letters proposed these lavishly expensive arrangements because the kingdoms of the Franks and Burgundians apparently lacked such refinements. Letters, however, from the collection of Sidonius Apollinaris make it clear that the water clock was not an unfamiliar piece of technology in Gaul and one must assume that the presumed absence of musicians in northern Gaul was a fiction.[58] Instead, the real object of the letter is the alignment of Boethius' reputation for learning in music with the appreciation for this discipline at Theoderic's court and Cassiodorus' ability to expound at length on the topic.

Even by the standards of the *Variae*, the Boethian disquisitions are unusual in that they do not support an administrative or legal decision. The correlation between digressive, encyclopaedic topics and administrative sentences forms a rhetorical strategy throughout the collection and Cassiodorus seems to have made an exception to that rule in the case of Boethius. However, what should be noted is that where the digressions do not support the narrative of the letter, the digressive material has become the purpose of the letter. That the digressive material drew heavily from the works of Boethius bears keeping in mind. In discussing music in letter 2.40, Cassiodorus entertained the same consideration of the fanciful and mythological aspects of the discipline as Boethius in *De institutione musica*. By contrast, Boethius chose a more sober approach for his *De institutione arithmetica*, where he strictly avoided such material when discussing mathematics, and Cassiodorus' treatment of the subject in letter 1.45 shows identical restraint.[59] The parallel in tenor with which

---

[56] Cassiodorus, *Variae* 1.45.3, 'sic enim Atheniensium scholas longe positus introisti, sic palliatorum choris miscuisti togam, ut Graecorum dogmata doctrinam feceris esse Romanam'; 1.45.3, 'deducens ad Romuleos senatores quicquid Cecropidae mundo fecerant singulare'.

[57] Cassiodorus, *Variae* 1.45.5–11.

[58] On *clepsydrae* (waterclocks), Sidonius Apollinaris, *Epistulae* 2.9.6 and 2.13.4.

[59] Pizzani, 'Lettere', 151; also on Cassiodorus' knowledge of music, Fridh, '*Variae* II.40', 43–51.

Cassiodorus discussed these disciplines was a conscious and conspicuous attempt to demonstrate a common cultural, and by extension moral, sensibility shared between Cassiodorus and Boethius.

Of course, the obvious rhetorical purpose for focusing attention on Boethius in the first two books of the *Variae* is that doing so effectively removed Cassiodorus from a narrative association with Boethius' condemnation. The entire structure of the *Variae* obscures Cassiodorus' presence in 524, the year of Boethius' execution and the second year of Cassiodorus' tenure as master of offices under Theoderic. Cassiodorus rarely supplies material (such as indiction dates) that would allow assigning letters to a particular date. The omission of dates becomes even more curious given the overt pretence of the *Variae* to representing Roman legal culture. The *Theodosian Code* specifically nullified any legal document lacking the annotation of day and year.[60] By contrast, only letters of the *Variae* dealing with financial matters supply indiction dates.

Mommsen rightly suspected that the bulk of letters in Book 5 pertain to Cassiodorus' tenure as master of offices from 523 to 526, the last of Theoderic's reign. Interestingly, the first and last two letters of Book 5 originated from Cassiodorus' quaestorship (507–11), not his mastership of the offices. Book 5 begins with diplomatic letters to the Warni and the Haesti which may have originally pertained to the solidification of Theoderic's foreign policy during either the conflict with Anastasius or the war in Gaul.[61] Similarly, the last two letters of Book 5 treat the diplomatic failure and escalating antagonism between the courts of Theoderic and Trasimund, the Vandal king. This was a specific moment that an audience familiar with the events of Theoderic's reign would have identified as pertaining to Cassiodorus' quaestorship.[62] Following Book 5, the 'historical narrative' of the *Variae* is broken by two books of *formulae*, after which Cassiodorus resumes in Book 8 with letters from the reign of Athalaric. Cassiodorus purposefully dislocated the letters attributable to his exercise of authority as *magister officiorum* during Theoderic's last years; the *Variae* unwillingly bear testimony to a shuffling of epistolary files that further removed Cassiodorus from connection with the death of Boethius.

---

[60] *Codex Theodosianus* 1.1.1.
[61] Compare Cassiodorus, *Variae* 3.3 to the Thuringians, Herulians and Warni, 5.1 to the Warni and 5.2 to the Haesti.
[62] Wolfram, *Goths*, 244–5, that troubles between the Ostrogoths and Vandals broke out in 511 as a result of Theoderic's intervention in Gaul; Martindale, *PLRE I*, 1117, also locates the rupture pertaining to these letters in 511.

But it was not enough to avert personal culpability for the deaths of Boethius and Symmachus. The *De consolatione* had portrayed a palatine government that was utterly incapable of supporting the public careers of men grounded in ethical wisdom. Indeed, Boethius complained that Wisdom itself had been forced to cower in hiding under the assault of a corrupt government.[63] In the hands of political detractors at the eastern imperial court, the indictment of the *De consolatione* could be used to obstruct the return to Ravenna of the palatine elite formerly indebted to Amal service. Thus it is in the context of attempting to rectify the reputation of state service at the broadest cultural level that the *Variae* show such interest in representing philosophical wisdom. More specifically, the *Variae* show sensitivity to Neoplatonic conceptions of political wisdom. It is highly probable that the events leading to Boethius' downfall were shaded by his attachment to Neoplatonic teaching and its visibility in his various works and that Cassiodorus fashioned the *Variae* to deflect an accusation of ignorance in such matters against the palatine elite.[64] Like the accusation of sorcery levelled against Apuleius in the late second century, the charges made by informers under Valentinian and Valens in the fourth century and Justinian's persecution of the Hellenes, such claims could be used to demonstrate the boorishness or tyrannical predilections of the accuser. The charge of sorcery levelled against Boethius in the course of his trial probably did take advantage of a common misunderstanding of a philosopher's interest in natural history.[65] Procopius seems to suggest that Boethius and Symmachus were denounced by those jealous of their eminence in learning, perhaps indicating the suspicions of the philosophically 'unenlightened'.[66] In an earlier treatise on the Trinity, Boethius decried the resentment and misunderstanding aroused by his studies among less-learned men:

Wherever I turn my eyes, they fall on either the apathy of the dullard or the jealousy of the shrewd, and a man who should cast his thoughts before such unnatural creatures of men, I will not say to consider but rather to trample under

---

[63] Boethius, *De consolatione philosophiae* 1.3.15–17, 'Nunc enim primum censes apud inprobos mores lacessitam periculis esse sapientiam?'

[64] On the debt of Boethius' works to Neoplatonism, Chadwick, *Boethius*, 16–22, 120–73, 225–47; Crabbe, 'Literary design', 237–41; Moorhead, 'Boethius' life', 22–32; Magee, 'Boethius'.

[65] For the episode concerning Apuleius, *Apologia* 3 and 36–7; for accusations against philosophers in the reigns of Valentinian and Valens, Ammianus Marcellinus, *Res Gestae* 29.1.41, 29.2.4, 29.2.6; more generally on this, Barnish, 'Martianus Capella', 105–8, on intellectual syncretism; Bowersock, *Hellenism*, 9–12, on the synonymous association of Greek culture with paganism; Lenski, *Failure of Empire*, 211–34, for an examination of the 'magic' trials under Valentinian and Valens.

[66] Procopius, *Wars* 5.1.32–34.

foot, would seem to bring discredit on the study of divinity. So I purposely use brevity and wrap up the ideas I draw from the deep questionings of philosophy in new and unaccustomed words such as speak only to you and to myself, that is, if you ever look at them.[67]

To an uninitiated audience, the 'new and unaccustomed words' drawn 'from the deep questionings of philosophy' could have been misinterpreted as the arcane linguistic paraphernalia of 'magical' practices.[68] Similarly, in a prefatory letter to another treatise, Boethius laments the outcome of such misunderstanding: 'I was, I admit, much put out, and being overwhelmed by the mob of ignorant speakers, I held my peace, fearing lest I should be rightly set down as insane if I held out for being sane among those madmen.'[69] Boethius addressed both of these prefatory letters to his father-in-law, Symmachus, who had himself presided over a sorcery trial involving fellow senatorial elite.[70]

Given the education possessed by Boethius and Symmachus, which they shared with their closest associates and which distinguished them from men of lesser social means, it becomes easy to understand how too deep an interest in Platonic philosophy could lead to suspicion and estrangement. Elite tolerance of and interaction with the classical intellectual tradition, at least in the realm of philosophical ideals, could leave members of the nobility vulnerable to accusations. The populace of Rome in the sixth century certainly proved itself more than capable of demonstrating violent intolerance for the cause of orthodoxy. One of Theoderic's harshest rebukes against the Senate resulted from the inability of the senators to prevent an attack on the Jewish synagogue in Rome.[71] The periodic 'discovery' of Manichaeans in the city of Rome seems to have been a common outlet for social and political tensions, spoken of with formulaic regularity in the *Liber Pontificalis*, including several instances in the sixth century.[72] Of the three instances occurring during Theoderic's reign, one took place in the time of the contested papacy of the bishop Symmachus (generally in the same period as the accusation of sorcery against Basilius and Praetextatus), and another occurred during the episcopacy of Hormisdas, in the same period as Boethius' trial. Papal elections had long proven to be opportunities for the

---

[67] Boethius, *De trinitate, praefatio* 13–20, trans. Stewart, Rand and Tester, *LCL*, 5; on this, Kirkby, 'Scholar', 57.
[68] On this, Brown, 'Sorcery', 126–7.
[69] Boethius, *Contra Eutychen et Nestorium, praefatio* 31–3, trans. Stewart, Rand and Tester, *LCL*, 75.
[70] Cassiodorus, *Variae* 4.22.   [71] Cassiodorus, *Variae* 4.43.
[72] *Liber Pontificalis* 33.2 (Miltiades), 40.2 (Siricius), 41.2 (Anastasius), 51.1 (Gelasius), 53.5 (Symmachus), and 54.9 (Hormisdas).

senatorial elite to further partisan politics by prescribing orthodoxy and proscribing rivals. Such scenarios had been evident from the time of the contested election of Damasus in the fourth century to that of the bishop Symmachus in the late fifth century. It would be difficult to suggest the extent to which an uninitiated audience could differentiate between Manichaeanism and Neoplatonic teachings, but there may be grounds to suggest that some similarities between the two could have been exploited by a party with hostile motivations. Both Neoplatonism and Manichaeanism shared a deep interest in natural history and astrology, interests closely associated with divinatory and magical practices.[73] Most importantly, Manichaeanism and Neoplatonism share a common basic separation between the material and spiritual, regardless of the fact that each system resolves the outcome of that separation for the individual in different ways.[74] Furthermore, most public officials were incapable of identifying Manichaeans doctrinally and by the sixth century the sect had become a generic epithet for heterodoxy, especially associated with sorcery through its origins in the near east.[75] Even Pope Symmachus was accused of Manichaeanism by Emperor Anastasius, inspiring an *Apologeticus adversus Anastasium Augustum* and probably provoking the Pope's own persecution of so-called Manichaeans.[76] The very diversity of Manichaean practices and tenets at Rome may have contributed to its becoming a blanket heterodoxy for anything doctrinally provocative.[77] Attempts of the sixth-century church to control or ban pervasive Christian practices such as the *sortes sanctorum* (Christian divination) reveal how difficult it was to prescribe a uniform religious life for Christians.[78] In Rome, where religious primacy was becoming a defining characteristic of the city, it was probably more expedient and desirable to identify the unreformed as Manichaean than as failed Christian.

Additionally, the accusation against Albinus had already been prejudiced by a religious dispute concerning doctrinal heterodoxy.[79] On those grounds, Boethius' decision to defend Albinus would have inevitably drawn his own interest in doctrinal matters into question. The issue of magic could have only clouded deliberation at Boethius' trial and it seems likely that, provided the insubstantial nature of the accusation

---

[73] Lieu, *Manichaeism*, 177–9.
[74] On Boethius' handling of this distinction, Starnes, 'Boethius', 27–38.
[75] Lieu, *Manichaeism*, 125–7, on the inability of officials to identify Manichaeans; 142–79, on the association of Manichaeanism with sorcery; 207–18, on the use of 'Manichaean' as a generic label for heterodoxy.
[76] Duchesne, *Liber Pontificalis*, 265, note 14.   [77] Lim, 'Unity', 240–8.
[78] Klingshirn, '*Sortes sanctorum*', 77–130.   [79] *Collectio Avellana* 173.

of treason, those opposed to senatorial involvement at the Ostrogothic court sought more condemning material to stack against Boethius. The lingering presence of 'pagan' interests at Rome during this period would have afforded opponents of senatorial involvement at the Amal court ample opportunity for such an accusation.[80] Cassiodorus was certainly aware of non-Christian traditionalists in Rome.[81] A similar case seems to have been arranged against an earlier *magister officiorum* in 470. A fragment from John of Antioch reports that this official, Romanus, was executed for sorcery. In his *Chronica*, Cassiodorus termed Romanus' offence ambiguously a 'capital crime against the state', illustrating the fine line that separated religious heterodoxy and political treason for the holders of high office.[82]

Symmachus, as the addressee of Boethius' *Tractates*, would logically fall under suspicion by association. The intimate terms in which Boethius described the secrecy that he shared with Symmachus in discussing divine matters in the *Tractates* could not have helped. Even in the *De consolatione*, Boethius insisted on inadvertently implicating his father-in-law:

Besides, the fact that my house hides no guilty secrets deep within, my friendship with good men, and the uprightness of my father-in-law . . . all these protect me against any suspicion of this crime. But they are so wickedly impious that it is actually from you [Lady Philosophy] that they derive their proof of this great charge; I shall appear to have been a close party to such a misdeed precisely because I am steeped in your learning and trained in your ways.[83]

This is all very reminiscent of the false allegations made against Apuleius on account of his philosophical interest in investigating nature and the report of Ammianus Marcellinus on the misunderstanding of philosophical inquiry by officials and the resultant persecution of philosophers.[84] A common thread between Ammianus and the Manichaeans recorded in the *Liber Pontificalis* is the burning of 'dangerous' texts. Ammianus makes it clear that the texts in question were of a philosophical nature, typically treatises of the various liberal arts and law. It is impossible to tell how many of the books heaped and burned before St Peter's doors were actually the doctrine of Mani and how many were extracts of Plato or Aristotle. Like the difference between 'magic' and traditional religious practice, the difference between classical learning and

[80] Chastagnol, *Le Sénat*, 51; Bertolini, *Roma*, 65–7; Pietri, 'Aristocratie', 421–5.
[81] Cassiodorus, *Expositio Psalmorum* 103.13 and 103.16.
[82] Cassiodorus, *Chronica* 1289, 'His conss. Romanus patricius affectans imperium capitaliter est punitus'; discussed in MacGeorge, *Warlords*, 246.
[83] Boethius, *De consolatione philosophiae* 1.4.145–52, trans. Tester, *LCL*, 157.
[84] Ammianus Marcellinus, *Res Gestae* 29.1.41, 29.2.4, 29.2.6.

the arcane could be subjected to various interpretations depending on the manner in which it was presented and depending on the temperament of the audience.[85]

As the following chapters will explain, the pervasive sensitivity of the *Variae* to Neoplatonic conceptions of government and justice was the medium by which the letters communicated the ethical background of palatine elites visible in their daily habits. This presentation responded to the historical circumstances of Boethius' death in which a political audience had proven unable or unwilling to distinguish between an interest in Neoplatonic doctrine and malevolent cultic practice. It was Cassiodorus' intention that the *Variae* transpose the image of a philosophically alert bureaucratic elite over that of the benighted palatine elite of the *De consolatione*. This was all the more imperative because the eastern bureaucratic elite at this time constructed its own ideological contest with Justinian in precisely the same terms as had Boethius – that only elites with the appropriate intellectual background could properly exercise political authority and legal wisdom. The *De consolatione* was deeply indebted to the Neoplatonic ideal of state service.[86] In fact, Boethius' *De consolatione* portrayed Theoderic's court as an antithesis of the philosophical ideals found in the *Dialogue on Political Science*.[87] Where the *Dialogue* attempted to define the best possible type of government in which the ruler was philosophically sensitive and carefully observed hierarchy to prevent conflict between social orders, the description of Theoderic's court in the *De consolatione* focused on internecine rivalry and selfish ambition that was unregulated by the discipline of a wise and just ruler.

On the contrary, Cassiodorus constructed the *Variae* to display not only that the Italian bureaucratic elite had performed service to the state under a philosopher king (Theoderic), but that when the quality of kingship diminished at the Amal court (under Theodahad and Witigis), the bureaucratic elite had maintained its traditional and ethical bearing. It is the genius of the *Variae* that they responded broadly to allegations made against the Amal court in the *De consolatione* and appealed to support from the eastern bureaucratic elite by maintaining the appearance of a disorganized collection of letters. Its 'variousness' provided it with a screen against being perceived as an actively polemical treatise, which in fact it was. A wry comment in the *Historia Augusta* makes clear just how susceptible to scrutiny and suspicion a formal history could be: 'Well

---

[85] On the historical subjectivity of *superstitio*, Markus, *Signs*, 130–3; Bowes, *Private Worship*, 44–8.
[86] Chadwick, *Boethius*, 16–22; Matthews, 'Boethius', 36; cf. Boethius, *De consolatione philosophiae* 1.4.18–25.
[87] Crabbe, 'Literary design', 237–41.

then, write as you will. You will be safer in saying whatever you wish, since you will have as comrades in falsehood those authors whom we admire for the style of their histories.'[88] The seemingly natural disorder of the *Variae* was, in fact, a tessellated historical narrative. The further back the audience stood to take in the whole account, the better the jewelled epistolary fragments revealed a coherent image of state service in Ostrogothic Italy.

---

[88] *Historia Augusta, Vita Aureliani* 2.2, '"Scribe", inquit, "ut libet. Securus quod velis dices, habiturus mendaciorum comites, quos historicae eloquentiae miramur auctores,"' trans. Magie, *LCL*.

PART III

Reading the Variae *as political apologetic*

INTRODUCTION

When Cassiodorus and the remnants of the Amal court arrived in Constantinople, prospects for securing political patronage were poor. The distrustful scrutiny of Justinian's court, the memory of senatorial conflict with the Amals and the presence of other prominent Italian émigrés hostile to the idea of 'Gothic' rule in Italy presented substantial obstacles. With the visible presence of the Anicii and other prominent members of the western senatorial elite in Constantinople, Justinian had little reason to grant concessions to Italian émigrés who had been affiliated with the Amal court at a more intimate level. At the same time, Cassiodorus' introduction to the literary milieu of Constantinople and his interaction with officials of the eastern administration would reveal a far more dynamic political environment than that which had existed in Ravenna. Compared to the court of the Amals, the culture and apparatus of the eastern administration may have indeed seemed 'Byzantine' in the complexity both of its operation and of the loyalties of its personnel. Among other things, Cassiodorus probably came to appreciate that it was the subtlest of critiques that survived to reach the widest audience. Isolated from the highest avenues of political redress at the eastern court, Cassiodorus instead appealed to that faction of the eastern political elite that was dissatisfied with Justinian's regime. By drawing from salient themes of the eastern political discourse and using those themes to construct an ideological portrait of Italy under Amal rule in the *Variae*, Cassiodorus advertised that the western palatine elite had been cut from the same intellectual and moral cloth as the eastern bureaucracy. At stake was the reputation and future political involvement of officials from the former Amal court and the support that they might receive from eastern officials in deciding the kind of government that would take shape at Ravenna after the conclusion of the Gothic War.

In this context, the *Variae* fulfilled the traditional role of a classical history by advancing a model that celebrated the period of Amal governance in Italy. At the same time, by masquerading as an official dossier of daily palatine activities, the *Variae* avoided official censure. The variety of the collection fractured its own concrete ideological statement into hundreds of seemingly innocuous events that revealed a deliberate programme only after a thorough and complete reading. Barnish has already noted that the impression of officialdom and grandeur mattered more than the actual content of the letters and that the deeper, intended meaning of the letters was meant to be 'detected' by an audience sensitive to the exegesis of literature.[1] Given Cassiodorus' later religious vocation and retirement at Vivarium, it is possible to surmise that the political agenda of the *Variae* ultimately failed. Either the political conditions at Constantinople proved too inflexible for Cassiodorus to influence or Cassiodorus' rhetorical strategy proved too abstruse even for an audience weaned on Zosimus and Procopius. Nonetheless, examining the *Variae* as the trace evidence of Cassiodorus' reception and engagement with the political discourse at Constantinople tells much about the interaction of literature and philosophical ideals in the political culture of the sixth century.

The remaining chapters trace the ideological structure of the *Variae* in detail, noting where salient themes contested Justinianic imperial theology and where they spoke to affiliation with the culture of the eastern bureaucracy. The programmatic nature of the political ethos that saturates the *Variae* has already been the subject of much scholarly commentary.[2] The chief contribution of the present interpretation will be in locating the origins of the thematic strands of that ethos in the context of Justinian's highly controversial reign. Traditionalism was certainly commonplace as a core political doctrine in any period or region of Roman and post-Roman history, but the semantics constituting 'tradition' were often determined by the blend of social, political and religious culture that formed an audience's conceptual background. In the case of the *Variae*, the presentation of traditionalism was aimed at contesting the notion from Justinianic propaganda that Italy had become 'barbarized'. More importantly, traditionalism in the *Variae* was structured by concepts strikingly similar to the polemical lines drawn by the traditionalist

[1] Barnish, 'Sacred texts', 368–9.
[2] Löwe, 'Cassiodor', 424–32; Barbieri, 'Cassiodoro', 295–301; Martino, 'Gothorum laus', 31–45; Krautschick, *Cassiodore*; Sirago, 'Goti nelle *Variae*', 179–97; Scivoletto, 'Cassiodoro', 3–24; Lepelley, 'Eloge', 33–47; Barnwell, *Roman West*, 167–9; Barnish, *Cassiodorus*, xxviii–xxix; Giardina, 'Progetto delle *Variae*', 45–76; Heather, 'Ostrogothic Italy', 326–30; Jouanaud, 'Pour qui Cassiodore', 721–41; Tartaglia, 'Elementi', 59–69; Amory, *Ostrogothic Italy*, 43–82; Silvestre, 'Uso politico', 93–105; Kakridi, *Cassiodors Variae*, 24–33; Barnish, 'Roman responses', 7–22; Bjornlie, 'A reappraisal'.

faction of the eastern elite. Taken as a whole, the fragmented comments concerning jurisprudence in the *Variae* articulate a position that contended with the notion of the ruler's right to countermand fixed legal and administrative practice. The keen sensitivity to legal and administrative 'tradition' portrayed in the *Variae* also had a firm basis in Neoplatonic philosophical thought. Articulating legal traditionalism with Neoplatonic concepts advanced the cause of Cassiodorus and his political dependents in two ways: first, it demonstrated that the western palatine elite had maintained the intellectual and ethical norms of the political group from whom they sought support (the eastern bureaucracy); second, portraying the same philosophical grounding that Boethius had espoused as a devotee of Neoplatonic thought refuted the philosopher's claim, rendered immortal in the *De consolatione*, that moral excellence could not co-exist in with palatine service under a king.

Chapter 7

LITERARY ASPECTS OF THE *VARIAE*

THE PREFACES AND AUDIENCE OF THE *VARIAE*

One of the chief obstacles to understanding the purpose of the *Variae* has been the difficulty of establishing a historically viable relationship between Cassiodorus and his intended audience. The frustrating reticence of important contemporary witnesses to Ostrogothic Italy who failed to mention Cassiodorus (authors such as Boethius, Ennodius, Arator and Procopius) has contributed to the impression that Cassiodorus wrote within a literary oubliette, disconnected from a wider audience except as the ghostwriter of briefs from the Amal chancery.[1] In the absence of commentary from external sources which might have shed light on why and for whom Cassiodorus compiled the *Variae*, authorial intent must be unpacked by examining from within the text itself how Cassiodorus anticipated the expectations of his intended audience. That Cassiodorus would have tuned his text to the sensitivities of a particular audience follows the fundamental precepts for writing that any educated author of the classical and late antique periods would have internalized since Cicero first described the ideal orator.[2] The precepts for addressing a piece of literature to a particular public audience dictated that an author mould his text, at least in its initial premises, to the anticipated expectations of the audience.[3] The two prefaces that Cassiodorus supplied for the *Variae* (one commencing Book i and the other commencing Book ii) are particularly important in this respect. The very fact that

---

[1] As examples of this line of thinking, Auerbach, *Literary Language*, 258–9; Petrucci, *Writers*, 32; note, however, Barnish, 'Maximian', 16–32, has attempted to insert Cassiodorus into a wider literary network.

[2] On the 'inscribed reader' as the kind of reader anticipated by a text who would be ideally equipped 'to catch every nuance and every allusion', Feeney, 'Horace', 19.

[3] Cicero, *Orator* 8.24; for a similar expression from the fourth century, Gregory of Nazianzus, *Epistulae* 51; see Kaster, 'CICERO', 250–65; for examples of Cicero's reception as a pedagogical gold standard in classical and late antiquity, Pliny the Elder, *Naturalis Historia* 7.31; Quintilian, *Institutio Oratoria* 10.1.37–123 and 10.5.2–31; Lactantius, *Divinae Institutiones* 1.15.6, 1.17.3, 3.14.10; Ambrose, *De officiis*; Jerome, *Epistulae* 22.30; Augustine, *De doctrina christiana*; Cassiodorus, *Variae*, first preface 16.

the inclusion of two lengthy prefaces represents a departure from traditional epistolography invites the audience of the *Variae* to consider them closely.[4] It is true that Pliny and Sidonius offered explanations for their collections each in the first letter addressed to a close colleague, but these explanations are submerged within the framework of a presumably original letter and certainly do not elaborate on the decision to publish a collection to the extent of Cassiodorus' prefaces.

Most examinations of the *Variae* have, a priori, regarded the collection as fossilized artefacts of the chancery at Ravenna, a view that reduces the role played by rhetorical design that is so pronounced in revised collections.[5] On the contrary, Cassiodorus' prefatory comments provide a tantalizing glimpse of the political context of his letter collection and hint at a rhetorical strategy in the portrayal of public service that depended on his audience's appreciation of communal representation in the epistolary genre. Just as Pliny asked his audience to imagine his collection as disorganized material drawn from a neglected bureau, Cassiodorus understood the need to maintain balance between the 'realism' of his collection as artefacts of service at the Amal chancery and the rhetorical purpose of the epistolary tradition.[6] The prefaces allowed Cassiodorus to draw attention to features that the *Variae* shared with the epistolary tradition, in particular the sense of community, moral consensus and collaboration so common to other classical and late antique epistolary collections.

Unlike typical epistolary collections, Cassiodorus' letters were not portrayals of private life. Instead, it was Cassiodorus' purpose to demonstrate the values of a collaborative community engaged in public life. This difference required explanation to an audience conditioned by centuries of an epistolary tradition that focused on the presentation of private lives. In compiling a collection of administrative pronouncements, where governmental mandate might be assumed to eclipse the purpose of the author, Cassiodorus risked diluting the portrayal of a collaborative social structure (*amicitia*) that was so fundamental to other letter collections.[7] In

[4] Bjornlie, 'Amicitia', 135–54.
[5] Hasenstab, *Variensammlung*, 5–7; Fridh, *Opera*, 1–5; O'Donnell, *Cassiodorus*, 56–102; Krautschick, *Cassiodore*, 113; Vidén, *Roman Chancery*, 71–3; MacPherson, *Rome*, 193; Barnish, *Cassiodorus*, xxx–xxxii; Gillett, 'Cassiodorus' *Variae*', 38–42.
[6] Pliny, *Epistulae* 1.1; on the lively influence of Pliny's letters in late antiquity, Cameron, 'Pliny's letters', 289–98.
[7] For Cassiodorus as the architect of state propaganda in the *Variae*, Hasenstab, *Variensammlung*, 8–9; Courcelle, *Histoire*, 206; O'Donnell, *Cassiodorus*, 86; Barbieri, 'Cassiodoro', ix–xv; Reydellet, *Royauté*; Scivoletto, 'Cassiodoro', 4; Viscido, *Studi*, 16–25; Jouanaud, 'Pour qui Cassiodore', 722; for opinions which regard the *Variae* as the product of Amal policy, Nickstadt, *De Digressionibus*, 38–9; Goffart, review, 989; Moorhead, '*Libertas*', 161–8; MacPherson, *Rome*, 40 and 169; Barnish,

contrast to other collections, the dispositive finality of legal decisions and administrative directives represented in the *Variae* did not present the same opportunity for demonstrating interactive participation in a deliberative process. Even the diplomatic letters adopt a character more appropriate to overt declarations of Amal state policy than to the sensitive exchange that one would expect to find between foreign states.[8] The exception to the overtly declaratory nature of the diplomatic letters is the dossier of letters exchanged between the last Amal rulers and Justinian's court after the death of Amalasuntha; this change of character has a rhetorical function that receives consideration in a later chapter.

Attention to certain correspondences between the content of Cassiodorus' prefaces and the wider cultural function of epistolary collections provides a crucial key to understanding the message embedded in the *Variae*. Cassiodorus' two prefaces are modestly lengthy affairs, requiring eighty-eight and forty-eight lines respectively, in the *MGH* edition. Because Cassiodorus devoted more attention to these prefaces than to any individual letter, they demand the attention of an audience attempting to understand the nature of the collection and the aims of its author. The first preface begins with a fairly common topos in ancient literature – a dialogue between Cassiodorus and certain anonymous associates who insist that he publish his letters for posterity. Predictably, Cassiodorus objects on the grounds that the turbulent activity of palatine service did not provide him with the opportunity to observe an appropriately decorous style.[9] Cassiodorus then explains how his interlocutors marshalled an argument against his objection, claiming that because he held such demanding posts as quaestor and praetorian prefect, his letters would serve as unadulterated witnesses to the probity of his service to the state[10] and would complement the dignity of his previous literary works.[11] Cassiodorus eventually capitulates and under protest agrees to publish his letters, but for two chief reasons: for the edification of those who in future generations would enter palatine service and, more importantly, to rectify the reputations of those who served with him under the Amal regime – that is, the same interlocutors persuading him to assemble the collection.[12] Cassiodorus then continues to explain

---

Cassiodorus, xxviii–xxix; Meyer-Flugel, *Bild der Gesellschaft*, 48; Gillett, 'Cassiodorus' *Variae*', 38–42.

[8] Cassiodorus, *Variae* 1.1, 1.46, 2.1, 2.41, 3.1, 3.2, 3.3, 3.4, 4.1, 4.2, 5.1, 5.2, 5.43, 5.44, 8.1, 9.1, 10.1, 10.2.

[9] Cassiodorus, *Variae, praefatio* 1.4–5; on the trope of hasty writing, Janson, *Prefaces*; Conybeare, *Paulinus*, 2–24.

[10] Cassiodorus, *Variae, praefatio* 1.8.   [11] Cassiodorus, *Variae, praefatio* 1.11.

[12] Cassiodorus, *Variae, praefatio* 1.8–9; note a similar sentiment in Pliny, *Epistulae* 1.8.6.

the structure of the collection in twelve books, his decision to name them the *Variae*, and the relation of that decision to classical precepts of style.

The second preface elaborates on the theme of hurried composition, in effect denying any attempt at rhetorical arrangement on Cassiodorus' part and strengthening the claim of the collection's authenticity. This preface also enters into an interesting discussion of the different readings that the *Variae* will receive by men of leisure and men constrained by governmental duties.[13] Cassiodorus then introduces an associate, Felix, 'that most wise man whose advice I share in every situation', as one of the interlocutors responsible for persuading Cassiodorus to publish his letters.[14] Cassiodorus explains the different circumstances of letters in the last two books – that he wrote them in his own name as praetorian prefect – and he concludes by stating that his colleagues requested that he next embark on the production of a treatise concerning the nature of the soul (the *De anima*).

Cassiodorus' prefatory discussions provided his audience with a number of reference points that allowed them to understand the *Variae* in the context of their experiences as readers of classical literature. It is first important to note the connection that his prefaces make with the cultural function of epistolary collections. In his own words, Cassiodorus decided to correct the record of public service, 'so that the coming generation might recognize as worthy the guiltless deeds of a clear conscience'.[15] Cassiodorus used the words *inemptam actionem*, here translated as 'guiltless deeds', with the understood emphasis of sixth-century Latin on judicial corruption, implying his concern with professional reputation. The dialogue in which this concern unfolds deploys the clearly recognizable language of *amicitia*. Cassiodorus' interlocutors were his *amici*, who urged him out of esteem (*dilectionem*) for his ability, who reproved his hesitation out of affection (*ex affectione*), and for whom he committed himself dutifully to hardship (*ex officiosissimo labore*).[16] Publishing a collection of letters at the behest of close colleagues is a theme that the *Variae* share with earlier epistolary collections. Pliny the Younger and Sidonius Apollinaris both explained their collections in terms of the obligations

[13] Cassiodorus, *Variae, praefatio* 11. 2.

[14] Cassiodorus, *Variae, praefatio* 11.4, 'accipiat viri prudentissimi Felicis praesumptione factum, cuius participatus sum in omni causa consilium'.

[15] Cassiodorus, *Variae, praefatio* 1.1, 'ut ventura posteritas et laborum meorum molestias, quas pro generalitatis commodo sustinebam, et sinceris conscientiae inemptam dinosceret actionem'; cf. Barnish, *Cassiodorus*, 1–5.

[16] Cassiodorus, *Variae, praefatio* 1.2, *praefatio* 1.12, *praefatio* 11.8.

of *amicitia*.[17] Expressions of *amicitia* within the context of literary correspondence portrayed communal consensus on the set of ethical virtues
found in the collection.[18] It was equally important to Cassiodorus that
he frame the *Variae* with the concept of shared social obligation, but
the bureaucratic corporatism that served as *amicitia* for elite members
of late imperial palatine service was in some ways very different from
the milieu of elite *otium* represented by Pliny and Sidonius. Members of
this network of professional friendships defined their culture through
the ritually formalized hierarchy of political patronage. The prestige
of their culture was governed by a carefully coded language of submission
to authority. These differences necessitated that Cassiodorus enact the
traditional dialogue between author and urging friend in an even more
elaborate fashion than that found in earlier collections. Doing so was a
means for Cassiodorus to reassure his audience that traditional *amicitia*,
and its moral imperatives, were equally operative in elite bureaucracy.

When Cassiodorus described Felix as one among those compelling
him to publish, his sense of obligation to this man derived from the
certitude that Felix was 'purified by the sincerity of good character,
outstanding in the knowledge of law, distinguished in the aptness of his
diction, young with the maturity of age, a charming disputant, and a man
of proportionate refinement in speaking, who preferred to discharge the
affairs of state by finding a favourable outcome by his own labour'.[19] In
other words, Felix cherished the traditions of learning and deportment
consistent with the ideals of *paideia* and *mos maiorum*, and for his sake
and the sake of others like him Cassiodorus undertook the defence of
their service to the state. It seems apparent that Cassiodorus described
in Felix the ideal civil servant and that this was an individual portrait of
the collectivity of Cassiodorus' bureaucratic colleagues. It is also possible
that in dedicating the *Variae* to Felix, Cassiodorus named a patron for his
effort to repair the reputation of the palatine elite. It is not inconceivable
that Cassiodorus' companion was closely associated with the family of
the only other Felix named in the letters of the *Variae*, one Flavius Felix,
the *vir illustris*, western consul of 511 and the scion of a noble family
from Gaul.[20] The first three letters of Book 2 of the *Variae* describe the

---

[17] Pliny, *Epistulae* 1.1; Sidonius, *Epistulae* 1.1; on the influence of Pliny and Sidonius on the *Variae*,
Bjornlie, 'Amicitia'.

[18] Bjornlie, 'Amicitia'.

[19] Cassiodorus, *Variae*, *praefatio* 11.5, 'Etenim vir primum est morum sinceritate defaecatus, scientia
iuris eximius, verborum proprietate distinctus, senilis iuvenis, altercator suavis, mensuratus elo-
quens: qui necessitates publicas eleganter implendo ad favoribilem opinionem suo potius labore
perduxit.'

[20] Cassiodorus, *Variae* 2.1, 2.2, and 2.3; PLRE II, 462–3.

recent repatriation of the family of Flavius Felix to Italy and letter 2.3 embellishes the family line by mentioning the consulship of a former Gallic Felix.[21] This previous Felix can only be Flavius Constantius Felix, consul of 428, identified as having familial connections with the family of Ruricius of Limoges and as being the father of the Gallic emperor Avitus, and hence having a strong connection to Sidonius Apollinaris, the son-in-law of that emperor.[22] This connection to the family of Flavius Felix is tantalizing because it implies the influence of a Gallo-Roman aristocrat from a family already familiar with the social and political significance of an epistolary reputation.

Further developing the construct of epistolary *amicitia*, Cassiodorus in the second preface explained how, upon completing the twelve books of letters, his associates again compelled him to write, this time a treatise on the soul so that it might be understood by what faculty he was able to expound so much concerning affairs of the state in the *Variae*.[23] The *De anima* of Cassiodorus is a text richly indebted to Neoplatonic thought and provides a glimpse into the philosophical dimension of bureaucratic service by describing the substance of the soul according to its capacity to understand the natural world around it.[24] Cassiodorus appended the *De anima* to the *Variae* and, in his later *Expositio psalmorum*, he called it the thirteenth book of the *Variae*.[25] In the preface of the *De anima*, Cassiodorus repeats how, after completing the *Variae*, he again embraced the interests of his colleagues, whom he described as 'the sweet confraternity of my friends'.[26] The combined interest of Cassiodorus and these associates in both the political record (the *Variae*) and the capacity of the soul for moral discernment (the *De anima*) formed a bridge between the two texts and made a profound statement about the political culture that they shared and which the *Variae* idealized. In short, the *Variae* were intended to portray a historical model for a community of the bureaucratic elite, while the *De anima* provided a means for understanding the moral erudition of that community.

Cassiodorus explicitly mobilized the concept of a historicizing ideal (*modo historico colore*) and the moral ideal of elite tradition (*consuetudine*

---

[21] Cassiodorus, *Variae* 2.3.2. [22] Mathisen, *Ruricius*, 20–22; Settipani, *Continuité*.
[23] Cassiodorus, *Variae*, *praefatio* 11.7.
[24] On the *De anima*, Halporn, '*De Anima*', 39–109; DiMarco, 'Fonti', 95–117; Halporn and Vessey, *Cassiodorus*.
[25] Cassiodorus, *Expositio Psalmorum* 145.2.
[26] Cassiodorus, *De anima* 1, 'Cum iam suscepti operis optato fine gauderem, meque duodecim voluminibus iactatum quietus portus exciperet, ubi etsi non laudatus certe liberatus adveneram, amicorum me suave collegium in salum rursus cogitationis expressit.'

maiorum) in his first preface.[27] Interestingly, Cassiodorus called Pliny the Younger an *orator et historicus* in his earlier *Chronica*. It may be that, by the sixth century, audiences had come to read epistolary collections as histories.[28] It is certainly the case that the *Collectio Avellana*, which appeared somewhat later in the sixth century, had the same intent.[29] The connection between the *Variae* and the historical, testamentary nature of epistolary collections received further emphasis in the parallel made in the first preface between Cassiodorus' *Gothic History* and the *Variae*. Cassiodorus' interlocutors draw attention to the twelve books that Cassiodorus wrote in the service of recording the history of the Goths and it is shortly after that that he describes the structure of the *Variae* in twelve books.[30] Cassiodorus' letter collection was meant to be read as an authentic, historical record of state service in which expressions of epistolary *amicitia* assured the readers of the *Variae* that the ethical virtues portrayed within individual letters represented the entire palatine community.

It is also apparent from the prefaces that Cassiodorus intended the *Variae* to court the opinion of a wider external audience. The very fact that Cassiodorus wrote his prefaces in the form of a dialogue implies a third party as an audience, one external to his bureaucratic *amici*. He addresses this audience directly in the first preface, shifting to the vocative and referring to them in apostrophe as *legentes*, readers, and asking their forgiveness for what may be a blemished style that should have received censure from those urging him to write (his colleagues).[31] In the second preface, Cassiodorus again addresses this third party, this time as *diserti*, recognizing the learned men whom he expected would scrutinize the *Variae* as a record of the probity of his associates.[32] Thus the prefaces observe a distinction between the intended audience of the collection and Cassiodorus' *amici*, those with whom he portrayed the quotidian duties

---

[27] Cassiodorus, *Variae, praefatio* 1.9, 'Tu enim illos assumpsisti vera laude describere et quodam modo historico colore depingere. Quos si celebrandos posteris tradas, abstulisti, consuetudine maiorum, morientibus decenter interitum.'

[28] Cassiodorus, *Chronica* 756, 'His conss. Plinius Secundus Novocomensis orator et historicus insignis habetur, cuius ingenii plurima opera extant.'

[29] The publication of the *Collectio Avellana* as a collection is generally assumed to follow shortly after the date of the latest letter, *Epistula* 83 dated to 14 May 553, making it roughly contemporary with the *Variae*; note that *Collectio Avellana* 1 commences the collection with a historical narrative (*Gesta*) and continues with *epistulae* and *libelli* addressed to recipients in the manner of an epistolary collection.

[30] Cassiodorus, *Variae, praefatio* 1.11 and 1.13.

[31] Cassiodorus, *Variae, praefatio* 1.12, 'Nunc ignoscite, legentes, et si qua est incauta praesumptio, suadentibus potius imputate, quia mea iudicia cum illo videnter facere, qui me decreverit accusare.'

[32] Cassiodorus, *Variae, praefatio* 11.8, 'Modo parcite diserti, favete potius inchoantes: nam si nihil mereor eloquentiae munere, considerandus sum potius ex officiosissimo labore.'

of state service. In making this distinction, Cassiodorus appealed to the didactic nature of more traditional epistolary collections and invited his audience to evaluate the merit of bureaucratic service at the level of their collectively shared values. The bureaucratic corporatism displayed in the prefaces, which continues in individual letters, was the *amicitia* of palatine service. It was this form of *amicitia* that Cassiodorus intended his audience to understand as the 'substance' of collegiality and consensus which made the *Variae* legible as a picture of an idealized community. Far from acknowledging the *Variae* as a project outside the ambit of traditional epistolography, the prefaces advertised the rhetoric of consensus and friendship so fundamental to the reading of a letter collection. This effort was understandably necessary given that Cassiodorus wanted his audience to apply the same attitudes toward reading a traditional epistolary collection to what was, in fact, a very unusual specimen of the genre.

One final aspect of how Cassiodorus conditioned his audience for reading the *Variae* needs to be considered. Unlike Sidonius, Cassiodorus did not invoke the ghosts of past epistolary masters in order to invite his audience to make comparisons between the *Variae* and other epistolary collections. He instead constructed in his prefaces the re-enactment of communal *amicitia* and obligation. Doing so provided a thematic context familiar to ancient audiences as being the proper framework of an epistolary collection. Cassiodorus furthermore invoked the ghosts of Horace and Cicero, although not as epistolary exemplars. This needs to be understood as a subtle invitation for his readers to frame the *Variae* further with their knowledge of the works pertaining to these two authors. In a sense, the names of these authors and references to particular works were windows that opened onto an intellectual landscape in which the *Variae* were firmly embedded. Both authors were notable in the art of epistolary writing. However, Cassiodorus referred to Cicero at the end of each preface in connection with his discussion of proper style (not his letters), a subject that will receive more attention later in the chapter.[33]

With respect to Horace, Cassiodorus' reference was specific and grounded in the sixth-century reception of his poetic precepts. The western consul of 527 and *comes domesticorum* Vettius Mavortius had undertaken copying and amending Horace's *Epodes* with an otherwise

---

[33] Cassiodorus, *Variae, praefatio* 1.16, 'Neque enim tria genera dicendi in cassum prudens definivit antiquitas', an indirect reference to Cicero's *Orator*; and more directly, *praefatio* 11.8, 'qui tantis rei publicae necessitatibus occupatus sic vacare potui sub urentibus curis si me gloriari contigisset fluminibus Tullianis'.

unattested Securus Melior Felix, quite probably the same Felix of Cassiodorus' second preface.[34] Securus Felix is noted in the subscript to manuscripts of Horace as *vir spectabilis, comes consistorianus* and *rhetor urbis Romae*, all epithets appropriate to a high-ranking official serving in the *officium* of a praetorian prefect. Because such projects often captured the attention of a specific literary community, Cassiodorus' interest in Horace probably had much to do with how he identified himself with the literary interests of a specific circle of palatine colleagues. The specificity of Cassiodorus' reference to Horace played an additional role in conditioning how an audience should read the *Variae*. Horace's name appears at the very outset of the first preface, where Cassiodorus explicitly asks his readers 'to reflect upon the words of Horace, who advises as to the danger that hasty speech might incur'.[35] Theodor Mommsen attributed this advice to Horace's epistle 1.18.71, 'a word uttered immediately flies irretrievable', which, if true, fits with Cassiodorus' concern about overly hasty publication.[36] Interestingly, this particular letter from Horace is more concerned with the nature of obligation and the possible compromise of virtue in friendships, a subject which reflects Cassiodorus' own purpose in publishing the *Variae*. Later in the preface, Cassiodorus again draws attention to Horace by repeating the poet's mandate, this time from his *Ars Poetica*, not to publish a work until nine years have lapsed after composition, the idea again being that the premature publication of a work is irrevocable.[37] By mentioning Horace's dictum concerning nine years, Cassiodorus may have implied that he had laboured over the production of the *Variae* for a great deal of time. If so, it should not be taken as a reference to the period of thirty years of public life which the individual letters presumably span, but rather to the amount of time required for the revision of individual letters and arrangement of the collection as a whole. The manner in which Cassiodorus described the completion of the *Variae* in his preface to the *De anima* suggests that his earlier complaints about hurried composition pertained more to the

[34] *PLRE* II, 'Vettius Agorius Basilius Mavortius 2', 736–7; the subscription to a manuscript of Horace's *Epodes* reads, 'Vettius Agorius Basilius Mavortius v.c. et inl[ustris], ex com[ite] dom[esticorum], ex cons[ule] ord[inario], legi et ut potui emendavi, conferente mihi magistro Felice oratore urbis Romae'; cf. *PLRE* IIIA, 'Felix 1', 481, identified as the *consiliarius* of Cassiodorus, and *PLRE* IIIA, 'Securus Memor Felix', 481, identified in the manuscript as 'v[ir] sp[ectabilis], com[es] consist[orianus], rhetor urb[is]'.
[35] Cassiodorus, *Variae, praefatio* 1.2, 'Addebam debere illos Flacci dicta recolere, qui monet, quid periculi vox praecipitata posit incurrere.'
[36] Mommsen, *MGH AA XII*, 3; Horace, *Epistulae* 1.18.71, 'et semel emissum volat irrevocabile verbum'.
[37] Cassiodorus, *Variae, praefatio* 1.4, 'Nonus annus ad scribendum relaxatur auctoribus'; Horace, *Ars Poetica* 386–9, 'Si quid tamen olim scripseris, in Maeci descendat iudicis auris et patris et nostras, nonumque prematur in annum, membranis intus positis.'

time in which he wrote the original letters than to the time in which he assembled the collection. The latter was an occasion of more laborious deliberation.[38]

More importantly, Cassiodorus' attraction to the *Ars Poetica* probably reflected his interest in the receptiveness of his audience to the importation into epistolary prose of precepts from outside the genre. The *Ars Poetica* itself is deeply concerned with the boundaries of genre and avoiding transgressions of genre in the eyes of an audience.[39] Horace's opening metaphor of the painter who creates a monstrosity by conjoining the incongruous body parts of various animals was the subject of commentary by classical scholars from Quintilian in the first century to Porphyry in the third and should have been a familiar topic to any learned audience even in the sixth century.[40] The metaphor set the tone for Horace to challenge the notion of a rigidly circumscribed definition of genre. According to the *Ars Poetica*, novelty in literary form should be tolerated within appropriate measure.[41] Horace acknowledged that Nature had fitted men with the linguistic skill to mirror their conditions, in both poetry and oratory, and that to offer a presentation inconsonant with the natural state threatened to bring odium upon the author.[42] Nevertheless, he further noted that even though authors were bound to follow the presentation of themes which audiences would recognize, new themes might be introduced so long as they were consistent with some aspect that the audience could reference.[43] Indeed, Horace advocated avoiding slavish imitation through the introduction of novel themes which, although new, maintained a certain balance and consistency with established tradition.[44] It was the task of the author to anticipate his audience by navigating the course between clever invention and familiar discourse.[45] To that end, Horace advocated blending the precepts of poetry with those of oratory.[46]

Horace's discussion concerning experimentation with literary form would have resonated particularly strongly for Cassiodorus, who was, in a sense, inventing a new venue for the display of epistolary *amicitia*.

---

[38] Cassiodorus, *De anima* 1, 'Recently, I rejoiced in the longed for completion of a work that I had undertaken, when after having been tossed about by the task of composing the twelve books [of the *Variae*], I was welcomed into the peaceful harbor', trans. in Halporn and Vessey, *LCL*, 237.

[39] Frischer, *Shifting Paradigms*, 61–73.

[40] Horace, *Ars Poetica* 1–14; on discussions by Quintilian and Porphyry, Frischer, *Shifting Paradigms*, 70–2.

[41] Horace, *Ars Poetica* 46–51.

[42] Horace, *Ars Poetica* 108–13; a similar sentiment at 60–72 and 153–78.

[43] Horace, *Ars Poetica* 119–27, esp. 119.   [44] Horace, *Ars Poetica* 128–35.

[45] Horace, *Ars Poetica* 240–3.   [46] Horace, *Ars Poetica* 333–4.

Horace's concept of the literary hybrid was quite relevant to the incorporation into the epistolary genre of concepts derived from another genre important to the *Variae*, namely encyclopaedic writing. Indeed, certain sentiments in the *Ars Poetica* seem tailor-made for Cassiodorus' purpose in assembling the *Variae*. When Horace writes, 'I would advise one who has learned the imitative art to look to life and manners for a model, and draw from there living words', this was precisely Cassiodorus' intent – to depict an ideal drawn from a 'historical record', albeit one formed using the skill of invention, seamlessly blending, as Horace said, 'facts with fiction'.[47] Surely the irony of Horace's statement that he would teach poets something concerning the very public affairs of 'office and duty' was not lost on Cassiodorus, who sought to provide a model of bureaucratic deportment through letters written not in his own name, but in those of Amal rulers.[48] Indeed, if Cassiodorus was aware of Horace's biography, it may be that Horace served as something of a personal inspiration for him in the turbulent years at the end of his official public life. Horace had served under Augustus as a quaestor's clerk and had assisted the emperor in writing his correspondence when Augustus was overwhelmed by the duties of state.[49] Of keen interest to Cassiodorus would have been the fact that, even under the weight of such an intimate association with the emperor's household, Horace had managed to carve out a reputation for himself as something more than simply an emperor's amanuensis.

THE RHETORICAL PURPOSE OF *VARIETAS*

It is clear from the structure of the *Variae* and from the material included within the collection that Cassiodorus intended his audience's familiarity with several different literary traditions to shape their reception of a record of palatine culture at Ravenna. Just as a reader of Cassiodorus' prefaces would recognize the tradition of epistolary *amicitia* as a theme suggesting a purpose for the *Variae*, so too the prefaces served to call to mind the literary tradition of encyclopaedic writing in a way that would condition a reader's understanding of the content of the letters (notably the encyclopaedic digressions embedded in letters throughout the collection). The discursive range of material included within the *Variae* indicates that Cassiodorus intended the collection to reflect the

---

[47] Horace, *Ars Poetica* 151–2, 309–18; trans. Fairclough, *LCL*, 463 and 477.

[48] Horace, *Ars Poetica* 306–8, 'munus et officium, nil scribens ipse, docebo, / unde parentur opes, quid alat formetque poetam, / quid deceat, quid non, quo virtus, quo ferat error'.

[49] Suetonius, *Vita Horati* 484 and 487; on Horace as an *apparitor*, or minor imperial functionary, Nichols, 'Social status', 109–22.

Reading the Variae as political apologetic

tradition of the encyclopaedic miscellany which, like epistolary writing, depended as a genre upon a specific conceptual framework prescriptive for readers. The actual encyclopaedic content appears in the form of digressive material inserted with seeming randomness throughout the *Variae*.[50] Every book of the collection includes one or more letters in which the main theme has become an opportunity to digress in an extended treatment of history and legend, the liberal arts, natural history or geography. More pervasively, a multitude of smaller inclusions – allusions to classical and Christian literature, etymologies and metaphor referring to nature – contribute to the fabric of a more sustained presentation of encyclopaedic knowledge which establishes a pattern for, and has a cumulative effect on, the reading of the *Variae*. The diversity of this material represents, *pars pro toto*, a kind of intellectual universality for the political elite that complements notions of Italy's political totality emphasized elsewhere in the letters.[51]

In the same manner that the prefaces draw attention to the theme of *amicitia* from epistolary culture, they also referenced the tradition of encyclopaedic writing. As Cassiodorus explained it, he owed much to conversations shared with a class of governmental elite who collaborated to preserve an understanding of the classical literary heritage.[52] One of the more active agents of that learned circle was the Felix addressed in the second preface. It is entirely conceivable that Felix was responsible for attuning Cassiodorus to the didactic value of drawing upon a tradition of encyclopaedic writing. In addition to collaborating with Mavortius on Horace's *Epodes*, Felix had emended his copy of Martianus Capella in 534, demonstrating an interest in works of an encyclopaedic nature. This interest was likely an expression of familial tradition: Cassiodorus acknowledged that the father of Flavius Felix (the consul) was an avid reader of Greek natural histories and a commentator on the *artes liberales*, two types of works indebted to a tradition of encyclopaedic writing.[53]

---

[50] A simple list of letters including digressive material, both full disquisitions and brief references, provides an idea of the overall impact on the collection as a whole: *Variae*, 1.2, 1.3, 1.4, 1.10, 1.12, 1.13, 1.17, 1.21, 1.24, 1.27, 1.30, 1.35, 1.37, 1.38, 1.39, 1.40, 1.45, 1.46, 2.3, 2.14, 2.15, 2.16, 2.19, 2.21, 2.22, 2.28, 2.39, 2.40, 3.5, 3.24, 3.27, 3.29, 3.47, 3.48, 3.50, 3.51, 3.52, 3.53, 4.34, 4.36, 4.47, 4.50, 4.51, 5.1, 5.2, 5.3, 5.4, 5.17, 5.21, 5.33, 5.34, 5.39, 5.42, 6.3, 6.5, 6.18, 6.21, 7.5, 7.6, 7.15, 7.18, 7.46, 8.12, 8.13, 8.18, 8.22, 8.30, 8.31, 8.32, 8.33, 9.2, 9.3, 9.6, 9.14, 9.21, 9.22, 9.24, 9.25, 10.4, 10.6, 10.11, 10.29, 10.30, 11.1, 11.7, 11.10, 11.14, 11.15, 11.36, 11.38, 11.40, 12.2, 12.3, 12.4, 12.5, 12.11, 12.12, 12.14, 12.15, 12.18, 12.19, 12.20, 12.22, 12.24, 12.25, 12.28.

[51] Cassiodorus, *Variae* 1.1.3, 'cuncta Italiae membra'; 1.18.2, 'imperium Italiae'; 2.41.3, 'regnum Italiae'; 9.20.1, 'universos fines Italiae'; 9.24.9, 'Italico orbe'; similarly noted by Barnish, '*Cuncto Italiae*', 329.

[52] Cassiodorus, *Variae, praefatio* 1.1.   [53] Cassiodorus, *Variae* 2.3.3–4.

This particular intellectual interest is pronounced in the prefaces of the *Variae*. Cassiodorus named his collection in the tradition of other encyclopaedic works where the *varietas* of the material achieved a kind of unity.[54] The title *Variae* encapsulated a complex conceptual landscape in the same manner of other titles in the genre – *Musae*, *Silvae*, *Lectiones*, *Confusae*, *Prati*, *Coniectanea* and *Noctes* – to mention but a few. These titles subordinated variety to some form of organizational concept, indicating that heterogeneity of material and lack of formal structure contributed harmoniously to a holistic image. Unlike the monster that Horace ridiculed for its unseemly arrangement of body parts, *varietas* was the fabric of thematic unity and had rhetorical purpose. And unlike Horace's monster, which could be noted from a glance as something disproportionate and unreal, the harmony of *varietas* must be found in careful and comprehensive reading, which allowed the audience to appreciate how the various 'topographical' features of the conceptual landscape related one to another. In connection with the choice of title, Cassiodorus explained that he had arranged the collection 'so that, although the attention of the reader is hastened along by the diversity of subject matter, nevertheless, understanding is secured when it reaches the end'.[55] Cassiodorus plainly made the connection between the variety of material and the overall didactic effect of reading the work as a whole. It was expected that the reader should detect thematic patterns in the *varietas* of the collection.[56] In short, *varietas* was not merely variety, but variety with thematic purpose. The expectation that an ancient audience should read even a tessellated text like the *Variae* as a kind of narrative performance is not unusual.[57] Nonetheless, the unconventional use of administrative briefs to construct a work with the rhetorical function of *varietas* required some additional, prefatory explanation.

The difference between the *Variae* and other works of encyclopaedic writing is addressed indirectly in the second preface, where Cassiodorus refers to the rather commonplace theme of tension between leisure (*otium*) and business (*negotium*), alternating periods of differentiated activity in which members of the elite were expected to engage. *Otium* was a concept that specifically connoted time for cultural pursuits, particularly the study of literature and philosophy such as envisaged in sympotic

---

[54] On *varietas* in classical and post-classical writing, Carruthers, '*Varietas*'.

[55] Cassiodorus, *Variae*, *praefatio* 1.13, 'bis sena librorum ordinatione composui, ut, quamquam diversitate causarum legentis intentio concitetur, efficacius tamen rapiatur animus, cum tendit ad terminum'.

[56] Carruthers, *Craft*, 136–7.

[57] As noted by Carey, *Pliny's Catalogue*, 1, with respect to Pliny the Elder; and König and Whitmarsh, 'Ordering knowledge', 32, with respect to the *Onomasticon* of Pollux.

dialogues or Pliny the Younger's portrayals of literary recitals. The anti-thetical concept, *negotium*, likewise had a specific meaning. *Negotium* described those activities undertaken out of duty to clients, peers or the state. Symmachus drew attention to the potentially problematic ethical distinction between the two concepts in the first letter of his collection, where he promised to grant as much attention to his leisured pursuits as to official business.[58] For Aulus Gellius, a noted encyclopaedic author, the distinction between *otium* and *negotium* served to delimit his audi-ence. Writing the *Noctes* had been an activity performed in the interstices between spates of *negotium* and Gellius intended it to serve as intellectual diversion for others likewise unencumbered by public duties.[59] It does not appear that Gellius thought that the leisured class alone was intellectually elevated and worthy of his books. Gellius recognized that his collection would also be ideally convenient as literary refreshment for those who were accomplished in the liberal arts but who were currently involved in a stage of life occupied with official duties (*vitae negotiis occupatos*).[60] Gellius does, however, insist that a certain kind of person, one given over to *negotium* who was poorly educated, would react negatively to his work and should therefore not approach his books.[61]

Cassiodorus also plays with this theme in his prefaces. As previously noted, Cassiodorus attempted in the first preface to excuse himself from publishing his collection on the grounds that his official duties (*negotium*) had rendered his style imperfect (a complaint that he shared with the encyclopaedist Pliny the Elder).[62] In the second preface, however, Cas-siodorus returned to this theme and inverted the critique, stating that men occupied with public service should not expect the kind of literary polish that one acquired through the study of ancient authors (*praecepto veterum*), a pursuit that was the product of *otium*. In fact, Cassiodorus continued, because *negotium* was a matter of duty, men similarly involved (*occupa-tus*) in service to the state should take a view favourable to Cassiodorus' efforts, indicative as they are of his dedication to official matters.[63] Cas-siodorus' position in the second preface represents more than an attempt to defend his written style; it clearly signals the intended audience of the *Variae*.[64] Cassiodorus' statement assumes that men occupied with state service (*occupati*), rather than the leisured reader (*otiosi*), would read

---

[58] Symmachus, *Epistulae* 1.1.   [59] Aulus Gellius, *Noctes Atticae*, *praefatio* 1 and 12.
[60] Aulus Gellius, *Noctes Atticae*, *praefatio* 12.   [61] Aulus Gellius, *Noctes Atticae*, *praefatio* 19–20.
[62] Cassiodorus, *Variae*, *praefatio* 1.4; cf. Pliny the Elder, *Historia Naturalis*, *praefatio* 18, for a similar statement.
[63] Cassiodorus, *Variae*, *praefatio* 11.1–3 and, more pointedly, *praefatio* 11.8.
[64] Contra Kakridi, *Cassiodors Variae*, 16–21.

the collection and relate to Cassiodorus' dedication to matters of duty, rather than style. In this way, by employing the same rhetoric found in Gellius' preface, Cassiodorus staged his project as a specimen of encyclopaedic writing, albeit one intended for an audience more interested in the kind of administrative material found in the *Variae*. Indeed, the second preface continues by implying that words rendered by someone hampered by frequent demands should be trusted more for their lack of artifice.[65]

In the course of Cassiodorus' discussion of this topic, an interesting verbal parallel arises between the two prefaces. In the first preface, Cassiodorus stated that the diversity of material in the *Variae* would aid the reader's understanding, 'so that, although the attention of the reader is hastened along by the diversity of subject matter [*diversitate causarum*], nevertheless, understanding is secured [*rapiatur*] when it reaches the end'.[66] However, Cassiodorus used an almost identical construction in the second preface while describing how the public official was seized with a plethora of obligations, *occupatus autem qui rapitur diversitate causarum*.[67] In each case, that of the reader and the public official, the attention of the mind has been seized (*rapere*) by *diversitas causarum*, a phrase that refers both to the variety of topics contained in the *Variae* and to the variety of obligations dependent upon the dedication of public officials. It would seem that, contrary to his protest of having submitted before his reader a collection lacking in artistic polish, Cassiodorus has subtly aligned the theme of the didactic value of *varietas* of the letters with the intellectual culture of the governmental elite.

Cassiodorus further defined the intended audience of the *Variae* in the prefatory discussion of appropriate style. Like the apology for difficult circumstances of composition, Cassiodorus introduced the theme of written style in the first preface and continued the discussion in the second. In the first preface Cassiodorus had stated that the title *Variae* also correlated with his use of more than one style for addressing a variety of people.[68] Cassiodorus further mentions the three styles of oratory recommended by the ancients for different occasions, describing in brief the *subtilis*, *mediocris* and *gravis* styles.[69] For Cassiodorus, stylistic variation referred to the diverse levels of understanding among the original recipients of his letters, a conception of literary style that he would have

---

[65] Cassiodorus, *Variae, praefatio* 11.3–4.
[66] Cassiodorus, *Variae, praefatio* 1.13, 'composui, ut, quamquam diversitate causarum legentis concitetur, efficacius tamen rapiatur animus, cum tendit ad terminum'.
[67] Cassiodorus, *Variae, praefatio* 11.2. [68] Cassiodorus, *Variae, praefatio* 1.15, 'varias personas'.
[69] Cassiodorus, *Variae, praefatio* 1.16, 'tria genera dicendi'.

received through the *De doctrina christiana* of Augustine.[70] Responding
to Cicero's precepts from *Orator*, Augustine shifted the meaning of style
away from the Ciceronian definition, where the nature of material used in
a speech determines the choice of diction. Instead, Augustine aligned the
three classical styles to the varied levels of understanding in the audience
to whom he addressed his treatise: the modest for those who were ignorant of instruction, the middle for those who had received instruction
but required encouragement, and the high for those who understood
the instruction and yet refused to obey.[71] For Augustine, the three styles
corresponded to the respective learning needs of these audiences, not
to a tone of deportment dictated by the nature of the material. It is
clear from the second preface that Cassiodorus was aware of Cicero's
status in matters of style, but Cassiodorus' interest in Cicero was here
directed at the relationship between reading and eloquence.[72] Cicero is
not mentioned in the first preface where Cassiodorus discusses the styles
of oratory. It appears that, following Augustine, Cassiodorus related his
choice of style in the letters to the instructional needs of an audience,
stating that 'a topic is treated in one way for those glutted with much
reading, in another way for those sustained by a moderate appetite and
in another way for those persuaded by a meagre flavour of literature, so
that they would avoid the kind of style that pleases learned men'.[73]

It has long been noted by modern readers of the *Variae* that Cassiodorus' letters do not reflect styles carefully differentiated by importance
of occasion or status of recipient. Instead, Cassiodorus' letters demonstrate a remarkable degree of consistency in terms of syntax, grammar
and vocabulary.[74] Nevertheless, Cassiodorus purposefully mobilized the
topic of differentiated styles. Toward the end of his first preface, Cassiodorus notes that, for the audience of the collection, he would 'render
the modest style humbly and the middle style not brazenly', but he
explicitly avoids the presumption (*praesumptio*) of speaking in the grand

---

[70] On Cassiodorus' exposure to the works of Augustine: O'Donnell, *Cassiodorus*, 119–58;
Quacquarelli, 'Elocutio', 385–403; Prinz, 'Cassiodor', 562, and 'Illuminismo', 4; Astell, 'Cassiodorus', 48; Halporn and Vessey, *Cassiodorus*, 21.
[71] Augustine, *De doctrina christiana*, *praefatio* 3–4, on the levels of learning; *De doctrina* 4.96, on three
corresponding styles; Augustine is working with Cicero, *Orator* 101.
[72] Cassiodorus, *Variae*, *praefatio* 11.8.
[73] Cassiodorus, *Variae*, *praefatio* 1.15, 'Aliter enim multa lectione satiatis, aliter mediocre gustatione
suspensis, aliter a litterarum sapore ieiunis persuasionis causa loquendum est, ut interdum genus
sit peritiae vitare quod doctis placeat.'
[74] Fridh, *Études*, 82; Fridh, *Terminologie*, 18; O'Donnell, *Cassiodorus*, 74; for other linguistic studies of
the *Variae*, Skahill, *Syntax*; Zimmerman, *Vocabulary*; Suelzer, *Clausulae*; Vidén, *Roman Chancery*;
contra Momigliano, 'Cassiodoro', 3, who accepted Cassiodorus' prefatory comment on style at
face value.

style.[75] This indicates that, like Gellius, Cassiodorus intended the *Variae* for an attentive and sympathetic audience, the *diserti* of his preface, not those intransigent in their beliefs who would criticize his work. The assumed criticism of a reader not engaged in public service, in contrast to the *occupatus* who is attentive to diverse things (*diversitate causarum*), corresponds to the two audiences who would be receptive to the humble and moderate styles. Others, receptive only to the grand style on account of their intransigence, Cassiodorus will not address. The repeated theme of style in both prefaces and the pointed opposition of *otiosus* and *occupatus* in the second preface indicate that Cassiodorus designed the *Variae* for a specific audience.[76]

As suggested by the prefaces, Cassiodorus' engagement with a tradition for *varietas* was programmatic in nature. It lent a thematic consistency to the portrayal of the quotidian habits of the bureaucratic elite, but it may also function more expansively, situating the *Variae* as one within a triad of texts each similarly concerned with levels of interpretation. The *Variae*, *De anima* and the *Expositio psalmorum* each refer to one another in their prefaces and it may be that Cassiodorus conceived of these three works in particular as a loosely connected whole. The second preface of the *Variae* announces the composition of *De anima* and Cassiodorus' introduction to the *De anima* confirms the completion of the *Variae*. Cassiodorus opened his preface to the *Expositio psalmorum* with mention of Ravenna and the cares of secular life.[77] Each text shares a similar structure: twelve books in the *Variae*, twelve questions on the soul in *De anima* and twelve themes to explicate in the treatment of the Psalms.[78] While it would be precipitous to claim that Cassiodorus had planned all three texts in advance, it is nonetheless possible to acknowledge that as a whole, these works reflect Cassiodorus' deep interest in interpretative reading. The relation of the *De anima* to the *Variae* in this respect is particularly evident.[79] In his *Expositio psalmorum*, Cassiodorus assigned the *De anima* a

---

[75] Cassiodorus, *Variae, praefatio* 1.18, 'Quapropter humile de nobis verecunde promittimus; mediocre non improbe pollicemur; summum vero, quod propter nobilitatem sui est in editiore constitutum, nos attigisse non credimus. Verum tamen sileant praesumptiones illicitae.'
[76] Cassiodorus, *Variae, praefatio* 11.1, 'quod constat otiosus debere, nemo potest occupatos exigere'; *praefatio* 11.2, 'verum hoc mihi obicere poterit otiosus... occupatus autem'.
[77] Cassiodorus, *Expositio psalmorum, praefatio*.
[78] Note a similar emphasis placed on numeric arrangement of a text in Cassiodorus' *Institutiones, praefatio* 2.1–3, where the thirty-three chapters of Book 1 and the seven chapters of Book 2 have biblical signification.
[79] Note the emphasis given to the thematic nature of the number twelve at *De anima* 17, 'And so we have closed our little work with the number twelve, which adorns the heavens with a variety of constellations... so that rightly even this calculation, which is consecrated in such great arrangements of natural things, might be joined to the interpretation of the soul', trans. in Halporn and Vessey, *TTH*, 280.

position as the thirteenth book of the *Variae*, strengthening the thematic connection between the two texts and inviting consideration of how the encyclopaedic digressiveness, the *varietas* of the *Variae*, may provide a potential thematic linkage between the texts.[80] The second preface of the *Variae* similarly strengthens the connection. Cassiodorus states that after completing the twelve books of the *Variae*, his friends compelled him to speak about the substance of the soul and its virtues, so that they might learn something about that very element by which he had declaimed so much.[81] And in the first section of *De anima*, Cassiodorus explained that these same friends wished to rid themselves of ignorance concerning the soul, so that they might understand how knowledge is gained.[82] Both statements refer to a particular capacity of the soul required for learning, a concern attested in Cassiodorus' discussion of style which influenced the didactic nature of his *varietas*. The thematic connection between the two texts may have been further implied when Cassiodorus stated that he had arranged the variation of material in the *Variae* such that it would carry the reader to the end of the collection, presumably to the second preface, where he announced the *De anima*.[83] The stated purpose of the *De anima* to reveal how the soul perceives the world's mysteries, found both in the second preface of the *Variae* and in the *De anima*, implies that Cassiodorus intended the *De anima* to exercise a hermeneutic function with respect to reading the *Variae*. Indeed, Cassiodorus' later work in the *Expositio* assumes that variety invited contemplation and interpretation.[84] Stated simply, *varietas* had pedagogical purpose. The manner in which that *varietas* appeared in the encyclopaedic digressions of the letter collection also set it apart from the genre with which the *Variae* are more commonly associated in modern scholarship – legal writing.

THE *VARIAE* AND THE LATE ANTIQUE CHANCERY

One of the prevailing trends in the study of the *Variae* has been to examine the connection that the collection has to a late Roman chancery tradition of legal writing. Such studies have emphasized the attachment that the *Variae* bear to an established tradition of writing edicts, rescripts and dispositive letters and have contributed much to our current understanding of how the letters of the *Variae* reflect an awareness of an administrative

---

[80] Cassiodorus, *Expositio psalmorum* 145.2.   [81] Cassiodorus, *Variae, praefatio* 11.7.
[82] Cassiodorus, *De anima* 1.   [83] Cassiodorus, *Variae, praefatio* 1.13.
[84] Cassiodorus, *Expositio Psalmorum, praefatio* 10 and 15.

literary style.[85] However, writing within the idiom of the late Roman chancery tradition does not necessarily equate to being a product of a late Roman chancery.[86] That the *Variae* possess a quality that is simultaneously epistolary, encyclopaedic and legalistic needs to be understood as the stage setting of a textual performance. As noted previously, the risk that Cassiodorus faced was that his audience would not appreciate the manner in which the *Variae* was intended to represent the communal nature of values portrayed in the letters. Emphasizing the debt of the collection to epistolary tradition ensured that the ethical themes found in the letters would be recognized as the 'persona' of a community, not an individual. The digressive quality of the collection also played an important role, projecting a universal scope for the ethical knowledge of the community. Likewise, the legal and administrative attribution of the letters required preservation and played an equally performative role, demonstrating the enactment of those ethical themes in quotidian bureaucratic activities. As will be elaborated upon later, the treatment of law was polemically charged and a crucial factor in the contemporary context of Cassiodorus' publication of the *Variae*. Nevertheless, despite the interdependence of epistolarity, *varietas* and legalism as 'rhetorical voices' in the *Variae*, the unique manner of their interaction sets the *Variae* apart from direct correspondence with a living chancery tradition. The unprecedented nature of the *Variae* suggests that Cassiodorus had deliberately constructed a unique style for the presentation of the bureaucratic elite in the process of revising and editing the individual letters that he incorporated into the collection.[87]

Viewing the *Variae* as a text divorced from the rhetorical modes present in other epistolary and encyclopaedic collections has contributed to the predominant assumption that the *Variae* are purely documentary in nature. The least-questioned assumption is that letters of the *Variae* had circulated as 'artefacts' among a circle of bureaucratic elite prior to Cassiodorus' assembling them into a collection, a view that presupposes that the letters of the collection are authentic to the occasion in which they were written for the original recipients and that they comprise a record of the actual moment. The administrative and legal language

---

[85] Boak and Dunlap, *Administration*; Zimmerman, *Vocabulary*; Fridh, *Études*; Fridh, *Terminologie*; Carney, *Bureaucracy*; Conso, 'Formula', 265–86; Vidén, *Roman Chancery*; Pferschy, 'Urkunden-formulars', 1–128; Barnish, *Cassiodorus*, xxi–xxiii; Gillett, 'Cassiodorus' *Variae*', 37–50; Barnish, 'Sacred texts', 362–70.

[86] De Salvo, 'Politica', 99–113, has already noted that the *formulae* included in Books 6 and 7 of the collection constitute an innovation in the late antique chancery tradition.

[87] Hinted at in Pferschy, 'Cassiodor', 253–73.

found in the *Variae* does, to a degree, resonate with the character of the Amal chancery. The rescripts rendering decisions to officials vested with legal power conform to what is known of the process for obtaining legal verdicts. The dispositive letters used to direct the performance of various administrative activities have aims within the legal competence of bureaucratic functionaries. The several edicts scattered throughout the collection assume a tone consistent with former imperial decrees found in epigraphic and documentary evidence. And the frequent examples of diplomatic communication are certainly in evidence as being common currency in the late antique and early medieval political theatre. Moreover, the *Variae* frequently refer to a wider body of legal writing consistent with administrative writing. This textual legal record appears almost as a palimpsest in terms such as *leges principum, ius Romanum, regulas constitutas, leges priscorum, constituta divalia, constitutum veterum sanctionum* and *constituta priscorum.*[88] Although a specific imperial constitution is mentioned only once, the diversity of vocabulary used in reference to an abstract legal tradition conforms to the style of administrative writing by avoiding precise legal terminology (jargon).[89]

This residue that the *Variae* possess from the letters' original function as administrative briefs does not, however, qualify the collection as an unadulterated product of the chancery. The apparatus that truly removes the *Variae* from consideration as a chancery record is the digressive material threaded through individual letters. Nowhere else in the late antique or early medieval corpus of legal documents does there exist a comparable assemblage of such material. The closest analogue to the *Variae* is the book of imperial correspondence collected as the *Relationes* of Symmachus.[90] Although similarly concerned with public matters and written from the perspective of an urban prefect of Rome, the *Relationes* do not project a cultural model as coherently as do the *Variae.* Encyclopaedic interest and digressions are absent from the *Relationes* and nowhere else in evidence, suggesting that the literary nature of the *Variae* was not transmitted through an established administrative style.

The *Theodosian Code* supplies another possible antecedent for a received chancery style in Italy, although here too the style is thoroughly restrained.[91] By itself, this proves little since it was the explicit purpose of the *Theodosian Code* to delete extraneous material from imperial

---

[88] For examples, Cassiodorus, *Variae* 1.1.3, 1.27.1, 2.4.1, 2.18.1, 2.27.1, 2.27.2, 2.28.4, 3.8.2, 3.43.1, 4.12.3, 4.25.2, 4.42.4, 6.25.1, 8.13.4, 8.13.5–6, 9.19.2, 9.24.8, 10.6.5, 10.7.1, 11.7.4, 11.8.1, 11.8.2, 12.21.3–4.

[89] Cassiodorus, *Variae* 9.18.1, 'sanctio divi Valentiniani'; Honoré, 'Theodosian Code', 135–40.

[90] Barrow, *Prefect.*

[91] On muted rhetorical style in the *Code*, Harries, 'Superfluous verbiage'.

decrees in an attempt to create a clear and lucid legal text embodying the pronouncements of emperors since Constantine. An introductory constitution prescriptive for the kind of material to be included in the *Theodosian Code* prohibited the sort of repetitious and excessive rhetorical features that abound in the *Variae*.[92] In the editorial process the jurists responsible for compiling the *Code* between 429 and 437 expunged any superfluous material surviving from the original promulgations – so much so that modern scholars have been hard pressed to reconstruct the original contexts for many of the *Code's* constitutions.[93] Moreover, Cassiodorus would have been aware of this stylistic prescription. Given the role of the *Theodosian Code* as a social contract between the eastern imperial court and the senatorial elite, it is difficult to imagine that Cassiodorus would not have had access to the final edited copy.[94] A law of AD 443 decreed that copies of the *Code* should be produced and at Ravenna the dissemination of these copies would have been the special concern of the praetorian prefect.[95] It is fair to assume that Cassiodorus' nomination as praetorian prefect in 533 brought him in contact with a copy of the *Theodosian Code*, if not earlier when he served as *consiliarius* (legal adviser) during his father's tenure as praetorian prefect from AD 503 to 507. Hence any digressive material that formed the legal style prior to 437 could not have provided an antecedent for the *Variae* through the *Theodosian Code*.

Where the *Theodosian Code* does not represent what may be considered a 'living' chancery style, the imperial *Novellae* provide better comparanda for the kind of administrative style that might have influenced the Amal chancery.[96] As imperial decrees promulgated by emperors (from Theodosius II to Anthemius) after the completion of the *Code*, the *Novellae* preserve many of the stylistic features that the unforgiving editorial eye of jurists eliminated from the original constitutions of the *Code*.[97] The more effusive style found in these edicts indicates that emperors communicated law to the public with more rhetorical flourish than the laconic style of the *Code* would suggest. The *Novellae* have elaborate structures consisting of sometimes heavily abstracted *proemia* that provide a moral foundation for the topic of the constitution, a *narratio* delivering the specific circumstances requiring legal attention and a *dispositio* announcing the action to be taken. As noted by scholars attentive to legal form, the *Variae* preserve these same structural features, a correspondence that

92 *Codex Theodosianus*, 1.1.6.1.
93 Honoré, 'Theodosian Code', 160; Matthews, *Theodosian Code*, 20 and 160.
94 On the *Theodosian Code* as communication between the imperial court and the senatorial elite, Schmidt-Hofner, 'Ehrensachen', 209–43.
95 *Codex Theodosianus* 1.1.2; see also Matthews, *Theodosian Code*, 31 and 49.
96 *Novellae*, trans. in Pharr, 477–572.   97 Matthews, *Theodosian Code*, 160.

provides the best evidence for a 'living' chancery style.[98] Something of this administrative style seems to have been active in letters exchanged between the Pope in Rome and the eastern imperial court, as witnessed in select letters of the *Collectio Avellana*.[99] A minor but apparent difference between earlier documents issued from the imperial court and the *Variae* is that the constitutions generally end with a *conclusio* describing the means for executing the legal decision arrived at in the *dispositio* of the text. In the *Variae*, the *conclusio* often returns to the moral reasoning expressed in the *proemium*, using an epigrammatic phrase as closure and bringing circularity to the letter. The closing statements of letters in the *Variae* suggest a degree of rhetorical polish not usually observed even in the imperial *Novellae*.

What is not found in the various imperial enactments is the sort of digressive material evident in the *Variae*. While the *Novellae* sometimes employ brief allegorical statements in the *proemia*, this in no way compares with the full-blown disquisitions and references to antique authorities which appear throughout the *Variae* and pertain more properly to the tradition of encyclopaedic writing. Just as the epigrammatic *conclusiones* lend individual letters of the *Variae* circularity and conceptual completion, the encyclopaedic range of the digressive material scattered among the letters lends unity of form to the collection as a whole. In the case of the *Novellae*, one finds only three digressive examples, limited to brief statements, not the fully developed topics found in the *Variae*.[100] Interest in encyclopaedic material is similarly absent from the *Collectio Avellana*.

Even in the light of the elaborate structural style shared between the *Variae* and the earlier *Novellae*, there is firm evidence that the administrative style employed at the Amal court assumed, on a more regular basis, the kind of restraint found in the *Theodosian Code*. The *Edictum* of Theoderic, dating from the early period of Theoderic's reign, consists of what are obviously brief abridgements, with at least the intent of preserving the sense of the law, from select constitutions of the *Theodosian Code*.[101] The *proemium* of the text states quite plainly that Theoderic had before him a law code of trusted authority when he dictated the contents of his own *Edictum*.[102] The statutes of the *Edictum* are straightforward and

[98] Fridh, *Terminologie*, 39–59; Vidén, *Roman Chancery*, 120–53; Pferschy, 'Cassiodor', 263–7; Kakridi, *Cassiodors Variae*, 34–51.
[99] Pferschy, *Formular*, 188.   [100] *Novellae* 1.3.1, 7.3, 16.1.1 of Theodosius II.
[101] On the *Edictum*, Moorhead, *Theoderic*, 75–6; Amory, *Ostrogothic Italy*, 78–82; Lafferty, 'Law', 337–64; more generally on the relationship between the *Theodosian Code* and 'barbarian' law codes, Matthews, 'Roman law', 31–44, and Matthews, '*Interpretationes*', 11–32.
[102] *Edictum Theodorici Regis*, proemium.

functional pronouncements, lacking both epideictic embellishment and any attempt to incorporate the abstract principles upon which the law may have been based. The *Edictum* probably provides the best indication that, at least by the sixth century, the routine expression of law did not normally take the form of elaborate, epistolary treatises.[103]

By comparison, the general edicts preserved in the *Variae* have a very different character.[104] Each edict approaches the topic concerned through the exposition of a *proemium* that provides a theme underpinning the nature of governance, such as relief for the oppressed or the psychology of punishment, and relates that theme to the *narratio* which follows.[105] At times, the edicts include play on words, such as the edict issued at Como offering a reward for the return of a stolen statue, 'We assign a golden price to a bronze commodity, and we bestow a metal far more precious than that which we should want to find.'[106] More substantially, five of these edicts employ digressions on natural history and legal history, directly address personifications and biblical descriptions, and cite classical literature as a source of authority, material for which there is no precedent in external evidence for a living chancery style.[107] Interestingly, a passage from the *Variae* describing the qualities appropriate for a legal advocate suggests that, by Cassiodorus' day, restraint of expression served as an ideal in the Amal chancery. Letter 5.40 explains that Cyprian advanced to the office of *comes sacrarum* because he was 'accustomed to relate the confused quarrels of agitated claimants with a particularly well-defined and clear summary', that he 'disentangled cases with such ease . . . what orators could hardly obtain from jurors with the most carefully constructed rhetoric, [he] was proven to obtain . . . by clear pleading', and that it was his practice to 'summarize the probable verdict with clear brevity'.[108]

The sentiment expressed in Cyprian's nomination explains the terse brevity found in other administrative documents from the Ostrogothic period. For example, the *Epistolae Theodericianae* comprise a dossier of

---

[103] Contra Amory, *Ostrogothic Italy*, 78–82, who finds the palatine context of the *Edictum* to be analagous to that of the *Variae*.

[104] Cassiodorus, *Variae* 2.25, 2.36, 9.2, 9.18, 11.8, 11.11, 11.12, 11.40, 12.13, 12.28.

[105] Cassiodorus, *Variae* 2.25.1 and 9.18.1 respectively.

[106] Cassiodorus, *Variae* 2.36.2, 'damus in aeneo compendio aureum munus; et metalla quam invenire possumus pretiosiora largimur'.

[107] Cassiodorus *Variae* 9.2.1, 9.2.5, 11.40.7–8, for natural history; 11.8.1, for legal history; 11.40.3–6, for personification; 12.28.7 and 12.28.10, for biblical descriptions; and 9.2.5, for classical citation.

[108] Cassiodorus, *Variae* 5.40.2–4, 'Interpellantium siquidem confusas querelas distincta nimis ac lucida relatione narrabas . . . te ita facile contigit expeditum, ut quod illi vix possunt artificiosis schamatibus a iudicibus obtinere, tu probareris a principe puris allegationibus impetrare . . . tu suggestionem lucida brevitate concluderes'; cf. Barnish, *Cassiodorus*, 87–8.

letters from Pope Gelasius to members of Theoderic's court concerning
various issues between 494 and 496. The final letter included in the
dossier was a decree from Theoderic to the Senate concerning the misuse
of church property at Rome, which Mommsen dated to 507, precisely
when Cassiodorus served the chancery in the capacity of quaestor.[109]
While Gelasius' letters and Theoderic's decree do enjoy some expansive
flourish in the *proemium*, they are explicit and functional in a way not seen
in the *Variae*. Attention is given to a thorough explication of the facts,
not to the circularity of moral allusions. While some of Gelasius' letters
appear fragmentary, the influence of imperial administrative writing on
the papal scrinium has long been noted.[110] The survival of protocols in
Theoderic's decree (such as do not survive for the *Variae*) would seem
to authenticate an administrative style shared between the Amal court
and the papal scrinium that was contemporary with Cassiodorus and that
favoured clear and direct expression over the style found in the *Variae*.[111]
When compared to letters addressed by Theoderic to the Senate in the
Variae, the stylistic disparity between 'documents' of the *Variae* and other
materials generated by the Ostrogothic chancery becomes even more
apparent. The *Variae* contain some eighteen letters addressed to the Senate
by Theoderic, dealing with a wide range of topics – the appointment
of consuls and other magistrates, various causes of urban unrest in the
city of Rome, the collection of taxes, the disposition of public lands
and criminal cases.[112] Each letter reflects the dignity of the Senate with
ornate rhetorical embellishment. The seriousness of the topic seems to
have influenced the stylistic form very little. By comparison, the letter
from Theoderic contained in the *Epistolae Theodericianae* is a rather bald
specimen, although its subject matter is clearly no less weighty. As a very
crude measurement of this difference, the letters addressed to the Senate
in the *Variae* average over thirty lines each in the *MGH* edition, while
the letter from the *Epistolae Theodericianae* required only twelve in the
same edition.

This same distinction between the *Variae* and a current administrative
practice may be made through another set of *comparanda* that have much
in common with the *Variae* in terms of historical context. The fifty-nine
documents edited by Jan Tjäder (the *Ravenna Papyri*) address a range
of legal matters including property ownership, payment disputes and
wills collected in the ecclesiastical archive of Ravenna from the mid-fifth

[109] *Epistolae Theodericianae Variae*, in Mommsen, *MGH AA XII*.
[110] Noble, 'Literacy', 82–108.   [111] Especially *Ep. Theod.* 3 and *Ep. Theod.* 6.
[112] Cassiodorus, *Variae* 1.4, 1.13, 1.30, 1.43, 1.44, 2.3, 2.16, 2.24, 2.32, 3.6, 3.12, 3.31, 4.4, 4.16, 4.43, 5.4, 5.22, 5.41.

century to the eighth.[113] Of these, approximately thirty may be dated to a period that would allow comparison with the *Variae*.[114] The most common feature of these documents is their strictly non-literary and legal nature. Several of these features demonstrate continuity in the production of legal documents from the mid-fifth century to the end of the sixth. The regular use of protocols and the inclusion of signatory witnesses in many of these documents demonstrate an attempt to conform to certain uniform standards that a legal forum (such as the governmental chancery) would recognize as having official legitimacy.[115] In many of these documents what may be considered a case narrative has been constructed using the statements of individual witnesses; statements copied from original documents; and the inclusion of inventories of goods, properties or prices relevant to the particular case.[116] The *Ravenna Papyri* originating in the period of Ostrogothic control of Ravenna bear traces of all of these features, indicating continuity with habits of legal writing from the fifth and later sixth centuries.[117] Although these documents were drafted for private individuals (some on behalf of chancery magistrates, but most on behalf of private citizens or members of the clergy) and not as official communication from the governmental chancery, they nevertheless have the same utilitarian simplicity of Theoderic's *Edictum* and *Epistolae Theodericianae*. They are, furthermore, full of the kind of detail (especially inventories) lacking in the *Variae* which speaks to their being the kind of document that had real (as opposed to rhetorical) legal and administrative function.

The cumulative comparison of the *Variae* to other legal and administrative documents is telling. The edicts contained within the *Variae* bear little resemblance to the *Edictum* of Theoderic. Similarly, the more quotidian administrative communications of the *Variae* retain the purely superficial stylistic elements of the imperial *Novellae*, more than do the *Epistolae Theodericianae*, while failing to represent the essential elements of a usable legal document as found in the *Ravenna Papyri*. The *Ravenna Papyri* themselves seem to represent antecedents for the legal and administrative language found later in Lombard Italy and Frankish Gaul from

[113] For the critical introduction, Tjäder, *Papyri Italiens*, 13–165.
[114] Tjäder dated *Ravenna Papyri* 1, 10–11, and 59 to between 433 and 490; *Ravenna Papyri* 12, 29 and 47–8 fall between 491 and 539; *Ravenna Papyri* 30–2 originate in 540, although it is not certain whether they were written before or after Witigis admitted Belisarius to the city; *Ravenna Papyri* 2–9, 13–14, 16, 20, 33–7, 43, 49 and 55 date from 541 to 600.
[115] For example, *Ravenna Papyri* 1, 5, 7 8, 10, 13–15, 29, 30–7, 43, 47–8.
[116] For personal statements and quoted documents, *Ravenna Papyri* 1, 4–5, 7–8, 10, 15–16, 29, 31, 33; for inventories, *Ravenna Papyri* 1, 8, 10, 20, 29–31, 33, 35–7, 43, 47–8.
[117] Especially *Ravenna Papyri* 29 and 47–8.

the seventh to ninth centuries.[118] The attention to legal details and essentially non-literary nature of the later, early medieval legal culture can be located in the writing habits that also produced the *Ravenna Papyri* and which the *Variae* assiduously avoid.

The unavoidable conclusion is that Cassiodorus consciously drew from what was by his day an administrative style no longer in currency. In other words, the chancery style found in the *Variae* was affected, not derived from habitual, contemporary usage. In fact, studies seem to indicate that, for Cassiodorus, each letter represented an opportunity to mine a wide array of earlier sources, both official records and literary works.[119] Taken as evidence for careful preparation in writing, the resonances of earlier sources in the *Variae* would stand in contradiction to the position taken in both of Cassiodorus' prefaces, in which he claims that the continual disturbance of court duties prevented him from giving attention to literary refinement. Some scholars have taken this protest at face value, noting hasty composition in what appear to be syntactical errors and an inconsistent use of titulature.[120] However, what would seem attributable to a lack of revision may instead indicate Cassiodorus' awkwardness in attempting to write in a manner that was classicizing in comparison to contemporary usage in the western chancery. The style encountered in Cassiodorus' *Chronica* bears little resemblance to that of the *Variae* and probably comes closer to reflecting a living chancery style, something especially evident in the brevity of the preface. Written in 519 for the consulship of the heir presumptive, Eutharic, the *Chronica* is a specimen of writing composed for an auspicious occasion at the Amal court that would presumably warrant the full pomp of rhetorical flourish. Because Cassiodorus was presumably out of office between 511 and 523, he could claim no interruptions to his literary *otium*. Instead, the flat annalistic style found in the *Chronica* appears to bear witness to an altogether different stage of literary maturity from letters in Books 1 to 5 of the *Variae*, which represent a span of Cassiodorus' public life from 507 to 526. This suggests that Cassiodorus wrote the *Variae* in an artificial diction gleaned from his reading of law, not its actual usage. The legal and administrative records surviving from late antiquity simply do not provide a precedent for a text of the same nature as the *Variae* that would support the notion of a *longue durée* continuity in administrative writing habits. At best, Cassiodorus

[118] McKitterick, *Carolingians*, 25–75; Everett, *Literacy*, 163–234.
[119] Rocca, 'Cassiodoro', 234; Martino, '*Gothorum laus*', 42–3; Leopold, '*Consolando*', 828–36; Csaki, '*Variarum*', 56; Fridh, '*Variae* II.40', 46–7; Lepelley, 'Eloge', 35–8; Colace, 'Lessico'; Fauvinet-Ranson, 'Amalasonthe', 277; Pizzani, 'Lettere', 151; Gasti, 'Spunti', 136–40.
[120] Barnish, *Cassiodorus*, xvii.

seems to have adopted a language similar to that of the earlier *Novellae*, not that of a functioning administration.[121] Even where similarities between the *Variae* and an earlier protocol for legal and administrative writing may be located, they are at best superficial.

[121] Contra Fridh, *Terminologie*, 3 and 62; Pferschy, 'Cassiodor', 267; Fauvinet-Ranson, 'Amalasonthe', 305; but note that Reydellet, *Royauté*, 190–1, hesitates to align the *Variae* too closely to legal writing.

Chapter 8

ANTIQUITAS *AND* NOVITAS

THE LANGUAGE OF GOOD GOVERNANCE
IN THE VARIAE

JUSTINIANIC LAW AS *NOVITAS*

The most prominent feature of the *Variae* is their presentation of a coherent traditionalist personality for Amal governance in Italy. The exercise of law was fundamental to the formulation of a political persona for any government, but by portraying the Amal court (and its various agents) *in medias res* in the daily processes of law and administration, Cassiodorus engaged with one of the most politically charged topics of the day – Justinian's codification of Roman law. The priority that Justinian gave to the new codification is evident in the timing of the project. In 528, just months after his accession, Justinian had commissioned the group of jurists who revised and combined three previous bodies of Roman law in the new *Codex Iustinianus*. The opening language of the *Codex* reveals how imperative the project was to Justinian's legitimacy:

> Therefore we had in mind to publish this in perpetual force . . . that learned advocates as much as the litigants should all know that it is in no way permitted in court cases to cite constitutions from the three ancient codes . . . or from those which at present are called new constitutions, but it is necessary to use only constitutions included in our Code, with those charged with the crime of forgery who would dare to act against this injunction when the citation of constitutions from our Code should suffice.[1]

The new *Codex*, in effect, made Justinian's name the only legitimate source of legal process and even prescribed death for those who would presume to use previous formulations of the law. In 530, with the *Codex* completed, Justinian again sought to emphasize his station at the pinnacle

---

[1] *Codex Iustinianus, praefatio* 2.3, 'Hunc igitur in aeternum valiturum iudicio tui culminis intimare prospeximus, ut sciant omnes tam litigatores quam disertissimi advocati nullatenus eis licere de cetero constitutiones ex veteribus tribus codicibus, quorum iam mentio facta est, vel ex iis, quae novellae constitutiones ad praesens tempus vocabantur, in cognitionalibus recitare certaminibus, sed solis eidem nostro codici insertis constituionibus necesse esse uti, falsi crimini subdendis his, qui contra haec facere ausi fuerint, cum sufficiat earundem constitutionum nostri codicis recitatio adiectis etiam veterum iuris interpretatorum laboribus ad omnes dirimendas lites.'

216

of a juridically ecumenical society by ordering the jurists to compose an explanation for the principles of legal theory (the *Institutionum Iustiniani*). Again, the opening language of this text emphasized Justinian as the absolute arbiter and subordinated previous jurisprudence to the standing of old-fashioned pretensions to legal knowledge:

We directed them specifically to this common purpose: that they should gather under our authority and direction the principles of law, so that it should be permitted for you not to learn the earliest origins of the laws from ancient stories, but to approach them with imperial illumination, just as the portals of your soul should receive nothing erroneous and nothing placed out of context, but only what pertains to the very evidence of the matter.[2]

As a companion to the *Institutionum*, the jurists at the same time commenced the *Digesta*, a compilation of the pronouncements of earlier jurists resolving various contradictions in the law. The urgency of this project is manifest. The *Digesta* alone required the redaction of an estimated three million lines of legal text into a document of 150,000 lines arranged in fifty chapters.[3] The combined *Codex*, *Institutionum* and *Digesta* were completed and packaged (in what is now called the *Corpus Iuris Civilis*) in 533. By the time the major cities of the Mediterranean (including Rome and Carthage) received the final, revised version of the *Corpus* in 534, Justinian's ambition to pair imperial legal unity with the political reunification of the Roman Empire was already well advanced.[4] Indeed, Justinian's interest in law was one element in a triad of imperial unity – legal, political and religious – upon which he based his legitimacy as emperor.[5]

Even before the completion of the full *Corpus*, the *Codex* served as a platform for the steady stream of new legislation that emerged during Justinian's reign. Where the *Codex* and *Digesta* abridged and, where necessary, reconciled pre-existing legal texts, Justinian's *Novellae* introduced often abrupt interventions in legal tradition, many written by Justinian's own hand.[6] Between 529 and 542, Justinian promulgated 291

---

[2] *Institutionum Iustiniani*, *praefatio* 3, 'Convocatis specialiter mandavimus, ut nostra auctoritate nostrisque suasionibus component institutiones, ut liceat vobis prima legum cunabula non ab antiquis fabulis discere, sed ab imperiali splendore appetere, et tam aures quam animae vestrae nihil inutile nihilque perperam positum, sed quod in ipsis rerum optinet argumentis accipiant.'

[3] Humfress, 'Law in practice'.

[4] Belisarius claimed Carthage in September 533, the complete *Corpus Iuris Civilis* arrived in North Africa and Rome in November 534, Belisarius and Mundus began the campaign against the Ostrogoths in Sicily and Dalmatia in December 535. On the receipt of the new codification in the west, Humfress, 'Law and legal practice', 164.

[5] *Institutionum Iustiniani*, *praefatio* 1; Humfress, 'Law and legal practice', 161–84; Ando, 'Religion', 126–45.

[6] Honoré, *Tribonian*, 31–9.

new constitutions, with a significant bulk enacted in the decade following the final completion of the *Corpus* (535–42).[7] These new constitutions treated a diverse range of topics, from private law (such matters as legacies and marriage) to institutional law (such as those concerning the competences of magistrates).[8] Although, at a practical level, the flood of new legislation sought to streamline administrative procedure and eliminate the financial incentives for corruption, the sheer volume announced the re-orientation of eastern imperial society on the divinely inspired wisdom of the new emperor. Statements articulating that divine inspiration were everywhere present in the *Corpus* and the *Novellae* and received further support through the exegetical work of Junillus.[9] The frequency of Justinian's legal programme demanded recognition of the emperor as the concrete, rather than the abstract, source of legal authority. Each successive *Novella* was posted at stational locations in Constantinople and prefectural capitals such as Antioch and Alexandria. Copies also circulated among public officials, lawyers and teachers.[10] The visibility of the *Novellae* in public life and in the discourse of professionals interjected the personality of Justinian into quotidian legal affairs where the magistrate or functionary of civil service typically provided a face for legal authority. This change was particularly abrupt for the bureaucracy, where association with the personal will of previous emperors whose constitutions had established administrative practices had lost their particularity and had been replaced, over time, by notions of tradition and custom.[11] For elites of the eastern Mediterranean whose personal interests were intimately tied to the perceived stability of law, Justinian's intervention was unsettling. The not infrequent vacillation in the imperial interpretation of specific legal problems in successive *Novellae* did not increase faith in the process of revising the old with the new.

The dramatic change in the orientation of the legal culture threatened officials and their professional dependents with the potential loss of a traditional source of public authority. As has been discussed, the resultant indictment against Justinian's regime is evident in the polemical literature of the period. According to Procopius, Justinian's codification did not remove confusion and contradictions, nor did it rectify inequities embedded in the Roman legal tradition, as many of Justinian's

---

[7] For the chronology of the *Novellae*, Honoré, *Tribonian*, 105–38.
[8] Sirks, 'Colonate', 120–43, treats an example of the social and economic changes attempted by Justinian's new legislation.
[9] For example, *Digesta, proemium*; *Novella* 1, *praefatio*; cf. Junillus Africanus, *Instituta Regularia Divinae Legis Libri Duo* 2.5.
[10] Lanata, *Legislazione*, 109–28.　　[11] Pazdernik, 'Justinianic ideology', 189–91.

Novellae claimed.[12] Instead, Justinian's legal activity was viewed as legislative *novitas*, the perversion of traditions that had structured the Roman state. Indeed, just the opposite of the vision of ecumenical imperial stability propounded by Justinian, the series of new laws was seen as a sustained attempt to destabilize the state at every turn: 'For everything was thrown into confusion in every part and nothing thereafter remained fixed, but both the laws and the orderly form of the government were completely overturned by the confusion that ensued.'[13] At a rhetorical level, Procopius' attention to continually changing law was a manner of characterizing Justinian personally. Complaints about legal innovation were a standard means in ancient literature of representing the capricious mental state of the ruler. It also suggested that the emperor's understanding of justice (which, as an abstract principle, was traditionally held to be constant and universal) was deeply flawed. It was axiomatic that a state governed by a ruler who tampered with the legal tradition was likely to experience the injustices of a tyranny:

And in no law or contract was there left any effective power resting upon the security of the existing order, but everything was turned to a reign of increasing violence and confusion, and the government resembled a tyranny, yet not a tyranny that had become established, but one rather that was changing every day and constantly beginning again. And the decisions of the magistrates seemed like those of terrified men whose minds were enslaved through fear of a single man.[14]

For John Lydus, who was similarly preoccupied by the character of Justinian's reign, innovation was a contravention of the deep-seated reverence for ancient custom (*mos maiorum*), the mastery of which was the basis for elite status. In Lydus' estimation, change equated to the demise of tradition and the deterioration of benefits associated with the management of the state:

With the greatest part, perhaps indeed all, of the traces of the wisdom of the ancients wiped away, one cannot continue to remain without tears when one realizes from what is set out below how formerly the law preserved freedom for the citizenry and how numerous were the blessings from which people of our day have gradually been excluded.[15]

---

[12] For examples of Justinian's claim, *Novella* 7, *praefatio*; *Novella* 23, *praefatio*; *Codex Iustinianus*, *praefatio* 2.1.

[13] Procopius, *Anecdota* 7.7, trans. Dewing, *LCL*, 79; for other references to the confusion of Justinian's legal innovations, *Anecdota* 7.31, 9.51, 11.1–2, 13.20–21, 14.9–10, 27.33, 28.16, 29.15; on references to specific *Novellae* in the *Anecdota*, see Kaldellis, *Procopius*, 150–9.

[14] Procopius, *Anecdota* 7.31–32, trans. Dewing, *LCL*, 87.

[15] John Lydus, *De magistratibus* 3.11.1–2, trans. Carney, *Bureaucracy*, 70.

Similar lamentations permeate Lydus' *De magistratibus*. Although they tend to frame a conflict with Justinian's authority in ethical terms, it is clear that Lydus understood the more concrete threat that legal innovation posed for the safeguards to elite property, wealth and rights that had accumulated over centuries.[16]

Accusing Justinian of innovation allowed Procopius and John Lydus to attach the critique of the emperor to an extended discourse that viewed departure from the traditions for which the elite acted as patrons as a sign of moral failure. In the context of traditional elite norms, willingness to innovate had always been a token for the lack of suitability for public life and for potential radical rupture in the political order. Sallust in his *Bellum Catilinae* noted that the insanity of Catiline was manifest in his willingness to break with established elite order and offer radical change to the undeserving:

This insanity was not confined to those who were implicated in the plot, but the whole body of the commons through desire for change favored the designs of Catiline. In this very particular they seemed to act as the populace usually does; for in every community those who have no means envy the good, exalt the base, hate what is old and established, long for something new, and from disgust with their own lot desire a general upheaval.[17]

Although broad in its implication for governmental and societal rupture, *novitas* had a much stronger association with poor legal judgement. Quintilian equated *novitas* with disregard for legal custom as a matter of simple definition.[18] In the assessment of a ruler, legislative *novitas* had a sharper meaning. The biographer of Marcus Aurelius identified the excellence of the emperor by the fact that he resisted the temptation to innovate in law, 'he engaged rather in the restoration of old laws than in the making of new and even kept near him prefects with whose authority and responsibility he framed his laws'.[19] The emphasis that the biographer gives to the emperor working within the constraints of legal custom and in consultation with advisers (presumably representative of the elite orders) reflects the anxiety that the governmental elite had concerning a ruler who might act arbitrarily with respect to the law. In petitioning

---

[16] For other similar statements, John Lydus, *De magistratibus* 1.12.5, 1.20.4–5, 1.28.5, 2.12.1–2, 3.12.1, 3.68.1–5; on Lydus' rebuke of legal changes, Maas, *John Lydus*, 5–7.

[17] Sallust, *Bellum Catilinae* 37.1–3, trans. Rolfe, LCL, 63.

[18] Quintilian, *Declamationes Maiores XIX*, 7.4, 'Quam multa, dii deaeque, non minus sunt iusta, quam lex, exigit quarundam invidia rerum, ut vinci se magnitudo patiatur. Et quicquid accidisse mireris, tantundem poscit in ultione novitatis.'

[19] *Historia Augusta, Vita Marci Antonini* 11.10, trans. Magie, LCL, 163.

Theodosius, Symmachus found it convenient to remind the emperor tactfully that imperial authority depended on the trust that the senatorial elite placed in imperial decrees and that continued trust depended, in turn, on the emperor operating within acceptable legal limits.[20]

The consequence of an emperor breaking faith with the political elite and legislating too far beyond the bounds of the legal custom that preserved the rights of the elite was readily visible in the sixth century with Zosimus' handling of the memory of Constantine. According to Zosimus, Constantine's break with the traditions of the state began as a result of his lack of comprehension of natural law, which should have prevented him from murdering his son and wife.[21] This misunderstanding of natural order, ancient custom and law proved to be his fundamental flaw as a ruler and resulted in a cascade of consequential failures and departures in governing the state: rejecting the traditional religion of the state for a new religion which offered him absolution for his crimes, abandoning Rome for a new capital after incurring the wrath of the people by embracing Christianity, the enervation of the army at games in the new capital and finally the loss of battles.[22] The weakness that Zosimus noted in Constantine's character and which prevented him from understanding the simplest level of law (natural law) had direct consequence in his administration of the state. Zosimus blamed Constantine for confusing the 'ancient and established magistracies', abandoning the frontier to 'barbarians', imposing unjust taxes and squandering revenues.[23] Negative portrayals of Justinianic *renovatio* by Procopius and John Lydus have much in common with Zosimus' interpretation of Constantinian *novitas*. The pejorative portrayals of Constantine and Justinian were both heavily informed by a long tradition that located more pervasive governmental failure in a tendency toward legal innovation. Justinian's court was well aware that such intensive legal activity could expose the regime to precisely this kind of criticism. Scattered throughout the *Novellae* are expressions of concern for the custodianship of law's antiquity.[24] It is perhaps because Justinian and his jurists blatantly plastered such a shallow veneer of *antiquitas legis* on startling departures from established legal custom that Procopius and Lydus dwelled on the rampant 'confusion' that attended Justinian's legal programme.

---

[20] Symmachus, *Relationes* 30.4, 'de cuius responses iugi honore mansuris vestrae clementiae fas est esse iudicium; nos venerari potius quam interpretari oracular divina consuevimus'.
[21] Zosimus, *Historia Nova* 2.29.   [22] Zosimus, *Historia Nova* 2.29–32.
[23] Zosimus, *Historia Nova* 32–3, on magistracies; 34, on the frontiers; 38, on taxes and state expenses; trans. Green and Chaplin.
[24] For example, *Novella* 1, *praefatio* 1; *Novella* 4, *praefatio* 4; *Novella* 97, *praefatio*; *Novella* 140.1.

ANTIQUITAS LEGIS IN THE VARIAE

As a long-established feature of ancient political discourse, juxtaposing the flaws of *novitas* with the virtue of antique tradition offered Cassiodorus a firm platform for the portrayal of the Amals as conservators of tradition. The prominent statement made by the *Variae* for the continuation of imperial legal tradition under the Amals has long been noted in modern scholarship as a compositional strategy of the letters. What has not received consideration is the extent to which the contemporary polemic concerning Justinian and legal innovation influenced the ideological statement of the *Variae*. It is clear from contemporary sources that the topic of legal tradition occupied a prominent place in the conflict that attempted to interpret Justinian's reputation as either *novitas* or *renovatio*. The level of political communication between Rome, Ravenna and Constantinople ensured that it had been a topical subject probably since Justinian first decreed the revision of the legal system in 528. First as praetorian prefect of Italy and then as a refugee in Constantinople, Cassiodorus was in a position to witness first-hand the reaction of the capital's political elite to successive promulgations, especially during the height of Tribonian's controversial tenure as a jurist from 535 to 541.[25] Jean-Louis Jouanaud has already suggested that the twelve books of the *Variae* correspond, at least superficially, to the structure of Justinian's *Codex*. Jouanaud has furthermore suggested that this was part of an apologetic strategy that sought reconciliation with the imperial court.[26] Although it takes into account the intersection of eastern politics and the legal personality of the *Variae*, Jouanaud's explanation does not identify the truly startling manner in which the *Variae* contest Justinianic jurisprudence, particularly the interpretation of natural law. The difference between the legal personalities of the *Variae* and Justinian's propaganda which focuses on an interpretation of nature and natural law will receive fuller attention in the following chapter. For now it suffices to point out that it is precisely that difference, and Cassiodorus' treatment of natural law, that drew the *Variae* within the orbit of Neoplatonic thought and a polemical eastern discourse. It was a textual persona crafted as an appeal to the sensitivities of the eastern traditionalist elite. How the *Variae* formulated the 'traditionalism' of western bureaucratic culture

---

[25] Honoré, *Tribonian*, 105–17, that Tribonian contributed to most of the drafting of legislation from 529 to the Nika Revolt in 532; 117–38, that Tribonian's direct contribution to Justinian's legislation continued through his deposition from public office and after his reinstatement until 541.

[26] Jouanaud, 'Pour qui Cassiodore', 722–41.

can be reconstructed by examining the way in which the concepts of *antiquitas legis* and *novitas* interact in the collection.

For a text with such a traditionalist ideology, the *Variae* almost never refer to an actual Roman code recognized as having legal authority. Only one letter comes close to citing a specific imperial constitution. In an edict attributed to Athalaric concerning the unlawful seizure of private property, the king commands the renewal of a 'decree of the divine Valentinian . . . long grievously neglected'.[27] Mommsen suggested that the antecedent was a law of Valentinian II from 389, although Barnish has since offered a *Novella* of Valentinian III from 440 as a more likely choice.[28] In either case, Cassiodorus' letter does not cite a source for the law, nor does it excerpt text from either the appropriate passage of the *Theodosian Code* or the *Novella*. A similar comparison may be made to *Variae* 11.39, in which Cassiodorus treats Bruttium's tax contribution. The letter orders a reduction in the annual contribution and is aware that an earlier imperial constitution had similarly reduced the amount.[29] Nevertheless, Cassiodorus did not cite a specific legal text or excerpt language from the sources that informed him about the particular case history. The absence of fragments of legal text recycled from legitimate codes is particularly surprising, given the pervasive linguistic habit of the period in which writers regularly excerpted from older texts in order to establish authority.

This is not to suggest that the *Variae* neglect the presentation of *antiquitas legis*; quite the opposite, reverence for the Roman legal tradition in the *Variae* is pervasive and diverse in expression. But rather than referring to specific constitutions that already had the force of law (as is seen in the *Novellae* of the *Theodosian Code*), the *Variae* deploy only oblique references to a disembodied Roman legal tradition.[30] Cassiodorus described this legal tradition with a host of quasi-technical terms such as *constituta priscorum* and *iura antiquorum*.[31]

[27] Cassiodorus, *Variae* 9.18.1, 'severitate legum et nostra indignatione damnamus statuentes, ut sanctio divi Valentiniani adversum eos diu pessime neglecta consurgat'; cf. Barnish, *Cassiodorus*, 116–20.
[28] Theodor Mommsen, *MGH AA XII*, 283, on *Codex Theodosianus* 4.22.3; Barnish, *Cassiodorus*, 117, on *Novella* 8 of Valentinian III.
[29] Cassiodorus, *Variae* 11.39.5, 'Nam cum mille ducenti solidi annuis praestationibus solverentur, ad mille eos regia largitate revocavi'; on the correspondence of this letter to *Codex Theodosianus* 14.4.4 and *Novella* 36 of Valentinian III, Barnish, 'Pigs, plebeians', 166–85.
[30] For example, *Novellae* 8.2, 10.3, 11.1, 16.1, 18.3, 21.5, 32.1, 33.1, 35.1 and 35.13 of Valentinian III reference either the constitutions of former emperors or the *Theodosian Code*.
[31] For examples, Cassiodorus, *Variae* 1.1.3, 1.27.1, 2.4.1, 2.18.1, 2.27.1, 2.27.2, 2.28.4, 3.43.1, 4.10.3, 4.12.3, 4.12.3, 4.42.4, 6.4.5, 6.25.1, 8.13.4, 8.13.5–6, 9.15.1, 9.19.2, 9.24.8, 10.6.5, 10.7.1, 11.7.4, 11.8.1, 11.8.2, 12.21.3–4.

The variousness and lack of specificity with which Cassiodorus referred to a legal tradition require consideration. It is certainly conceivable that Cassiodorus avoided citing specific constitutions of the *Theodosian Code* because, in compiling his collection after 535, the use of the *Theodosian Code* outside its new context in the *Corpus Iuris Civilis* was technically illegal. However, if Cassiodorus' concern had been compliance with Justinian's new codification, it becomes equally difficult to explain the complete absence of any reference to a text from the Justinianic *Corpus*, which arrived in Rome (and presumably Ravenna) in November of 534. Two letters of the *Collectio Avellana* in which Pope John (533–5) and Pope Agapetus (535–6) cite language from the *Codex Iustinianus* indicate that the emperor's new codification was in circulation.[32]

The omission of legal language from the Justinianic *Corpus* in the *Variae* is particularly curious given the timing and function of various public posts held by Cassiodorus. Although his tenure as quaestor and master of offices pre-dated the commencement of Justinian's codification, both offices were by nature intimate with the exercise of law. Especially as quaestor, Cassiodorus was responsible for formulating pronouncements in a language consistent with the requirements of law. Legal expression from the *Theodosian Code* should be expected in the letters of Books 1–3, which correspond to his quaestorship.[33] As praetorian prefect from 533, Cassiodorus held the greatest judicial and administrative competence in Italy (with the exception of the king). It is certainly the case that some jurists and magistrates avoided technical terms in the course of writing and that this reflects training in classical rhetoric, but it has already been observed that the *Variae* do indeed affect a chancery style.[34] Given that the *Corpus Iuris Civilis* arrived in Rome in November of 534 and open hostilities did not erupt between Ravenna and Constantinople until December 535, the complete absence of reference to the *Corpus* from earlier letters of Cassiodorus' prefecture seems all the more deliberate.[35]

The more likely explanation is that Cassiodorus employed a legal diction that refrained from specificity while at the same time capturing the nostalgia for old Roman legal custom. The use of terms such as

---

[32] *Collectio Avellana* 84.7–21 (John to Justinian) and 91.8–22 (Agapetus to Justinian) contain language from *Codex Iustinianus* 1.1.7–8.

[33] On the quaestorship's intimacy with law and the legal background of quaestors, Harries, 'Roman quaestor', 148–72; Honoré, *Law*, 11–18.

[34] On the avoidance of technical terms in the writing of some legal experts, Voss, *Recht und Rhetorik*, 50–7; Honoré, *Law*, 20–2.

[35] On the receipt of the new codification in the west, Humfress, 'Law and legal practice', 164; by comparison, the *Theodosian Code* had been completed in November 437, and presented to the Senate of Rome in December 438, Matthews, *Theodosian Code*, 6–7.

*reverentia priscarum legum, verita sanctionis, priscum ius, sententiae pruden-
tium* and *decreta veterum* communicated veneration for tradition (the spirit
of law) rather than a bookish compliance with legal details (the letter of the law). As a habit of legal expression sustained throughout the
collection, it has a more personal character that speaks to concern for
custom handed down from the mores of the ancients. Custom, or *consuetudo*, was a recognized feature of Roman legal culture which depended
on the authority and interventions of the literary elite who served as
conservators of cultural memory.[36] Being a product of collective cultural memory, *consuetudo* allowed a more flexible range of interpretation
than precisely annotated legal texts and presented more opportunities
for reaching consensus.[37] In short, by studiously avoiding the citation of
contemporary legal texts, the *Variae* suggested a legal culture that showed
deference to personal interaction between the court of the Amals and
the educated elite of Italy. Hence Cassiodorus accorded Theoderic an
old-fashioned respect for custom: 'we should preserve the customs of
antiquity [*consuetudinem antiquam*]'.[38] The ideology of the *Variae* accepted
that the traditional habits practised by men of virtue were the source of
text-based laws, 'for you the books of the ancients and the deeds of your
forebears are the same'.[39] Long-standing custom had the force of law in
the *Variae* and the administration conducted its business and settled disputes 'according to traditional practice'.[40] Thus the *Variae* communicated
the sensitivity of the Amal regime to *consuetudo* and advertised how governance had avoided any injunctions contrary to customary legal rights
and practices.[41] In this sense, the *Variae* project the notion of a consen-
sual compact between the Amal state and the governed. The collective
agency of *consuetudo* which suggests negotiation and degrees of concession at the level of personal interaction also takes an abstracted didactic
quality as *provida antiquitas* ('foresightful antiquity'), an almost universal
agency which instructed the state in the habits of lawful administration.[42]
In contrast to the Justinianic *Corpus*, which sought to constrain through

---

[36] Harries, *Law and Empire*, 31–5.   [37] Harries, *Law and Empire*, 47–68.

[38] Cassiodorus, *Variae* 3.39.1, 'Aequitatis ratio persuadet, ut exercentibus laetitiam publicam consuetudinem servemus antiquam'; cf. Barnish, *Cassiodorus*, 64–5.

[39] Cassiodorus, *Variae* 8.20.6, 'aequales tibi sunt libri veterum et actions parentum'; also 1.44.4,
'numquam maiori damno periclitati sunt mores, quam cum gravitas Romana culpatur'.

[40] Cassiodorus, *Variae* 3.8.2, 'secundam morem veterem'; similarly, 3.39.2, 'Quapropter . . . quae
mos priscus indulserat, cum praestante tempore munificentia sit pro lege'; 8.24.1, 'Itaque flebili
aditione causamini hoc fuisse longae consuetudinis institutum.'

[41] For example, with respect to the Senate, Cassiodorus, *Variae* 1.41.1, 'hoc enim praecipientes
nihil imminuimus sacro ordini de solita auctoritate iudicii'; 4.25.3, 'secundum priscam consuetudinem', and 5.22.2, 'maioris natu auctoritate'.

[42] Cassiodorus, *Variae* 4.19.2, 'Siliquatici namque praestationem, quam rebus omnibus nundinandis
provida definivit antiquitas'; and similarly, 4.33.2 and 4.35.1, 'provida antiquitas'.

definition the traditional latitude with which the literary elite handled the law, the *Variae* treated law as dependent upon the code of deportment favoured by the elite (*consuetudo*) and provided it with a universal and unalterable personality (*antiquitas*).

Cassiodorus formulated perhaps the most salient statement concerning *consuetudo* and *novitas* in an edict written in his own name (letter 11.8) in which he provided a brief disquisition on the history of law.[43] As an edict addressed to the 'provinces' of Italy, the letter supplies something of a contract for the type of governance that subjects could expect from Cassiodorus as praetorian prefect and the kind of obedience that he anticipated in return. The foundational principle underlying Cassiodorus' conception of an equitable social contract was a statement concerning legal custom and innovation. The edict begins:

It was the custom of the ancients to decide new laws so that successive rulers would add whatever seemed lacking for the people; now, however, it suffices for a ruler of good conscience to observe the decrees of the ancients. Formerly, the original stock of humanity was roused by this novelty, when they realized that the governance of their own lives depended on another man's will; but then whichever laws were not doubted to have been soundly constituted by the ancients became fixed. Therefore do the laws suffice for us, if only that particular inclination should be found lacking.[44]

Cassiodorus here encapsulated the conception of law that is found throughout the *Variae*. The edict acknowledges the necessary novelty of early imperial constitutions which derived from the specific needs of the people, but, having satisfied these needs, law became fixed as custom. The laws enacted in former times had acquired moral strength through continuous usage and had proven efficacious in the maintenance of good habits, to the extent that innovation, *novitas*, should now be eschewed entirely. Thereafter, the legal custom inherited from antiquity obviated the need for further innovation and should suffice for a wise ruler. Cassiodorus restates this principle several times in the edict, advising the 'provincials' to 'be content with the laws of the fathers' and to 'be fully in favour of custom and free from novelty'.[45] The

---

[43] For previous comments, Bjornlie, 'A reappraisal', 155–7.

[44] Cassiodorus, *Variae* 11.8.1, 'Priscorum mos fuit nova iura decernere, ut succedenti populo aliquid quod omissum videbatur adiungerent; nunc autem sufficiens satis conscientiae veterum decreta servare. Erat ante genus hominum sub hac novitate sollicitum, dum regulam vitae suae in aliena cognoscerent voluntate pendere; modo vero unusquisque novit fixum, quod ab antiques plenissime non dubitat constitutum. Sufficiunt ergo vobis iura, si non desit voluntas eximia.'

[45] Cassiodorus, *Variae* 11.8.2, 'legibus patriis estote contenti'; and 11.8.4, 'Estote tantum ad consueta solliciti, de novitate securi.'

didacticism of these statements demonstrates Cassiodorus, and by extension the bureaucratic elite serving the praetorian office, as having full
command of traditional jurisprudence. It was a legal traditionalism that
reinforced the role of the elite as cultural stewards who preserved custom, but it also acknowledged the consensus and co-operative agreement
necessary for civic harmony. It was a juridical principle that made little
allowance for the kind of legislative authoritarianism seen in Justinian's
vision of a society of law.

THE VIRTUE OF CONSERVING THE PAST

Cassiodorus further developed the contrast between the *Variae* and Justinian's legislative agenda by emphasizing the tension between *antiquitas*
as something requiring constant vigilance to preserve and the corrosive
influence of *novitas* on legal tradition. Cassiodorus portrayed the Amal
court as the primary agent safeguarding the cultural force of antiquity
and ensuring the continuity of prosperity. Cassiodorus encapsulated this
sentiment neatly in a letter pertaining to the disturbances that frequently
attended public spectacles, 'For there is nothing that we want to preserve
for you more eagerly than the discipline of your ancestors, so that whatever has been praiseworthy since antiquity might increase even more
under us.'[46] Even with respect to the enactments of a deceased king in
territory newly conquered by the Ostrogoths (Alaric II in Gaul), the
principle of avoiding innovation remained ascendant, 'For why should
we topple previous arrangements, where there is nothing that we ought
to correct?'[47] The preference for continuing trusted practice as opposed
to beginning something new was also reinforced as an abstract principle
that could be located in a person's ethical disposition. Hence the letter
appointing Cyprianus to the Senate notes, 'The continued employment
of a good man is prized by nature itself, since it must be praised less for
commencing the plans of good things than for preserving them.'[48]

In one of his more charming letters, Cassiodorus included a disquisition on the origin of papyrus that again described the seamless

---

[46] Cassiodorus, *Variae* 1.31.3, 'Nihil est enim, quod studiosius servare vos cupimus quam vestrorum veterum disciplinam, ut, quod ab antiquis laudabile semper habuistis, sub nobis potius augeatis'; and 3.39.1, 'Aequitatis ratio persuadet, ut exercentibus laetitiam publicam consuetudinem serve-mus antiquam.'

[47] Cassiodorus, *Variae* 4.17.1, 'Definitam rem ab antiquo rege, quam tamen constat rationabiliter esse decretam, nulla volumus ambiguitate titubare, quia decet firmum esse quod commendatur probabili iussione. Cur enim priora quassemus, ubi nihil est quod corrigere debeamus?'

[48] Cassiodorus, *Variae* 8.22.2, 'Natura ipsa boni adhibita perserverantia pretiatur, quia minus est laudanda incipere quam bonorum propositum custodire.'

relationship between universal order (embodied in nature) and *antiquitas* as a kind of ethical principle. The letter explains how provident natural processes (the growth of reeds that allow the production of papyrus) allowed for the accumulation of ancient knowledge and constancy of governance:

> Antiquity, that governess of all affairs, mindful of the many occupations of our bureau, so diligently prepared that the abundant supply of documents should not fail . . . to the extent that the public bureau ought to preserve in commendable perpetuity the integrity of its faithfulness [to the public good]. The bureau, knowing not mortal defect, ever increases in annual accumulation, continually accepting the new and preserving the old.[49]

Pairing the Nilotic permanence of reed growth to the bureaucratic accumulation and preservation of documents, the letter draws attention to the ethical considerations of documentary custodianship entrusted to public officials.[50] The natural continuity of papyri and the state bureau preserved ancient wisdom (*prudentium sensa servantur*), facilitated judicial rulings (*iudices multis profutura decernerent*) and obviated the opportunity for corruption (*ademptus est impudentissimus exactionibus locus*).[51] In the spirit of conserving *antiquitas* for the benefit of society, papyri and the bureau preserved a faithful account of human deeds, 'For even if our memory retains the subject, it alters the words; on paper, however, it is stored securely so that it may be heard always with consistency.'[52] The *Variae* combine as a single concept the veneration of antiquity, natural order and political order. Thus formulated, traditionalism was to be found in the extent to which preservation was preferred over change and adulteration. The virtue of continuity with the past is apparent in another letter appointing a scribe to the bureau: 'See what ancient trust and daily efficiency is entrusted to you . . . the ancient voice of documents, when it will have been delivered from your sanctum without corruption . . . Be

---

[49] Cassiodorus, *Variae* 11.38.1, 'Moderatrix rerum omnium diligenter consideravit antiquitas, ut, quoniam erat plurimis per nostra scrinia consulendum, copia non deesset procurata chartarum'; further on, 11.38.6, 'quatenus scrinium publicum integritatem fidei suae laudabili debeat perpetuitate servare. Quod defectum inter mortalia nesciens annua cumulatione semper augescit, nova iugiter accipiens et vetusta custodiens'; cf. Barnish, *Cassiodorus*, 159–60.

[50] Cassiodorus, *Variae* 11.38.2, 'Pulchrum plane opus Memphis ingeniosa concepit, ut universa scrinia vestiret quod unius loci labor elegans texuisset. Surgit Nilotica silva.'

[51] Cassiodorus, *Variae* 11.38.1, 'cum iudices multis profutura decernerent . . . Ademptus est impudentissimus exactionibus locus: specialiter a damnis exemit propter quos principis humanitas dedit'; 11.38.3, 'Nam quid tale in qualibet cultura nascitur, quam illud, ubi prudentium sensa servantur?'

[52] Cassiodorus, *Variae* 11.38.5–6, 'quotiens desiderium lectoris invenerit: humanorum actuum servans fidele testimonium, praeteritorum loquax, oblivionis inimica. Nam memoria nostra et si causas retinet, verba commutat; illic autem secure reponitur, quod semper aequaliter audiatur'.

a transcriber, not an inventor, of ancient enactments.'[53] As in letter 11.38
concerning papyri, emphasis is again placed on avoiding *novitas* as the
antithesis of *antiquitas*, and *antiquitas* is characterized as the source of a
natural political order embodying moral governance.

The seamless blending and interdependence of key concepts – nature,
antiquity, political order, moral order – is a characteristic feature of the
Variae. The mores inherited from antiquity provide structure for the
maintenance of an idealized political and moral order. Destabilizing one
concept would threaten the presentation of a harmonious whole and
reinforces how these concepts participate in a necessary natural order.
The obvious antithesis to this carefully formulated system is innovation.
Although *novitas* appears only infrequently in the *Variae* as an explicitly defined concept, the persistent attention given to the concept of
conservation ensured that innovation was understood as the potential
destabilizing force. In the letter appointing Cassiodorus' father to the
patriciate, Cassiodorus recounts how the *novitas* of Theoderic's reign
had temporarily permitted uncertainty and potential disturbance among
the provinces of Italy.[54] Presumably it was the host of old-fashioned
virtues decorating the elder Cassiodorus which allowed him to recognize
Theoderic's arrival not as a novelty, but as the arrival of a conservator
of tradition.[55] As recounted in another letter, by the end of his reign
Theoderic had so comported the state that his death would not present a
similar opportunity for *novitas*.[56] The *Variae* certainly give the impression
that Amal policies had avoided subjecting the provinces to novel changes
in administration.[57] More importantly, the *Variae* give the impression that
it was the continuity of office holders who maintained an attachment to
antiquitas and prevented the abrupt emergence of *novitas*. The *Variae* offer
clear statements that the appointment of magistrates of the appropriate
moral calibre was the surest safeguard against the disruption of *novitas*:
'We bestow this post on those best suited as conservators, which we
believe is preferable.'[58] Conversely, the *Variae* also portray the odium of

[53] Cassiodorus, *Variae* 12.21.3–4, 'Vide quod tibi committitur antiqua fides et cotidiana diligentia . . . vox antiqua chartarum cum de tuis adytis incorrupta processerit . . . Translator esto, non
conditor antiquorum gestorum.'
[54] Cassiodorus, *Variae* 1.3.3, 'In ipso quippe imperii nostri devotus exordio, cum adhuc fluctuantibus
rebus provinciarum corda vagarentur et neglegi rudem dominum novitas ipsa pateretur'; cf.
Barnish, *Cassiodorus*, 6–8.
[55] For example, Cassiodorus, *Variae* 1.3.4.
[56] Cassiodorus, *Variae* 8.6.2.   [57] Cassiodorus, *Variae* 4.26.2.
[58] Cassiodorus, *Variae* 1.42.4, 'Illa, quae potiora credimus, ad conservandum melioribus damus et
in quibus sustinere damna non patimur, fidelioribus profecto mentibus applicamus'; similarly,
2.16.4, 3.17.3, 8.14.2.

public offices conferred in a manner not in keeping with the sanction of antiquity.[59]

Perhaps the strongest statement made by the *Variae* with respect to how the Amal court exercised the preservation of tradition in the appointment of officials may be found, ironically, in one of Cassiodorus' own literary innovations – the two books of *formulae* included in the collection.[60] Books 6 and 7 of the *Variae* contain seventy-two letters providing models for the appropriate form of address used in magisterial appointments and administrative decrees. A similar assemblage appears nowhere else in earlier classical or post-classical literature. According to his first preface to the *Variae*, Cassiodorus intended these *formulae* to relieve his successors of the shame caused by a written style that was harried by the urgent demands of state:

> But I have not been able to permit others to endure that which I often experienced in bestowing offices; that is, speeches written hastily and without polish, which were demanded so suddenly that it seemed hardly possible to write it. And so I have included *formulae* for all the official posts in the sixth and seventh books so that however late I might take care for my own reputation, I might assist my successors in the near future.[61]

Several aspects of this passage bear consideration. First, the claim of hurried composition conforms to the rhetoric by which Cassiodorus attempted to deflect blame for the censure his collection might arouse. It also conforms to the presentation of his political dependents as *occupati*, officials who ascended in station through devoted service to the state and who were not to be confused with the *otiosi* appointed to temporary tenures from the senatorial elite.

More importantly, Cassiodorus' inclusion of the *formulae* relates directly to his belated concerns for his own reputation and the reputations of his political dependents. At the very least, the *formulae* provided a putative record for the comprehensive maintenance of traditional public

---

[59] For example, Cassiodorus, *Variae* 2.28.4 and 9.24.1.

[60] On Cassiodorus' *formulae*, Conso, 'Formula', 265–85; De Salvo, 'Politica', 99–113; Prostko-Prostynski, 'Chronoligie', 503–8.

[61] Cassiodorus, *Variae, praefatio* 1.14, 'Illud autem sustinere alios passi non sumus quod nos frequenter incurrimus in honoribus dandis, impolitas et praecipites dictiones, quae sic poscuntur ad subitum, ut vix vel scribi posse videantur. Cunctarum itaque dignitatum sexto et septimo libris formulas comprehendi, ut et mihi quamvis sero prospicerem et sequentibus in augusto tempore subvenirem: ita quae dixi praeteritis conveniunt et futuris, quia non de personis, sed de ipsis locis quae apta videbantur explicui'; cf. Barnish, *Cassiodorus*, 1–5.

offices and functions of the state under the Amals. Book 6 commences with a *formula* for the most antique of offices (soon to become defunct under Justinian) – the consulship. From there, the book continues in a manner that preserves, more or less, a hierarchy of public distinction, moving to letters of appointment for the patriciate, the praetorian prefecture, the urban prefecture, the quaestorship, the mastership of the offices, and an assortment of other high palatine posts. The *formulae* include both purely titular appointments and the offices holding real competence over various palatine bureaus. Book 7 continues the hierarchical progression with minor *comitivae*, prefectures of provinces and specific cities, and includes *formulae* for the maintenance of a host of services that were components of the late Roman state (mints, arms factories, aqueducts).

As a composite, the contents of Books 6 and 7 represent the full panoply and complexity of late Roman governance. Taking into account that John Lydus' history of the magistracies represented wider anxiety concerning the deterioration of antique traditions associated with public offices, Cassiodorus' *formulae* respond with calculated precision to the political discourse of the eastern capital by demonstrating the mobilization of the western state under obedience to *antiquitas*. Furthermore, the *formulae* of appointment to office are arranged according to the prestige traditionally accorded to the recipient by the office and irrespective of whether the post was titular or functional. Hence the *otiosi* and *occupati* who would hold these respective offices have not been segregated and share alternating positions of eminence. In the years following the fall of the Amal court at Ravenna when the political climate at Constantinople had become particularly polarized for different groups of Italian émigrés, the blending of status and station was probably calculated to relieve notions of a previous 'class conflict' at Ravenna. The fact that the list of public appointments begins with two honours granted to the senatorial elite which did not require administrative function (the consulship and the patriciate) was also probably calculated to understate tension between the two groups. Even seemingly extraneous material that does not play a role in portraying the hierarchy of state service contributes subtly to the image of state continuity according to a particular character that, in itself, is responsive to the eastern polemic. Summonses to court; requests for discharge from state service; notices to collect taxes and grant tax remissions; appointment of legal guardianship; and confirmations of matrimony, legitimacy and property rights are all included at the end of Book 7 to demonstrate the range of the state's concerns. Compared to the recent Justinianic legislation which determined intimate matters such as marriage, legitimacy and property rights according to the new and final letter of the law, Cassiodorus' *formulae* suggest (once again, as with the attention paid to *consuetudo*) that matters intimate to the individual could be handled on a basis of personal interaction.

Another indication that Cassiodorus intended the *formulae* to contribute to the traditionalist ideology of the *Variae* is their distance from anything that could be recognizable as a functioning documentary tool for bureaucratic writing. As previously mentioned, as *formulae*, the letters assembled in Books 6 and 7 have no direct antecedent in the literary or documentary tradition of classical or late antique writing. Closely analogous, however, and indeed a possible inspiration for Cassiodorus' books of *formulae*, is Justinian's *Digesta*. Book 1 of the *Digesta* contains a series of chapters dedicated to public posts in descending order of dignity from senators to tax assessors.[62] Each chapter assembles the redacted statements of earlier jurists concerning the public post under consideration and thereby compiles a profile of that post's qualifications, traditional duties and limits to competence. Shorn of stylistic flourish, the *Digesta* was functional as a handbook in a way that the *formulae* of the *Variae* were not. Instead, Cassiodorus' *formulae* often show far greater concern for the historical or even quasi-mythical origins of a public office than for actual administrative duties.[63] Even where attention is given to function, that function is usually provided only as justification for the more elaborate discourse concerning the proper moral qualifications and deportment required of the post. For example, the *formula* of the *Variae* concerning the urban prefect of Rome states the following concerning the judicial function of that office:

It is indeed grand to be the most celebrated man, but even grander to render judgement over celebrated men. This Senate, glorious by its remarkable reputation, is deemed to have a president, whom the world beholds pronouncing laws. And here it happens that those men enjoying complete power in the Senate tremble to pronounce their own cases in your presence. Indeed it is also known that this constraint must be excercised with discretion, so that they would elect to bind themselves to the laws that are known to have been established by them. This constraint is shared in common with us, but with this singular exception, that we are not able to be subjected to others who would judge us. Behold so many learned men and consider how you would advise them to dread the shame of transgression. You settle disputes among those whom you know to be your betters. Hence establish your reputation, so that all men of that noble

---

[62] Justinian, *Digesta* 1.9, senators; 1.10, duties of the consul; 1.11, duties of the prefect of the praetorian guard; 1.12, duties of the urban prefect; 1.13, quaestor; 1.14, praetors; 1.15, prefect of the city guard; 1.16, proconsul and legate; 1.17, prefect of Egypt; 1.18, governor; 1.19, procurator; 1.20, juridicus; 1.21, one to whom jurisdiction is delegated; 1.22, assessors.

[63] For example, Cassiodorus, *Variae* 6.1.1–3, on the history of the consulship; 6.2.1–2, on the history of the patriciate; 6.3.1, on the biblical origins of the praetorian prefecture.

congregation might accept your judgement. And above all show deference to the consulars. As first man you pronounce sentence, and you will appear as one who must be respected in that chamber of Liberty, where you are permitted to evaluate those chief men of the world vested with offices. What man is able to perceive the dark stain of vice who knows himself to be among so many lamps of virtue? Does not virtue recoil from hate? Close yourself to desire for favours. It is inevitable that you would hold the public's favour, if you should promise nothing secretly. It would be an exceptionally great and singular commendation if judges would not accept [the bribes] that many strain to offer. Not only Rome is entrusted to your authority, although in it is included the whole world, but the ancient rights also permit you to extend your jurisdiction within one hundred miles of the city, lest the mural trench confine the judge of such a city when Rome possesses everything.[64]

While the letter certainly acknowledges the fact that the urban prefect has judicial responsibilities in Rome, emphasis is placed on the particular style of public comportment necessary for the post. Deference to senatorial dignity and an incorruptible moral disposition receive primary attention. This in itself makes a strong claim for continuity with the requirements for public office received from antiquity, where it was assumed that the most traditional prerequisite was moral probity.

In fact, the letter discusses the moral disposition of the candidate almost to the complete exclusion of practical details concerning the post. This becomes particularly apparent when compared to the very different statement concerning the urban prefecture in the *Digesta*: 'All criminal matters whatsoever have been successfully claimed by the prefecture of the city as its own domain, and not only the crimes which are committed within the city but also those which have been committed outside

---

[64] Cassiodorus, *Variae* 6.4.1–5, 'Grande est quidem procerem esse, sed multo grandius de proceribus iudicare. Senatus ille mirabili opinione gloriosus probatur habere praesulem, quem mundus suspicit iura condentem; eoque fit ut illi utantur in senatu potestate perfecta, qui apud te trepidant dicere proprias causas. Verum haec quoque modestia cognoscitur esse praedicanda, ut optent se legibus teneri, quae ab ipsis sciuntur potuisse constitui. Quae res pro parte nobis absolute communis est; sed hac sola ratione discreti, quod alteri subdi non possumus, qui iudices nos habemus. Respice tot doctos viros et considera, quale sit his aliquid dicere nec erroris verecundiam formidare. De talibus disceptas, quos tibi cognoscis esse potiores. Sic ergo locum tuum tracta, ut omnes te iudicem honoratae congregationis agnoscant. Consides supra omnes scilicet consulares; sententiam primus dicis; et in illa Libertatis aula reverendus aspiceris, in qua commissos habere mundi primarios approbaris. Quis iam de obscuro vitio cogitare possit, qui se inter tot morum lumina esse cognoscit? Vis odium non recipere? Studium a te gratificationis exclude. Publicum amorem necesse est habeas, si secretius nil promittas. Erit nimirum magnum et singulare praeconium, si iudices non accipiant, ubi sunt qui multum dare contendant. Dicioni tuae non solum Roma commissa est, quamvis in illa contineantur universa, verum etiam intra centesimum potestatem te protendere antiqua iura voluerunt, ne tantae civitatis iudicem muralis agger includeret, cum Roma omnia possideret.'

the city but [*sic*] anywhere in Italy.'[65] Following this introduction, the *Digesta* continues with a detailed list of the specific conditions in which cases may be brought before the urban prefect: for example, when a slave claims asylum at a statue of the emperor, when a freedman has behaved arrogantly toward his former master, when tutors have proven incompetent, when moneylenders have committed fraud, and so on.[66] Similarly, the treatment in the *Digesta* details the kinds of urban service which fall under the prefect's supervision, such as public spectacles and the livestock market.[67] The office is treated systematically and with a specificity that confirms the didactic (as opposed to rhetorical) intent of the *Digesta* as a whole.

The functionality visible in Merovingian formularies of the seventh and eighth centuries also casts in higher relief the purely rhetorical purpose of Cassiodorus' *formulae*.[68] Again, where *Variae* are preoccupied with describing public offices in abstracted terms that present the attachment of the western bureaucracy to an ethical tradition, later *formulae* such as found in the *Formulary* of Marculf are brief and specific with respect to the function of different offices. Whether or not the *Variae* inspired later formularies, it is evident that Cassiodorus did not fashion them as the kind of document that would convey actionable information within a functioning administration.

THE ETHICS OF PUBLIC BUILDING

The *Variae* also engage with the polemics of *antiquitas* and *novitas* by taking a position in the ancient discourse concerning the ethics of public building. In a tradition that extends from Hellenistic orators to Cicero's *De legibus*, ancient authors formulated critiques of political figures by drawing attention to their building projects.[69] Moralizing attacks against building projects struck at the heart of a public official's right to claim membership among the elite. The euergetistic habit of the urban elite had always included the sponsorship of building projects. The construction of new edifices offered obvious benefits by employing the lower orders, but it also provided the amenities that set urban life apart from the rustic. The political, religious and cultural aspects of civic identity that developed around the use of such buildings literally ensured the enrolment of political figures among the 'founding fathers' of the community. In

---

[65] Justinian, *Digesta* 1.12.1, trans. Watson, 28–9.
[66] Justinian, *Digesta* 1.12.2–9.   [67] Justinian, *Digesta* 1.12.11–12.
[68] On Merovingian formularies, Zeumer, *MGH Form.*; Rio, *Formularies*; Rio, *Legal Practice*.
[69] Edwards, *Politics*, 137–72.

this sense, Livy's account of the founding of Rome did not merely stitch together the accumulated dedicatory evidence visible on monuments at the beginning of Augustus' reign. Livy drew upon contemporary notions of political power to reconstruct the development of Roman political and religious institutions in an architectural narrative. Civic identity conflated the political and religious customs embodied in the *loci* of urban spaces, most of which were attached to the memory of prominent individuals.

As part of the apparatus that substantiated political power, an individual's contribution to the urban fabric of the city was vulnerable to the same invective as moral character. In fact, architectural ambitions could be evaluated on the same ethical grounds as moral character. Questioning the contribution of a project could invalidate an individual's political efficacy. Often the most effective means of challenging the moral foundation of building was to suggest that it ran contrary to the traditional needs of the urban populace. Hence suggesting that a building was an innovation and an inversion of the natural order could impugn the political reputation of its sponsor. Especially potent was the accusation that a project perverted or contested nature at some level.[70] For Seneca the Elder, luxurious building attempted to compete with nature and its artificiality was an indication of lapsed judgement in matters of social order:

> For who could delight his mind with such debased imitations if he knew the reality? . . . Small minds have no room for great things. So they pile up masses of masonry even on the seashore, stop up bays by heaping earth in the depth of the ocean. Others let the sea into the land by means of ditches. For truly they do not know how to enjoy anything real, but in their sickness they need unnatural fakes of sea or land out of their proper places to delight them. Do you still wonder that, in their disdain for the natural, they now don't even like children – except those of others?[71]

Seneca's complaint is against the extravagant lifestyles of the wealthy and their neglect of traditional domestic culture. By drawing attention to how their opulent estates attempt to replicate a false nature, Seneca is able to impugn their understanding of a wider social order – especially one based on natural law. Such a critique was particularly incisive against rulers, where a failure to understand the fundamentals of natural law ('right and wrong') could have disastrous results. Perhaps the most spectacular case in point is the manner in which Tacitus handles Nero's construction of the new imperial complex after the great fire of 64. With a wide swathe of the valley between the Palatine, Esquiline and Caelian hills in

---

[70] Edwards, *Politics*, 146; also, Purcell, 'Town and country', 185–203.
[71] Seneca the Elder, *Controversiae* 2.1.13, trans. Winterbottom, *LCL*, 219.

ruins, Nero did not assume the euergetistic responsibilities of an urban benefactor and restore the city for the people. Instead, he constructed the type of private palace and luxury gardens that typify the depraved tyrant. The descriptions of forced nature used by Tacitus correspond to the intended image of a ruler so utterly lacking in an understanding of the natural order that the traditional social order is also jeopardized:

Nero turned to account the ruins of his fatherland by building a palace, the marvels of which were to consist not so much in gems and gold, materials long familiar and vulgarized by luxury, as in fields and lakes and the air of solitude given by wooded ground alternating with clear tracts and open landscapes. The architects and engineers . . . had the ingenuity and the courage to try the force of art even against the veto of nature and to fritter away the resources of a Caesar.[72]

It is important to bear in mind that the ancient discourse concerning building did not define a specific category of architecture as being particularly unethical. Nero's project had usurped the city for an individual's use, thereby inverting the normal relationship of the euergetistic benefactor. But Tacitus could also construct a more general critique of Roman imperial society (that is, the society of Romans under emperors) which targeted the same building projects offered to the urban populace by traditional Romans of yore:

In order that a population scattered and uncivilised, and proportionately ready for war, might be habituated by comfort to peace and quiet, he would exhort individuals, assist communities, to erect temples, market-places, houses . . . and little by little the Britons went astray into alluring vices: to the promenade, the bath, the well-appointed dinner table.[73]

The feature common to Nero and the Britons was not a specific kind of building but the disruptive agency of *novitas*. With Nero, innovation had taken the form of creating a false wilderness within the mural bounds. For the Britons, the novelty had been the introduction of urban fabric (Roman-style temples, fora, porticos, baths and villas) in support of leisured lifestyles. In both cases, Tacitus linked *novitas* to the widespread disruption of social norms.

The late antique political discourse sustained an interest in the polemics of building that contrasted innovative projects with those supportive of the public good. Ever the traditionalist, Zosimus defined Constantine as an innovator by describing the emperor's architectural projects in an unfavourable light: 'he expended the public treasury in unnecessary and unprofitable buildings [and] he likewise built some which in a short time

[72] Tacitus, *Annales* 15.42, trans. Jackson, *LCL*, 279.
[73] Tacitus, *Agricola* 21, trans. Hutton, *LCL*, 67.

were taken down again, because erected hastily, they could not stand long'.[74] Unlike the foundation of tradition upon which Livy's Rome was built, Constantine's contribution to Roman history was flawed by virtue of its hasty rise. The insubstantial quality of the buildings was a token of Zosimus' estimation of the emperor. Zosimus' negative characterization of Constantinian building may have also been a reaction to the tradition of praising church building established in Eusebius' *Vita Constantini*.

Justinian's reign was particularly susceptible to this line of critique. Sweeping legislative activity and administrative reforms almost immediately after his accession combined with an ambitious aspiration to build. So intense was Justinian's interest in urban monumentalization that it provided enough material for Procopius to celebrate the subject in his *Buildings* (completed around 550).[75] Justinian's architectural patronage was particularly visible in the environs of Constantinople, where the destruction of the Nika Revolt had cleared the ground for new building. In many respects, his projects conformed to the profile of the traditional urban benefactor by focusing on the protection and amenities of urban life.[76] Thus mural fortification and hydrology projects receive much attention in *Buildings*.[77] Where Justinian's impact on urban fabric perhaps surpassed his predecessors' was in religious building. Churches sponsored in whole or in part by Justinian and Theodora may be found in Constantinople, Ephesus, Antioch, Jerusalem, Bethlehem and Ravenna, placing Justinian's reign on a par with that of Constantine for religious building.[78] In a very real sense, Justinian's interest in church fabric was an analogue to his interest in legal text in terms of understanding how he advertised the conception of a politically and religiously unified empire.

For contemporaries opposed to Justinian's ideology of state, the emperor's preoccupation with building was an index of his propensity for innovation. The extent to which the ancient discourse concerning *antiquitas* and *novitas* conflated a social and political order with natural order ensured that maligning Justinian's building projects would contribute to his portrayal as a fundamentally flawed ruler incapable of apprehending the difference between 'right and wrong'. Although in *Buildings* Procopius enumerated Justinian's projects with the high rhetoric of

---

[74] Zosimus, *Nova Historia* 2.10, trans. Green and Chaplin.

[75] See Elsner, 'Rhetoric', 33–57, on Procopius' *Buildings*.

[76] In general on public building programmes in the late fifth and early sixth centuries, Krautheimer, *Three Capitals*; Liebeschuetz, *Decline*; Alchermes, 'Art', 343–75; Haarer, *Anastasius*, 230–45.

[77] For example, on aqueducts, Procopius, *Buildings* 1.11.10–14, 2.3.25, 2.5.11, 2.10.7, 2.10.22, 3.3.8, 3.7.1, 4.9.16, 4.11.13, 5.2.3, 5.3.1, 5.3.19, 5.9.36, 6.2.11; for a fuller treatment of Procopius' *Buildings*, Cameron, *Procopius*, 84–112.

[78] Alchermes, 'Art', 355–66.

panegyric, the view taken in the *Anecdota* is more reminiscent of Tacitus' handling of Nero:

He also saw fit to throw much money into certain buildings along the sea, seeking to put constraint upon the incessant surge of the waves. For he kept moving outward from the beach by piling up stones, being determined to compete with the wash of the sea, and, as it were, seeking to rival the strength of the sea by the sheer power of wealth.[79]

Procopius follows the established convention of portraying novelty and excess in building as the hubris of contending with nature. That these 'senseless buildings' derived from the confiscated wealth of free citizens (possibly the persecuted Hellenes) only served to underscore the causal relationship between a flawed understanding of the natural order (moral failure), *novitas* and societal rupture.[80] Procopius later identifies the 'senseless' projects as 'buildings over the sea' and new palaces in the suburbs:

And yet he squandered a great mass of money for no good reason on buildings over the sea and other senseless structures, building new ones in all parts of the suburbs, as if the palaces in which all the earlier emperors had been content to live throughout their lives could not contain his household.[81]

The 'buildings over the sea' probably refer to the many churches that Justinian sponsored throughout the eastern Mediterranean, while 'palaces' in the suburbs correspond to Justinian's construction in a suburb of Constantinople (Sycae), which the *Chronicon Paschale* claimed was renamed Justinianopolis.[82] More interesting is the way that Procopius' statement concerning palaces resonates, again, the Tacitean Nero, whose palace and personal entertainment consumed the city of Rome. Procopius made it quite clear that Justinian entertained his misguided interests at the expense of the genuine and pressing needs of the urban populace. Justinian's 'senseless' projects had claimed priority, for example, over repairs to the aqueducts that watered Constantinople, forcing the public baths to close and creating a shortage of drinking water.[83] Similarly, Procopius berated Justinian for his mismanagement of revenues in provincial cities, which required cities throughout the eastern empire to abandon the customary

---

[79] Procopius, *Anecdota* 8.7–8, trans. Dewing, *LCL*, 93.
[80] Procopius, *Anecdota* 11.3, notes that Justinian used the properties of persecuted citizens to fund both 'senseless buildings' and gifts to barbarians, possibly a reference to the gold used to secure the 'Eternal Peace' with Persia; trans. Dewing, *LCL*.
[81] Procopius, *Anecdota* 26.23; trans. Dewing, *LCL*, 311.
[82] *Chronicon Paschale* 528; Whitby, 'Historical writing', note 338.
[83] Procopius, *Anecdota* 26.23–25.

provisions for public buildings and caused the neglect of theatres, hippo-dromes and circuses.[84] Ultimately, the complaint about building in the *Anecdota* imposes an inversion of the traditional euergetistic habit. Instead of building for the benefit of the urban populace, Justinian 'squandered a great mass of money for no good reason' and allowed new construction to take priority over repairs to older and more useful forms of infras-tructure. Furthermore, Justinian's 'dysfunctional' approach to euergetism contended with the natural order of things, which, because human soci-ety was an extension of a divinely intended harmony, meant that it would necessarily be harmful to the public cause.

As previously noted, the designation of a building project as useful or harmful to public needs is usually arbitrary. The pejorative quality was drawn from the fact that it represented, at some level, a departure from the trusted habits of *antiquitas*. Fortifications, palaces and churches were not intrinsically innovative except that, in the case of many among the elite of Constantinople, they were associated with the 'non-traditional' aims of Justinian's policies – the confiscation of property as a part of the persecution of the Hellenes, changes in administrative and financial poli-cies and changes in the religious definition of who participated in empire. That this means of interpreting Justinian's reign was fairly widespread as a texture of the political discourse is evident in the sources. In terms very similar to those of Procopius, John Lydus pointedly praised baths, markets and aqueducts as the kinds of amenity that had *formerly* enriched life in the cities.[85] By contrast, he offered a less approving statement con-cerning palaces, particularly the building that became the official 'lair' for the debaucheries of John the Cappadocian in his capacity as praetorian prefect.[86]

Most commentators of the sixth century recognized that the discourse that attempted to read governmental virtue (or the lack thereof) into building programmes had serious political consequences. Marcellinus Comes, who was very sensitive to the cross-currents of Constantinian association, composed a geography (no longer extant) of Jerusalem and Constantinople that provided a detailed account of the disposition of the churches and other Christian sites. Such an account, possibly inspired by the attention paid to Constantine's building in the *Vita Constantini*, provided the perfect opportunity to further the rehabilitation of Con-stantine's reputation on the same grounds that Zosimus had sought to soil it. The surviving reference to Marcellinus' geography comes from

---

[84] Procopius, *Anecdota* 26.5–8.
[85] John Lydus, *De mensibus* 3.23, from Maas, *John Lydus*, 18, note 49.
[86] John Lydus, *De magistratibus* 2.21.1–4.

Cassiodorus, who probably understood its polemical value.[87] If inspired by Eusebius' treatment of Constantinian building, Marcellinus' geography laid a foundation for praising Justinian for the building programmes that he undertook (as a continuator of Constantine) in Constantinople and throughout the eastern Mediterranean. The fact that Procopius was responsible for a treatise that built on that foundation (*Buildings*) only underscores how polemical and treacherous this discourse was. Writing even later, Evagrius noted in the same breath that Justinian had obtained the property of others through greed and corruption, while he had also raised many magnificent churches for the care of the needy.[88] In a sense, Evagrius attempted to reconcile competing traditions concerning Justinian's reputation as a builder.

THE *VARIAE* IN CONTRAST

The portrayal of Amal building in the *Variae* appears everywhere sensitive to the eastern discourse that sought to tarnish Justinian's reign. Although the classical discourse on the polemics of building never developed a clearly defined typology for construction projects that were appropriate for the attention of rulers, the *Variae* take a conservatively utilitarian position concerning projects that should consume the resources of the state. Similar to the sentiment of Procopius' comments in the *Anecdota*, the *Variae* tend to give the impression that the Amals only indulged in building that had utilitarian purpose. Projects receiving royal sponsorship included the mural fortification of cities,[89] the repair of ports,[90] the restoration of baths[91] and derelict granaries,[92] the repair of sewers[93] and aqueducts,[94] and the construction of workshops.[95] Importantly, Cassiodorus addressed the greater majority

---

[87] Cassiodorus, *Institutiones*, 1.25.1, 'Marcellinus of whom I have already spoken should also be read with equal care. He described in minute detail the cities of Constantinople and Jerusalem in four books', trans. Halporn, *TTH*, 157.

[88] Evagrius, *Historia Ecclesiastica* 4.30.

[89] Cassiodorus, *Variae* 1.17, fortifications at Dertona; 1.25, repair of city walls at Rome; 1.28, measures to collect stones for walls; 2.7, restoration of walls; 2.34, concerning funds for city walls at Rome; 3.44, walls at Arles; 3.48, fortifications at Verruca; 3.49, fortifications at Catana; 5.9, walls at Tridentum; 12.17, fortifications at Ravenna.

[90] Cassiodorus, *Variae* 1.25, the dockyards at Rome.

[91] Cassiodorus, *Variae* 2.37, the baths at Spoleto; 2.39, the springs at Aponus; 4.24, baths of Turasum.

[92] Cassiodorus, *Variae* 3.29, granaries 'ille et ille', presumably at Rome, 'in ea praesertim urbe, ubi cuncta dignum est constructa relucere'.

[93] Cassiodorus, *Variae* 3.30, sewers at Rome; 8.29 and 8.30, sewers at Parma.

[94] Cassiodorus, *Variae* 3.31, aqueducts at Rome; 4.31, an unspecified aqueduct; 5.38, aqueducts at Ravenna; 7.6, aqueducts at Rome.

[95] Cassiodorus, *Variae* 4.30, workshops at Rome to contribute to the restoration of the city.

of letters dealing with construction to the restoration of existing edifices, such as baths and aqueducts, or the fitting of older structures to new use. An excellent example is the rehabilitation of a derelict portion of the Forum Romanum through the construction of workshops and living quarters:

It is indeed fitting that each person consider the increase of his own country, but especially those whom the state has attached to itself with the highest honours, since it is the nature of things that one who is seen to undertake greater things necessarily ought to accomplish more. And so, you have asked in the petition sent to us that permission be granted for building workshops upon the portico of Curva, which fittingly encloses the Forum in the manner of a courtyard, being situated near the Domus Palmata, so that a building for private habitation may be extended and the appearance of newness may arise from the ancient city. Let it thus happen, that what has been able to decline from negligence should be seen sustained by the diligence of inhabitants, since the ruin of buildings is easily accomplished by removing the careful attention of residents and that which the presence of men does not look after quickly sunders with the ripening of age. Thence we, who desire the city to be comported with the brilliance of rising buildings, grant the requested opportunity, unless the project impedes either public utility or its comeliness. For this reason, expect to commence untroubled by legalities, so that you may furnish Roman workshops and both the worthy tenant and the completed work may commend the author. For there is no other undertaking by which one is better able to be acknowledged for both the inspiration of wisdom and the practice of munificence.[96]

Although strictly speaking a new construction, the project promised to restore the ancient heart of Rome to its traditional social and economic rhythms. The conservatism of these building and renovation projects is often expressed in various terms connoting *utilitas publica*, or the advantage to the common good.[97] In this way, the support of the Amal court for building merges with a deeper ideological stream of legislative and

[96] Cassiodorus, *Variae* 4.30.1–3, 'Decet quidem cunctos patriae suae augmenta cogitare, sed eos maxime, quos res publica sibi summis honoribus obligavit, quia ratio rerum est, ut eum necesse sit plus debere, qui visus est maiora suscipere. Porrecta itaque supplicatione testatus es Curvae porticus, quae iuxta domum Palmatam posita forum in modum areae decenter includit, superimponendis fabricis licentiam condonari, ut et privatarum aedium habitatio protendatur et antiquis moenibus novitatis crescat aspectus. Ita fit, ut, quod per incuriam poterat labi, manentum videatur diligentia sustineri, quia facilis est aedificiorum ruina incolarum subtracta custodia et cito vetustatis decoctione resolvitur, quod hominum praesentia non tuetur. Unde nos, qui urbem fabricarum surgentium cupimus nitore componi, facultatem concedimus postulatam, ita tamen, si res petita aut utilitate publicae non officit aut decori. Quapropter rebus speratis securus innitere, ut dignus Romanis fabricis habitator appareas perfectumque opus suum laudet auctorem. Nulla enim res est, per quam melius possit agnosci et prudentis ingenium et largitatis effectus.'
[97] Cassiodorus, *Variae* 1.17.1, 1.28.3, 2.7, 3.29.2, 3.31.4; on *utilitas publica* as an aspect of the ideology of the *Variae*, Barbieri, 'Cassiodoro', ix–xv; Scivoletto, 'Cassiodoro', 3–24; Colace, 'Lessico', 159–76.

administrative decisions made on behalf of utility to the state and the common weal of the governed.[98]

The level of attention that the *Variae* give to *utilitas publica* is simply a refined aspect of a larger picture that attempted to communicate complete devotion to *antiquitas* as a model for good governance. Like showing deference to the inviolability of ancient legal custom, maintaining careful distance from *novitas* in building also advertised a moral predisposition and becomes a part of the political persona communicated by the *Variae*. The message is consistent at every level in the *Variae*. In a letter addressing something as minor as the theft of a bronze statue in Como, Cassiodorus found the opportunity to interject the core ideology that was to be understood as the character of governance in Italy: 'It is grievous to our reign that the accomplishments of the ancients vanish, especially when we desire to increase the adornment of cities daily.'[99] Grander projects involving urban fabric, such as public baths, adopted the same posture that was concerned to restore the present day to the pristine quality of antiquity: 'we want to join the wonders reported of the ancients to the reputation of our reign, since such are an increase to royal glory when nothing diminishes under us?'[100]

The contrast between *novitas* and *antiquitas* was so embedded in the ethical considerations concerning building that Cassiodorus could even risk drawing attention to the obvious paradox of restoration. Letter 4.24 called a portico that had fallen into disrepair 'that which awaits the splendour of restoration, so that, in a kind of confusion, the face of novelty is returned to something mature with antiquity and something renewed would arise'.[101] The near-contradiction is strikingly similar to Cassiodorus' recognition in letter 11.8 that while imperial law had formerly been innovation, it has since taken on the grandeur of custom. The parallel underscores how Cassiodorus intended this attitude toward building to be understood as pervasive in all aspects of governance. Statements containing this sentiment were deployed equally in reference to

[98] Cassiodorus, *Variae, praefatio* 1.1, *praefatio*, 1.6, 1.24.1, 1.29.1, 1.45.1, 2.5.1, 2.6.1, 2.16.4, 2.20.1, 2.23.1, 2.30.3, 2.31.3, 2.32, 3.25.2, 3.26.1, 3.27.3, 3.34.1, 4.16.1, 4.38.3, 4.41.3, 4.47.2, 5.5.1, 5.6.1, 5.7.1, 5.9.1, 5.14.9, 5.17.6, 5.18.1, 5.31.1, 6.12.2, 7.32.1, 7.33.1, 8.2.9, 8.3.4, 8.10.8, 10.13.6, 11.1.8, 11.4.3, 11.8.5, 11.37.1, 12.1.5, 12.2.6, 12.6.3.
[99] Cassiodorus, *Variae* 2.35.1, 'Acerbum nimis est nostris temporibus antiquorum facta decrescere, qui ornatum urbium cottidie desideramus augere.'
[100] Cassiodorus, *Variae* 2.39.1, 'Si audita veterum miracula ad laudem clementiae nostrae volumus continere, quoniam augmenta regalis gloriae sunt, cum sub nobis nulla decrescunt, quo studio convenit reparari quod etiam nostris oculis frequenter constat offeri?' Also 3.30.1, 3.44.1, 4.31.1.
[101] Cassiodorus, *Variae* 4.24.1, 'quae iam longo situ squalor vetustatis obnuverat, splendorem reparationis expetere, ut rebus antiquitate confusis novitatis facies adulta reddatur'; similarly 4.30.2.

the preservation of buildings, law and institutional culture.[102] The result was the portrayal of a government with harmonious consistency.

Another manner in which the *Variae* speak to traditionalism through the subject of buildings and urban fabric is in spoliation. A scattering of letters in the collection are concerned with the disposition of fallen stonework and the quarrying of derelict buildings.[103] The history of urban spoliation certainly had a long representation in late antique legislation, where emperors recurrently expressed their interest in limiting the harvesting of materials from defunct public monuments in order to maintain the integrity of the fabric of urban institutions.[104] Such legislation as found in the *Theodosian Code* responded to a widespread aesthetic value placed on the sculptural and architectural elements of public buildings which encouraged their removal and reinstallation in private property.[105] The core of that aesthetic value was the eclecticism of *mos maiorum* and the notion that embedding fragments of ancient building in a new structure could 'capture' the prestige of *antiquitas*. Even in public architecture sponsored by emperors, the reappropriation of materials from a previous age had more to do with maintaining an attachment to *antiquitas* than with the logistical ease of reuse. A sampling of this habit may be seen in the later mural fortification of Rome, where the incorporation of architectural features such as funerary monuments (the Pyramid of Cestius) and triumphal arches (Porta Appia and Porta Tiburtina) actually complicated mural defence rather than augmented it. Late antique cities had a long history in which the reuse of materials formed a vital part of the visual symbolic language of the urban environment. From the earlier imperial tondi implanted into the Arch of Constantine to the harvesting of ancient columns for use in late antique churches, the spoliation of materials from older sites created continuity with *antiquitas* in new contexts. Of course, as seen in the *Theodosian Code*, unsanctioned spoliation was discouraged for fear that the original context for *antiquitas* (at the material level) would disappear altogether. Like the more literary *mos maiorum*, the spoliation of ancient urban fabric required the mediation of authority.

---

[102] Cassiodorus, *Variae* 3.31.1, 'Quamvis universae rei publicae nostrae infatigabilem curam desideremus impendere et deo favente ad statum studeamus pristinum cuncta revocare', concerning the administrative duties of the Senate.

[103] Cassiodorus, *Variae* 1.28, 2.7, 3.9, 5.8.

[104] On legislation concerning spoliation, Alchermes, 'Spolia', 167–78; Dubouloz, '*Loca publica*', 53–74.

[105] See, in particular, Majorian's *Novella* 4 of 458, which deals with widespread opportunities to harvest prestigious components of urban fabric after the Vandalic sack of Rome; on the development of an aesthetic that encouraged spoliation, Brenk, 'Spolia', 103–9; Elsner, 'Culture of spolia', 149–84; Hansen, *Appropriation*.

Reading the Variae as political apologetic

Letters from the *Variae* provide a model for how authority mediated and safeguarded the cultural heritage of *antiquitas* and *mos maiorum*. When combined with the veneration of *antiquitas* and *mos maiorum* expressed in the *Variae*, letters concerning the spoliation of buildings become the exercise of a kind of virtue. Deciding in which context it was proper to disassemble the past required the discernment of a wise and culturally sensitive ruler (and, by extension, a discerning government). As demonstrated to the Senate in a sharp rebuke concerning the removal of bronze and lead from public structures and the quarrying of stone from temples, the *Variae* could vigorously discourage the systematic pillaging of public monuments.[106] But in as much as spoliation could be conducted as a means of preserving *antiquitas* in a new context, it was also encouraged:

Let those blocks of marble which lay torn down and neglected throughout the city be set aside for those chosen for such work and be added to the building of the walls, so that a venerable fortification might return something to public beauty and that stones cast about under ruins should thus adorn.[107]

Similarly, in a letter directing the citizens of Aestunae to collect derelict columns and marble for transportation to Ravenna, the hierarchy that values the new relative to the old has been preserved. Old materials are to be retrieved in order that something new may preserve *antiquitas* and thereby retain the grandeur of the past:

Indeed, it is our intention to build new things, but even more to protect ancient things, since we are likely to acquire no less praise for the preservation of things than for their foundation. Consequently, we desire to erect modern buildings without impairing those of the previous age; for it is not deemed acceptable to our sense of justice that anything becomes disadvantaged for the sake of others. And so, we have discovered that columns and marble stone, having been cast down by the envy of great age, now lie without use in your town. And since it profits nothing to protect anything carelessly cast aside, they ought to rise up, revived for adornment, rather than to show sorrow in the memory of the preceding age ... contrive by any means to haul the above-mentioned columns and marble slabs to Ravenna, so that, by a lovely craftsmanship, a forgotten likeness may once again be returned to fallen marbles and that which

---

[106] Cassiodorus, *Variae* 3.31.4, 'Aes praeterea, non minimum pondus, et quod est facillimum direptioni, molissimum plumbum, de ornatu moenium referuntur esse sublata, quae auctores suos saeculis consecrarunt. Aes enim Ionos Thessaliae rex, plumbum Mida regnator Phrygiae repererunt. Et quam miserum est, ut unde famam providentiae alii susceperunt, nos opinionem neglegentiae incurrisse videamur? Templa etiam et loca publica, quae petentibus multis ad reparationem contulimus, subversioni fuisse potius mancipata.'

[107] Cassiodorus, *Variae* 2.7, 'Et ideo illustris sublimitas tua marmorum quadratos, qui passim diruti negleguntur, quibus hoc opus videtur iniunctum in fabricam murorum faciat deputari, ut redeat in decorem publicum prisca constructio et ornent aliquid saxa iacentia post ruinas.'

244

had been blackened by neglect should be able to reclaim that quality of shining antiquity.[108]

An identical formulation of the past in a present context can be found in Paulinus' statement concerning a new church dedicated to St Felix which eclipsed the function of the older basilica, 'For novelty in the old is . . . as useful an adornment as age in the new.'[109] Cassiodorus employed a term unusual in late antique Latin, *modernus* ('modern'), to connote the novelty of desiring the new, but even here the attraction of something new is carefully subordinated to the prestige of *antiquitas*. In fact, throughout the *Variae*, Cassiodorus uses the term *modernus* in contraposition to *antiquitas*, with the understanding that 'modernity' was proper only in as much as it was informed by or modelled on the past. In contrast to absolute rupture with the past represented by *novitas*, Cassiodorus used *modernus* as a concept for 'the new' that was consistent with the ethos of the *Variae*.[110] The new should only receive attention in the service of maintaining antiquity. In fact, antiquity should be preserved to the extent that it takes on the 'shining' aspect of the new. To do otherwise would violate the same profound sense of the appropriate that also informs the exercise of justice: 'it is not deemed acceptable to our sense of justice that anything becomes disadvantaged for the sake of others' (*incommodum nostrae iustitiae non . . . acceptum*).[111]

The proper bounds of the traditional and modern receive further definition in the *Variae* with respect to palace construction, a subject of interest in the political discourse of Constantinople. One of the earliest letters in the collection (1.6) announces the construction of a new palace basilica at Ravenna that was to be dedicated with the name of Hercules. The letter is addressed to Agapitus, the urban prefect of Rome, who has

---

[108] Cassiodorus, *Variae* 3.9.1–3, 'Propositi quidem nostri est nova construere, sed amplius vetusta servare, quia non minorem laudem de inventis quam de rebus possumus adquirere custoditis. Proinde moderna sine priorum imminutione desideramus erigere; quicquid enim per alienum venit incommodum, nostrae iustitiae non probatur acceptum. In municipio itaque vestro sine usu iacere comperimus columnas et lapides vetustatis invidia demolitos; et quia indecore iacentia servare nil proficit, ad ornatum debent surgere redivivum quam dolorem monstrare ex memoria praecedentium saeculorum . . . supra memoratas platonias vel columnas ad Ravennatem civitatem contradat modis omnibus devehendas, ut conlapsis metallis oblitterata facies reddatur iterum de arte pulcherrima et quae situ fuerant obscura, antiqui nitoris possint recipere qualitatem.'

[109] Paulinus of Nola, *Carmen* 28.173–176; trans. Hansen, *Appropriation*, 257; for greater elaboration, Hansen, *Appropriation*, 247–60.

[110] Cassiodorus, *Variae* 3.3.5, 'modernis saeculis moribus ornabantur antiquis'; 3.9.1, 'proinde moderna sine priorum imminutione desideramus erigere'; 4.51.2, 'antiquorum diligentissimus imitator, modernorum nobilissimus institutor'; 11.1.19, 'Ordo flagitat dictionis Augustarum veterum pompam moderna comparatione excutere.'

[111] Cassiodorus, *Variae* 3.9.1–3.

been asked to dispatch marble workers to Ravenna for the purpose of adorning the structure:

It is fitting that a prince should consider which efforts would enrich the state and it is worthy indeed for a king to adorn a palace with building. For it is not fitting that we should yield to the ancients with respect to adornment, when we are not unequal to the prosperity of those ages. On this account, I have commenced the massive undertaking of the Basilica of Hercules in the city of Ravenna, to which antiquity contributed a suitable name.[112]

At first glance, the letter seems to stumble across a carefully observed dichotomy consistently present elsewhere in the collection, and indeed the letter seems aware of this problem. The proposed basilica would be a new construction and an ornament to Theoderic's reign as opposed to being something ancient and utilitarian and thereby deserving of preservation. Resolution to this problem is found in the name of the edifice, which *antiquitas* supplied, rendering it a more suitable undertaking.

Dedicating the basilica with the name of Hercules was more than a superficial means of explaining the inconsistency of patronizing a new palace complex. The name has direct relevance to the ideological purpose of the building or, more exactly, the ideological function that the building served in the *Variae*.[113] At present Ravenna contains no archaeological trace of a structure identifiable as a Basilica of Hercules.[114] Furthermore, the only textual reference to the building is found in the *Variae*. Agnellus' *Liber Pontificalis Ecclesiae Ravennatis*, an otherwise detailed source of information for the urban structures of sixth-century Ravenna, is silent on the matter. As such, the various suggestions which attach the basilica either to the intra-mural palace of Theoderic or to a proposed circus complex are speculative.[115] It may be that Cassiodorus intended the letter to signal the proximity of the western palatine elite to a Neoplatonic brand of political traditionalism. The name of Hercules recognized the ancient imperial formulation of political theology by which emperors paralleled the political dependencies of *caesares* to *augusti* with the divine relationship of Hercules to Jupiter. Senior emperors (*augusti*) as late as Diocletian styled themselves symbolically as 'Jupiter' while the junior

---

[112] Cassiodorus, *Variae* 1.6.1–2, 'Decet principem cura quae ad rem publicam spectat augendam, et vere dignum est regem aedificiis palatia decorare. Absit enim ut ornatui cedamus veterum, qui inpares non sumus beatitudine saeculorum. Quapropter in Ravennati urbe basilicae Herculis amplum opus aggressi, cuius nomini antiquitas congrue tribuit.'

[113] On the admonitory symbolism of Hercules in a later, Carolingian context, Nees, *Tainted Mantle*.

[114] On the subject of the *Basilica Herculis*, Dyggve, 'Basilica Herculis', 75–78; Deichmann, *Ravenna*, 41; Ward-Perkins, *Building*, 162–3; Johnson, 'Theoderic's building', 73–96; Kennell, 'Hercules' basilica', 159–75; Deliyannis, *Ravenna*, 123–4.

[115] For the problems with either interpretation, Deliyannis, *Ravenna*, 119–24.

authority of their protégés (*caesares*) was represented through symbolic attribution to 'Hercules', the divine son. In this way, the highest level of imperial political structure assumed a familial intimacy that was reinforced by association with divine (and universal) harmony. This manner of representing imperial authority ended with Constantine. Thus a *Basilica Herculis* represents a specifically pre-Constantinian piece of imperial political language that acknowledged the Amals and the western palatine elite as occupying a position subordinate to the eastern emperor and court. The statement blended well with the political traditionalism embedded in the first letter of the *Variae*, which claimed that Theoderic's rule was a lawful imitation of the eastern emperors:

And therefore, most pious of emperors, it is becoming to your authority and dignity that we ought to strive for civic harmony with you, we who have thus far benefited from your affection. For you are the most sublime dignity of all kingdoms, you the beneficent defender of the entire world, whom all other rulers rightfully admire, since they recognize something to pertain particularly to you alone. We especially know this, who by divine providence have learned in your state that manner by which we are able to govern the Roman people equitably. Our rule is an imitation of yours, the exemplary form of the only good empire having been set on display. However much we follow you, so much do we outstrip other nations.[116]

Letters 1.1 and 1.6, when combined, offer a reference to a non-Christian divine political order that would have appealed to the philosophically and politically traditionalist Hellenes of the eastern bureaucracy. Significantly, evidence of the symbolic political value of Hercules was present in sixth-century Constantinople. The forum built by Theodosius I was ringed by columns fashioned to represent the club of Hercules.[117]

As a piece of the rhetoric with which Cassiodorus intended to impress an eastern audience, the ideological subordination of the western court to the eastern capital is strengthened by the fact that other known Amal palaces outside Ravenna are thoroughly muted in the *Variae*. It is well known from the *Anonymus Valesianus* that Theoderic completed three palace complexes that integrated imperial *aula*, portico, bath and theatre

---

[116] Cassiodorus, *Variae* 1.1.2–3, 'Et ideo, piissime principum, potentiae vestrae convenit et honori, ut concordiam vestram quaerere debeamus, cuius adhuc amore proficimus. Vos enim estis regnorum omnium pulcherrimum decus, vos totius orbis salutare praesidium, quos ceteri dominantes iure suspiciunt, quia in vobis singulare aliquid inesse cognoscunt, nos maxime, qui divino auxilio in re publica vestra didicimus, quemadmodum Romanis aequabiliter imperare possimus. Regnum nostrum imitatio vestra est, forma boni propositi, unici exemplar imperii: qui quantum vos sequimur, tantum gentes alias anteimus. Hortamini me frequenter, ut diligam senatum, leges principum gratanter amplectar, ut cuncta Italiae membra componam.'
[117] Ricci, 'Recenti restauri', 465–6.

at Ravenna, Verona and Pavia.[118] Similarly, the *Valesianus* noted how Theoderic had provided for the maintenance of one of the imperial palaces at Rome, certainly a fact warranting advertisement had the political climate been neutral toward palaces.[119] However, the only extensive reference to a palace complex in the *Variae* is a *formula* for the *curator palatii*, the caretaker of the palace. The *formula* carefully manages any disruption that it may have caused to the ideology of the *Variae* by suggesting that the Amals enjoyed architectural tastes similar to those of Justinian. The *formula* embeds discussion of the palace in a very tradition-oriented disquisition concerning the ancient architectural knowledge of Euclid, Archimedes and Metrobius.[120] The letter is primarily concerned to communicate that building undertaken by the Amals, including the palace, has been informed by the dictates of antiquity, 'so that only the newness of the buildings should distance them from the work of the ancients'.[121] The *novitas fabricarum* and *fundare novitatem* discussed in the letter conveniently call to mind the criticism against Justinian.[122] But by qualifying the desire to build something new by the fact that the court architect had learned from ancient scholars, the letter assures the audience that the western court maintained a careful attachment to *antiquitas*. Once again, it is not the case that palaces were thought to be intrinsically bad, but it was necessary (in light of the eastern polemic) to qualify any *novitas* associated with new construction at Ravenna with the sanction of *antiquitas*.

CHURCH BUILDING IN THE *VARIAE*

Another manner in which the *Variae* demonstrate sensitivity to an eastern polemic of building is by maintaining absolute silence with respect to the building of churches.[123] It is certainly the case that church building was a regular subject of interest in late antique literature. Writers of the fifth and sixth centuries spoke of the

---

[118] *Excerpta Valesiana* 71.   [119] *Excerpta Valesiana* 67.   [120] Cassiodorus, *Variae* 7.5.2–4.
[121] Cassiodorus, *Variae* 7.5.4–5, 'Decorum magisterium, propositum omnino gloriosum in tam longas aetates mittere, unde te debeat posteritas ammirata laudare . . . Quapropter quicquid ad te pertinet, ita decenter, ita firmiter volumus explicari, ut ab opere veterum sola distet novitas fabricarum.'
[122] Cassiodorus, *Variae* 7.5.4, 'Nam sicubi aut civitatem reficimus aut castellorum volumus fundare novitatem vel si construendi nobis praetorii amoenitas blandiatur, te ordinante ad oculos perducitur quod nobis cogitantibus invenitur.'
[123] Similarly noticed by Brogiolo, 'Ideas of town', 108, that the flourish of sixth-century religious building, especially at Ravenna, is not evident in the *Variae*.

construction of churches with relish and in great detail.[124] Closer to home for Cassiodorus and the Amals, Ennodius dedicated two poems to church building and discussion of the foundation of new churches is a regular structural feature of the *Liber Pontificalis*.[125] Of course, these are examples of church building absent the patronage of a secular ruler. In the east, there was a long tradition begun by Eusebius of praising the support that church building received from emperors, but under Justinian the involvement of the emperor in church building became seen as a distraction from the proper affairs of the state by the conservative intellectual elite of Constantinople. The absence of church building in the *Variae* needs to be understood as a specific facet of the ideological presentation of the collection that was tied to the eastern polemic. The omission of the subject from the *Variae* can only have been intentional as church building was among the premier interests of the Amals at Ravenna that would have required extensive communication to marshal material resources. Agnellus noted that Theoderic and the Amals had been responsible for the construction of seven churches in Ravenna and its neighbouring suburbs, Caesarea and Classe.[126] Although these churches maintained an Arian theological orientation until the late 560s, it is not probable that this would have caused Cassiodorus to suppress their mention in the *Variae*. Cassiodorus elsewhere refers to a Goth who was possibly a member of the Arian clergy.[127] Additionally, the *Variae* present the Amals as amply attentive to the affairs of the 'orthodox' church and matters concerning its clergy.[128] The chief difference between Justinian's involvement in church affairs and the presentation of the Amals and churches of Italy in the *Variae* was one of agency. In the majority of letters touching on the administration of the church or church property, the Amals figure as the recipients of petitions seeking intervention or resolution.[129] In others involving the criminal activity of members of the clergy, the Amals refer sentencing to a higher authority in the ecclesiastical order, such as a bishop.[130] By contrast, church building for a secular ruler implied

---

[124] Paulinus of Nola, *Carmen* 28; Sidonius Apollinaris, *Epistulae* 3.1, 4.15, 6.12; Ennodius, *Epistulae* 96, 97, 98; Gregory of Tours, *Decem Libri Historiarum* 1.31, 1.32, 2.14, 2.15, 2.16, 2.17.

[125] Ennodius, *Carmena* 2.9 and 2.60; *Liber Pontificalis* 50–61, covering the period from Popes Felix III to Vigilius (483–555), mention the construction of twelve basilicas.

[126] Agnellus, *Liber Pontificalis Ecclesiae Ravennatis* 86.

[127] Cassiodorus, *Variae* 2.17, 'pro sorte quam Butilani presbytero nostra largitate contulimus'.

[128] Cassiodorus, *Variae* 1.9, 1.26, 2.8, 2.29, 2.30, 3.7, 3.14, 3.37, 3.45, 4.18, 4.20, 4.31, 4.34, 4.44, 8.8, 8.15, 8.24, 9.5, 9.15, 9.16, 10.34, 11.2, 11.3, 12.13, 12.20, 12.27.

[129] For example, Cassiodorus, *Variae* 2.29, in answer to a petition from bishops concerning property in Sicily; 2.30, in answer to a petition from the church to appoint a *defensor ecclesiae* for the poor; 4.20, concerning the seizure of church property; 8.15, concerning a request from the clergy of Rome to intervene in a contested papal election.

[130] For example, Cassiodorus, *Variae* 1.9.3, 4.18.2, 8.24.

patronage and the potential for a certain degree of intervention in matters of religion.

The absence of church building from the *Variae* seems related to Cassiodorus' sensitivity to the eastern political polemic surrounding Justinian in Constantinople. This polemic probably did not begin to emerge until after the first Hellene purge of 529. Interestingly, the *Variae* contain three letters that may represent Cassiodorus' active suppression of the attention that the Amals gave to church building and, if genuine, these letters would have originated at the beginning and end of the Amal regime. The first letter has already been discussed. It is quite possible that the *Basilica Herculis* mentioned in letter 1.6 was in fact one of the Amal churches of Ravenna described in terms that masked the religious associations of the structure. The very term *basilica* was almost universally used for 'church' by the sixth century, while the sort of civic halls from which churches originally derived their form were referred to as *aulae*.[131] The church of Sant'Apollinare Nuovo, built by Theoderic, is probably the best candidate. It was certainly a massive enough undertaking and it shared a precinct with Theoderic's *palatium* complex, in which case Cassiodorus could speak of it as an adornment of the palace. The church was itself the central component of a religious complex that included a baptistery. Both sustained damage in the late seventh and mid-eighth centuries, for which reason it was restored on both occasions and the original mosaic programme of the apse has been lost.[132] Had the original programme borne any resemblance to that of the chapel in the orthodox episcopal complex (constructed in the same period between 494 and 520), the name *Basilica Herculis* acquires additional meaning.[133] Within the narthex of the Capella Arcivescovile is a sixth-century mosaic of Christ dressed as a soldier and bearing an emperor's imperial cloak. Trampled and submissive under the feet of the Christ figure are the serpent and lion, which recalls the biblical triumph of David in the Psalms.[134] These were also the symbolic attributions of Hercules, who wrestled a serpent as a child and bore the hide of the Nemean lion. It is quite probable that the portrayal of Christ as a martial figure blended the two associations. Christ figured as Hercules and their parallel associations with divine fathers and imperial power structures might have warranted Cassiodorus' rather

---

[131] On this distinction, Deliyannis, *Ravenna*, 350.

[132] Agnellus, *Liber Pontificalis Ecclesiae Ravennatis* 89 and 119; on Sant'Apollinare Nuovo, Deliyannis, *Ravenna*, 146–74.

[133] On the Capella Arcivescovile, Deliyannis, *Ravenna*, 188–96.

[134] Psalm 90:12–13, 'in manibus portabunt te ne forte offendas ad lapidem pedem tuum / super aspidem et basiliscum ambulabis et conculcabis leonem et draconem'.

figuratively naming a church dedicated by Theoderic to Christ as the *Basilica Herculis*.[135]

The second indication that the *Variae* possibly suppress discussion of church building is found in two letters (10.8 and 10.9) situated in the last book written in the name of the Amals. Letter 10.8 introduces the subject of certain unspecified building preparations undertaken at Ravenna by Amalasuntha and Theodahad with Justinian's involvement. The letter mentions a particular Calogenitus whom Justinian sent to Ravenna, probably as an architect or mosaicist.[136] It is tempting to read in these arrangements the faint outline of diplomatic relations revolving around the ongoing construction of San Vitale, the final decorative programme of which bore the stamp of the triumphant entry of Justinian and eastern orthodoxy into Ravenna.[137] If this is indeed the case then Cassiodorus may have purposefully included letters alluding to the interference of Justinian in Italian affairs even at the level of public building. A suppressed reference to San Vitale, a structure more reminiscent of Justinianic churches in Constantinople such as the Hagia Sophia or SS Sergius and Bacchus than of basilica-style churches such as Sant'Apollinare Nuovo, may have been intended to remind an eastern audience that Justinian's interventionist policies (and building) extended beyond Constantinople. At any rate, the sheer allusiveness and ambiguity of these two letters certainly did not lend themselves to instructing a bureaucratic audience in forms of chancery writing, and some other motive for their inclusion must be assumed.

CIVILITAS

The care that Cassiodorus took to present a 'politically correct' relationship between Amal governance and the physical space of cities in the *Variae* is but one aspect of a wider programmatic presentation. As seen in the *Variae*, the subjects of law, administration, magisterial competence and even urban planning were all carefully regulated by a form of traditionalism that accepted *antiquitas* as the model of good governance. Which antiquity from the *longue durée* of the Roman past should be

---

[135] Agnellus, *Liber Pontificalis Ecclesiae Ravennatis* 86, preserves the original dedicatory inscription, 'Theodericus Rex hanc ecclesiam a fundamentis in nomine domini nostri Yhesu Christi fecit'; discussed in Urbano, 'Donation', 73–6.

[136] Cassiodorus, *Variae* 10.8.2, 'Et ideo mansuetudinem vestram reverenter salutans harum portitorum illum ad excellentiae vestrae beneficia destinavi, ut marmora vel alia necessaria quae quondam Calogenitum comparare feceramus.'

[137] On this subject in general, Von Simpson, *Sacred Fortress*, 1–37; on the possible completion of San Vitale before the arrival of Bishop Maximian, Andreescu-Treadgold and Treadgold, 'S. Vitale', 716–21.

consulted is never defined. Instead, expressing a mental habit that was receptive to the lessons of the past and resistant to breaks with tradition seems to be the central message. Adherence to this kind of traditionalism is expressed as a kind of virtue in the *Variae*. It was more than one of the personal virtues that described the moral base of an individual; instead, it was a communal virtue upon which the moral base of an entire society depended. The *Variae* offered a model in which the acceptance of tradition ensured continuity with the same society that had witnessed the rise and prosperity of the Roman Empire. The notion that tradition bound a society in peaceful harmony was expressed with the term *civilitas*, which appears in the *Variae* with striking regularity.[138] Although not unique to the *Variae* as a term embodying social harmony, it appears in the *Variae* more regularly and with more specificity than in other sources.[139] The term *civilitas* provides a specifically urban meaning for social harmony. It embodies notions of civic and governmental apparatus, urban community and the unobstructed function of law. The meaning of *civilitas* ('civic harmony') derives from its lexical association with the concepts of *civis* ('citizen') and *civitas* ('a city with status recognized by central government'). As such, *civilitas* was a form of public harmony which was enjoyed by cities and citizens and depended on mutual participation in a specifically urban culture mediated by government. Hence respect for legal and administrative traditions, especially office holding and the behavioural norms associated with the duty of office holding, is a vital component in the representation of a society regulated by *civilitas*.

It is the particularly urban character of traditionalism (of which *civilitas* is the product) found in the *Variae* that would have been aimed at rehabilitating the reputation of Amal government. As they were portrayed in the eastern imperial propaganda, the Amals laboured under association with 'barbarian' military bands recruited from the uncultivated frontier of more rustic provinces. By demonstrating the command that the Amals possessed over legal and magisterial tradition, a proper understanding

---

[138] Cassiodorus, *Variae* 1.11.2, 1.27.1, 1.30.3, 1.32.2, 1.44.2, 2.24.5, 2.29.2, 3.24.4, 3.34.2, 4.16.1, 4.17.3, 4.27.5, 4.33.1, 4.39.5, 4.44.1, 5.4.2, 5.26.2, 5.31.1, 5.37.1, 6.5.5, 7.1.4, 8.2.2, 8.33.1, 9.14.8, 9.18, 9.18.1, 9.19.3, 10.14.1, 10.18.3, 12.5.6; for discussions of *civilitas* as ideology, Momigliano, 'Italian culture', 217; Martino, '*Gothorum laus*', 31–45; Scivoletto, 'Cassiodoro', 3–24; Lepelley, 'Eloge', 33–47; Amory, *Ostrogothic Italy*, 43–46, 116–18; Kakridi, *Cassiodors Variae*, xxx; Halsall, *Migrations*, 332; for an excellent survey of the development of urban identity in the Ostrogothic period, Fauvinet-Ranson, 'Patrimoine monumental', 205–16.

[139] For example, Ennodius in his *Panegyricus* to Theoderic employed the term *civilitas*, but in a much more general sense of a 'peaceful society': Ennodius, *Panegyricus* 3.11, 'Educavit te in gremio civilitatis Graecia praesaga venturi'; 4.15, 'Quis hanc civilitatem credat inter familiares tibi vivere plena executione virtutes?'; 20.87, 'Sed inter proeliares forte successus, quibus omnes instruis et concilias omina secunda vincendi, civilitatis dulcedini nil reservas?'

of the ethical bounds of urban culture and the value of the classical intellectual heritage, the *Variae* neutralized the piece of eastern imperial propaganda by which Justinian had promoted the Gothic War.

It is also worth repeating that any concern that Cassiodorus may have had about portraying the Amal government at Ravenna was inflected by the eastern polemic concerning *antiquitas* and *novitas*. In his history of the church of Ravenna, Agnellus recorded a poem written in the decorative mosaic of the Orthodox Baptistry of Neon, one of the early fifth-century bishops of Ravenna. The first two lines of the poem offered a challenge to the notion of hallowed antiquity: 'Withdraw, ancient name, antiquity yield to novelty! Behold, the glory of the renewing fountain glitters more nobly.'[140] Although the poem attributed to Neon refers to discarding the old in the context of spiritual renewal, the very public location of the inscription and its contrast of *novitas* and *vetustas* indicate that the discourse concerning the suitability of antiquity as a model was far more complicated in Ravenna than the rhetoric of the *Variae* suggests. If the concept of *novitas* lingered in Ravenna as a positive cultural force, particularly in relation to the history of Ravenna as a new capital, then this may provide yet another reason to locate the rhetoric of the *Variae* more securely in an eastern polemic.

---

[140] Agnellus, *Liber Pontificalis Ecclesiae Ravennatis* 28, 'Cede, vetus nomen, novitati cede vetustas! Pulchrius ecce nitet renovati gloria Fontis.'

Chapter 9

NATURA AND LAW IN JUSTINIAN'S *NOVELLAE* AND THE *VARIAE*

SIXTH-CENTURY CULTURAL DEBATES

The sixth-century debates concerning building, law, classical letters and tradition were not abstract academic disagreements. Although often discussed in abstract terms in late antique sources, these debates were vigorous confrontations, the resolution of which eventually determined the intellectual and political culture of the early Middle Ages. At stake was the extent to which an elite class that justified its status through association with traditional *paideia* would determine the criteria for political participation. Traditionalist elites would always enjoy political participation in a state that justified itself in terms drawn from the lexicon of classical ideas concerning law and justice, civic duty and honour, and the relation of individuals to the state. However, it was during the late antique period, more than ever before, that other forms of elite membership challenged what had been a relatively stable model for exercising urban authority. Militaristic definitions of authority had been in close competition with concepts emerging out of a strictly urban and literary model throughout the history of the Roman Empire. Although it had often proven relatively easy for a political elite groomed in the intellectual culture of *paideia* to assimilate military tradition, the resolution of this competition was never firmly achieved. Tension between military and urban tradition had always been present to some degree, but in many ways it is possible to speak of the militaristic definition of political elite as having finally become ascendant in the west during the fifth and sixth centuries. Similarly, the other competing conception for elite status found with Christian bishops and ascetics had increasingly been a factor since the third century. The emerging conception of Christian leadership challenged and in many ways altered the social, economic and political behaviour of the traditional Roman elite.

As competing styles of leadership, the specifically military and religious identities of late antiquity did not require 'traditional' urban elite status to justify their role in political participation. In simple terms, the military *comes* of the fifth and sixth centuries need not learn Virgil and Cicero in order to compete for status in the *consistorium*.[1] Similarly, the bishop competed for the attention of the urban populace using a subtly different semiotic palette than did the classically educated elite.[2] In many cases, the resolution of competition was found in deeper modes of assimilation. In the same way that the traditional urban elite could claim to preside over military traditions preserved in literature, the same traditional elite had become deeply entrenched in Christian leadership. Indeed, many families would completely shed the more secular brand of urban leadership in preference for its ecclesiastical analogue.

As the most visible participants in an imperial society, late antique emperors had steadily adopted a style that blended traditional urban, military and religious conceptions.[3] Given the robust influence of Christianity, emperors participated in certain secular traditions only with difficulty. By the sixth century, imperial leadership had shed the more irreconcilable symbolic associations to the extent that it was easier to portray the emperor as an enlightened Christian warrior than as a Platonizing Christian. This transition was facilitated by the extent to which Christian leadership at the local level had already adopted many of the characteristics of traditional urban leadership. The classical components of urban leadership that had been selectively rejected in the portrayal of Christian urban leadership were also being pared away, in the fifth and sixth centuries, from the portrayal of the Christian emperor. Justinian's conflict with the bureaucracy was as much a contest to control the legitimating processes in Constantinople as it was a final stage in the *longue durée* refinement of the emperor's public image. That image would be triumphant and unconquered in war and ascendant over an ecumenical Christian society in which 'tradition' was not contested.

Removing the generation of what constituted tradition from the hands of elites devoted to the *antiquitas* of classical *paideia* began with the formulation of a new kind of jurisprudence. In this sense, the promulgation of the Justinianic law codes was an assertive rather than a corrective or compilatory act. By editing, correcting and systematizing ancient law, Justinian's court claimed full and uncontested authority over the laws that defined the eastern Roman empire as a state. It was particularly by

---

[1] Procopius, *Wars* 5.2.12, reports that the Gothic nobility did not consider instruction in letters appropriate for a king's education.

[2] Brown, *Power and Persuasion* and *Poverty and Leadership* on the development of this new style of religious leadership.

[3] For the representation of earlier ideals of emperorship, Noreña, *Imperial Ideals*.

correcting the 'muddle' of the legal tradition that Justinian asserted his right to determine what would constitute tradition. Such an assertive act undermined the intellectual basis of a significant segment of the political elite who had been trained as repositories of *paideia* and who had enjoyed the authority to adjudicate law according to interpretations founded on the preservation of antique lore. The *Novellae* were probably the most widely distributed and publicly visible documents of Justinian's legal programme and, as such, they spearheaded Justinian's attempt to promote a new conception of the state that would shed dependence on the bureaucracy for generating state ideology.

THE NEW NATURAL LAW AND THE CLASSICAL
TRADITION OF *NATURA*

The negative reaction to Justinian's new laws attests to how disruptive they were to bureaucratic agency. That the *Novellae* adopted the rhetoric of *reverentia antiquitatis* probably indicates that this negative reaction had been anticipated. The first *Novella* after the completion of the new legal code (from January of 535) claimed to restore the virtue of ancient law: 'But because we have found a great number of the former laws neglected, we have decided to restore them, thereby fittingly showing honour to the dead as much as offering protection to the living.'[4] Similarly, later *Novellae* claimed 'to examine and understand what ancient law wills' and to decree 'in agreement with antiquity'.[5] Thus the *Novellae* regularly claimed that alterations to law had been made in consultation with the authority of the past.[6] Tribonian was particularly adept at embedding historical references in the *Novellae* to this end. More frequently, however, the *Novellae* engaged in a ruthless evisceration of past authority. Previous imperial constitutions were considered 'cruel and unworthy of the temperance of our age'.[7] The ancient law deserved preservation or revival only after being subjected to the corrective agency of a Christian emperor.[8] The theme of improving the past appears throughout the

[4] *Novellae Iustiniani*, *Novella* 1, *praefatio* 1, 'Sed quoniam ita positas leges iam plerumque neglectas invenimus, reparare eas iudicavimus oportere et tam viventibus praebere ex eis cautelam quam morientibus hinc exhibere honorem.'
[5] *Novella* 97, *praefatio*, 'Cogitatio facta est nobis nuper perscrutari et agnoscere, quid volens nobis antiqua lex'; *Novella* 140.1, 'sancimus . . . ut antiquitus consensu'.
[6] Maas, 'Roman history', 19–25.
[7] *Novella* 2, *praefatio*, 'valde crudeliter habere constitutiones illas et indigne clementia nostrorum temporum'.
[8] *Novella* 4, *praefatio*, 'Legem antiquam positam quidem olim . . . rursus revocare et ad rempublicam reducere . . . putavimus, non simpliciter eam, sicut iacebat, ponentes (erat enim quaedam ei pars omnino non discreta), sed cum competenti et deo placito distribuentes augmento.'

256

Novellae.[9] For Justinian, antiquity was venerable only to the extent that it remained compatible with his times. Centring the source of juridical agency on the person of the emperor and away from the concept of antiquity even allowed Justinian to countermand his own legislation: 'For it is not shameful to us if we should devise something even better than what we have previously commanded, to decree something and then make a suitable correction, rather than wait for law to be corrected by others.'[10] The reaction against what was perceived as the arbitrary and sometimes contradictory nature of Justinian's legislation required official response. It is clear from the earliest *Novellae* that Justinian's court was sensitive to criticism directed at his legal programme. As stated in a *Novella* from August of 536, 'It has come to our attention that certain persons have fallen into baseless doubt concerning what we have decreed.'[11] In response, Justinian's jurists formulated a legal theory flexible enough to counter widespread criticism and still allow the emperor to legislate according to the needs of the state irrespective of what tradition might dictate. The basis of this legal theory was a new definition of natural law.

How the *Novellae* contested an established classical formulation of natural law has already received compelling treatment from a number of scholars.[12] The present study need only outline the basic premises of the legal theory embedded within the *Novellae* and draw attention to its departure from classical conceptions of 'nature' as a basis for thinking about law and morality. Ancient jurisprudence had a long-established tradition that considered the laws binding society in terms of their connection to an almost intangible system of 'natural law'. It is true that classical thought never produced an entirely stable definition of nature (particularly its relation to the divine and to human society) and natural law. The concept of 'nature' was susceptible to permutation and often possessed an ambivalent personality. For example, nature as an agent in human affairs could represent both *providentia* (wisdom informed by divine will) and *saevitia* (primal savagery).[13] Nature was a concept that

---

[9] *Novella* 7, *praefatio*, 'Unam intentionem hanc semper ponimus, omne quicquid prius imperfectum aut confusum videbatur, hoc et expurgare et perfectum ex imperfecto declarare'; for discussions of how Justinian clothed his introduction of new legislation as the renovation of the past, Humfress, 'Law and legal practice', 170–1; Pazdernik, 'Justinianic ideology', 201.

[10] *Novella* 22, *praefatio*, 'Non enim erubescimus, si quid melius etiam horum quae ipsi prius diximus adinveniamus, hoc sancire et competentem prioribus imponere correctionem nec ab aliis expectare corrigi legem.'

[11] *Novella* 19, *praefatio*, 'Pervenit ad nos dubitationem vanam quibusdam incidisse, si, quod sanctum est a nobis'; Humfress, 'Law and legal practice', 175, points out how the preface to *Novella* 60 also demonstrates a defensive attitude toward popular criticism of Justinian's stream of legal emendation.

[12] Thurman, 'Juridical nature', 77–85; Lanata, *Legislazione*; Maas, 'Roman history'.

[13] Noted by Beagon, *Roman Nature*, 37–42.

could be readily used to portray the antithesis of civilization, but it also represented a primal manifestation of divine order.

Despite the sometimes contradictory shades of meaning attributed to *natura*, several consistent features emerged out of a formal philosophical discourse concerned with the relation of humanity to a wider onto-logical setting. Aristotle elaborated a full conception of 'nature' as a *sensible* world of material things (apprehended through sensory percep-tion) and an *intelligible* world of the essential principles (apprehended only by the intellect) that pertain to material things. This dual mirroring was governed by a divinely inspired system in which the constituent com-ponents of the universe served as elements of a divine 'world' harmony. Hence the sensible world included celestial bodies, topographical features and meteorological events, plants and animals, rocks and minerals and humans. At the intelligible level, the world consisted of principles that governed the actions of all these material things; hence the movement of celestial bodies, the latent properties of inanimate objects, the growth of plants and the behaviour of animals were reified as components of a total universe. The psychological (or moral) characteristics of humans fell within this framework and, by extension, so too did the manner in which humans organized themselves into societies (particularly with institutions).[14] Because this harmony of sensible form and intelligible purpose was divinely inspired, nature as a system was both universal and eternal. The Platonic and Aristotelian study of nature accepted that the various physical things possessed interior (moral) natures that were har-monized and governed by universal principles. The wisdom acquired through the study of philosophy was a kind of perspicacity that allowed the mind's eye to penetrate the external, material natures of things in order to understand the interior, metaphysical (spiritual) natures that governed them. By studying the physical principles of nature's various components, one came eventually to understand the non-physical princi-ples that were in harmony with divine purpose. Virtue or 'correct living' patterned on the intelligible principles of creation became the property of one thus enlightened.

Later Hellenistic Stoicism transmitted the idea of the natural world as a metaphysical system to the Romans, for whom it became formu-lated as *ius naturae* ('natural law') and attained the sense of being that which is in agreement with the dictates of divinely inspired universal har-mony. Cicero was one of the principal vectors for that transmission. The emphasis that Cicero placed on *ius naturae* in his *De republica, De legibus,*

---

[14] For Aristotle's formulation of nature, Waterlow, *Nature*, 1–92; Cooper, *Knowledge and Nature*, 107–29.

De officiis, De amicitia, the *Academica* and the *Disputationem Tusculanarium* signals his engagement with Plato, Aristotle and the Stoics.[15] According to Cicero, the pursuit of wisdom at its most ancient foundation began with the contemplation of nature.[16] More specifically, the investigation of the natural world facilitated the understanding of moral goodness.[17] The scope of such inquiry should include contemplation of everything from the motion of the stars to the depths of the seas.[18] Because nature models what is good, examination of such matters teaches proper conduct and reveals the true form of virtue.[19] Cicero appealed to the concept of *ius naturae* to explain everything that pertained to the proper conduct of an individual and the proper governance of a society. Cicero's insistent reference to *ius naturae* when discussing morality, custom, institutions and religion underlines his conviction that Roman culture and Roman institutions mirrored divine providence.[20] More importantly, natural law inhered in all humans, but it acted as a point of reference for human laws only in as much as a society was just and guided by wisdom. The assertion that Roman law was founded on *ius naturae* validated the presumed perfect rationality and divine providence of the Roman state.

Although not directly concerned with Roman law, Pliny's *Historia Naturalis*, the various moral works of Seneca and the *De natura animalium* of Aelian show the same interest in representing 'nature' as the foundation of a universal and divine moral system to which human society is intimately connected.[21] For Pliny, the concepts *natura, mundus* and *deus* were consonant with one another.[22] As a unified entity, Pliny's *divina natura* was eternal, ineffable and the ultimate expression of *ratio*, with which humanity maintained a close harmony.[23] Without the diversity and wonders of nature, it would not be possible to know how close human morality and institutions had come to following divine *ratio*.[24] Similarly, Seneca's work is predicated on the assumption that the processes of the natural world (*iurae naturae*) correspond to divine arrangement and that an understanding of those processes reveals the proper model for moral behaviour.[25] Hence the moral lessons of Seneca's *Naturales*

---

[15] Note especially Cicero's discussion of *ius naturae* as a principle superior to human customs at *De legibus* 1.6–12; *De natura deorum* 1.14, 2.14.31; *De finibus* 4.7.

[16] Cicero, *Disputationum Tusculanarium* 5.3.8–9.

[17] Cicero, *Disputationum Tusculanarium* 5.24.68–25.70; esp. 5.24.68, 5.24.69, 5.25.70.

[18] Cicero, *Disputationum Tusculanarium* 5.23.69.

[19] Cicero, *Disputationum Tusculanarium* 5.25.71; similarly, *Academica* 1.5.19–20.

[20] Rawson, *Cicero*, 154; Asmis, 'Natural law', 1–31.

[21] Beagon, *Roman Nature*, 26–54; Carey, *Pliny's Catalogue*, 19–26; Inwood, *Reading Seneca*, 225–48.

[22] Carey, *Pliny's Catalogue*, 19–20.   [23] Beagon, *Roman Nature*, 26–54.   [24] Conte, *Genres*.

[25] For example, Seneca the Younger, *Epistula* 90.34; *De providentia* 1.2; *Naturales Quaestiones* 3.15.3, 3.16.4, 3.29.3, 3.29.7, 6.1.12, 7.12.4, 7.25.3.

Quaestiones inevitably follow from observations concerning rainbows, lightning, the hidden sources of waters, clouds, earthquakes and comets. Seneca's prefatory comments to the *Naturales Quaestiones*, in particular, reveal the expectation that *natura* was a portal through which the mind's eye accessed the divine purpose woven into the material fabric of the world which the wise take as instruction for proper living:

> That special virtue which we seek is magnificent, not because to be free of evil is in itself so marvellous but because it unchains the mind, prepares it for the realization of heavenly things, and makes it worthy to enter into association with God. The mind possesses the full and complete benefit of its human existence only when it spurns all evil, seeks the lofty and the deep and enters the innermost secrets of nature. Then as the mind wanders among the very stars it delights in laughing at the mosaic floors of the rich and at the whole earth with all its gold.[26]

Similarly, the even less formal and weakly structured *De natura animalium* of Aelian also depends on the assumption that nature possessed moral content. In Aelian's case, the virtues of sagacity, shrewdness, justice, temperance, bravery, affection and familial piety could be found in the habits of animals.[27] Although Pliny, Seneca and Aelian show no interest in discussing how *ius naturae* informs human institutions as directly as did Cicero, the pronounced association between knowledge of the natural world and moral knowledge formed a necessary antecedent to a formulation of law as the reflection of *ius naturae*. An indication that Pliny understood this connection is found in his inclusion of the plastic arts as the ultimate extension of the physical (sensible) natural world with which the *Historia Naturalis* is mainly concerned. It is worth speculating on whether a similar *Historia* concerned with the spiritual (intelligible) natural world would have terminated with more purely intellectual arts, notably rhetoric and law. The range of intellectual topics with which authors of encyclopaedic literature such as Aristotle, Varro and Martianus Capella engaged suggests as much.

CLASSICAL *NATURA* AND THE DIVINE

The implicit assumption that nature possessed moral meaning is found in another context yet further removed from formal philosophical discourse. Probably the most obvious expression of Roman attitudes toward

---

[26] Seneca the Younger, *Naturales Quaestiones* 1, *praefatio* 6–7, trans. Corcoran, *LCL*, 7; similar statements at *praefatio* 1.1, 1.3, 1.12, 1.16–17; *praefatio* 3.11 and 3.18.

[27] Aelian, *De natura animalium, epilogue.*

nature (and one little discussed in modern scholarship) is found in divinatory practices.[28] A considerable amount of Roman religious activity was predicated on the belief that various aspects and manifestations of nature served as a medium by which the arrangement of divine order could be read. The observation of birds (*auspicia*), the reading of entrails from sacrificial victims (*haruspices*) and the interpretation of meteorological and 'wondrous' natural phenomena (*prodigia*) were all based on the same assumption that the natural world was a kind of performed text, the proper reading of which would reveal the meaning of specific acts that had been choreographed into a divine harmony. Although Romans could speak of such religious practices as 'old-fashioned', reports of divination were a regular apparatus of narrative in histories and biography where they speak to an audience with a profound sensitivity to the notion that the visible natural world was encoded with invisible messages. Livy, for example, constructed a narrative for the rise of Rome that made ample use of the outcomes of portents which he recorded out of 'conscientious scruple' (*quaedam religio*).[29] Likewise, Suetonius anticipated that his audience would accept the notion that the lives of Roman emperors were imprinted on the performed text of the natural world.[30] Pliny certainly accepted that natural phenomena and unusual events involving animals were modes of communication that had impact on the moral lives of humans.[31] Roman authors expressed the assumption that human morality was bound to a wider *natura* (both physical and metaphysical) perhaps most pungently when human morality failed. Lucan portrayed the convulsion of the natural world as the most profound means of communicating the magnitude of rupture in political order represented by civil war. Not only was civil war mirrored by the inversion of properties native to the elements, but nature itself contended against the progress of the war.[32] Lucan, of course, found the ultimate expression of the moral failure of civil war in describing how Pompeius Sextus rejected licit forms of divination and instead sought prophecies from notorious Thessalian witches who practised their art by countermanding the laws of nature.[33]

The intellectual culture of late antiquity inherited this highly abstracted manner of thinking about the relationship between human morality

---

[28] For a recent contribution on the subject, Rasmussen, *Public Portents*.

[29] Livy, *Ab urbe condita* 43.13.2, 'Ceterum et mihi vetustas res scribenti nescio quo pacto antiquus fit animus et quaedam religio tenet, quae illi prudentissimi viri publice suscipienda censuerint, ea pro indignis habere, quae in meos annales referam.'

[30] For example, Suetonius, *Divus Caesar* 81.3; *Divus Vespasianus* 5.2.

[31] Pliny the Elder, *Historia Naturalis* 2.113, 11.55, 17.243, 17.244, 31.7; Beagon, *Roman Nature*, 146–58; Conte, *Genres*, 88–9.

[32] For example, Lucan, *De bello civile* 1.72–80 and 9.700–838.

[33] Lucan, *De bello civile* 6.413–588; especially 6.428–429, 6.461–465, 6.469–491.

and the natural world. For someone in the late fourth century like Symmachus, nature still represented the first source of wisdom and, more importantly, it represented a single universal harmony:

> It is reasonable that whatever each of us worships is really to be considered one and the same. We gaze up at the same stars, the sky covers us all, the same universe compasses us. What does it matter what practical system we adopt in our search for the truth? Not by one avenue only can we arrive at so tremendous a secret.[34]

The transmission of texts from the earlier Roman periods to late antiquity certainly had much to do with the continuity of conceptions of a common divine fabric that underlay the material diversity of the universe. For example, Symmachus, Ausonius, Ammianus Marcellinus, Macrobius, Martianus Capella, Isidore of Seville and Bede, among Latin authors, read and admired Pliny's *Historia Naturalis*.[35] It is certainly the case that late antique Christian authors incorporated classical assumptions about *natura* and *ius naturae* in their reflections on the sensible and intelligible natural world. Indeed, the literary practices that Christians applied in the exegesis of holy scripture by and large derived from a classical tradition for extracting the hidden (intelligible) meaning from the literal (sensible) form of the word.[36] As early as Clement of Alexandria, and certainly by the fourth century with Basil of Caesarea and Gregory of Nyssa, eastern Christian writers adopted a view of nature that was fully consonant with classical thinking (with the noted exception concerning creation).[37] The natural world represented the unity of a divine purpose and the connection between humanity and nature was moral. Indeed, the exegesis of biblical texts in which the representation of nature called for allegorical and anagogical interpretation contributed to the richly diverse use of nature as metaphor in patristic literature.

CHRISTIAN INTEREST IN *NATURA*

Among Christian authors writing in the Latin west, the attachment to an essentially Platonic and Aristotelian conception of nature was no less pronounced. Although nature had been replaced by scripture as the ultimate source of wisdom, creation was nonetheless consistent with the word of God and could be consulted in an inquiry into God's will. In his *De doctrina christiana*, Augustine stressed the importance of learning

---

[34] Symmachus, *Relatio* 3.10, trans. Barrow, *Prefect*, 41.
[35] John Healy, *Pliny the Elder: Natural History*, xxxvi–xxxvii.
[36] Simonetti, *Biblical Interpretation*, 89–119.
[37] Wallace-Hadrill, *Patristic View of Nature*, 102–27; Clark, 'Cosmic sympathies', 319–25.

about things of the natural world as a complement to the exegetical study of scripture:

> In the same way I can see the possibility that if someone suitably qualified were interested in devoting a generous amount of time to the good of his brethren he could compile a monograph classifying and setting out all the places, animals, plants and trees, or the stones and metals, and all the other unfamiliar kinds of objects mentioned in scripture.[38]

According to Augustine, all things enjoyed a role in the divine harmony and even 'animals and physical matter find a voice through those who contemplate them'. Such contemplation granted access to a higher order of truth.[39] Hence, as Augustine's prescription from the *De doctrina christiana* makes clear, the investigation of the natural world was still held to grant access to moral understanding even in a Christian context, albeit through deepening the understanding of the 'kinds of objects mentioned in scripture'. It should be noted that the kind of text Augustine has in mind ('a monograph classifying and setting out all the places, animals, plants and trees, or the stones and metals') probably resembles a Christian version of the *Historia Naturalis* of Pliny the Elder.

Interestingly, Ambrose of Milan had already accomplished something approximating Augustine's request sometime during the last decades of the fourth century with his *Hexameron*. The basic structure of the *Hexameron* provided an explication of the biblical days of creation. More importantly, though, Ambrose cultivated natural history as a form of revelation. The imprint of Greek patristic interest in providing a Christian explanation for natural history is heavy, particularly that of Basil of Caesarea, who composed *Homiliae in Hexameron* in around 370. In Ambrose's version, nature possessed a definite and determined arrangement, even if it sometimes seemed inscrutable to humans. Furthermore, as an expression of divine will, nature was imbued with moral meaning and humanity, as a consequence of its place in creation, shared with the natural world the same moral schematics. For Ambrose, the explication of natural phenomena and the habits of creatures had concrete didactic value. Exempla from nature formed a pattern that provided moral instruction for attentive people.[40] In a very definite sense, Ambrose followed the attitude toward nature found in Pliny the Elder, Seneca and Aelian by finding in the explication of nature a medium suitable for discussing human mores. Ambrose certainly viewed human political institutions as

---

[38] Augustine, *De doctrina christiana* 2.141, trans. Green, 123.
[39] Augustine, *Confessiones* 5.1, trans. Chadwick, *LCL*, 72; similarly, *De ordine* 1.2.
[40] Ambrose, *Hexameron* 5.5.12–14.

resonating something of nature's harmony. In the course of describing how birds flying in formation take it in turn to lead and follow, the *Hexameron* also describes the ideal state:

From the beginning men began in this manner to establish a political system based on nature, with the birds as models. Thus there was equal participation in both labor and office... Here was an ideal state where no one became accustomed to unbroken power. Again, no one was intimidated by a long period of servitude, because advancement, due to interchange of office and to the fitting measure of its duration, appeared all the more supportable in that it resulted in the establishment that each one would have a share in the task of government.[41]

Where Ambrose departed from Pliny's view of nature was in his conviction that nature harmonized both virtues and vices for human edification, thus providing *exempla* for both the right and wrong sorts of behaviour. Pliny did note certain antipathies in nature in order to elaborate the notion of an orchestrated harmony which included carefully balanced antipodes.[42] As moral *exempla*, however, individual elements of creation were neutral. It was the system of relationships that carried meaning. For Ambrose, specific animals signified either good or evil moral content that was directly transmittable to humans as *exempla* – 'Fish, then, are either good or bad.'[43] The fact that the *Hexameron* included the fall of Adam in his discussion of the days of creation underscores that Ambrose viewed nature as the mirror of humanity's imperfection. Closer to Cassiodorus' own generation, Christian interest in the instructional value of nature seems to have remained compelling in the west. A letter from Fulgentius of Ruspe to an otherwise unknown correspondent, Scarila, demonstrates how questions concerning nature formed a normal part of Christian instruction.[44] More importantly, the connection between nature and governance by law remained a valid referent. A mid–fifth-century bishop, Valerianus of Cimelium, noted in a sermon on biblical law that the universal laws of nature shared a common origin with the written laws of humanity:

So vast is the system of control that even the constellations run their courses, with all those recurring changes of their unwearying journey, inside the confines of periods set by law . . . Clearly, nature, having no intelligence of her own, would be throwing everything into the greatest confusion, were not the system of control governing the world . . . We have mentioned these matters for a definite

---

[41] Ambrose, *Hexameron* 5.15.52, trans. Savage, 201.
[42] Pliny, *Historia Naturalis* 8.29, 8.71, 8.90, 8.206, 10.195, 10.203, 10.207, 11.279, 16.227, 17.239, 20.1, 20.28, 24.1–4.
[43] Ambrose, *Hexameron* 5.6.15, trans. Savage, 170.   [44] Fulgentius of Ruspe, *Epistula* 10.

purpose: that you may learn to keep the Gospel precepts and obey the divine commandments.[45]

Such a formulation was not confined to those trained in a patristic tradition. Secular authors of the sixth century also maintained an interest in describing nature, man and law in terms that presumed the presence of a single, co-ordinating principle. Thus Fulgentius (the Mythographer) expressed in his *De aetatibus mundi et hominis* the assumption of a teleological harmony shared by the natural world and humanity:

In this way, man because he progresses, the world because it exists, and the number of letters because it comes to this total, a harmonious distribution can be discovered in my book; as you observe the connecting links of its contents arranged in natural order, you discover both [*sic*] a full description of men's ways, a clear picture of natural laws, and the range of letters in congruence with them.[46]

Although cryptic, and concerning the arrangement of his text, Fulgentius explicitly linked human habits (*hominum mores*) to a law derived from the natural order of things (*mundi dilucidos ordines*). It is clear that the natural world and human society were not to be considered in separate conceptual categories.

NEOPLATONIC INTEREST IN *NATURA*

Although concepts pertaining to nature and natural law clearly filtered into the intellectual culture of the sixth century, the content was often based on the rather diffuse reception of general notions about nature. By contrast, Neoplatonism maintained a discourse well into the sixth century that had refined the articulation of a much more precise system for thinking about *natura* or *physis*.[47] Where Christian thought accepted an understanding of nature as having an ambivalent character that agreed with the Christian doctrine concerning original sin, Neoplatonic nature had become even more idealized as a conceptual zone.[48] The earlier and more purely Platonic view that elevated humans in a cosmic hierarchy on the basis of their ability to reason began to acknowledge that animals too had an awareness of the divine and even held a certain piety toward

---

[45] Valerianus, *De bono disciplinae* 1–2, trans. Ganss.
[46] Fulgentius, *De aetatibus mundi et hominis, praefatio* 4, trans. Whitbread, 188–9.
[47] Clark, 'Cosmic sympathies'; Remes, *Neoplatonism*, 77–100; Charadonna and Trabattoni, *Physics*; Martijn, *Proclus*.
[48] Lanata, *Filosofi*, 41–3, that the shift in Platonic thinking visible in late antiquity was a reaction against Christian ideas about the divine; this distinction is touched upon by Clark, 'Cosmic sympathies', 319.

natural laws.[49] For Porphyry, animals possessed a weaker form of reasoning while at the same time they obeyed natural law. Porphyry and later Iamblichus described plants and animals as having a 'cosmic sympathy' for the dictates of divine will.[50] Later Neoplatonic philosophers maintained the earlier formulation of nature as a 'cosmology of world-harmony', but this notion of universal harmony became reified with a detached personality as the 'cosmic soul'.[51] Plotinus in particular formalized the structure of intelligible nature as a hierarchy of virtues.[52] The base of this hierarchy was formed by moral virtues characteristic of specific manifestations of the natural world ('natural virtues') exemplified in particular by specific animals.[53] Above these natural virtues resided the 'ethical virtues' acquired through habituation to the natural virtues. Eventually, one obtained 'political virtue' through the exploration of self-guided reason and this became the first stage of 'divinization', or the assimilation of the self to the transcendent intellect of the 'cosmic soul'.[54] Simplicius maintained a firm attachment to this line of Neoplatonic thought right up to the closure of the Neoplatonic school at Athens in 529.[55] Even after the closure of the Academy, strong resonances of Neoplatonic doctrine concerning nature, law and the state appeared at the heart of Constantinopolitan political culture in the *Dialogue on Political Science*. The *Dialogue* includes a fairly lengthy excursus that describes the unity of the sensible (physical) sun with the intelligible (divine) sun in order to illustrate how the organizational principle of the physical universe mirrors the divine organizational principle.[56] This arrangement has direct relevance for the investigation of what form the ideal (intelligible) form of government should take. According to the *Dialogue*, the ruler interested in following an 'imperial science' patterned on the divine ideal should 'obtain this from analogy with works of divine craftsmanship'.[57] The *Dialogue* prescribed learning the 'nature of man' from comparison with the attributes and behaviours of plants and animals. It is significant that after describing how the state should be modelled on the natural world, the *Dialogue* continues by elaborating on how this ideal state should maintain its structure with laws.[58] The implication that human laws should derive from

---

[49] Lanata, *Filosofi*, 43, citing Celsus, *On true doctrine* 4.23, 4.69, 4.74–75, 4.78, 4.85, 4.88, 4.98–99.
[50] Clark, 'Cosmic sympathies', 310–17; again in Clark, 'Animal passions', 88–93.
[51] For example, Plotinus, *Enneads* 4.4.40; 'cosmology of world-harmony' in Markus, *Signs*, 127.
[52] On this, O'Meara, *Platonopolis*, 39–48.   [53] Plotinus, *Enneads* 1.3.6.18.
[54] Plotinus, *Enneads* 1.2; similar formulations found in Porphyry, *Sententiae*, and Iamblichus, *De mysteriis*.
[55] Baltussen, *Simplicius*, 68–87.   [56] *Dialogue on Political Science* 5.119–122.
[57] *Dialogue on Political Science* 5.5–8, on modelling the ideal state on the natural world; trans. Bell, *TTH*, 146–7.
[58] *Dialogue on Political Science* 5.17–21.

a stable and fixed conception for *ius naturae* is a startling challenge to the legal rhetoric emerging from Justinian's court at precisely the same time.

The Neoplatonic emphasis on the synchronization of political and legal culture with a universal cosmic harmony had a profound influence on the bureaucratic elite of Constantinople, particularly in terms of how they justified their elevated status. It may also explain, at least in part, why Justinian's legal programme weighed so heavily against the idea of natural law (and its nebulous interpretation in the hands of philosophically minded bureaucrats) as a source of legal authority that had the potential to contest the will of the emperor. It is precisely this link between Neoplatonism and bureaucratic habits of thinking about law and nature that not only formed a cornerstone of bureaucratic corporatism at Constantinople but also cast the bureaucracy under suspicion during the reign of Justinian.[59] For Justinian to arrogate imperial authority to himself, he first had to contend with a legal culture that had allowed the accretion of so much political authority to the bureaucracy. Although the legal expressions found in the *Novellae* declared that legal changes had been made according to ancient custom and in consultation with natural law, the *Novellae* also offered a dramatically different interpretation of nature. According to the *Novellae*, nature was not a universal constant, but rather it existed in a state of constant flux.[60] Mutability in nature was the constant factor and this mutability explained the inconsistencies of human behaviour.[61] The *Novellae* use the terms *varietas* (and its Greek cognate *poikilia*) and *novitas* with some frequency to describe an almost rampant changeability in nature that required constant adjustments to law that were not arbitrary or contradictory, but in keeping with the continually changing course of nature.[62] Rather than innovating, the activity of the prudent legislator merely attempted to maintain pace with the periodic fluctuations that affected human behaviour. The central claim of Justinianic legislation was that because human behaviour fluctuated over time with nature, constant variation in law was not only necessary, it was also a practice that maintained close contact with nature and divine will.[63] In effect, nature as an expression of God's design necessitated departures from conformity with antiquity.[64]

---

[59] A point made by Lanata, *Legislazione*, 229–33.
[60] *Novella* 74, *praefatio*; *Novella* 84, *praefatio*; similarly, *Novellae* 6, 13, 22, 28, 39, 49, 60, 69, 73, 88, 137.
[61] *Novella* 39, *praefatio*; *Novella* 49, *praefatio*; on this, Lanata, *Legislazione*, 14–17 and 165–222; Maas, 'Roman history', 29–30.
[62] On the use of *varietas* and *poikilia* in the *Novellae*, Lanata, *Legislazione*, 170.
[63] *Novella* 18, *praefatio*; *Novella* 73, *praefatio*.   [64] *Novella* 107, *praefatio*.

NATURA IN THE VARIAE

It is easy to appreciate how the characterization of nature in the *Novellae* had the potential to become instantly polemical. Where *varietas* in the long-standing classical and Neoplatonic definition of nature had served to emphasize harmony (just as it had in classical and late antique encyclopaedic literature), the *varietas* of nature in the *Novellae* was a force disruptive of human affairs. By extension, nature was guilty of *novitas*, not the emperor. It is also easy to appreciate how the polemics of *varietas* in the *Novellae* may have provided inspiration for Cassiodorus' *Variae*. The title *Variae* by itself was extremely polemical in as much as it referred to the concept of *varietas* as an organizational agency. From the perspective of a traditionalist governmental audience, where the *Novellae* represented new interventions (innovations) in the history of Roman jurisprudence, the content of the *Variae* represented a traditionalist governmental style and presented a record of legal practice based on the very theoretical basis of nature that the *Novellae* contested. It must be emphasized that the *Variae* contain nothing that could be construed as legal innovation, despite the presumed novelty of a 'barbarian' regime in Italy. Cassiodorus intended the *Variae* to demonstrate that Italy as a political system contained the same *varietas* as the natural world and that the traditional system of justice exercised in Italy was consonant with a *ius naturae* that found harmony in *varietas*, not discord. In essence, the *Variae* claim that the Amal regime had a correct understanding of nature which allowed the exercise of justice that was consonant with ('true') universal principles. This correct understanding of universal principles also presented Amal rule as in continuity with the divine provenance of traditional Roman governance.

Cassiodorus accomplished this polemical rejoinder by arranging an encyclopaedic array of *exempla* pertaining to the broad classical definition of 'natural history' in a manner that supported the legal and administrative decisions found in the *Variae*. Modern commentators on the *Variae* have already recognized the role of natural history in constructing the image of a society based on universal law.[65] Cassiodorus' approach claims originality by virtue of the fact that he incorporated what was traditionally the subject of philosophical or theological speculation into the living testament of a government's administrative record. Unlike the often abstracted principles of Justinian's legislation, the *Variae* provided a witness for how legal decisions were based in natural law and placed the deliberations over those decisions in the mouths of Amal

---

[65] Reydellet, *Royauté*, 193–5; Scivoletto, 'Cassiodoro', 6; Barnish, 'Sacred texts', 363.

rulers, demonstrating how decisions were made in consultation with the dictates of nature and antiquity.

Cassiodorus used nature as exempla in over fifty letters, and while this represents only a portion of the 468 letters in the collection, the distribution, repetition and prominence of these disquisitions have a forceful effect.[66] The combination of an unbroken chain of almost incidental references to nature with a score of more fully developed treatments was intended to make a cumulative impression on the reader. And while the causal relationship between an exemplum from nature and the *sententia* of a letter is not always overt, the association is established persistently enough that its message would have been unmistakable to anyone familiar with *ius naturae* as a legal concept. The message would have been especially clear to an audience familiar with Justinian's *Novellae*.

The first example of nature appears almost immediately in the collection (1.2) and addresses the very issue of nature's variability. Directing a certain agent named Theon to investigate delays in the harvesting of the purple pigment used to manufacture *purpura* for royal vestments, the letter claims that the shellfish producing the dye cannot vary from its nature, so the fishermen must be at fault and deserve the severity of the law:

Because the quality of the shellfish is not variable, if there is still a vintage from its press, the blame will undoubtedly lie with the workers, on account of whom no wealth has been obtained. However, when a carefully trained worker tinctures strands of white silk in those reddened fonts, it ought to have the most faultless purity of body, since the inner nature of such material is said to flee from pollution.[67]

The letter contrasts the fixed nature of the shellfish and dye with the unreliability of the fishermen, demonstrating quite neatly how human activities ought to be weighed in consideration, with *natura* as a constant element, not a variable one. The purity of the ink, as a raw element of *natura*, possesses both physical and moral qualities. The ink discharges 'a princely rain of fiery liquid' which also possesses 'the most faultless

---

[66] Cassiodorus, *Variae* 1.2.1–4, 1.10.3–4, 1.12.3, 1.13.3, 1.21.3, 1.24.3, 1.35.2–4, 1.37.3, 1.38.2, 1.40.1, 1.45.5–11, 1.46.3, 2.14.2–5, 2.19.2–3, 2.21.1, 2.39.2–11, 2.40.2, 2.40.6–8, 3.29.1, 3.47.2–5, 3.48.2–3, 3.51.5–6, 3.52.4, 4.36.2, 4.47.5, 4.50.1–7, 4.51.3–4, 5.33.2, 5.34.2–3, 5.39.1, 8.12.4–5, 8.30.2–3, 8.31.1–7, 8.32.1–3, 8.33.5–8, 9.2.1–5, 9.6.3–6, 9.24.8, 10.29.2–4, 10.30.1–8, 11.10.1–3, 11.15.1–5, 11.36.2–3, 11.38.1–5, 11.40.7–8, 12.3.1, 12.4.3–5, 12.11.1, 12.14.1–5, 12.15.1–5, 12.22.2–5, 12.25.1–2, 12.28.1.

[67] Cassiodorus, *Variae* 1.2.4, 'Quod si conchyliorum qualitas non mutatur, si torcularis illius una vindemia est, culpa nimirum artificis erit, cui se copia nulla subtraxit. In illis autem rubicundis fontibus cum albentis comas serici doctus moderator intinxerit, habere debet corporis purissimam castitatem, quia talium rerum secreta refugere dicuntur immunda.'

purity of body, since the inner nature of such material is said to flee from pollution'.[68] As such, it is even more suitable as a measure of human behaviour. Furthermore, the letter digresses further by explaining the history of dye production:

Indeed the process was discovered with such ease and short work. When a dog excited with hunger crushed in his jaws the shellfish cast upon the Tyrian shore, naturally his mouth, overflowing with the ensanguined moisture, was stained with the miraculous pigment. And so the occasion led men to an unexpected skill, and practising the example they undertook to dedicate the fine skill to their princes.[69]

The letter refers to two important sources of authority found throughout the *Variae*: that of *natura* and *antiquitas*. In this particular letter the two sources of authority are not discrete. *Antiquitas* has established the habit of imitating *natura*. The attributes of *antiquitas* and *natura* have also combined to express an idealized political order, which imitates the natural order. The purity of the substance 'distinguishes the one ruling with an ensanguined darkness, it makes the lord conspicuous and distinguishes him from all mankind, lest it be permitted to mistake princes at sight'.[70] In fact, the essential nature of the substance is so well fitted to its function within the political order that it is proven inseparable from that function: 'Once the dye spread through the cloth, it is [more] likely to be destroyed with the garment, before it fades out of the fabric.'[71] Thus the inner and exterior qualities (purity and permanence respectively) signify and distinguish a political order accepted since antiquity. Thus Theoderic's command that the purple cloth arrive on a timely basis is consonant with the dictates of nature, antiquity and correct government.

An identical scenario appears in letter 1.35, a letter written in Theoderic's name that complains about delays in the shipment of grain to Ravenna. The letter sites the 'measured arrangement of nature' which has provided weather suitable for transport, whereby the fault must lie

---

[68] Cassiodorus, *Variae* 1.2.2, 'aquarum copia resolutus imbrem aulicum flammeo liquore laxaverat'.
[69] Cassiodorus, *Variae* 1.2.7, 'Verum talis tantaque res quam facili legitur inventa compendio! Cum fame canis avida in Tyrio litore proiecta conchylia impressis mandibulis contudisset, illa naturaliter umorem sanguineum defluentia ora eius mirabili colore tinxerunt. Et ut est hominibus occasiones repentinas ad artes ducere, talia exempla meditantes fecerunt principibus decus nobile dare rem, quae substantiam noscitur habere mediocrem.'
[70] Cassiodorus, *Variae* 1.2.2, 'nigredo sanguinea regnantem discernit, dominum conspicuum facit et praestat humano generi, ne de aspectu principis possit errari'.
[71] Cassiodorus, *Variae* 1.2.3, 'Haec cum infecta semel substantia perseverat, nescit ante subtrahi quam vestis possit absumi.'

with corrupt ships' masters rather than with nature or the law.[72] Indeed, the letter even tests other possible factors from nature that might have prevented the shipment – the retarding weight of remoras and barnacles on the hull of the ship or the enervating touch of eels which may have bitten the sailors.[73] But the letter eventually discounts these phenomena, noting their possibility only in the sense of moral interpretation: 'I believe that these sailors who are unable to move themselves have acquired such an affliction. But to them the impediment of the remora is venality, the bite of the conch is insatiable greed, the eel is the pretence of fraud.'[74] Because the only possible 'natural' explanations would contradict another evident aspect of nature (providential weather), these natural explanations have been translated into moral causes ascribed to the sailors. Once again, nature provided the constant standard by which the actions of men should be measured.

The letter to Theon concerning purple dye, however, is given particular prominence by virtue of its position within the collection. The preceding letter (and the first in the collection) is addressed to the emperor Anastasius, in which Theoderic expresses the indebtedness of his own rule to the example of the eastern empire. As a pair, letter 1.1 to Anastasius and letter 1.2 make an interesting introduction to the *Variae*. In essence, the letters serve to declare that the Amal court had followed two important *exempla* in establishing its government of Italy – the model of eastern *imperium* on the one hand and *natura* on the other. Letter 1.2, however, makes it clear that although the tradition (*antiquitas*) for the extraction of *purpura* began at Tyre, nature had fitted Italy with its own source for princely raiment at Hydron.[75] In an interesting contraposto of historical and political realities, letter 1.2 acknowledges that the historical production of the imperial colour was a novelty in Italy (having been preceded first by the east). However, despite the deference to eastern imperial rule found in letter 1.1, the availability of *purpura* in Italy makes the autonomous *imperium* of Amal rule a consequence of *natura rerum*, a concept that was particularly contested in connection with Justinian's reign.

---

[72] Cassiodorus, *Variae* 1.35.2, 'Et ideo frumenta publica, quae de Calabro atque Apulio litoribus per cancellarium vestrum aestatis tempore consuerant destinari, nec autumno venisse modis omnibus permovemur, cum solis reflexus australia signa discurrens, naturae ordine modificatus.'

[73] Cassiodorus, *Variae* 1.35.3–4.

[74] Cassiodorus, *Variae* 1.35.4, 'Credo talia incurrerunt, qui se movere non possunt. Sed echinais illis impedimentosa venalitas est, concharum morsus insatiata cupiditas, torpedo fraudulenta simulatio. Ipsi enim studio pravo faciunt moras, ut occasiones incurrere videantur adversas.'

[75] Cassiodorus, *Variae* 1.2.7.

Another example in which nature seems to dictate the appropriate course of action appears in a letter (4.50) addressed to the praetorian prefect Faustus concerning assistance for the province of Campania following an eruption of Mount Vesuvius. In this letter, Theoderic readily agrees with a request to grant a remission on taxes in this region, provided that the prefect obtains proof of natural devastation. The letter continues with a brief disquisition on the beneficial aspects of volcanic eruption. Such an event 'is not entirely unbearable; the volcano sends laden signs ahead, so that the adversities may be more tolerably endured'. Additionally, an eruption contributes to the fertility of the soil, such that 'it will soon produce various shoots and restore this great expanse, which only shortly before had been wasted'.[76] The point seems to be that, although a portent, the eruption of Vesuvius does not warrant a rupture in the normal course of taxation. Once again, there is the presentation of parity between state and nature. A volcanic eruption was predictable, and even beneficial to the land, much in the same manner as the relation of taxation to the state. What could have been described as a case of nature in flux warranting a change in policy was normalized without the alteration of fiscal practices. This particular line of reasoning need not be taken as consistent throughout the *Variae*. Other letters follow a different course of resolution and allow remission on various imposts and taxes based on the natural quality of the region under consideration. In contradiction to the decision made for Campania, Como was relieved of a burdensome obligation to the *cursus publicus* because of the beauty of the region, 'since everything beautiful is too tender for toil, and those who habitually enjoy sweet delights easily feel the burden of affliction'.[77] More reasonably, a region such as Rhegium could win a dispensation from taxes on account of the difficulty of producing grain there.[78] In each case, the administrative decision is described in terms of a consideration of whether the demands of the state properly mirror nature. At one level,

---

[76] Cassiodorus, *Variae* 4.50.3, 'Sed non in totum durus est eventus ille terribilis; praemittit signa gravia, ut tolerabilius sustineantur adversa'; and 4.50.5, 'sed fertiles harenas, quae licet diuturna fuerint adustione siccatae, in varios fetus suscepta germina mox producunt et magna quadam celeritate reparant, quae paulo ante vastaverant'. See Leopold, '*Consolando*', for a different treatment of this letter; note that Leopold interprets this letter as Cassiodorus' attempt to reconstruct the imperial version of a letter of consolation, missing the consequence of *natura* as a stable theme throughout the *Variae*.

[77] Cassiodorus, *Variae* 11.14.6, 'Quapropter incolis harum rerum iure parcitur, quando amoena omnia delicata sunt ad labores et facile onus afflictionis sentient, qui uti suavibus deliciis consuerunt'; *Variae*, 12.15.1–5, a similar reason is used in removing certain obligations from Squillace; cf. Barnish, *Cassiodorus*, 154–6.

[78] Cassiodorus, *Variae* 12.14.1–5.

deciding the fiscal contribution of a region based on its natural resources is simply practical. But the letters in the *Variae* also include consideration at the level of intelligible resources. For example, the citizens of Como have been so fitted to the region that they no longer have the interior capacity to bear burdens. The point of the letter was to demonstrate the agency that nature had with respect to legal and administrative decisions. Although it certainly made sense to suspend taxes in a region stricken by natural disaster, the role of nature as a determinant in governance was the chief message.

NATURA AS THE SOURCE OF TRADITION AND MORAL GOVERNANCE

In keeping with the tradition of *ius naturae*, the *Variae* characterize nature as the source of knowledge, particularly with respect to how the liberal arts had been fashioned from the study of the natural world. The subject of human knowledge appears famously in those letters addressed to Boethius. Letter 1.10 finds the origins of arithmetic in the certitudes of heavenly motion:

For that which is called arithmetic has established a sure rationale among the uncertainties of the world, just as we know it has in the heavens...O the revelation of the wise! O the foresight of the ancients! Such a thing is carefully worked out, which naturally adorns human usage and so symbolically contains the secrets of nature.[79]

As an art of human devising with no less antiquity than law, arithmetic was capable of mirroring the dimensions of nature with its calculations; the 'sands of the sea, the drops of rain, the stars of the sky each delimited with quantifiable number', each measurement demonstrating human arts to be sublime by virtue of imitating nature.[80] Similarly, in letter 1.45 to Boethius, engineering is described as an imitation of nature first claimed by antiquity: 'O the inestimable excellence of the craft, which succeeds in making the secrets of nature common when it claims only to play! . . . The whole of the disciplines of learning, every endeavour of the learned, as far

---

[79] Cassiodorus, *Variae* 1.10.3–6, 'Haec enim quae appellatur arithmetica inter ambigua mundi certissima ratione consistit, quam cum caelestibus aequaliter novimus; evidens ordo, pulchra dispositio, cognitio simplex immobilis scientia, quae et superna continet et terrena custodit . . . O inventa prudentium! O provisa maiorum! Exquisita res est, quae et usui humano necessaria distingueret et tot arcana naturae figuraliter contineret'; cf. Barnish, *Cassiodorus*, 12–14.

[80] Cassiodorus, *Variae* 1.10.4, 'quantitate numerabili harena maris, guttae pluviarum, stellae lucidae concluduntur'.

as they are able, seeks to know the power of nature.'[81] And again, letter
2.40 to Boethius becomes an opportunity to celebrate the confluence of
ancient learning which modelled music on 'the hidden recesses of nature',
calling to mind the intelligible side of *natura* whose harmony governs the
virtues enjoyed by humanity.[82] In this way, Cassiodorus portrayed human
knowledge (of which law forms a portion) as correct when it derived
from the learning of ancients, which itself derived, ultimately, from the
correct understanding of nature. In the course of appointing an adviser
for a military *comes*, letter 8.12 digressed on the origins of grammar,
where the very letters of the alphabet purportedly derived from nature:
'For even today, cranes, which gather in flocks, describe the shapes of the
alphabet by nature's instruction.'[83] Such portrayals often appeared with
the seeming randomness that allowed encyclopaedic literature to claim
to be 'natural' representation.

Given how the *Variae* find in the natural world patterns for the various liberal arts, other human institutions similarly become dependent
on association with natural models. Much of this material appears only
as passing metaphor. For example, Cassiodorus compared the induction
of new candidates to public office to grafting young shoots or germinating seeds.[84] Similarly, good civil administration was compared to the
husbandry of a good farmer: 'It is fitting that the provinces . . . should be
comported according to the laws and good character, since it is truly the
kind of life that is bound by a righteous order . . . For thus the experienced
cultivator clears away his own field of thorny scrub.'[85] Hence nature in
the *Variae* is seen to govern the institutional activities of humanity in its
diverse forms. Monumental building projects and urban domiciles were
seen and interpreted through comparison to counterparts in the natural
world.[86] Even the construction of a military encampment was dictated by

---

[81] Cassiodorus, *Variae* 1.45.9–10, 'O artis inaestimabilis virtus, quae dum se dicit ludere, naturae praevalet secreta vulgare! . . . Universae disciplinae, cunctus prudentium labor naturae potentiam, ut tantum possint, nosse perquirunt'; cf. Barnish, *Cassiodorus*, 20–4.

[82] Cassiodorus, *Variae* 2.40.3, 'mutat animos artifex auditus, et operosa delectatio haec cum de secreto naturae tamquam sensuum regina tropis suis ornata processerit'; also, 2.40.6; cf. Barnish, *Cassiodorus*, 38–43.

[83] Cassiodorus, *Variae* 8.12.5, 'Nam et hodie grues, qui classe consociant, alphabeti formas natura inbuente describunt, quem in ordinem decorum redigens, vocalibus consonantibusque congruenter ammixtis, viam sensualem reperit, per quam alta petens ad penetralia prudentiae mens posit velocissima pervenire'; cf. Barnish, *Cassiodorus*, 102–4.

[84] Cassiodorus, *Variae* 1.12.3, 1.13.3, 3.29.1.

[85] Cassiodorus, *Variae* 5.39.1, 'Decet provincias regno nostro deo auxiliante subiectas legibus et bonis moribus ordinari, quia illa vita vere hominum est, quae iuris ordine continetur. Nam beluarum ritus est sub casu vivere; quae dum rapiendi ambitu feruntur, inprovisa temeritate succumbant. Agrum suum denique a dumosis sentibus doctus purgat agricola, quia laus excolentis est, si agreste solum dulcissimis fructibus amoenetur'; similarly, 11.36.2–3.

[86] Cassiodorus, *Variae* 1.21.3, 3.51.5–6, 4.36.2, 8.30.2–3.

the providential terrain supplied by nature and anticipated by the habits of animals preparing their own defences.[87]

More importantly, and closer to the purpose of law, the *Variae* also display exempla from nature as instruction for the moral behaviour of men. The introduction of young men to the rigours of warfare finds its antecedent in the *Variae* with raptors training for flight.[88] In contrast to preparedness in war, the *Variae* also offer exempla for the sociability of men, for which reason they should prefer the social habits of birds to the solitary allurements of a private estate.[89] Similarly, the chastity of beasts instructs men to honour the rights of matrimony.[90] The fidelity of parents to their young is compared to the devotion of birds to their offspring: 'What will be expected from men, when this devotion is recognized as innate among birds?'[91] Even the vulture provides a kind of patronage of birds of lesser stature that would instruct the slave not to murder his master.[92] The disruptive activities of humans are more readily contrasted with a stable system of natural order: 'It is a kind of piety to confound those who are shown to have involved themselves in crimes against the order of nature.'[93] Because the temperament of a man convicted of murder corresponds to that of a salamander, a creature given over to the heat of internal passions, letter 3.47 sentences him to exile on a volcanic island.[94] The character of another man is ascribed the deceptive appearance of the chameleon and the fractured personality of a faceted gem on account of his deception.[95] And since the sentencing of a crime often corresponds to the 'personality' of some feature represented in the natural world, imprisonment too has its place in the natural order. In fact, within the 'natural history' depicted in the *Variae* there are even natural exempla of creatures accomplished in escaping various snares that provide the moral justification for cancelling prison sentences.[96] It bears consideration that finding a 'natural' antecedent for pardoning criminals obviates any question whether the original sentence was unjust.

As noted with respect to the pure quality of *purpura* in letter 1.2, the capacity of nature to prescribe the moral bounds of human behaviour was related to the idea of nature's purity as an unadulterated manifestation of the divine harmony of creation. Waters in particular enjoyed this

---

[87] *Variae* 3.48.2–5.   [88] Cassiodorus, *Variae* 1.24.3, 1.38.2, 1.40.1.
[89] Cassiodorus, *Variae* 8.31.7 and 9.2.1–5.   [90] Cassiodorus, *Variae* 1.37.2 and 5.33.2.
[91] Cassiodorus, *Variae* 2.14.5, 'Quid ergo homines facere debebunt, quando hanc pietatem et in avibus inesse cognoscunt?'; cf. Barnish, *Cassiodorus*, 27–8.
[92] Cassiodorus, *Variae* 2.19.2–3.
[93] Cassiodorus, *Variae* 2.14.5, 'quando genus pietatis est in illos distringere, qui contra naturae ordinem sceleratis se docentur actionibus miscuisse'.
[94] Cassiodorus, *Variae* 3.47.2–5.   [95] Cassiodorus, *Variae* 5.34.2–3.
[96] Cassiodorus, *Variae* 11.40.7–8.

association with elemental purity. In letter 2.39, Theoderic orders the architect Aloisius to restore the buildings pertaining to the springs at Aponus to their former glory. In the course of describing the wondrous appearance of this spring, the letter depicts a certain moral capacity for moderation possessed by the waters. This moral quality at first seems attributable to the enhancements of human engineering:

O the ever miraculous genius of its creator, that the heat of a natural passion should thus be restrained for the advantage of the human body, so that what would be capable of causing death in its original form [the waters], thus moderated by learning, should bestow both health and delight![97]

However, further along in the letter, the moral quality of the water is clearly more profound than the intervention of an architect. Indeed, it would seem that the 'creator' from the passage above (God) has taught the waters, not a craftsman:

But even as this very pool becomes more calm, the waters stunned with a kind of practice of restraint by which men are refreshed, if a woman should enter it, it boils over, and therefore the use of the pool has been appropriately arranged for either one or the other sex.[98]

This ability to impose modesty on the bathers is attributed to 'evidence of its perception, the pervasive purity of the boiling waters'.[99] From this prescient purity the waters are able to perform the miracle of moral judgement:

For example, should someone by chance presume to pollute the natural purity of the waters with a single hair from a stolen sheep, what is by necessity immersed in the burning waters would boil away rather than he should succeed at cleaning it. O how the waters should receive due reverence for their secrets, when they not only possess feeling, but also stand possessed of righteous judgement and what fails to be resolved in human altercations is given over to be decided by the equitability of the pools. Silent nature here speaks, and when it judges,

---

[97] Cassiodorus, *Variae* 2.39.3, 'O magistri mirandum semper ingenium, ut naturae furentis ardorem ita ad utilitatem humani corporis temperaret, ut quod in origine dare poterat mortem, doctissime moderatum et delectationem tribueret et salutem!'
[98] Cassiodorus, *Variae* 2.39.6, 'Sed ut ipsum quoque lavacrum mundius redderetur, stupenda quadam continentiae disciplina in undam, qua viri recreantur, si mulier descendat, incenditur, propterea qui et ipsis altera exhibitio decora collata est; scilicet ne ardentium aquarum fecundissimum locum non crederent habuisse, unde plurima largiretur, si uterque sexus uno munere communiter uteretur.'
[99] Cassiodorus, *Variae* 2.39.7, 'Haec perenitas aquarum intellegendi praestat indicium per igneas terrae venas occultis meatibus influentem imitus in auras erumpere excocti fontis inriguam puritatem. Nam si naturae fuisset illud incendium, sine interitu substantiae non esset amissum; sed aquae material sensibilis, sicut peregrinum contraxit ignem, sic iterum nativum facile recepit algorem.'

it pronounces by certain means a sentence that excludes the perfidy of him denying [the charge].[100]

A similar phenomenon occurs in letter 8.32 regarding a stream near Squillace, where Cassiodorus described waters that respond to the human voice as though imbued with agency, 'A remarkable force, an unheard-of property that waters are stirred by the voice of men and, as though they responding to the words called out in human speech, they murmur I know not what.'[101] The marvel of this phenomenon derived from the moral force of nature, 'the purity of its very waters'.[102] It is because of a similar purity that the waters at Marcellianum are able to respond in chorus to the prayers of the bishop.[103]

The portrayal of a moral quality in nature allowed the *Variae* to communicate *exempla* not only for how the behaviour of men ought to be judged, but also for the proper administrative policies of the government. The extent to which the Amal regime actually thought in terms of nature as the background for the handling of legal and administrative matters is doubtful. However, the inclusion of these *exempla* at least portrayed a style of governance that was sensitive to the antiquity of an intellectual culture that had formulated the state and its legal apparatus as an extension of a natural order of divine arrangement. More importantly, the inclusion of nature in the *Variae* speaks to more immediate engagement with a contemporary discourse. One of the last letters of Cassiodorus' collection advances a pointed riposte to the new Justinianic legal theory which sought to diminish the authority of nature as a source of moral *exempla*. Presumably written in response to a request for the remission of taxes on account of a poor harvest, Cassiodorus took the opportunity to compose a small treatise on natural history, the focus of which seems to be that 'unnatural' events actually occur within the normal course of nature. The letter begins,

Often are those men troubled who anticipate the changing order of things, since those things which are occasionally deemed contrary to habit are often full of portent. For nothing happens without reason, nor does the world operate

---

[100] Cassiodorus, *Variae* 2.39.11, 'Nam si quis forte pecus furatum pilis natives solito more spoliare praesumpserit, undis ardentibus frequenter inmersum necesse est ut ante decoquat quam emundare praevaleat. O vere secretarium iure reverendum, quando in his aquis non solum sensum, sed etiam verum constat esse iudicium et quod humana nequit altercatione dissolvi, fontium datum est aequitate definiri. Loquitur illic tacita natura, dum iudicat, et sententiam quodam modo dicit, quae perfidiam negantis excludit.'

[101] Cassiodorus, *Variae* 8.32.3, 'Nova vis, inaudita proprietas aquas voce hominum commoveri, et, quasi appellatae respondeant ita hominum sermonibus provocatae, nescio quid inmurmurant.'

[102] Cassiodorus, *Variae* 8.32.2, 'et aquarum ipsarum virtute mirabilis'.

[103] Cassiodorus, *Variae* 8.33.5–8.

according to casual occurrences, but whatever we observe to come to an end occurs as a divine plan.[104]

Embedded within this excursus is an affirmation of the reliability of nature. Even though nature may produce portents inspiring awe, these events should not be considered to occur outside the plan of things, for which reason nature is not fickle or unreliable, at least not in the sense of deviating from a providential plan. This becomes clearer further on when, after discussing a rather rich panoply of natural portents, Cassiodorus then states, 'But lest these recent events [*praesens causa*] torment you with great uncertainty, turn to a consideration of natural history [*naturalium rerum*] and that which seems obscure to the crowd because of its stupendous nature will become a thing fixed by natural order [*ratione certum*].'[105] The statement assures the reader that even seemingly disruptive natural events have a definite and fixed place within a natural harmony. Cassiodorus addressed this letter to a deputy minister (*agens vices*) of the praetorian prefecture and the exhortation to consult the natural history to which the commons lack access reinforces the notion that such matters of legal and administrative interpretation should rest in the hands of a philosophically enlightened bureaucratic elite. Even more provocative, Cassiodorus contrasts the normal course of natural events with the truer cause for alarm, 'When kings would change their own laws [*constituta*], men are paralysed lest affairs should proceed in a manner other than that to which they had become accustomed.'[106] Although Cassiodorus does not elaborate on this train of thought, the comparison suggests that while change in the natural world is temporary and follows some divine plan, the changes wrought by rulers in their laws had profounder consequences. Cassiodorus' use of *induti* suggests that such alterations in custom were the product of a surface (sensible) reading of nature that was ignorant of a deeper, intelligible order. Indeed, almost as proof evident that natural disasters contained nothing inconsonant with the course of law, letter 12.28 (the final letter of the collection) cheerfully announces the same famine to have been a providential gift allowing

---

[104] Cassiodorus, *Variae* 12.25.1, 'Plerumque solliciti fiunt, qui mutatos rerum ordines intuentur, quia saepe portendunt aliqua, quae consuetudini probantur adversa. Nihil enim sine causa geritur nec mundus fortuitis casibus implicatur, sed quicquid venire videmus ad terminum, divinum constat esse consilium. Suspenuntur homines, cum sua reges constituta mutaverint, si aliter induti procedunt quam eorum usus inoleverat. Quis autem de talibus non magna curiositate turbetur'; cf. Barnish, *Cassiodorus*, 179–81.

[105] Cassiodorus, *Variae* 12.25.5, 'Sed ne te praesens causa magna haesitatione discruciet, ad considerationem revertere naturalium rerum et fit ratione certum, quod stupenti vulgo videtur ambiguum.'

[106] Cassiodorus, *Variae* 12.25.1, 'Suspenduntur homines, cum sua reges constituta mutaverint, si aliter induti procedant quam eorum usus inoleverat.'

the ruler to demonstrate his generosity: 'Penury has granted praise to our king from the provinces; fields have been made barren, so that the wealth of the lord might become manifest.'[107] So long as nature was understood by the ruler as a sort of divine economy, governance could not help but maintain a harmonious relationship with divine will.

CASSIODORUS' SOURCES FOR *NATURA*

The sources that Cassiodorus drew from for his natural exempla provide some insight into the politics of weaving natural history into the 'public record' of the Amal government. The connection between Cassiodorus' use of animals as moral exempla and the *Hexameron* of Ambrose has been noted by a number of scholars.[108] Given the political culture common to Milan and Ravenna, it certainly makes sense that Ambrose would have a prominent reputation as a moral figure in Cassiodorus' literary milieu. Indeed, Cassiodorus demonstrated broad familiarity with the works of Ambrose in his *Institutions*, where the *Hexameron* numbered among the texts that Cassiodorus noted as important to understanding the significance of creation.[109] Furthermore, some of the more curious attributes that Ambrose noted as pertaining to specific animals in the *Hexameron* also drew Cassiodorus' attention in the *Variae*. For example, both Ambrose and Cassiodorus described the peculiar habit of the sea urchin, which clings to pebbles as ballast in advance of storms. However, in spite of this thematic similarity, Cassiodorus' treatment lacks the kind of verbal reminiscence that would allow a firm attribution of the passage to Ambrose.[110] The story of the urchin can also be found in Eustathius' Latin translation of Basil's *Hexameron*, which Cassiodorus also praised in his *Institutions*. In fact, Cassiodorus praised Eustathius' *Hexameron* at greater length than he did the *Hexameron* of Ambrose, noting that Eustathius

---

[107] Cassiodorus, *Variae* 12.28.1, 'Quis nesciat providentiam divinam usibus nostris aliqua velle subducere, ut humanum posit animum comprobare ... data est provinciis in regis nostri laudem penuria; steriles facti sunt agri, ut ubertas domini posit agnosci.'

[108] Nickstadt, *De Digressionibus*, 29–36; Zumbo, '*Excursus* zoologici', 194.

[109] Cassiodorus, *Institutiones* 1.1.3–4, mentions the *Hexameron* of Ambrose; 1.4.1, on Ambrose's *Explanatio Super Psalmos*; 1.16.3 and 1.16.4, on Ambrose's *De fide*; 1.28.4, on Ambrose as a church father who had mastered the study of secular letters in his own works.

[110] Cassiodorus, *Variae* 3.48.4, 'echini, qui sunt mella carnalia, costatilis teneritudo, croceae deliciae divitis maris, dum futures tempestates agnoverint, loca mutare cupientes, quia illis pro levitate corporis nandi nulla fiducia est, lapillos, quibus pares possunt esse, complexi, quadam anchorarum ponderatione librati scopulos petunt, quos fluctibus vexandos esse non credunt'; Ambrose, *Hexameron* 5.9.24, 'Echinus, animal exiguum, vile ac despectibile, maritimum loquor, plerumque index futurae tempestatis aut tranquillitatis adnuntius solet esse navigantibus. Denique cum procellam ventorum praesenserit, calculum validum arripit eumque velut saburram vehit et tamquam ancoram trahit, ne excutiatur fluctibus.'

had managed to rival the eloquence and genius of Basil. Cassiodorus also seems to have been more familiar with Eustathius' work and he described in some detail the contents of Basil's nine books, which he knew through Eustathius' translation.[111] Nonetheless, Cassiodorus' version of the sea urchin also appears to have been independent of that of Eustathius at a lexical level.[112]

Such thematic coincidences with the two authors of the Latin *Hexameron* are not infrequent in the *Variae*. Ambrose referred to the ability of tiny remoras to retard the movement of ships under full sail and Cassiodorus amplified this theme with the addition of the conch and the eel.[113] Similarly, both Ambrose and Cassiodorus described the civic morality of cranes, whose rotation in flight resembles an idealized political order:

Cranes know how to practise moral concord, among whom none seeks to be foremost, since they do not have an ambition for inequity. They take watch in turn, they protect each other with shared caution, each supports the other. Thus distinction is taken away from none, while everything is preserved in common. Even their flight is arranged with equal alternation; the last becomes the leader and the one that holds primacy does not refuse to be last. Thus they are obedient to a kind of shared association without kings; they obey without an overlord and they serve without terror.[114]

In many respects, Cassiodorus here appears to have paraphrased a fuller passage from the *Hexameron* of Ambrose.[115] Cassiodorus' description of parent hawks which goad their young out of the nest with buffets from their wings also appears to have an antecedent in Ambrose, although once again an obvious lexical link is lacking.[116] And finally, Cassiodorus' description of the elephant bears several features in common with similarly lengthy treatments in the *Hexameron* of both Ambrose and Eustathius.[117]

The *Variae*'s lack of verbal dependence on the *Hexameron* contrasts with the obvious thematic connection and needs to be explained. It could be the case that Cassiodorus' excursuses on natural history were completely independent of the *Hexameron* and instead drawn from a literary culture

---

[111] Cassiodorus, *Institutiones* 1.1.1.   [112] Eustathius, *Hexameron* 7.741.5.

[113] Ambrose, *Hexameron* 5.10.31; Cassiodorus, *Variae* 1.35.3.

[114] Cassiodorus, *Variae* 9.2.5, 'Grues moralem noverunt exercere concordiam, inter quas nullus primatus quaeritur, quia iniquitatis ambitus non habetur. Vigilant vicissim, communi se cautela custodiunt, ipse pastus alternus est. Sic honor nullis adimitur, dum omnia sub communione servantur. His etiam volatus vicaria aequalitate disponitur; ultima fit prima et quae primatum tenuit, esse posterior non recusat. Sic quadam communione sociatae sibi sine regibus obsequuntur, sine dominatu parent, sine terrore famulantur.'

[115] Ambrose, *Hexameron* 5.15.50–51.

[116] Cassiodorus, *Variae* 1.24.3; Ambrose, *Hexameron* 5.18.59.

[117] Cassiodorus, *Variae* 10.30.1–8; Ambrose, *Hexameron* 6.5.31–35; Eustathius, *Hexameron* 9.751.5.

where certain topics were treated with stock thematic tropes. Such an explanation would certainly apply to late antique literary culture, but the *Institutions* make it clear that Cassiodorus was definitely familiar with each *Hexameron*. This leaves the possible explanation that Cassiodorus knew and borrowed from the *Hexameron*, but that he chose to paraphrase the material. Here a difficulty arises in conflict with the established literary habit, which preferred to establish the *mos maiorum* of a text through the inclusion of verbal fragments from literary antecedents, which the *Variae* lack.[118] The fact that other Latin sources for natural history (such as Pliny's *Historia Naturalis* and Virgil's *Georgics*) do not correspond to specific themes in the *Variae*, in the way that the *Hexameron* does, seems to indicate that Cassiodorus preferred to use Ambrose and Eustathius as sources for natural history, but that he deliberately distanced himself from acknowledging these texts in the *Variae*. This can be explained by the fact that Cassiodorus had a polemical reason for distancing the *Variae* from a specifically Christian and Justinianic reading of nature. As noted previously, the Neoplatonic treatment of nature differed from the patristic in one important respect. For theologians such as Augustine, Ambrose and Eustathius, nature was inextricably tied to the consequence of original sin and hence nature contained both good and evil. The denial of corruption in nature was, in a very real sense, a denial of the Christian concept of grace. Hence in theological treatments nature provided exempla for virtuous behaviour and for wickedness. Similar to the jurisprudence of the *Novellae*, Eustathius noted the moral pitfalls that abounded in the sheer variety [*varietas*] of the natural world:

Just as with the multitude of fish, those who strenuously seek to please rulers are changeable with a variety of dispositions; neither holding firm with one design, they present themselves one way to some and differently to others, he has a disposition that is modest with the chaste and flaunting luxury with the self-indulgent, thus habits fitted to particular circumstances... Flee therefore the variability of his habits and pursue rather truth, sincerity and innocence since the serpent is changeable... We ought not, therefore, to blame all fish, but there are even some to praise and imitate.[119]

---

[118] On the practice of embedding of excerpted fragments in a new text and its relation to a literary *mos maiorum*, Chin, *Grammar and Christianity*, 11–38.

[119] Eustathius, *Hexameron* 7.740.3, 'Tales sunt qui summatibus obsequentes assidue, mentis varietate mutantur; nec in uno proposito perdurantes, alios atque alios se demonstrant, pudicitiam cum castis, luxuriam cum libidinosis exercentes, et omnino ut cuiusque mens fuerit, ita proprios aptantes mores... Fuge igitur eiusmodi morum varietatem, et sectare potius veritatem, sinceritatem, innocentiam, quoniam et vipera varia est... Non ergo totos pisces debemus arguere, sed etiam certos quosque laudare atque imitari.'

This passage appears after Eustathius' lengthy discussion concerning the varied habits of fish. Ambrose came to the same conclusion, albeit discussed in different terms, when writing about fish in his *Hexameron*.[120] Both authors traced their interpretation of nature to the Greek theological discourse through Basil of Caesarea.

The theological discourse on nature and creation was a sharp departure from the way in which Neoplatonic thinking defined the natural world. The difference hinged on how the natural world could be interpreted as a source of moral knowledge. For the late antique theologian, nature was pregnant with both divine virtues and the signs of humanity's fall from grace. This interpretation clearly validated the Justinianic arrogation of legal authority by reinforcing the notion that nature was temperamental, inconstant and in need of a Christian exegete to sort its varied moral meanings in order to produce correct law. Cassiodorus' formulation of nature in the *Variae* differed from that of the theological tradition, even where he borrowed material from Ambrose and Eustathius. Cassiodorus tended to refer to nature as an absolute constant that functioned in a strictly ordered manner; departures could only be considered unnatural innovation and, where it concerned law and administration, bad governance. In short, nature in the *Variae* could not supply contradictory *exempla*. As will be demonstrated, understanding the *exempla* of nature did, however, still require the mediation of attentive wisdom.

---

[120] Ambrose, *Hexameron* 5.6.15, 'Piscis ergo es, o homo. Audi quia piscis es: simile est regnum caelorum reti misso in mare, quod ex omni genere piscium congregavit . . . sunt ergo et boni et mali pisces; boni servantur ad pretium, mali statim ardent.'

Chapter 10

READING GOOD GOVERNANCE IN THE
VARIAE AND THE *DE ANIMA*

DISCERNING PROBITY

It is through the presentation of nature, and more specifically by present-ing an understanding of nature operative in governmental decisions, that the *Variae* attempted to rehabilitate the reputation of state service in Italy. Notably the portrayal of legal and political culture in the *Variae* stands in direct opposition to Justinianic propaganda. Where Justinian's *Novellae* justified legal innovations by defining nature as changeable, the *Variae* based legal and administrative decisions on the universal constancy of nature. Pairing the stability of nature with the antiquity of legal custom contested the Justinianic rationale for tampering with tradition. Further-more, the manner in which Cassiodorus blended discussions of nature with commentary on the literary tradition established a model in which *natura* had informed *antiquitas*. In essence, the *Variae* suggest quite force-fully that *reverentia antiquitatis* was a means of accessing *natura rerum*, which was itself a source of universal truth and pure legal reasoning. Thus, in contrast to the exaggerated *divina electio* of Justinian's propaganda, which sought to create a position for the emperor as the chief exegete of Roman society and eliminate the mediation of governmental intellectual elite, Cassiodorus responded with a formulation that emphasized a collective intellectual tradition (not the person of the emperor) as the source of good governance.[1]

Thus the *Variae* positioned Cassiodorus and the bureaucratic elite of Italy in a very specific ideological context. Where the eastern emperor *dictated* matters concerning nature and law, the Amals and the palatine elite of Italy *received* law from learned ancient custom that was itself informed by nature and the harmonious system that orchestrated nature. Because this system was essentially a moral order, the recurring attention to nature in the *Variae* also served to demonstrate the moral suitability

---

[1] On *divina electio*, Brown, 'Elites', 328.

283

of western palatine service. In addition to showing respect for a venerable intellectual tradition, the recurrent use of metaphor and digression
pertaining to nature was intended to reveal to the audience of the *Variae*
that members of the governing class in Italy could 'read' the moral value
contained in nature. That is, the explication of nature was also a demonstration of acuity in a kind of spiritual 'sight' that revealed the moral
contours of universal order that were embedded in the natural world.
By extension, the ability to perceive the moral meaning of the natural
world implied the ability to read the moral quality of people, particularly
people engaged in government.

In order to communicate this elaborate message, the *Variae* depended
on the reception of an extended intellectual history that found in the
study of *natura* the source for understanding moral goodness. The process
of discovery by which the natural world revealed the hidden (intelligible) moral meaning of divine arrangement formed a common thread
from Platonic and Aristotelian to Neoplatonic thought.[2] The Epicurean
Lucretius, the Stoic Seneca and the Christian Augustine all claimed that
one perceived moral truths in the natural world through a kind of spiritual vision of the mind.[3] For Seneca, only the wise possessed the ability to
penetrate the external, material natures of things in order to understand
their interior relation to the divine.[4] For Augustine, too, the divine order
of the natural world was obscured to the eyes of the body, but would
become apparent to the vision of a mind that was properly educated.[5]
An earlier author whom Augustine admired, Apuleius of Madauros,
composed an elegant performance of this relationship between vision
of the natural world and spiritual health in his *Metamorphoses*. Apuleius
described the young Lucius whose mind was so inflamed with the desire
for illicit knowledge (magic) that his bodily eyes were incapable of perceiving things in their true nature:

With my anxiety and my excessive passion to learn the rare and the marvel-
lous... I was on tenterhooks of desire and impatience alike, and I began to
examine each and every object with curiosity. Nothing I looked at in that city
seemed to me to be what it was; but I believed that absolutely everything had
been transformed into another shape by some deadly mumbo-jumbo: the rocks I
hit upon were petrified human beings, the birds I heard were feathered humans,

---

[2] On the soul seeing the invisible divine order of nature, Hansen, *Appropriation*, 202–19.
[3] Lucretius, *De rerum natura* 1.1114–1117; Seneca the Younger, *Naturales Quaestiones* 1, *praefatio* 3
and *praefatio* 12.
[4] Seneca, *Epistulae* 90.34.
[5] Augustine, *De ordine* 1.2; *De vera religione* 30.55; 32.59–60; *De civitate dei* 8.5 and 11.2.

the trees that surrounded the city wall were humans with leaves, and the liquid in the fountains had flowed from human bodies.[6]

After many trials, Lucius is finally relieved of his faulty vision through divine revelation, whereupon the sights of the natural world take on a more wholesome aspect:

This was the end of the holy revelation, and the invincible divinity now withdrew into herself. At once I was quickly released from sleep . . . the cloud of dark night was banished and the sun arose all gold . . . Beyond my own private joy, everything seemed to be so filled with happiness that I could feel every sort of animal, and all the houses, and even the day itself rejoicing with bright faces. For a sunny and calm day had come close on the heels of yesterday's frost, so that even the songbirds were enticed by the spring warmth to sing lovely harmonies, soothing with their charming greetings the mother of the stars, parent of the seasons, and mistress of the whole world. Why, even the trees . . . loosened by the southerly breezes and glistening with leaf-buds, rustled sweet whispers with the gentle motion of their arms . . . the sea, now calm, lapped quietly against the shore. The sky too . . . shone bare and clear with the brilliance of its own true light.[7]

Where Lucius' vision had previously conveyed a world where the birds, trees and waters had been clothed with a sinister aspect, after experiencing spiritual rejuvenation the world suddenly appeared in 'its own true light', with the majesty of natural harmony unobscured by his troubled mind. Although Apuleius dressed his *Metamorphoses* with second-century middle Platonism and religiosity, the extent to which access to divine wisdom was signified by precocious vision of the natural world was not lost on late antique Christians. From Athanasius' *Life of Antony* to Bede's *Life of Cuthbert*, the special virtues of 'holy men' were legible to a wider audience through their ability to communicate with and control the portion of creation invisible to most of humanity. 'Supernatural' powers such as banishing demons and curing disease assumed that the individual blessed with holy wisdom could 'see' the cause of the unseen forces troubling the body or mind.[8]

In the case of secular rulers, having such an acuity of mental vision that one could penetrate the secrets of nature and thus gain access to an understanding of justice in its true state added a sacral quality to

---

[6] Apuleius, *Metamorphoses* 2.1, trans. Hanson, LCL, 59.

[7] Apuleius, *Metamorphoses* 11.7, trans. Hanson, LCL, 305–7.

[8] Athanasius, *Vita Antonii* 48, 51, 57, 58, 64; episodes in which Anthony wrestled with 'unseen' demons and cured disease became paradigmatic for later hagiographers such as Sulpicius Severus, Ennodius of Pavia, Gregory of Tours, Gregory the Great and Bede; note Markus, *Signs*, 3, that 'reading the world' and 'reading scriptures' were tandem components of a coherent narrative for the late antique Christian audience.

political legitimacy. The lack of such prescience had long been a topos used by Roman historians to impugn poor rulers. Suetonius claimed that Nero had brought about his own downfall first by scorning customary rites and then by failing to interpret the signs intended for him on the eve of his death.[9] Likewise, Domitian famously misinterpreted portents pertaining to his own murder and the Emperor Carus perished by disregarding the oracles.[10] By contrast, the emperors Vespasian and Hadrian were distinguished in later tradition by their ability to cure disease.[11] Each exemplum, both positive and negative, depended on the audience's understanding of the importance, at least at the ideological level, of a ruler's sensitivity to *natura*. It is doubtful whether contemporary political audiences expected living emperors to cure disease or read random portents in nature; rather, these exempla were part of a postmortem semiotics that exemplified the moral merit of each emperor's life.

Such literary topoi drew from a more formal intellectual tradition that had maintained strong continuity in the pairing of governance and nature in philosophical discourse. Plato formulated the ideal ruler as a philosophically sensitive king who, having perfect mental vision, was capable of seeing absolute truths in the spiritual side of nature. According to Plato, knowledge of these truths would guide the king in preserving natural law in the institutions that governed human activity.[12] Dio Chrysostom similarly described an ideal ruler whose exercise of justice was the corollary of his position in a state that was an imitation of universal order and harmony.[13] These notions concerning the ruler and prescient access to the divine arrangement of the universe remained the dominant formulation of ideal governance. Plotinus in the third century maintained that the ideal ruler should have an intellect trained in philosophy so that it would be capable of perceiving the intelligible world that revealed the moral purpose of all material things.[14] In the fourth century, Themistius articulated something of a reiteration of Diogenes, who found in the king 'law embodied, a divine law which has come down from on high . . . a providence of that nature closer to earth'.[15] Thus in late antiquity, the role of the emperor as the focal point of natural order transfigured him as one of the constant forces of nature. Several Latin panegyrics likened Constantine to an elemental force in the operation of the empire.[16] In later panegyric, the seas preserved Anastasius from destruction because

---

[9] Suetonius, *Nero* 56.   [10] Suetonius, *Domitianus* 16; Aurelius Victor, *De Caesaribus* 38.4–6.
[11] Suetonius, *Divus Vespasianus* 6.2–3; *Scriptores Historiae Augustae, Vita Hadriani* 25.1–4.
[12] Plato, *Republic* 5.473–480; 6.484.   [13] Dio Chrysostom, *Discourse on Kingship* 1.66–68.
[14] Plotinus, *Enneads* 5.8.10–13; discussed in Digeser, 'Religion', 68–84.
[15] Themistius, *Oratio* 5.64b; trans. Heather and Moncur, *TTH*.
[16] *Panegyrici Latini* 6.11.2–3; 6.13.3; 12.9.5; 12.22.1–2.

the emperor was the embodiment of law.[17] Again in Cassiodorus' generation, Plato's seminal description of the ruler who was spiritually prescient
and attentive to the lessons of the natural world found a clear voice in
the *Dialogue on Political Science*. The *Dialogue* called for a ruler who was
'the philosophical emperor and the imperial philosopher'; someone who
would rule in accordance with the divine order mirrored in the physical
arrangement of the world.[18] Importantly, it was precisely this ideal of
Plato's *Republic* that Boethius questioned as doubtful.[19]

PROCOPIUS AND READING NATURE

The currency of this discourse concerning temporal rulership and divine
arrangement in nature clearly influenced the manner in which Procopius
portrayed political events during Justinian's reign. Ever the clever commentator, Procopius offered his own perspective of this discourse by
restricting the attribution of this ability to interpret nature to 'barbarian'
kings. In doing so, Procopius used the portrayal of the prescient 'barbarian' ruler as a foil with which to compare the efficacy of Justinian.
Tacitus had similarly attributed to 'barbarians' the ability to see the divine
in nature as a component of his wider critique of Roman society and its
claim to the enjoyment of divine providence.[20] Procopius, however, portrayed 'barbarian' rulers as thoughtful readers of nature's hidden messages
with much more consistency. According to one story, Attila circum-
vented the protracted siege of Aquileia by reading a prophecy in the
flight of a stork that had nested in the fortifications, 'for [Attila] was most
clever at understanding and interpreting all things'.[21] Attila's insight into
the nature of things stands in contrast to the misguided uncertainty of
Valentinian III, who in the immediately preceding section of the *Wars*
asked a subordinate adviser 'whether he had done well in putting Aetius
to death'.[22] Based on the structure of Procopius' narrative, the emperor's
lack of vision precipitated the fall of Aetius and set the stage for Attila's
conquest of Aquileia. The story of Attila and the stork also appears in
Jordanes' *Getica*, perhaps indicating that Procopius drew from a stock
of fifth-century narratives concerning the famous Hunnic king.[23] The
repeated attribution, however, of similar stories to more recent 'barbarian' kings suggests a more programmatic narrative design in the *Wars*. For
example, the Vandal king Geiseric predicted that Marcian would claim

---

[17] Priscian, *De laude Anastasii Imperatoris* 270–9.
[18] *Dialogue on Political Science* 5.123, trans. Bell, *TTH*, 171; cf. Plato, *Republic* 473d.
[19] Cf. Plato, *Republic* 473d; Boethius, *De consolatione philosophiae* 1.4.19–21.
[20] Tacitus, *Germania* 9.   [21] Procopius, *Wars* 3.4.29–35, trans. Dewing, *LCL*, 43–5.
[22] Procopius, *Wars* 3.4.25–28, trans. Dewing, *LCL*, 41–3.   [23] Jordanes, *Getica* 42.220.

the imperial office by noting the shadow cast over him by an eagle, 'since [Geiseric] was an exceedingly discerning person, [he] suspected that the thing was a divine manifestation'.[24]

As has already been discussed, Procopius portrayed Theoderic as a ruler imbued with a sense of justice that was both prophetic, by virtue of his ability to read signs in nature, and innate, by virtue of his unlettered state of education. In describing Theoderic in this way, Procopius responded to an important feature of the contemporary political discourse. It was perhaps because of the polemical nature of this discourse that Procopius even depicted a bad 'barbarian' king, Theodahad, as being able to foresee the destruction of Gothic power in Italy by reading the *sortes* in swine.[25] In another instance, the otherwise obscure leader of the Warni, Hermegisclus, was capable of receiving prophecy through communication with nature and even predicted his own death through the croaking of a bird.[26] For Procopius, like Tacitus before him, the 'barbarian' was the material with which one framed a critique of imperial rule.

The manner in which Procopius framed 'barbarian' prescience as a critique of Justinian comes into sharper focus with the prophecy that foretold Italy's eventual submission to a eunuch.[27] The prophecy, which Procopius claimed to have learned from a Roman senator, was an interpretation of a 'prodigy' in which a rustic steer attempted to mount a bronze bull in the Forum Romanum. The story was clearly intended to communicate the final debasement of the Romans that would occur with the arrival of Narses toward the end of the Gothic War. More importantly, the story allowed Procopius an opportunity to evaluate the source of Justinian's discernment: Procopius stated that Justinian sent Narses to Italy either because the emperor's judgement had perceived the future or because chance had decided the matter.[28] Procopius described Justinian's decision with purposeful ambivalence, 'the reason why this was the wish of the emperor was explicitly evident to no one in the world; for it is impossible that an emperor's purpose be discovered except by his own will'.[29] Such ambivalence does not compare favourably to the clear discernment that Procopius ascribed to 'barbarian' kings. The fact that Justinian speaks only once in the *Wars* also contributes to an unfavourable comparison between the ambiguity of his discernment and that of mere 'barbarians'. Although Procopius regularly constructed the narrative of the *Wars* around the direct speech of Romans and 'barbarians', Justinian

---

[24] Procopius, *Wars* 3.4.2–10, trans. Dewing, *LCL*, 35–7.   [25] Procopius, *Wars* 5.9.1–7.
[26] Procopius, *Wars* 8.20.13–15.   [27] Procopius, *Wars* 8.21.5–22.
[28] Procopius, *Wars* 8.21.18–20.   [29] Procopius, *Wars* 8.21.6–7, trans. Dewing, *LCL*, 273.

maintains a mute presence.[30] The one speech that Procopius attributed to
Justinian proved to be patently false; Justinian claimed that if Theodahad
submitted Italy to the emperor's authority, he would 'never repent having made us friends instead of enemies'.[31] Where Justinian's discernment
appears ambiguous and even flawed in the *Wars*, the *Anecdota* reveal an
emperor actively opposed to the natural order, on account of which God
visited natural disasters on the empire.[32] In short, Procopius' treatment
of Justinian's reign was heavily influenced by a contemporary discourse
dealing with the innate capacity of the ruler to understand the dictates of
natura and to arrange human activities in congruence with the universals
contained therein.

CASSIODORUS AND THE PORTRAYAL OF READING PROBITY

Cassiodorus was certainly sensitive to this abstracted, exegetical manner
of reading *natura* against moral meaning. In his later work, the *Expositio
psalmorum*, Cassiodorus echoed Augustine's description of the inner eye
of the mind which penetrates hidden layers of meaning: 'By directing
your mind's eye through [the Psalms'] thin texture, you can easily gaze
into their hidden depths. Who would regard all these explanations and
these differing expressions as superfluous? It is wicked to believe that the
divine Scriptures contain any idle matter.'[33] The *varietas* of nature had
meaning and consequence in the *Expositio*. The fact that Cassiodorus
could compare the different shades of meaning in words of religious
text to the variety of shades visible in the natural world (the refracted
colours of jewels, the plumage of birds, the hues of the chameleon)
reinforces the notion of variety in the natural world as being imbued
with moral meaning.[34] The reference to visual capability underscores
the harmonious pairing of the sensible material and intelligible spiritual
aspects of *natura*. It also emphasizes the notion that this moral landscape
was legible to a reader of the natural world who possessed the appropriate
mental acuity (wisdom). The frequent use of exempla from nature in
reference to matters of governance in the *Variae* makes a very concrete

---

[30] A curious fact noted by Cameron, *Procopius*, 145.
[31] Procopius, *Wars* 5.6.22–26, trans. Dewing, *LCL*, 57.
[32] Procopius, *Anecdota* 13, *passim*, on the instability and contradictory nature of Justinian's mind;
18.1 and 18.36–37 on Justinian's unnatural and demonic character which was the cause of various
catastrophes in the empire.
[33] Cassiodorus, *Expositio Psalmorum*, praefatio 10.20–25, trans. Walsh, 33; on the influence of Augustine on Cassiodorus' *Expositio*, Astell, 'Cassiodorus', 37–75.
[34] Cassiodorus, *Expositio Psalmorum* 52.7.187–200; cf. Heydemann, 'Christian *gentes*', 5.

claim concerning the sensitivity of the Amal court to universal good. The explication of natural history in the *Variae* was a strategy that intimated the capacity of Amal rulers to 'read nature'.

Cassiodorus employed a vocabulary throughout the *Variae* that emphasized the active and ever-searching judgement of Amal rulers. Where Procopius rendered Justinian voiceless and possessed of doubtful wisdom, Cassiodorus attempted to reveal the mind of the ruler as it scrutinized the virtues of men and compared them to what nature had instructed, thereby allowing the ruler to pronounce decisions in accordance with nature's moral meaning. For example, Cassiodorus described Theoderic as the ideal philosopher king who sought the source of wisdom and justice in *natura*: 'The most perspicacious investigator inquires after the course of the stars, the depths of the ocean, and the mysteries of springs, such that the most diligent of men, by his scrutiny of the nature of things, would appear to be a kind of philosopher clad in purple.'[35] It is perhaps on this account that Cassiodorus intimated in the same letter that Theoderic had intimacy with future events, 'for whatever his mind perceived, always became a fact, and by a miraculous exercise of wisdom, he never doubted that what he had foreseen would occur accurately in the future'.[36] Cassiodorus attributed Theoderic's wisdom to the study of the natural world and his management of human affairs was correspondingly providential. Similarly, Athalaric consulted 'writers of natural history', blending *natura* with *antiquitas* as a source of moral authority in order to assign correctives to the ills of wider society.[37] Thus the *Variae* articulate the ruler's awareness of the natural world as the mental apparatus of his understanding of governance. Such expressions inevitably link the judgement of the ruler to the common weal of the realm:

The mind of the ruler is the source of public distinction and such as the judgement of the lord will be, thus does it give rise to the image of liberty; it is easier that, if it is proper to say, nature would err than that the prince would be able to shape a republic dissimilar to himself.[38]

---

[35] Cassiodorus, *Variae* 9.24.8, 'Stellarum cursus, maris sinus, fontium miracula rimator acutissimus inquirebat, ut rerum naturis diligentius perscrutatis quidam purpuratus videretur esse philosophus'; cf. Barnish, *Cassiodorus*, 124–7.

[36] Cassiodorus, *Variae* 9.24.2, 'Cum futuris rebus eum crederes habere tractatum; nam quod concepisset animus, reddebat semper effectus miroque sapientiae studio non habebat dubium, quod veraciter praevidebat esse venturum.'

[37] Cassiodorus, *Variae* 9.2.5, 'Quarum morem scriptores rerum naturalium contuentes politiam quondam inter ipsas esse commemorant, quas civico affectu vivere cognoverunt.'

[38] Cassiodorus, *Variae* 3.12.1, 'Publici enim decoris mater est mens regentis et quale fuerit dominantis arbitrium, talem parit libertatis aspectum. Facilius est quippe, si dicere fas est, errare naturam quam dissimilem sui princeps posit formare rem publicam.'

It is important that Cassiodorus here touches upon the notion of nature in error only to demonstrate its incomprehensibility for the king. This was a direct contradiction of Justinianic legal theory placed in the mouth of Theoderic supposedly before Justinian's accession.

From intimacy with *natura*, the scope of application of royal wisdom expands and appears in various affirmations of its ability to apprehend the truth in different spheres of social and political life: 'Our mind . . . being impassioned for the cares of the republic and scrutinizing the intentions of diverse peoples is often struck by the complaints of the people.'[39] Such a statement recalls the restless preoccupation of Theodosius II in a *Novella*, 'with our divine perception, we are studying the affairs of the human race day and night'.[40] Cassiodorus, however, presented a far more complex and sophisticated symbolic palette by which the audience of the *Variae* should understand governmental decision making. Cassiodorus folded references to *natura* and *antiquitas* in the *Variae* with such frequency that, although not mentioned in every letter, a comprehensive reading of the collection (as Cassiodorus encouraged his readers to undertake in his first preface) provides a cumulative assurance that all governmental decisions in Italy had the same morally sound foundation.

By far the most consequential and evident sign of morally sound judgement in the ruler was to be found in the selection of candidates for public office, a topic that was dear to the reputation of Cassiodorus and his political dependents. The scrutiny of the ruler nowhere else appears more active in the *Variae* than in discerning the integrity of men selected for public positions: 'our intuition, that spy of virtues, sees in you this quality'.[41] A formula for the *comitiva patrimonii* declares that the princely understanding of moral matters has its foundation in the clear perception of *natura*, 'And therefore be attentive to this, pursue virtue, since no man is able to deceive the prince who is proven best at investigating the nature of things even in you.'[42]

The claim that *natura* was legible to the attentive ruler both in the natural world and in the hearts of men underpins the entire apologetic strategy of the *Variae*, which sought to counter what was to Boethius the impossibility of a moral palatine service. The extent to which the *Variae* mirror the virtue of the ruler and nominees to office, so common in the

---

[39] Cassiodorus, *Variae* 1.30.1, 'Animum nostrum, patres conscripti, rei publicae curis calentem et diversarum gentium consilia perscrutantem pulsavit saepius querela populorum.'

[40] *Novellae* of Theodosius, 16.1.1, *praefatio*, trans. Pharr, 501.

[41] Cassiodorus, *Variae* 1.22.2, 'Haec in te speculator virtutum noster sensus inspexit'; similarly, 1.12.1, 3.6.6, 6.9.3, 6.16.3, 9.22.2, 10.4.4.

[42] Cassiodorus, *Variae* 6.9.4, 'Et ideo ad quas provecti estis, studete virtutibus, quia nemo potest principem fallere, qui etiam rerum naturalium causas in vobis optime probatur inquirere.'

classical discourse of *amicitia*, furthers this apologetic strategy. According to the *Variae*, the individual appointed to office reflected the character of the ruler: 'Our attention scrutinizes these men, and we rejoice in these found with the treasure of good habits, in whom the grace of our countenance is imprinted just as in the fashioned image granted for public honours.'[43] The 'fashioned image', whether a consular diptych or a statue, connoted the sense that such an appointment was a public display not only of the dignity of the recipient of office, but also of the character of the ruler. And even here, the *Variae* found an antecedent for that mirrored moral quality in *antiquitas*. In a letter from Athalaric to the new quaestor Ambrosius, Cassiodorus reminded the audience that the mirroring of virtues in political relationships had achieved an earlier ideal with Trajan and Pliny the Younger.[44] However, even while emphasizing how appointed officials shared the same moral qualities as the ruler, there is the unavoidable sense that the judgement of the ruler has played the dominant role, almost in the sense of fashioning the character of the official from the appropriate raw material. In reflecting on his own public career, Cassiodorus stated, 'for such judgements [of the Amals] have not discovered my merits, but created them'.[45] Philostratus made the same sort of statement concerning authority and agency when describing the career of Antipater of Hierapolis, who proved himself praiseworthy under a good emperor (*ab epistulis Graecis* for Septimius Severus) and disastrous under a bad emperor (governor of Bithynia under Caracalla).[46]

The appointment of virtuous men to public offices substantiated the efficacy of royal judgement and, in effect, demonstrated it to be in accord with nature. Perceiving the inner qualities of men was an exercise of the ability to read the moral quality of the natural world, especially since in theory the moral substance of humanity did not differ from that of the wider natural landscape. The long continuity of classical literature signified the possession of virtue by assigning to an individual the ability to discern the inner nature and virtues in others. This gift of discernment was also a pronounced topos in religious literature describing holy

[43] Cassiodorus, *Variae* 1.4.2, 'Hos viros nostra perscrutatur intentio; his morum thesauris gaudemus inventis, in quibus velut figuratis honorum vultibus clementia nostrae serenitatis exprimitur'; similarly, 1.22.3, 2.34.1, 4.3.1, 8.22.2.
[44] Cassiodorus, *Variae* 8.13.4, 'Habemus sequaces aemulosque priscorum. Ecce iterum ad quaesturam eminens evenit ingenio. Redde nunc Plinium et sume Traianum'; cf. Barnish, *Cassiodorus*, 8–12.
[45] Cassiodorus, *Variae* 11.1.3, 'haec non audemus [Cassiodorus] falsa dicere, sed confitemur esse potiora; nam talia iudicia non invenerunt merita, sed fecerunt; neque enim nos inde iactamus, qui intellegimus dominos nostros humilia voluisse sustollere, ne videantur inmeritis tam ingentia praestitisse'; similarly, 1.3.1, 1.41.1, 1.43.1, 1.43.4, 9.22.1; cf. Barnish, *Cassiodorus*, 145–50.
[46] Philostratus, *Lives of the Sophists* 2.24.607.

Christians, who were said to possess the ability to read the souls of others by virtue of their own spiritual excellence.[47] At one level, as Sidonius Apollinaris testified, knowing the soul of another was simply a precondition of enjoying true harmony (*amicitia*) with that individual.[48] At another level, the individual possessed of true wisdom read the character of a soul in the same manner as reading the moral landscape of the physical world. Late antique hagiography commingled the saint's ability to perceive human nature with miracles involving the control of nature so thoroughly as to leave no doubt for his audience that human moral substance and nature were woven into the same fabric.

With respect to Cassiodorus, this means that the *Variae* offered the means for an audience to appreciate Amal governance in Italy at a moral level. By describing how Amal rulers 'read' the moral aptitude of appointees to the palatine court, Cassiodorus demonstrated to the audience of the *Variae* the virtue in the Amals which permitted them to judge others at such an interior level.

THE *DE ANIMA* AND THE SOUL AS THE INSTRUMENT OF READING PROBITY

Cassiodorus appended the *De anima* to his letter collection as a means of ensuring that his audience would read the *Variae* with an eye toward moral interpretation.[49] His first preface to the *Variae* hints that the act of reading the collection involved exposure to moral meaning:

Moreover, you conceal, such as I may say it, the image of your mind, where each age to come would be able to admire you. Indeed, it often happens that the father begets a son different from himself, while it is scarcely possible that the written style be found inconsonant with the will. Therefore such an offspring is plainly a more reliable witness, for what is born from the secret of a man's breast is considered a more truthful representation of its source.[50]

Cassiodorus directed the attention of his readers to the subtler, moral message contained in the *Variae* by appending the *De anima* to the collection as a sort of instructional manual or, more precisely, as a treatise that

[47] Gaddis, *Religious Violence*, 207; Rapp, *Holy Bishops*, 56–74.
[48] Sidonius Apollinaris, *Epistulae* 7.14.
[49] For selected studies of Cassiodorus' *De anima*, Halporn, '*De Anima*', 39–109; DiMarco, 'Fonti', 93–117; Mauro, 'Cassiodoro', 219–49; Halporn and Vessey, *Cassiodorus*.
[50] Cassiodorus, *Variae, praefatio* 1.10, 'Celas etiam, ut ita dixeram, speculum mentis tuae, ubi te omnis aetas ventura possit inspicere. Contingit enim dissimilem filium plerumque generari: oratio dispar moribus vix potest inveniri. Est ergo ista valde certior arbitrii proles: nam quod de arcano pectoris gignitur, auctoris sui posteritas veracius aestimatur'; also discussed in Kakridi, *Cassiodors Variae*, 51–7.

bore a direct relation to how the *Variae* should be read and interpreted. The second preface of the *Variae*, which declares Cassiodorus' intention to write a treatise on the soul for the same audience that requested his letters, establishes a framework for the two works to be read together. It is, furthermore, implicit in the first section of the *De anima* that knowledge of the soul would enhance the reader's understanding of material in the *Variae*:

Recently I rejoiced in the longed for completion of a work that I had undertaken, when after having been tossed about by the task of composing the twelve books [of the *Variae*], I was welcomed into the peaceful harbour to which I had come perhaps without praise but at least free from care. Yet the sweet throng of my friends has once again urged me out into the sea of thought, asking that since I have the ability to disclose the mysteries of matters so great, I should clarify certain obscurities that I had found both in sacred and secular literature about the substance and activities of the soul. "Furthermore", they say, "it would be very foolish for us to let ourselves remain ignorant of the soul, the source of much of our knowledge, as though it were something separate from us, since it is useful for us first of all to understand how we gain knowledge."[51]

In a temporal sense, Cassiodorus differentiates the *Variae* and the *De anima* as distinct phases of writing, noting the exhausting and somewhat troubled completion of the one and the unfettered commencement of the other. However, it would also seem apparent from the urging of Cassiodorus' *amici* that his explanation of the soul was a prerequisite for understanding the content of the *Variae*; understanding the nature of the soul was the sine qua non for understanding anything else pertaining to creation. In fact, this seems to be the intent of Cassiodorus' learned *amici*, that after comprehending the 'substance and activities of the soul', they may then penetrate the deeper meaning of nature:

The motions of the planets in the heavens and the harmonious movements of the stars down the sky . . . the height of the aether, the size of the earth, the cloud-borne rains, raging hailstorms, the quakes of solid ground, the nature of wandering winds, the depths of the unsteady sea, the powers of green plants and the combinations of the four elements dispersed throughout the body.[52]

Similarly, the *De anima* states that 'the soul . . . ponders unceasingly views of the nature of things, thinks deeply about heavenly phenomena, investigates nature intensively and aspires to comprehend deeper knowledge of its own creator'.[53] According to the *De anima*, the investigation of

[51] Cassiodorus, *De anima* 1.1–9, trans. Halporn, *TTH*, 237.
[52] Cassiodorus, *De anima* 1.14–28, trans. Halporn, *TTH*, 237–8.
[53] Cassiodorus, *De anima* 4.21–24, trans. Halporn, *TTH*, 243; similarly, 4.71–73.

the material world was a natural preoccupation of the soul, which had an innate proclivity to apprehend its own moral substance in the rest of creation.

In short, Cassiodorus structured an exchange between himself and his palatine *amici* by which the soul would be explained in such a way as to promote further understanding of *natura*, the classical source of wisdom. Cassiodorus' response to his colleagues is a predictable expression of reluctance, because 'these themes were not suitable for imperial rescripts such as I had recently dealt with, but for deep and recondite investigations that clearly require not these our corporeal ears, but the acute and purest hearing of the inner man'.[54] This would seem to undermine any claim that the *De anima* served as a hermeneutic for the *Variae*, except that Cassiodorus' protest is obligatory rather than convincing. In fact, his protest was probably intended to discourage the casual reader, while strengthening the rhetorical framework that linked the *Variae* to the *De anima*, and would be noticeable to the more careful reader. As Cassiodorus continued to explain, 'Discussion about the soul is not so easy because it is by means of the soul we know how to explain countless facts.'[55] This statement recalls the pervasive encyclopaedism and the importance of *varietas* embedded in the *Variae*.

Cassiodorus' explanation for how the soul understands the moral content of *natura* forms a thematic connection between the *Variae* and the *De anima*. However, a number of scholars have instead seen the *De anima* as a profound break from Cassiodorus' interest in public life.[56] It is true that Cassiodorus drew more heavily from religious sources in composing the *De anima* than he had in the *Variae*. Although the *Variae* contain references to biblical characters, scriptural text is nowhere present.[57] In the *De anima*, it appears that Cassiodorus was influenced at least in part by patristic conceptions of the soul and he seems to have borrowed from Augustine and possibly from Claudianus Mamertus.[58] But in the period when Cassiodorus composed the *De anima*, Neoplatonic interest in producing commentaries on the soul had reached a peak. Aristotle's *De anima* supplied the raw material for the late antique commentaries on the soul. The treatises of Iamblichus and Augustine demonstrate both

---

[54] Cassiodorus, *De anima* 2.1–4, trans. Halporn, *TTH*, 239.
[55] Cassiodorus, *De anima* 2.4–5, trans. Halporn, *TTH*, 239.
[56] Gillett, 'Cassiodorus' *Variae*', 40; Mauro, 'Cassiodoro', 220; Halporn and Vessey, *Cassiodorus*, 19; Kakridi, *Cassiodors Variae*, 149; Markus, *Signs*, 83; note, however, that Barnish, *Cassiodorus*, xxiv–xxv, accepts thematic connection between the *Variae* and the *De anima*.
[57] Barnish, 'Sacred texts', 369, 'The bulk of scriptural allusions in the Variae are . . . like the classical, concealed – to be detected, and then, perhaps, interpreted only by those who had developed an ear for such things.'
[58] DiMarco, 'Fonti', 95–117.

the pervasive interest in defining the soul and the divergent paths those interpretations would take.[59] By the early sixth century, a new generation of interest in the soul had arrived, centred on the Neoplatonic school at Athens, where commentaries were produced by philosophers such as Priscian of Lydia and Simplicius.[60] The *Solutiones* of Priscian in particular come close to the central theme of the *Variae* by prefacing an encyclopaedic treatment of natural phenomena with a study of the soul.[61] Even the commentary offered by John Philoponus, a provocative Christian from Alexandria, was a response to the essentially Aristotelian interpretation of the soul espoused in contemporary Athens.[62] In particular, the Neoplatonic conception of the soul emphasized the hierarchic relationship between the soul and political virtues.[63] The influence of Neoplatonic thinking in the political culture of Constantinople and the prescriptive nature in which Neoplatonic treatises on the soul discussed political structure had the potential to make any discussion of the soul a polemical issue. In the light of the sixth-century intersection of interests in both the soul and governmental structure, it would seem that Cassiodorus' interest in composing a *De anima* had less to do with Christian piety than with exposure to eastern discourses and concern for his public life.[64]

The internal linkages that Cassiodorus established between the *Variae* and his *De anima* speak to an interest in the 'spiritual' interpretation of governance common to Neoplatonic thought. Beyond the more mechanical linkage established by cross-referencing the *De anima* and the *Variae* in their respective prefaces, the thematic correspondences are particularly important. As mentioned, the *De anima* expresses an interest in making the soul the focal point in the interpretation of nature. Additionally, the *De anima* sustains the concept of *varietas* as an organizational feature of knowledge and nature. Where *varietas* serves as a chief characteristic of the natural world in the *Variae*, in the *De anima* Cassiodorus extended the concept to include the exuberant diversity of human society:

[59] Iamblichus, *De anima*; Augustine, *De immortalitate animae, De quantitate animae, De natura et originae animae*.
[60] On the Athenian trajectory of Neoplatonic interest in the explication of the soul during the sixth century, Hadot, *Néoplatonisme*, 189–202; Blumenthal, 'John Philoponus', 62; Siorvanes, *Proclus*; Gritti, *Proclo*; De Haas, 'Priscian of Lydia', 756–63; as an example, Simplicius, *In libros Aristotelis De anima commentaria*.
[61] De Haas, 'Priscian of Lydia', 756–9.
[62] John Philoponus, *In Aristotelis De anima libros commentaria* and *De aeternitate mundi contra Proclum*; Sorabji, 'John Philoponus', 1–40.
[63] Hadot, *Néoplatonisme*, 153–6; Siorvanes, *Proclus*, 6–20.
[64] Also on the Neoplatonic influence on the *Variae* and *De anima*, Kakridi, *Cassiodors Variae*, 143–56.

divinity alone brings order out of diversity and at the same time makes everything clear by consistent rules. And so, endowed with abundant reason . . . the soul discovered the alphabet and advanced the uses and disciplines of the various arts and sciences, surrounded states with protective walls, created garments of various kinds, diligently forced the earth to produce better crops, rushed across the deep waters on winged ships, cut through huge mountains for the convenience of travellers, enclosed ports in a semicircular shape for the use of ships, adorned the earth with beautifully arranged structures.[65]

The *De anima* extends the concept of *varietas* to include the institutions and accomplishments of human society as a part of *natura*, much as Pliny the Elder included human arts in his natural history. The implication is that the soul not only facilitates the interpretation of the natural world, but also governs an understanding of human institutions and affairs as a part of that 'natural' harmony. In these terms, good governance becomes a consequence of a proper understanding of the soul.

The theme of how the soul 'reads' the moral quality of other souls also has direct bearing on the *Variae* as a record of governmental quality. In particular, this function of the soul elevates the appointment of palatine officials above 'profane' activity to the exercise of spiritual virtue. Cassiodorus described this process in its baser, mechanical form when he discussed how the inner virtues of a man could be read in his behaviour and physiognomy:

For just as the rising sun reveals the colours of objects at night's flight, thus will the quality of your character not conceal itself from careful princely scrutiny. Your mind will lay bare to our eyes and ears. We recognize the character of servants in their countenance and in their voice. If an expression is tranquil, if the voice is calm, we believe the reason to be the most morally upright. For we do not consider to be justice anything that is said confusedly. For which reason your test of him ruling will be thought to speak, since those who are able to put forth their own speech are unable to conceal their own intention. Indeed, words of men are the mirror of the heart, since it is demonstrated that what is believed to agree with good character is itself read in its very actions. The proud man is apparent by his swaggering gait; the wrathful man is declared by the seething of his eyes; a crafty man always prefers the view of the ground; a fickle man possesses a wandering of the eyes; the greedy man is revealed by hands hooked inward as though talons. And therefore be attentive to this, pursue virtue, since no man is able to deceive the prince who is proven best at investigating the nature of things even in you.[66]

---

[65] Cassiodorus, *De anima* 4.84–93, trans. Halporn, *TTH*, 246.

[66] Cassiodorus, *Variae* 6.9.3–4, 'Nam sicut sol ortus corporum colores fugata nocte detegit, ita se morum tuorum qualitas assidue viso principe non celabit. Mens tua et oculis nostris patebit et auribus. In vultu et in voce cognoscimus servientium mores. Si facies tranquilla, si vox moderata

This same conception appears in the *De anima* where he describes the physical characteristics of good and wicked men in an attempt to demonstrate how divine purpose designed the body to act as a receptacle specifically expressive of its content (the soul).[67] Although the soul might disguise itself with various bodily trappings, its true nature was always discernible to someone who understood virtue. Cassiodorus' attention to this topic is not out of place in other formulations of the relationship between inner nature and physical characteristics found in the ancient world.[68] The tradition of observing the appearance and physical habits of individuals as indices to the character of the soul dates to Hippocrates. It found articulate philosophical exponents in Aristotle and later in Polemo.[69] Among historians, the habit of thinking of the body as a 'legible' surface for the imprint of spiritual traits appeared in authors as diverse in intellectual background as Sallust, Ammianus Marcellinus and John Malalas.[70] Christian bishops did not shy away from the theory in its more classical form even while hagiographers could accentuate the holiness of their subjects by inverting bodily semiotics.[71] More significantly, Boethius' final treatise intimated the same opinion that wickedness was visible in the characteristics of corrupt officials. The sensitivity with which the *Variae* portray 'reading' nature in public officials has much to do with the extent to which Boethius condemned palatine service in various terms of 'bestiality':

In this way, then, whatever falls from goodness, ceases to be; wherefore evil men cease to be what they were — but that they were men till now their still surviving form of the human body shows — and therefore by turning to wickedness they have by the same act lost their human nature . . . The violent plunderer of others'

suggesserit, credimus esse probatissimas causas; quicquid enim turbulenter dicitur, iustitiam non putamus. Quapropter pensabit loqui tuum dominantis examen, quando nequeunt proprias tegere voluntates, qui suos possunt proferre sermones. Speculum siquidem cordis hominum verba sunt, dum illud moribus placere creditur, quod ipse sibi ad agendum legisse monstratur. Superbus quin etiam varicatis gressibus patet; iracundus luminum fervore declaratur; subdolus terrenum semper amat aspectum; leves inconstantia prodit oculorum; avarus obuncis unguibus explanatur. Et ideo ad quas provecti estis, studete virtutibus, quia nemo potest principem fallere, qui etiam rerum naturalium causas in vobis optime probatur inquirere'; similarly, 3.6.3, 8.14.3, 8.17.4.

[67] Cassiodorus, *De anima* 11–13.

[68] Brown, *Power and Persuasion*, 59–61, on physiognomy, inner character and political authority; Beagon, *Roman Nature*, 113–19, on the tradition of physiognomy as an extension of nature's semiotic language; Gleason, *Making Men*, 55–8, on reading the body as a revelation of the mind; Kokoszko, *Descriptions*, 18–52; Boys-Stones, 'Physiognomy', 19–124.

[69] Nussbaum and Rorty, *Essays*; Blumenthal, *Aristotle and Neoplatonism*; Polansky, *Aristotle's De Anima*; Swain, 'Polemon', 125–201.

[70] Sallust, *Bellum Catilinae* 15.3–5; Ammianus Marcellinus, *Res Gestae* 15.8.16; note too *Panegyrici Latini* 6.17.3.

[71] Ambrose, *Hexameron* 6.58; Ennodius of Pavia, *Vita Epiphanii* 13–16.

wealth burns with avarice; you would say he was like a wolf. The wild and restless man exercises his tongue in disputes; you will compare him to a dog. The secret trickster rejoices that he succeeds in his frauds; let him be on a level with the little foxes. He that cannot govern his anger roars; let him be thought to have the spirit of a lion. The timorous and fugitive is afraid of things not fearful; let him be reckoned like a deer. The stupid sluggard is numb; he lives an ass's life. The fickle and inconstant changes his pursuits; he is no different from the birds. A man is drowned in foul and unclean lusts; he is gripped by the pleasure of a filthy sow.[72]

The discussion of physical characteristics in the *De anima* provided one level for understanding how the moral content of the soul was imprinted visibly on the individual. As previously noted, *De anima* claimed that the soul perceived the moral meaning of the natural world.[73] More importantly, though, because the soul was formed of the same moral substance as the rest of creation, it more readily perceives 'the spiritual to which it recognizes itself to be similar in form.'[74] Thus because the soul was made of the moral substance of divine creation, it possessed the ability to recognize virtue and goodness in another soul. By extension, it was spiritual virtue that allowed good Amal rulers to recognize the moral content of the natural world and their subjects.[75]

CONSCIENTIA AND SPIRITUAL LIGHT

Cassiodorus elaborated on this relationship between the soul and external *natura* by defining the material of the soul. The *De anima* described the soul as a receptive substance that became infused with the quality of either good or evil activities, 'And so we are wise when we conduct ourselves well because of divine enlightenment and we are foolish when blinded by the mists of misdeeds.'[76] The characteristic of the soul that displays the record of conduct is *conscientia*. A soul with good conscience, *conscientia*, will have concern for the maintenance of its unblemished quality and will avoid association with souls of inferior quality.[77] With similar emphasis on the idea of *conscientia*, Cassiodorus stated at the beginning of his first preface to the *Variae* that he had gathered his letters 'so that the coming generation might recognize as worthy the disinterested deeds of a clear

---

[72] Boethius, *De consolatione philosophiae* 4.3.47–69, trans. Tester, *LCL*, 335.
[73] Cassiodorus, *De anima* 4.   [74] Cassiodorus, *De anima* 4.21–24, trans. Halporn, *TTH*, 243.
[75] Tartaglia, 'Elementi', 61–4, similarly notes that the *Variae* locate justice in the personal virtue of the Amals, although without connection to the theme of nature.
[76] Cassiodorus, *De anima* 4.159–160, trans. Halporn, *TTH*, 250.
[77] Cassiodorus, *De anima* 4.120–124.

conscience [*libera conscientia*] and the burden of my duties, which I had endured for the sake of the common advantage'.[78] The emphasis on *conscientia* forms a tangible link between the spiritual in the *De anima* and the governmental in the *Variae*. In essence, Cassiodorus' use of *conscientia* in the *Variae* allowed him to portray temporal governance as a moral matter. Variations on the concept of *conscientia* fill the letters of the *Variae* and seem to form a substrate tissue that allows the judgement of the ruler and actions taken on behalf of the state to be understood as spiritual activity. In its plainest sense, *conscientia* indicates men lacking guilt with respect to past actions.[79] However, it more frequently appears in the *Variae* as an abstracted moral quality of the soul and as the purity of intention recognizable by others of like nature. Thus defined, *conscientia* acts as the hallmark by which the Amal rulers recognize men of good character among their subjects. It was a quality that allowed them to act as arbiters in the dispensation of honour and distinction where deserved. The *Variae* reified *conscientia* as a substance that signified moral integrity, much as the colour purple signified royal or imperial bearing.

The importance of *conscientia* to the moral basis for appointment to office accounts for the frequency with which it and references to the soul appear in the *formulae* of Books 6 and 7.[80] The *conscientia* of a public official is physically visible to a good ruler.[81] The *conscientia* that a ruler detects in those promoted to public service is more than an individual's awareness of personal defects and past transgressions. It is expressed as an innate characteristic possessed by an individual from birth, 'just as you are endowed with good conscience'.[82] The *conscientia* has moral force in the activity of a public official, determining the kind of judge that he would be, 'a man who would disperse the clouds of corruption with the light of good intention'.[83] It is also *conscientia* that allows a ruler to preserve the observance of law and permits, through a kind of emanation of the substance, his magistrates to accomplish the same through an

---

[78] Cassiodorus, *Variae, praefatio* 1.1.
[79] Cf. Ammianus Marcellinus, *Res Gestae* 15.8.2, 'Addebantque noxarum conscientia stimulante complures'; *Historia Augusta, Vita Aurelii* 14.2–3, 'ut mihi gratias ageret res publica et conscientia mea'; Ennodius of Pavia, *Panegyricus* 11.57, 'Nullum de honoribus tetigit desperatio, quem iuverunt deprecantem bona conscientiae.'
[80] Cassiodorus, *Variae* 6.5.4, 6.9.6, 6.12.2, 6.15.4, 6.17.4, 6.20.4, 6.21.3, 6.22.2, 7.2.1, 7.32.1, 7.35.1.
[81] Cassiodorus, *Variae* 8.18.2, 'Aequo gradu eloquentia tua atque conscientia pariter incedebant; nullus iudicum quod in te corrigere posset invenit. Accessit enim venustas oris et castitas animi.'
[82] Cassiodorus, *Variae* 8.21.5, 'sicut es conscientia praeditus'.
[83] Cassiodorus, *Variae* 4.4.2, 'qui venalitatis obscura animi claritate refugiat'; similarly, with respect to an official's capacity as a judge, 1.44.2, 'purissimum testem'; 3.11.3, 'pretiosum puritatem conscientiae'; 8.18.5, 'bonae conscientiae'; 10.14.4, 'bona conscientia'; 10.28.1, 'nota conscientia'; 11.4.1, 'conscientiam'.

understanding of equity.[84] Indeed, *conscientia* seems to have actual legal agency in the *Variae*: 'let proven justice resolve this case with the careful examination of its own good conscience'.[85] This, of course, relates to the *De anima*, where Cassiodorus named justice foremost among the political virtues of the soul.[86] It is with this connection between *conscientia* and justice in mind that Cassiodorus asked 'various bishops' to intercede on his behalf on the occasion of his nomination to the praetorian prefecture:

> You, who are a spiritual father, who beholds the author of all things with an illuminated mind, do pray diligently to the sacred Trinity on my behalf, so that it would cause the ready candle placed in my mind to shine forth, to the extent that nothing seen within me should fail and that it might reveal the appearance of others to me. For what does it benefit a judge [of men] to be transparent to others, if he is still rendered obscure to himself? Let one for whom it is proper to elevate to the tribunal bestow the dignity of good conscience. Let him render the judge unimpeded, lest he wrong the man wandering astray.[87]

Here Cassiodorus approached a more expansive definition of *conscientia* as that quality of the soul that allows a man to perceive right and wrong. He articulated this in much the same way in a letter addressed to Pope John on the same occasion:

> Let that rational strength of the soul offer us counsel; let the face of truth glowing emerge, lest bodily blindness cloud our mind; let us follow what is within, lest we become lost to ourselves; let wisdom which is wise in its own truth instruct us; let that which shines with heavenly clarity illuminate us.[88]

Cassiodorus seeks the element of the soul imbued with 'true wisdom' that will guide him during his execution of an office upon which the fate of other men will invariably depend. The wisdom to which Cassiodorus

---

[84] Cassiodorus, *Variae* 11.8.1, 'nunc autem sufficiens satis conscientiae veterum decreta servare'; 11.9.4, 'Instar nostrae geritis dignitatis, si vos conscientiae puritate tracteris'; 11.16.2, 'quia ubi conscientiam fas est intendere, inde debet sermo iudicis inchoare'.

[85] Cassiodorus, *Variae* 3.45.2, 'conscientiae suae probata iustitia causam diligenti examinatione discutiat'.

[86] Cassiodorus, *De anima* 7.1–4; cf. Plato, *Republic* 1.352–356, 4.432–435, 4.473–480, on governance as the means and end of justice; and 2.369 and 4.435, on the direct correspondence between the extent of justice in men governing and the 'nature' of the state.

[87] Cassiodorus, *Variae* 11.3.1–2, 'Vos autem spiritales parentes, qui auctorem rerum illuminata mente conspicitis, pro me sanctae trinitati sedulo subplicate, ut splendere laetum faciat in medio positum candelabrum, quatenus nec mihi interior desit visus et de me aliis pandatur aspectus. Numquid proderit iudicem aliis esse perspicuum, si sibi potius reddatur obscurus? Dignitatem conscientiae donet, qui tribunalia praestare dignatus est. Facitat inoffensum iudicem, ne damnet errantem.'

[88] Cassiodorus, *Variae* 11.2.3, 'Vigor ille rationabilis animae nobis consilium praestet; facies veritatis albescat, ne mentem nostram innubilet caligo corporea; sequamur quod intus est, ne foris a nobis simus; instruat quod de vera sapientia sapit; illuminet quod caelesti claritate resplendet'; cf. Barnish, *Cassiodorus*, 150–2.

refers bears all the characteristics of the *conscientia* that grants the soul its ability to perceive moral goodness or baseness in others.

The use of light as imagery to describe this quality is more than a descriptive metaphor. The *De anima* defines the substance of the soul as light: 'Authorities have said that this substance has a fiery quality . . . We would, however, be correct in calling it instead a light because it was created in the image of God.'[89] For Plato, this spiritual light was the agency of the soul's recognition of truth, and hence it was essential to the exercise of justice.[90] Furthermore, authors from Aristotle to Pliny acknowledged that the light forming the soul was the same raw substance that formed the intelligible structure (the divine harmony) of the cosmos.[91] In late antiquity, even Christian theological discourses had become accustomed to discussing spiritual purity as 'light', primarily through exposure to Neoplatonic ideas concerning the soul.[92] Gregory of Nazianzus regularly used the imagery of illumination to connote a state of moral purification that allows one to perceive the divine, 'and where there is a keeping of commandments there is a purification of the flesh, that cloud that covers the soul and does not allow it to see the divine light'.[93]

In the *Variae*, the use of light as a metaphor for public service is pronounced and serves to locate governmental service within the 'intelligible' framework of the moral universe. At the simplest level of representation, light occurs as an epithet describing the honour in which a man bathes for having distinguished himself in public service. But even at this simple level, *lumen* has a spiritual quality recognized by the attention of the ruler: 'we have been especially desirous of this, in order that ornaments [*lumina*] of worth should adorn your assembly [the Senate] . . . Our attention scrutinizes these men'.[94] Similar expressions appear throughout the *Variae*.[95] A man who advances from one office to another is said to have the characteristic of 'a bright sun, which having accomplished an undertaken day, may then [advance] to illuminate yet another with

---

[89] Cassiodorus, *De anima* 5.1–2 and 5.11–13, trans. Halporn, *TTH*, 252.
[90] Plato, *Republic* 6.508; also *Phaedo* 109–11.
[91] Aristotle, *De anima* 1.2.404b.15; Pliny the Elder, *Naturalis Historia* 2.24.95.
[92] Beeley, *Gregory of Nazianzus*, 72–90, on the connection between Platonic philosophy and Christian theology; 90–113, on the the concept of divine light.
[93] Gregory of Nazianzus, *Theological Oration* 39.8–10; trans. Beeley, *Gregory of Nazianzus*, 69–70.
[94] Cassiodorus, *Variae* 1.4.2, 'ut collegium vestrum ornent lumina dignitatum, quando decenter augmenta patriae reddunt, qui aulica potestate creverunt. Hos viros nostra perscrutatur intentio'; cf. Barnish, *Cassiodorus*, 8–12.
[95] Cassiodorus, *Variae* 1.27.1, 1.41.1, 1.42.2, 2.3.3, 3.6.2, 3.12.1, 3.33.1.

the pleasantness of its brilliance'.[96] Cassiodorus elsewhere emphasized the correlation between public offices and heavenly configuration, the components of which are traditionally understood as bodies of light:

While it is fitting that your assembly should always radiate with native splendor, it is nonetheless rendered more brilliant by the extent that it is increased with the illumination of public offices. For heaven itself glows more with the abundance of stars and from that numerous beauty it returns a wondrous grace to those gazing at it.[97]

Cassiodorus clearly intended this imagery to elide conceptions of the divinely inspired arrangement of nature and the temporal order of governance: 'It is clearly nature's design that an abundance of blessings delight us more.'[98] As in the natural world, the operation of this spiritual light has discernible properties. Because the ability to exercise political virtues innate to the soul (justice, wisdom, temperance and fortitude) depends on holding office, it is a natural conclusion in the *Variae* that the ruler, who is vested with the capacity to perceive these qualities in men, should dispense appointments and therefore figure as a source of spiritual illumination.[99] Revealingly, Theodahad did not bathe in his own brilliance, but rather drew it from Amalasuntha, his partner in rule who was more sensitive to *conscientia*.[100] Those who shared in the salubrious illumination of the ruler received an opportunity to increase the public virtues of their own spiritual light, 'you who shine with distinguished position are now permitted to accomplish nothing in obscurity'.[101] Such officials in turn shed a similar grace on those associated with them, thus perpetuating a natural political order.[102] The extent to which this political order depended on the virtues of distinguished individuals, at least as it is articulated in the *Variae*, is apparent in the relative lack of self-determinism of the greater majority of subalterns:

[96] Cassiodorus, *Variae* 1.13.3, 'Habetis certe evidens nostrum in hac parte iudicium, ut post illius apices culmen ad alteram conscenderet dignitatem . . . sereni solis consuetudinibus aestimandus, qui licet susceptum diem peragat, alterum tamen eadem gratia claritatis illuminat.'
[97] Cassiodorus, *Variae* 8.19.1, 'Licet coetus vester genuino splendore semper irradietur, clarior tamen redditur quotiens augetur lumine dignitatum. Nam caelum ipsum stellis copiosissimis plus refulgent et de numerosa pulchritudine mirabilibus intuentibus reddit decorum.'
[98] Cassiodorus, *Variae* 8.19.1, 'Naturae siquidem insitum est, ut bonorum copia plus delectet'; also, 10.3.2.
[99] Cassiodorus, *Variae* 8.23.1, 6.23.2, 9.24.11.   [100] Cassiodorus, *Variae* 10.4.4–5.
[101] Cassiodorus, *Variae* 7.38.1, 'Quapropter nihil iam obscurum agere patiaris, qui clarissimatus dignitate resplendes.'
[102] Cassiodorus, *Variae* 8.10.1.

It is the custom for civil servants to submit willingly to the authority of those holding office, since they lack public distinction of their own. [Instead], they sparkle in alternating light, they shine with dependent strength, and in those who have no right to their own illumination, there seems to be a certain reflected image of the true office.[103]

Finally, it is probably best to consider Cassiodorus' use of light as the signifier of moral political activity in terms of his exposure to a predominant eastern discourse. This kind of imagery does appear in literature from the west in the sixth century, but never with this kind of programmatic density. For example, Avitus of Vienne described the emperor's majesty in terms of the diffusion of light on two occasions.[104] However, rather than a regular feature of Avitus' writing, this imagery probably represents a style adopted on the occasion of diplomatic correspondence between the Burgundian and eastern courts. It would be mistaken to conclude that Avitus was an isolated example of this type of imagery in the west, but for sheer density of representation, the eastern Mediterranean should be considered a likelier influence on Cassiodorus. The Neoplatonic literature of the Greek east maintained a steady connection to the idea of the goodness and purity of the soul radiating like 'living light'.[105] In his commentary on the *Timaeus* of Plato, Proclus considered light to be the connective tissue of the universal hierarchy.[106] Furthermore, the luminous quality of the soul was considered by Damascius to be the most elevated and the purest aspect of human conscience.[107] More generally, the concept of 'divine light' even determined features of design in eastern art and architecture.[108] Another source for this manner of describing political culture which is much more contemporary with Cassiodorus' work on the *Variae* and *De anima* is the *Dialogue on Political Science*. The *Dialogue* described imperial authority as 'political illumination', which poured from the ruler and was then mediated through successive tiers of office holding.[109] The similarity to the formulation of mediated 'political' light in letter 6.15 of the *Variae* is striking. Somewhat later than Cassiodorus, a more voluble example of this kind of political imagery appears in a work composed at the eastern court after Justinian's death.

---

[103] Cassiodorus, *Variae* 6.15.1, 'Vices agentium mos est sic iudicum voluntatibus oboedire, ut suas non habeant dignitates. Splendent mutuato lumine, nituntur viribus alienis et quaedam imago in illis esse videtur veritatis, qui proprii non habent iura fulgoris.'

[104] Avitus of Vienne, *Epistulae* 46 and 78.

[105] For example, Porphyry, *Vita Plotini* 13 and 22; Marinus, *Vita Procli* 3; on Proclus' use of the spiritual light of the soul in his *Hymns*, Saffrey, 'Neoplatonist spirituality', 258.

[106] Siorvanes, *Proclus*, 241–2.   [107] Hadot, *Néoplatonisme*, 182–84.

[108] For example, Procopius' comments on the Hagia Sophia as a source of divine light, *Buildings* 1.1.29–30 and 42.

[109] *Dialogue on Political Science* 5.58–61.

Corippus' panegyric to Justin II displays a fulsome array of court figures as luminous, celestial bodies.[110] Closer to the usage found in the *Variae*, Corippus described the operation of a political order in terms of cosmic illumination:

Everything is as bright [as Olympus], everything as well ordered in its numbers, as shining with light: just as the golden shining stars in the curving sky accomplish their courses poised on their own measure, number and weight, and remain firm in fixed retreat, and one light shines over all; all the stars yield to its superior flames and they feed on the fire of their monarch, by which they lie eclipsed.[111]

Given the later date of Corippus' work and his proximity to the eastern court, it may be that the rampant light imagery present in his panegyric to Justin II represents an attempt by the court to appropriate a language conciliatory to the bureaucratic ethos after Justinian's death. Whether or not the *Dialogue* was a direct influence on Cassiodorus or Corippus, it is certain that, in terms of the sheer density of representation, both the *De anima* and light in the *Variae* reflect Cassiodorus' exposure to the political discourse of the eastern capital.

Cassiodorus offered his audience a fully developed model for the spiritual nature of temporal governance through the combined reading of the *Variae* and the *De anima*. The use of *conscientia* to describe moral quality and light imagery to describe a political order collapsed distinctions between the sensible and intelligible world and allowed governance in Italy to be read as a moral system operating in tandem with divine providence. On the one hand, this formulation reflected directly on the reputation of the Amal rulers in whose names Cassiodorus articulated it. The repetitive use of verbs that imply perception and understanding, especially *videre*, heightens the sense that public administration functioned daily as a visual exercise of reading the moral character of people against an intuition sensitive to the processes of the natural world.[112] However, there is another level of interpreting this ideological construction of the *Variae* which is implicit in the fact that Cassiodorus himself wrote these letters and, in a sense, acted as their narrator in his prefaces. As shall be seen, presenting the Amal government as philosophically enlightened also had the effect of amplifying the spiritual quality of bureaucratic corporatism in Italy.

---

[110] On the emperor described as a source of heavenly light, Corippus, *In laudem Iustini Augusti Minoris* 1.249, 2.189–195, 2.299, 3.70–84, 4.240–245; on court members as lesser lights, 2.285–295, 3.219–230, 4.90–130, 4.365–374.

[111] Corippus, *In laudem Iustini Augusti Minoris* 3.179–187, trans. Cameron.

[112] Macpherson, *Rome*, 201.

Chapter 11

THE *VARIAE* AS APOLOGETIC NARRATIVE

CASSIODORUS AND SELF-PRESENTATION

Cassiodorus completed the *Variae* with two books of letters written under his own name as praetorian prefect and separated them from the rest of the collection with a second preface. By dividing the collection in this manner, the letters of these last two books communicate the ethical personality of the praetorian prefecture independent of Amal governance.[1] The first letters included in Book 11 were carefully selected for that purpose. Letter 11.1, addressed to the Senate at Rome, announces Cassiodorus' appointment to the praetorian prefecture by Amalasuntha. Unlike any other in the collection, this letter provides something of a 'state of the union address', framing the moment of Cassiodorus' appointment by recalling the prosperity of Amal governance under Theoderic and noting the providential nature of regime change that occurred with the accession of Amalasuntha and her son, Athalaric. The letter cites the former defeat of the Franks and Burgundians, and then the recently successful campaign against the eastern emperor Justin in the Balkans.[2] More importantly, the letter provides a panegyric to Amalasuntha, making it apparent that Theoderic's daughter (rather than his grandson) ruled Italy.[3] The tenor with which Cassiodorus praised Amalasuntha is highly reminiscent of the praise that Theoderic received as a 'purple-clad king'.[4] Amalasuntha's erudition, eloquence, fluency in languages and political discernment receive careful attention.[5] Her mastery, in particular, of ancient wisdom and the languages of the Greeks, Romans and Goths makes her something of a 'universal' monarch who surpasses the previous exemplar for female rule (Galla Placidia) and combines all

---

[1] On the ethics of ancient office holding, Lendon, *Honour*; Sivonen, *Roman Magistrate*.
[2] Cassiodorus, *Variae* 11.1.10–13.
[3] Cassiodorus, *Variae* 11.1.4; on this letter, Fauvinet-Ranson, 'Amalasonthe', 267–308.
[4] Cassiodorus, *Variae* 11.1.17, 'Quid ergo de animi firmitate loquar, qua vicit et philosophos valde praedicatos?' Cf. Barnish, *Cassiodorus*, 145–50.
[5] Cassiodorus, *Variae* 11.1.6–10, especially 11.1.6 and 11.1.7.

the qualities (*felicitas, patientia, mansuetudo, aequitas, forma, castitas, fides, pietas,* and *sapientia*) of former Amal rulers.[6] In so praising Amalasuntha's merits, the letter reveals the moral qualities that had been passed to Cassiodorus, as though through spiritual emanation, by his appointment, 'for such judgement did not discover my merits, but created them'.[7] Although the remaining letters of Books 11 and 12 purportedly represent the span of Cassiodorus' tenure as praetorian prefect (533–8) under Athalaric, Theodahad and Witigis (for whom he composed letters in Books 8–10), the moral reputation of his prefecture maintained a virtual tether to Amalasuntha's wisdom and discernment.

After this first address to the Senate, Cassiodorus continued with a series of letters requesting the blessing of the Pope and bishops of Italy (letters 11.2–3), which he followed immediately with exhortations to various officers under his command concerning the kind of moral probity demanded by their positions (letters 11.4–7).[8] The sequence of letters was particularly well suited to demonstrate Cassiodorus' own receptiveness to instruction in matters of governmental virtue and his responsibility for transmitting that governmental virtue to others.[9] Shortly after, Cassiodorus included his general edict outlining the administrative governance of Italy (letter 11.8). In this way, Cassiodorus' prefecture can be seen to gather moral strength first from Amalasuntha's appointment, then through assent of the Senate and finally through the spiritual blessing of the Pope and bishops of Italy. The appeals for spiritual guidance from the Pope and bishops of Italy complemented the manner in which Cassiodorus acted as a political patron, ensuring the morality of governance as it flowed from the praetorian prefect to his subalterns, both the staff of his *officium* and the agents (*cancellarii*) that he assigned to act on his behalf throughout the provinces. Just as Cassiodorus requested prayer for the wisdom to govern virtuously, so too did he provide moral advice for his subordinates:

---

[6] Cassiodorus, *Variae* 11.1.9–10, comparison to Galla Placidia; 11.1.19, comparison to former Amals.

[7] Cassiodorus, *Variae* 11.1.3, 'nam talia iudicia non invenerunt merita, sed fecerunt'.

[8] Cassiodorus, *Variae* 11.1, Cassiodorus to the Senate; 11.2, to Pope John; 11.3, to the bishops of Italy; 11.4 and 11.5, to Ambrosius, deputy of the praetorian office; 11.6, to Johannus, Cassiodorus' *cancellarius*; 11.7, to all magistrates of the provinces.

[9] Cassiodorus, *Variae* 11.1.2, 'Primum, ut hoc putemus utile quod honestum, ut nostros actus quasi pediseque semper iustitia comitetur et quod a continenti principe non emimus, nulli turpiter venditemus'; 11.2.3, 'Vigor ille rationabilis animae nobis consilium praestet; facies veritatis albescat, ne mentem nostram innubilet caligo corporea; sequamur quod intus est, ne foris a nobis simus; instruat quod de vera sapientia sapit; illuminet quod caelesti claritate resplendet. Talem denique iudicem publicus actus excipiat'; 11.3.1, 'Vos autem spiritales parentes, qui auctorem rerum illuminata mente conspicitis, pro me sanctae trinitati sedulo subplicate, ut splendere laetum faciat in medio positum candelabrum, quatenus nec mihi interior desit visus et de me aliis pandatur aspectus.'

Behold where antiquity saw fit to place you: you who bask in such brilliance at every turn will be seen from all directions. Therefore, turn your ears and heart to our admonition; fasten in your mind everything that we have commanded. Let none of these words pour through you as though through an open pipe which appears full only so long as the water flows in it. Be rather a vessel, so that you would preserve what is heard because you would not pour forth what was received; since it will profit nothing, if whatever words have crossed the thresholds of your ears should please and [yet] they should not fasten themselves in the chambers of your heart.[10]

The passage encapsulates Cassiodorus' role as a dispenser of offices received from antiquity and as the arbiter of the moral requirements suitable for each post. Cassiodorus' exhortations for moral deportment echo the same sentiment read in the letters of Theoderic and Athalaric. They also communicate the notion that virtuous conduct is something more than a basis for future remuneration; the conduct of the subordinate official reflects the very nature of his political patron: 'If you would act with the purity of good conscience [*conscientiae puritate*], you will accomplish the equivalent of our own public position.'[11] Cassiodorus' admonition to his subordinates and his general edict to Romans and Goths complete the model of moral emanation.

Cassiodorus' prefecture had also received a moral inheritance through the *antiquitas* of the offices that he held while advancing through the ranks of palatine service. According to the ideology portrayed in the *Variae*, these offices had been carefully preserved by Amal governance. It was perhaps in an attempt to destabilize the notion that the Amals were non-Roman interlopers that Cassiodorus traced the antiquity of at least one office (the praetorian prefecture) not to Roman, but to biblical tradition:

For when Pharaoh, the king of Egypt, was vexed by strange dreams concerning the threat of future famine and human counsel was unable to disclose the meaning of such phantoms, the blessed man Joseph was found, who would both predict the future accurately and most providently support a threatened populace. This very man it was who first consecrated the insignia of this office; the same man ascended to that carriage so deserving of respect; he was elevated

---

[10] Cassiodorus, *Variae* 11.6.6, 'Vide quo te antiquitas voluerit collocari; undique conspieris, qui in illa claritate versaris. Proinde ad nostra monita aures animumque converte; fige menti omnia quae iubemus; non te tamquam vacuam fistulam dicta perexeant, quae tamdiu plena conspicitur, quamdiu in eam undae influere posse noscuntur. Esto potius conceptaculum, quod audita custodias, quod suscepta non fundas; qua nihil proderit, si auribus tuis transitura placeant et in cordis sinibus se omnia non defigant'. Similar exhortations for moral conduct in 11.5, 11.9, 12.2, 12.3, 12.13, 12.21.

[11] Cassiodorus, *Variae* 11.9.4, 'Instar nostrae geritis dignitatis, si vos conscientiae puritate tractetis'; similarly, 11.4, 11.6.4, 12.1.1.

to this peak of glory so that his wisdom might bestow on the people what the might of the ruler was unable to provide. For it is from this example that even now the prefect is called the father of governance; and today the voice of the crier calls out that very name, admonishing the judge lest he should permit himself to be dissimilar [in any way].[12]

By comparing the praetorian prefecture with the secular position of the prophet Joseph, Cassiodorus again illustrated the state administrative apparatus in its spiritual aspect. In effect, palatine service had been prefigured in biblical times, not Roman. In as much as the Christian church was an extension of biblical word, the bureaucracy was now an extension of an original priesthood begun under Joseph. In supporting an institution with putatively biblical origins inherited by the Romans, the Amals had become coeval with the Romans.

The allusion to Joseph as the progenitor of the praetorian prefecture was particularly incisive as a reminder that palatine service had a moral tradition that extended well beyond both Amal and Roman governance.[13] This was not, however, intended as a declaration of religious independence from the non-orthodox Amals; rather, the lack of more overt scriptural reference in the *Variae* suggests the portrayal of a more abstract concept of bureaucratic priesthood. Cassiodorus similarly described the quaestorship in terms reminiscent of a priesthood. Cassiodorus phrased the office of quaestor as 'the glory of letters, the temple of civic harmony, the progenitor of every public distinction, the very household of restraint, and the seat of every virtue'.[14] The notion of a temple housing virtuous letters conflates easily enough with the idea of a church.

The frequent use of *conscientia* in the *Variae* similarly contributed to the idea of palatine service as a kind of priesthood. By comparison, the term *conscientia* appears in the *Novellae* on five occasions.[15] In each case, the term was used in reference to the clergy, which may indicate that Cassiodorus' notion of governmental spirituality had already been

---

[12] Cassiodorus, *Variae* 6.3.1–2, 'Nam cum Pharao rex Aegyptius de periculo futurae famis inauditis somniis urgeretur nec visionem tantam humanum posset revelare consilium, Ioseph vir beatus inventus est, qui et futura veraciter praediceret et periclitanti populo providentissime subveniret. Ipse primum huius dignitatis infulas consecravit; ipse carpentum reverendus ascendit; ad hoc gloriae culmen evectus, ut per sapientiam conferret populis quod praestare non potuerat potentia dominantis. Ab illo namque patriarcha et nunc pater appellatur imperii; ipsum hodieque resonat vox praeconis, instruens iudicem, ne se patiatur esse dissimilem'. Cf. Barnish, *Cassiodorus*, 94–6.

[13] Barnish, 'Roman responses', 14–15.

[14] Cassiodorus, *Variae* 6.5.5, 'Atque ideo prudentiae vel eloquentiae tuae fama provocati quaesturam tibi, gloriam litterarum, civilitatis templum, genetricem omnium dignitatum, continentiae domicilium, virtutum omnium sedem . . . deo praestante concedimus'; cf. Barnish, *Cassiodorus*, 96–7.

[15] Noted in Archi and Colombo, *Novellae*, 524.

influenced by the desire to represent bureaucratic corporatism as a kind of priestly brotherhood. Cassiodorus certainly deepened this impression by his frequent use of the term *caritas*, which carried specifically Christian connotations for a bond made in the mutual enjoyment of spiritual enlightenment.[16] In the *Variae*, however, rather than a Christian substitute for *amicitia*, the term *caritas* appears in all manner of address between political actors. Drawn from the discourse of Christian spirituality, *caritas* in the political context of *Variae* becomes a part of the vocabulary of spiritually enlightened governmental confraternity.

Thus rhetorical and semiotic affirmations of probity served to assure the audience of the *Variae* and *De anima* that palatine service, not just the Amals, preserved a sacred tradition for ethical governance. A crucial message of the *Variae* was that under deteriorating conditions, officials in Italy maintained respect for the antiquity of law and strictness in demanding the exercise of virtues appropriate for public office. As will be discussed, the *Variae* portrayed the kingship of Theodahad and Witigis as a period of impaired governance in Italy.[17] Thus the *Variae* claim in very deliberate terms that, even if the Amal court had continued on its course of deterioration without the interruption of the Gothic War, the palatine officials vested with the administration of the state would have maintained the integrity of moral governance. The ideology of the *Variae* provided a living testimony and future promise (*ventura posteritas*) for how the antiquity of institutions could maintain the semblance of imperial government even in a political system that was otherwise relatively weak and theoretically dependent on personal contact with a king.[18] The collection's articulation of a 'natural political order' removed governance from the sphere of fallible personal interests and placed it within the framework of institutional corporatism based on the exercise of virtue and tradition.

It is important to note that, although the recurrent symbolism of light suggests Neoplatonic emanation and downward refraction, the *Variae* also display the agency of the bureaucracy as having a crucial role in the ethical system of government. Cassiodorus assigned a portion of this agency to himself while announcing his appointment to the praetorian prefecture in two letters (9.24 and 9.25) written for Athalaric. Where

---

[16] For examples of *caritas* in this context, Cassiodorus, *Variae* 1.1.6, 1.4.11, 1.43.5, 1.44.1, 2.16.5, 2.41.3, 3.6.7, 3.49.1, 4.5.1, 5.17.4, 7.3.2, 7.3.5, 7.11.2, 8.1.5, 8.3.5, 8.23.4, 9.5.1, 9.5.3, 9.18.4, 10.10.1, 10.12.3, 10.18.2, 10.21.1, 10.23.2, 10.25.1, 11.1.4, 11.5.1, 11.11.1, 11.13.4.

[17] On how the general disposition of letters according to the rule of each monarch was intended to display the decline of the character of Amal rulers, Krautschick, *Cassiodor*, 136; Meyer-Flugel, *Bild der Gesellschaft*, 43; Bjornlie, 'A reappraisal', 143–79.

[18] Cassiodorus, *Variae, praefatio* 1.1.

Book 11 commences with an announcement of the same appointment written in Cassiodorus' name, Book 9 ends with Athalaric's announcement to Cassiodorus and the Senate. However, the difference in tone between the announcements of Books 9 and 11 is remarkable. While writing in his own name, Cassiodorus clearly displayed the debt that he owed to the character of Amalasuntha. Letters 9.24 and 9.25, however, strongly suggest Cassiodorus' tutelage of Theoderic in matters of governmental wisdom. Letter 9.24 praises Cassiodorus for nothing less than Theoderic's philosophical instruction, with special advertence to matters of natural history.[19] Letter 9.25 extended Cassiodorus' advice to matters of state: 'The truth and eloquence of his words have guided the mind of the one ruling, to whom [Cassiodorus] thus referred every matter, so he himself [the king] should wonder at who accomplished it.'[20] In both letters it is manifest that Cassiodorus' virtuous nature had commended him to the Amal court. The arrangement of these letters suggests that the royal mind had identified Cassiodorus' character and Cassiodorus in turn 'supported the heavy foundation of royal character with the strength of . . . eloquence'.[21] The shift in agency, from the portrayal of Cassiodorus as an agent of instruction in Book 9 to Cassiodorus' deference to the agency of royal vision in Book 11, demonstrates an economy of virtuous reciprocity that was, in fact, the cornerstone of the political system advocated in the *Dialogue on Political Science*. The placement of these letters also served to exclude Theodahad and Witigis from this system of reciprocity. By ending Book 9 and commencing Book 11 with letters pertaining to the same event, Book 10, which contains letters written for Theodahad and Witigis, seems to reside outside the system of moral interdependence. The strong continuity that Books 11 and 12 have with themes present in books pertaining to the reigns of Theoderic and Athalaric (under Amalasuntha's regency) suggest to the audience of the *Variae* that the palatine bureaucracy was quite capable of maintaining continuity with the ancient mores of governance, even under deeply flawed kings.

THEODAHAD AS A RHETORICAL FOIL

The treatment of Theodahad and Witigis in the *Variae* stands in sharp contrast to the treatment of Theoderic, Athalaric and Amalasuntha and

---

[19] Cassiodorus, *Variae* 9.24.8.
[20] Cassiodorus, *Variae* 9.25.1, 'Trahebat regnantis animum veritas et disertitudo dictorum, cui sic omnia retulit, ut miraretur ipse qui fecit'; cf. Barnish, *Cassiodorus*, 127–30.
[21] Cassiodorus, *Variae* 9.24.3, 'dum molem tantam regalis ingenii facundiae tuae viribus sustineres'; cf. Barnish, *Cassiodorus*, 124–7.

strongly suggests a calculated and rhetorical portrayal. Theoderic obviously provided the gold standard for the height of Amal governance as a philosopher king and *imperator* of a hegemony of 'barbarian' kingdoms. The *Variae* also suggest that Athalaric maintained the essential semblance of Theoderic's government. For example, the first letter appearing in the name of Athalaric (8.1) was addressed to the emperor Justin in the same terms with which Theoderic addressed Anastasius at the beginning of the collection (1.1). Both letters acknowledge the diplomatic necessity of good relations between the east and the west and both declare previous justifications for hostility forfeit. The *Variae* also commence Athalaric's reign with a succession of letters requesting oaths of fidelity.[22] These letters confirm the seamless transition of loyalty from Theoderic to Athalaric. They also advertise the territorial extent of Amal control in the west, which Amalasuntha maintained in Athalaric's name through the continuation of Theoderic's policies.[23] In short, the *Variae* intended Theoderic, Amalasuntha and Athalaric to be understood as the continuity of traditional and morally fit governance under the Amals.

Book 10 presents a different image of Amal governance. Amalasuntha appears only briefly, and for the express purpose of introducing Theodahad as the next ruler in succession after the premature death of Athalaric.[24] The only other letters assigned to Amalasuntha are brief and highly cryptic – one to Justinian concerning building arrangements (presumably in Ravenna) and the last a perfunctory greeting to the Empress Theodora.[25] Although the letters featuring Amalasuntha are limited in thematic scope, it is clear enough from the praise lavished on her in the letter announcing Cassiodorus' promotion (11.1) that Theodahad's reign was an abrupt departure from former Amal governance. Cassiodorus portrayed the debased nature of Theodahad's governance in a number of ways. First, letters announcing his accession as king emphasize his dependence on Amalasuntha. In the letter announcing his elevation to Justinian, Theodahad states, 'For I am most determined not to deviate in the least bit from the judgement of one who shines with the light of

---

[22] Cassiodorus, *Variae* 8.2, to the Senate; 8.3, to the Roman people; 8.4, to the Romans in Italy and Dalmatia; 8.5, to the Goths in Italy; 8.6, to Liberius as prefect of Gaul; 8.7, to the Gauls; 8.8, to Victorinus and the clergy of Milan; also, a series of appointments seems to have in mind this same idea of fidelity after succession, 8.9–8.11, the Goth Tuluin as patrician; 8.12, Arator as Tuluin's partner in administration; 8.13–8.14, Ambrose as quaestor; 8.16–8.17, Opilio as count of the sacred largesse; 8.20, Avienus as praetorian prefect; 8.21–8.22, Cyprian as patrician.

[23] Cassiodorus, *Variae* 11.1.10, 'Sub hac autem domina, quae tot reges habuit quot parentes, iuvante deo, noster exercitus terret externos: qui provida dispositione libratus nec assiduis bellis adteritur nec iterum longa pace mollitur.'

[24] Cassiodorus, *Variae* 10.1 and 10.3, Amalasuntha on the confirmation of Theodahad's accession.

[25] Cassiodorus, *Variae* 10.8 to Justinian and 10.10 to Theodora.

wisdom, since she both disposes her own kingdom with remarkable order
and she preserves the agreeability promised to all with firm strength.'[26]
The letter even contains admission that Amalasuntha had attempted to
correct Theodahad's character prior to allowing him to share the throne,
'I first felt her justice, so that I might then arrive at the grace of her
advancement. For, as you know, she caused me to plead my cases with
private citizens under common law.'[27] The idea that Theodahad had been
morally ill-suited to rule prior to Amalasuntha's influence is strengthened
in letter 10.5, where Theodahad must advise his personal servant that the
kind of behaviour that had been acceptable prior to Theodahad's assumption of royal dignity was no longer tolerable. According to the report of
the *Variae*, Theodahad's 'virtue' was truly a recent mint.[28]

Similarly, Cassiodorus clouded Theodahad's reputation with respect to
his role as an executor of diplomatic relations. The *Variae* characterized
Theoderic's reign, in part, by demonstrating his influence over a wide
range of western 'barbarians' and a carefully managed posture of non-
conciliatory deference toward the eastern empire. According to letter
11.1, Amalasuntha and Athalaric apparently maintained this diplomatic
personality. In direct contrast, the entirety of Theodahad's diplomatic
record in the *Variae* is entangled by obscure correspondence with the
eastern court, which serves only to illustrate Theodahad's sycophancy.[29]
On the domestic front, Theodahad's reputation fares just as poorly. Book
10 contains a 'dossier' of letters to the Senate and the people of Rome
that narrates a sequence of events in which Theodahad first sequestered
senatorial hostages at Ravenna (presumably after Amalasuntha's murder)
and then imposed a garrison on Rome.[30] Where Theoderic had played
a stern fatherly role in his relationship with the Senate, Theodahad is
shown to behave in such a heavy-handed manner that he eventually
must offer pledges of his own good faith, a reversal of power relations
when compared to the oaths required by Athalaric.[31]

[26] Cassiodorus, *Variae* 10.2.2, 'Ab eius enim iudicio me nullatenus deviare certissimum est, quae
tanta sapientiae luce resplendent, ut et propria regna mirabili dispositione componat et promissam
cunctis gratiam robusta firmitate custodiat.'
[27] Cassiodorus, *Variae* 10.4.4, 'cuius prius ideo iustitiam pertulit, ut prius ad eius provectionis
gratiam pervenirem. Causas enim, ut scitis, iure communi nos fecit dicere cum privates'.
[28] Cassiodorus, *Variae* 10.5.1–2, 'Et ideo praesenti iussione praecipimus, ut quicumque ad domum
nostram noscitur pertinere . . . nullis praesumptionibus insolescat . . . Mutavimus cum dignitate
propositum et si ante iusta districte defendimus, nunc clementer omnia mitigamus.' Cf. Barnish,
Cassiodorus, 132–3.
[29] Cassiodorus, *Variae* 10.2, 10.9, 10.15, 10.19–26; note Gillett, *Envoys*, 180–1, that the dossier of
letters to Justinian and Theodora is 'the most disproportionate in the distribution of diplomatic
correspondence throughout the *Variae*'.
[30] Cassiodorus, *Variae* 10.13, 10.14, 10.18.   [31] Cassiodorus, *Variae* 10.16 and 10.17.

THEODAHAD'S FAILED VISION

The *Variae* call into question the moral efficacy of Theodahad's administration most effectively by tampering with the theme of 'reading' nature that was so carefully constructed in letters pertaining to earlier Amals. In particular, two letters concerning the illness of a Gothic *comes* (10.29) and the restoration of bronze elephants at Rome (10.30) illustrate the failure of Theodahad's judgement. These two letters feature disquisitions on natural history that Cassiodorus crafted to reveal Theodahad's skewed insight into the relationship between *natura* and political harmony.[32] Of the twenty-four letters attributed to Theodahad in the *Variae*, only letters 10.29 and 10.30 display excursuses of the type seen elsewhere in the collection and for that reason may be regarded as exemplary of the way Cassiodorus chose to portray Theodahad's thinking. According to letter 10.30, Theodahad directed the urban prefect of Rome to restore certain statues of elephants which had fallen into disrepair along the Via Sacra. Presumably as an opportunity to demonstrate his erudition as well as his attention to civic tradition, the letter develops into an extended disquisition on the natural history of elephants. Read within the context of public relations between the Amal court at Ravenna and the senatorial elite of Rome, such a display of literary cultivation and concern for the monumental past of the city corresponds well with the general tenor of the letter collection as a whole. Both the style of the letter, reflecting as it does the traditions of classical learning, and its concern for the material preservation of antiquity advertise Theodahad's *romanitas*. Treated as an authentic document, the letter could be read as a fragment of the propaganda generated by the chancery at Ravenna to encourage the continued support of the traditional Roman aristocracy for what was a distant court prone to be seen as semi-barbaric.[33]

This interpretation would seem to make sense, except that Cassiodorus fashioned in this letter a natural history that satirizes the elephant rather than shows it as a creature worthy of public celebration. In this way, Cassiodorus portrayed a rupture in the previous Amal sensitivity to the relationship between the natural world and public life. The letter describes the elephant as an unwieldy slave, remarkable only for its mass, which submits itself to menial tasks. Its tottering size renders the elephant barely capable of independent motion and requires the governance of and foddering by a master, not unlike the contemporary city of Rome, which was

---

[32] On the rhetorical function of these two letters, Bjornlie, 'A reappraisal'.
[33] On the portrayal of semi-barbarism in court politics, Moralee, 'Maximus Thrax', 55–82.

dependent upon annonarial provisioning administrated from Ravenna.[34] It is possible to see the elephant of this letter as an allegory for the governance of the ancient capital, which Theodahad entrusted to the urban prefect, the addressee of the letter:

Even for living elephants, which, while in a kind of genuflection, will have lent their enormous limbs to the human occupation of felling trees, a false step is dangerous; those with their full bulk lying prostrate are unable to rise by their own strength, evidently because their feet are not articulated with joints, but they stand continually rigid and unbending in the manner of columns. Whenever such a great mass lies on the ground, then you would believe them to be more crafted of metal [than flesh], because you would behold living creatures unable to move themselves. They lie overcome as though lifeless bodies: you would deem dead what you should not doubt to be living. And after the fashion of collapsed buildings, they know not how to quit willingly a place that they were able to occupy by their own support. Such terrible size is unequal to the minutest ant, when it does not enjoy the blessing that is apparently granted by nature to the least animal. They rise with human assistance, by whose skill they are cast down. Even a brute beast, mindful of this favour, knows itself to have been restored to its own footing; indeed it accepts as master one whom it knows to have assisted it. It moves at the pace set by that very governor, willingly takes sustenance from him and, what exceeds the intelligence of all four-legged animals, it does not hesitate to honour on sight the one whom it knows to be the ruler of all affairs.[35]

Far from a beast that would ennoble the city of Rome, the elephant of this letter has 'ulcerous skin', for which reason, Cassiodorus explained, lepers barred from passing city gates received their name, an ironic observation given the prestigious location of the statues within the *pomerium* of the

---

[34] For evidence of continued annonarial distributions in Rome in the sixth century, the *Excerpta Valesiana* 12.67, and Cassiodorus, *Variae* 6.18 and 11.5.

[35] Cassiodorus, *Variae* 10.30.2–3, 'Nam et vivis ipse casus adversus est, qui, dum in genus cubationis, arte hominum succisis arboribus, ingentia membra commiserint, toto pondere supinati nequeunt propriis viribus surgere, quos semel contigerit corruisse, scilicet quia pedes eorum nullis inflectuntur articulis, sed in modum columnarum rigentes atque incurvabiles iugiter perseverant. Ibi tanta mole prostrati sunt, ut tunc magis metallicos possis credere, cum se vivos aspicias non movere. Iacent superstites similitudine cadaverum: mortuos putes, quos vivos esse non dubites et more cadentium fabricarum, nesciunt locum sponte relinquere, quem suis membris potuerint occupare. Magnitudo illa terribilis nec formicis minutissimis par est, quando beneficium non habet naturae, quod ultima videntur animalia meruisse. Humano solacio consurgunt, cuius arte iacuerunt. Belua tamen suis gressibus restituta novit memor esse beneficii: in magistrum quippe recipit quem sibi subvenisse cognoscit: ad ipsius arbitrium gressus movet, ipsius voluntate cibos capit, et, quod omnem intelligentiam quadrupedum superat, non dubitat primo aspectu adorare quem cunctorum intellegit esse rectorem'. Note how the treatment of elephants by Ambrose in *Hexameron* 5.31–35, to which Cassiodorus' description is indebted, makes several comparisons to buildings.

city.[36] The elephant also has a truculent disposition and a propensity for retaliating against perceived insults in distinctly rancorous fashion.[37] Of the virtues assigned to the elephant by Pliny the Elder, such as a sense of honour and respect for religion, Theodahad's elephants possess only the barest traces.[38] As a letter directed to the leading official of Rome, its content was not particularly laudatory, nor does it explain how the characteristics of the live elephant render its bronze counterparts worthy of restoration.

In contradistinction to the careful association of public building with good governance and *reverentia antiquitatis* consistently repeated in *Variae*, this letter portrays Theodahad's concern for the restoration of bronze elephants which were, given their treatment, of questionable symbolic value. Although the letter is at least superficially concerned with the preservation of antiquity, Theodahad's project allocated state resources to the repair of superficial ornamentation while neglecting the more functional urban fabric of the surrounding Forum Romanum. This seems particularly egregious considering the symbolic capital embodied in the higher-profile buildings of the Roman Forum.[39] Theodahad's concern for the monumental centre of Rome seems to reflect a certain ambivalence toward the grandeur of its past; the opening statement of the letter claims that the Via Sacra had been dedicated to various questionable beliefs, *multis superstitionibus*.[40] Theodahad's interest in elephants seems especially frivolous when compared to Theoderic's earlier concern for the *utilitas* of the Forum, expressed in letter 4.30, which ordered the construction of workshops intended to renew the appearance and usefulness of the area.[41] It would seem that Theodahad failed to understand the imperative of *reverentia antiquitatis* and *utilitas publica*, the sentiments

---

[36] Cassiodorus, *Variae* 10.30.7, 'Cutis huius ulcerosis vallibus exaratur, a qua transportaneorum nefanda passio nomen accepit, quae in tantam duritiam solidatur, ut putes esse osseam cutem'; Cassiodorus here apparently referred to *elephantiasis* as a locution for leprosy, a usage he shares with Pliny the Elder, Augustine and Vegetius.

[37] Cassiodorus, *Variae* 10.30.5–6, 'Quod si aliquis praebere contempserit postulata, vesicae collectaculo patefacto tantam dicitur alluvionem egerere, ut in eius penatibus quidam fluvius videatur intrare, contemptum vindicans de fetore. Nam et laesus servat offensam et longo post tempore reddere dicitur, a quo iniuriatus esse sentitur.'

[38] Cf. Pliny the Elder, *Naturalis Historia* 8.1–3, and Cassiodorus, *Variae* 10.30.3; Cassiodorus' discussion is similarly distinct from Solinus, *Collectanea rerum memorabilium* 25.1–15, which reproduces Pliny's moral interpretation of the elephant while differing significantly in other respects.

[39] On the urban fabric at the monumental centre of Rome in this period, Marazzi, 'Last Rome', 279–303; Augenti, 'Palatine Hill', 44–9; Coates-Stephens, 'Housing', 239–59; Ward-Perkins, *Building*, 38–48; Whitehouse, Barker, Reece and Reese, '*Schola Praeconum*', 53–101.

[40] Cassiodorus, *Variae* 10.30.1, 'Relationis vestrae tenore comperimus in via sacra, quam multis superstitionibus dicavit antiquitas'; on pejorative associations of *superstitio*, Bowes, *Private Worship*, 44–8.

[41] Cassiodorus, *Variae* 4.30.2.

so central not only to the urban projects of his predecessors but to their entire conception of good governance.

The letter becomes even more profoundly awkward when consideration is given to Theodahad's political position at the time.[42] As previously discussed, the period of Theodahad's rule following Amalasuntha's murder witnessed an escalation of political uncertainty and a cascade of diplomatic blunders with both the senatorial elite at Rome and Justinian's court. The novel presence of a Gothic garrison at Rome and the sequestering of senatorial hostages at Ravenna contrasts markedly with Theodahad's professed concern for the antique trophies of the ancient capital. Theodahad's difficulties on the front of foreign relations with the eastern imperial court also render questionable the appropriateness of his interest in public ornamentation. The terseness of his correspondence (10.19–26) with the eastern court was not in keeping with the diplomatic decorum found, for example, in the very first letter of the collection – Theoderic's letter to Anastasius. The change in tone speaks to political uncertainty and even a degree of desperation. Indeed, the last letter in this series (10.26) makes it clear that prominent inhabitants of Italy had begun to appeal to Justinian concerning their disagreements with Theodahad's court.[43] If Theodahad's letter concerning the bronze elephants was actually delivered, it coincided with the eve of the Gothic War and the fall of Amal rule in Italy. Given the political conditions of Theodahad's reign, illustrating his putative concern for elephants in the *Variae* served as an indictment of the general ineptitude of his political thinking at the time.

This portrayal of Theodahad as a dysfunctional ruler appears in another letter concerned with the body politic and natural history. Letter 10.29 grants leave of absence to a military commander, the otherwise unattested *comes* Wisibad, permitting him to travel to the springs of Bormio where he was to recuperate from a debilitating case of gout. This letter differs little in its general context from several others in the collection in which Ostrogothic rulers granted discharges to public officials for reasons of personal health. Several letters written in the name of Theodahad's more celebrated predecessor, Theoderic, imply that such dispensations from official duty were routine practice.[44] A similar letter written for Athalaric (9.6) elaborated on concern for the health of a court official. In the case of letter 9.6, dismissal from duty entailed a lengthy disquisition on the

[42] Mommsen, *MGH AA XII*, dated letter 10.30 *c.* 535–6.
[43] Cassiodorus, *Variae* 10.26, offers Theodahad's response to Justinian concerning complaints about the taxation of monastic property in Italy.
[44] Cassiodorus, *Variae* 3.21 to Faustus, *vir illustris* and senator at Rome; 5.36 to Starcedius, *vir spectabilis* serving some military function warranting the donative.

healthful effects of the natural surroundings of Baiae, particularly its restorative waters. The letter was an opportunity to demonstrate the king's correct understanding of *natura rerum*, especially the relationship between the purity of nature and its capacity to heal.[45] As previously discussed, similar treatments appear in other letters which allow Amal rulers to expound on the miraculous properties of natural springs at Aponus (1.39), Squillace (8.32), and Lucania (8.33).

The letter attributed to Theodahad, however, presents thinking on *natura rerum* that is altogether different and rather unsettling. Instead of describing the recuperative benefits of Bormio, this letter draws attention to the degenerative process of the disease as it wages war on the human body:

We fulfill your request with a medicinal injunction, so that we might restore with the blessing of a command that health which we rightly expect to find in you. For it does not avail that this disease should disarm such a warlike man with the tyrannies of grievous affliction, by which means it forces virile limbs to seize up with an infusion of punishing fluid and increasingly fills pliant ligaments with a stone-like swelling. When it knows everything else to be rendered useless, it seeks the hollow cavities of the joints where, spreading slowly, it creates stones from standing water, as though from a swamp, and the wandering disease constricts with the unsightly rigidity of something solid what nature had granted the grace of bending. This unhealthy suffering and insufferable health binds anything supple, contracts the nerves and causes a body that has been stricken with no mutilation to shorten. It withers the measure of the body by fastening upon the limbs and it is noticed less by those who feel nothing to have been removed. The assistance of the limbs is removed from those who survive; the living body is unable to move and thus reduced to senseless members; a man is no longer able to move by his own accord, but is carried by the motion of someone else. This condition is known to be a living death worse than any torment and one who was unable to avoid the final outcome of such punishment is considered to have had the better lot. For indeed, the sickness departs, but it leaves only a remnant of strength and, in a novel example of misfortune, the suffering seems to withdraw while the diseased man does not cease to be sick. Even the weighted limbs of debtors are occasionally freed from torture; but the chains of this disease, once it will have been able to fasten on to a captive, are not known to release him for the rest of his life. Departing, it leaves a ruinous token of its presence and after the manner of barbarian tribes, having claimed the hospitality of the body, it protects its own claim with violence, lest a hostile wholesomeness should perhaps dare to return there, where such a savage entity has laid hold.[46]

---

[45] Cassiodorus, *Variae* 9.6.2–3.

[46] Cassiodorus, *Variae* 10.29.1–4, 'Desiderium tuum remediali iussione sanamus, ut sospitatem, quam merito in te quaerimus, iussionis beneficio compleamus. Absit enim, ut bellicosissimum

The letter takes a keen interest in disease as an inversion of nature, especially in describing how the disease reverses the natural properties of the body, filling pliant tissues with stone-like swelling. Cassiodorus ingeniously employed *commutatio* to demonstrate how disease reverses the natural condition, provoking liquids to arrest, *arescere*, and tissue to swell, *replere*, thereby inverting the properties of fluids and solid matter. As described in the letter, the progression of the disease has strong parallels with the body politic. The references to debt bondage, the accommodation of barbarians on private property and tyranny all describe a society at odds with itself and suggest an inversion of Theodahad's understanding of nature and government.[47] Indeed, the traditional understanding of gout as a metaphor for moral failure may imply that Theodahad rewarded an undeserving public servant with a holiday.[48]

Although these letters accord with Cassiodorus' use of natural history as digressive material, it is also apparent that Cassiodorus impugned Theodahad's political thinking by distorting his understanding of nature. These digressions aggravated a carefully constructed theme in the *Variae* by which justice and the appropriateness of legal and administrative decisions were explained by comparing the consequence of human behaviour to positive *exempla* from nature. Letters 10.29 and 10.30 are the only examples of Theodahad's attempt to apply a philosophical understanding of the natural world to governing. They are also the last letters attributed to him in the collection. As depicted in the *Variae*, Theodahad shows interest in reading nature like other Amals; but like Trimalchio, who misconstrues being Roman at every level, so too does Theodahad only succeed at aping the good ruler. Procopius, too, seems to draw attention

virum tyrannis gravissimae calamitatis exarmet, quae miro modo membra virentia infusione poenalis umoris cogit arescere nodosque mobiles replet marmoreo tumore crescentes. Cum norit alia cuncta vacuare, iuncturae petit concavas lacunas, ubi palustri statione pigrescens saxa perficit de liquore et quae ad decorem inflexionis natura laxaverat, in turpissimum rigorem peregrina soliditate constringit. Haec passio insanabilis et sanitas passibilis ligat solutos, contrahit vivos et decrescere facit corpora, quae nulla sunt mutilatione truncata. Constantibus membris proceritatis mensura perit et minor cernitur, cui nihil subductum esse sentitur. Subtrahuntur superstiti ministeria membrorum; corpus vivum est nec movetur et inter insensibilia redactum iam non proprio voto, sed motu fertur alieno. Haec viva mors supra omnia tormenta sana dicitur et melius habere fertur, qui evasisse causam tanti periculi non probatur. Desederat quidem dolor, sed dimittit reliquias fortiores et, novo infelicitatis exemplo, passio videtur abscedere et aeger non desinit aegrotare. Appendia ipsa cruciatis debitoribus aliquando solvuntur; ista enim vincula sunt quae, cum semel potuerint illigare captum, nesciunt in tota vita dissolvere. Infelicia signa relinquit abscedens et more gentium barbararum hospitium corporis occupatum suis indiciis violenta defendit, ne ubi ferox ista coepit succedere, adversa illuc iterum sanitas audeat fortassis intrare.'

47 Cassiodorus, *Variae* 10.29.2, 'ut bellicosissimum virum tyrannis gravissimae calamitatis exarmet'; and 10.29.4, 'et velut duobus auxiliis congregates in medium missa superatur'.
48 Cameron, *Last Pagans*, 279–81.

to Theodahad's philosophical interests merely in parody. In the *Wars*, Theodahad's interest in Plato contrasts markedly with his devotion to wealth and his lack of engagement in public life. Procopius mirrored this incongruity in a comment that he attributed to Justinian's envoy, Peter the Patrician, who informed Theodahad that (perhaps specifically in his case) the philosophical life was ill-suited to kingship.[49]

RHETORICAL ARRANGEMENT IN THE *VARIAE*

Cassiodorus' portrayal of Theodahad as a dysfunctional ruler had a concrete purpose in the arrangement of letters in the *Variae*. The first nine books of the *Variae* contain letters written by Cassiodorus in the names of rulers from an earlier and, as portrayed in the collection, more successful period of Amal governance. Through the overt demonstration of interest in natural history, Cassiodorus implied that the government of Italy under these rulers was dictated by *pura conscientia*. By contrast, Book 10 contains letters written in the names of Theodahad and Witigis, rulers under whom relations with Constantinople and the senatorial elite at Rome suffered. Corresponding to the apparent deficiency in their political acumen – especially evident in Theodahad's misreading of the use of natural history and public building – the portrayal of *pura conscientia* disappears. Compared with letters of the *Variae* which detailed the enactments of earlier rulers, letters ascribed to Theodahad presented his reign as a grossly diminished affair. Where Theodahad was a genuine Amal and required repudiation according to the same semiotics that had elevated Theoderic and Athalaric, Witigis received less attention in the *Variae*. An Amal only through usurpation and marriage, Witigis received attention only in the last five letters in Book 10. The purpose of Witigis' letters in the collection is rhetorical. The brevity and lack of coherent ideological content illustrate the extent of decline in kingship at Ravenna.

In direct contrast to the letters of Book 10, the last two books of the collection depicting Cassiodorus' activities as praetorian prefect under Amalasuntha, Theodahad and Witigis present the image of continuity in ethical governance, now in the hands of dedicated officials. In character with the ideological programme of the *Variae*, Cassiodorus demonstrated how the proper understanding of natural phenomena permitted the ethically sound exercise of judicial and administrative authority even when the king was demonstrably void of such understanding. In his capacity as praetorian prefect, Cassiodorus referred an ill servant to more healthy surroundings by explaining the salubrious benefits of nature, rather than

---

[49] Procopius, *Wars* 5.3.1–2 and 5.6.6–13.

fixating on the degenerative process of disease, as in Theodahad's letter.[50] In similar disquisitions of Books 11 and 12, Cassiodorus emphasized the regularity of public service and administrative practices through comparisons with nature. In a letter to the *cancellarius* of Samnium (11.36), Cassiodorus compared the course of a career in public service to the regularity of planetary courses. Similarly, decisions to collect or remit taxes often appear after consideration of the natural resources of a particular region; the speculative musings of a natural historian of the classical tradition determined such matters, not the record-keeping tabulation of an accountant.[51]

Indeed, letters of the last two books of the *Variae* make the case that the moral probity of palatine officials in Italy assured the regularity of traditional administrative practices. Cassiodorus constructed this continuity with the repetition of numerous vignettes representing the kinds of administrative activity under his personal supervision that had concerned the earlier Amal rulers. These letters include accounts of Cassiodorus' involvement in providing provisions for the city of Rome, regulating prices and weights, rendering judgement in legal cases and attention to building through the repair of roads and bridges.[52] The transition from royal to prefectural governance is so seamless that Cassiodorus even speaks of his *cancellarius* in the same terms in which an Amal considered his quaestor, 'thus it is proven that the mind of the president of an office is depicted through you'.[53] A significant feature of this portrayal is the sense that duty to state service and a genuine affection for tradition take precedence over the attachments of personal loyalty. In discussing the provisions that antiquity has allotted to the citizens of Rome, Cassiodorus stated, 'We would readily concede our own resources to be depleted rather than we should allow those of the Romans to diminish, not so that I would capture popular favour and applause, but so that, with God's assistance, I might fulfill the duty of my appointment.'[54] With

---

[50] Cassiodorus, *Variae* 11.10.

[51] Cassiodorus, *Variae* 11.38, paper; 12.4, wine; 12.11, provisions for Rome; 12.12, wine; 12.14, grain; 12.15, provisions for the cursus publicus; 12.22, *garum*; 12.24, wine, oil and grain; 12.25, taxes.

[52] Cassiodorus, *Variae* 11.5, 11.39, 12.11, on provisions for Rome; 11.11, 11.12, 11.16, on prices and weights; 12.9, for a legal case; 12.18 and 12.19, for building.

[53] Cassiodorus, *Variae* 11.6.3, 'Actus enim tui iudicis opinio est et sicut penetrale domus de foribus potest congruenter intellegi, sic mens praesulis de te probatur agnosci'; concerning the quaestor, 6.5.2, 'Haec nostris cogitationibus necessario familiariter applicatur, ut proprie dicere posit quod nos sentire cognoscit; arbitrium suae voluntatis deponit et ita mentis nostrae velle suscipit, ut a nobis magis putetur exisse quod loquitur.'

[54] Cassiodorus, *Variae* 11.5.3, 'In nobis facilius consentimus excedi quam Romanorum utilitates patiamur imminui; non ut favorem captem plausumque popularem, sed ut iuvante deo meum in illis compleam dilectionis arbitrium.'

similar emphasis on duty to the fulfilment of public service, Cassiodorus instructed another *cancellarius* with the following words:

> Those [public servants] allotted to labours gleam with the practice of that very thing, which always renders men educated; labours, let me call them harsh masters and relentless teachers, through which anyone may be made more cautious, when dangers are feared to be incurred. Let someone be educated in oratory, and another be taught in some other discipline; nonetheless, that man who is honed in the devotion of continuous service is rendered the more learned.[55]

The statement agrees with the ethic, visible in the writing of someone like John Lydus, by which an eastern official educated in a theology of political science would instruct subordinates.

Another concordance between royal and prefectural governance appears in the nomination of officials to office. A group of letters in Book 11 constitutes what appear to be *formulae* for offices conferred by the praetorian prefect.[56] The majority of these letters have not been addressed to specific recipients and a fair portion of them include not only instructions to assume office, but also the dignities received by the official leaving that post.[57] Cassiodorus elsewhere elaborates on the principle of the regular advancement of officials through the serried ranks of bureaucratic corps in a way that would have assured his audience that public service had achieved the indissoluble fixedness of an institution:

> For why should a civil servant of public works endure anything insecure after such uncertainties of service? Such a man has vowed to preserve the reputation of the prince by being vigilant in repeated duties, since he excels others in [observing] oaths of service. For he has continually obeyed imperial commands and so that he might display reverence for the praetorian seat, he became obedient to the prefect as soon as that man began to exercise the distinguished title. Therefore, to hinder such a man is sinful, since no man should be harassed after a victory.[58]

---

[55] Cassiodorus, *Variae* 11.37.3, 'Splendescunt usu ipso laboribus attributi, qui reddunt homines semper instructos; labores, inquam, violenti magistri, solliciti paedagogi, per quos cautior quis efficitur, dum incurri pericula formidantur. Erudiatur quis forensibus litteris; alter qualibet disciplina doceatur; ille tamen instructior redditur, qui actu continuae devotionis eruditur.'

[56] Cassiodorus, *Variae* 11.17–35.

[57] Cassiodorus, *Variae* 11.18–19, departing from and advancing to the *cornicularius*; 11.20–21, the same with respect to the *primiscrinius*; 10.31–32, the *primicerius singulorum*.

[58] Cassiodorus, *Variae* 11.35.1–2, 'Cur enim agentum in rebus miles officii post tot laboris incerta aliquid patiatur ambiguum, qui crebris actionibus excubando ideo principis nomen habere promeruit, quia militiae sacramentis ceteros antecellit? Observavit enim iugiter imperialibus iussis et ut reverentiam praetorianae sedis extolleret, tunc ad eius venit obsequium, quando vocabulum coepit habere praecipuum. Tales ergo tardare piaculum est, quia post palmam nemo dilatus est.'

According to Cassiodorus, the virtuous execution of duties in public service, although onerous, provides one of the only certainties in a life of varied fortunes, 'For which reason is public service certain in an insecure life.'[59] The solid and unperturbed fixity of civil service in the *Variae*, much like the stability of nature, would have been a source of comfort for officials, eastern or western.

Cassiodorus composed this elaborate arrangement in the *Variae* to oppose the accusation that philosophical wisdom could not flourish in the palatine service of Italy. Not only do the Amals converse with the educated men of Italy on matters of abstruse learning, especially seen in the disquisitions on the liberal arts, but the many digressions on natural history also demonstrate their capacity to 'read nature' and thereby derive judicial decisions from the very source of justice.[60] Where Boethius complained about the injustice and avarice of servants of the court, the *Variae* demonstrate the harsh stance of the Amals against the corruption of officials.[61] Where Boethius lamented that a philosophical predisposition for providing service to the state had brought him low, the *Variae* explicitly make good service on behalf of the state a pre-condition for the favours of the king.[62] In fact, the phrase *pro utilitate publica* appears more frequently without lexical variation than almost any other phrase used repetitively in the *Variae*.[63] Indeed, it was for this very purpose (*utilitas publica*), that Boethius had undertaken an active public position and the account rendered in the *Variae* makes it clear that philosophy had found a safe home in the governance of Italy.[64] More importantly, where Boethius claimed that he had committed the truth of

---

[59] Cassiodorus, *Variae* 11.36.1, 'Qua de re sub incerta vita certa militia est nec habet quod posit metuere, qui ad designatum tempus inoffense meruit pervenire'; similarly, 11.37.1; cf. Barnish, *Cassiodorus*, 157–9.

[60] Cassiodorus, *Variae* 1.10, 1.45, 2.3, 2.40, 3.52, 4.51, 8.12, 9.21, 10.6, 11.36, 11.38, for letters with digressions dedicated to the liberal studies.

[61] Boethius, *De consolatione philosophiae* 1.4.34–53; Cassiodorus, *Variae* 3.20, 3.26, 3.27, 3.30, 3.46, 4.27, 5.30, against persecution of private persons by public officials; 2.29.2, 3.28.2, 4.4.2, 5.15.2, 5.19.1, 11.7, 11.8.3, 11.36.4–5, 12.1, 12.6, 12.16.4, more generally concerning corruption.

[62] Boethius, *De consolatione philosophiae* 1.4.18–21, 'Atqui tu hanc sententiam Platonis ore sanxisti: beatus fore res publicas, si eas vel studiosi sapientiae, contigisset'; Cassiodorus, *Variae* 1.3.5, 1.4.3, 1.10.1, 1.21.1, 1.22.1, 1.24.1, 1.36.1, 1.42.1, 1.43.1, 2.1.1, 2.6.1, 2.15.4, 2.28.1–2, 2.40.17, 3.5.2, 3.16.3, 3.19.1, 3.23.1, 3.28.1, 4.3.1, 5.18.1, 5.19.1, 5.21.2, 5.40.1, 8.11.3, 11.15.1, 11.37.1, for expressions of reciprocity whereby the ruler and servant alike are rewarded for good public service.

[63] Cassiodorus, *Variae, pro utilitate publica* and its several variants, *praefatio* 1.1, *praefatio* 1.6, *praefatio* 1.8, 1.17.1, 1.24.1, 1.28.3, 1.29.1, 1.45.1, 2.5.1, 2.6.1, 2.16.4, 2.20.1, 2.23.1, 2.30.3, 2.31.3, 2.32, 3.25.2, 3.26.1, 3.27.3, 3.29.2, 3.34.1, 4.16.1, 4.38.3, 4.41.3, 4.47.2, 5.5.1, 5.6.1, 5.7.1, 5.9.1, 5.14.9, 5.17.6, 5.18.1, 5.31.1, 6.12.2, 7.32.1, 7.33.1, 8.2.9, 8.3.4, 8.2.9, 8.3.4, 8.10.8, 10.13.6, 11.1.8, 11.4.3, 11.8.5, 11.37.1, 12.1.5, 12.2.6, 12.6.3.

[64] Boethius, *De consolatione philosophiae* 1.4.18–31.

events to record for the scrutiny of posterity in his *De consolatione*, Cassiodorus offered a competing truth for the attention of a more immediate posterity.[65]

In addition to defending his personal public record against libel from countrymen hostile to Amal rule, the *Variae* made an overt appeal to a specific group of eastern officials in order to gather support for the return of Italian officials to the administration of government at Ravenna. The themes with which Cassiodorus appealed to this audience – *reverentia antiquitatis*, a naturalistic conception for the basis of law, the connection between the spirit of governance and the moral character of officials – reveals his sensitivity to the hardships that eastern civil servants endured as a result of Justinian's reforms. Above all, Cassiodorus appealed to their sense of bureaucratic corporatism as an assurance that, in the hands of its native service elite, the fundamental character of administration in Italy had differed little from that of its eastern counterpart. The message was something that could inspire both exiled western officials and disaffected eastern bureaucrats. The ideology of the *Variae* professed that the corporatism of educated service elites could survive the depredations or inadequacy of nearly any ruler, whether it was a Theodahad or a Justinian.

The purpose of the *Variae* was the depiction of a healthy palatine administration at Ravenna that was in the hands of men steeped in an understanding of their own moral obligation to the state as an abstract ideal. The religious and moral elements of Cassiodorus' last two books contributed to the vague notion of a 'priesthood' of state service, something that would have appealed to the sensitivities of an eastern bureaucratic audience. It is important to keep in mind that Cassiodorus communicated this message during the twilight of the western administration in which he had served. In fact, after 540, that administration existed only as a memory and a future possibility. Procopius recorded how the administrative practices to which Italy had become accustomed under emperors continued without interruption under the Amals and immediately fell into desuetude upon the arrival of Justinian's protégé, the logothete Alexander.[66] Alexander's corruption succeeded in alienating the Italian population mainly through his handling of taxation and property rights.[67] He exacerbated the situation by withholding the

---

[65] Boethius, *De consolatione philosophiae* 1.4.86–88, 'Cuius rei seriem atque veritatem, ne latere posteros queat, stilo etiam memoriaeque mandavi'; Cassiodorus, *Variae, praefatio* 1.1, 'ut ventura posteritas et laborum meorum molestias, quas pro generalitatis commodo sustinebam, et sinceris conscientiae inemptam dinosceret actionem'.
[66] Procopius, *Anecdota* 26.26–30.   [67] Procopius, *Wars* 7.1.28–33.

payment of troops and thereby provoked lawless rapine in Italy by eastern imperial forces.[68] Procopius' *Anecdota* explicitly paralleled the suffering of native Italians with Justinian's administrative settlement in North Africa, where corrupt officials mulcted the native population with severe taxation and provoked the garrisoned soldiers to mutiny on account of a poorly managed remuneration.[69] Procopius detailed the manner in which Justinian's agents attempted to incorporate North Africa into the fiscal administration of the eastern empire, a process ultimately causing, in Procopius' opinion, the impoverishment of the people and the political instability of the region.[70] Justinian's administration in Constantinople failed to grasp the realities of land ownership in North Africa and succeeded only in alienating first the native North African landowners and then eastern imperial soldiers who had married landowning women.[71] While Procopius reported these events later than could have influenced Cassiodorus' compilation of the *Variae*, the conduits of communication between North Africa and Italy would have made palatine officials at Ravenna well aware of the administrative consequences of Justinian's territorial conquest. The *Liber Pontificalis* and the history of Victor of Vita both mention how Rome had absorbed refugees from North Africa during the reign of Geiseric.[72] This earlier exodus established channels of communication that encouraged further immigration to Italy during Justinian's conquest and reorganization of North Africa. Procopius noted how Amalasuntha's *comes* in Campania received soldiers deserting from Belisarius' army in North Africa.[73] In fact, the *Variae* disclose how Cassiodorus' activities as praetorian prefect just prior to the Gothic War included making arrangements for the integration of North Africans as landowners in Italy.[74] Report of the reforms that Justinian imposed on North Africa (*Novella* 36) probably filtered through refugees and through official channels to Ravenna on the very eve of the Gothic War. Moreover, the substantial presence of North Africans in Constantinople ensured that the subject of the African settlement remained vigorous in the political discourse after Cassiodorus' arrival there. Recent work on

[68] Procopius, *Wars* 7.9.1–6.
[69] Procopius, *Anecdota* 18.1–12 on North Africa, especially 18.10–12, on tax assessments; 18.13–22 on Italy, especially, 18.14–15.
[70] In addition to Procopius, *Anecdota* 18.1–12, cf. also *Wars* 4.14.8–21, on the mutiny over land distribution.
[71] Modéran, 'Vandales en Afrique', 113–17.
[72] *Liber Pontificalis* 53.11; Victor of Vita, *Historia Persecutionum* 1.15, how Geiseric caused a 'great throng' of clergy and noblemen to immigrate to Italy; on the diaspora of North Africans to Italy, Conant, 'Mediterranean communications', 5–14.
[73] Procopius, *Wars* 5.3.15.   [74] Cassiodorus, *Variae* 12.9.

Cassiodorus' *Institutions* has demonstrated how Justinian's conquests may have predisposed Cassiodorus' political sympathies along geographical boundaries, particularly with respect to North Africa.[75]

In August of 554, Justinian issued his *Constitutio Pragmatica*, detailing how émigrés would resume life upon their return to Italy and the rights they could expect under the emperor's governance. The articulation of topics within the *Constitutio* speaks heavily of co-operation between Justinian's court and those Italians who collaborated in replacing the Amal regime at Ravenna. The document promised open routes of travel between Italy and Constantinople and unrestrained access to Justinian's court.[76] The preponderance of attention given to taxation and property rights in the *Constitutio* confirms that those Italians at Justinian's court had placed the postwar settlement of Italy at the forefront of their political agenda.[77] The *Constitutio* also attempted to restore some semblance of normalcy to the administration of Italy in terms of the competence of its local officials.[78] However, mention of the government at Ravenna is glaringly absent from this document. In this respect, the former palatine elite of Ravenna seem to have lost their positions. In fact, the combined confirmation of landowning privileges for Italians and the absence of provisions for the restructuring of public life at Ravenna may have articulated what was, in effect, forced retirement for many of the officials who had served under the Amals. Compiling his *Variae* in the late 530s or early 540s, Cassiodorus could not have foreseen the kind of redress offered by the *Constitutio* in 554. But the concern for taxation and office holding in letters of Books 11 and 12 seems to reflect sincere anxiety that Italy might share in the experience of North Africa, which it did for a time. Taxation appears in the last two books of the *Variae* as the single most consuming activity of Cassiodorus' praetorian prefecture. The model provided by these letters is one governed by a balance between the necessity of serving the state and moderation in executing

---

[75] Chazelle, 'Three Chapters', 161–205.

[76] *Constitutio Pragmatica* 27, 'Viros etiam gloriosissimos ac magnificos senatores ad nostrum accedere comitatum volentes sine quocumque impedimento venire concedimus, nemine prohibendi eos habituro licentiam, ne senatoribus nostris vel collatoribus debitus introitus quodammodo videatur excludi.'

[77] *Constitutio Pragmatica* 2, concerning property granted by Totilla; 3, concerning property documents destroyed during the war; 4, claims made on the property of fugitives; 9, that tax collection should be left to the magistrates of individual provinces and not to higher offices (presumably not to Byzantine administrators); 10, that the payment of taxes should take place according to the customary schedule; 12 and 14, concerning the culpability of tax collectors for fraud and extortion.

[78] *Constitutio Pragmatica* 23, that military magistrates should not become involved in civil cases and that such cases should be left to civil judges.

the requisites of antique governance: 'Just as we do not want the fiscal burden to become heavier for any reason, thus do we also consider, with God's approval, the prescribed payments to be completed within the constituted amount of time.'[79] Hence Cassiodorus' tenure as praetorian prefect offers examples for both the rigorous enforcement of taxation and its remission owing to circumstances of hardship.[80] The message is one that Cassiodorus and other Italian palatine refugees probably hoped that eastern imperial officials would appreciate – an understanding that taxes were important as a necessary expression of public devotion, but a devotion tempered with equal necessity by moral discernment.

Cassiodorus' other main concern, office holding, appears in the last books with equal pungency. Unfortunately, as seen in the *Constitutio Pragmatica*, the cumulative message of the *Variae* had less impact on the final disposition of postwar Italy. In this sense, it must be conceded that the *Variae* represent an elaborate rhetorical text that ultimately failed in its purpose. The *Variae* proved either too subtle or not subtle enough to counter the exigencies of war, politics and literary polemic at Constantinople.

As a final suggestion for interpreting Books 11 and 12, it may be that in portraying the character of the Italian administration under declining Amal kingship, Cassiodorus was articulating an indictment against what the Gothic War had brought to an abrupt end. Although the personal virtue of individual rulers had diminished in the person of Theodahad, the *Variae* suggest that the administration itself was more than capable of continuing a legacy for just and moral governance that had been handed down from antiquity. On the whole, the *Variae* imply that, contrary to the recently coined Justinianic notion that the imperial west had ended in 476, the 'empire' in Italy would have survived irrespective of 'barbarian' kingship. Thus the *Variae* suggest something in the nature of a debt owed to those officials who had kept antiquity alive in Italy in spite of Gothic 'barbarity'. Pliny had similarly used the last book of his epistolary collection to demonstrate how elite culture survived in spite of the way that imperial patronage had come to dominate political life in Italy. Book 10 of Pliny's collection opens a window into the confidential world of palatine service that is both necessary and separate from the more familiar social discourse of what constitutes a good Roman life in the first nine

---

[79] Cassiodorus, *Variae* 11.7.4, 'Quapropter sicut fiscalia onera nulla occasione volumus aggravari, ita constitutis temporibus praefinitas illationes praecipimus deo iuvante compleri.'

[80] Cassiodorus, *Variae* 12.2, 12.8, 12.10, 12.16, on the enforcement of taxation; 12.5, 12.7, 12.14, 12.27, on remission.

books. Cassiodorus seems to have inverted the paradigm established by Pliny. The first ten books of the *Variae* set the stage for normality in Italian governance in the same way that Pliny's first nine articulated the decorum of Roman private life. However, where Pliny used his last book to demonstrate the interaction of a Roman citizen with imperial administration, Cassiodorus portrayed a kind of Roman public life that existed beyond the direct influence of the ruler.

Chapter 12

CONCLUSION

Innovative traditionalism and its consequence

Authority in the sixth century was intimately bound to notions of received tradition, despite the degree of social change that separated the sixth century from the earlier Roman Empire. Scarcely a corner of the post-classical Roman world could be found in the sixth century that had not been dramatically altered by some aspect of the social, political, economic, religious and aesthetic transformations of late antiquity. That being the case, the attachment to tradition seen in modes of exercising or representing authority (whether political, religious or intellectual) becomes all the more startling. The vibrant experimentation and adaptations of late antiquity were inseparable from the mediation of a vocabulary for traditional ideals. The habit by which sixth-century elites studiously copied and edited texts from a host of classical 'forebears' illustrates continued interest in preserving that vocabulary in only one spectrum of late antique life (the textual). As a collective of loosely interdependent concepts, the idea of tradition was astonishingly flexible, as is evident in the ease with which it could be applied to a variety of contexts and appropriated by new agents of authority. At one horizon of the post-classical world, the prefatory lament of Gregory of Tours, that no writers remained who could render the past in the antique tradition, served to condition, quite evocatively, an audience's perception of his own authority as an author. The same dependence on representations of the stewardship of antique tradition is visible at the other horizon, the eastern Roman empire, where Justinian's *renovatio*, with its implicit emphasis on the recovery of past imperial glory, similarly mobilized an audience's perception of authority in a political context. Absolute definitions for what actually constituted 'tradition' rarely mattered as much as making the claim to tradition at the appropriate moment and in the appropriate setting. For example, the sixth-century Frankish king Chilperic sought to impress Gallo-Roman bishops by displaying gifts received from the eastern emperor, illustrating just one particular context in which connection with tradition, even in a vaguely defined sense, had value. It made little difference that these gifts (gold medallions) commemorated spectacles at the Hippodrome, a feature of imperial culture that had vanished from Gaul by this date.[1]

Chilperic's display of gold medallions is also illustrative of the importance of channels of communication between Constantinople, as a source of imperial tradition, and a wider post-Roman world. This kind of communication clearly mattered for 'successor' kingdoms centred on places like Carthage, Ravenna and Paris. It was even more important for Constantinople, where the maintenance of traditional expressions of imperial authority was a continuous performance that stressed the relation of the imperial capital to the extended boundaries of the former Roman Empire. Justinian's interests in North Africa, Italy and Spain were inseparable from the presentation of imperial tradition (and authority) at Constantinople. Justinianic reconquest has often been portrayed in modern scholarship as a last attempt to arrest the progression of 'decline and fall' in the west. What has not been emphasized enough is that these attempts to restore western provinces to imperial control were the culmination of intensive communication between Constantinople and former governing centres of the western Mediterranean. Communication of this nature happened at many levels – diplomatic communication between royal and imperial courts, legal communication embodied in the codifications of reformed Roman law, negotiation concerning religious disputes, the transfer of artistic and architectural themes, the exchange of literary works among elite groups and even waging war. Such communication inevitably involved claims concerning authority, agency and dependency based on proximity to tradition. With respect to Italy, communication between Rome, Ravenna and Constantinople became particularly intense in the period during which the Amal and imperial court advanced haltingly toward open conflict. The urgency of much of this communication comes into sharp relief in Procopius' history of the wars, in the letters of the *Collectio Avellana* and in Cassiodorus' *Variae*.

This book has recast the *Variae* as a text that Cassiodorus composed not, as has previously been assumed, as the résumé of governmental policies and a culture that was uniquely Ostrogothic, but as a text that owes its thematic characteristics to powerful currents of exchange between the eastern and western centres of authority. The *Variae* claimed a definite position in cultural debates about law and tradition, nature and knowledge, and governmental morality; the particular contours of these debates, as seen in the *Variae*, were often contingent upon the representation of imperial tradition and authority in the east. This is hardly surprising given that Cassiodorus was exposed to these themes in public

1 Gregory of Tours, *Decem Libri Historiarum* 6.2.

offices that filtered communication between Rome, Ravenna and Constantinople at many levels. More specifically, this book has argued that the policies by which Justinian attempted to generate legitimacy for his reign instead precipitated a vigorous polemic about imperial tradition to which Cassiodorus was exposed. This polemic was certainly already well developed by the time that Cassiodorus assumed the responsibilities of the praetorian prefecture. The polemic had become 'formalized' (in the sense of adopting specific rhetorical themes) through literary critiques of Justinian's reign that emerged either just before or during Cassiodorus' period in Constantinople. We shall never know with certainty whether Cassiodorus compiled the *Variae* in Italy, sometime just before or after the fall of Ravenna, or later, after arriving in Constantinople. Given the nature of political communication between Italy and Constantinople and the urgency of the war for the palatine elite, it actually makes little difference. It is equally likely that Cassiodorus composed the *Variae* either in Italy to impress the eastern officials that he assumed would arrive after the war or in Constantinople for proponents of the political polemic whom he hoped would influence the postwar settlement. In either context, Cassiodorus, as the former praetorian prefect of Italy, was well informed about the political culture at Constantinople. Likewise, whether in Italy or Constantinople, the resolution of the Gothic War was a pressing matter for the former palatine elite of Ravenna. Prior scholarship has largely assumed a priori that eastern affairs did not influence the manner in which the *Variae* portray governance in Italy, even when any reconstruction of the authorial context (Italy or Constantinople) must acknowledge that Cassiodorus compiled the collection during what was the longest and possibly the most disruptive war waged in the history of ancient Italy.

The present study has suggested a new means for understanding the *Variae* by taking into account Justinian's reign and the Gothic War as the most formative circumstances for Cassiodorus' publication of an epistolary collection. The inclusive dates of this study, from 527 to 554, reposition the *Variae* within a broader context of the political interaction initiated by Justinian's accession in 527 and the continued political aspirations of Cassiodorus and other palatine elites which did not find proper closure until the resolution of the Gothic War in 554. Dominant themes in the letters of the *Variae* that correspond with the debates that animated the political polemic of Constantinople supply the links between narratives (of Constantinople and Italy) that have often been discussed in mutually exclusive terms.

This book suggests that Cassiodorus fashioned in the *Variae* an image of palatine governance that was attuned to Constantinopolitan debates about legitimacy and tradition in order to make the governmental elite of Ravenna appear suitable for return to office after the conclusion of the Gothic War. The elaborate rhetorical purpose of the *Variae* required adopting a number of novel literary forms intended, ironically, to communicate seamlessly the attachment of the palatine elite of Ravenna to tradition. Nowhere in the epistolary record of antiquity have other letter collections required laboured prefaces of the sort that accompany the *Variae*. The *formulae* and encyclopaedic disquisitions of the *Variae* are also entirely unprecedented in previous administrative and legal writing. The *De anima* and its close heuristic relation to the encyclopaedic content of individual letters similarly represent an innovation in the literary record of antiquity. As the product of a society in which authority was communicated through at least symbolic attachment to tradition, an explanation for the striking departures of the *Variae* from established modes of writing has been long overdue. In each case, it has been found that the prefaces, the *formulae*, the encyclopaedic digressions and the *De anima* were integral to the common purpose for which Cassiodorus compiled the *Variae*.

Finally, the argument of this book should be understood as a necessary qualification to the manner in which the *Variae* have informed studies of sixth-century Italy, but it is certainly not a vitiation of those contributions. The core content of the *Variae* – the actual legal and administrative issues forming the purpose of the majority of individual letters – could hardly represent inventions of Cassiodorus. In all likelihood, Cassiodorus retained copies of the substantial record of letters that he had written in official capacity, as had Pliny the Younger and Symmachus before him. When Ravenna fell to Belisarius, Cassiodorus' copies of this corpus naturally remained in his possession whether he was at Rome, Ravenna or Constantinople. As an assemblage of individual letters, the corpus provided source materials capable of being rearranged and interpolated in a manner suitable to Cassiodorus' more immediate purpose during the Gothic War. The composition of the prefaces, the addition of the *formulae*, the elaboration of older letters with new encyclopaedic material and, in select cases, the inclusion of forgeries constituted the editorial process with which Cassiodorus revised the older dossier to deliver a new message. This means that the *Variae* must be understood as having content with layered contexts. Like the historical record of late antique Italy in a larger sense, where archaeological evidence reveals one layer of social, economic and cultural realities and textual evidence often provides a rhetorical veneer of political and cultural presentation, so too the *Variae* are part historical reality and part rhetorical presentation. The task of studying late antique Italy through the lens of the *Variae* must involve separating these layers into independent contexts – the late Roman chancery of Ravenna on one hand and a political response to the Gothic War on the other. When the rhetorical content of the *Variae* is properly filtered, it may very well be the case that a different understanding of the political and economic development of late antique Italy will begin to emerge.

BIBLIOGRAPHY

PRIMARY SOURCES

Aelian, *De natura animalium*, ed. M. Valdés, L. Fueyo and L. Guillén, *Claudianus Aelianus: De natura animalium* (Berlin, 2009); ed. and trans. A. Scholfield, *Aelian: On the Characteristics of Animals*, LCL (Cambridge, Mass., 1958)

Agapetus, *Advice to the Emperor*, trans. P. Bell, *Three Political Voices from the Age of Justinian: Agapetus – Advice to the Emperor; Dialogue on Political Science; Paul the Silentiary – Description of Hagia Sophia*, TTH (Liverpool, 2010); ed. R. Riedinger, *Agapetos Diakonos: Der Fürstenspiegel des Kaisers Justinianos* (Athens, 1995)

Agathias, *Historiarum libri quinque*, ed. and trans. J. Frendo, *Agathias: The Histories* (Berlin, 1975)

Agnellus, *Liber Pontificalis Ecclesiae Ravennatis*, ed. D. Deliyannis, *Agnelli Ravennatis Liber Pontificalis Ecclesiae Ravennatis*, CCSL (Turnhout, 2006); trans. D. Deliyannis, *The Book of Pontiffs of the Church of Ravenna* (Washington, DC, 2004)

Ambrose, *De officiis*, ed. and trans. I. Davidson, *Ambrose: De officiis* (Oxford, 2001)
  Hexameron, ed. C. Schenkl, *Sancti Ambrosii Opera*, vol. *1*, CSEL (Leipzig, 1897); trans. J. Savage, *Saint Ambrose: Hexameron, Paradise, and Cain and Abel* (New York, 1961)

Ammianus Marcellinus, *Res Gestae*, ed. W. Seyfarth, *Ammiani Marcellini Rerum Gestarum Libri Qui Supersunt* (Stuttgart, 1999); ed. and trans. J. Rolfe, *Ammianus Marcellinus, vols. 1–III*, LCL (Cambridge, Mass., 1935–9)

Apuleius, *Apologia*, ed. J. van der Vliet, *Lucii Apulei Madaurensis Apologia, sive De Magia Liber et Florida* (Leipzig, 1900); trans. H. Butler, *The Apologia and Florida of Apuleius of Madaura* (Oxford, 1909)
  Metamorphoses, ed. and trans. J. Hanson, *Apuleius: Metamorphoses, vols. 1–II*, LCL (Cambridge, Mass., 1989)

Aristotle, *De anima*, ed. and trans. W. Hett, *Aristotle: On the Soul; Parva Naturalia; On breath*, LCL (Cambridge, Mass., 1986)

Athanasius, *Vita Antonii*, trans. R. Meyer, *St. Athanasius: The Life of St. Antony* (New York, 1950); ed. J. Migne, *S. Athanasii, Opera Omnia Quae Exstant, vol. II*, PG (Paris, 1857)

Augustine, *Confessiones*, ed. L. Verheijen, *Aurelii Augustini Opera, vol. 1.1*, CCSL (Turnhout, 1981); trans. H. Chadwick, *Saint Augustine: Confessions* (Oxford, 1998)
  De civitate dei, eds. B. Dumbart and A. Kalb, *Aurelii Augustini Opera, vols. XIV.1–2*, CCSL (Turnhout, 1955); ed. and trans. G. McCracken, W. Green, D. Wiesen,

Bibliography

P. Levine and E. Sanford, *Augustine: City of God, vols. I–VII*, LCL (Cambridge, Mass., 1957–72)

De doctrina christiana, ed. and trans. R. Green, *Augustine De Doctrina Christiana* (Oxford, 1995)

De immortalitate animae, ed. W. Horman, *Sancti Aurelii Augustini Opera, vol. I.4,* CSEL (Vienna, 1986)

De natura et origine animae, ed. C. Urb and J. Zycha, *Sancti Aurelii Augustini Opera, vol. VIII.1,* CSEL (Vienna, 1913)

De ordine, ed. W. Green, *Aurelii Augustini Opera, vol. II.2,* CCSL (Turnhout, 1970)

De quantitate animae, ed. W. Horman, *Sancti Aurelii Augustini Opera, vol. I.4,* CSEL (Vienna, 1986)

De vera religione, ed. J. Martin, *Aurelii Augustini Opera, vol. IV.1,* CCSL (Turnhout, 1962)

Aulus Gellius, *Noctes Atticae*, ed. and trans. J. Rolfe, *The Attic Nights of Aulus Gellius, vols. I–III,* LCL (Cambridge, Mass., 1970–84)

Aurelius Victor, *De Caesaribus*, ed. F. Pichlmayr, *Sexti Aurelii Victoris Liber De Caesaribus Praecedunt Origo Gentis Romanae et Liber De Viris Illustribus Urbis Romae Subsequitur Epitome De Caesaribus* (Stuttgart, 1911); trans. H. Bird, *Sextus Aurelius Victor: Liber De Caesaribus,* TTH (Liverpool, 1994)

Avitus of Vienne, *Epistulae*, ed. R. Peiper, *MGH AA,* vol. VI.2 (Berlin, 1883); trans. D. Shanzer and I. Wood, *Avitus of Vienne: Letters and Selected Prose,* TTH (Liverpool, 2002)

Boethius, *Contra Eutychen et Nestorium*, ed. and trans. H. Stewart, E. Rand and S. Tester, *Boethius: The Theological Tractates; The Consolation of Philosophy,* LCL (Cambridge, Mass., 1918)

De consolatione philosophiae, ed. L. Bieler, *Anicii Manlii Severini Boethii Philosophiae Consolatio* (Turnhout, 1957); ed. and trans. S. Tester, *Boethius: The Theological Tractates; The Consolation of Philosophy,* LCL (Cambridge, Mass., 1973)

De institutione arithmetica, ed. G. Friedlein, *Anicii Manlii Torquati Severini Boetii De Institutione Arithmetica Libri Duo; De Institutione Musica Libri Quinque; Accedit Geometria Quae Fertur Boetii* (Leipzig, 1867)

De institutione musica, ed. G. Friedlein, *Anicii Manlii Torquati Severini Boetii De Institutione Arithmetica Libri Duo; De Institutione Musica Libri Quinque; Accedit Geometria Quae Fertur Boetii* (Leipzig, 1867)

De trinitate, ed. and trans. H. Stewart, E. Rand and S. Tester, *Boethius: The Theological Tractates; The Consolation of Philosophy,* LCL (Cambridge, Mass., 1918)

Cassiodorus, *Chronica*, ed. T. Mommsen, *MGH CM,* vol. XI.2 (Berlin, 1894)

De anima, ed. J. Halporn, *Magni Aurelii Cassiodori Senatoris Opera, vol. I,* CCSL (Turnhout, 1973); trans. J. Halporn, *Cassiodorus: Institutions of Divine and Secular Learning; On the Soul,* TTH (Liverpool, 2004)

De orthographia, ed. H. Keil, *Grammatici Latini,* vol. VII (Leipzig, 1880)

Epithalamium, ed. T. Mommsen, *MGH AA,* vol. XII (Berlin, 1894)

Expositio psalmorum, ed. M. Adriaen, *Magni Aurelii Cassiodori Senatoris Opera, vols. II.1–2,* CCSL (Turnhout, 1958); trans. P. Walsh, *Cassiodorus: Explanation of the Psalms, vols. I–III* (New York, 1990)

Historia Tripartita, ed. R. Hanslik, *Historia Ecclesiastica Tripartita* (Vienna, 1952)

335

Institutiones divinarum et saecularium litterarum, ed. R. Mynors, *Institutiones Divinarum et Saecularium Litterarum* (Oxford, 1937); trans. J. Halporn, *Cassiodorus: Institutions of Divine and Secular Learning; On the Soul, TTH* (Liverpool, 2004)

Ordo generis Cassiodororum, ed. J. O'Donnell, *Cassiodorus* (Berkeley, 1979) 259–66; ed. A. Galonnier, *Anecdoton Holderi ou Ordo Generis Cassiodororum: Éléments pour une étude de l'authenticité boëcienne des Opuscula Sacra* (Paris, 1997)

Variae, ed. T. Mommsen, *MGH AA*, vol. xii (Berlin, 1894); ed. Å. Fridh, *Magni Aurelii Cassiodori Senatoris Opera*, vol. i, CCSL (Turnhout, 1973); trans. S. Barnish, *Cassiodorus: Variae, TTH* (Liverpool, 1992)

Cassius Dio, *Historia Romana*, ed. and trans. E. Cary, *Dio's Roman History, vols. i–ix*, LCL (Cambridge, Mass., 1982–95)

Cicero, *Academica*, ed. and trans. H. Rackham, *Cicero: De Natura Deorum; Academica*, LCL (Cambridge, Mass., 1994)

De finibus, ed. and trans. H. Rackham, *Cicero: De Finibus Bonorum et Malorum*, LCL (Cambridge, Mass., 1971)

De legibus, ed. and trans. C. Keyes, *Cicero: De Re Publica; De Legibus, LCL* (Cambridge, Mass., 1977)

De natura deorum, ed. and trans. H. Rackham, *Cicero: De Natura Deorum; Academica*, LCL Cambridge, Mass., 1994)

Disputationum Tusculanarium, ed. and trans. J. King, *Cicero: Tusculan Disputations*, LCL (Cambridge, Mass., 1971)

Orator, ed. and trans. H. Hubbell, *Cicero: Brutus; Orator, LCL* (Cambridge, Mass., 1971)

Chronicon Paschale, trans. M. Whitby and M. Whitby, *Chronicon Paschale: 284–628 AD, TTH* (Liverpool, 1989); ed. L. Dindorf, *Chronicon Paschale ad Exemplar Vaticanum, vols. i–ii, CSHB* (Bonn, 1832)

Codex Theodosianus, ed. and trans. C. Pharr, *The Theodosian Code and Novels and the Sirmondian Constitutions: A Translation with Commentary, Glossary and Bibliograpy* (Princeton, 1952)

Collectio Avellana, ed. O. Guenther, *Epistulae Imperatorum Pontificum Aliorum, CSEL* (Vienna, 1895)

Corippus, *In laudem Iustini Augustini Minoris*, ed. and trans. Averil Cameron, *In laudem Iustini Augusti Minoris, Libri IV* (London, 1976)

De ceremoniis, ed. J. Reiskii, *De Ceremoniis Aulae Byzantinae Libri Duo, vols. i–iii, CSHB* (Bonn, 1829–40)

Dialogue on Political Science, trans. P. Bell, *Three Political Voices from the Age of Justinian: Agapetus – Advice to the Emperor; Dialogue on Political Science; Paul the Silentiary – Description of Hagia Sophia, TTH* (Liverpool, 2009); C. Mazzucchi, *Menae Patricii cum Thoma Referendario De Scientia Politica Dialogus* (Milan, 1982)

Dio Chrysostom, *Discourses on Kingship*, ed. and trans. J. Cohoon, *Dio Chrysostom: Discourses, vols. i–v, LCL* (Cambridge, Mass., 1932–56)

Edictum Theodorici Regis, ed. F. Bluhme, *MGH Leges*, vol. v (Hannover, 1875)

Ennodius of Pavia, *Carmena*, ed. F. Vogel, *MGH AA, vol. vii* (Berlin, 1885)

Epistulae, ed. F. Vogel, *MGH AA, vol. vii* (Berlin, 1885)

Panegyricus, ed. and trans. C. Rohr, *Der Theoderich-Panegyricus des Ennodius* (Hannover, 1995); ed. and trans. S. Rota, *Magno Felici Ennodio: Panegirico del Clementissimo Re Teoderico* (Rome, 2002)

Bibliography

Paraenesis Didascalia, ed. F. Vogel, *MGH AA, vol.* VII (Berlin, 1885)
Vita Epiphanii, ed. F. Vogel, *MGH AA, vol.* VII (Berlin, 1885); trans. G. Cook,
    The Life of Saint Epiphanius by Ennodius (Washington, DC, 1942)
Epistolae Theodericianae Variae, ed. T. Mommsen, *MGH AA, vol.* XII (Berlin, 1894)
Eugippius, *Vita Severini*, ed. H. Sauppe, *MGH AA, vol. 1.2* (Berlin, 1877); trans. L.
    Bieler, *Eugippius: The Life of Saint Severin* (Washington, DC, 1965)
Eunapius, *History*, ed. and trans. R. Blockley, *The Fragmentary Classicizing Historians*
    of the Later Roman Empire: Eunapius, Olympiodorus, Priscus and Malchus, vol. II:
    Text, Translation and Historiographical Notes (Liverpool, 1983)
Eusebius, *Historia Ecclesiastica*, ed. and trans. K. Lake, *Eusebius: The Ecclesiastical*
    History, LCL (Cambridge, Mass., 1959)
    Vita Constantini, trans. Averil Cameron and S. Hall, *Eusebius, The Life of Con-*
    stantine: Introduction, Translation and Commentary (Oxford, 1999); ed. F. Winkel-
    mann, *Über das Leben des Kaisers Konstantins* (Berlin, 1975)
Eustathius, *Hexameron*, ed. J. Migne, *S. Basilii, Opera Omnia Quae Exstant, vol.* II,
    PG (Paris, 1888)
Evagrius, *Historia Ecclesiastica*, trans. M. Whitby, *The Ecclesiastical History of Evagrius*
    Scholasticus, TTH (Liverpool, 2002); ed. J. Bidez and L. Parmentier, *Ecclesiastical*
    History (London, 1898)
Excerpta Valesiana, ed. and trans. J. Rolfe, *Ammianus Marcellinus, vol.* III, LCL
    (Cambridge, Mass., 1952)
Formulary of Marculf, ed. K. Zeumer, *MGH Form.* (Hannover, 1886); trans. A. Rio,
    The Formularies of Angers and Marculf: Two Merovingian Legal Handbooks, TTH
    (Liverpool, 2008)
Fredegar, *Chronica*, ed. B. Krusch, *MGH SRM, vol.* II (Hannover, 1888)
Fulgentius, *De aetatibus mundi et hominis*, ed. R. Helm, *Fabii Planciadis Fulgentii*
    Opera (Leipzig, 1898); trans. L. George Whitbread, *Fulgentius the Mythographer*
    (Columbus, 1971)
Fulgentius of Ruspe, *Epistulae*, ed. J. Fraipont, *Sancti Fulgentii Episcopi Ruspensis*
    Opera (Turnhout, 1968); trans. R. Eno, *Fulgentius: Selected Works* (Washington,
    DC, 1997)
Gesta Theoderici, ed. B. Krusch, *MGH SRM, vol.* II (Hannover, 1888)
Gregory of Nazianzus, *Epistulae*, trans. A. Malherbe, *Ancient Epistolary Theorists*
    (Atlanta, Ga., 1988); ed. J. Migne, *S. Gregorii Theologi, Opera Quae Exstant*
    Omnia, vols. I–IV, PG (Paris, 1857)
    Theological Oration, trans. C. Beeley, *Gregory of Nazianzus on the Trinity and the*
    Knowledge of God: In Your Light We Shall See Light (Oxford, 2008)
Gregory of Tours, *Decem libri historiarum*, ed. B. Krusch, *MGH SRM, vol. 1.1*
    (Hannover, 1884)
    Gloria martyrum, ed. and trans. R. van Dam, *Gregory of Tours: Glory of the Martyrs*,
    TTH (Liverpool, 1988)
Gregory the Great, *Dialogorum*, ed. and trans. A. Mondadori, *Gregorio Magno: Storie*
    di Santi e di Diavoli (Dialoghi), vols. I–II (Belluno, 2005)
Historia Augusta, ed. and trans. D. Magie, *Scriptores Historiae Augustae, vols. I–III*, LCL
    (Cambridge, Mass., 1967)
Horace, *Ars Poetica*, ed. and trans. H. Fairclough, *Horace: Satires, Epistles and Ars*
    Poetica, LCL (Cambridge, Mass., 1978)

Bibliography

Epistulae, ed. and trans. H. Fairclough, *Horace: Satires, Epistles and Ars Poetica*, LCL (Cambridge, Mass., 1978)

Epodes, ed. and trans. N. Rudd, *Horace: Odes and Epodes*, LCL (Cambridge, Mass., 2004)

Iamblichus, *De anima*, ed. and trans. J. Finamore and J. Dillon, *Iamblichus, De Anima: Text, Translation and Commentary* (Leiden, 2002)

De mysteriis Aegyptiorum, trans. E. Clark, J. Dillon and J. Hershbell, *Iamblichus, De Mysteriis* (Atlanta, Ga., 2003)

Isidore of Seville, *Historia Gothorum Vandalorum Suevorum*, ed. T. Mommsen, *MGH CM, vol. II* (Berlin, 1892)

Jerome, *Epistulae*, ed. and trans. F. Wright, *Select Letters of St. Jerome*, LCL (Cambridge, Mass., 1954)

John of Ephesus, *Historia Ecclesiastica*, trans. R. Payne-Smith, *The Third Part of the Ecclesiastical History of John of Ephesus* (Oxford, 1860)

John Lydus, *De magistratibus*, ed. and trans. T. Carney, *On the Magistracies of the Roman Constitution: De Magistratibus* (Lawrence, 1971)

De mensibus, ed. R. Wuensch, *Liber de Mensibus* (Leipzig, 1898)

De ostentis, ed. C. Wachsmuth, *Liber de Ostentis et Calendaria Omnia* (Leipzig, 1897)

John Malalas, *Chronographia*, trans. E. Jeffreys, M. Jeffreys and R. Scott, *The Chronicle of John Malalas* (Melbourne, 1986); ed. H. Thurn, *Corpus Fontium Historiae Byzantinae* (Berlin, 2000)

John of Nikiu, *Chronicle*, trans. R. Charles, *The Chronicle of John, Bishop of Nikiu* (Oxford, 1916)

John Philoponus, *De aeternitate mundi contra Proclum*, ed. H. Rabe, *John Philoponus: De Aeternitate Mundi Contra Proclum* (Leipzig, 1899)

In Aristotelis De anima libros commentaria, ed. M. Wallies, *Ioannes Philoponus: In Aristotelis De Anima Libros Commentaria* (Berlin, 1909)

Jordanes, *Getica*, ed. T. Mommsen, *MGH AA, vol. v.1* (Berlin, 1882); trans. C. Mierow, *The Gothic History of Jordanes* (Princeton, 1915)

Romana, ed. T. Mommsen, *MGH AA, vol. v.1* (Berlin, 1882)

Josephus, *The Jewish War*, ed. and trans. H. Thackeray, *Josephus: The Jewish War*, *vols. I–III*, LCL (Cambridge, Mass., 1926)

Joshua the Stylite, *Chronicle*, trans. F. Trombley and J. Watt, *Chronicle of Pseudo-Joshua the Stylite*, TTH (Liverpool, 2001); ed. W. Wright, *Joshua the Stylite: Chronicle Composed in Syriac AD 507* (Cambridge, 1882)

Junillus Africanus, *Instituta Regularia*, trans. M. Maas, *Exegesis and Empire in the Early Byzantine Mediterranean* (Tübingen, 2003); ed. Heinrich Kihn, *Theodor von Mopsuestia und Junilius Africanus als Exegeten* (Freiburg, 1880)

Justinian, *Codex Iustinianus*, ed. P. Krueger, *CIC, vol. II* (Berlin, 1904)

Constitutio Pragmatica, ed. R. Schoell, *CIC, vol. III* (Berlin, 1904)

Digesta, ed. T. Mommsen and P. Krueger, *CIC, vol. I* (Berlin, 1904); ed. and trans. A. Watson, *The Digest of Justinian, vols. I–II* (Philadelphia, 1985)

Institutionum Iustiniani, ed. P. Krueger, *CIC, vol. I* (Berlin, 1904)

Novellae, ed. R. Schoell, *CIC, vol. III* (Berlin, 1904)

Lactantius, *Divinae Institutiones*, ed. and trans. P. Monat, *Lactance: Institutions Divines, Livres I–II* (Paris, 1986–7)

Libanius, *Orationes*, ed. and trans. A. Norman, *Libanius: Selected Works, vols. I–II, LCL* (Cambridge, Mass., 1977)

Liber Pontificalis, ed. A. Duchesne, *Le Liber Pontificalis: Texte, Introduction et Commentaire* (Paris, 1886); trans. R. Davis, *The Book of Pontiffs (Liber Pontificalis): The Ancient Biographies of the First Ninety Roman Bishops to AD 715, TTH* (Liverpool, 1989)

Livy, *Ab urbe condita*, ed. and trans. B. Foster, *Livy, vols. I–XIV, LCL* (Cambridge, Mass., 1948–61)

Lucan, *De bello civile*, ed. and trans. J. Duff, *Lucan: The Civil War: Books I–X (Pharsalia), LCL* (Cambridge, Mass., 1957)

Lucretius, *De rerum natura*, ed. and trans. W. Rouse and M. Smith, *Lucretius: De Rerum Natura, LCL* (Cambridge, Mass., 1992)

Malchus, *History*, ed. and trans. R. Blockley, *The Fragmentary Classicizing Historians of the Later Roman Empire: Eunapius, Olympiodorus, Priscus and Malchus, vol. II: Text, Translation and Historiographical Notes* (Liverpool, 1983)

Marcellinus Comes, *Chronicon*, ed. J. Migne, *S. Prosperi Aquitani Opera Omnia; Idatii et Marcellini Comitis Chronica, PL* (Paris, 1861); trans. B. Croke, *The Chronicle of Marcellinus: A Translation and Commentary* (Sydney, 1995)

Marinus, *Vita Procli*, ed. and trans. H. Saffrey and A. Segonds, *Marinus: Proclus ou sur le bonheur* (Paris, 2001)

Novellae (Theodosian), ed. and trans. C. Pharr, *The Theodosian Code and Novels and the Sirmondian Constitutions: A Translation with Commentary, Glossary and Bibliography* (Princeton, 1952)

Olympiodorus, *History*, ed. and trans. R. Blockley, *The Fragmentary Classicizing Historians of the Later Roman Empire: Eunapius, Olympiodorus, Priscus and Malchus, vol. II: Text, Translation and Historiographical Notes* (Liverpool, 1983)

Panegyrici Latini, ed. and trans. C. Nixon and B. Rogers, *In Praise of Later Roman Emperors: The Panegyrici Latini* (Berkeley, 1994)

Paul the Deacon, *Historia Romana*, ed. H. Droysen, *MGH SRG* 2 (Berlin, 1879)

Paulinus of Nola, *Carmena*, trans. A. Ruggiero, *Paolino di Nola: I Carmi* (Naples, 1996); ed. G. de Hartel, *S. Paulini Nolani Opera, vols. I–II, CSEL* (Leipzig, 1894)

Philostratus, *Lives of the Sophists*, ed. and trans. W. Wright, *Philostratus: Lives of the Sophists; Eunapius: Lives of the Philosophers, LCL* (Cambridge, Mass., 1998)

Photius, *Bibliotheca*, ed. R. Henry, *Bibliothèque, vols. I–IX* (Paris, 1959–91)

Plato, *Phaedo*, ed. and trans. H. Fowler, *Plato: Euthyphro, Apology, Crito, Phaedo, Phadrus, LCL* (Cambridge, Mass., 1960)

Republic, ed. and trans. P. Shorey, *Plato: The Republic, vols. I–II, LCL* (Cambridge, Mass., 1930)

Pliny the Elder, *Historia Naturalis*, ed. and trans. H. Rackham, *Pliny: Natural History, vols. I–X, LCL* (Cambridge, Mass., 1938)

Pliny the Younger, *Epistulae*, ed. and trans. B. Radice, *Pliny the Younger: Letters, vols. I–III, LCL* (Cambridge, Mass., 1969)

Panegyricus, ed. and trans. B. Radice, *Pliny the Younger: Letters, vols. I–III, LCL* (Cambridge, Mass., 1969)

Plotinus, *Enneads*, ed. and trans. A. Armstrong, *Plotinus, vols. I–VII, LCL* (Cambridge, Mass., 1966–88)

Porphyry, *Vita Plotini*, trans. G. Carratelli, *Porfirio: Vita di Plotino ed Ordine dei suoi Libri* (Naples, 1946)

    Sententiae, ed. and trans. L. Brisson et al., *Porphyry: Sentences: Études d'introduction, texte grec et traduction française, commentaire* (Paris, 2005)

Priscian, *De laude Anastasii Imperatoris*, trans. P. Coyne, *Priscian of Caesarea's De Laude Anastasii Imperatoris: Translated with Commentary and Introduction* (Leweston, 1991)

Priscus, *History*, ed. and trans. R. Blockley, *The Fragmentary Classicizing Historians of the Later Roman Empire: Eunapius, Olympiodorus, Priscus and Malchus*, vol. II: *Text, Translation and Historiographical Notes* (Liverpool, 1983)

Procopius, *Anecdota*, ed. and trans. H. Dewing, *Procopius*, vol. VI, LCL (Cambridge, Mass., 1935)

    Buildings, ed. and trans. H. Dewing, *Procopius*, vol. VII, LCL (Cambridge, Mass., 1954)

    Wars, ed. and trans. H. Dewing, *Procopius*, vols. I–V, LCL (Cambridge, Mass., 1914–28)

Pseudo-Dionysius of Tel-Mahre, *Chronicle*, trans. W. Witakowski, *Pseudo-Dionysius of Tel-Mahre: Chronicle (Known Also as the Chronicle of Zuqnin) Part III*, TTH (Liverpool, 1996)

Quintilian, *Declamationes*, ed. and trans. D. Shackleton Bailey, *Quintilian: The Lesser Declamations*, vols. I–II, LCL (Cambridge, Mass., 2006); trans. L. Sussman, *The Major Declamations Ascribed to Quintilian* (Frankfurt am main, 1987)

    Institutio Oratoria, ed. and trans. D. Russell, *Quintilian: The Orator's Education, Books 1–2*, vols. I–IV, LCL (Cambridge, Mass., 2001)

Ravenna Papyri, ed. J. Tjäder, *Die Nichtliterarischen Lateinischen Papyri Italiens aus der Zeit 445–700*, vols. I–II (Uppsala, 1955)

Rutilius Namatianus, *De reditu suo*, ed. L. Mueller, *Claudii Rutilii Namatiani de Reditu Suo Libri II* (Leipzig, 1870)

Sallust, *Bellum Catilinae*, ed. and trans. J. Rolfe, *Sallust*, LCL (Cambridge, Mass., 1921)

Seneca the Elder, *Controversiae*, ed. and trans. M. Winterbottom, *The Elder Seneca: Declamations*, LCL (Cambridge, Mass., 1974)

Seneca the Younger, *De providentia*, ed. N. Lanzarone, *L. Annaei Senecae Dialogorum Liber I De Providentia* (Florence, 2008)

    Naturales Quaestiones, ed. and trans. T. Corcoran, *Seneca: Naturales Quaestiones*, vols. I–II, LCL (Cambridge, Mass., 1971–2)

Sidonius Apollinaris, *Epistulae*, ed. and trans. W. Anderson, *Sidonius: Poems and Letters*, LCL (Cambridge, Mass., 1936)

Simplicius, *In libros Aristotelis De anima commentaria*, ed. M. Hayduck, *Simplicius: In Libros Aristotelis De Anima Commentaria* (Berlin, 1882)

Socrates Scholasticus, *Historia Ecclesiastica*, ed. and trans. G. Hansen, P. Périchon and P. Maraval, *Socrate de Constantinople: Histoire ecclésiastique* (Paris, 2004)

Solinus, *De mirabilibus mundi*, ed. T. Mommsen, *Collectanea rerum memorabilium* (Berlin, 1895)

Suda, ed. A. Adler, *Lexicon (Sudae Lexicon)*, vols. I–V (Leipzig, 1928–38)

Suetonius, *Lives of the Caesars*, ed. and trans. J. Rolfe, *Suetonius*, vols. I–II, LCL (Cambridge, Mass., 1914)

Bibliography

Vita Horati, ed. and trans. J. Rolfe, *Suetonius, vols. I–II*, LCL (Cambridge, Mass., 1914)

Symmachus, *Epistulae*, ed. O. Seeck, *MGH AA, vol.* VI (Berlin, 1883)
  Relationes, trans. R. Barrow, *Prefect and Emperor: The Relationes of Symmachus, AD 384* (Oxford, 1973)

Tacitus, *Agricola*, ed. and trans. M. Hutton and M. Ogilvie, *Tacitus: Dialogus; Agricola; Germania*, LCL (Cambridge, Mass., 1970)
  Annales, ed. and trans. J. Jackson, *Tacitus: The Histories; The Annals, vols. I–IV*, LCL (Cambridge, Mass., 1925–56)
  Germania, ed. and trans. W. Peterson, *Tacitus: Dialogus; Agricola; Germania*, LCL (Cambridge, Mass., 1963)

Themistius, *Orationes*, trans. P. Heather and D. Moncur, *Politics, Philosophy and Empire in the Fourth Century: Select Orations of Themistius*, TTH (Liverpool, 2001); ed. H. Schenkl, G. Downey and A. Norman, *Themistii Orationes, vols. I–III* (Leipzig, 1965–74)

Theophanes Confessor, *Chronica*, trans. C. Mango and R. Scott, *The Chronicle of Theophanes Confessor: Byzantine and Near Eastern History, AD 284–813* (Oxford, 1997); ed. C. de Boor, CSHB (Leipzig, 1883)

Valerianus, *Homiliae de bono disciplinae*, ed. J. Migne, *S. Chrysologi Archiepiscopi Ravennatis Opera Omnia Sequuntur Sanctorum Valeriani et Nicetae*, PL (Paris, 1894); trans. G. Ganss, *Saint Peter Chrysologus: Selected Sermons, and Saint Valerian: Homilies* (Washington, DC, 1953)

Vegetius, *Epitoma rei militaris*, ed. L. Stelten, *Flavius Vegetius Renatus: Epitoma Rei Militaris* (New York, 1990); trans. N. Milner, *Vegetius: Epitome of Military Science*, TTH (Liverpool, 1993)

Victor Tonnennensis, *Chronica*, ed. T. Mommsen, *MGH CM, vol.* II (Berlin, 1892)

Vigilius, *Epistulae et Decreta*, ed. J. Migne, *Magni Aurelii Cassiodori Senatoris, Opera Omnia, Praecedunt Vigilii Papae, Gildae Sapientis et Pelagii Papae Scripta Universa*, PL (Paris, 1865)

Vulgate Bible, *Biblia Sacra Iuxta Latinam Vulgatem Versionem, vols. I–XV* (Vatican, 1926–78)

Walahfrid Strabo, *De imagine tetrici*, ed. P. de Winterfeld, *MGH Poet., vol.* II (Berlin, 1884)

Zachariah of Mytilene, *Historia Ecclesiastica*, trans. F. Hamilton and E. Brooks, *The Syriac Chronicle Known as That of Zachariah of Mitylene* (London, 1899)

Zonaras, *Epitome historiarum*, ed. L. Dindorf, *Ioannis Zonarae Epitome Historiarum* (Leipzig, 1868–75)

Zosimus, *Nova Historia*, ed. L. Mendelssohn, *Zosimi Comitis et Exadvocati Fisci Historia Nova* (Leipzig, 1887); trans. W. Green and T. Chaplin, *The History of Count Zosimus, Sometime Chancellor of the Roman Empire* (London, 1814); trans. R. Ridley, *Zosimus, New History: A Translation with Commentary* (Sydney, 1982)

SECONDARY LITERATURE

Ahl, F., 'The art of safe criticism in Greece and Rome', *American Journal of Philology* 105.2 (1984) 174–208

Bibliography

Aiello, V., 'Cassiodoro e la tradizione su Costantino', in Leanza, *Cassiod.* (Soveria Mannelli, 1993) 131–57

Alchermes, J., 'Spolia in Roman cities of the late empire: legislative rationales and architectural reuse', *Dumbarton Oaks Papers* 48 (1994) 167–78

'Art and architecture in the age of Justinian', in Maas, *CC Just.* (Cambridge, 2005) 343–75

Amici, A., 'Cassiodoro a Costantinopoli: *da Magister Officiorum a Religiosus Vir*', *Vetera Christianorum* 42 (2005) 215–31

Amory, P., *People and Identity in Ostrogothic Italy, 489–554* (Cambridge, 1997)

Ando, C., 'Pagan apologetics and Christian intolerance in the ages of Themistius and Augustine', *Journal of Early Christian Studies* 4.2 (1996) 171–207

'The administration of the provinces', in D. Potter, ed., *The Blackwell Companion to the Roman Empire* (Oxford, 2006) 177–92

'Religion and *ius publicum*', in C. Ando and J. Rüpke, eds., *Religion and Law in Classical and Christian Rome* (Stuttgart, 2006) 126–45

Andreescu-Treadgold, I., and W. Treadgold, 'Procopius and the Imperial Panels of S. Vitale', *Art Bulletin* 79 (1997) 716–21

Archi, I., and A. Colombo, eds., *Legum Iustiniani Imperatoris Vocabularium Novellae, Pars Latina, Tomus 2* (Milan, 1977)

Arslan, E., 'La monetazione dei Goti', *Corso di Cultura sull'Arte Ravennate e Byzantinea* 36 (1989) 17–59

Asmis, E., 'Cicero on natural law and the laws of the state', *Classical Antiquity* 27.1 (2008) 1–33

Astell, A., 'Cassiodorus's *Commentary on the Psalms* as an *Ars rhetorica*', *Rhetorica* 17.1 (1999) 37–75

Athanassiadi, P., 'Apamea and the Chaldaean Oracles: a holy city and a holy book', in Smith, *Phil. Soc.* (Swansea, 2005) 117–43

Athanassiadi, P., and M. Frede, eds., *Pagan Monotheism in Late Antiquity* (Oxford, 1999)

Auerbach, E., *Literary Language and Its Public in Late Latin Antiquity and in the Middle Ages* (New York, 1965)

Augenti, A., 'Continuity and discontinuity of a seat of power: the Palatine Hill from the fifth to the tenth century', in J. Smith, ed., *Early Medieval Rome and the Christian West* (Leiden, 2000) 43–54

Baltussen, H., *Philosophy and Exegesis in Simplicius: The Methodology of a Commentator* (London, 2008)

Banaji, J., *Agrarian Change in Late Antiquity: Gold, Labor and Aristocratic Dominance* (Oxford, 2001)

Barbieri, G., 'La concezione politico-economica di Aurelio Cassiodoro', in *Verona in Età Gotica e Longobarda* (Verona, 1982) 295–301

Barnes, T., 'Panegyric, history and hagiography in Eusebius' Life of Constantine', in R. Williams, ed., *The Making of Orthodoxy* (Cambridge, 1989) 94–123

Barnish, S., 'The Anonymus Valesianus II as a source for the last years of Theoderic', *Latomus* 42.3 (1983) 572–96

'The genesis and completion of Cassiodorus' *Gothic History*', *Latomus* 43.2 (1984) 347–54

Bibliography

'Martianus Capella and Rome in the late fifth century', *Hermes* 114.1 (1986) 98–111

'Taxation, land and barbarian settlement in the western empire', *Papers of the British School at Rome* 54 (1986) 170–95

'Pigs, plebeians and *potentes*: Rome's economic hinterland, *c.* 350–600', *Papers of the British School at Rome* 55 (1987) 157–85

'Transformation and survival in the western senatorial aristocracy, *c.* AD 400–700', *Papers of the British School at Rome* 56 (1988) 133–50

'The work of Cassiodorus after his conversion', *Latomus* 48 (1989) 157–87

'Maximian, Cassiodorus, Boethius, Theodahad: literature, philosophy and politics in Ostrogothic Italy', *Nottingham Medieval Studies* 34 (1990) 16–32

Cassiodorus: Variae (Liverpool, 1992)

'*Religio in stagno*: nature, divinity and the christianization of the countryside in late antique Italy', *Journal of Early Christian Studies* 9.3 (2001) 387–402

'Sacred texts of the secular: writing, hearing and reading Cassiodorus' *Variae*', *Studia Patristica* 38 (2001) 362–70

'*Cuncto Italiae membra componere*: political relations in Ostrogothic Italy', in Barnish and Marazzi, *Ostrogoth.* (Woodbridge, 2007) 317–37

'Roman responses to an unstable world: Cassiodorus' *Variae* in context', in S. Barnish, L. Ruggini, L. Cuppo, R. Marchese and M. Breu, eds., *Vivarium in Context* (Vicenza, 2008) 7–22

Barnwell, P., *Emperor, Prefects and Kings: The Roman West, 395–565* (Chapel Hill, 1992)

Barrow, R., *Prefect and Emperor: The Relationes of Symmachus, AD 384* (Oxford, 1973)

Bartsch, S., *Actors in the Audience: Theatricality and Doublespeak from Nero to Hadrian* (Cambridge, Mass., 1994)

Bauman, R., *The Crimen Maiestatis in the Roman Republic and Augustan Period* (Johannesburg, 1967)

Beagon, M., *Roman Nature: The Thought of Pliny the Elder* (Oxford, 1992)

Becker, A., 'The dynamic reception of Theodore of Mopsuestia in the sixth century: Greek, Syriac and Latin', in S. Johnson, ed., *Greek Literature in Late Antiquity: Dynamism, Didacticism, Classicism* (Burlington, 2006) 29–48

Beeley, C., *Gregory of Nazianzus on the Trinity and the Knowledge of God: In Your Light We Shall See Light* (Oxford, 2008)

Bell, P., *Three Political Voices from the Age of Justinian: Agepetus, Advice to the Emperor; Dialogue on Political Science; Paul the Silentiary, Description of Hagia Sophia* (Liverpool, 2009)

Bertolini, O., *Roma di Fronte a Bisanzio e ai Longobardi* (Bologna, 1941)

Bierbrauer, V., *Die Ostgotischen Grab- und Schatzfunde in Italien* (Spoleto, 1975)

Bjornlie, S., 'What have elephants to do with sixth-century politics? A reappraisal of the "official" governmental dossier of Cassiodorus', *Journal of Late Antiquity* 2.1 (2009) 143–71

'*Amicitia* in the epistolary tradition: the case of Cassiodorus' *Variae*', in K. Mustakallio and C. Krötzel, eds., *De Amicitia: Friendship and Social Networks in Antiquity and the Middle Ages* (Rome, 2010) 135–54

Blair-Dixon, K., 'Memory and authority in sixth-century Rome: the *Liber Pontificalis* and the *Collectio Avellana*', in K. Cooper and J. Hillner, eds., *Religion, Dynasty and Patronage in Early Christian Rome, 300–900* (Cambridge, 2007) 59–74

Blumenthal, H., 'John Philoponus and Stephanus of Alexandria: two Neoplatonic Christian commentators on Aristotle', in D. O'Meara, *Neoplatonism and Christian Thought* (Albany, 1982) 54–63

    Aristotle and Neoplatonism in Late Antiquity: Interpretations of the De Anima (London, 1996)

Boak, A., and J. Dunlap, *Two Studies in Later Roman and Byzantine Administration* (New York, 1924)

Bodel, C., 'Un chef germain entre Byzance et l'Italie: L'épitaphe d'Asbadus à Pavie (Suppl. It. 9.15)', in M. Ghilardi, C. Goddard and P. Porena, eds., *Cités ital.* (Rome, 2006) 91–100

Borchert, S., 'Das Bild Theoderichs des Großen in der Chronik des sogenannten Fredegar', in S. Kolditz and R. Müller, eds., *Geschehenes und Geschriebenes: Studien zu Ehren* (Leipzig, 2005) 435–52

Bowersock, G., *Hellenism in Late Antiquity* (Ann Arbor, 1990)

Bowes, K., *Private Worship, Public Values and Religious Change in Late Antiquity* (Cambridge, 2008)

Boys-Stones, G., 'Physiognomy and ancient psychological theory', in S. Swain, ed., *Seeing the Face, Seeing the Soul: Polemon's Physiognomy from Classical Antiquity to Medieval Islam* (Oxford, 2007) 19–124

Brenk, B., 'Spolia from Constantine to Charlemagne: aesthetics versus ideology', *Dumbarton Oaks Papers* 41 (1987) 103–9

Brennan, C., 'Gentilician permanence and strategy over seven centuries?', *Journal of Roman Archaeology* 9 (1996) 335–9

Brock, S., 'The conversations with the Syrian orthodox under Justinian (532)', *Orientalia Christiana Periodica* 47 (1981) 87–121

Brogiolo, G., 'Ideas of the town in Italy during the transition from antiquity to the Middle Ages', in G. Brogiolo and B. Ward-Perkins, eds., *The Idea and Ideal of the Town between Late Antiquity and the Early Middle Ages* (Leiden, 1999) 99–126

Brown, Peter, 'Sorcery, demons and the rise of Christianity: from late antiquity into the Middle Ages', in Peter Brown, ed., *Religion and Society in the Age of Saint Augustine* (London, 1972) 119–46

    The World of Late Antiquity: AD 150–750 (New York, 1989)

    Power and Persuasion in Late Antiquity: Towards a Christian Empire (Madison, 1992)

    'Elites in Late Antiquity', *Arethusa* 33.3 (2000) 335–45

    Poverty and Leadership in the Later Roman Empire (Hanover, 2002)

Brown, Thomas, *Gentlemen and Officers: Imperial Administration and Aristocratic Power in Byzantine Italy, AD 554–800* (Rome, 1984)

Brubaker, L., 'Memories of Helena: patterns of imperial female matronage in the fourth and fifth centuries', in L. James, ed., *Women, Men and Eunuchs: Gender in Byzantium* (London, 1998) 52–75

Bruhn, J., *Coins and Costume in Late Antiquity* (Washington, DC, 1993)

Burns, T., *A History of the Ostrogoths* (Bloomington, 1984)

Cameron, Alan, 'The fate of Pliny's letters in the late empire', *Classical Quarterly*, New Series 15.2 (1965) 289–98

'The end of the ancient universities', *Cahiers d'histoire mondiale* 4 (1966) 653–73

'The date of Zosimus' *New History*', *Philologus* 113 (1969) 106–10

Claudian: Poetry and Propaganda at the Court of Honorius (Oxford, 1970)

Circus Factions: Blues and Greens at Rome and Byzantium (Oxford, 1976)

'The house of Anastasius', *Greek, Roman and Byzantine Studies* 19 (1978) 259–76

The Last Pagans of Rome (Oxford, 2011)

Cameron, Alan, and D. Schauer, 'The last consul: Basilius and his dyptich', *Journal of Roman Studies* 72 (1982) 126–45

Cameron, Averil, 'The "scepticism" of Procopius', *Historia* 15.4 (1966) 466–82

Agathias (Oxford, 1970)

'Cassiodorus deflated', *Journal of Roman Studies* 71 (1981) 183–6

Procopius and the Sixth Century (New York, 1985)

'The construction of court ritual: the Byzantine Book of Ceremonies', in D. Cannadine and S. Price, eds., *Rituals of Royalty: Power and Ceremonial in Traditional Societies* (Cambridge, 1987) 106–32

'Education and literary culture', in Averil Cameron and P. Garnsey, eds., *Cambridge Ancient History XIII, The Late Empire, AD 337–425* (Cambridge, 1998) 665–707

'Old and new Rome: Roman studies in sixth-century Constantinople', in P. Rousseau and M. Papoutsakis, eds., *Transformations of Late Antiquity: Essays for Peter Brown* (Burlington, 2009) 15–36

Canepa, M., *The Two Eyes of the Earth: Art and Ritual of Kingship between Rome and Sasanian Iran* (Berkeley, 2009)

Cappuyns, D., 'Cassiodore', in A. Baudrillart, ed., *Dictionnaire d'histoire et de géographie ecclésiastiques, vol. XI* (Paris, 1949) 1349–1408

Carey, S., *Pliny's Catalogue of Culture: Art and Empire in the Natural History* (Oxford, 2003)

Carney, T., *Bureaucracy in Traditional Society: Romano-Byzantine Bureaucracies Viewed from Within, vols. I and II* (Lawrence. Kan., 1971)

Carruthers, M., *The Craft of Thought: Mediation, Rhetoric and the Making of Images, 400–1200* (Cambridge, 1998)

'Varietas: a word of many colours', *Poetica* 41 (2009) 11–32

Cavallo, G., 'La circolazione libraria nell'eta di Giustiniano', in G. Archi, ed., *L'Imperatore Giustiniano: Storia e Mito* (Milan, 1978) 203–20

'La cultura a Ravenna tra corte e chiesa', in O. Capitani, ed., *Le Sedi della Cultura nell'Emilia Romagna: L'Alto Medioevo* (Milan, 1983) 29–51

Cavarría, A., and T. Lewit, 'A bibliographical essay', in W. Bowden, L. Lavan and C. Machado eds., *Recent Research on the Late Antique Countryside* (Leiden, 2004) 3–51

Cecconi, G., *Governo Imperiale e Élites Dirigenti nell'Italia Tardoantica: Problemi di Storia Politico-Amministrativa (270–476 d.C.)* (Como, 1994)

Cekalova, A., 'Der Nika-Aufstand', in F. Winkelmann, ed., *Volk und Herrschaft im Frühen Byzanz: Methodische und quellenkritische Problem* (Berlin, 1991) 11–17

Chadwick, H., *Boethius: The Consolations of Music, Logic, Theology and Philosophy* (Oxford, 1981)

Chaniotis, A., 'The conversion of the temple of Aphrodite at Aphrodisias in context', in J. Hahn, S. Emmel and U. Gotter, eds., *From Temple to Church: Destruction and Renewal of Local Cultic Topography in Late Antiquity* (Leiden, 2008) 243–73

Bibliography

Charadonna, R., and F. Trabattoni, eds., *Physics and Philosophy of Nature in Greek Neoplatonism* (Leiden, 2009)

Chastagnol, A., review of Ruggini (1961), *Journal of Roman Studies* 53 (1963) 210–12
Le Sénat romain sous le Règne d'Odoacre: Recherches sur l'épigraphie du Colisée au Ve siècle (Bonn, 1966)

Chauvot, A., *Procope de Gaza, Priscien de Césarée, Panégyriques de l'Empereur Anastase Ier* (Bonn, 1986)

Chazelle, C., 'The Three Chapters Controversy and the biblical diagrams of Cassiodorus' *Codex Grandior* and *Institutions*', in Chazelle and Cubitt, *Crisis Oik.* (Turnhout, 2007) 161–205

Chin, C., *Grammar and Christianity in the Late Roman World* (Philadelphia, 2008)

Christie, N., 'Barren fields? Landscapes and settlements in late and post-Roman Italy', in G. Shipley and J. Salmon, eds., *Human Landscapes in Classical Antiquity: Environment and Culture* (London, 1996) 256–75
From Constantine to Charlemagne: An Archaeology of Italy, AD 300–800 (Burlington, 2006)

Christensen, A., *Cassiodorus, Jordanes and the History of the Goths: Studies in a Migration Myth* (Copenhagen, 2002)

Clark, G., 'Cosmic sympathies: nature as the expression of divine purpose', in G. Shipley and J. Salmon, eds., *Human Landscapes in Classical Antiquity: Environment and Culture* (London, 1996) 310–18
'Animal passions', *Greece and Rome* 47.1 (2000) 88–93

Coates-Stephens, R., 'Housing in early medieval Rome, AD 500–1000', *Papers of the British School at Rome* 64 (1996) 239–59

Codoñer, J., 'Prokops "*Anecdota*" und Justinians Nachfolge', *Jahrbuch der Österreichischen Byzantinistik* 53 (2003) 47–82

Colace, P., 'Lessico monetario in Cassiodoro: simbologia della moneta e filosofia del linguaggio', in Leanza, *Cassiod.* (Soveria Mannelli, 1993) 159–76

Collins, R., *Di Fredegar-Chroniken* (Hannover, 2007)

Conant, J., 'Europe and the African cult of saints, circa 350–900: an essay in Mediterranean communications', *Speculum* 85.1 (2010) 1–46

Conso, D., 'Sur le sens de *Formula* dans les *Variae* de Cassiodore', *Revue de philologie de littérature et d'histoire anciennes* 56.2 (1982) 265–86

Conte, G., *Genres and Readers: Lucretius, Love Elegy and Pliny's Encyclopedia* (Baltimore, 1994)

Conybeare, C., *Paulinus Noster: Self and Symbols in the Letters of Paulinus of Nola* (Oxford, 2005)

Cooper, J., *Knowledge, Nature, and the Good: Essays on Ancient Philosophy* (Princeton, 2004)

Cooper, K., *The Fall of the Roman Household* (Cambridge, 2007)

Cooper, K., and J. Hillner, eds., *Religion, Dynasty and Patronage in Early Christian Rome, 300–900* (Cambridge, 2007)

Corcoran, S., 'Two tales, two cities', in J. Drinkwater and B. Salway, eds., *Wolf Liebeschuetz Reflected* (London, 2007) 193–209
'Anastasius, Justinian and the pagans: a tale of two law codes and a papyrus', *Journal of Late Antiquity* 2.2 (2009) 183–208

Courcelle, P., *Histoire littéraire des grandes invasions germaniques* (Paris, 1964)

Crabbe, A., 'Literary design in the *De consolatione philosophiae*', in M. Gibson, ed., *Boethius: His Life, Thought and Influence* (Oxford, 1981) 237–41
Croke, B., 'The misunderstanding of Cassiodorus, *Institutiones* I.17.2', *Classical Quarterly* 32.1 (1982) 225–6
'AD 476: the manufacture of a turning point', *Chiron* 13 (1983) 81–119
'Cassiodorus and the *Getica* of Jordanes', *Classical Philology* 82.2 (1987) 117–34
'Theodor Mommsen and the Later Roman Empire', *Chiron* 20 (1990) 159–89
Count Marcellinus and His Chronicle (Oxford, 2001)
'Dynasty and ethnicity: Emperor Leo I and the eclipse of Aspar', *Chiron* 35 (2005) 147–203
'Jordanes and the immediate past', *Historia* 54.4 (2005) 473–94
'Justinian's Constantinople', in Maas, *CC Just.* (Cambridge, 2005) 60–86
'Procopius' *Secret History*: rethinking the date', *Greek, Roman and Byzantine Studies* 45 (2005) 405–31
Csaki, L., '*Variarum* I.X of Cassiodorus as a program of monetary policy', *Florilegium* 9 (1987) 53–64
Curran, J., *Pagan City and Christian Capital: Rome in the Fourth Century* (Oxford, 2000)
Dagron, G., *Naissance d'une capitale: Constantinople et ses institutions de 330 à 451* (Paris, 1974)
Emperor and Priest: The Imperial Office in Byzantium (Cambridge, 2003)
Daryaee, T., 'The Persian Gulf trade in late antiquity', *Journal of World History* 14.1 (2003) 1–16
Daube, D., 'Ne quid infamandi causa fiat: the Roman law of defamation', in G. Moschetti, ed., *Atti del Congresso Internazionale di Diritto Romano e di Storia del Diritto*, vol. III (Milan, 1951) 411–50
De Haas, F., 'Priscian of Lydia and Pseudo-Simplicius on the soul', in L. Gerson, ed., *The Cambridge History of Philosophy in Late Antiquity*, vol. II (Cambridge, 2010) 756–64
Deichmann, F., *Ravenna: Hauptstadt des spätantiken Abendlandes I: Geschichte und Monumente* (Wiesbaden, 1969)
Deliyannis, D., 'The mausoleum of Theoderic and the seven wonders of the world', *Journal of Late Antiquity* 3.2 (2010) 365–85
Ravenna in Late Antiquity (Cambridge, 2010)
'Ravenna, St. Martin and the Battle of Vouillé', *Illinois Classical Studies* 33 (in press)
Demougeot, E., 'La carrière politique de Boèce', in L. Obertello, ed., *Atti Congresso Inernazionale di Studi Boeziani* (Rome, 1981) 97–108
Dench, E., *Romulus' Asylum: Roman Identities from the Age of Alexander to the Age of Hadrian* (Oxford, 2005)
De Salvo, L., 'Politica commerciale e controllo dei mercati in eta teodericiana: su alcune 'formulae' cassiodoree', in Leanza, *Cassiod.* (Soveria Mannelli, 1993) 99–113
Diesenberger, M., 'Hair, sacrality and symbolic capital in the Frankish kingdoms', in R. Corradini, M. Diesenberger and H. Reimitz, eds., *The Construction of Communities in the Early Middle Ages: Texts, Resources and Artefacts* (Leiden, 2003) 173–212

Digeser, E., 'Religion, law and the Roman polity: the era of the Great Persecution', in C. Ando and J. Rüpke, eds., *Religion and Law in Classical and Christian Rome* (Stuttgart, 2006) 68–84

DiMarco, M., 'Scelta e utilizzazione delle fonti nel *De Anima* di Cassiodoro', *Studi e Materiali di Storia delle Religioni* 51 (1985) 95–117

Drake, H., *Constantine and the Bishops: The Politics of Intolerance* (Baltimore, 2000)

Drijvers, J., 'Eusebius' *Vita Constantini* and the construction of the image of Maxentius', in H. Amirav and B. Romeny, eds., *From Rome to Constantinople* (Leuven, 2007) 11–27

Dubouloz, J., 'Acception et défense des *loca publica*, d'après les *Variae* de Cassiodore: Un point de vue juridique sur les cités d'Italie au VIe siècle', in M. Ghilardi, C. Goddard and P. Porena, eds., *Cités ital.* (Rome, 2006) 53–74

Durliat, J., 'Cité, impôt et integration des barbares', in W. Pohl, ed., *Kingdoms of the Empire: The Integration of Barbarians in Late Antiquity* (Leiden, 1997) 153–79

Dyggve, E., 'Excursis sulla "Basilica Herculis" ricordata da Cassiodorus', *Corsi Rav* 2 (1957) 75–8

Edwards, C., *The Politics of Immorality in Ancient Rome* (Cambridge, 1993)

Edwards, M., *Neoplatonic Saints: The Lives of Plotinus and Proclus by Their Students* (Liverpool, 2000)

Elsner, J., 'From the culture of *spolia* to the cult of relics: the Arch of Constantine and the genesis of late antique forms', *Papers of the British School in Rome* 68 (2000) 149–84

    'The rhetoric of buildings in the *De aedificiis* of Procopius', in L. James, ed., *Art and Text in Byzantine Culture* (Cambridge, 2007) 33–57

Evans, J., *The Age of Justinian: The Circumstances of Imperial Power* (London, 1996)

Everett, N., *Literacy in Lombard Italy, c. 568–774* (Cambridge, 2003)

Fauvinet-Ranson, V., 'Portrait d'une regente: un panegyrique d'Amalasonthe (Cassiodorus, *Variae* 11.1)', *Cassiodorus* 4 (1998) 267–308

    'Le devenir du patrimoine monumental Romain des cités d'Italie à l'époque ostrogothique', in M. Ghilardi, C. Goddard and P. Porena, eds., *Cités ital.* (Rome, 2006) 205–16

Feeney, D., 'Becoming an authority: Horace on his own reception', in L. Houghton and M. Wyke, eds., *Perceptions of Horace: A Roman Poet and His Readers* (Cambridge, 2009) 16–38

Festy, M., 'L'Histoire auguste et les Nicomaques', in *Historiae Augustae Colloquium* (Bari, 2007) 183–95

Flower, H., *The Art of Forgetting: Disgrace and Oblivion in Roman Political Culture* (Chapel Hill, 2011)

Fotiou, A., 'Dicaearchus and the mixed constitution in sixth-century Byzantium: new evidence from a treatise on "political science"', *Byzantion* 51.2 (1981) 533–47

    'Plato's philosopher king in the political thought of sixth-century Byzantium', *Florilegium* 7 (1985) 17–29

Fowden, G., 'The pagan holy man in late antique society', *Journal of Hellenic Studies* 102 (1982) 33–59

    'Sages, cities and temples: aspects of late antique Pythagorism', in Smith, *Phil. Soc.* (Swansea, 2005) 145–70

Bibliography

Frakes, J., *The Fate of Fortune in the Early Middle Ages: The Boethian Tradition* (Leiden, 1988)

Francovich, R., and R. Hodges, *Villa to Village: The Transformation of the Roman Countryside in Italy, c. 400–1000* (London, 2003)

Frendo, J., 'Three authors in search of a reader: an approach to the analysis of direct discourse in Procopius, Agathias and Theophylact Simocatta', in C. Sode and S. Takacs, eds., *Novum Millenium: Studies on Byzantine History and Culture* (Burlington, 2001) 123–35

Fridh, Å., *Études critiques et syntaxiques sur les Variae de Cassiodore* (Göteborg, 1950)

Terminologie et formules dans les Variae de Cassiodore: Études sur le développement du style administratif aux derniers siècles de l'antiquité (Stockholm, 1956)

Magni Aurelii Cassiodori Senatoris Opera, Pars I (Turnhout, 1973)

'Cassiodorus' digression on music, *Variae* II.40', *Eranos* 86 (1988) 43–51

Frischer, B., *Shifting Paradigms: New Approaches to Horace's Ars Poetica* (Atlanta, 1991)

Gaddis, M., *There Is No Crime for Those Who Have Christ: Religious Violence in the Christian Roman Empire* (Berkeley, 2005)

Galinsky, K., ed., *The Cambridge Companion to the Age of Augustus* (Cambridge, 2005)

Galonnier, A., *Anecdoton Holderi ou Ordo Generis Cassiodororum: Elements pour une étude de l'authenticite boëcienne des Opuscula Sacra* (Paris, 1997)

Boèce: Opuscula Sacra I (Paris, 2007)

Garnsey, P., 'Roman patronage', in S. McGill, C. Sogno and E. Watts, eds., *From the Tetrarchs to the Theodosians: Later Roman History and Culture, 284–450 CE* (Cambridge, 2010) 33–54

Garzya, A., 'Cassiodoro e la grecita', in Leanza, *Att. Sett.* (Soveria Mannelli, 1986) 118–30

Gasti, F., 'Spunti in materia di *naturalis historia* nelle *Variae* di Cassiodoro', *Cassiodorus* 6–7 (2001) 133–50

Giardina, A., 'Le due Italie nella forma tarda dell'impero', in A. Giardina, ed., *Societa Romana e Impero Tardoantico: Istituzioni, Ceti, Economie* (Rome, 1986) 1–30

'Cassiodoro politico e il progetto delle *Variae*', in *Teoderic.* (Spoleto, 1993) 45–76

Cassiodoro Politico (Rome, 2006)

Gillett, A., 'The date and circumstances of Olympiodorus of Thebes', *Traditio* 48 (1993) 1–29

'The purposes of Cassiodorus' *Variae*', in A. Murray, ed., *After Rome's Fall: Narrators and Sources of Early Medieval History* (Toronto, 1998) 37–50

'Rome, Ravenna and the Last Western Emperors', *Papers of the British School at Rome* 69 (2001) 131–67

Envoys and Political Communication in the Late Antique West, 411–533 (Cambridge, 2003)

Gizewski, C., *Zur Normativität und Struktur der Verfassungsverhältnisse in der späteren römischen Kaiserzeit* (Munich, 1988)

Gleason, M., *Making Men: Sophists and Self-Presentation in Ancient Rome* (Princeton, 1995)

Goffart, W., 'Zosimus, The First Historian of Rome's Fall', *American Historical Review* 76.2 (1971) 412–41

Review of Krautschick, *Speculum* 60.4 (1985) 989

349

Bibliography

The Narrators of Barbarian History, AD 550–800: Jordanes, Gregory of Tours, Bede and Paul the Deacon (Princeton, 1988)

'Jordanes's *Getica* and the disputed authenticity of Gothic origins from Scandinavia', *Speculum* 80.2 (2005) 386–97

Goltz, A., *Barbar, König, Tyrann: Das Bild Theoderichs des Großen in der Überlieferung des 5 Bis 9 Jahrhunderts* (Berlin, 2008)

Gray, P., 'The legacy of Chalcedon: christological problems and their significance', in Maas, *CC Just.* (Cambridge, 2005) 215–38

Greatrex, G., 'The Nika Riot: a reappraisal', *Journal of Hellenic Studies* 117 (1997) 60–86

Rome and Persia at War, 502–532 (Leeds, 1998)

'Procopius the outsider?', in D. Smythe, ed., *Strangers to Themselves: The Byzantine Outsider* (Aldershot, 2000) 215–28

'Lawyers and historians in late antiquity', in R. Mathisen, ed., *Law, Society and Authority in Late Antiquity* (Oxford, 2001) 148–61

'Recent work on Procopius and the composition of *Wars* VIII', *Byzantine and Modern Greek Studies* 27 (2003) 45–67

Grey, C., 'Revisiting the "problem" of "*agri deserti*" in the late Roman empire', *Journal of Roman Archaeology* 20.1 (2007) 362–76

Grierson, P., and M. Blackburn, *Medieval European Coinage, vol. 1: The Early Middle Ages (5th–10th Centuries)* (Cambridge, 1986)

Gritti, E., *Proclo: Dialettica, Anima, Esegesi* (Milan, 2008)

Gruber, J., *Kommentar zu Boethius, De Consolatione Philosophiae* (Darmstadt, 1984)

Haarer, F., *Anastasius I: Politics and Empire in the Late Roman World* (Cambridge, 2006)

Haas, C., *Alexandria in Late Antiquity: Topography and Social Conflict* (Baltimore, 1997)

Hadot, I., *Le problème du néoplatonisme alexandrin: Hiéroclès et Simplicius* (Paris, 1978)

Haldon, J., 'Economy and administration: how did the empire work?', in Maas, *CC Just.* (Cambridge, 2005) 28–59

Hällström, G., 'The closing of the Neoplatonic school in AD 529: an additional aspect', in P. Castrén, ed., *Post-Herulian Athens: Aspects of Life and Culture in Athens, AD 267–529* (Helsinki, 1994) 145–57

Halporn, J., 'Magni Aurelii Cassiodori Senatoris Liber *De Anima*: introduction and critical text', *Traditio* 16 (1960) 39–109

Halporn, J. and M. Vessey, *Cassiodorus: Institutions of Divine and Secular Learning; On the Soul* (Liverpool, 2004)

Halsall, G., 'Childeric's grave, Clovis' succession and the origins of the Merovingian kingdom', in R. Mathisen and D. Shanzer, eds., *Society and Culture in Late Antique Gaul: Revisiting the Sources* (Aldershot, 2001) 116–33

Barbarian Migrations and the Roman West, 376–568 (Cambridge, 2007)

Hannestad, K., 'Les forces militaires d'après la Guerre gothique de Procope', *Classica et Mediaevalia* 21 (1960) 136–83

Hansen, M., *The Eloquence of Appropriation: Prolegomena to an Understanding of Spolia in Early Christian Rome* (Rome, 2003)

Harl, K., *Coinage in the Roman Economy, 300 BC to AD 700* (Baltimore, 1996)

Harries, J., 'The Roman imperial quaestor from Constantine to Theodosius II', *Journal of Roman Studies* 78 (1988) 148–72

Law and Empire in Late Antiquity (Cambridge, 1999)

'Superfluous verbiage? Rhetoric and law in the age of Constantine and Julian', *Journal of Early Christian Studies* 19.3 (2011) 345–74

Harrison, M., *A Temple for Byzantium: The Discovery and Excavation of Anicia Juliana's Palace–Church in Istanbul* (London, 1989)

Hasenstab, B., *Studien zur Variensammlung des Cassiodorus Senator: Ein Beitrag zur Geschichte der Ostrogothenherrschaft in Italien* (Munich, 1883)

Heather, P., 'Cassiodorus and the rise of the Amals: genealogy and the Goths under Hun domination', *Journal of Roman Studies* 79 (1989) 103–28

Goths and Romans, 332–489 (Oxford, 1991)

'The historical culture of Ostrogothic Italy', in *Teoderic.* (Spoleto, 1993) 317–53

'New men for new Constantines', in P. Magdalino, ed., *New Constantines: The Rhythm of Imperial Renewal in Byzantium, 4th–13th Centuries* (Cambridge, 1994) 11–33

'Theodoric king of the Goths', *Early Medieval Europe* 4.2 (1995) 145–73

'Fourth-century *foedera* and *foederati*', in W. Pohl, ed., *Kingdoms of the Empire* (Leiden, 1996) 57–74

'Roman and Goth in the kingdom of the Ostrogoths', in H. Goetz, ed. *Regna et Gentes* (Leiden, 2003) 86–134

'*Foedera* and *foederati* of the fourth century', in T. Noble, ed., *From Roman Provinces to Medieval Kingdoms* (London, 2006) 292–308

The Fall of the Roman Empire: A New History of Rome and the Barbarians (Oxford, 2006)

'Goths in the Roman Balkans, *c.* 350–500', in A. Poulter, ed., *The Transition to Late Antiquity on the Danube and Beyond* (Oxford, 2007) 163–90

Hedrick, C., *History and Silence: Purge and Rehabilitation of Memory in Late Antiquity* (Austin, Tex., 2000)

Heinzelmann, M., *Gregory of Tours: History and Society in the 6th Century* (Cambridge, 2001)

Hen, Y., *Roman Barbarians: The Royal Court and Culture in the Early Medieval West* (New York, 2007)

Hendy, M., 'From public to private: the western barbarian coinages as a mirror of the disintegration of late Roman state structures', *Viator* 19 (1988) 29–78

Heydemann, G., 'Biblical Israel and the Christian *gentes*: social metaphors and the language of identity in Cassiodorus' *Expositio psalmorum*', in G. Heydemann and W. Pohl, eds., *Strategies of Identification: Early Medieval Perspectives* (Turnhout, 2012)

Hobsbawm, E., and T. Ranger, eds., *The Invention of Tradition* (Cambridge, 1983)

Hodgkin, T., *The Letters of Cassiodorus: Being a Condensed Translation of the Variae Epistolae of Magnus Aurelius Cassiodorus Senator* (London, 1886)

Holmes, C., 'Political literacy', in P. Stephenson, ed., *The Byzantine World* (London, 2010) 137–48

Honoré, T., *Tribonian* (Ithaca, 1978)

'The making of the Theodosian Code', *Zeitschrift der Savigny-Stiftung für Rechtsgeschichte, Romanistiche Abteilung* 103 (1986) 134–68

Law in the Crisis of Empire, 379–455 AD: The Theodosian Dynasty and its Quaestors, with a Palingenesia of Laws of the Dynasty (Oxford, 1998)

Bibliography

Humfress, C., 'Law and legal practice in the age of Justinian', in Maas, *CC Just.* (Cambridge, 2005) 161–84

'Law in practice', in P. Rousseau, ed., *A Companion to Late Antiquity* (Malden, 2009) 377–91

Hunger, H., *Prooimion: Elemente der byzantinischen Kaiseridee in den Arengen der Urkunden* (Vienna, 1964)

Inwood, B., *Reading Seneca: Stoic Philosophy at Rome* (Oxford, 2005)

James, E., 'Gregory of Tours and the Franks', in A. Murray, ed., *After Rome's Fall: Narrators and Sources of Early Medieval History* (Toronto, 1998) 51–66

Janes, D., *God and Gold in Late Antiquity* (Cambridge, 2011)

Janson, T., *Latin Prose Prefaces: Studies in Literary Conventions* (Stockholm, 1964)

Jeffreys, E., 'Writers and audiences in the early sixth century', in S. Johnson, ed., *Greek Literature in Late Antiquity: Dynamism, Didacticism, Classicism* (Burlington, 2006) 127–39

Jeffreys, E., M. Jeffreys and R. Scott, *The Chronicle of John Malalas* (Melbourne, 1986)

Johannes, H., 'Die Zerstörung der Kulte von Philae: Geschichte und Legende am ersten Nilkatarakt', in J. Hahn, S. Emmel and U. Gotter, eds., *From Temple to Church: Destruction and Renewal of Local Cultic Topography in Late Antiquity* (Leiden, 2008) 203–42

Johnson, M., 'Toward a history of Theoderic's building program', *Dumbarton Oaks Papers* 42 (1988) 73–96

Jones, A., 'The constitutional position of Odoacer and Theoderic', *Journal of Roman Studies* 52 (1962) 126–30

The Later Roman Empire, 284–602: A Social, Economic, and Administrative Survey, 2 vols. (Baltimore, 1964)

Jones, A., and J. Martindale, *The Prosopography of the Later Roman Empire, vol. 1* (Cambridge, 1971)

Jones, C., 'Apollonius of Tyana in Late Antiquity', in S. Johnson, ed., *Greek Literature in Late Antiquity: Dynamism, Didacticism, Classicism* (Burlington, 2006) 49–64

Jouanaud, J., 'Pour qui Cassiodore a-t-il publié les *Variae*?', in *Teoder.* (Spoleto, 1993) 721–41

Kakridi, C., *Cassiodors Variae: Literatur und Politik im ostgotischen Italien* (Leipzig, 2005)

Kaldellis, A., 'The religion of Ioannes Lydos', *Phoenix* 57.3 (2003) 300–16

'Identifying dissident circles in sixth-century Byzantium: the friendship of Prokopios and Ioannes Lydos', *Florilegium* 21 (2004) 1–17

Procopius of Caesarea: Tyranny, History and Philosophy at the End of Antiquity (Philadelphia, 2004)

'Republican theory and political dissidence in Ioannes Lydos', *Byzantine and Modern Greek Studies* 29 (2005) 1–16

'The works and days of Hesychios the Illoustrios of Miletos', *Greek, Roman and Byzantine Studies* 45 (2005) 381–403

'The date and structure of Prokopios' *Secret History* and his projected work on church history', *Greek, Roman and Byzantine Studies* 49 (2009) 585–616

Kaster, R., *Guardians of Language: The Grammarian and Society in Late Antiquity* (Berkeley, 1988)

'Becoming "CICERO"', in P. Knox and C. Foss, eds., *Style and Tradition* (Stuttgart, 1998) 250–65.

Kelly, C., 'Later Roman bureaucracy: going through the files', in A. Bowman and G. Woolf, eds., *Literacy and Power in the Ancient World* (Cambridge, 1994) 161–76

Ruling the Later Roman Empire (Cambridge, Mass., 2004)

'Bureacracy and government', in N. Lenski, ed., *The Cambridge Companion to the Age of Constantine* (Cambridge, 2006) 183–204

Kennell, S., 'Hercules' invisible basilica (Cassiodorus, Variae 1.6)', *Latomus* 53.1 (1994) 159–75

Kirkby, H., 'The scholar and his public', in M. Gibson, ed., *Boethius: His Life, Thought and Influence* (Oxford, 1981) 44–69

Kitchen, T., 'Italia and Graecia: west versus east in the rhetoric of Ostrogothic Italy', in C. Kelly, R. Flower and M. Williams, eds., *Unclassical Traditions, vol. II: Perspectives from East and West in Late Antiquity* (Cambridge, 2011) 116–30

Klingshirn, W., 'Defining the *sortes sanctorum*: Gibbon, Du Cange and early Christian lot divination', *Journal of Early Christian Studies* 10.1 (2002) 77–130

Kokoszko, M., *Descriptions of Personal Appearance in John Malalas' Chronicle* (Łódź, 1998)

König, J., and T. Whitmarsh, 'Ordering Knowledge', in J. König and T. Whitmarsh, eds., *Ordering Knowledge in the Roman Empire* (Cambridge, 2007) 3–39

Krautheimer, R., *Three Christian Capitals: Topography and Politics* (Berkeley, 1983)

Krautschick, S., *Cassiodor und Die Politik seiner Zeit* (Bonn, 1983)

Lafferty, S., 'Law and society in Ostrogothic Italy', *Journal of Late Antiquity* 3.2 (2010) 337–64

LaFleur, R., 'Horace and *onomasti komodein*: the law of satire', *Aufstieg und Niedergang der Romischen Welt: Geschichte und Kultur Roms im Spiegel der neueren Forschung* 31.3 (1981) 1790–7

Lamma, P., *Oriente e Occidente nell'Alto Medioevo* (Padua, 1968)

Lanata, G., *Legislazione e Natura nelle Novelle Giustinianee* (Naples, 1984)

Filosofi e Animali nel Mondo Antico (Geneva, 1992)

Lee, A., 'The empire at war', in Maas, *CC Just.* (Cambridge, 2005) 113–33

Lendon, J., *The Empire of Honour: The Art of Government in the Roman World* (Oxford, 1997)

Lenski, N., *Failure of Empire: Valens and the Roman State in the Fourth Century* AD (Berkeley, 2002)

ed., *The Cambridge Companion to the Age of Constantine* (Cambridge, 2006)

Leopold, J., '*Consolando per edicta*: Cassiodorus, *Variae* IV.50 and imperial consolations for natural catastrophes', *Latomus* 45.4 (1986) 816–36

Lepelley, C., 'Un eloge nostalgique de la cite classique dans les *Variae* de Cassiodore', in C. Lepelley, ed., *Haut moyen-age: Culture, éducation et société* (Paris, 1990) 33–47

Liebeschuetz, J., *Decline and Fall of the Roman City* (Oxford, 2001)

Liebs, D., 'Roman law', in Averil Cameron, B. Ward-Perkins and M. Whitby, eds., *Cambridge Ancient History XIV, Late Antiquity, Empire and Successors, AD 425–600* (Cambridge, 2000) 244–52

Lieu, S., *Manichaeism in the Later Roman Empire and Medieval China* (Tübingen, 1992)

'From history to legend and legend to history: the medieval and Byzantine transformation of Constantine's *Vita*', in S. Lieu and D. Montserrat, eds., *Constantine: History, Historiography and Legend* (London, 1998) 136–76

Lieu, S., and D. Montserrat, eds., *From Constantine to Julian: Pagan and Byzantine Views – A Source History* (New York, 1996)

Lim, R., 'Unity and diversity among western Manichaeans: a reconsideration of Mani's sancta ecclesia', *Revue des études augustiniennes* 35 (1989) 231–50

Lizzi, R., *Vescovi e Strutture Ecclesiastiche nella Città Tardoantica: Italia Annonaria nel IV–V Secolo d.C.* (Como, 1989)

    La Conversione dei 'Cives', l'Evangelizzazione dei 'Rustici': Alcuni Esempi fra IV e VI Secolo (Spoleto, 2009)

Löwe, H. 'Cassiodor', *Romanische Forschungen* 60.3 (1948) 424–32

Maas, M., 'Roman history and Christian ideology in Justinianic reform legislation', *Dumbarton Oaks Papers* 40 (1986) 17–31

    ed., *John Lydus and the Roman Past: Antiquarianism and Politics in the Age of Justinian* (London, 1992)

    Exegesis and Empire in the Early Byzantine Mediterranean: Junillus Africanus and the Instituta Regularia Divinae Legis (Tübingen, 2003)

    'Roman questions, Byzantine answers', in M. Maas, ed., *CC Just.* (Cambridge, 2005) 1–27

MacCormack, S., 'Change and continuity in late antiquity: the ceremony of "adventus"', *Historia* 21.4 (1972) 721–52

    Art and Ceremony in Late Antiquity (Berkeley, 1981)

McCormick, M., *Eternal Victory: Triumphal Rulership in Late Antiquity, Byzantium and the Early Medieval West* (Cambridge, 1986)

McEvoy, M., 'Rome and the transformation of the imperial office in the late fourth–mid-fifth centuries AD', *Papers of the British School at Rome* 78 (2010) 151–92

MacGeorge, P., *Late Roman Warlords* (Oxford, 2002)

McKitterick, R., *The Carolingians and the Written Word* (Cambridge, 1989)

    History and Memory in the Carolingian World (Cambridge, 2004)

    'Roman history in the early Middle Ages', in C. Bolgia, R. McKitterick and J. Osborne, eds., *Rome across Time and Space: Cultural Transmission and the Exchange of Ideas, c. 500–1400* (Cambridge, 2011) 19–34

MacMullen, R., *Corruption and the Decline of Rome* (New Haven, 1988)

MacPherson, R., *Rome in Involution: Cassiodorus' Variae in Their Literary and Historical Setting* (Poznań, 1989)

Magee, J., 'Boethius' *Consolatio* and the theme of Roman liberty', *Phoenix* 59.3 (2005) 348–64

    'Boethius', in L. Gerson, ed., *The Cambridge History of Philosophy in Late Antiquity*, vol. II (Cambridge, 2010) 788–812

Malmberg, S., 'Above the gate: symbols on the gate and the gate as symbol at Rome, Ravenna and Constantinople', in S. Birk, T. Kristensen and B. Poulsen, eds., *Using Images in Late Antiquity* (Oxford, 2012)

Malosse, P., 'Libanius on Constantine again', *Classical Quarterly* 47.2 (1997) 519–24

Mango, C., *Le développement urbain de Constantinople (IVe–VIIe siècles)* (Paris, 1985)

Marazzi, F., 'The destinies of the late antique Italies: politico-economic developments of the sixth century', in R. Hodges and W. Bowden, eds., *The Sixth Century: Production, Distribution and Demand* (Leiden, 1998) 119–59

'Rome in transition: economic and political changes in the fourth and fifth centuries', in J. Smith, ed., *Early Medieval Rome and the Christian West* (Leiden, 2000) 21–39

'The last Rome: from the end of the fifth to the end of the sixth century', in Barnish and Marazzi, *Ostrogoth.* (Rochester, 2007) 279–303

Markus, R., *Signs and Meanings: World and Text in Ancient Christianity* (Liverpool, 1996)

Christianity and the Secular (Notre Dame, 2006)

Markus, R., and C. Sotinel, 'Introduction', in Chazelle and Cubitt, *Crisis Oik.* (Turnhout, 2007) 1–14

Marrou, H., *A History of Education in Antiquity* (Madison, 1956)

Martijn, M., *Proclus on Nature: Philosophy of Nature and Its Methods in Proclus' Commentary on Plato's Timaeus* (Leiden, 2010)

Martindale, J., *The Prosopography of the Later Roman Empire, vol.* II: AD 395–527 (Cambridge, 1980)

The Prosopography of the Later Roman Empire, vol. III A: AD 527–641 (Cambridge, 1992)

The Prosopography of the Later Roman Empire, vol. III B: AD 527–641 (Cambridge, 1992)

Martino, P., '*Gothorum laus est civilitas custodia* (Cassiodorus *Variae* 9.14.18)', *Sileno* 8 (1982) 31–45

Mathisen, R., 'Patricians as diplomats in late antiquity', *Byzantinische Zeitschrift* 790 (1986) 35–49

Ruricius of Limoges and Friends: A Collection of Letters from Visigothic Gaul (Liverpool, 1999)

Matthews, J., *Western Aristocracies and Imperial Court, AD 364–425* (Oxford, 1975)

'Anicius Manlius Severinus Boethius', in M. Gibson, ed., *Boethius: His Life, Thought and Influence* (Oxford, 1981) 15–42

Laying Down the Law: A Study of the Theodosian Code (New Haven, 2000)

'Roman law and barbarian identity in the late Roman west', in S. Mitchell and G. Greatrex, eds., *Ethnicity and Culture in Late Antiquity* (London, 2000) 31–44

'The *Interpretationes* of the *Breviarium*', in R. Mathisen, ed., *Law, Society and Authority in Late Antiquity* (Oxford, 2001) 11–32

Mauro, L., 'Cassiodoro e l'antropologia', in M. Silvestre and M. Squillante, eds., *Mutatio Rerum: Letteratura Filosofia Scienza tra Tardo Antico e Altomedioevo* (Naples, 1997) 219–49

Meier, M., *Das andere Zeitalter Justinians: Kontingenzerfahrung und Kontingenzbewältigung im 6. Jahrhundert n. Chr.* (Göttingen, 2003)

Menze, V., *Justinian and the Making of the Syrian Orthodox Church* (Oxford, 2008)

Merrills, A., and R. Miles, *The Vandals* (Malden, 2010)

Metlich, M., *The Coinage of Ostrogothic Italy* (London, 2004)

Meyer-Flugel, B., *Das Bild der Ostgotisch-römischen Gesellschaft bei Cassiodor: Leben und Ethik von Römern und Germanen in Italien nach dem Ende des Weströmischen Reiches* (New York, 1992)

Mierow, C., *The Gothic History of Jordanes* (Princeton, 1915)

Millar, F., 'Rome, Constantinople and the near eastern church under Justinian: two synods of C.E. 536', *Journal of Roman Studies* 98 (2008) 62–82

'Linguistic co-existence in Constantinople: Greek and Latin (and Syriac) in Acts of the Synod of 536 CE', *Journal of Roman Studies* 99 (2009) 92–103

Mitchell, K., and I. Wood, eds., *The World of Gregory of Tours* (Leiden, 2002)

Mitchell, S., and P. van Nuffelen, eds., *Monotheism between Pagans and Christians in Late Antiquity* (Leuven, 2010)

eds., *One God: Pagan Monotheism in the Roman Empire* (Cambridge, 2010)

Modéran, Y., 'L'établissement territorial des Vandales en Afrique', *Antiquité tardive* 10 (2002) 87–122

'L'Afrique reconquise et les Trois Chapitres', in Chazelle and Cubitt, *Crisis Oik.* (Turnhout, 2007) 39–82

Momigliano, A., 'Cassiodorus and the Italian culture of his time', *Proceedings of the British Academy* 41 (1955) 207–36

'Cassiodoro', in A. Ghisalberti, ed., *Dizionario Biografico degli Italiani* (Rome, 1960) 1–9

ed., *The Conflict between Paganism and Christianity in the Fourth Century* (Oxford, 1963)

Moorhead, J., 'Boethius and Romans in Ostrogothic service', *Historia* 27.4 (1978) 604–12

Libertas and *nomen romanum* in Ostrogothic Italy', *Latomus* 46.1 (1987) 161–8

Theoderic in Italy (Oxford, 1992)

'Cassiodorus on the Goths in Ostrogothic Italy', *Romanobarbarica* 16 (1999) 241–59

'Totila the Revolutionary', *Historia* 49.3 (2000) 382–6

'Boethius' life and the world of late antique philosophy', in J. Marenbon, ed., *The Cambridge Companion to Boethius* (Cambridge, 2009), 13–33

Moralee, J., 'Maximinus Thrax and the politics of race in late antiquity', *Greece and Rome* 55.1 (2008) 55–82

Morony, M., 'Economic boundaries? Late antiquity and early Islam', *Journal of Economic and Social History* 47.2 (2004) 166–94

Morosi, R., 'I *comitiaci*, funzionari romani nell'Italia Ostrogota', *Quaderni Catanesi* 3.5 (1981) 77–111

'I saiones, speciali agenti di polizia presso i Gothi', *Athenaeum* 59 (1981) 150–65

Neale, J., *A History of the Holy Eastern Church: The Patriarchate of Alexandria, vol. II* (London, 1847)

Nees, L., *A Tainted Mantle: Hercules and the Classical Tradition at the Carolingian Court* (Philadelphia, 1991)

Nelis-Clément, J., *Les beneficiarii: Militaires et administrateurs au service de l'empire (1er s.a.C.–VIe s.p.C.)* (Bordeaux, 2000)

Nichols, M., 'Social status and the authorial personae of Horace and Vitruvius', in L. Houghton and M. Wyke, eds., *Perceptions of Horace: A Roman Poet and His Readers* (Cambridge, 2009) 109–22

Nicks, F., 'Literary culture in the reign of Anastasius I', in S. Mitchell and G. Greatrex, eds., *Ethnicity and Culture in Late Antiquity* (London, 2000) 183–203

Nickstadt, H., *De Digressionibus Quibus in Variis Usus Est Cassiodorus* (Marburg, 1921)

Noble, T., 'Literacy and the papal government in late antiquity and the early Middle Ages', in R. McKitterick, ed., *The Uses of Literacy in Early Mediaeval Europe* (Cambridge, 1990) 82–108

Bibliography

Noreña, C., *Imperial Ideals in the Roman West: Representation, Circulation, Power* (Cambridge, 2011)

Nussbaum, M., and A. Rorty, eds., *Essays on Aristotle's De anima* (Oxford, 1992)

Obertello, L., 'La morte di Boezio e la verita storica', in L. Obertello, ed., *Atti Congresso Internazionale di Studi Boeziani* (Rome, 1981) 59–70

O'Donnell, J., *Cassiodorus* (Berkeley, 1979)

'Liberius the patrician', *Traditio* 37 (1981) 32–71

The Ruin of the Roman Empire (New York, 2008)

O'Meara, D., ed., *Neoplatonism and Christian Thought* (New York, 1982)

'The Justinianic dialogue *On Political Science* and its Neoplatonic sources', in K. Ierodiakonou, ed., *Byzantine Philosophy and Its Ancient Sources* (Oxford, 2002) 49–62

Platonopolis: Platonic Political Philosophy in Late Antiquity (Oxford, 2003)

'A Neoplatonist ethics for high-level officials: Sopatros' letter to Himerios', in Smith, *Phil. Soc.* (Swansea, 2005) 91–100

Paratore, E., 'Cassiodoro nella cultura del suo tempo', in Leanza, *Cassiod.* (Soveria Mannelli, 1993) 19–25

Paschoud, F., *Zosime: Histoire nouvelle, Tome I, Livres I et II* (Paris, 2003)

Pazdernik, C., 'Justinianic ideology and the power of the past' in Maas, *CC Just.* (Cambridge, 2005) 185–212

Perl, E., *Theophany: The Neoplatonic Philosophy of Dionysius the Areopagite* (New York, 2007)

Petersen, H., 'Livy and Augustus', *Transactions of the American Philological Association* 92 (1961) 440–52

Petrucci, A., *Writers and Readers in Medieval Italy: Studies in the History of Written Culture* (New Haven, 1995)

Pferschy, B., *Formular und Formeln: Studien zur Typologie der Variae des Cassiodorus Senator* (Vienna, 1982)

'Cassiodors Variae: individuelle Ausgestaltung eines spätrömischen Urkundenformulars', *Archiv für Diplomatik* 32 (1986) 1–128

'Cassiodor und die Ostgotische Konigsurkunde', in *Teoder.* (Spoleto, 1993) 253–73

Pietri, C., 'Le Sénat, le people chrétien et les parties du cirque à Rome sous le Pape Symmaque (498–514)', *Mélanges d'archeologie et d'histoire* 78 (1966) 123–39

'Aristocratie et société cléricale dans l'Italie chrétienne au temps d'Odoacre et de Théodoric', *Mélanges de l'École française de Rome* 93 (1981) 417–67

'Les aristocraties de Ravenne (V–Vis)', *Studi Romagnoli* 34 (1983) 643–73

Pietri, C., and L. Pietri, *Prosopographie chrétienne du Bas-Empire II: Prosopographie de l'Italie chrétienne (313–604)* (Rome, 2000)

Pizzani, U., 'Le lettere di Teoderico a Boezio e la mediazione culturale di Cassiodoro', *Cassiodorus* 4 (1998) 141–61

Polansky, R., *Aristotle's De anima* (Cambridge, 2007)

Polara, G., 'La letteratura in Italia nel VI secolo', in M. Silvestre and M. Squillante, eds., *Mutatio Rerum: Letteratura Filosofia Scienza tra Tardo Antico e Altoedioevo* (Naples, 1997) 11–36

Potter, D., *The Roman Empire at Bay, ad 180–395* (London, 2004)

'The unity of the Roman Empire', in S. McGill, C. Sogno and E. Watts, eds., *From the Tetrarchs to the Theodosians: Later Roman History and Culture, 284–450 CE* (Cambridge, 2010) 13–32

Price, R., 'The Three Chapters Controversy and the Council of Chalcedon', in Chazelle and Cubitt, *Crisis Oik.* (Turnhout, 2007) 17–37

Prinz, F., 'Cassiodor und das Problem Christlicher Aufgeklarheit in der Spätantike', *Historische Zeitschrift* 254.3 (1992) 561–80

'Cassiodoro e il problema dell'illuminismo cristiano nella tarda antichita', in Leanza, *Cassiod.* (Soveria Mannelli, 1993) 3–18

Prostko-Prostynski, J., 'Zur Chronoligie der Bücher VI und VII den Variae von Cassiodor', *Historia* 53.4 (2004) 503–8

Purcell, N., 'The *apparitores*: a study in social mobility', *Papers of the British School at Rome* 51 (1983) 125–73

'Town in country and country in town', in E. MacDougall, ed., *Ancient Roman Villa Gardens* (Washington, DC, 1987) 185–203

'The "ordo scribarum": a study in the loss of memory', *Mélanges de l'École française de Rome* 113 (2001) 633–74

Quacquarelli, A., 'La elocutio di S. Agostino nelle riflessioni di Cassiodoro', *Augustinianum* 25 (1985) 385–403

Rance, P., 'Narses and the Battle of Taginae (Busta Gallorum) 552: Procopius and sixth-century warfare', *Historia* 54.4 (2005) 424–72

Rapp, C., 'Hagiography and monastic literature', in *Cristianita d'Occidente e Cristianita d'Oriente (Secoli VI–XI)* (Spoleto, 2004) 1228–77

'Literary culture under Justinian', in Maas, ed., *CC Just.* (Cambridge, 2005) 376–97

Holy Bishops in Late Antiquity: The Nature of Christian Leadership in an Age of Transition (Berkeley, 2005)

Rasmussen, S., *Public Portents in Republican Rome* (Rome, 2003)

Rawson, E., *Cicero: A Portrait* (London, 1975)

Remes, P., *Neoplatonism* (Berkeley, 2008)

Reydellet, M., *La royauté dans la littérature latine de Sidoine Apolinaire à Isidore de Séville* (Rome, 1981)

Ricci, A., 'I recenti restauri alla Belgrat Kapi nellemura terrestri di Costantinopoli', *Milion* 2 (1990) 465–6

Rike, R., *Apex Omnium: Religion in the Res Gestae of Ammianus* (Berkeley, 1987)

Rio, A., *The Formularies of Angers and Marculf: Two Merovingian Legal Handbooks* (Liverpool, 2008)

Legal Practice and Written Word in the Early Middle Ages: Frankish Formulae, 500–1000 (Cambridge, 2009)

Robinson, P., 'Dead Boethius: sixth-century accounts of a future martyr', *Viator* 35 (2005) 1–19

Rocca, R., 'Cassiodoro e la *historia ludorum*', *Romanobarbarica* 5 (1980) 225–37

Rubin, B., *Prokopios von Kaisareia* (Stuttgart, 1954)

Ruggini, L., *Economia e Società nell'Italia Annonaria': Rapporti fra Agricoltura e Commercio dal IV al VI Secolo d.C.* (Bari, 1961)

'Pubblicistica e storiografia bizantine di fronte alla crisi dell'impero romano', *Athenaeum* 51 (1973) 146–83

Bibliography

'Nobilita romana e potere nell'eta di Boezio', in L. Obertello, ed., *Atti Congresso Internazionale di Studi Boeziani* (Rome, 1981) 73–96
'Societa provinciale, societa romana, societa bizantina in Cassiodoro', in Leanza, *Att. Sett.* (Soveria Mannelli, 1986) 245–61
Ruscu, D., 'The revolt of Vitalianus and the "Scythian Controversy"', *Byzantinische Zeitschrift* 101.2 (2008) 773–85
Saffrey, H., 'Neoplatonist spirituality: from Iamblichus to Proclus and Damascius', in A. Armstrong, ed., *Classical Mediterranean Spirituality: Egyptian, Greek, Roman* (New York, 1986) 250–65
Said, E., *Orientalism* (London, 1978)
Salaman, M., ed., *Paganism in the Later Roman Empire and in Byzantium* (Cracow, 1991)
Salzman, M., 'Reflections on Symmachus' idea of tradition', *Historia* 38.3 (1989) 348–64
   The Making of a Christian Aristocracy: Social and Religious Change in the Western Roman Empire (Cambridge, Mass., 2002)
   'Rethinking pagan–Christian violence', in H. Drake, ed., *Violence in Late Antiquity* (Burlington, 2006) 265–85
Sanfilippo, M., 'Cassiod. Orat. Rell. p. 470, II. 16–21 Traub', *Quaderni Catanesi* 4.8 (1982) 460–4
Sarris, P., *Economy and Society in the Age of Justinian* (Cambridge, 2006)
Scheibelreiter, G., 'Justinian und Belisar in Fränkischer Sicht: zur Interpretation von Fredegar, *Chronicon* II 62', in W. Hörandner, ed., *Byzantos* (Vienna, 1984) 267–80
Schmidt-Hofner, S., 'Ehrensachen: Ranggesetzebung, Elitenkonkurrenz und die Funktion des Rechts in der Spätantike', *Chiron* 40 (2010) 209–43
Schott, J., *Christianity, Empire and the Making of Religion in Late Antiquity* (Philadelphia, 2008)
Schouleer, B., 'Le déguisement de l'intention dans la rhétorique grecque', *Ktema* 11 (1986) 257–72
Scivoletto, N., 'Cassiodoro e la "retorica della cita"', *Giornale Italiano di Filologia* 38 (1986) 3–24
Scott, R., 'Malalas, *The Secret History* and Justinian's Propaganda', *Dumbarton Oaks Papers* 39 (1985) 99–109
   'The image of Constantine in Malalas and Theophanes', in P. Magdalino, ed., *New Constantines: The Rhythm of Imperial Renewal in Byzantium, 4th–13th Centuries* (Cambridge, 1994) 57–71
Settia, A., 'Le fortificazioni dei Goti in Italia', in *Teoderic.* (Spoleto, 1993) 101–31
Settipani, C., *Continuité gentilice et continuité familiale dans les familles sénatoriales romaines: Mythe et réalité* (Oxford, 2000)
Shanzer, D., 'Ennodius, Boethius and the date and interpretation of Maximian's *Elegia III*', *Rivista di Filologia e di Istruzione Classica* 111.2 (1983) 183–95
   'The death of Boethius and the "Consolation of Philosophy"', *Hermes* 112.3 (1984) 352–66
   'Two clocks and a wedding: Theoderic's diplomatic relations with the Burgundians', *Romanobarbarica* 14 (1996) 225–58

'Interpreting the Consolation', in J. Marenbon, ed., *The Cambridge Companion to Boethius* (Cambridge, 2009) 228–54

Shaw, G., 'Theurgy: rituals of unification in the Neoplatonism of Iamblichus', *Traditio* 41 (1985) 1–28

Theurgy and the Soul: The Neoplatonism of Iamblichus (University Park, Penn., 1995)

Silvestre, M., 'Cassiodoro e l'uso politico della storia', in M. Silvestre and M. Squillante, eds., *Mutatio Rerum: Letteratura Filosofia Scienza tra Tardo Antico e Altomedioevo* (Naples, 1997) 93–105

Simonetti, M., *Biblical Interpretation in the Early Church: An Historical Introduction to Patristic Exegesis*, trans. J. Hughes (Edinburgh, 1994)

Simoni, F., 'La memoria del regno ostrogoto nella tradizione storiografica carolinga', in P. Delogu, *Le Invasioni Barbariche nel Meridione dell'Impero: Visigoti, Vandali, Ostrogoti* (Soveria Mannelli, 2001) 351–75

Siniossoglou, N., *Plato and Theodoret: The Christian Appropriation of Platonic Philosophy and the Hellenistic Intellectual Resistance* (Cambridge, 2008)

Sinnigen, W., 'Administrative shifts of competence under Theoderic', *Traditio* 21 (1965) 457–66

Siorvanes, L., *Proclus: Neo-Platonic Philosophy and Science* (Edinburgh, 1996)

Sirago, V., 'I Goti nelle Variae di Cassiodoro', in Leanza, *Att. Sett.* (Soveria Mannelli, 1986) 179–97

'Operazioni militari in Calabria durante la Guerra Gotica', in Leanza, *Cassiod.* (Soveria Mannelli, 1993) 115–29

Sirks, B., 'From the Theodosian to the Justinian Code', *Atti Dell'Accademia Romanistica Costantiniana* 6 (1986) 265–302

'The colonate in Justinian's reign', *Journal of Roman Studies* 98 (2008) 120–43

Sivonen, P., *Being a Roman Magistrate: Office-Holding and Roman Identity in Late Antique Gaul* (Helsinki, 2006)

Skahill, B., *The Syntax of the Variae* (Washington, DC, 1934)

Smith, J., *Europe after Rome: A New Cultural History 500–1000* (Oxford, 2005)

Sorabji, R., 'John Philoponus', in R. Sorabji, ed., *Philoponus and the Rejection of Aristotelian Science* (London, 1987) 1–40

'Divine names and sordid deals in Ammonius' Alexandria', in A. Smith, ed., *The Philosopher and Society in Late Antiquity* (Swansea, 2005) 203–13

Sotinel, C., 'Emperors and popes in the sixth century: the western view', in Maas, *CC Just.* (Cambridge, 2005) 267–90

'The Three Chapters and the transformations of Italy', in Chazelle and Cubitt, *Crisis Oik.* (Turnhout, 2007) 85–120

Speck, P., 'Wie dumm darf Zosimus sein? Vorschläge zu seiner Neubewertung', *Byzantinoslavica* 52 (1991) 1–14

Starnes, C., 'Boethius and the development of Christian humanism: the theology of the *Consolatio*', in *Atti Congresso Internazionale di Studi Boeziani* (Rome, 1981) 27–38

Stein, E., 'Deux questeurs de Justinien et l'emploi des langues das ses Novelles', *Bulletin de la Classe des lettres de l'Académie de Belgique* 23 (1937) 365–90

Suelzer, M., *The Clausulae of Cassiodorus* (Washington, DC, 1944)

Swain, S., 'Polemon's *Physiognomy*', in S. Swain, ed., *Seeing the Face, Seeing the Soul: Polemon's Physiognomy from Classical Antiquity to Medieval Islam* (Oxford, 2007) 125–201

Syme, R., *The Roman Revolution* (Oxford, 1939)

Tartaglia, L., 'Elementi di ideologia politica nelle Variae di Cassiodoro', *Filologia Antica e Moderna* 6 (1994) 59–69

Thurman, W., 'A juridical and theological concept of nature in the sixth century AD', *Byzantinoslavica* 32.1 (1971) 77–85

Townsend, W., 'The so-called Symmachan forgeries', *Journal of Religion* 13 (1933) 165–74

Treadgold, W., *The Early Byzantine Historians* (New York, 2007)

Troncarelli, F., *Tradizioni Perdute: La 'Consolatio Philosophiae' nell'Alto Medioevo* (Padova, 1981)
   'Boezio a Costantinopoli: testi, contesti, edizioni', *Litterae Caelestes* 3 (2008) 211–31

Urbano, A., 'Donation, dedication and *damnatio memoriae*: the Catholic reconciliation of Ravenna and the church of Sant'Apollinare Nuovo', *Journal of Early Christian Studies* 13.1 (2005) 71–110

Van Dam, R., *The Roman Revolution of Constantine* (Cambridge, 2007)

Van de Vyver, A., 'Cassiodore et son oeuvre', *Speculum* 6 (1931) 244–92

Van den Berg, R., 'Live unnoticed: the invisible Neoplatonic politician', in Smith, *Phil. Soc.* (Swansea, 2005) 101–15

Vanderspoel, J., 'Cassiodorus at *patricius* and *ex patricio*', *Historia* 39 (1990) 499–503
   Themistius and the Imperial Court: Oratory, Civic Duty and Paideia from Constantius to Theodosius (Ann Arbor, 1995)

Vera, D., 'Proprietà terriera e società rurale nell'Italia Gotica', in *Teoderic.* (Spoleto, 1993) 133–66

Vidén, G., *The Roman Chancery Tradition: Studies in the Language of the Codex Theodosianus and Cassiodorus' Variae* (Goteborg, 1984)

Viscido, L., 'Sull'uso del termine barbarus nelle "Variae" di Cassiodoro', *Orpheus* 7.2 (1986) 338–44
   Studi sulle Variae di Cassiodoro (Calabria, 1987)

Vitiello, M., '"Cassiodoriana": Gli *Excerpta Valesiana*, l'*adventus* e le *laudes* del principe Teoderico', *Chiron* 86 (2006) 113–33
   Il Principe, Il Filosofo, Il Guerriero: Lineamenti di Pensiero Politico nell'Italia Ostrogota (Stuttgart, 2006)
   'Cassiodorus anti-Boethius?', *Klio* 90.2 (2008) 461–84

Von Simpson, O., *Sacred Fortress: Byzantine Art and Statecraft in Ravenna* (Chicago, 1948)

Voss, W., *Recht und Rhetorik in den Kaisergesetzen der Spätantike: Ein Untersuchung zum nachklassischen Kauf- und Übereignungsrecht* (Frankfurt am Main, 1982)

Wallace-Hadrill, A., *Rome's Cultural Revolution* (Cambridge, 2008)

Wallace-Hadrill, D., *The Greek Patristic View of Nature* (Manchester, 1968)

Wallace-Hadrill, J., *The Fourth Book of the Chronicle of Fredegar with its Continuations* (Westport, 1960)

Wallis, R., *Neoplatonism* (New York, 1972)

Walsh, P., *Cassiodorus: Explanation of the Psalms, vols. I–III* (New York, 1990)

Wander, S., 'Cypress plates and the *Chronicle* of Fredegar', *Dumbarton Oaks Papers* 29 (1975) 345–6

Ward-Perkins, B., *From Classical Antiquity to the Middle Ages: Urban Public Building in Northern and Central Italy, AD 300–850* (Oxford, 1984)

 'Continuists, catastrophists and the towns of post-Roman northern Italy', *Papers of the British School at Rome* 65 (1997) 157–76

 The Fall of Rome and the End of Civilization (Oxford, 2005)

Wataghin, G., 'Christianization et organization ecclésiastique des campagnes: l'Italie du nord aux IV–VIII siècles', in G. Brogiolo, N. Gauthier and N. Christie, eds., *Towns and Their Territories between Late Antiquity and the Early Middle Ages* (Leiden, 2000) 209–34

Waterlow, S., *Nature, Change and Agency in Aristotle's Physics: A Philosophical Study* (Oxford, 1982)

Watts, E., 'Justinian, Malalas and the end of Athenian philosophical teaching in AD 529', *Journal of Roman Studies* 94 (2004) 168–82

 'Student travel to intellectual centers: what was the attraction?', in L. Ellis and F. Kidner, eds., *Travel, Communication and Geography in Late Antiquity: Sacred and Profane* (Burlington, 2004) 13–23

 'Where to live the philosophical life in the sixth century? Damascius, Simplicius and the return from Persia', *Greek, Roman and Byzantine Studies* 45 (2005) 285–302

 City and School in Late Antique Athens and Alexandria (Berkeley, 2006)

 'Three generations of Christian philosophical biography', in S. McGill, C. Sogno and E. Watts, eds., *From the Tetrarchs to the Theodosians: Later Roman History and Culture, 284–450 CE* (Cambridge, 2010) 117–33

Wes, M., *Das Ende des Kaisertums im Westen des Römischen Reichs* (Rijswijk, 1967)

Westerink, L. 'Philosophy and medicine in late antiquity', *Janus: Revue internationale de l'histoire des sciences, de la médecine, de la pharmacie et de la technique* 51.3 (1964) 169–77

Whitby, M., 'Greek historical writing after Procopius: variety and vitality', in Averil Cameron and L. Conrad, eds., *The Byzantine and Early Islamic Near East: Problems in the Literacy Source Material, vol. 1* (Princeton, 1989) 25–37

 'John of Ephesus and the pagans: pagan survivals in the sixth century', in M. Salaman, ed., *Paganism in the Later Roman Empire and in Byzantium* (Cracow, 1991) 111–31

 'Images for emperors in late antiquity', in P. Magdalino, ed., *New Constantines: The Rhythm of Imperial Renewal in Byzantium, 4th–13th Centuries* (Cambridge, 1994) 83–93

 'The violence of circus factions', in K. Hopwood, ed., *Organised Crime in Antiquity* (Swansea, 1999) 229–53

 The Ecclesiastical History of Evagrius Scholasticus (Liverpool, 2000)

Whitehouse, D., G. Barker, R. Reece, D. Reese, 'The *Schola Praeconum* I: the coins, pottery, lamps and fauna', *Papers of the British School at Rome* 50 (1982) 53–101

Whittaker, C., *Rome and Its Frontiers: The Dynamics of Empire* (London, 2004)

Wickham, C., review of Cecconi (1994), *Journal of Roman Studies* 86 (1996) 238–9

 Framing the Early Middle Ages: Europe and the Mediterranean, 400–800 (Oxford, 2005)

Wildberg, C., 'Philosophy in the age of Justinian', in Maas, *CC Just.* (Cambridge, 2005) 329–30

Williamson, G., *Eusebius: The History of the Church from Christ to Constantine* (London, 1965)

Wolfram, H., *History of the Goths* (Berkeley, 1979)

Wood, I., 'Fredegar's fables', in A. Scharer and G. Scheibelreiter, eds., *Historiographie im frühen Mittelalter* (Vienna, 1994) 359–66

  The Merovingian Kingdoms, 450–751 (New York, 1994)

  'Review: Cassiodorus, Jordanes and the History of the Goths', *Historisk Tidsskrift* 103.2 (2003)

  'Theoderic's monuments in Ravenna', in Barnish and Marazzi, *Ostrogoth.* (Woodbridge, 2007) 249–63

Wood, P., *'We Have No King but Christ': Christian Political Thought in Greater Syria on the Eve of the Arab Conquest (c. 400–585)* (Oxford, 2010)

Woolf, G., *Tales of the Barbarians: Ethnography and Empire in the Roman West* (Malden, 2011)

Zanker, P., *The Power of Images in the Age of Augustus* (Ann Arbor, 1988)

Zimmerman, O., *The Late Latin Vocabulary of the Variae of Cassiodorus: With Special Advertense to the Technical Terminology of Administration* (Washington, DC, 1944)

Zumbo, A., 'Sugli *excursus* zoologici nelle Variae di Cassiodoro', in Leanza, *Cassiod.* (Soveria Mannelli, 1993) 191–7

INDEX

Index

Milan, 13, 29, 30, 44, 131, 140, 279
Mommsen, Theodor, 19–21, 174, 178, 197, 212, 223
Mundus, 73

Narses, 288
natura
  in Christian literature, 262–5
  in classical literature, 258–62
  in Neoplatonic thought, 265–7
  moral discernment of, 283–99
  in the *Variae. See Variae*
natural law, 99, 101, 257–60
Neoplatonism, 52, 53–9, 101–2, 113–15, 179–83, 265–7, 281, 284, 295–6, 302, 304
  and the *Variae. See Variae*
Nicaea, Council of, 70–1
Nika Revolt, 36, 72–7, 78–9, 91, 97, 101, 105, 107, 109, 113, 117, 121, 137
Nonnos of Panopolis, 57
North Africa, 11, 36, 66, 72, 78, 82, 98, 102, 125, 126, 129, 134, 143, 159, 325, 326, 330
Novellae, Justinianic, 69–70, 217–21, 256–8, 267–8, 281, 283, 309
Novellae, Theodosian, 209–11, 213, 223–4, 291

Odoacer, 10, 93, 134–5, 138, 144, 159, 167–8
O'Donnell, James, 21
Olybrius, 134, 137, 141
Olympiodorus of Thebes, 55
Opilio, 140, 166–7
Ordo generis of Cassiodorus. *See* Cassiodorus
Origen, 103
Orosius, 87
Ostrogoths. *See* Amals, government of
otium/negotium, 48, 133, 201–5, 231–2

paganism, 8, 52–3, 56–8, 65–7, 115, 118–20, 179–83, 260–1
palatine service, development of, 41–4
palatine service, eastern, 44–59, 62–81
  exceptores, 45, 53, 62–4, 76–7
  excubitores, 45–6, 60–1
  in imperial polemic, 82–5, 267
  scholares, 44–5, 46, 53, 61–2, 76, 89
  scriniarii, 63, 64, 69, 118
palatine service, western
  of Ravenna, 31–3
  social relations with senatorial elite, 127–34
Paul the Deacon, 158
Pelagius, deacon of Rome, 147, 149
Persia, Sasanian, 8, 67, 76, 82, 102, 106–7, 120, 121
Peter the Patrician, 108, 145–6, 320

Philostratus, 292
Phocas, praetorian prefect, 117
Photius, 100
Plato, 53–4, 101, 182, 259, 286–7, 302, 304
Pliny the Elder, 202, 259–60, 261, 262, 263–4, 281, 297, 302, 316
Pliny the Younger, 190, 193, 195, 202, 292, 327–8
Plotinus, 56, 266, 286
Polemo, 298
Pompeius, 73, 77, 80, 96
Porphyry, 56, 198, 266
Primasius, 99
Priscian, 35, 64, 84, 130, 135–6
Priscian of Lydia, 296
Proba, 135
Proclus, 55, 114, 304
Procopius, 20, 36, 38, 41, 46, 57, 72, 73, 76, 79, 83, 85, 87–9, 94, 109–17, 120, 121–3, 125, 126, 142, 144–5, 147–8, 151–2, 154–5, 156, 157, 179, 186, 189, 218–19, 221, 237–40, 290, 319, 324–5, 330
  background and aims, 102–9
  on the Gothic War, 12–14, 18, 20, 27, 29
  and nature, 287–9
Pseudo-Dionysius of Tel-Mahre, 65
public building, ideology of, 86–9, 128–9, 170–1, 234–40, 316–17
  churches, 248–51
  in the *Variae. See Variae*
public spectacle, 87–9, 91–2, 109, 120–1, 128–9, 168, 170–1
Pulcheria, Empress, 71

Quintilian, 198

Radegund, 158
Ravenna
  in Gothic War, 13, 14, 17, 21, 26, 29, 35
  government at, 10–11, 129–34, 143
  palatium of Theoderic, 1–2, 250
  San Vitale. *See* Saint Vitale, church of
  Sant'Apollinare Nuovo. *See* Saint Apollinare Nuovo, church of
  as setting for polemic, 1–3, 94–7, 312, 314, 317, 326
Ravenna Papyri, 212–14
Rome, 10
  in Gothic War, 12–13, 35, 149
  sack of, 14, 87, 92, 147
  Senate of, 10–11, 129–34, 141–2, 149
Romulus Augustus, 16, 93, 135, 159, 168
Ruggini, Lellia, 87
Ruricius of Limoges, 194
Rusticiana, 134, 147, 149

Index